By Rexford G. Tugwell

HOW THEY BECAME PRESIDENT

THE LIGHT OF OTHER DAYS

THE ENLARGEMENT OF THE PRESIDENCY

THE ART OF POLITICS

THE DEMOCRATIC ROOSEVELT

A CHRONICLE OF JEOPARDY

THE PLACE OF PLANNING IN SOCIETY

THE STRICKEN LAND

THE BATTLE FOR DEMOCRACY

THE INDUSTRIAL DISCIPLINE AND THE
GOVERNMENTAL ARTS

INDUSTRY'S COMING OF AGE

REDIRECTING EDUCATION
(*editor and co-author*)

AMERICAN ECONOMIC LIFE AND THE
MEANS OF ITS IMPROVEMENT
(*editor and co-author*)

THE TREND OF ECONOMICS
(*editor and co-author*)

HOW
THEY BECAME
PRESIDENT

Thirty-five Ways to the White House

by

REXFORD G. TUGWELL

SIMON AND SCHUSTER 102075
New York

*For
Tyler and Franklin*

CONTENTS

Introduction   11

PART ONE: *The Thirty-five Ways*   19

George Washington   21
John Adams   31
Thomas Jefferson   42
James Madison   53
James Monroe   63
John Quincy Adams   75
Andrew Jackson   86
Martin Van Buren   99
William Henry Harrison   110
John Tyler   122
James Knox Polk   131
Zachary Taylor   143
Millard Fillmore   155
Franklin Pierce   166
James Buchanan   178
Abraham Lincoln   188
Andrew Johnson   206
Ulysses S. Grant   219
Rutherford Birchard Hayes   233
James A. Garfield   247
Chester Alan Arthur   259
Grover Cleveland   270
Benjamin Harrison   285
William McKinley   295
Theodore Roosevelt   308
William Howard Taft   323
Woodrow Wilson   339
Warren Gamaliel Harding   356
John Calvin Coolidge   370

7

Herbert Clark Hoover — 386
Franklin Delano Roosevelt — 403
Harry S. Truman — 423
Dwight David Eisenhower — 438
John Fitzgerald Kennedy — 456
Lyndon Baines Johnson — 474

PART Two: *Choosing the Best of the Ways* — 501

Rules and Exceptions — 503
What Is Striven For — 508
The Uses of Exactitude — 511
Successes Are Worked For — 513
Some Uniformities — 515
Some Handicaps — 517
Some Advantages — 520
Lawyers, Generals, and Businessmen — 525
The Prevalence of Diversity — 528
The Attraction of Leadership — 532
The Selection Process — 536
Guiding Suggestions — 539
Devices and Their Uses — 542
The Reluctant Seldom Succeed — 545
Whig-Republicans and Democrats — 551
On Taking Positions — 555
Politics and Ethics — 558
The Evolution of Instruments — 561
Finding a Leader — 563
Toward Better Candidates — 567
New Questions, New Techniques — 569

Politics cannot be learned once for all from a text book, or the instruction of a master. What we require to be taught on that subject is to be our own teachers.

—JOHN STUART MILL
Inaugural Address at
St. Andrews, 1867

INTRODUCTION

M ANY PRESIDENTS have complained about the burdens of office and
have longed aloud for the sweet release of retirement. Some,
wise about the trials of public life, have anticipated their immolation
with foreboding. The first of them did that. Washington, about to be
sworn in, said that his movement to the chair of government would
be accompanied by feelings not unlike those of a culprit going to the
place of execution. And others have said, after induction, that the
office was a prison and its disciplines inhuman.

There have indeed always been those who would make the sacrifice.
Professor McBain once said about this, somewhat wryly, that history
did not record many instances of available candidates who shunned the
high office because of the injustice of its exactitudes—or, he added, for
any other reason.[1] But it must really be admitted that its duties are
beyond any man's capacity. They were this from the first, as Washington knew they would be, and have become immensely more so as
time has passed.

One of the worst of the Presidential trials is the duel that goes on
between the image makers around the central symbolic figure and
those who reject the version preferred by his supporters. The man
himself is wearied by the constant care he must take to cultivate the
character prescribed for him—or that he has assumed. Since the source
of his power is involved, he can never relax; but the battering is brutal.
Those who would destroy him are ingenious, energetic and persistent.
He must touch up his portrait every day and defend it from defilers.

This is mostly his own fault. He has represented himself as the kind
of person who could meet the Presidential requirements and has shaped
his image accordingly. It was because of this that a majority voted for
him. If they had not he would not be there. But he can never forget
that nearly half—usually—voted for someone else.[2] And he must

---

[1] *The Living Constitution*, New York, 1937, 117.
[2] Thirteen Presidents had a minority of the votes cast, one of them, Wilson,
twice. That is more than one-third of the thirty-five.

wonder constantly whether he has gained or lost in their regard. Every word and every action must be measured by its effect on the next poll and, indeed, on the next election. All this—and much else—goes to make the Presidency an inhuman ordeal.

There are students of the office who enumerate a dozen or more identifiable phases of the whole Presidential duty. Only a few need be mentioned to show that no one person can possibly perform all of them, much less do so satisfactorily. As he runs for office he is the designated representative of his party and he remains that after election, in addition to being (with his Vice-President) the one official who must represent the whole nation even though he has been preferred by only part of it. This projects him at once into two situations of diametric opposition.

Nevertheless he must quickly take up the duties of leadership in both foreign and domestic policy. He will be a participant in legislating—so much a participant that he is sometimes called Chief Legislator. And he is Commander in Chief of the armed forces.

These are awesome undertakings; yet there are others. It is for him to see that the laws of the largest social organism in the world are properly executed.

And, besides, he is expected to be the guide and mentor of the people, their conscience, calling them to better ways, reminding them of their duties to one another, to other peoples, and to posterity.

With all this confronting them it is no wonder that Presidents have been driven to complain. Yet there is always someone, newly elected, to ride with an outgoing President up Pennsylvania Avenue, and stand in the January cold of East Capitol Square to take the prescribed inaugural oath. This newcomer is always experienced in public life. He may not have made a career in politics, but often he has; and certainly he has watched predecessor Presidents endure the trials of office. He knows its rigors. He has survived an exhausting competition with others who would stand in his place if they could. He has created and gained acceptance for a character he must now enlarge.

What he undertakes is assumed in spite of knowing that no one can do what is required of him. Both the expectation that someone can be found to do what no man can do, and the faith that he will be found by the process we use, are unreal dogmas. Even those professionals who operate the machinery often expect something to result that is quite unlikely. They, like the rest of us, are bemused by the democratic dream. Under its influence they—and all of us—are quite capable of cherishing the complete contradiction that a fallible procedure will always have good results. Vice-President Marshall once illustrated this paradox by saying that as a good Democrat he believed that his party was always right—but that he knew that it wasn't so. In just this way Americans believe that their parties, conventions and campaigns can and will inevitably produce the superman we need—but they know it isn't so. They have not done so in the past and they will be less able to do so in the future.

What follows here tries to penetrate the myth and to discover the reality. It considers briefly each of the successful approaches to the White House in our past. It is meant to emphasize what we *know*, as contrasted with what we *believe*. If the belief were not so determined, some existing arrangements would long ago have been changed; and we may well have come to a time when changes are imperative, when dreams must give way to reality. This is one excuse for such an examination.

But, besides this, I hope it may be of use to those among a new generation of eligibles who, looking at the Presidency, may wonder if it can be attained, and if so, how. They will have been told that any young person may aspire to it. Like Napoleon's corporal who carried a marshal's baton in his knapsack, each is supposed to have a Presidential commission in his briefcase. This again, we older ones know, is not so. Only a few among many eager aspirants have been successful, and only a few could possibly have succeeded.

What qualifications enabled the successful to emerge on top? What traits or circumstances favored them over their competitors? These thirty-five histories, it is hoped, will furnish some answers to these questions.

So far as first elections are concerned, it is intended to ignore the glamor and affection that comes to Presidents once they are inducted, and to examine their situation and their behavior before they were chosen. Re-elections occur in quite different circumstances; some Presidents, but not all, go on to second terms. In these contests the glamor and affection—or the disillusion—must be taken into account; incumbents have to run on their records; and challengers have it to contend with.

At any rate, we shall try to uncover as many likenesses and differences among the successful as the data will permit for this purpose; we shall not care whether the candidate, once he attained office, proved to be capable. Whether he was weak or strong, inspiring or dull, popular or indifferently regarded, his experience in getting there will be of equal interest. Among the weak and dull (but not necessarily unpopular), Grant and Harding are usually listed first; but their coming to office was at least as interesting in a professional sense as Jackson's or Wilson's, these being usually regarded as strong and inspiring.

It seems, indeed, that the most competent operations—from the technical point of view—have resulted in the poorest product. This in itself raises a question important to democracy: whether there may not be an inherent defect in political efficiency as we measure it. It might be so. If the professionals could elect just anyone, they would prefer a candidate they could manage easily, not one with originality and force; such a one might escape from control. It has happened in the past, and preventing it is a serious consideration with insiders.

The possibility that pliant candidates are looked for is an argument for devices that will obstruct such a result. Political reformers have always regarded the convention as a bosses' meeting. They often say that what it takes to be nominated in one of them is drastically different from what it takes to perform well in office. What truth there is in these observations we shall see.

There have been forty-four elections. These have placed in the Presidency thirty-one different individuals. Four others reached the office from the lesser one of Vice-President (when a President died), but were not elected to succeed themselves (Tyler, Fillmore, Andrew Johnson, and Arthur). Theodore Roosevelt, Coolidge, Truman and Lyndon B. Johnson went on to a term of their own, and so are included in the list of those elected. The total, of course, is thirty-five. It is intended to consider all the instances of reaching office whatever the means or circumstances may have been.

There have been many treatises about Presidents and the Presidency, realistic enough, some of them, so that the myths about the men and the office ought long since to have vanished. But at least one still persists, because we cling to the ideal of equality—that the office seeks the man. Where all are equals it is still felt that no one has a superior capability. The natural extension of this view is that surprised individuals are chosen by their peers. It is almost indecent to suggest that they themselves have worked and plotted to be chosen. Everything that happens in the real world contradicts this conception; but subconsciously we still allow it to influence us.

Following the distinction between believing and knowing, we know that as power accretes its value rises, and that an office is much desired because of what can be done with it. It satisfies an instinct to dominate, to manipulate others, and to dispose of favors. Men will work to attain such positions. We know too there are conglomerates of interest centering in candidates. They are no longer individuals when they have been marked for preferment. They belong to something outside of, and far larger than, themselves. The party, the insiders of the party, have an interest to be served. Power for these professionals is profitable. Its disposal has tremendous possibilities they know how to enlarge and develop. We may like to believe this is not so, but we know that it is.

Believing and knowing come together, however, in the recognition that the Presidency is the nation's supreme office; however the incum bent arrived there, he is vested with our loyalty to the nation he now heads. What we believe him to be we know he can become, and we expect that he will. He will not be able to do the impossible; but he can try mightily to fulfill our hopes. We shall inquire whether the successful contenders waited passively for their suitability to be recognized or whether they have set their hopes on attaining it far ahead, and strained, sacrificed, compromised and labored to achieve it. And we shall look further. If they have not conformed to the stereotype, but have schemed and labored to gain the prize, how did they go about it?

For studying this process it would have been appropriate to have taken a sequence of campaigns for the governorship of a state or the mayoralty of a city. Some elements are the same whatever the elective office, but a good many are different. The larger the area and the constituency, the more dazzling the glamor, the deeper the complexity. Not only are the impinging possibilities increased in number, but each is invested with a vast and glowing potential. One who looks covetously at the Presidency must think of many issues that stretch the best-informed and most capable minds. He must at least acknowledge that they exist even if he avoids them; and avoidance itself may have consequences.

But for the student, the Presidential sequence has the attraction of immensity, of range and of consequence. There is an intense interest in the individual who holds the office. He is under constant scrutiny. His words, and even the intonations of his words, are analyzed for meaning. His intentions are important. His actions may be, for his constituents, devastating or rewarding.

It cannot be expected that successful aspirants will have acted within firm rules gained from study. They may have been guided by calculation, perhaps; by analysis of a special sort, also; but not by any but the most general *rules*. There has not yet been time; there is not enough precedent; they cannot have deduced from predecessors what they themselves ought to do. And as for us, students, thirty-five is not a large number. We may be able to uncover the beginnings of uniformity, hints of the best behavior; but our sample is still small, and our conclusions must be cautious.

We should expect, besides, that even if strategies can be seen to have been deliberately formulated and tactics developed, circumstances will have been unruly. Society changes; people change; opponents change; and the establishment of confidence is essentially a mysterious business. We may have to say that it is not a technique to be learned but a talent to be born with.

The first election was in 1788; and in each since that time there has been at least one loser as well as a winner. Usually there have been several losers in the campaign itself and, of course, many more in the

preliminaries. Among those who might have been chosen are some of
the most dazzling figures in our history—such as Hamilton, Jay and
Burr at the very beginning. Some of these came very close to being
chosen. John Jay, for instance, was a qualified statesman who in his
time had, possibly, as much influence on policy as anyone except
Washington himself. Yet, because his life was lived in Washington's
shadow, and because his own performance had become unpopular at
the moment when he might have been eligible, he never even came
close to selection.[3]

One preliminary lesson from such experience is plain enough: an
individual who very early develops clear and forceful ideas about
public policy, who expresses them without reservation and has become
clearly identified with them, takes the risk that the circumstances may
change. If the policy subsequently is thought to be unsuitable, he becomes unpopular. This happened to Jay. On a diplomatic mission to
Britain he negotiated a treaty thought to betray a bias against France
and in favor of Britain. France was at the moment in great favor, and
all talk of his candidacy was silenced. Adams, who was the Vice-President, was chosen. He was possibly even more prejudiced in favor of
the British as against the French, but he was not caught in an embarrassing tangle at an inopportune time.

Aaron Burr, who was Hamilton's contemporary and rival, made a
much closer approach than Hamilton. He became Vice-President and
was for a time, in the early months of 1801, apparently about to become President. He was tied with Jefferson and lost only because
Hamilton, who controlled Federalist votes in the House of Representatives, regarded him as more of a rascal than Jefferson. There is some
temptation to conclude from this example that being a scoundrel is
conducive to being almost, if not quite, successful. But generalizations
of this sort are dangerous without a good deal of data; and there have
not been many Burrs.

The names just mentioned—those of Washington and Jefferson, who
became Presidents, and those of Hamilton, Jay and Burr, who did not
—belong to the first years of our Republic. The lessons to be learned
from their experiences, so remote from us in time, may not at first seem
relevant. There were difficulties of electioneering that we can only
imagine, what with the hardships of travel and the time it required,
the absence of means of communication and the like; and the issues of
that time were discussed in language that seems to us to have a kind of
archaic quality. Yet many of the differences tend to disappear when
they are reflected on, except, of course, the physical ones.

---

[3] About those who made bids but failed, or at least some of them, Charles
Judah and George Winston Smith have written in *The Unchosen* (New York,
1962).

People did gather, listen to speeches, and join in discussion; and they did make up their minds. They were sovereign then as now (although a smaller percentage of them could share the sovereignty, since there were qualifications for suffrage that many could not meet); and they were apt to have the last say if not the first one. Presently the machinery so carefully devised to keep them from really deciding matters would be modified to allow a choice between two—or perhaps among several—candidates. Suffrage would become universal and voting would be more direct.

In order to be quite clear about this inquiry into the approach and accession of the thirty-five, let me say what it is not. It is not a history of elections in the United States or a history of the Presidency. Neither is it a series of biographical sketches. It is a little of each, but only as much as is necessary to a much narrower purpose—to find out something about the attaining of the office.

One thing more—those who get to the White House have to consider the problem of staying there. Several Presidents could not stay on when they wanted to very much—the Adamses, Van Buren, Fillmore, Pierce and Arthur are examples. There is therefore a problem not only of further ambition but of methodology. If an incumbent hopes to succeed himself he must study ways to do it. These will be different from those which got him there in the first place. This is obvious. And the eight who were elected once but were not re-elected would seem to show that there is even more difficulty about it.

Many individuals face the first problem: nomination by a responsible party. Fewer face the second: being elected after being nominated. Only some of those who are nominated and elected are forced to consider the third: renomination. The processes of elimination are still severe. Death has intervened for no less than eight. And senility overtook Buchanan while he was in office. So that for only some two-thirds of those who have become President has the third problem arisen. But for them there was still a fourth: re-election. This would seem also to be special. It was not solved by Adams, by Van Buren, by Cleveland (once; he succeeded in a second attempt), by Taft or by Hoover. Then for some there have been further choices and further problems. Washington and his immediate successors held to a self-imposed two-term limit; Grant sought a third but found himself blocked; and both Theodore Roosevelt and Coolidge were equivocal. Franklin D. Roosevelt ignored what had become a fairly firm precedent. His ignoring it precipitated a constitutional amendment to make what had been a tradition a complete prohibition. So future Presidents (unless the Constitution is again amended) may have the four enumerated crises to surmount, but there will be no further ones after re-election to a second term.

This inquiry is directed to the first and second of these problems, with less consideration for the third and fourth. These last are worth a study in themselves; but far fewer individuals are concerned. What is of most interest is the ways of attaining rather than the ways of staying. It may be that putting together even so small a number as thirty-five may tell us something about how the Presidency is won.

R.G.T.

The University of Puerto Rico

PART ONE

The Thirty-five Ways

George Washington
1732–1799

Born at Wakefield, Westmoreland County, Virginia
Became first President in 1789 at 57

HISTORY

1743	Father died.
1748	Began surveying in the West.
1752	Inherited Mount Vernon.
1753	Sent on a winter mission to the Ohio Country as a militia major.
1754	Went West again with soldiers at the beginning of the Seven Years' War, now spreading to America.
1755	Served on the staff of General Braddock.
1759	Married Martha Custis, a widow of 27.
1775	Appointed Commander in Chief of the Continental Army.
1781	Accepted the surrender of Cornwallis at Yorktown.
1783	Returned his commission to the Continental Congress.
1787	Presided over the Constitutional Convention.
1789	Inaugurated as President (Vice-President, John Adams). No opponent.

1789–91   Undertook prolonged tours both North and South.
1792   Re-elected.
1797   Retired to Mount Vernon.
1799   Died on December 14 at 67.

OF ALL the statesmen in American history, Washington has most conspicuously the characteristics of simplicity, steadfastness, integrity, and absolute devotion to his country to such a degree that they dominate all his other traits. For a long time these traits obscured the more human side of his nature. We know more about that now; and it has relieved the austerity and coldness of the older portrait and has revealed an appreciation of his own worth, perhaps to be described as vanity; but nothing has changed the impression that when he had a decision to make about public policy it was made in complete detachment and with only the public interest in view.

There is hardly another among about-to-be-Presidents who did not admit the considerations we ordinarily call politics to his approach. We do not hold this against the others. If they had not been mindful of these matters they might not have become President at all. But Washington was different. It is necessary to recall about him that the political arts were deliberately forsworn.

One of the most important of these arts is that of concealing intentions. This may require resort to a duplicity not to be justified by any other necessity. Actions must be taken when they become vital, and often they must not be published in advance. It is very difficult to reach the upper levels of leadership without resorting to this deliberate deception. And it is equally difficult to remain there without its further use. But Washington did not use it to get there. This alone, if there were no other characteristics, would set him apart from all the rest.

This abstention was not because of ignorance. He had used the technique with excellent results during his generalship of the American armies. Howard Swiggett, writing about him as a military leader and commenting on his employment of spies, even double spies, to fool the British Commander, Lord Howe, said of him, "If the object had not been noble, some characteristics which animated him would be called guile and duplicity."

Guile, amounting to duplicity, is, however deplorable, a usual and accepted resort. Nevertheless, judged by the criteria we accept in other occupations, it is thoroughly reprehensible. It has often been remarked that a statesman who in his private life is a paragon of virtue, who would neither steal nor lie, will do both for his country without the slightest hesitation and with every sign of being convinced that he has only done his duty. He will expect it to be approved, and more often than not it will be.

But, to be clear, we must recognize this conduct for what it is. It may be patriotic, but it is wrong by our professed rules; and nothing can make it right. This is said to emphasize this as one of the sacrifices necessary to a practical political career—that is, unless we accept the example of Washington rather than that of his successors. Washington's conduct shows that principle *need not* be sacrificed to attain office. But if it is not to be sacrificed, the aspirant must be a Washington, and Washingtons are scarce. He was unusual not only because he had a rocklike character, but because he operated in very unusual circumstances. The right combination might appear, but certainly a recurrence is so unlikely that dependence on it is impractical. It is much more usual to accept the necessity of public immorality. Politicians say to themselves that if the object is noble, the means, however ignoble, may be justified. Professionals, however, keep matters straight in their own minds. Nothing, in their regard, is more detestable than a hypocrite. This recalls Lincoln Steffens' view that a knowing rascal is almost an honest one.

The practical criterion is applicable to other political leaders and even to Washington as a military man, but not to Washington the potential President, nor to him, either, in office. He scorned such resorts. He stood where he stood on every conceivable question without equivocation or desire to evade. There were occasions when he would not explain. But this was because partisans were trying to confuse the public about him, and he thought the public ought to—and did— know where he stood.

There is every evidence that his policies were, in fact, well and widely understood. In a way they had the same quality as his public character. Having so purified himself, he stood stark and alone in a kind of majesty. Anyone could guess what his attitude would be on any matter before him. This might well have been fatal in any other circumstances, but in the infant days of the Republic, a man mightier than the state he served, with an integrity towering above that of the Congress, the courts, or any associate he might have, was what was direly needed. He would stand between his people and all threats from abroad and from within. And in those days the environment must often have seemed to be mostly hostile. Nothing was yet secure in tradition or by reputation. The nation was regarded by other nations as hardly worth noticing. There were no guiding rules for public policy; no one knew what the new Republic's legislature might do next. But Washington the other nations respected; and Washington would be a guarantee of governmental reason.

We have only to look at the other statesmen who were his contemporaries to understand why he was unanimously, almost spontaneously, agreed on. Consider Franklin, who might have been an alternative. He was a revered elder. His services to the young nation had been as valuable as Washington's. He was old, and wise and clever. That was just it; besides having grown somewhat feeble, he was clever; Washington, in contrast, was not only commandingly virile, he was dense and slow. He had none of Franklin's openness to the flood of new ideas, none of his happiness with experimentation, none of his wide appreciation of nature, human and other. He was a man of the soil, at home on his acres, a careful manager of his estate. He loved the fields and forests. By preference he spent his days in the saddle, considering as he rode through the lanes how one or another of his farms could be made more productive.

He had only one vision outside a Mount Vernon made into a model estate—that was a nation in which numerous Mount Vernons could be developed and made secure. Of course he thought in strategic terms as became a General. He saw that the land to the west must come under the same rule as the seaboard states. He had surveyed some of that land; he had fought to keep the French out of it when he was still a loyal subject of the King; he had invested heavily in it as a private individual and had done all he could to encourage its development.

But he did not become President to protect his investments beyond the Alleghenies. He became President to protect the nation he had fought for; and that involved development toward the West. This was a sound conception. If one of the European empires had permanently possessed the land beyond the Alleghenies, the small states crowded against the seaboard would have declined, by contrast, to minuscule influence in the world. They might even have disappeared.

This large view of his was allied with his single-mindedness and simplicity. The West should belong to the United States. This was understood by everyone when he was chosen. He stood not only for certainty and security but for expansion. And Americans even so early were incorrigible expanders. Those were times, however, when two powerful European nations were engaged in a struggle which seemed likely to divide the world. And among the prizes were the vast domains on three sides of the States. The resolve that they should go to neither seemed sheer effrontery. But Washington had weight enough to make it seem feasible. If anyone could do it, he could.

It is interesting to consider how he must have arrived at his clear and ineluctable conceptions: independence, union, and expansion.

It has been suggested that humiliating experiences with British army officers when he was serving with them in the trans-Allegheny campaigns against the French and Indians may have been responsible for his opposition to British rule in America. And there does seem to have been in his persistence through so many years and against such odds a deep grounding in revulsion. He was utterly convinced that independence was right, that Americans could not live with honor, and would never be allowed to prosper, as a colony.

Yet he appears as much an English gentleman as any Englishman could possibly be. He was the very model of a country squire with fixed attitudes who only left his favorite pursuits to serve his nation, and then reluctantly and temporarily. The British seem to have recognized this and to have felt a certain pride in him. What he had done was in a tradition they had created. He had fought for decent treatment and vindicated an instinct for justice. The Germanic King may have regarded him as a traitor; but that was not the reaction of most of the King's subjects.

The young George had not had an easy life, and if when he was grown he was independent, almost to the point of intractability, it was because he had overcome so many handicaps in demonstrating his right to command. When the British officers rejected his advice and pursued the tactics of their texts to ridiculous defeat in the Allegheny forests, he lost forever any feeling of inferiority he might have developed. They were parade-ground soldiers. The same arrogance, pursued into statecraft, would reduce the colonials to permanent inferiority.

If he had this suggestion planted in his mind during his experience in the West as a young officer, it had material for amplification in subsequent years as the British policies developed. The rule was: everything for the mother country, nothing for the colonists. What provoked the outright rebellion was taxes that outraged merchants and shipowners. It is possible to justify these as a due contribution to the expense of protection from the French and Indians. But they had been decided on without consultation; and no more provoking slogan was ever devised than "taxation without representation." It was very foolish to have alienated the most powerful people in the colonies.

It is very probable that the importers and the shippers, who were most enraged about the taxes, were rather synthetic American patriots. Most of them would much rather have won their point and remained British. They were far from generous when it came to supporting the revolutionary armies. And perhaps most of them felt, when actual fighting began, that their commercial indignation had got out of hand and betrayed them. Washington, as Commander in Chief, had to contend with their strong impulse toward appeasement as well as with the British armies. But he was a planter, not a merchant; and this made all the difference. He was steadfast; and the fearsomeness of Imperial power broke against the rock of his resolution. Americans must not tolerate British rule; that was his resolve; and in the end he had his way.

We can see, also, how he came quite naturally to his concept of union. This was due to a later but no less formative experience with government by loosely federated sovereign states and an executive which was a feeble arm of the legislature.

When the war had been won and he had retired to Mount Vernon, and the Continental Congress, so hopelessly inefficient during the war, fell into even more irresponsible ways, it was mostly because the states would allow it so little authority. From 1783, when he surrendered his commission, the dangers of a divided and feeble government became more and more apparent. The individual states were inclined to exclusiveness and, even worse, to discriminations against each other. Commerce among them could not move freely and no agreed policy concerning trade with other nations could be arrived at. The United States, not being really united, fell lower and lower in the esteem of the world's statesmen. John Adams, in Europe on various missions, was frantic over unpaid debts he had negotiated. There were years when the Congress did not meet at all, and when it did the states would not settle the debts contracted by its officials. The Confederation seemed likely to fall apart, and soon.

Washington was among those who sponsored a meeting at Annapolis in 1786 to consider freeing commerce among the states. Nothing of much importance resulted from this except a recommendation for another meeting in 1787. It was this later one that became the Constitutional Convention. What was accomplished in Philadelphia resulted from deliberately exceeding terms of reference, something the more timid delegates objected to but which was stoutly supported by the advocates of a strong union.

Washington is known to have been among those who wanted a central government with enlarged powers. He probably would have liked a monarchy, and he consented only with reluctance to legislative checks upon the Executive. But in spite of deep discouragement at some points in the discussion, such as when he wrote to Hamilton that "men of local views" seemed likely to prevent any considerable accomplishment, he was fairly satisfied with the result. He knew that the framework of the Constitution depended for much of its character on its shaping in practice. His willingness to become the first President was doubtless influenced by this perception. His investment in the new government was already extensive. He would give more years of his life to shaping its early traditions.

He had studied government in his careful way. He found in Adams' ideas, voluminously set out in messages from Europe, and in his enormous treatises, a compromise he could accept between popular rule and advantages for an elite. He did not think all men were equal, but he did think they had rights. And the structure worked out in Philadelphia made sure, he thought, that capable men would run the government and that they would run it justly.

Like others of his contemporaries, he thought of government as an instrument. The American people, by molding it and using it, could go on to a great destiny. The nation would grow and expand. The government must be capable of containing and expressing this development. Americans had for centuries been pushing against the wilderness. Washington was symbolic of this, and the citizens felt proud and confident in selecting him.

It was fortunate that in the first elections there was no contest. There simply was not the organization to accommodate a campaign. This was more true, naturally, of the first than the second. By 1792 some progress had been made. But in 1788—when the election should have been held—the Congress spent so much time arguing about the comparatively trivial matter of a location for the national capital that provision for the Presidential election was neglected. The late states had only just got around to ratifying the Constitution—New Hampshire, the crucial ninth one, ratified in June (New York and Virginia followed) and the Congress could not meet until after that. An election for November could have been authorized. But actually the debate over the capital city went on until September. By that time it was apparent—communications and transport being what they were— that January 1789 would be the earliest possible time for an election. When the resolution declaring that the Constitution was duly ratified and authorizing the choosing of Presidential electors was passed, the states had as yet made no preparation whatever. And since the Constitution provided that each state should arrange for election "in such manner as its Legislature may direct," these bodies had to meet and debate about procedures.

It was intended that the legislatures should provide for popular elections, not that they should themselves elect. Some attempt to set up popular voting was made in New Hampshire, Massachusetts, Pennsylvania, Maryland, and Virginia; but even after these elections in New Hampshire and Massachusetts the legislatures finally chose the electors. There was almost no voting in Pennsylvania, Maryland, and Virginia; there seemed to be no interest. In New York there arose a controversy between the houses of the legislature, and no electors were chosen. And Rhode Island and North Carolina had not yet ratified. So these three states did not participate at all.

Washington was elected in this rather unsatisfactory way by 69 electors from 10 states, when there should have been 91 from 13 states. To complete the story of tardiness and indifference, the legislature of the Confederation, before adjourning, had provided that the new Congress of the United States should meet on the first Wednesday of March to proclaim the election results. But a quorum did not gather until April 6. On that day the electoral votes were counted and Washington and Adams were declared elected.

Adams became Vice-President because he had the second highest number of electoral votes (34), the next highest being John Jay (with 9). At that time each elector voted for two Presidential candidates, a method changed by constitutional amendment in time for the election of 1804, when Presidential and Vice-Presidential candidates were differentiated.

All this irregularity, amounting to illegality, might have broken up the Union at the outset if there had been any contest. But there was not. Washington was so universally regarded as the nation's first citizen that his selection was natural and unquestioned. There seem to have been suggestions that Franklin or Adams might be chosen, but they were very faint and were not encouraged by Franklin and not very hopefully regarded by Adams, although he believed in his heart that he would have been a better choice. Never again would there be quite this unanimity. Monroe's second election would approach it, perhaps, but even that would not be nearly so foregone a result.

No one looking forward to a Presidential canvass can learn much from Washington's experience. He never had to think of getting into office, to say nothing of staying there—the second election was also uncontested. But one can learn that the political arts are unnecessary to a man of character and reputation whose place in the nation has become for some reason impregnable. There could be other reasons for this impregnability than those which created the Washington who was "the father of his country." But it is hard to imagine them. And no one else has ever attained the same ranking in his countrymen's hearts. Even the compassionate Lincoln, now held second to Washington among Presidents, had a hard political life. He was reviled in proportion to his goodness. Washington had his enemies. They were mostly men who had suffered from his rigid uprightness. The outright Tories who had disagreed with him were exiled; but there were others who had been disciplined during the hard years of the Revolution. Toward the last he felt himself hardly used by the rising Democratic-Republicans; but there was never any real question about his integrity.

A man who, almost alone, had furnished the hard core of determination that independence should be achieved could not, when he had won, be harmed by common malice. He was beyond its reach. He had struggled with an irresolute and divided Continental Congress influenced by competing committees; he had had to build a new army every spring during a long war; he had had to fight an enemy superior in numbers, in quality, and in training, by coming to grips only when he could achieve temporary advantages. By a masterly tour de force, he had gathered around Yorktown his own and the assisting French forces, by land and by sea, bottling up Cornwallis and his army without possibility of reinforcement. And with a spectacular show of formal military protocol he had accepted, with a dignity that established his figure forever among men of honor, the surrender of his enemy.

Washington won his two elections at Yorktown, a much better place to win them than on the hustings. Others have won by gaining a somewhat similar renown; but none would achieve such commanding respect that no alternative seemed in the least reasonable.

John Adams
1735–1826

Born in Braintree, Massachusetts
Became second President in 1797 at 61

HISTORY

1755	Graduated from Harvard.
1755–58	Taught school.
1758	Admitted to the bar.
1764	Married Abigail Smith.
1770	Defended soldiers of the Boston Massacre.
1774–77	Member of the Continental Congress.
1778–79	Diplomatic missions to France.
1780	Member of Massachusetts Constitutional Convention.
1785–88	Minister to Great Britain.
1789	Elected Vice-President.
1792	Re-elected Vice-President.
1796	Elected President (Vice-President, Jefferson); opponent, Jefferson.

31

1798   Signed Alien and Sedition Acts and prepared for war with France.

1800   Concluded peace with France. Moved from Philadelphia to Washington and became the first occupant of the White House. Defeated for re-election by Jefferson.

1826   Died in Braintree on July 4 at 90.

WHEN JOHN ADAMS was elected to the Presidency in 1796 a consuming envy of Washington was partially assuaged. It had tormented him for years, but especially since the beginning of his Vice-Presidency seven years before. There are many references to this jealousy in his diary and in his letters. He knew it to be shameful, and watching Washington hold the nation together, he had been well enough aware that it was something he could not have done. Still he could not quite conquer his envy.

This was allied with another failing he was often accused of by his enemies, and sometimes admitted. He was incorrigibly vain. He would wonder—in conversation or at length in his diary—whether this was really a defect of character. What he really believed was that it was justified by his courage, his intelligence, and his services to the nation. Why these virtues were not more generally acknowledged, he could not understand.

His worst time had been during his Vice-Presidency. He had not at first understood that this was a stand-by office and that he was not really expected to be an active second in the government unless some disablement should remove the President. He had before him, as he presided over the Senate, some of the most stormily critical individuals in the country. His attempts to lecture them and to join in their debates were badly received. There was a suspicion of any formal display; and Adams loved show and thought it a most vital appurtenance of government, especially one just getting started and trying to impress other nations. He was accused—with some reason—of monarchical leanings. His finicking arguments about titles and procedures as the Senate shaped itself was part of this tendency.

His preference for institutions resembling those kingly ones to be seen in Britain and elsewhere was genuinely part of his governmental theory. He had a fear of partisanship, and he felt that the danger of violence and civic confusion was increased by frequent elections. He was certain, as he saw the excitement rise during his Vice-Presidency and come to a climax whenever an election was near, that the Constitution ought to have given all officials longer terms. He wrote to a friend that the civic disturbance bred by campaigning "tended to civil war," and went on to say that another convention was the only remedy:

> When bribery, corruption, intrigue, maneuver, violence, force shall render elections too troublesome . . . another convention must be called, [which] may prolong the period of Senators from six years to twelve or twenty or thirty or forty or for life, or if necessary propose the establishment of hereditary Senators.[1]

---

[1] Page Smith, *John Adams*, 2 vols. (New York, 1962), II, 791.

In the same letter he expressed even worse fears about Presidential canvasses and said he could conceive no other way to preserve liberty than to have a hereditary President. But on this particular subject he did say different things at different times. Perhaps because he was so often accused and felt so defensive as the weight of opinion during his later life turned toward more universal suffrage and as notions of equality spread, there are long passages in his papers defending his position. He seems, in fact, to have been somewhat frightened by his earlier vehemence in defending government by an elite and anxious to make it clear that he too was a revolutionist of the true breed. Perhaps what he wrote his friend Dr. Rush in 1790 was meant to be published. His letter was written because the desire for a monarchy was more and more often being charged to him, and because now he had a political future to protect:

"I am a mortal and irreconcilable enemy to monarchy," he said, and went on to deny that he had altered his opinions since 1776. "I am no friend to hereditary limited monarchy in America. This I know can never be admitted without an hereditary senate to control it, and an hereditary nobility or senate in America I know to be unattainable . . . "[2] He begged his friend, therefore, not to misrepresent him to "posterity."

If this sounds equivocal and unconvincing it is because he was turning away from something he had certainly once hoped for and still believed in. It had taken some hard lessons to convince him of the impracticality he now spoke of. There were more to come, too, before he would be cured of his longing for more glamorous trappings, more sonorous titles, and the pageantry he felt essential to office.

Following Adams' career as he progressed from being a Boston lawyer, protesting British misrule and injustice, to helping in the drafting of the Declaration, then service in the early Congresses, is easy for the student who will read. It is all there, in Adams' own words. And the outpouring of ideas, theories, the results of research, opinions on everything any man ever thought of, went on all his life. He would live to be ninety, and the flood seldom stopped even for a day. The volume became immense. And, of course, long before he finally laid down his pen, his son John Quincy would have begun to write.

In much of what Adams wrote there is a note of pain and puzzlement. He never learned patience with slower minds or tolerance of differing ones. And this tenderness, together with the nature of his theories of government, can only lead to the conclusion that, much as was owed him by the new Republic, he ought never to have become President. It might have been better if he had been appointed to the Chief Justiceship and Jay had succeeded Washington.

---

[2] *Ibid.,* 757.

But it must be recalled that when he was elected he had been Vice-President—a reluctant and dissatisfied one—for two terms and was bursting with suppressed ambitions. Hamilton, who knew well enough how difficult and thorny Adams was, only reluctantly consented to support him; but, everything considered, it did seem to him the best thing to do. This was important, as Adams was nervously aware, because Hamilton was now something of a political boss. His prestige as Washington's Secretary of the Treasury and the success of his schemes to stabilize the finances of the new nation had won him the regard of the conservatives—and this meant, of course, the Federalists. He was the recognized adversary of Jefferson, the leader of the Democratic-Republicans, and all his calculations were intended to keep Jefferson from becoming President. If this meant supporting Adams, he would even do that.

It is interesting to contrast the working methods of these two. Both had retired from the Cabinet, but Jefferson had gone quietly to Monticello, saying that he was through with the world of affairs, but all the time keeping up an immense correspondence and directing his rapidly growing party machine. He never appeared as a principal in any argument and emerged only at election time as the choice of the party's electors. Hamilton took his position at once as a prominent New York attorney, and began to organize and direct Federalist groups in all the states. They were however beginning to find themselves under attack by the more equalitarian leaders. These, by 1796, were, like Jefferson, under French influence, or at least so much in sympathy with the revolution in France that the conservative and Anglophile Federalists seemed more monarchical and anti-democratic than they really were. This election, indeed, is sometimes pictured as a contest between Britain and France carried out on the American scene.

But if Adams—and others like Hamilton and Jay among the Federalists—was excoriated as aristocratic and monarchical, it was mostly the exaggeration of election fervor. It is a fact of some significance that this first real election in the United States, with parties only partly formed, was as bitter and violent as any in our history. The name-calling, the imputation of foreign affiliation and corruption, the shouting and demagoguery, resorted to by both sides, were as extreme and unprincipled as though the political experience of years were being drawn on.

This was terribly disconcerting to Adams. He was now sixty-one and had been continuously in the service of his country, one way or another, for most of his adult life. His role in making the Revolution had been enlarged by the adoption of a government that represented the arrangements he had so carefully worked out. The balancing of powers, the creation of an executive, the two-chamber legislature, and the establishment of a judiciary were ideas he had fought for with pen and tongue for years. True, he had been abroad—on various diplomatic missions he had been in Europe for years just preceding the first election—when the Constitution had been written, and he had not been wholly satisfied with it; but it bore the marks of his labor. Since he was one creator of the government—in his own view, the most important one—he ought to have been given the Presidency, as Washington had, in recognition of his fatherhood. To have the savage opposition of the "mob" boiling up all around him was not only ungrateful but illustrated all the dangers he had warned his fellow countrymen about if the electorate was not restricted, elections seldom held, and the Executive not made strong to hold in check the unruly representatives of the lower House.

Adams knew as well as anyone how Washington had sustained the new nation through its first stumbling years, how he had given the Presidency form, and how he had prevented the French revolutionists from drawing the United States into the vortex of their confused terror. He acknowledged this, and his vain sensitivity was mollified by Washington's careful recognition of his position. He was always included in official events, social as well as governmental; and Abigail was encouraged to be friends with Martha. But still he was unhappy.

When during Washington's second term Jefferson launched his attempt to discredit Hamilton for the funding operation that enriched so many speculators even though it did once for all establish the nation's credit, Adams watched from the Vice-Presidency. Jefferson, acting through his busy seconds, even made approaches to impeachment; and when they failed there was not much he could do except to retire from the scene. When he established himself at Monticello, Adams said it was "simply to allow his reputation to grow until a clamor was raised for him to succeed Washington as President." Writing further to his son, he said that Jefferson thought by this step "to get a reputation of an humble, modest, meek man, wholly without ambition or vanity. . . . But if a prospect opens, the world will see and he will feel that he is as ambitious as Oliver Cromwell. . . ."

From such remarks, as Page Smith says, it was clear enough that already Adams thought of Jefferson as his real rival. "He wished and intended to succeed Washington and he watched with apprehension every move of his former friend . . . What he saw plainly disturbed him. Jefferson was a master of political maneuver, subtle, shrewd, tenacious, a politician . . . in the new style, resourceful in . . . exploiting every opportunity presented by the emerging democracy."[3]

Smith goes on to say that "Adams, as he girded himself for the contest that he foresaw, was perhaps already doomed. Certainly he was seriously inhibited by his image of himself as a man above

[3] *Ibid.*, 846.

politics, an independent man whose fiercely guarded integrity would not allow him to truck and bargain and scheme for the prize he so much desired."[4]

As the time actually approached when Washington would decide whether he would accept a third nomination or would retire, Adams' long-suppressed desire for the first place became an acute fever of worry and pessimism. He was now unhappily aging; he was fat and beset by many physical ills. His teeth were going, his eyes were dimming, he had knotted veins in his short legs, and his face was a caricature of the handsomeness it had had in his youth. He was irascible, contentious, inclined to be contemptuous with inferiors, and utterly unable to be genial or conciliatory. He was also poor. He had always fought poverty as a public official. The succeeding governments he had served, down to and including the new one under the Constitution, had all been parsimonious. His salary and allowances had never been enough to meet bare expenses. This, together with his rather high-flown idea of the state an official must maintain, especially an Ambassador in a foreign capital, had kept him in perpetual debt. Sometimes he was so pinched for funds that he threatened to return at once to private practice of the law, and he was always complaining, to anyone who might have influence, of his penurious state.

He was not the picture of a statesman, as Washington had been —wealthy, withdrawn, and dignified. Adams was furious in argument, impatient with opposition, and little respected except for his sharp intelligence. It is really no wonder that Hamilton thought of Pinckney as an alternative. He had at least some of Washington's presence, he was well-born, and he was sufficiently affluent.

It has to be recalled that there were no formal nominations in those years; also that the Electoral College was in the phase that was later revised. It was theoretically supposed that electors would be chosen in each state, that they would meet, and that they would cast two votes for individuals they themselves regarded as desirable. The division of opinion into two camps—radical and conservative, French and British, Democratic-Republican and Federalist—however unexpected, developed very rapidly in the new nation. Washington watched it with dismay. He held himself, as he believed, above what he called faction and tried his best to conciliate the contenders in his own official family. He knew he had failed when first Jefferson and then Hamilton left him and began to organize in opposition to each other. He still preserved his neutrality. But he made no appointments and gave no encouragement to those who were not in sympathy with the objectives of his administration. This meant that he favored the Federalists; it could not mean anything else.

[4] *Ibid.*, 847.

Even Washington was attacked before he left office; but the respect for him restrained the violent criticism any other might have suffered. It was the election after he had left the scene that first let loose the partisan storm. Its strength was not enough to keep Adams from succeeding then; but its force would grow, and Adams would not know how to combat it except in ways that made it worse; and it would cause the tragedy of his defeat for re-election.

Both times it was Jefferson who was his antagonist. But Hamilton resorted to a maneuver in 1796 that, when Adams heard of it, infuriated him. Hamilton had made up his mind that the Federalist candidate would have to be Adams in order to hold New England; but he secretly passed the word to his correspondents in all the states that Federalists should vote equally for Adams and Pinckney, saying that this would make Jefferson's defeat more certain. What he secretly hoped was that if the Southern Federalists voted solidly for Pinckney and the New Englanders split their vote Pinckney might be elected; but it did not happen. The Southerners stuck together; but so did the New Englanders; and Pinckney lost even the Vice-Presidency. The vote was Adams 71, Jefferson 68, Pinckney 59, and Burr 30.

It was a raging campaign that lasted until December, because not until then would the Electoral College meet. It was supposed that all those elected would stick to their party, but they did not have to; and there was some hope of last-minute influence. Jefferson and Adams remained all this time in retreat, Jefferson at Monticello and Adams at Braintree. Adams was sick with apprehension. His diary and letters express a black foreboding and presuppose that all his services to the nation were about to end in the unhappiness of retirement.

In ten of the sixteen states it was the legislatures which chose the electors, so the cross fire of propaganda probably had far less effect than it would later when they were chosen by popular vote. That he had only three more votes than Jefferson was considered a humiliation by Adams. But he was President and it remained to be seen what he could do in office.

Adams went into the Presidency neither a good Federalist nor a Democratic-Republican. He was not a good Federalist because he was not a businessman and not a capitalist. He was a farmer and a lawyer, and his sympathies were much the same as Jefferson's. In fact, they had found substantial agreement in former days when they had been colleagues. He was not pro-British either, as many Federalists were; he had not only suffered from British snobbishness in Boston before the Revolution when he was struggling to make a start in life and had no claim to upper-class distinction, but had been treated as an inferior when he had represented the newly independent nation in London. These were the reasons Hamilton did not trust him.

But he had no sympathy with Jefferson's philosophy. He had seen
the French disrupt their government and turn their nation into a confused and headless monster, unable to govern itself or to behave with
propriety abroad. Jefferson's faith in the goodness of human nature, he
thought infantile. Men were not equal; they were creatures of passion
and their government had to be one that checked their natural tend-
encies to exploit each other, to disrupt orderly procedures, and to
pursue their own interests regardless of others' rights. Any legislature
of direct representatives would exhibit these same defects. They
could not be trusted and must be checked by an upper house with
longer tenure and only an indirect responsibility to the voters. And
both must be balanced by an executive with such powers as might be
needed to make certain that reason and not passion prevailed, that the
public interest came first, and that the legislature did not fall into
confusion.

These were the ideas that Washington approved, also; and they were
the formative ones of the Constitution—although Adams would have
shaped the detail differently. It was fitting that he should follow Washington even if he was no model Federalist.

It was not yet understood that Presidents must necessarily be party
leaders. Washington had been one only in a lofty and almost unconscious way. And Adams had no liking for most of his fellow party
members—if he could be called a party member. He had not been
formally nominated because no one was; but he had been elected as a
Federalist, there was no doubt about that. And his refusal really to
recognize it was because he was unwilling to be President in any but his
own stubborn and highly principled way.

There was another reason why things very soon began to go wrong
for him. He was tactless and suspicious. He had a hair-trigger temper
and very often was sarcastic and unnecessarily sharp. These are not
the qualities of a politician or, indeed, of a leader of any sort. And
Adams promptly made more enemies than he could handle. He kept
Washington's Cabinet, and they soon were disaffected. If he was not
a party man, they were, and it was not long before they were looking
to Hamilton rather than to Adams for instructions.

This was Adams' situation when he ran head on into the French
complications which led to the Alien and Sedition Laws, the creation
of a standing army—and to a final disaffection among the voters that
discredited Federalism and brought Jefferson to the Presidency. It is
usually said that the Federalists' disaster in 1800 was their own fault.
The party members in the Congress went much too far in the Alien
and Sedition Acts. It was true that the Directory in France treated
the United States emissaries with unpardonable rudeness and attempted to interfere in inadmissible ways in domestic politics, but to

make mere disagreement with the government unlawful, and suspects subject to deportation, was to flout the very principles of the Revolution.[5]

It was this resort to extremity that gave Jefferson his opening. It must be said that Adams realized what was happening. It was differences over this that led to the dismissal of his holdover Cabinet. They were behaving as Hamilton thought they ought to regardless of Adams' orders. He saw that conciliation was called for and that the "undeclared war" ought to be ended. The Secretaries of State and of War delayed and hampered the carrying out of his policy. But when he dismissed them, it split the Federalists and alienated the Hamilton faction.

When the election approached, the Democratic-Republicans settled on Jefferson and Burr as their candidates. The Federalists would have liked to abandon Adams. Many of them had reason to dislike him. Hamilton, hearing of these disaffections and hoping to discover an alternate, went himself on an exploring journey. The trouble was that, although Adams had never been popular with the leaders, there was no other Federalist they liked better. In fact, no other available politician could hope to win. So he was made their choice again.

But neither Hamilton nor the other leaders worked hard for their nominee. And Hamilton did something of a very strange sort, calculated certainly to do far more harm than good. He wrote a pamphlet about Adams saying that he had "irrefragible proof of his unfitness" for the Presidency. Yet at the end he made the incredible statement that all the same he hoped no vote would be withheld from him. Aaron Burr got hold of the document and, as could be expected of Burr, published it. It was fatal.

This time Adams was defeated. The electoral vote was Jefferson and Burr each 73, Adams 65, Pinckney 64, and Jay 1.

If Adams is to be admired—and there are a multitude of reasons for admiring him—it is not because he was a politician. Perhaps he ought never to have become President. He never understood the people of the United States. He only understood the upper classes. He was elected because popular politics had not quite yet got started. But during his administration party work started under Jefferson's leadership and was so efficient that Adams was defeated for re-election.

---

[5] The Alien Act of June 1789 authorized the President to order deported all aliens regarded as dangerous or suspected of treasonable inclinations.

The Sedition Act of July made it unlawful to enter into unlawful combinations opposing the execution of laws or to aid any insurrection, riot, unlawful assembly or combination. Fines and imprisonment were prescribed for persons convicted of publishing any "false, scandalous, or malicious writing" bringing disrepute to the United States government, Congress, or the President.

Twenty-five persons were prosecuted and ten convicted—all Republicans.

This might be taken to show that political sensitivity is not essential for a first election but that it is for a second. But there is more to the Adams tragedy than this. He was the victim of a sweeping change, one that he did not understand and would always resent. He had a sharper intelligence than Jefferson and was morally Burr's superior; he was as far from being a popular idol as Hamilton; he was, indeed, far from wanting to be. Like Hamilton, he thought the people untrustworthy. They needed to be led and disciplined by those who were fitted for it by education, experience, and demonstration of fitness. They ought to recognize this and accept the direction of their betters. Their betters, it will be noticed, were not necessarily aristocrats. Washington belonged to a respectably second-rate landed family; and although Adams was a New England intellectual, he had come of a line of plain farmers, none of whom had been a leader or had shown unusual talent. But neither approved the passionate opposition to aristocracy of Sam Adams and Tom Paine, who were more representative of revolutionary ideas. There was a world of difference between John and his cousin Sam, the agitator who had been so hot for violent opposition to the British. John had been the cool and calculating lawyer, no less set on independence, but more reserved and respectable in his approach. Nevertheless, when it came to devising new institutions and arguing for new policies, John was relied on. He was a statesman. But with all his learning and his superior intelligence he was not fitted for political leadership.

The example of this early President showed clearly that those who assume the office but are unsuited for it will inevitably create tragedy for themselves and for the nation. But it was a lesson not learned. There were others to come, and some whose tragedies were more heartbreaking.

Adams was so humiliated and enraged by his defeat for re-election in 1800 that he refused to accompany Jefferson to the inaugural ceremonies, the only outgoing President who would ever do so for such a reason. He would live for twenty-five years in sullen and critical retirement, growing more and more crabbed. The single comfort of his old age was the career of his son, whom he would live to see in the President's House. That career would be no happier than his own had been, and for much the same reasons; but that he could not have known.

Perhaps it may be noted that in his very last years he was reconciled with Jefferson, with whom his disgust had been so uncontrollable; and one of the most thoughtful series of letters between American statesmen is that exchanged between them in age. They died on the same day in 1826. It was appropriate that it should have been the Fourth of July.

Thomas Jefferson
1743–1826

Born at Shadwell, Virginia
Became third President in 1801 at 57

HISTORY

1762	Graduated from William and Mary College.
1767	Admitted to the bar.
1768	Work begun at Monticello.
1769	Elected to the House of Burgesses.
1772	Married Martha Wayles Skelton (a widow).
1775–76	Member of the Second Continental Congress.
1776	Resigned from the Congress. Chairman of the committee to prepare Declaration of Independence. Elected to the Virginia House of Delegates.
1779	Elected Governor of Virginia.
1780	Re-elected Governor of Virginia.
1781	Resigned from Governorship.
1783	Elected to the United States Congress.
1784	Appointed Minister to France.

42

1785	Elected by the Congress to succeed Franklin as Minister to France.
1789	Appointed Secretary of State.
1793	Resigned as Secretary of State.
1796	Elected Vice-President.
1800	Elected President (Vice-President, Burr); opponents, Burr and Adams.
1804	Re-elected President (Vice-President, Clinton); opponent, Pinckney with King.
1809	Retired to Monticello.
1826	Died at 83.

THOMAS JEFFERSON rates as one of the cleverest practitioners of the political arts among the line of American Presidents. Only Jackson, Johnson, and the two Roosevelts can be compared with him. It is true that his first election was made easier by the ineptitude of John Adams—who, in addition to being a Federalist, seemed to have very little judgment about public opinion; even though it was the opinion of a small circle that counted most, he alienated them. But Jefferson in contrast abetted every circumstance favoring him. If history was on his side, he was always on the side of history.

The Federalists, who throughout the Washington and Adams administrations controlled the Congress, embroiled themselves with the French, who were by 1796 inclined to be contemptuous of the new nation they had helped to create. If possible, they were worse than the British about the impressment of American seamen and interference with commerce; and their envoys abused their diplomatic status and intrigued openly against Britain.

Washington did his best to be neutral in the war going on between the European giants; but he was so annoyed by the French representatives and so horrified by the revolutionary excesses in France that he found it difficult. Adams, following Washington, was formally neutral and had furiously opposed the British during his Ambassadorship. But he could not accept the horrors of revolution. Jefferson could. And since he could, he could use Adams' reluctance in his agitation against the Federalists and their President. This gradually became an appeal for violent opposition. And when Adams and the Congressional majority went so far as to pass the Alien and Sedition Acts their political credit was so diminished that they lost the Presidency and never regained it.

It might be noted that when these Acts were passed Washington was still alive and did not object. He disapproved the popular sentiment in favor of the French revolutionists; indeed, he had as little respect as Adams for popular attitudes in general. People ought to accept the judgment of their betters—that was the Federalist theory. Federalists evaded the question: Who are the betters? But in their own minds they had no doubts. In New England, they were the clergy, the professional practitioners, the large merchants, and the shipowners; in the South, they were the planters, the clergy, and others who had accumulated wealth. The clergy were perhaps the leaders among the Federalist stalwarts; but the merchants and planters were not far behind; and lawyers, as usual, were their representatives in political activity.

Jefferson usually defined himself as a deist or Unitarian. This infuriated the orthodox religionists of the Protestant sects so powerful in New England. But also he favored a society made up of small farmers, a kind of rural utopia, loosely organized, vigilant concerning individual rights, and eternally opposed to bigness in business or in agriculture. And there were more farmers than clergymen, lawyers, and merchants, even more who could vote under the restricted rules for suffrage. This gave him a constituency. If it could be activated it could be relied on.

Considering the size of the Monticello estate,[1] Jefferson's small-farmer position seems obviously a political one. He had a perennial quarrel with Hamilton, who believed in a strong centralized government and a well-disciplined people. They first exchanged words across Washington's Cabinet table, with Washington invariably coming down on Hamilton's side; and before the election of 1796, both had resigned to carry on their dispute by private agitation. Hamilton never concealed his views or his activities. Jefferson, then as always, preferred to be devious, to work through others—Madison and Monroe, for instance, and even such extremists as Freneau, the journalist. Only the Democratic-Republican insiders knew the extent of Jefferson's direction of partisan tactics from an ostentatious "retirement" at Monticello.

In 1796, Jefferson had to be content with second place. Washington's influence was still too strong to be overcome, and Democratic-Republican agitation had not yet had time to persuade a majority that Federalism was obsolete. Even then, however, it could be seen what way the drift was tending. The trouble with the Federalists, as with reactionaries in all times and places, was their small numbers. Any extension of the electorate brought in an enlarged opposition. Jefferson's appeal to the common man—the small farmer, the mechanic—infuriated conservatives. Seventeen ninety-six was already a year of passion and internal dissension. But 1800 was to be even worse, because the Federalists would see the end of their regime in clear prospect and lose all restraint in frantic attempts to re-establish their position.

Jefferson's intrigues were largely responsible for Adams' decline in favor. But there was also involved Hamilton's active distaste for Adams and his frequent dissent about questions of policy; and Hamilton was the most active and influential leader of the party. He thought the Alien and Sedition Laws complete political folly—as did John Marshall. Adams, therefore, did not have very effective support for re-election even from some of his own party: New York in 1800 divided its electoral vote equally between Jefferson and Burr; Adams got none of the 24 votes.

---

[1] Its size varied at different times. It was, however, never small.

There was an unpleasant surprise waiting for Jefferson as well as Adams when the electoral votes were counted. Aaron Burr of New York had exactly the same number—73—as Jefferson. Adams had 65 and was clearly defeated. But Burr had been intended by no one to be President. He had been the Democratic-Republican candidate for Vice-President.[2]

The peculiar operation of the Electoral College device (by which electors cast votes for two candidates and which was soon to be changed) had resulted in this tie. Burr should have resigned in Jefferson's favor, since it was clear that Jefferson was the intended President; but that was not the Burr way. Chance had placed him in a position to bargain for the nation's highest office, and the temptation was too strong. There followed a confused episode. The election was thrown into the House of Representatives by constitutional provision. The Federalists then tried to make a bargain with Jefferson; they would vote for him if he would continue Federalist financial policies, keep their officeholders, and maintain a strong navy.

This proposition was put to him by Adams himself; but Jefferson refused. There followed thirty-six ballots, during which the politicking was as intense as any later smoke-filled room ever saw. In the end, Bayard, one of the Federalists, cast a blank ballot, along with others from Vermont and Maryland, and thus gave Jefferson a majority. Hamilton, who disliked Jefferson but regarded Burr as impossible, was largely responsible for persuading his Federalist friends to vote for Jefferson. The Burr-Hamilton enmity was not new; but this incident exacerbated it.

So Jefferson and the Democratic-Republicans replaced Adams and the Federalists. Jefferson did not succeed in putting his ruralistic political philosophy into practice. The small farmer continued to be at a disadvantage, and business got such a momentum that it could never afterward be effectively subdued. Nevertheless, popular sovereignty had been reaffirmed. The change sometimes seemed to be from one of arrogant discipline to one of demagogic persuasion; but it could never afterward be questioned that the popular will was supreme.

That will might be a manipulated one, but there was always the possibility that it might reject efforts to manage it. In Jackson's day, its power would be crudely exercised, a reaction to be repeated several times when conservatives went too far in favoring business. Nevertheless, a major theme in American history would be the gradual accretion of power by industrialists and financiers. There would be periods when that power would be challenged (by Jackson, for instance, and by Bryan), sometimes successfully and sometimes not. Even when it was,

---

[2] Designated in spring by a Congressional caucus.

the champions of the people lacked the ability to establish effective controls, and presently progress toward business autonomy was resumed.

Jefferson was the first of several Presidents who, although honored in our history, did not actually understand the basic drift of American society and so appealed to a phantom symbolism. It might almost be said that American society was allowed to be shaped by blind forces. Its institutions were seldom created for any positive reason. They were nearly always intended to correct abuses grown so flagrant as to be intolerable. The interests to be controlled, in these instances, were invariably well entrenched in the Congress; and when they could not prevent attritions, they usually succeeded in diffusing or diverting them. So controls were never very effective. The rooting of the industrialists' influence in the fabric of government finally became an accepted virtue. We became a capitalist nation as well as a capitalist society.

It has to be said that this development began as Jefferson maneuvered for the Presidency. His hazy vision of a country devoted to agricultural pursuits formed a screen the Hamiltonian forces could work behind with perfect freedom. He was a political theorist and a lawyer. Under his influence the young nation adopted democratic manners but actually favored the moneyed interests. The Jeffersonian equality was not economic; it was all political. But it carried popular approval.

He had a fairly humble, but yet respectable, origin. His father died when Jefferson was fourteen,[3] and his journey to Williamsburg to begin his education was begun on horseback with his few possessions in a pack. Actually, as the eldest son (in a family of ten children) he had inherited the family farm. His mother was a Randolph, and so he belonged to a first family. But the farm, east of the Blue Ridge and on one of its foothills, had been cut out of the wilderness by his father, and Jefferson was always cramped because it produced so little cash. It was only by economical management and some skimping that he succeeded in his intention to become a lawyer.

At William and Mary College he was an absorbed student, ranging widely in his reading, achieving competence in the classics, in mathematics, and in philosophy. We also hear of him, as became his Randolph heritage, sitting with the Governor's company at dinner and conversing gravely with the elders. He was tall, thin, and sandy-haired; he was studious and clever, and his poverty was somehow minimized. He played the violin and talked well, as he would always do, of nature, of plantation management, and of public affairs. If his dress was plain, his manners were not.

---

[3] It must have seemed by then that a widowed mother was a necessity—both Washington and Adams had lost their fathers early.

The young man's progress from Williamsburg days would have been spectacular if it had not been so naturally undertaken and so quietly accomplished. He became a lawyer, a legislator, a Governor, and a diplomat. Even though his philosophy, when it developed, stood in complete contrast to that of his fellow lawyers and plantation owners, he appeared to be the personification of the Virginia gentleman. Like other upper-class Virginians, he wanted independence. But, unlike them, he was able to accept the "democratic excesses" to which independence would lead. He even believed in universal suffrage, which was far from gentlemanly. In a letter in 1800 (to Jeremiah Moor) he said: ". . . my opinion has always been in favor of it [universal suffrage] . . . I believe we may lessen the danger of buying and selling votes, by making the number of votes too great for any means of purchase: I may further say that I have not observed men's honesty to increase with their riches." But these were mature thoughts. He gave no offense to the company he sat with in Williamsburg as a student, nor for many years afterward.

Between his years of education and apprenticeship and his strike for the Presidency, Jefferson's faith in democracy was deepened and widened not only by his experiences at home but by years of residence abroad, mostly in France, where, unlike Adams, he developed a deep sympathy for the revolution. This carried over when he came back to be Washington's Secretary of State and was often the cause of difference between himself and the Federalist leaders—even Washington. And it was involved in his resignation from the Cabinet and his subsequent election first as Vice-President and then as President.

But besides his service abroad, he had behind him by 1800 election and re-election to the Governorship of Virginia and election to the Congress. Even before that he had been a member of the Continental Congress and—one of his best-known services—drafter of the Declaration of Independence.

He might also have written the final draft of the Constitution since he was so skilled, but he was abroad at the time (as was Adams) and could take no part. This, for his political ambition, was fortunate. He was able to say that he disapproved some of its provisions—the less "democratical" ones. But this he made no particular point of at the time and was able to take an oath to preserve it. It was in subtler disparagements of its operations that his disapproval was made known.

When he began seriously to assume the opposition leadership, he was fully matured and at the height of his influence. No cleverer candidate ever coveted the Presidency. There is no other who, in some respect, is not made to appear culturally deficient by comparison. It was no more than justified to call him "the sage of Monticello." That Monticello, by the way, was perpetually in process of becoming a finished product, embodying the new ideas Jefferson had gathered and pondered in France and elsewhere abroad. It is interesting that he operated a nail factory as well as farms and that it helped materially in paying the heavy expenses of maintenance. Even with slavery the estates hardly maintained themselves; and the improved practices, the machinery, and the newly introduced crops did not cause it to prosper. Like others of his sort, Jefferson was on the verge of bankruptcy most of his life.

His domestic life was saddened by the death of his wife in 1782; and his daughters' and his grandchildren's affection was no very good substitute. But money shortage and domestic sorrows seem to have been muted troubles. His fertile mind, ranging among his various proficiencies, and his eternal passion for the manipulation of public opinion were the sustainers of his life. He designed houses for his friends—as well as, later on, a campus for the University of Virginia. He was, for many years, President of the Philosophical Society founded by Franklin. He experimented with household gadgets; he wrote about botany, paleontology, and other scientific subjects; and altogether he had a full and satisfying life. The Presidency seems to us now to have been a natural climax.

The years preceding the election of 1800 are crowded with interest. As is true of all professionals, every activity was one calculated to forward his ambition. During the Congressional sessions, he presided over the Senate as Adams' Vice-President; but adjournment came early in spring, and from then until autumn he was usually at Monticello. In Washington, he lived in a boardinghouse, as members of the Congress often did in those days. Their families seldom came with them to the swampy, malarial city on the Potomac, whose streets were not paved and where there were more vacant lots than buildings. Jefferson ate at a common table with Democratic-Republican colleagues. That he was the leader, however, no one doubted. It was not evident in his dress, in his courteous manner, or in the display of Vice-Presidential perquisites. But unmistakable respect was shown for his adroit political suggestions. Democratic-Republicanism centered in him and it was rapidly forming an opposition to Federalism.

Jefferson made no speeches; but his conversations with supporters were frequent and intimate. These were not the people themselves; they were the leaders—demagogues, the Federalists said. But it has to be recalled that the demagogues had to address themselves, not to "the mob," as conservatives were always saying, but to a middle-income group. "The mob" could not vote.

When the Constitution went into effect, property qualifications had existed in all thirteen states. By 1800 there had been some progress toward widened suffrage; but Jefferson's constituents all had to be

persons who paid taxes. The qualifications were not specified in the
Constitution other than that they must be the same as those required
for electors of "the most numerous branch of the state legislature."
But no state had adopted universal male suffrage. Only eight had
abandoned property qualifications.

Jefferson's strategy was guided by this restriction. Whether he
would have liked to appeal to "the mob" or not, he was limited to
taxpayers; and this eliminated at least 25 per cent of adult males.

But the small farmers, especially those on the deep frontiers, the
tradesmen, and skilled workmen were open to his persuasion. The
trend toward widening would go on until, in Jackson's time, universal
male suffrage would be within sight. But such a constituency was not
available to Jefferson.

Most of the workers in Jefferson's enormous informal organization
had never seen or talked with him; yet its operations became daily
more effective. It would grow finally into such overwhelming numbers
that it would carry everything before it and persist for two decades.
He had for close associates the Virginians Madison and Monroe, almost
extensions of himself; in the various states there were such figures as
Gallatin and McKeon in Pennsylvania, George Clinton and Burr in
New York, John Taylor and Charles Pinckney in the Carolinas; and
below these there were the local bosses. Some of these were agitators
who spoke to farmers' meetings in the villages or to tradesmen in city
meeting rooms; some were pamphleteers; more were behind-the-scenes
manipulators of a sort so familiar in all political machines, workers at
the local level, arranging favors in exchange for votes, promising
patronage, and whispering scurrilous rumors about their opponents. It
was a deeply rooted organization.

His long campaign involved the fomenting of hate for the gentry, a
hate natural to frontier farmers and tradesmen who were at a disadvantage with big competitors. In inns, in country stores, and on the
streets of small towns, the grass-roots agitation never stopped. Jefferson's own correspondence with local leaders was enormous, and that of
his lieutenants was almost as large. This kind of operation was not new
in America—it is reminiscent of the Committees of Correspondence so
effective in pre-revolutionary days—but it was being used now by a
master politician reaching for power.

One of Jefferson's advantages was that of being the leader of a
cause. All political leaders like to regard their campaigns as causes, and
they are frequently blown up into "crusades." Jackson did this and
others followed, with less convincingness, right down to Eisenhower.
Eventually there would be a certain skepticism about the exalted
messianic role claimed for themselves by ambitious politicians; but in
1800 voters had not become immune by long usage. The Federalists,

from whom the nation had to be saved, had after all just been represented in the Presidency by Washington and Adams. They had leanings toward centralized government, with its administering confined closely to an elite, and were frightened by violent partisanship. But it was hard to contend that they were not patriots or that they meant to subvert the Bill of Rights. Washington might have put on some airs, and Adams might have tried to enlarge his dignities unduly; but they had given the new nation direction, they had sealed the Union, and they had held off foreign aggressors. Jefferson in power would have the same problems, and he would meet them with the same determination, even if with different devices. But to become President he had to pillory his predecessors and create the impression of a callous ruling class and a downtrodden people. He succeeded so well that Americans to this day frequently accept the same illusions that his contemporaries were so passionately convinced were facts.

The Federalists—as conservatives are so apt to do—accepted the terms of the struggle as he imposed them. They behaved in such ways as to confirm his most exaggerated claims. The result of this was that he not only had a cause of unusual emotional potential, but he also soon had enemies. If there is anything a democratic Presidential candidate needs as badly as to become the distinctive representative of a popular movement, it is a foil, a group of opposing politicians who can be excited and enraged by his effrontery. When they are thus agitated they become extreme and lose both temper and judgment. They appear to be exactly what the instigator says they are—enemies of popular causes, heartless exploiters, monopolists of power and office. They can be overcome only by a hero. And he is highly visible.

It was Jefferson's ultimate cleverness that he did not personally claim to be the needed St. George who would slay the dragon of Federalist privilege. His followers did it for him. They were carefully coached; their scripts were written for them; their every movement was calculated. Jefferson, however, appeared to be quietly presiding over the Senate, walking to and from his boardinghouse and taking his meals in pleasant company; or he was tending his estate at Monticello with his numerous grandchildren about him, conspicuously "retired" from political affairs. If he had been out in the open, he would have had to oppose Washington, Adams, Hamilton, Marshall, Jay, and other persons of enormous prestige. Washington especially was difficult to diminish in 1799; but even after his death he would be as formidable, almost, as he had been in life, so sacred was he among Americans. Yet he was first disparaged and then attacked, and he had retired a discouraged man. Adams did not have Washington's monumental popular reputation; and besides, he was an unattractive figure, corpulent, testy, opinionated, and always ready to instruct. But he had the Adams mind, and tangling with an Adams had seldom proved profitable. Hamilton stood in the background, the strong man of the Federalists. He too worked through persuasion and maneuver, with an enormous correspondence and a machine with governmental powers. But he was more apt to be drawn into controversy, as Jefferson never could. Hamilton's cleverness as a pamphleteer was always tempting him to go too far, so that he incurred reverse reactions. Jefferson bided his time, compared notes with his lieutenants, watched the Federalists rant and rave, and directed his orators and pamphleteers as they went about getting him ready for the President's House.

The most effective performance for the Federalists was that of the New York and New England divines. They reached extremes only professional orators could hope to equal. One William Linn of New York said Jefferson was plainly an infidel and a menace to true religion; he pictured a government headed by him in this way: "Infidels will surround him . . . Let him spend the sabbath in feasting, in visiting or receiving visits, in riding abroad, but never going to church; and frequent public worship will become unfashionable. Infidelity will become the prattle from the highest to the lowest condition of life . . ." He went on, as did others, to accuse Jefferson of every thinkable crime, *The Gazette of the United States* being their most used vehicle.

But the calumniators always got around to accusing him of being a conspirator, a fomenter of strife; and finally concentrated on a fulminating denunciation of democracy, saying that it was synonymous with anarchy, civil war, and desolation. "No wise man but discerns its imperfections . . . no honest man but proclaims its fraud," said one editor. Virginia was full of "mad democrats," a Bostonian wrote. And so it went, rising to a climax at election time. Jefferson, finally, became what he had intended to be—the representative democrat—made so by his accommodating enemies.

This, it will be seen, is the perfect model of a campaign, and as such deserves the most serious study. It is recommended as the first and almost the best of all the long line. It depended on perfect strategy and careful handling of tactics. It protected its principal, exposed only subordinates, and goaded the enemy to an extremism which lost more votes than "the cause" earned. It landed its conceiver and contriver in the White House and kept him there as long as he wanted to stay. And it cast his shadow far down into subsequent history. The next three Presidents would be more his successors than leaders in their own right.

There have been other first-rank politicians in our Republic, but none more deserving of our respect or more followed by aspirants than the Jefferson who led the Federalists into his carefully baited trap in 1800.

James Madison
1754–1836

Born at Port Conway, Virginia
Became fourth President in 1809 at 58

HISTORY

1772	Finished his education at Princeton with a postgraduate year.
1776	Member of the Williamsburg convention to draft a state constitution and the Virginia Declaration of Rights.
1776	Elected to the Virginia Assembly. Met Jefferson for the first time.
1778	Elected to the Virginia State Council.
1779	Elected by the Virginia Assembly to the Continental Congress.
1787	Delegate to the Constitutional Convention in Philadelphia.
1788	Member of the Virginia Ratifying Convention.
1789	Elected to the United States House of Representatives.
1794	Married Dolly Payne Todd.
1801	Became Jefferson's Secretary of State.
1808	Elected to the Presidency. (Vice-President, George Clinton); opposing ticket, C. C. Pinckney and Rufus King.

1812	Re-elected (Vice-President, Gerry); opponent, De Witt Clinton.
1817	Retired to Montpelier in Virginia.
1829	Delegate to the Virginia Constitutional Convention.
1836	Died at Montpelier.

THERE ARE SOME PEOPLE who, when they hear the name Madison, think of the War of 1812 and the disgrace of an invaded Washington with most of its public buildings burned; there are others who think of him as Washington Irving described him "—ah, poor Jeemy— he is but a withered little apple-john." But for our purpose here this depreciation is out of place. He did attain the Presidency, after having helped in creating the new nation. He was also re-elected. He was one of the most influential of the small number who shaped our institutions —after John Adams perhaps the most influential. He belonged among those who, following Jefferson, deplored the Federalist shape it seemed to be taking and worked for more equality and less control by the elite. It was fitting that he should succeed Jefferson in the Presidency. If he was withered, it was late in life.

He ardently desired the office; but so have most men in politics who felt they had a chance. It is expected, a tradition started by Jefferson. The individual who feels the call and does not pursue it denies himself a democratic right and others the opportunity of selection. It is not for him to say that he shall not gain the prize; it is for his fellow citizens to make that decision. They expect him to offer his past career and his future promise and to ask for judgment as to whether these are good enough. This is the Jeffersonian attitude.

It is true that able and upright men have often been unwilling to seek office. They would rather not be involved in the degrading activities that seem to them necessary for success. And it must be admitted that the political processes of democracy do often involve compromise, favoritism, and even corruption. That they need not, we can learn from Washington and some others. That such conditions do exist may be the result of a dogma never quite abandoned—the dogma of literal equality.

Jefferson, under the influence of the French Revolution, accepted this, and Madison, of course, was Jefferson's colleague. The Jeffersonians themselves were superior men with curiously low standards of public morality. They intrigued and bargained for office; they created and ran a corrupt political machine; they began the disparagement of the elite that would come to a climax with Jackson.

But Jefferson was a persuasive boss. He stayed in the background, taking advantage of processes he would not engage in himself. Madison was closer to the operating machinery. But even he was less a participant than a manager.

When Jefferson retired, the organization could keep itself intact only if it went on as it had been. Madison would not disturb it. Jefferson would have preferred Monroe; but when the party caucus opted for Madison he did not strenuously object. Madison's qualifications were not to be questioned. He had not only helped to form the government and served in its legislature, but had been Secretary of State. No one knew the Presidency better or had clearer ideas about its functioning.

It may be doubted, however, whether by 1808 these were the most influential reasons for his election. The widening of the electorate, begun before the old century ended, had progressed. Even taxpaying qualifications had been abandoned in New Hampshire in 1792 and in Georgia in 1798. And the one-third of the adult white males who were disfranchised when the Constitution was adopted was now reduced to perhaps one-fifth. There really was a popular vote.

It had not needed so considerable a reduction to defeat the Federalists. But the continuing trend had made it certain that they would never come back to power. Jefferson had taken advantage of this tidal movement, and so long as it went on rising it would maintain the Jeffersonians in power. Even when Jackson brought the frontier farmers and villagers into full play against the second Adams the quarrel was within the Democratic-Republican party. Jackson might be said to have re-established Jeffersonian democracy after some years of gradual erosion.

Madison was no Jackson—that is to say, he was not a popular hero, known in every gathering of citizens. But the powerful sponsorship of Jefferson was enough. The Democratic-Republican machine needed only word from Jefferson that Madison was acceptable. But the organization had little to do to elect him. The Federalists were reduced to impotence.

When Madison was Presidential candidate, he was not the same handsome figure he had been some years before. A life of continuous scholarly labor, exhausting discussion with contemporaries, and hard work, with little assistance, as Secretary of State had changed his appearance; but his luminous intelligence was unimpaired. He was no longer forceful; he had been subservient too long.

It has to be said that he altogether lacked that valuable characteristic of national leaders—presence. And it was a time when presence was especially needed. The nation was still weak, still treated with disrespect by the larger nations on all the borders; and its largely illiterate electorate was reluctant to accept any discipline at all beyond that needed for local order. And a government that asked for taxes to support large policies was suspect.

Jefferson's encouragement of these views had enlarged and spread them until they had become dangerous to the national security. There were by now no armed forces of any account, for instance, and foreign relations had to be conducted with no other support than reason, something the British, the French, and the Spanish ignored. And they were pressing.

But the election of 1808 was not affected by this weakness, which was, if anything, regarded as a virtue—because it was cheap and because it did not involve a strong central government to "interfere." Madison had helped Jefferson in bringing about the conditions that would make his own election easy.

He had several advantages; Jefferson would support him with the party machine not only for election but during his administration. He had assistance from the new elite of the Democratic-Republicans that by now so much resembled that of the old Federalists—and in fact included some of them or their descendants. (John Quincy Adams was one of these.) Then his long experience as a Congressman and Cabinet member made him at home with the upper level of bureaucracy, and when he appointed James Monroe to be his Secretary of State he not only ensured continued liason with Jefferson but brought his only real rival into his official family. What resources there were he knew about, and he was fully aware of the developing crisis he must face.

But he also had a helper by now well known to everyone and widely admired. This was his wife Dolly; who may possibly be set down as an instance of a luck regarded by his friends as unusual throughout his career. But when it is recalled that Dolly was the daughter of a boardinghouse keeper in Philadelphia, it has about it a suspicion of design—Dolly's design, perhaps, although Madison seems to have asked Burr to arrange their first meeting. At any rate, no man ever had a more valuable asset. "Little Jeemy," in his late fifties may have been shrunken and quite without sparkle, may have had a thin voice which fell away at the end of his sentences, and may often have seemed abstracted, almost distrait, but in his early forties he had been able to court Dolly successfully and had kept her devotion throughout a long marriage. There was either something *to* him or Dolly made something *of* him. The surviving stories of her opulent beauty and unfailing good nature make her seem far more glamorous than most of her successors in the President's House. Only Frances Cleveland and Jacqueline Kennedy would match her as an asset to a Presidential husband.

When Jefferson was picking a successor, as he could do without hindrance, Dolly must have been in his mind almost as much as James. He himself had presided over a lonely establishment except when one of his daughters came to visit; and they took no responsibility of the sort Dolly carried so competently. In fact, Dolly, when she was the wife of the Secretary of State, dressed them, advised them, and backed them up. She was nominally the second woman in Washington but actually came to be first in the second Jefferson term.

Jefferson was not really the plain man his show of commonness was meant to indicate. He had discriminating tastes, as anyone can see by looking at Monticello or the other houses he designed. But for political effect he made many sacrifices. He never finished or adequately furnished the President's House, for instance, and it remained for Dolly to do that when her husband succeeded Jefferson. It was a task that had to be done all over after the British burned it; but she presided as gracefully at Octagon House, where the Madisons moved temporarily, as she ever had in the mansion itself. The distraction and amusement she offered helped in the national forgetting after the humiliating war that might well have discredited Madison and the Democratic-Republicans.

Madison may have been, to a novelist's view, "a withered little apple-john" who looked like nothing at all beside his glowing wife in her Paris gowns and feathered headdress. But that was in the candlelit evenings, and that was not a political judgment. Actually he was clever in political maneuver, and, having worked with Jefferson himself so long, had acquired a vast experience. It is difficult now to determine whether Jefferson or Madison was responsible for the Virginians' long run of success.

Also, he had dealt continuously with foreign affairs since his youth; and his knowledge of constitutional law was superior to that of any man of his generation except John Adams. Then, too, he had the priceless habit of hard work. He slept little and often rose in the night to read, make notes, or finish a paper that was on his mind. And although he was no orator, he was extremely effective in discussion. The clarity of his mind and the orderliness of his exposition made up for a lack of floridity such as others possessed.

It was lucky that the little man who was five feet six and a fraction, who hesitated when he spoke, and who was so reluctant to attempt the oratory of politics, did not have to make a campaign such as would later become customary. A head for strategy, a shrewd appraisal of possibilities, a diligent cultivation of the Democratic-Republican local leaders—these sufficed.

One lesson we can learn from him is obvious. We have already learned part of it from John Adams. It is that it is not necessary to have the classic appearance of a Roman statesman; it is not necessary to be loquacious; it is enough to have a powerful sponsor and to follow faithfully the professional path to preferment.

Madison's running mates were George Clinton in his first election and Elbridge Gerry in his second. The men he defeated were Charles Cotesworth Pinckney and De Witt Clinton. It is about this time that we must begin to concern ourselves with defeated candidates—and with minor characters in general who have had parts in the historical drama which is always unfolding about the Presidency. These have their lessons for us, no less than those who succeeded.

George Clinton, for instance, who was the other Democratic-Republican candidate in 1808 and who can therefore be said to have run with Madison the first time, had already been Vice-President under Jefferson, and he was as well known as any public figure in the young nation. He was a native New Yorker who had served in the revolutionary army, had been a member of the Continental Congress, had been repeatedly Governor of New York, and had opposed the adoption of the Constitution on much the same grounds as afterward emerged in Jefferson's appraisals. As early as 1792 he had had some Democratic-Republican support for the Vice-Presidency. And when the Federalists had tried to elect John Jay to the Governorship in his place they had failed. This demonstrated Clinton's hold on his New York electorate, something so shrewd a politician as Jefferson was not likely to overlook.

It was convenient to substitute another New Yorker for Aaron Burr in 1804 and to continue him in 1808. As a political possibility, Clinton rather than Madison might have succeeded Jefferson; but the Virginians were unwilling to let go their hold, and specifically Jefferson regarded Madison's selection as a perpetuation of his own regime. Then, too, in 1808 Clinton was visibly growing old. He was sixty-nine to Madison's fifty-seven, and a rather heavy and overblown sixty-nine. But the choice of Clinton, both in the 1804 and 1808 elections, as the Vice-Presidential candidate offers an early illustration of what was later a customary practice—the use of the secondary office to strengthen the principal candidate's bid. There are various ways of using this device. Washington and Adams obviously appealed to two widely different electorates; Jefferson and Madison, in their choice of running mates, were following a precedent. But the Clinton election was an improvement. There was no hope of winning Massachusetts away from the Federalists by choosing a Massachusetts candidate; but there was a hope—and it had some success—of winning New York. And New York did at least split, 13 to 6 electoral votes.

Madison won easily in 1808. But in 1812 he did not win quite so easily. For one thing, George Clinton had died and the substitution of Gerry from Massachusetts did not help because New England could not be won anyway. But it was of more importance that, as the maneuvering for the nomination began, a crisis in foreign affairs was rapidly developing. Madison had followed Jefferson in trying to maintain a neutral policy as the European powers quarreled. But Napoleon was now reaching toward vaster conquests and Britain was rising to the challenge. Both were ruthless and neither saw any reason to consider the rights of so small and helpless a nation as the United States in another and distant part of the world.

The Federalists were by 1812 a war party; but their war would have been against France. To "protect American commerce," so important to New England, they had long advocated a big navy. Jefferson and Madison had sympathies for revolutionary France; but these sympathies did not run to intervention. And they allowed the armed forces almost to disappear. Madison's policy has sometimes been called a vacillating one; but what that means is that he tried to use diplomacy as a substitute for the threats he could not make.

The war Madison had to take responsibility for was one his predecessors had avoided by vigilance, by accepting humiliations without number, and by coldly appraising the young nation's strength rather than its temperature. There was usually a war party with more or less influence, and the Presidents and their Secretaries of State were always holding off foreign aggressions at the same time that they refused to be drawn into commitments they could not meet and did not want to prepare for. There had been twenty years of this when Madison sought election. There were now seventeen states; and Tennessee and Ohio in the then West had become the swing districts. They wanted war. He could not suppress or quiet the "War Hawks" led by Kentucky's Henry Clay. The more conservative East was overborne and the President—as other Presidents after him would do—gave in. In an unusual poetic response to the stimulation, he said that he would "throw forward the flag of the country, sure that the people would press forward to defend it."

That this was, in the circumstances, extreme folly cannot be denied. The nation had few well-trained military men, the barest skeleton of an army and navy, obsolete equipment, and depleted credit. What happened was strictly to be expected by anyone not deluded by such oratory as Clay and his colleagues were spouting so prodigally.

The beginning of the war cannot be said to have been undertaken very nobly or wisely. Madison made no effective defense against the clamor of the War Hawks, especially Clay and Calhoun, who day by day assailed the British to embarrass the President. The Federalists would be the gainers from this agitation within the Democratic-Republican party unless Madison gave in to the loud demands of his own supporters.

He did give in, however, before a decision had to be made on the Democratic-Republican nominee, and as a result was unanimously designated by the caucus held in May of 1812. In giving in, however, he had risked offending those who were opposed to war. These were the Eastern commercial interests. There was now a division between

East and West, with the South staying Jeffersonian; this pattern would often recur.

It was noticed that when the caucus was held in the spring of 1812 New York members did not attend. And presently opposition to Madison was manifested. Later in May a caucus of the New York State legislature put forward De Witt Clinton, who was a Democratic-Republican as his uncle had been. It was intended that he should run as an independent; but the Federalists, now reduced to a shadow, adopted him. They were ready to support even a Clinton if he could repair their fortunes—and if he was opposed to war with Britain. In September, at a conference of party leaders from eleven states, he was designated as the Federalist candidate, with Jared Ingersoll for Vice-President.

The campaign was one between the war and peace parties, and war won. War practically always wins. It may be foolishly undertaken, it may promise few results even if successful, and may be utterly beyond the national capacity; but it is invariably a political success until it is over. It elected Madison, and it defeated Clinton. From this experience the conclusion began to be borne in on the professionals that bombastic xenophobia pays. When Clinton, on the peace side, lost, it was the needless end of a career. He, rather than Monroe, might well have succeeded Madison in 1816. There was no great appeal in Monroe's bid, considering his past; and Clinton was an extremely popular figure. He had had a long secondary political career, but the support of the Federalists and his advocacy of peace when the drums were beating and the flags flying were fatal.

The Federalists carried New England for Clinton (except Vermont); Clinton's own popularity won New York; and New Jersey went to the Federalists because the legislature disregarded the popular vote and chose electors who voted for Clinton. As it was, Clinton had 89 electoral votes to Madison's 128.

Whether the same result would have been registered if the humiliations of the next three years could have been foreseen, no one can say. Military excitement allows no dissent. The national ego protects itself against reality much as an individual's does. What Madison thought of himself for having capitulated to the War Hawks, no one knows. He was re-elected; and in politics victory blots out the past with all its doubts about the means used to attain the desired result.

The outcome of the war was not so unfavorable to the United States as is often argued. Canada was not captured, it is true; but the West was conceded by the British and a century of expansion was made possible. Andrew Jackson, who had been selected to defend New Orleans, was given the chance to whip the same British army that had burned Washington. This made him a hero. The victory came well after peace had been made; nevertheless, it dimmed the memory of dismal defeats along the Canadian border and went some way toward excusing Madison for the disgrace of abandoning Washington to the British and seeing the Capitol and the White House burned.

The peace treaty, signed at Ghent, settled nothing. The issues made so much of by the War Hawks were not even mentioned in it. Canada, which brash untrained armies had set out to conquer, remained British. But as soon as the war stopped, a wave of prosperity drowned the wave of recriminations before it could swell to dangerous size.

Aside from any such consideration, Madison's espousal of war has to be recognized as a strategic move. To put oneself at the head of a developing popular cause is the second best of all ways to the Presidency. The first and very best is, of course, to be a Washington, the father of a people. But the next is to be the hero of a movement. Madison, in doing this, became something more than a successor to Jefferson.

James Monroe
1758–1831

Born in Westmoreland County, Virginia
Became fifth President in 1817 at 59

HISTORY

1780	Studied law with Jefferson after courses at William and Mary and service in the war with Washington.
1782	Elected to the Virginia Assembly.
1783	Elected to the Continental Congress.
1786	Present at the Annapolis Conference.
1787	Elected to the Virginia Assembly.
1789	Defeated by Madison for election to the First Congress.
1790	Elected to the United States Senate.
1794	Appointed Minister to France.
1799	Elected Governor of Virginia.
1803	Sent by Jefferson on a mission to France.
1810	Elected to the Virginia Assembly.
1811	Again Elected Governor of Virginia. Resigned Governorship to become Madison's Secretary of State.

1814	Became Secretary of War as well as State.
1816	Elected to the Presidency (Vice-President, Tompkins); opponent, Rufus King.
1820	Almost unanimously re-elected; only 1 adverse vote for J. Q. Adams (Vice-President, Tompkins).
1831	Died impoverished in New York.

O N OCTOBER 3, 1817, John Quincy Adams, recently returned from eight years abroad as a diplomat, and about to assume office as Secretary of State in Monroe's Cabinet, wrote the following passage in his diary:

> I had visits this morning from Mr. Levett Harris, Mr. Nourse, the Registrar of the Treasury, and Mr. Correa da Serra, the Portuguese Minister. Harris had just returned from visits to Mr. Jefferson, Mr. Madison, and President Monroe, and Correa was going to pay them. Correa says he calls them the Presidential Trinity. . . .

Ambassadors, if they are to further the interests of the governments they represent, need to be thus realistic. The Presidency from Jefferson's accession in 1801 until the end of Monroe's second term in 1825 was a trinitarian affair, and the Portuguese Minister knew what he was doing in consulting all three. Neither Madison nor Monroe made many consequential decisions without at least consulting with Jefferson. The decision for war had had Jefferson's acquiescence even if it had been reluctant. And it must be recalled that Monroe was Madison's Secretary of State (and became, in 1814, Secretary of War as well); it was a collaboration of long standing with Jefferson the respected senior.

Madison was eight years younger than Jefferson; Monroe was seven years younger than Madison. Their accessions to the Presidency exhibit the regularity normal to the differences in their ages: Jefferson was fifty-seven, Madison fifty-eight, and Monroe fifty-nine. When J. Q. Adams should succeed Monroe at fifty-seven, a norm would seem to have been established. These were in fact somewhat, but not notably, above the average (a little over fifty-five years).

Everyone interested in the American past must wish he could have seen the three Jeffersonians in company. To have watched them walking on the Pennsylvania Avenue of their day—not much more than a dusty or muddy village road—would have been something to remember. Jefferson and Monroe were much alike in looks; both were tall, rangy, and rawboned. Madison, between them, would have seemed deceptively insignificant. Actually his was the quickest intelligence of the three. One listening to a discussion among them would soon have discovered this. Jefferson would be the suggestive one, full of ideas, rather loose, ranging over a wide area. His was never a confined imagination; and he would be the least likely of the three to be limited by scruple in devising political schemes. Monroe would have been the slow one, lawyer-like, hesitant to conclude, but stubborn in argument. Madison's would have been the best-stocked memory, filled by long bouts of reading and close study; and his would have been the sharpest intelligence.

It may be suggested here that Madison's superior intelligence did not make him a better candidate or a better President than the other two. Most historians would probably rate him third in the area of action. It is something to take note of, that a high intelligence rating is not necessary for a Presidential aspirant. It does not follow that a high I.Q. is a disqualification, merely that other characteristics are necessary. Presumably they could be added ones as well as substitute ones; but this is something we may well explore after there is more evidence from other experiences as we go along. It could be that no really intelligent person could accommodate himself to the maneuverings and compromises necessary to political success; but we shall see. For now, simply note that a brilliant intellect is not a necessity.

Jefferson, Madison, and Monroe, with their different qualities, made a formidable trio; and now that it was Monroe's turn at the highest office, they had an enormous accumulated experience to call on. As we have noted, this experience was available and was used. When, too, it is recalled that J. Q. Adams was Monroe's Secretary of State, the whole must be admitted to have been an array of talent hardly equaled before or since. And Monroe was to be elected easily, to have a distinguished first term, and to go on quite easily into a second.

The ordeal of war was past; but the peace was to be exploited and the future of a vast nation charted; also, the old-world nations were to be put in their place. Monroe is, indeed, to later generations, one of the Presidents best known and most admired.

To understand how and why it was Monroe rather than someone else who became President in 1816, it is necessary to explore his early experiences. For instance, the companionship with Jefferson, so important to his success, began in his youth; and the identification with Virginia and then national, public life began as soon afterward as it very well could have begun. We must understand at once that besides the necessary sponsorship, he also had that inner-determined drive without which an ambitious politician seldom reaches the top, especially one who, like Monroe, was neither quick nor clever. He began to study law and administration with Jefferson (who was then Governor) when he was twenty-two; and when he was twenty-four he was elected to the legislature. This was the beginning of something that went on and on. Few politicians have been elected to so many different offices, and very few have been appointed to more different ones than Monroe subsequently occupied. He had all the experience anyone could have in public life.

The young man who started on this distinguished career by going to William and Mary College from the Oak Hill estate of his father in Westmoreland County would end, it is sad to say, in poverty and almost obscurity. Oak Hill would have gone to pay his debts. He would die an exile in New York City in the house of his son-in-law.

The end of Monroe, by the way, as of so many Presidents, raises a tantalizing question in the mind of the student. When the penalty of success was so often to reach old age in poverty and perhaps distress, what made the pursuit and the dedication so attractive? This question is discussed in another place and in a wider context. But we may note here that Monroe's is a conspicuous example of a neglect of former Presidents and Vice-Presidents that amounted almost to a punishment.[1]

A review of Monroe's career, like that of Madison, reveals a long dedication to public service through the law and politics. His was not a mind to cope with the elusive problems of constitution-building; but his advice was always sound and his loyalty beyond question. The Presidency was a normal culmination. He would be the last of the Jeffersonians, and he would preside over the last years of "good feeling."

Monroe's college years at William and Mary had been interrupted by war. In 1776 he went North as a First Lieutenant with the Third Virginia Infantry under orders of the Continental Congress. His regiment was to help Washington resist the British exploitation in New York of victory on Long Island. The march lasted a month in the heat and dust of back roads in full summer. He was under the immediate command of Captain William Washington; and in the same regiment John Marshall, later to be Chief Justice, was also a First Lieutenant. The regiment fought at White Plains and moved with the army across the river to Hackensack under British pressure—Lord Howe had 30,000 experienced troops to Washington's 16,000, and Washington was tormented by desertions, shortages, and lack of reinforcements—and on across New Jersey in autumn weather which was turning cold and rapidly became bitterly so. The British pursued, but cautiously, and Washington had time to collect the boats for the famous crossing of the Delaware.

Monroe's regiment was then sent to prevent British landings at Perth Amboy or New Brunswick, so he suffered all the hardship of that terrible winter retreat across New Jersey. On the night of December 11 the river was crossed. The operation was barely complete when the Hessians marched into Trenton with flags flying and music playing, in conspicuous contrast with the ragged rebels they were driving before them. But Washington did not accept defeat. Somehow his men found the fortitude to recross the icy Delaware at

---

[1] An Act of 1958 changed this situation somewhat by providing a pension of $25,000 and certain office expenses, but is still less generous than provisions for Justices and Generals who are allowed full salary until death.

Christmas time. The surprise of the Hessians was an incredible feat, made possible by the hardihood of such subordinates as William Washington, who was gravely wounded, and Monroe, who was hit but was luckily attended at once by a surgeon who "caught up the artery" and saved his life. The young man was not yet nineteen, but he was already a veteran of the Revolution's worst fighting.

After he recovered and had had a short leave, he became an aide to General Lord Stirling. He maintained this status until 1778, when some complication, not entirely clear, caused him to leave the army. He spent the winter in Philadelphia, where his uncle, Joseph Jones, was a member of the Congress. He may have been in financial trouble, since he had served without pay and had met all his own expenses. It is also guessed that he may have had an embarrassing love affair. He was certainly personable. The statue of him by Margaret Cresson now in the Monroe Law Office in Fredericksburg shows a clean firm jaw, a cleft chin, a pleasant mobile mouth, a prominent nose, and deeply hollowed eyes. It is the head of a responsible, thoughtful, but agreeable young man, sure of himself and ready for an important place in the world. He is known to have been a ladies' favorite—as Madison, for instance, was not.

Washington thought well of him. The Commander in Chief did in fact recommend him highly. In a letter to Colonel Archibald Cary, he mentioned a difficulty about introducing him "into the Continental line," but said that it was hoped that the state might enable him "to follow the bent of his military inclination." The General went on to say that if an event of that kind could take place it would give him particular pleasure.

A Lieutenant-Colonelcy in the militia followed; but the war was in its later stages and Virginia raised no more troops; so he stayed in Williamsburg, intending to study with George Wythe, who had been Jefferson's teacher. But it was then that he was made an aide to the Governor, who was Jefferson, and began a course of legal instruction.

Jefferson was notoriously lazy—one of John Adams' complaints about him—but, like many who are reputedly indolent, indefatigable in things that interested him. He thought the way to teach law was what later became familiar as the case-study method—as contrasted with Wythe's use of texts. He had real success with Monroe, at least, and, as often happens in such relationships, he became as much mentor as teacher. Monroe credited him with having taken over the direction of his life, and he was eternally grateful. It can be said that the debt was repaid with faithful service. The connection was never broken.

When Virginia was raided in 1780, he was made Colonel of an "emergency regiment," largely gathered by his own efforts. The regiment served with Steuben and Muhlenberg. The traitor, Benedict

Arnold, burned Richmond, and Lafayette was sent to oppose him. Cornwallis, retreating from the Carolinas, came up into Virginia; but Lafayette's able defense caused Cornwallis to take up the Tidewater position at Yorktown, where he was later trapped by Washington. As an incident of his movements, Cornwallis sent Tarleton to capture Jefferson at Monticello. Jefferson's escape was the occasion of a letter of congratulation from Monroe which seemed to ask for a military command. If this was his purpose he did not succeed, but spent the whole of the Yorktown period on one of his estates in King George County.

His neighbors in King George sent him as their Representative to the General Assembly in 1782. Jefferson congratulated him and said, answering a protest against his own withdrawal from Washington's Cabinet, "I have examined my heart to know whether it was thoroughly cured of every principal of political ambition." He found that after so many years, it was. "Public service and private misery are linked together," he said. Monroe probably did not take this any more seriously than Adams did. At any rate, he did not accept the withdrawal as a precedent for himself. He was just beginning his own government career. He had, in fact, been chosen to be a member of the Executive Council of the legislature.[2]

Monroe's military service deserves attention because this is a matter of importance to every ambitious politician in a war generation. To have a record of active participation is a real asset, and the lack of it a corresponding handicap. In Monroe's case, when he was a Presidential candidate many years later, Burr was to write slurringly of his record, saying that as a mere aide to Stirling he deserved no recognition for courage. This was obviously unfair; but by that time there was a later service to be cited as well as that with Washington; when the whole Federal government was demoralized in 1814, when the Generals disgraced themselves by their incompetence, and when President Madison was on the run, it was he who restored order and organized resistance.

Between the one service and the other, Monroe was repeatedly elected to the legislature, was a member of the Continental Congress and of the United States Senate, was twice Governor of Virginia, and was Minister to France, to Britain, and to Spain. Then in 1811, fateful year for the young nation, he became Madison's Secretary of State. He was a logical choice, considering his diplomatic service. He and Madison had perhaps been more rivals than friends, and he was not

---

[2] This Council of eight was important because post-Revolutionary legislatures were unwilling to allow Governors much power. A means for collaboration between the branches was necessary. Young John Marshall was a member of the Council at the same time. And he obviously meant to go on.

Madison's first choice; besides, he had not been conspicuously successful in his missions abroad. Still the appointment was owed him. He was
"the other Jeffersonian," one of the three, and destined to succeed
when Madison retired. Other considerations were not so important
as this.

He had made serious mistakes during Washington's Presidency. He
had been chosen as envoy to the new Republic of France because of
his connection with Jefferson, whose approval of French behavior was
well known, and had appeared in Paris just after the reign of terror
and the execution of Robespierre. On the stage of the National Convention, the President of that body embraced him; and he presented a
flag of the United States to hang with the tricolor of France. All
American conservatives, including Washington, were outraged by this
exhibition. They regarded the revolutionists with horror; and that an
envoy of their government should have been thus carried away by
sympathy with such a cause was an unforgivable offense. He was
presently recalled and came home indignant, so much so that when he
journeyed down into Virginia he deliberately passed Mount Vernon
without paying his respects. Also, he wrote a long tirade which not
only justified his own behavior but bitterly denounced Washington's
policies.

This last occurrence pleased Jefferson, naturally, and when he became President he again sent Monroe to Paris. On this occasion the
purchase of Louisiana was negotiated and some of Monroe's lost
prestige was recovered. It has to be noted, however, that he lost it
again in London when he negotiated a treaty that Jefferson refused
even to submit for ratification. That after this he emerged as Secretary
of State marks him as signally durable; and, indeed, durability was one
of his chief characteristics. In contrast with Jefferson, who always had
to act the common man and was never very convincing in the role,
Monroe had no need to act. He had no style, no flair. But he remained
steady. This gave him a reputation for reliability, always a most
important political asset. Voters on occasion like a man who seems to
them trustworthy and likely to stay put. Monroe was that kind of man.

There was an intellectual difficulty to be coped with as he
approached the Presidency: a complete reversal of Democratic-
Republican attitudes became necessary. Jefferson had been a states'-
rights man; but Madison and Monroe were forced by the expansion of
commerce and industry to become nationalists. Before Monroe succeeded Madison, Hamilton's Report on Manufactures had been
resuscitated and a protective tariff act had been passed; and in the
same year the Second Bank of the United States—modeled on Hamilton's—was established. The Democratic-Republican preference for
France and hatred of Britain were reversed, and outstanding contro-
versies were compromised.

Economic changes were transforming the country, and these political reverses were adjustments to the deeper movement. New England had been strongly separatist. That is to say, its adherence to the Union had been strongly tinged with a feeling that the states ought not to be controlled from any center in New York or Philadelphia. Now its manufacturers were finding that Federal tariffs were very useful.

On the other hand, Calhoun, who would presently become the loud expositor of states' rights in the South as the issues that were to cause the Civil War began to shape themselves, had been strongly nationalist. Calhoun himself had been one of the War Hawks who had given Madison no rest until he consented to fight for the national honor.

In fact, most of the statesmen—and all politicians—of the period spanning the War of 1812 would be unrecognizable by the end of Madison's administration. While Monroe was being fitted out for the Presidency, Jeffersonianism of the original school disappeared. Meade Minnegerode, in *Presidential Years, 1787–1860*,[3] commented on this:

> Except as surviving individuals, the Federalists had practically ceased to exist . . . Mr. Jefferson's Republicans were firmly in power—one faction or another seeking the advantage, the Livingstons, the Clintons, the followers of John Randolph, the new men in Congress, John Calhoun, Henry Clay—but now they were calling themselves Democrats, and it was a curious thing how Republican, how Federalist, almost, they had become with the years. . . .
>
> Mr. Jefferson's successors, in their mode of life, their social habits, and their intellectual attitude, had shown no lack of aristocratic instinct. The Madisons had restored the Presidential levees and pomps; the Monroes had brought fastidious elegance to their regime; the business of government remained primarily an occupation for gentlemen; the people at large had no more to do with it than the man in the moon.

Monroe, as Secretary of State, helped Madison formulate the policies of the New Nationalism, and it seemed to become the new men who so lately had been states'-righters and even proletarians. They were now interpreting the Constitution loosely. The Federal government could exercise many more powers than those specified for it—as John Marshall had said in some famous opinions that had infuriated Jefferson. In fact, Marshall, the old Federalist, who had been appointed by John Adams as a last lingering vestige of Federalism just as Jefferson came into office, was still Chief Justice. Madison and Monroe had made their peace with him. A long line of decisions was fixing the

[3] *N.Y.*, 1927, 126.

Federal powers at the maximum that could be needed for the nation's expansion. The jurisdiction of the states was being reduced to local matters.

That this should have been agreeable to Madison and Monroe does indeed seem a strange reversal. But besides economic changes at home, there were differences in the larger world before and after the dividing year of 1815. When the French and British made peace and the United States need no longer be torn between warring giants who respected no rights but their own, commerce could resume and grow.

Also, although the War of 1812 was in many ways ignoble from the American point of view, it had results which later caused it to be spoken of as a "second war of independence." At any rate, the nation suddenly seemed to assume a new stature. Because the pressures from abroad were removed, an entirely new orientation could take place. The domestic realignment was radical.

Cotton was King in the South and expanding westward. Because the crop was mostly sold abroad, its growers were free traders—just the opposite in interest, now, of the North. The Northwest was expanding and becoming politically important, and the trans-Appalachian country was filling up rapidly and exercising a fresh influence.

But all this was happening gradually. The new alignments would be seen to have hardened by Jackson's time. As Monroe succeeded Madison, there was a time of pause and retrospection. It was afterward called an "era of good feelings." This was deceptive; under the surface all of the antagonisms which were to break out in a fury of hatred within a decade were seething. But they were latent for Monroe. His electoral victories were to be notable for near unanimity—only one electoral vote would be registered against him in 1820—but it was a unanimity of puzzlement and indecision.

One reason for the deceptive political calm was that the divisions boiling up were within the Democratic-Republican party itself. The Federalists no longer were a party. Their unpatriotic behavior during the war had sometimes approached traitorousness, and this by itself would have discredited them. Federalism was, in fact, dead, never again to revive.

At any rate, whoever was the chosen candidate of the Democratic-Republicans was certain of election. Monroe had only to be put forward to win, and how could the protégé of Jefferson and Secretary of State to Madison be refused the nomination?

There was, nevertheless, some difficulty. King Caucus, as it was by now resentfully called, still prevailed. This custom of party legislators in the Congress meeting and choosing candidates had no legal justification, and it was resented by politicians in the states, who were frequently something less than friendly with the Washington legislators.

A substitute method—the party convention—would presently appear. But in Monroe's time Caucus was still King, and it was in the caucus that Monroe's pre-election troubles came.

There were two other contenders—Secretary of the Treasury Crawford of Georgia and Representative Henry Clay of Kentucky. These two had been among the advocates of war and its most determined supporters during Madison's administration. Crawford was much more popular than Monroe among the professional politicians. Against this undoubted preference, Monroe had the powerful support of both Madison and Jefferson. Among the administration family there was anxiety, not only because of Crawford's popularity but because of the rising opposition to the caucus. Clay had put himself at the head of the anti-caucus movement. He had not yet the stature of Crawford, being a younger man; and so he was not so strong a contender in this election as he would be in 1824 (in opposition to J. Q. Adams), but he was nevertheless a very prominent politician and had much support in the new trans-Appalachian country.

When the caucus met on March 12 only half the Democratic-Republican members showed up. It therefore adjourned to the sixteenth; and at that time, more being present, Clay offered a resolution saying that no candidates would be nominated. It failed; but it put him on record against the system he would actively oppose in 1824. Clay's resolution having been got out of the way, a choice between Crawford and Monroe was voted on. The vote was in favor of Monroe (65 to 54). There was still trouble; Crawford was strong in New York and New Jersey as well as in North Carolina, Kentucky, and Georgia; and public meetings in all these states were held to denounce Monroe as well as the caucus system. But since Monroe was a more or less official choice, there was after all no bolting, and the excitement soon died down.

The Federalists made no nomination, but Rufus King was the unofficially accepted candidate. In the election he carried only Connecticut, Delaware, and Massachusetts—a showing which ended all Federalist attempts to participate in national elections.

The Democratic-Republicans were still cohesive, still a party; but they would not be for long. The "era of good feelings" lasted long enough, however, to re-elect Monroe in 1820 in one of the most nearly unanimous of all American elections. There were several reasons for this. No other party had as yet succeeded the Federalists in opposition. The Democratic-Republicans could not refuse to re-elect their own President (although they would do so in the case of Monroe's successor); and Monroe had successfully completed the reversal from early Jeffersonianism, both at home and abroad. He represented, even if very generally, American aspirations to become a great nation both by expansion and by independence from outside interference.

For both these achievements his Secretary of State was at least as responsible as he. J. Q. Adams used his sharp, suspicious intelligence effectively in negotiations with larger and more powerful nations. When he was done, the United States had become the dominant—in fact, the only great—power in America; and the so-called American System had become possible through occupation of the vast lands in the West.

It was as fitting that Adams should succeed as it had been that Monroe should have followed Madison.

John Quincy Adams
1767–1848

Born in Braintree, Massachusetts
Became sixth President in 1825 at 57

HISTORY

Attended schools abroad during his father's various missions.

1781	Appointed secretary to Francis Dana, first envoy to Russia from the United States.
1787	Graduated from Harvard.
1790	Admitted to the bar.
1791	Began to write on politics.
1794	Appointed by Washington Minister to the Netherlands.
1797	Married Louisa Catherine Johnson, daughter of the American Consul at London.
1797	Appointed by his father Ambassador to Berlin.
1802	Elected to the Massachusetts Senate.
1803	Elected to the United States Senate.
1809	Appointed by Madison Minister to Russia.
1814	With Gallatin, Bayard, Russell, and Clay negotiated peace with Britain (Treaty of Ghent).

1815	Appointed Minister to Great Britain.
1817	Appointed Secretary of State by Monroe.
1824	Elected President (by the House of Representatives; Vice-President, Calhoun). Principal opponent, Jackson, who actually had more Electoral votes.
1828	Renominated but defeated by Jackson.
1830	Elected to the House of Representatives.
1848	Died after being stricken on the floor of the House.

THE PURCHASE of Louisiana and the subsequent development of the Ohio Valley lay behind much of the political maneuvering of the 1820's. But the effect of this on politics was complex. With Henry Clay as its representative this region was pressing for recognition and development. And New England, becoming a manufacturing and trading area, wanted tariff protection for its industries and for its commerce, but no improvements to be paid for by taxes.

J. Q. Adams was the leading New Englander—a sophisticated and experienced one—but still, like all Adamses, rooted in the stony Massachusetts soil. Then there was the Old South, now haunted by several consuming fears; of the competitors in more efficient cotton-growing areas around the Gulf of Mexico; of the tariffs wanted by New England (because these tended to shut off the imports that paid for the cotton exported from the South); and for the institution of slavery. The most popular politician was the large and genial William H. Crawford, Monroe's Secretary of the Treasury. Calhoun of South Carolina was ambitious, but Crawford was better liked.

The rivals, as 1824 approached, were, then, Adams of New England, Clay of the Ohio Valley, and Crawford of Georgia. Clay had invented a name to symbolize his appeal. He called it the American System. This had two elements: internal improvements—roads, canals, river improvements, and so on—and protection from foreign imports. All during the Monroe administration he had pushed his sectional ideas from his Speakership of the House, hoping that the East would support Western development in return for assistance in getting protective tariffs.

There was one difficulty about Clay's appeal. The West wanted cheap land on easy terms to draw population; the East would just as soon see Western growth restricted if it attracted labor wanted in mills and factories.

This sectionalism, growing more and more acute, with bargaining constantly taking place, destroyed the unity that had characterized Monroe's first administration.

The three rivals—Adams, Crawford, and Clay—suddenly had others as 1824 approached. Indeed in this campaign there were an unusual number of able and well-known contenders. Andrew Jackson suddenly appeared, for instance; a group of supporters persuaded the Tennessee legislature to endorse him for the Presidency in 1822; but not much attention was paid to his candidacy until 1824, when a Pennsylvania convention also endorsed him. By this time he had been elected to the United States Senate. This was against his expressed wish; but he did take his seat and voted, of course, for protection and for expanded public works.

Jackson was the surprise contender. Until now he had been a Tennessee character, a merchant, planter, frontier soldier, judge, and land speculator. He had been a military hero; but the picture drawn of him by the Tennessee politicians was fictitious. They presented him as a man of the people, democratic, common, a friend of the poor. That a swell of support for the irascible, ignorant, inexperienced amateur General should suddenly threaten to upset all political calculations was an unhappy development for the others. They hardly knew how to meet the threat.

De Witt Clinton's rise was not so sudden or so formidable. The new Erie Canal, about to be completed, was known as "Clinton's Ditch" and marked him as a promoter of internal improvements. It was thought that his New York support might carry over into the West, where other projects like the canal were wanted. Unluckily for him, he proved unable to control his own state. The "Albany Regency," Van Buren's machine, dominated the legislature, and the electors it selected were hostile to Clinton. He had the satisfaction of being re-elected Governor. But he was counted out of the Presidential race.

It seems strange that of all these able contenders it should have been Adams who emerged finally as President. The campaign of that year was confused and unsatisfactory. It was centered in personalities; yet its outcome would determine important national issues. Monroe, Adams' predecessor, had been President in a postwar interlude when domestic issues were simmering but not yet acute, and when foreign policy was important. Napoleon had been defeated in Europe, and the French attempt to dominate the continent had collapsed. The Holy Alliance, with Russia an important partner, had come into being and was reaching out for world domination. But immediately, and so far as the Western Hemisphere was concerned, Britain was again the important European power. Adams, as Secretary of State, had guided American policy as it sought adjustment to the changed European situation. This trial of his abilities showed how farsighted he was and how capable in representing his nation. The appreciation of his statesmanship was general.

But the very qualities that made him a successful Secretary of State might have been recognized as ones that would make him an unsuccessful President. These were much the same characteristics his father had had, and it might have been predicted that they would lead to the same sort of tragedy. He was gifted, well educated, and had enormous and varied abilities. He had made the Monroe administration a much more notable one than it would have been if he had not been responsible for its foreign relations.

It was fitting enough that he should be Monroe's successor if the Presidency could be regarded as the culmination of a career or the reward for service. But a President has to be more than the logical man, more even than the most foresighted or most dedicated one of his generation. He has to be a leader his people will trust and will follow, and who can persuade them to support his policies. He has to be their conscience, their guide, their mentor; and he has to make them love him for it.

So even if Adams was Monroe's logical successor; if his services to the nation had been many and selfless; if his program of expansion was one the nation ought to have pursued—he did not have the gifts necessary for national leadership. He was made President in a doubtful way; he was undermined by those who should have been his allies; and even in office he could not arouse people's affections.

The new voters (including the Westerners), who at that time were swelling the electorate, were strictly practical men, neither noble nor far-seeing. They were, rather, self-seeking and blind to the historical forces in motion all around them. They were on the make; they were grasping and self-centered. All this was not because the frontiersmen were bad people. They were simply people. They had come from good stock and they would produce a creditable posterity. But pushing into the woods and living in isolation, they had been separated from civilizing amenities. Their communities, such as they were, lacked churches, schools, and adequate communication with the world outside. Local government was slow to develop and was resented as it grew. As they acknowledged the need for some order, primitive governmental arrangements were adopted; but they wanted a minimum of limitation on their freedom of action, and they were reluctant to see formal institutions take shape. They became anti-intellectual and anti-civilizational.

To justify all this, they invented their own version of equalitarianism —a literal one: every man not only had equal rights, he had equal abilities; and this meant, of course, that no one could do any job better than anyone else.

It ought to be noted that this was not only a trans-Allegheny phenomenon. There were still in New England, but especially in New York, Pennsylvania, and the Carolinas, people pushing into new valleys and establishing new settlements. These were not very different from those being set up in the woods of Ohio, Tennessee, and Kentucky. There were few roads, and the winter months could be ones of nearly complete isolation; the communities were ingrown, intolerant of strangers; and the outside world was rejected and ignored. Adams as a traveled and sophisticated statesman had no appeal for them.

Yet by those who could be counted among the leading citizens—

even in the remote settlements—Adams' reputation for facing up to the great powers abroad was known, and his abilities were recognized.

As Monroe's Secretary of State he had dealt with Canning and Castlereagh, the British statesmen opposed to him, with consummate courage and skill. It must be remembered that the United States had been the only independent nation in the hemisphere in 1815, but that by 1824 both North and South America were freed from European domination; and most of the new nations, nominally at least, had become republics. As the colonial areas to the south achieved independence, new attitudes toward them had to be defined. Adams' policy as Secretary of State was one of fostering independence, supporting republican ideas, and making trade and association as free as possible.

His negotiations with the British in these matters were risky and complicated. The British were hopeful that, as the ferment and change worked itself out, much of the freed territory would end up in the Empire. That it did not is due to Adams more than anyone else. The most enduring rule to be established in this matter goes under the name "Monroe Doctrine"; but it might better be attributed to Adams.[1]

It is almost forgotten now that the Tsar, feeling his strength after Napoleon's defeat, was expanding in the Pacific. In 1821 he extended Russian claims from Alaska to north of the 51st parallel (now in Oregon) and declared the waters closed to others from there to the Bering Strait. But in July 1823, Adams told the Russian Minister that the New World was now to be considered out of bounds to further European aggression. In October the Russians presented a note challenging republicanism in general and refusing to recognize the independence movement in Latin America. President Monroe and others in the Cabinet were inclined to compromise, although they were enthusiastic about the struggle then going on for Greek independence from the Turks. Monroe, in his own draft of the famous message, proposed to recognize Greek independence as well as to reprove France for invading Spain. Adams was against this "meddling" in European affairs. What he wanted to do was to speak the American mind in a note to the Russians and make the United States the guardian of the hemisphere. The Doctrine was finally embodied in Monroe's message; but it was largely Adams who had established the principle before the whole world.

At the time there was not so much interest in this rebuke to the Holy Alliance as in the local issues leading to the impending election. But it did set Adams in a very high place. He was the man who would have to be beaten. The ambitious politicians who hoped to succeed Monroe recognized it.

---

[1] The declaration was contained, after some argument, in Monroe's message to the Congress in 1823.

This was, as always, both fortunate and unfortunate. Adams was in the lead; but he was also a target. And there began that disparagement of his qualities which would become a torrent of abuse during the campaign and especially after the election.

William H. Crawford seemed to be in the lead at first. He was recognized, even though a Georgian, as the heir to the Virginia tradition. Monroe had brought Adams into his Cabinet to please New England; this was necessary; but it was something else to allow the Presidency to pass to New England. Crawford could count on the South. But there was Clay. He was a Kentuckian and his American System had a formidable appeal. And there was Jackson, Clay's rival for frontier affections. Clay had the disadvantage of having so long a record and so definite a one. Jackson had the advantage of being an attractive personality but of having made no commitments. His followers could and did promise everything to everyone.

All four candidates were Democratic-Republicans; but all were nationalists too, although with some variation. There was no states'-righter among them; that heresy was already visible in the South after having died out in New England, but it was not yet a politically desirable position. Things were somewhat simplified when Crawford was incapacitated by a paralytic stroke; and, as it turned out, Clay was so poor a contender as to be eliminated from consideration. Jackson carried Pennsylvania and the Carolinas; Adams carried New England and most of New York.

It was not Adams' virtues or his claims that finally made him President; it was Clay's jealousy of Jackson, so compulsive that, ignoring instructions of the Kentucky legislature, he voted for Adams in the House balloting.

Frontier feuds could be thus savage. There were now twenty-four states; thirteen of them voted for Adams and eleven for Jackson; and Adams became President even though Jackson had fifty thousand more popular and fifteen more electoral votes than he. This frustration of the obvious popular will had to be paid for; and Adams paid for it in four years of humiliation as President and in catastrophic defeat for a second term.

Adams was sore at heart that this should be the reason for his election; and his Presidency would often show the marks of his hurt. The campaign of the Jacksonians looking toward 1828 was only fumblingly met by Adams and from the first it was a losing defense. Even his first entirely correct strategic move was turned against him. This was his appointment of Clay as Secretary of State. It might have been thought that by having Clay in his Cabinet and Calhoun as Vice-President he would have consolidated a hold on the South and the West. He being from New England, the resulting coalition ought to have been effective. It was, however, undermined from the first by the new breed of local politicians springing up everywhere to whom scruples were unknown and local issues more important than national ones. And for their machines it was control of offices and the other favors dispensed by the Federal government that they wanted.

These local struggles throughout the states had been going on under the surface during Monroe's "era of good feelings"; the levelers were beginning to win by 1824; they carried Pennsylvania for Jackson even so early, and they would reach a national majority in 1828.

Jackson, as Adams' rival and successor, came out of the frontier and represented its narrow isolationism with terrifying faithfulness. It was logical that he should come to power. And the time for it had really arrived when Adams became President.

Because Clay's influence in the House had given Adams the election, and because Adams promptly made him Secretary of State in his new Cabinet, one of those ramps which sometimes bulk very large in American political history was begun. It was said that Clay had traded the votes he controlled for the office Adams appointed him to. Adams characteristically considered that everyone should have known that this was not true—that it was not in his character to make such a trade. So he refused to acknowledge the charge.

As politics goes in the United States, there seems nothing unusually reprehensible about such an arrangement if it had been made. There have been many others of a similar sort.[2] But the fact was that John Quincy, like all the Adamses, had a finicky conscience and a rigid sense of public propriety. He never in his life had compromised in order to get ahead or even to forward the policies he believed in. The elastic view of the means necessary to important ends, so ordinary in politics, he could not accept. The only means available to him were those justifiable by his own stern standards. When asked to give his followers some leeway, he refused. It seemed to him demeaning that he should even be asked. It was his contemporary, Clay, who made the famous assertion that he would rather be right than President. It would have come much more appropriately from Adams. Clay was not so delicate as this remark would make him seem.[3]

---

[2] When, for instance, Lincoln was nominated in a trade for Cabinet posts; when F. D. Roosevelt was nominated by giving his Vice-Presidency to Garner of Texas; and when Eisenhower made his post-election deal with Senator Taft and filled his Cabinet with businessmen in exchange for conservative support.

[3] When they were fellow commissioners at Ghent in 1814, Adams' life of hard work and earnest service stood in the greatest contrast to Clay's dissolute behavior. Adams was often rising at daybreak when Clay was returning from an all-night celebration. Clay's conduct was always that of a belligerent, self-serving, overly-ambitious politician. That Adams made him Secretary of State in spite of this was due to his belief that Clay's public conduct was guided by a principle he did not acknowledge in private. But of course a curious code governed the

There is not the slightest doubt that this high-mindedness was more true of the younger Adams than of any other Presidential candidate—except his father. He was both right and President. But it has to be acknowledged that his rigid rightness and his subsequent failure as Chief Executive were interlocked and that the one was largely the cause of the other.

There is a conclusion from this to be tested as we go along. Is it true that a candidate, to be successful, must trade and deal and disregard all interests not high in the voters' regard? Certainly Adams' failure was largely caused by his refusal to be guided by the warnings of the politicians.

He was so extreme in his rejection of compromise with his principles that he was considered by contemporary party men to be very nearly a fool—and this in spite of his vast learning, his ripe wisdom, and his wide experience. Because he allowed himself to become the easy victim of malicious opponents who were fertile in devising calumnies, the electorate formed a picture of him precisely the opposite of what he was. When he lost his second election he was put down as a political innocent who deserved to lose.

His detractors said of him when he was President that his habits were extravagantly European,[4] that he was subject to undue influence from New England interests, that he was undignified in dress and deportment, yet that he aped foreign aristocrats, and that his wife (whom he had married abroad but who was the daughter of an American Consul) was a foreigner—all this besides the reiterated charges of a "deal" with Clay.

The immolation of this reserved, proud, and sensitive Bostonian intellectual, exposed to the full flow of broad frontier humor and the spitefulness of village gossip, is one of the most unjust in our history. Not that Adams' partisans did not return the fire of the Jacksonians in kind—they did, and they were quite as scurrilous as their opponents—but without the President's support they were not convincing. Besides, most of the stories they told about Jackson were true in contrast to what was being said about Adams. But because Jackson was the kind of hero the frontiersmen favored, being recognizably one of themselves risen to prominence, the faults complained of were regarded more as virtues than as sins. The drumfire of rumor and villification ruined Adams and brought Jackson to the President's House on a wave of perverse approval in 1828.

---

gentlemen of the frontier. It was the same one that Jackson defended so fiercely. It allowed dissolute living, but it forbade dishonesty; it was strong on "honor" but weak on probity. Adams believed Clay to be an honorable man by the standards of Kentucky.

[4] A billiard table in the White House was represented by the Jacksonians as proof of Adams' profligacy. They said it was a gambling device.

Yet as a statesman Adams stood, even before he was President, on a higher level than Monroe, and as President his policies for the nation were more farsighted. And he had insight as well as more foresight.

When Jackson had embarrassed the Monroe administration by his conduct during an irresponsible foray into Florida, Adams alone had vigorously defended his headstrong behavior. As Secretary of State he had rejected the offended protests of both the Spanish and the British. And it was Adams who had been responsible for Jackson's appointment as Governor of the territory and who, again, had been his advocate when he had embroiled himself with the retiring Spanish officials. Florida must belong to the United States; in foreign hands it would always be a base for intriguing adventurers; if Jackson was rough and even murderous in his conquest, he got it done. This essential Adams respected.

Jackson must have known that in Adams he had had a powerful friend when one was most needed; but this was something he would not acknowledge. It was no virtue in his eyes for Adams to have recognized his services and intervened to prevent reprimands for insubordination. On the contrary, he made capital of official displeasure. So Adams got no thanks for defending him.

It was as a candidate of the on-marching masses who were to take Washington like an invading army, expel its officeholders and occupy its posts, that Jackson's political power grew. The day of the intellectuals, chosen by the best and most responsible citizens, succeeding each other in orderly fashion as each was prepared and ready, came to an end with Adams. There would be no more of them. The next President at all comparable would be Wilson, far down the forthcoming years.

Adams was the unhappy victim of a movement usually called democratic but more accurately described as an equalizing one. The most important specific attacks were against the remaining restrictions on voting in the state constitutions. This increased the electorate by adding to it those most likely to be influenced by specious appeals and most likely to exchange their votes for favors or even for money. The high-mindedness of the Jeffersonian appeal for equal rights was debased in this new political expansion. Jackson not only imitated Jefferson but parodied him.

It was in the resulting chaos that the old leaders were discredited and disestablished. Everywhere new crowd manipulators began to show themsleves more and more boldly. They presently began to make alliances. They looked for a man of their own sort, one who would allow them their way in the localities, and to the extent necessary in Washington too. They chose Jackson, and it was a perfect choice.

When they did not succeed with him in 1824 they aimed at 1828; and then they buried the enfeebled opposition in a tidal wave of votes.

Adams saw what was happening; but within his principles he could not effectively combat the local machines. His ally, Clay, was outshone by Jackson. The Jacksonians' claim that Clay's electoral votes had been traded for the promise of the Secretaryship of State ran through the country like a blighting wind, and it served the purpose. Adams, scorning to combat so fantastic a version of his motives and intentions, was helpless. It was political murder.

There was no national issue to be fought out; but there were manufactured ones. The rising political bosses, Buchanan and Van Buren, in Pennsylvania and New York, circulated the story of the "deal," and they also treated several entirely laudable policies advanced by Clay and Adams as diversions to hide the "corrupt bargain." The furor over nothing was incredible; and Calhoun, presiding over the Senate as Vice-President, betrayed Adams by allowing suggestions of outrageous sorts to be made freely on the floor. At the mid-term election in 1826 the way things were going could be seen all too clearly. The Jackson forces won control of the House.

The drift was being hastened now by the South's rising reaction against nationalism. Sectionalism was coming into its own there, with Calhoun, the one-time nationalist, leading. And Jackson was pictured to the Southerners as fully committed to their view. That Jackson did nothing to stop the misrepresentations about Adams, and about his own position, showed the appetite he now had for the Presidency. There was no resort beyond the conscience of his supporters. And all the time he posed as the hero, eager to serve his country.

When the election came, Jackson carried all the South and the West, but also Pennsylvania and most of New York. Buchanan and Van Buren were now spoken of with awe. They were the new men, the powers behind the Jacksonian throne. The old man—he was only sixty-two, but so enfeebled as to seem much older—came to Washington as he had invaded Florida, unprepared, scornful of learning, vindictive, and with a clamoring mob as his escort. Adams left unnoticed, still full of pride, wounded to the quick, and fearful for his country's future.

He had found a way to the Presidency, but it was a way he could wish he had not taken.

Andrew Jackson
1767–1845

Born in Waxhaw, South Carolina
Became seventh President in 1829 at 61

HISTORY

1784	Began the study of law in North Carolina, but spent most of his time in sporting—cockfighting, horse racing, and carousing.
1788	Moved to Tennessee, where he continued a mostly sporting life.
1791	Married Rachel Robards, who mistakenly thought she was divorced; accused of a scandal he would always have to fight.
1796	Admitted to the bar; became a delegate to the Tennessee constitutional Convention; Elected to the House of Representatives.
1798	Became a justice of the Tennessee Supreme Court.
1801	Became a Major General of Tennessee militia.
1806–12	Lived as a country gentleman, planter, and land speculator.
1812–15	After the Battle of New Orleans was nationally recognized as a military hero.

86

1818	Conducted Seminole War in Florida.
1824	Defeated by Adams for the Presidency in a House election after gaining a popular plurality.
1828	Elected President (Vice-President, Van Buren). Principal opponent, Clay with Sergeant.
1832	Re-elected.
1837	Retired after seeing Van Buren elected.
1845	Died in Tennessee.

J ACKSON, as a figure in Presidential annals, seems to a later generation to have come storming into Washington at the head of a mob intent on seizing the government and using it for favors to his partisans. Actually he became much more important than the principal in a mob scene; his was a long, lingering influence on political mores. He taught new lessons even to those well schooled in Jeffersonian strategy and has been a hero of the Democratic party ever since. This, however, is not wholly because he captured the Presidency as he did; he was also a defender of the Union when disintegration seemed to be setting in. His mob may have been spoilsmen, but they were patriots too.

Between Jefferson's retirement and Jackson's accession there had been a fairly genteel two decades with Madison, Monroe, and Adams in the President's House, and this calm was supported by continuity in the Cabinet and a settled upper civil service. But democracy with frontier irresponsibility was, as has been indicated, boiling up; and this in 1828 was the more violent for having been frustrated in 1824. Jackson's assumption did have revolutionary overtones. But it was not intended to overthrow the government. It was more to enforce the principle of equality within the government and to seize its offices and favors.

Jackson's approach to the Presidency is best understood if his military orientation is kept firmly in mind. This is quite apart from the reasons he received so much adulation and was supported so loyally by the electorate even when his caprices were most conspicuous. When a President really achieves this sort of rapport with his public, his power is impervious to attack. This was true of Jackson, as it would also be true of Grant, of Roosevelt, and of Eisenhower. All three allowed conduct among subordinate officials that can only be described as deplorable; all three adopted policies which would not have been tolerated in any of their contemporaries; all developed serious and indefensible inconsistencies. And all this had no effect whatever on the loyalty of their enormous followings.

But naturally Roosevelt and, surprisingly, Grant did not exhibit any military traits either in approaching office or after attaining it. Jackson did. He conducted his political campaigns in military fashion and behaved toward his governmental associates as though they were subordinate officers.

A passage from *Generals in the White House*[1] illuminates this point:

> Jackson has given his name to a decade; "Jacksonian democracy" has become a familiar phrase, synonymous with the rise of the common

---

[1] By Dorothy B. and Julius Goebel, Jr. (New York, 1945) 82.

man . . . Yet, strange contradiction, his administrations have almost as
frequently been dubbed "the Reign of King Andrew Jackson." Indeed,
"King Andrew" was a favorite gibe flung out by his adversaries, a
paradox only to be resolved in terms of the man and his past experiences. Had his political enemies clung to the old epithet, military
chieftain, they would have come nearer to the truth, for Jackson the
General lived on in the Presidency. His administrations were to him—
and certainly to his opponents—a series of battles in which he exhibited
the same qualities that had distinguished his military career. In his own
view, he fought for the people and the union as before he had battled
for the Republic . . . Characteristically, a man was either a friend or a
foe. His military experience had confirmed this outlook; to some degree
this impaired his capacity for office. Convinced that he was meting out
retribution and not retaliation, he opened the doors of the Federal
Government to the spoils system. With the resolution of a Covenanter
and the determination of a conqueror, he introduced the new democratic principle of "rotation in office," and made the Federal service a
party province . . .

The account goes on to illustrate Jackson's military bent by his behavior while President. And it is true that in several notorious instances
he did act as a General might and not at all as a political leader. He
went after the enemy vigorously, demanded absolute discipline, never
forgave a defection, and rewarded the faithfulness of friends with promotions or favors.

But what is of equal importance to us here, he used the same technique when running for office. The opposing candidate was an enemy
to be beaten at all costs by any available tactic.

Even the high-minded Washington resorted to means in military
exigencies that he never used as a civil official. Jackson made no such
distinction. This accounts for his consent to the meannesses, the
double-dealings, the resorts to lies and innuendoes used by his forces in
besting Adams, Clay, Calhoun, White, Webster, and his other opponents. And this attitude had a twin, made allowable by the same indifference to morality in public life. The slogan most often used to
characterize his administration was "To the victor belongs the spoils."
Any means was justified by its end, especially if that end was one
Jackson favored. There never was a man more touchy about his honor,
more chivalrous in private life, more scrupulous about his obligations
—so much so that he was always quarreling heatedly with those who
had impugned his reputation in some way. In these quarrels he was
rough and unforgiving; but for himself, he scorned tricks, subterfuges,
and deviousness. But all this was his private character. As a public man
he acted, and condoned the acting of others, in ways utterly at vari-
ance with such principles, and especially when an active "battle" was

going on. Then any resort that weakened the enemy or strengthened his own forces was justified.

It was consistent with this, too, that to him issues always appeared in blacks and whites. There were no grays. His side was "right," the other side was "wrong," and this was a judgment no one could question without arousing his anger. Because his enemies were wicked, they must not only be defeated but punished.

Some passages in the Jackson story inspire admiration for the originality of his mind, his energy in action, and his devotion to the Union. Others can only be defended as integral to a character with mostly admirable qualities. It is perhaps something American in Jackson that later generations have found so attractive even when his conduct was undoubtedly deplorable. In many ways he was a brawling ignoramus whose leveling instincts brought all that was thoughtful and fine into contempt because it was beyond his experience. But he had vigor, originality, and stamina. The tall frontiersman, whose fists and pistols were too ready, who detested a coward, who liked low company, and who thought effeteness a despicable quality, was a man for his times. He was the hero of an irresponsible electorate; and when he came to Washington, they came along with him—thousands of them.

The stories told of the mob's behavior when these partisans came to see him inaugurated in 1829 have the flavor of the backwoods. They came straight from the villages and farms, their boots heavy with mud, their appetites for food and liquor rapacious; they took over the President's House, swamped its facilities, broke its furniture, destroyed its hangings, and lay drunk in its corners and on its lawns.

According to an eyewitness account:

> It was a glorious day for the *sovereigns*, who assembled here to the amount of 15 or 20,000 . . . After the ceremony the old chief retired to the Palace where he had a regular Saturnalia. The mob broke in, in thousands . . . one uninterrupted stream of mud and filth . . .
>
> They crowded around the President until he was only saved from bodily harm by some gentlemen, who made a circle in front of him . . . he was glad to escape by a side entrance . . . The rabble fell on the refreshments, jostling the waiters as they appeared at the doors, breaking the china and glassware, standing in muddy boots on damask covered chairs, spoiling the carpets and creating such a press that . . . windows were used for exits . . .[2]

But the invasion was real, and the invaders stayed a long time. The government service would not recover from the attack of the spoilsmen for many years, because they would, in fact, have changed

---

[2] Quoted in J. S. Bassett, *The Life of Andrew Jackson*, 2 vols. (1911), II, 424.

American institutions to fit their desires. Only very gradually toward the middle of the next century would the merit system again replace that of jobs given for party work. A long evolution of civilized institutions had to raise the general level of literacy, and so the informed discussion of public affairs, before the change could take place. Washington was, for all that time, a welter of claimants for jobs, with fitness almost the last consideration. Successive Presidents resisted when they could; but actually their defenses were weak. Lincoln, in 1860, and even later Presidents, down to the eighties, would be heard to complain bitterly that so much time and energy should have to be spent in pacifying rapacious job seekers; hardly any remained, they said, for serious public business. Jackson perhaps doubted the wisdom of his hasty conclusions about Presidential behavior; but he never said so. Admitting mistakes was not in character for him.

The spoils system did not actually begin with Jackson; but it was as he took office that equality became a fetish and was extended to the claim that anyone was fit for any job. The only admissible question was whether a reward had really been earned by party service. It was by holding out the promise of a free grab for Federal perquisites that Jackson's managers overwhelmed the opposition. No election for decades thereafter would be free of the competition in promises between ins and outs. The outward appearance might be somewhat more seemly, but the real election work would be done by those who expected pay—in appointments, in contracts, in wanted legislation, or in leniency from the executive departments. This was generally known, of course; and if "politics" became a derogatory word in the American vocabulary, it was a deserved reputation, earned in the Jackson era. For decades the public service would not be a respectable career. It would be a low employment, and anyone involved in it would hardly be acceptable in decent company.

When Jackson was elected, he was no longer young. He had, for a long time, been in ill health, the result of his wilderness campaigns with their fevers, dysenteries, and debilitating hardships, and of the serious wounds he had suffered in two duels. The penalties of a misspent youth and manhood were upon him. He was irascible and vengeful, incapable of sustained study or thought, and, so far as administration was concerned, very much in the hands of the singularly unscrupulous familiars who had got him elected. He allowed them to begin at once the getting rid of everyone, or nearly everyone, who had served in the outgoing administration, and the appointing of their own followers. This the Jacksonians dignified as "rotation"; their enemies called it "proscription."

Because of the offense to conservative sensibilities involved in this, the other reasons for Jackson's prominence and popularity tend to be

overlooked even now. It is not too often recalled that it was not the
promise of spoils that first made him eligible in people's minds. It was
the success he had had as a militia General. He had been a brilliant
amateur; and an uneducated, crude, and violent people saw in him the
justification of their own characteristics. It was not necessary to be a
student, to live respectably, to devote time and care to the public
business. This was something that could be attended to when horse
races, cockfights, and all-night gambling sessions allowed.

Jackson never went to school; he became a lawyer and a judge, even
of the State Supreme Court, without any legal training to speak of. In
smaller wars, he had been a dashing volunteer Captain before his spectacular victory at New Orleans. It was this defeat of the British, so
badly needed to restore American morale, that made him a national
hero.

There was a political group in Tennessee who saw in the Jackson
reputation the enormous potentialities that afterward developed; and
it was they who got the state legislature to pass a resolution suggesting
his candidacy. It was they also who began the attacks on Adams that
destroyed his reputation. He was most criticized actually because he
advocated reasonable tariffs and an expansion of public improvements.
The fact was that Jackson had also favored these policies. But the
appeal was to narrow-mindedness, cupidity, and localism. Adams was
a national man. Jackson would lift the frontier into power and prosperity. The ensuing campaign was hypocritical and unscrupulous; but it
was a complete success.

This election illustrates the potency of a professional organization
with spoils in view. The election, of course, was pictured in advance
as a people's victory, and so successfully that the defection from
Adams ran all the way from the bottom to the top of American political life. His aloof rectitude was completely vulnerable to the undermining effect of the long-continued villification.

As the new regime began, Jackson proved not to be so wild a man
as Eastern conservatives had feared. He made no changes of importance
in the government's administrative organization, only in its personnel.
He was, in fact, very little interested in operations and tended to leave
the running of the government to his subordinates. This made an
opportunity for a group of familiars who came to be known collectively as the "Kitchen Cabinet," a term frequently useful in subsequent
years.[3]

Very few Presidents have been gifted administrators; some have

---

[3] The names usually mentioned among those in Jackson's Kitchen Cabinet included W. B. Lewis, Amos Kendall, and A. J. Donelson (his private secretary);
and after 1830, F. P. Blair, editor of *The Globe;* but two members of the regular
Cabinet were also usually spoken of as belonging to the inside group. These were
John H. Eaton, Secretary of War (whose marriage was the cause of so much
bickering), and Martin Van Buren (Secretary of State), Jackson's closest adviser.

been lamentably weak ones. And Kitchen Cabinets, or groups of assistants, often ones not holding office, are necessary in such circumstances.

But Jackson did not allow the determination of policy to escape his supervision. It became evident before long that definite attitudes were developing. They would constitute his platform for re-election. They were also the basis for opposition. And out of this opposition, with Adams and Clay as its leaders, a new political group would arise—the Whigs.[4]

Thus the Democratic-Republican party, after smothering the Federalists, broke into two parts. Jackson's part became the long-lasting Democratic party and the opposition became first Whig, then just before the Civil War, Republican. Jackson's shadow would thus be lengthened, with Whig intervals, to thirty-two years. This rivals the run of the Jeffersonians.

The policies he adopted that became the issues he chose to fight on were very soon being publicized. The first of these was strict constructionism. Since this would maximize the powers of the states and reduce those of the Federal government, it involved also a reduction of Federal spending for public improvements. If this seems a curious attitude for a dashing conqueror out of the West to assume, it must be remembered that this has always been the kind of policy developed by demagogues. They profess concern for "grass-roots" control and make impassioned pleas for states' rights.[5]

Strict constructionism left all the old Clay-Adams policies to the Whigs, and they came to be thought of as representing expansionism, a protective tariff, sound money, and conservation. These would prove in the long run to be the wise—the only possible—ideas for the vast

---

Jackson's attitude toward his regular Cabinet was responsible for the development of this group of unofficial advisers. He did not accept them as a consultative body but treated them as subordinates in military fashion. He did not even have regular Cabinet meetings.

[4] The Whigs would function, as we shall see, until 1856, meanwhile winning two elections, that of W. H. Harrison (with Tyler), and Taylor (with Fillmore). Both Harrison and Taylor died in office. Their terms were served out by Vice-Presidents; neither of these was elected to succeed himself, one because he would not, the other because he could not.

[5] Jackson had some difficulty with this issue. He had formerly favored Federal financing for improvements; he now made a rather fine distinction between those which were clearly local and those having national importance. The veto of the so-called Maysville Road Bill, inspired by Van Buren, made the administration's case. It would have paid for an internal Kentucky road; and it was supposed to have been sponsored by Clay to embarrass Jackson. But Jackson's massive popular support was not shaken by his refusal. The veto was an embarrassment to Calhoun, also, who had sponsored the internal improvements so necessary in the Carolinas if the West was to be reached. Calhoun and Van Buren were from the first rivals for the succession to Jackson, and Van Buren scored heavily on this issue. Especially, he consolidated his position as a right-hand adviser to the President.

national development that was to come. But the Jacksonians rejected
them and had popular support in doing so. The Whigs would never
really command more than a temporary majority and never be able
to implement their plans. It would not be until after the Civil War that
national interests would regain the influence on men's mind they once
had had.

The Jacksonian period was one of rapid change in party management. The widening of the franchise, the illiteracy of the voters, and
the lack of communications made possible party machines run by a
few insiders. Very soon this developed into the full-blown boss system.
So far as Presidential politics was concerned, the Congressional caucus
was discredited and was abandoned in 1824. How, then, were candidates for election to be chosen? Voters could hardly be expected
simply to write in their choices. In 1828 the legislatures of the states
took it upon themselves to put forward candidates; there were also
some party "conferences" and a few state conventions. But the finally
accepted device was one originated in 1831 by the Anti-Masonic party,
a temporary minority group—the representative party convention.
Jackson and Van Buren instantly grasped its possibilities. They initiated its use in 1832, and the Whigs followed in 1840. It would be
used thenceforth by all parties. It was not until 1848, however, that a
National party committee was set up by the Democrats, and even then
it did little but call conventions. Formal party organization developed
only gradually.

Intense activity had arisen every four years since Jefferson's time;
now it began to focus on the convention. And this institution immediately began to have a profound effect on the Presidency. The President now became much more formally a party leader; he was no
longer merely the embodiment of policies or attitudes; he was the
overlord. Once he was elected, also, he had a new orientation; he must
manage things so that his renomination for a second term would be
facilitated. Even after that, his hold on the party must be maintained
for its effect on Congressional discipline and so that he could influence
the choice of a successor.

Not all Presidents have desired to succeed themselves; and there
arose a fashion of announcing on accession that they would not seek
re-election. It grew out of the feeling that all offices ought to be
shared out, even the Presidency. It was a severe handicap, as the wiser
Executives saw. Power dissipates as its end comes into view, and subordinates become unruly. So presently sharing disappeared from among
the pervasive ideas of politics.[6] James K. Polk would be one of these

---

[6] But it undoubtedly had some influence on the rise of the movement ending
in the ratification of the Twenty-second Amendment to the Constitution fixing
two terms as the limit for a President. This, however, was also a reaction against

renouncers, as we shall see; but it was Jackson, the first of the Presidents under the organized party system with universal suffrage, who really set the pattern for his ablest successors. He wanted the second term.[7]

Jackson may have had a narrow view of Federal obligations, but he did not have a narrow view of the Presidency or of his responsibilities as a leader. He saw more clearly even than his predecessors, who had been such distinguished lawyers, the difference between the Presidential system of our Constitution and the Parliamentary-Cabinet system as practiced in Britain. He insisted strenuously that his powers were co-equal with those of the Congress. This was because he too had been elected,[8] and as for the Supreme Court, he refused to agree that it had any power whatever to limit or define his behavior.

Jackson did not come to Washington with these ideas; he developed them in office. But when they took hold, he held to them tenaciously; and his pugnacious determination was thoroughly approved by the electorate. This was bitterly resented by the Congress and especially the Senate. It would be a source of irritation, sometimes becoming a critical issue, for a long time to come. It would torment Lincoln in his day and almost lead to his successor's impeachment. It would result in substantial failure for Wilson's peace plans, and it would force the liquidation of much of F. D. Roosevelt's New Deal. It was a quarrel inherent in the Constitution so soon as a strong President should assert the powers derived from his independent position.

As with other Presidents who followed him, this was a principal issue in Jackson's claim to a second term. It was said of him that he was dictatorial and that he reduced the Congress to subserviency. He ac-

---

F. D. Roosevelt's four elections; it was sponsored by the Republicans in the aftermath of World War II.

[7] Cf. Basset, *op. cit.*, 477:

Jackson took his immense popularity for approval of his policy . . . He considered his own ideas the people's ideas. No President kept a more watchful eye on Congress to see that they did not violate the will of the people. Excluded from congressional halls by custom, through friends he kept well informed of all that transpired there. Either A. J. Donelson or Major Lewis was usually there and made quick report to the Chief. Thus the leader added to the ordinary feeling of party loyalty the force of a mild terror, increasing the coherence of his own party and embittering the attitude of his opponents.

[8] He stated this very clearly in 1832 in his veto of a bill for rechartering the national bank he so hated. It had been pushed by Clay as a kind of challenge, and the veto itself showed his confidence in his hold on the people. But embedded in it was an unexpected paragraph defining the Executive power:

Each public officer who takes an oath to support the Constitution swears that he will support it as he understands it, and not as it is understood by others. . . . The opinion of the judges has no more authority over Congress than the opinion of Congress has over the judges, and on that point the President is independent of both.

cepted the issue; the people believed that he, far more than the Congress, was representing their interests. And it would nearly always be so in the Executive-Legislative struggle. That assertiveness of this sort is useful in gaining second terms was demonstrated by Adams' failure and Jackson's success. Much of a President's real hold depends on his active leadership. He must bend ambitious legislative rivals to his will. He must even seek opportunities for quarreling with them. And he must, on carefully selected issues, appeal to the people for support. He can count on their disposition to rally behind a hero; and if the affair is well conducted, it will enable him to subdue his opponents. They will retreat sullenly; but they will retreat.

Jackson was the first President after Washington to establish so firm a protective relationship with the electorate that even his enemies assessed it as unassailable and challenged it only on extreme provocation. The size of his 1832 majority shows what a hold he had on their loyalty. He was nominated unanimously, and in the election he gained 219 electoral votes to Clay's 49. His support came from every part of the country, even New England.

We shall see this same feeling develop for Lincoln, for F. D. Roosevelt, and for Eisenhower. It is the most mysterious of all political phenomena and the most irresistible. But the conditions for its development are unusual and complex. The President must grow to be of heroic size, but not necessarily in the military way; neither Lincoln nor F. D. Roosevelt was a General, although Washington and Jackson were. But he must be given stature by leadership in a national crisis, usually war. And then there must be political finesse, at least in the beginning, as the myth takes shape. In Jackson's case, the military reputation and the irritable integrity were ready-made; the political finesse was supplied by the Kitchen Cabinet, Martin Van Buren doing much of the scheming.

This kind of relationship with the electorate, it must be emphasized, is not necessary to a candidate; it has, in fact, usually developed during incumbency, sometimes quite unexpectedly; again as in the case of Lincoln and F. D. Roosevelt. Most successful aspirants have not had it, and there have been some who, without it, have gone on to second terms; but it is the safest relationship because it is the most difficult to undermine in the inevitable vicissitudes of the second four years. If it is at all attainable it ought to be grasped and cultivated. But if it is not, there are other ways. Many statesmen, and some of the wisest, such as the Adamses, had no possibility of reaching such a rapport with the voters. If, nevertheless, they became President, as we have seen that both Adamses did, they were unsuccessful in the larger sense.

We shall see others, as we go along, who suffered from the same political difficulties: intellectualism, reserve, thorny integrity, stiffness, and pride. Some, like Cleveland and Wilson, overcame their handicaps. Others, like Taft and Hoover, failed to do so. It is one of the most interesting of all the phases of Presidential candidacy.

Then, too, it is instructive to study the kinds of issues most useful in establishing the protector-symbol. We can see them quite clearly in the Jackson case, and we can see as well how they were handled to produce the maximum effect. When Jackson had retired to the Hermitage, a worn but irrepressibly fiery old man, he was still the father of his people. His opinions were sought, babies and cities were still named after him, and his policies were those of his successor, even though thoroughly discredited. He even named the two party candidates who followed him.

His last annual message in December 1836 had overtones of satisfaction. He felt that what he had stood for had been achieved. The issues he had defined and set out to meet in 1829 had been resolved. The movement for internal improvements with Federal financing had been damped down; the tariff had had a reasonable compromise solution; the American System of Clay and Adams had been checked; the Bank of the United States, against which he had conducted a hammer-and-tongs battle and which he regarded as the citadel of Eastern privilege, was in liquidation; American prestige in foreign affairs was heightened (even if their conduct under his management had lacked something of dignity); and the national debt was extinguished by increased revenues. Beyond these achievements, and having promise for the kind of future he wanted for the country, the Democratic party was firmly established on a wide foundation and the successor of his choosing was in the White House. His enemies had been defeated and he himself as a patriarch stood high in the regard of his people.

Of all these issues, the most useful in so anchoring Jackson in popular affection that no attack could shake his majority was his vendetta with the Bank. And this does, indeed, illustrate with textbook perfection what has come to be a recognized truism of politics: an ambitious man must have a suitable enemy. It is not possible here to describe the battle of the Bank. It must be enough to say that this institution was private but had been chartered by the government in 1816; and that it had vast powers involving credit and the issuance of currency. It was profitable to "the financiers" and a source of irritation to borrowers. Debtors, as always, wanted to pay their debts in cheap money; creditors wanted them paid in hard money. The Bank was naturally controlled by the leaders. It was believed to exploit the many borrowers for the benefit of the few creditors.

The financiers had the same function in the Jackson campaign that they would have just a century later in F. D. Roosevelt's. They had the virtue of always being there to be denounced and attacked; how-

ever many times they are beaten, they are never destroyed. Their
natural enemies among the voters are an immense number; they themselves are few. Both Jackson and Roosevelt made masterly use of this
convenience.

Bankers are vulnerable. They are, to begin with, invariably conservative. They are therefore apt to resist change and to defend existing
arrangements. A political leader has only to suggest reform, wait for
them to react, and then denounce them as exploiters. It has always
worked.

Jackson got all the political credit the bankers could yield him. He
was the people's champion against the money power. But he left
things worse than he had found them. He had abolished the Bank but
had put nothing in its place. And the financial chaos of the succeeding
years was his legacy to his successor. One of the worst panics and subsequent depressions of the many suffered by the economy during the
nineteenth century occurred in 1837, just after he retired. The old
man in the Hermitage felt no responsibility. He had never understood finance anyway. But it was probable that his successor did. Van
Buren was a smarter man than Jackson, and much more a statesman.
But he never attained such a hold on the electorate, consummate politician that he was, as Jackson so effortlessly won and kept.

Martin Van Buren
1782–1862

Born in Kinderhook, New York
Became eighth President in 1837 at 54

HISTORY

1801	After attending village schools and reading law, became a law clerk in New York City.
1803	Licensed to practice in Kinderhook.
1807	Married kinswoman Hannah Hoes. Admitted to practice in the State Supreme Court.
1808–13	Moved to Hudson, became Surrogate; was very active in Democratic-Republican politics.
1812	Elected to the State Senate.
1816	Active in the election of Tompkins to the Vice-Presidency. Re-elected to the Senate. Attorney General of New York State.
1819	Removed from his position by Clinton. Wife died.
1820	Aided Federalists to elect Rufus King to the United States Senate and opposed Clinton, who, however, was re-elected.

99

1821	Elected to the United States Senate with the help of his "Bucktail" machine, known as the "Albany Regency."
1828	Eulogized Clinton and then ran for Governor to keep his "Bucktails" in power; resigned after winning.
1829	Appointed Secretary of State in Jackson's Cabinet.
1831	Resigned and was appointed Minister to Great Britain; appointment rejected by the Senate.
1832	Elected Vice-President with Jackson.
1836	Elected President (Johnson, Vice-President); opponent, W. H. Harrison.
1840	Renominated by the Democrats but defeated by Harrison.
1844	Unsuccessful candidate for the Democratic nomination.
1848	Unsuccessful Free-Soil nominee for President.
1862	Died at Kinderhook.

Jackson's handling of the Georgia and South Carolina defiances of Federal powers was the worst complication Van Buren had to deal with in planning to succeed in 1836. Georgia's expulsion of the Cherokees seems to us now a callous and cruel act. To have dispossessed the long-settled Indians and to have moved them far to the west into a strange and barren environment was to deprive them of long-established rights and condemn them to poverty in a strange land. Moreover, in *Worcester* vs. *Georgia* and in other cases, Chief Justice Marshall and his Court had held that the Georgia laws asserting sovereignty over the Indians were repugnant to the Constitution. But Jackson was equally unmoved by the Indian wrongs and by the Court's decisions; he was an old Indian fighter and he regarded his Presidency as a Commander in Chief's position. He was rumored to have said, "John Marshall has made his decision—now let him enforce it." In spite of protest and Court decree, he withheld Federal interference, and the Indians were summarily dispossessed.[1]

Van Buren, standing aside, watched as the Georgia incident was followed by that of South Carolina. In January of 1830, the Webster-Hayne debate in the Senate had alerted the whole country to a long-simmering issue. Disaffection throughout the South was rapidly spreading, and Calhoun was now openly advocating extreme states' rights.[2]

It was at a Jefferson Day dinner in 1830 that Jackson gave notice that he would stand no more nonsense from the nullificationists. There had been fulsome praise of Calhoun that evening, and the President had had enough of it. He rose and proposed a toast: "Our Union: it must be preserved."[3]

Yet the trouble persisted. In 1832, the South Carolina legislature actually passed nullification resolutions, and the Governor was authorized to use force to prevent Federal action. Another series of resolutions denounced Jackson and proclaimed the right of secession. The

---

[1] It is to be noted that Jackson's indifference to the Court's dictum was later considered one of the bulwarks of the Presidency. But this was another matter. The President vs. the Judiciary was not the same thing as the Federal Government vs. the States.

[2] No mention has been made of the tariff issue. But it must be noted that differences about it were among the most serious in acerbating the North-South quarrel. The North wanted protection for its infant manufactures; the South wanted markets abroad for its cotton and tobacco, which could not be maintained if they could not be paid for by foreign goods. The South was rapidly working up a grievance against the tariffs passed by a Congress controlled by the North.

[3] At Hayne's request his toast was amended for publication to "Our Federal Union. . . ."

South Carolinians had obviously presumed, because of the Georgia case, that no Federal intervention would take place. They were never more mistaken. Jackson at once made military dispositions, and in his following message to the Congress said the famous words: "Disunion by armed force is treason."

There followed one of the nation's great debates. It went on for months in the Congress, in the press, and in state legislatures. No one thought or spoke of anything else. But in the end a Force Bill was passed and South Carolina, giving in, rescinded the Ordinance of Nullification. Civil war had been postponed. But also no one knew where Van Buren stood.

It was on the Bank issue that he was caught. Abolition of the Bank was so much a part of Jackson's political apparatus, and it seemed so thoroughly popular an issue, that Van Buren was drawn into it in Jackson's train. When it failed, he had become President. He could not set up another institution without complete and public reversal of his position. Without it, the depression was very slow to retreat. He resorted to the Sub-Treasury—a caretaker institution—which looked like doing something, but really was not. And politically it was futile; he was crushed in the jaws of an issue that, with all his cleverness, he had not seen closing on him. He had been too busy with strictly political maneuvers to consider strategy. He turned out to be the third of the Presidents who could not get for himself a second term—a curious fact, because he was a thorough and—until then—successful politician, as neither Adams had been.

Two of the clearest and most significant lessons in this matter of ascent to the Presidency become available in the case of Van Buren. One of these is that a really commanding occupant of the office can designate his successor but that the choice may not be satisfactory. The other is that political finesse can carry an individual into office but is not enough in itself to keep him there more than one term.

At least two other examples of designation come to mind at once— that of John Adams by Washington and the much later one of Taft by Theodore Roosevelt. Neither was well suited to office, and neither was re-elected. Another case, that of Madison, designated by Jefferson as a successor, is not so clear. He was not an effective executive, but he was re-elected.

In the Van Buren instance, the lesson is particularly sharp because of his ability to dodge trouble. He is still supposed to have been one of the cleverest political manipulators in our history. His contemporaries called him "the Red Fox of Kinderhook" and spoke of him as "the Little Magician." He had been precocious too, so that his experience was a long one. He had been a delegate to a political convention before he was of age, had been appointed a county Surrogate at twenty-five, elected to the New York Senate at thirty, appointed Attorney General of the state at thirty-four, and at thiry-eight had been elected to the United States Senate.

This record, remarkable as it is, does not adequately convey his effectiveness. He was the head of the so-called Albany Regency, which controlled state politics and was influential nationally for many years; and he was one of the early Tammany chieftains. He was the first of the campaign managers. Webster said of him that no ten men had done so much to elect Jackson. He was not the first of the party bosses—Jefferson was that—but he was a pure example of the breed.

Someone said of Van Buren that he was the first President to get to the White House in gumshoes. And it is true that he got there by cleverness and manipulation. He took every advantage of the situation, including the dependence on him of Jackson, who had begun by making him Secretary of State. This in itself was the culminating one in a series of moves. During the three months preceding his appointment to the Department of State, he had been elected to the Governorship of New York, had resigned from the Senate to assume that office, and then had been made a member of Jackson's Cabinet. These were three dazzling pinnacles to have occupied in so short a time. But with his instinct for underemphasizing his own importance, he made as little as possible of the whole matter.

Then, when Jackson was quite clear that he wanted him as successor, he schemed to remove himself from the quarrels building up about the President's cantankerous person and became Minister to Great Britain. But the Senate, seeing through the maneuver, refused him confirmation, thus indulging its malice toward the Presidency and its support of its own presiding officer, Calhoun, who was becoming more and more committed to policies divergent from Jackson's—particularly on the issue of union. This gave Jackson and Van Buren the opportunity for a spectacular coup. Van Buren displaced Calhoun as candidate for Vice-President in 1832 and was overwhelmingly elected along with Jackson. He therefore was able to preside for four years over the body which had humiliated him. When he was nominated to succeed Jackson, his revenge was complete.

So far, so good. But when it came to re-election, all the Van Buren cleverness was insufficient. The strategy had been wrong; the consequences were upon him, and he was defeated. He kept on trying and even became a Free-Soil candidate in 1848, but he never again succeeded.

It is often said of him that he reached the Presidency by appointment almost as much as by election. This is a view which neglects his persistent and careful cultivation of political colleagues and his control of the party machinery. His party had become, by 1835, a formidably efficient force, made strong by patronage. It was fortunate for Van

Buren that this was so, because Jackson's influence was rapidly waning. He was as popular with the people as ever; but the bosses always look ahead and not behind. It is true, too, that Little Van (or Matty Van, as he was known among his Tammany Bucktails) had hopeful rivals among the Democrats. He had checked the ambitions of too many of them; they might come together in opposition. This danger was relieved so far as the Democratic nomination went; Calhoun and White were drawn off into the new coalition of Whigs. And the decisive influence in Van Buren's unanimous nomination by his party was, after all, the demand of the imperious old General that he be allowed to name his successor.

It is no secret that Van Buren played sycophant in several matters in which the General's heart was more engaged than his head. And he followed into inconsistencies of policy that still puzzle those who try to make some sense of the contradictions. Illustrative of this last was the allowing of Georgia to expel its Indians in defiance of Federal law and then coming down hard on South Carolina when that state presumed on the Georgia precedent. Besides these, the Bank issue was a Jacksonian vagary which became a heated issue and divided the country. In this, too, Van Buren stood with Jackson; and it was because of this that he ran head on into the depression of 1837 and saw the small farmers—who were being dispossessed—and the workers—who were unemployed—turn against him. These had been Jackson's devoted political slaves; but their ownership was not transferrable, and they abandoned Van Buren.

The Peggy O'Neill affair illustrates the sycophancy so characteristic of the Jackson-Van Buren relationship. Peggy was the lively daughter of a Washington innkeeper and had caught the eye of John Eaton, Jackson's Secretary of War. Peggy was already married, but presently her sailor husband committed suicide and left her free. Eaton promptly married her, and then the imbroglio began. For Peggy, whether she deserved it or not, had the reputation of being a lady of easy virtue. It was irrelevant that she pleased Eaton, bore him children, and continued to please him. Feminine society boycotted her, and this included, among others, the wives of Jackson's Cabinet.[4]

The old General was furious. His own wife, Rachel, had been subjected to calumny in the past. She had married him without taking pains to confirm her divorce from her first husband. And Jackson had fought, even dueled, with those to whom this seemed a reflection on her morals. Naturally, in the kind of campaign Jackson precipitated, this old story had been retold with embellishments. And just before

---

[4] The atmosphere of dissension was intensified when Jackson became convinced that his enemies, Clay and Calhoun, were enlisted on the side of Peggy's detractors.

his inauguration she had died, leaving him bereft and sore. In his mind, the ostracism of Peggy Eaton was associated with his own Rachel's immolation. It was with emotional zeal and complete forgetfulness of consequences that the President told his associates they must curb their wives. Either they would accept Peggy or take the consequences. They tried; but their wives behaved pretty much as they pleased, and Jackson was frustrated. It was this that led to the Cabinet reorganization of 1831.

It happened that Van Buren, being Secretary of State and therefore first among the Cabinet, was also a widower, his wife having died, leaving him with four sons. There was no woman in his household. The freedom this gave him, together with his natural suavity and blandness, enabled him to pretend that Peggy was a lady worthy of the most delicate and assiduous attentions. He said nothing to persuade others that their behavior was unjust; but the contrast of his own kindness with the cruelty of others touched the President. After the Eaton affair, nothing could persuade Jackson that Little Van was not the soul of chivalry; and for him such a virtue implied all the others.

The lesson in this for explorers of paths to the President's House is fairly plain. Sycophancy pays if the principal in the case controls the disposition of important favors. There is the subordinate consideration, carefully observed by Van Buren, that finesse must be used. It is easy to go too far, for instance, in aspersing others who choose another course. This is one of those matters of more or less, however, which cannot be taught; it has to be felt.

Van Buren had a careful and logical mind along with his Dutch persistence and coolness, and it must have given him some trouble to follow Jackson's nullification challenge, just as it must also to justify his inconsistencies in other matters involving strict or loose construction of the Constitution. At one moment Jackson seemed a states'-righter; the next, he was trumpeting that any challenge to the Union was treason. At one moment he seemed to favor public improvement with Federal funds; the next, any such suggestion was outrageous. But difficult as this must have been for the calculating Van Buren, he managed it.

It was willingness to accept Jackson as he was, and his ability to avoid commitment, that persuaded Jackson. Van Buren must succeed to the Presidency. Between them, they found a way to arrange it—the national convention.

Dissatisfaction with the Congressional caucus had already been taken advantage of by hopeful candidates who could control their state legislatures. A simple resolution in one of those bodies would serve for nomination. But when party control spread, this kind of tour de force was hardly allowable. The bosses needed some practical method of management. The ephemeral Anti-Masonic party first found it in a meeting of delegates from several states. The rivals for political influence were not too happy about being repeatedly outwitted, and if it had not been for the institution of the convention, even Jackson might not have been able to manage his designation of a successor. He got the legislature of New Hampshire to propose the change, saw to it that the party press supported it, and had delegates chosen who would accept advice from him. They were told when they assembled that "unless they wanted a quarrel with the General" they had better favor Van Buren. And, not daring to oppose the old party dictator, this was what they did.

It is interesting that at this first Democratic convention a two-thirds rule was passed which would not be repealed until 1936. It would have grave consequences in many divided conventions. Its most important historical effect would be to give the South, which could not have a nominee, at least a veto. No candidate could be chosen, until the rule was abrogated, to whom the Southerners had objection.

Since the convention proved amenable in 1832, the Jackson-Van Buren team decided to use it for 1836, when Jackson was to retire. When he determined that Van Buren should succeed him, he began to prepare the way by writing a letter to a friend, who duly published it, suggesting a convention whose delegates would be "fresh from the people"—a deliberate aspersion on legislative "nominations." Then the two of them went to work, as national political leaders have done ever since, to see to it that committed delegates were chosen. The Baltimore convention of 1836 was a complete success—that is to say, Van Buren was unanimously nominated. The opposition in that year did not convene.[5] Four years later, however, there was a full-dress convention in Harrisburg of all the dissidents. By now they called themselves Whigs, and their leaders were quite as adept as the Democrats at political manipulation; indeed, they defeated their teachers.

This convention of 1840 nominated W. H. Harrison, who had been defeated in 1836. John Tyler, who was not even a member of the party, although he was a delegate to the convention, was the designated Vice-Presidential candidate; and since General Harrison did not live long, he became President by this curious chance. The party had no

---

[5] The opposition did not have enough common purpose even to meet in 1836. Harrison was nominated by two state conventions at Harrisburg, one an Anti-Masonic group and the other made up of disaffected Democrats. But Daniel Webster was nominated by the Whig legislature of Massachusetts, and Hugh L. White was nominated by the legislatures of Tennessee and Alabama. That White could be nominated in Jackson's own state shows the decline in his power, as well as White's popularity. He was equally popular in other Southern states. Harrison got 73 electoral votes to White's 26 and Webster's 14. This lead gave him a start on the nomination for 1840, although he was by then getting on in years.

agreed policy and so could write no platform at its conventions, and for a good reason: any attempt to discuss issues would have disrupted the proceedings at once. The largest of the groups which had come together to oppose the Democrats were the remnants of the Federalists, the National Republicans who were followers of Clay and Adams, and the Anti-Masons. These, together with Calhoun and his supporters, still smarting from his replacement as Vice-President by Van Buren in 1832, were such a heterogeneous lot that it is not hard to understand why they kept strictly to the expedient and negative and never attempted constructive proposals. They had nothing in common except hatred of the Democrats.

This hatred, however, was a fiery one which kept its partisans together through several campaigns. Its bosses had a facility superior even to Van Buren's for manipulating public opinion. They knew precisely how to undermine their opponents; but also, rather surprisingly, they produced an invention—a thoroughly professional one, not perhaps to be defended on principle, but one which was nevertheless effective. General Harrison was made the first of the "log-cabin" Presidents. The descendant of Virginia aristocrats, himself a General and territorial official, was pictured as a frontier ignoramus, uncouth and ignorant. To be sure, the Whigs only took advantage of a clumsy Democratic attempt at ridicule. It was they who first said that Harrison had a log-cabin origin and was a hard-cider drinker. They were trapped by their own cleverness. It was a log-cabin and hard cider campaign, and it elected Harrison.

Van Buren earned his humiliation. It had always been his policy to evade issues, on the well-known principle that any position taken might offend some voters but that any issue evaded could only be held against him by inference. He was, among American Presidents, the original fence-sitter. His fence-sitting was, however, a much-followed precedent. Evasion would become almost as characteristic of Presidential candidates as the phony bonhomie, whose symbol among the cartoonists would be hand shaking and baby-kissing. These tricks, and many others, were encouraged by Van Buren's success with them.

But there was a clear illustration of the possible penalties in his defeat after one term. The way had been prepared by a severe depression, which came upon the economy even before Jackson had arrived back home at the Hermitage. Hard times were the Whigs' opportunity. People were miserable and frightened, and it was only necessary to make out that Van Buren was responsible. Actually the abolition of the Bank and the resulting financial chaos were Jackson's responsibilities; but Van Buren was heir to the disaster. And his response after attempts to evade had failed—the Sub-Treasury system—did not help. Anyway, the bill setting it up was delayed for several years, and the

long, hard process of recovery without governmental interference had
to be struggled through.

Van Buren's evasiveness was more successful in another field—that
of the growing asperity between North and South. We have seen that,
following Jackson, Van Buren would seem to be allied with those who
favored a strong Union. But he and Jackson had nevertheless been
strict constructionists. If the Federal government had only those powers enumerated in the Constitution, slavery was a matter to be determined by the states—an internal matter. This was a dividing issue
which would grow sharper very rapidly; but Van Buren was successful in evading efforts to make him take any clear stand.

It is sometimes said that this is a fortunate habit of political leaders
and of political parties too. When each party contains within itself
many diverse opinions on issues likely to divide the nation, neither
group can come into control of the government and force its will on
the other before opinion has gone overwhelmingly in one or the other
direction. On the slavery and nullification issues, so prominent in the
years from 1828 to 1860, it was a long time before a party could be
captured by either side. Eventually the Southern interest would become identified with the Democratic party and the North with
Republicanism. This was after the issue had hardened into one which
extremists on either side would not compromise. It is possible to see
how, with more moderation and less political heat, even this awful
ordeal by force could have been avoided.

On the other hand, trimming, on the Van Buren pattern, went
further than mere moderation. Jacksonian firmness had stopped nullification effectively once; its further use might have been better than
letting the Southerners believe that Unionists would never resort to
strong measures. It was only at the very last that the Northerners'
determination became clear; until then, secession seemed to the nullification politicians a threat they could use for blackmail.

Evasion is useful; but there comes a time when a choice has to be
made. What is required then is that the choice shall be one which
results in the public good. Otherwise, the penalties of failure will be
exacted. In Van Buren's case, the failure of the Bank policy brought
quick disaster. In the instance of temporizing with Southern disaffection—which ran on to secession—the trimming went on too long.
When the conflict had sharpened, the processes of politics would be
inadequate for a solution. The South by then would be sunk in a kind
of self-pitying hypnosis, convinced of oppression and Northern ill will,
but at the same time believing that the Northerners would not actually
resort to force. They were so used to doughfaces in the Federal
government that a sudden hardening of unionist sentiment seemed
impossible.

We need not deduce from this that the processes of politics are always inadequate to meet such challenges. From Jackson to Lincoln, there was not one political leader with that touch of genius needed to create a following, unite a majority, and enforce its will.

Van Buren left the Presidency a defeated and discredited man. He had done the institution a damage it would be long recovering from. But if politicians had had the wit to learn it, his experience was a definitive demonstration that the Presidency is best earned rather than inherited.

William Henry Harrison

1773–1844

Born in Charles City County, Virginia
Became ninth President in 1841, at 68

HISTORY

1791–96	Entered the army after attending Hampden-Sydney College for three years; campaigned against Indians under Washington and Anthony Wayne.
1795	Married Anna Tuthill Symmes.
1798	Resigned from the army with the rank of Captain. Became Secretary of the Northwest Territory.
1799	Territorial delegate in the United States Congress.
1800	Appointed Governor of Indiana Territory.
1811	Defeated Tecumseh in the Battle of Tippecanoe.
1812–14	Commissioned Major General of Kentucky Militia in the War of 1812; commissioned Brigadier General, then Major General, U.S. Army.
	Defeated the British in the Battle of the Thames. Resigned from the army and was appointed Commissioner to treat with the Indians.

110

1816	Elected to the Congress.
1819	Elected to the Ohio Senate.
1825	Elected to the United States Senate.
1828–36	Served briefly as Minister to Colombia, then retired to a farm at North Bend, Ohio, and became recorder and clerk of the County Court.
1836	Unsuccessful Whig candidate for President.
1840	Elected President (Vice-President, Tyler); opponent, Van Buren with Johnson.
1841	Died in office.

I T IS a little difficult to distinguish the two Van Buren-Harrison contests in 1836 and 1840 by any significant advantages one candidate
had over the other. In the first, Van Buren won; in the second, Harrison won. If we say that Van Buren got to be President in 1836 by
apple-polishing (as American locution has it), we have to say that
Harrison got there in 1840 as a puppet of the party professionals. But
both statements are too simple. Van Buren was more than a sycophant,
and Harrison was more than a tool of the Whig politicians.

As for Van Buren, we have seen how under study he escapes from
any easy stereotype. So does Harrison. It is true that he had less
impact as President than any other occupant of that office. But his
getting there is quite as instructive as that of any who served longer.
This is especially true because he figured in two campaigns and
improved the technique of losers who go on to become winners. There
is always something admirable about such an achievement. And it
contrasts interestingly with the failure of those who came close once
but whose second tries were *not* successful. Some of these were Harrison's contemporaries. Among them were Webster, Calhoun, and Clay,
politicians as prominent as it is possible to be without actually reaching
the top.

It is a partial explanation of Harrison's success to recall that he, and
not Van Buren, inherited Jackson's glamor and generally moved into
people's hearts as Jackson withdrew. It was ridiculous for Jackson to
solicit affection for Van Buren and to endow him with power. That
slick operator, who dodged and trimmed so successfully, had really no
original appeal of his own. A Democratic majority made him President
because Jackson wished it; but they would not keep him there. When
it was clear that he had little popular appeal, a more Jackson-like
figure was turned to—another frontier General with the repute of
victory upon him. He stood for none of Jackson's policies, of course;
but the way he attracted acclaim shows how small a part issues play in
such choices when a hero is available.

A later generation would experience much the same phenomenon in
the popularity of Eisenhower as Roosevelt's successor. If Eisenhower's
success was not because of his Republicanism, neither was Harrison's
because he was a Whig. Harrison probably discovered his Whiggish-
ness only just in time for his candidacy—as Eisenhower did his
Republicanism. Harrison's election was a thoroughly professional job.
There was no nonsense about principle. Such things were hardly mentioned; neither were large public issues. This was the Whig way. It
sufficed to win twice; but it could not keep the party alive for long.

There never was such buncombe as was invented in 1840; but also there never was such a general willingness among the voters to accept what they knew to be false. They were introduced to a General who would substitute for Jackson, and they had had enough of Van Buren, what with hard times and Presidential evasions. But there can have been very few who could have adduced a defensible reason for their votes in favor of Harrison.

This was an example destined to influence professionals from then on. The Eisenhower campaign of 1952 was certainly in direct descent from Harrison's in 1840, and in between there were others. The rule they deduced was: have a glamorous non-political candidate, avoid issues, and smear the opposition. Following it does nothing toward building a party organization or establishing a tradition for the future. But politicians are often very shortsighted. One victory at a time seems to satisfy them.

The Whig leaders found Harrison the ideal candidate for what they had in mind. He was the kind of prominent man who has found it possible to be, until the very last, apolitical. He had never in his life cast a vote before he was nominated for the Presidency. What were the contemporary professionals thinking of to permit such an elbowing aside of men who understood the significance of the office, to whom it was the supreme attainment, infinite in reward, by one who reached for it as an amateur? Perhaps the answer to this is that organized politics and professional politicians are widely considered to be disreputable. And only in exceptional circumstances is the electorate willing to have its highest representative office occupied by an individual who must have done what any politician must do who works his way up the organization ladder. If the professionals can play on this suspicion they are quite willing to do it. They have no pride of occupation.

Some career politicians have made it. We have seen Jefferson and Van Buren arrive; we shall see others, such as Garfield, Harding, and Coolidge; and we shall find cause to doubt whether the untainted amateur is as good a President as the professional. One of the least competent Presidents was Grant—another who never had voted—and one of the most eminent was Lincoln, who was an organization politician from early youth. But the smell of corruption does haunt organization headquarters. And some of the shrewdest party managers have put forward candidates who have made a show of drawing their skirts away and pretending to scorn the processes they are allowing to lift them toward positions of power.

Professional claimants will step aside, if necessary, to assist the party in winning. If their sense of realism tells them that the times call for a candidate who is a complete amateur, they will make way for one who seems to meet the specifications. If he catches on, they must hope that he is one they can manage. He may have his sticking points; and it is true that the Presidency often makes even the most tractable candidates difficult in further transactions with the bosses. This effect can be observed in soft and even deliquescent characters. In those who are the stuffed-shirt type there is apt to be aroused a lively sense of duty, and this too may be very awkward. Nevertheless, the political process settles inevitably into experienced hands. And even Presidents must accept the fact. It is probable that Harrison was a paragon of stuffed-shirtism who would have given his managers real trouble if he had lived; there was a hint of that in his rejection of the inaugural address Webster wrote for him. That Webster proffered it shows the contempt of the old hand for the amateur. That it may not have been justified, we can guess. The old man insisted on writing his own speech. True, Webster was allowed to work it over, but it was, after all, Harrison's own. Nothing could have exposed more clearly to the discerning the character of the recent contest than this address. The man who had been pictured as the common log-cabin, hard-cider candidate stepped forward with an elaborate production, filled with erudite allusion, addressed to the fundamentals. It was prolix, even tedious, in its classical references. It was this, in fact, that led Webster to remark about the revision he was allowed to make that in shortening it he had "killed a dozen Roman consuls dead as smelts."

Harrison was not to live long enough to show his capacity as President; but he was certainly the front for, and the beneficiary of (if a man can be said to benefit from something which killed him), a campaign of cynical deceit.

It is interesting to note a historians' verdict, more than a century later, on the campaign of 1840:

> The campaign of 1840 was the jolliest presidential election America has ever known. Van Buren suffered from the same buncombe that he had used against Adams in 1828; and the Whigs had plenty of money to influence the numerous unemployed. . . . Van Buren was pictured with cologne-scented whiskers, drinking champagne out of a crystal goblet at a table loaded with costly viands and massive plate. An unlucky sneer in a Democratic newspaper, to the effect that Harrison would be content with a log cabin and plenty of hard cider, gave opportunity for effective contrast. It became the log-cabin, hard-cider campaign. There were log-cabin badges and log-cabin songs, a *Log Cabin* newspaper and log-cabin clubs, big log cabins where the thirsty were regaled with hard cider that the jealous Democrats alleged to be spiked with whisky; little log cabins borne on floats in procession, with latch-string out . . .

Huge balls, supposed to represent the gathering majority, were rolled by men and boys from village to village and state to state, singing as they rolled:

> What has caused this great commotion, motion, motion,
>   Our country through?
> —It is the ball a-rolling on, for
> (*Chorus*) Tippecanoe and Tyler too:—
>   Tippecanoe and Tyler too.
> And with them we'll beat little Van, Van, Van,
> Oh! Van is a used-up man![1]

This was the scene, and these were the tactics.

Emerson the philosopher remarked about this time that the Democrats seemed to have the best principles and the Whigs the best men. There was a good deal in this. Others described the difference as one between people with wealth and position and those who were ignorant and irresponsible. It is remarkable how closely the Whigs did resemble their forerunners, the Federalists. It was beginning to be apparent that this was a persistent polarization in the United States—one party attracted the men of property and influence, and the other tended to gather unto itself the disadvantaged, the debtors, the little people. It would continue to be so.

Other issues would sometimes create diversions attracting adherents to one or the other side until the weight seemed to establish a new alignment. This happened when the Democratic party was maneuvered into identification with the South, leaving the Union cause to the Republicans. For a century to come there would be a "Solid South"— that is, white Southerners, without regard to class differences, would always vote Democratic. The complications following from this would together form a hard ideological lump in an otherwise fairly fluid series of coalitions determined by economic interests.

The Democrats could not always command the votes of the worker and the small farmer. They had to shape their policies in every campaign to attract them, and they did not always succeed. But this was their normal constituency. And the Republican party, succeeding the Whigs, as the Whigs had succeeded the Federalists, became the party of business, of the better people, of those who had education and culture. The Democrats were a party of demagogues and mobs, of bosses and delivered votes, and of municipal and state corruption. But it was

---

[1] *Growth of the American Republic,* Samuel Eliot Morrison and Henry Steele Commager (New York, 1930 and later), I, 556–57.

also the party of welfare measures and of opposition to monopoly and privilege.

Any such contrast is too sharply drawn to be more than very generally defensible. But the vast irrelevancy of the Civil War should not be allowed to confuse a real and persistent tendency toward polarization. Democrats would be more or less disreputable for a generation after their identification with states' rights and with the Copperheads, who, during the Civil War, would oppose the Union by conspiracy. This identification had about it, most of the time, the same false character as the Whig campaign of 1840; but Republicans, like Whigs, would always have the money necessary to create and perpetuate illusions. They would hire publicists in other campaigns just as freely as they hired the men and boys to roll the big balls about the country in 1840; and in other campaigns, as in that one, they would have a certain success. Often the success would be due to the same sort of popular eagerness to be fooled that put Harrison in the White House.

There was certainly, from the very first, in American political parties, this tendency, massive and irresistible, toward adhesion for reasons of social distinction; but there was a counter tendency too. The same historians who were just quoted speak of it as beginning with the Harrison nomination, which

> was a milepost in the evolution of the presidency. Wise politicians realized that when sectional issues threatened the national parties, they could nominate a 'favorite son' such as Webster, or a statesman with a definite policy such as Clay, only at a risk of alienating other members of the party alliance, and losing the election.[2]

It can be seen that there was a constant effort being made to escape the definite tagging of the party with a class label. Political managers mean to attract votes, not to repel them. Their instinct is to offer something for everyone at all open to persuasion, and to avoid argument likely to raise anyone's hackles. But they have never been able to escape altogether the general orientation of their party. They always have a platform, however ambiguously worded, to contend with; and this discloses what they would rather conceal. But they can and do attempt to find uncommitted, wholly ambiguous candidates. The historians say of this:

> Since 1840 successful presidential candidates have not been prominent and experienced statesmen, but military heroes or relatively obscure men who have not had time to make enemies. Only by inadvertence, as

---

[2] *Ibid.*, 555.

in the case of Lincoln and the Roosevelts, did the President prove to be
a man of outstanding ability.[3]

This is an appalling statement. But it cannot truthfully be said to
be an exaggeration. And if it is not, it reinforces the thesis that any
fellow of reasonably good appearance may set out to become President
with some hope of success. At least he is not disqualified because he
cannot discern in himself the qualities of sublimity we like to associate
with the Presidency. The kind of people realistic politicians look for
may very well be just the kind of person an ordinary man perceives
himself to be, even though there may be the most serious doubt about
his qualifications.

Harrison was the first of these ordinary men. He may not have been
so stupid as the politicians believed. But there is no doubt that this
ordinariness was an attraction for Thurlow Weed, then so potent a
boss, and for his professional colleagues. They were able to shape him
as a public figure and set him in contrast with the already existing
characters who were so much more prominent—Clay, Webster, and
Calhoun.

Our inquiry, then, about Harrison's arrival at the President's House
requires us to ask about his ancestry, his career, and his reputation, all
in relation to the specific situation of 1840.

The Harrisons arrived in Virginia toward the middle of the eighteenth century. They were prominent citizens almost from their first
coming, and their ancestral seat was one of the earliest of the conspicuous Virginia country houses. The President's father, Benjamin,
was well known all during the Revolution as one of the ardent pro-
testers of English rule. He was elected to the House of Burgesses
while very young and was one of those who signed the remonstrances
of 1774. Afterward he was a delegate to the Continental Congress and,
still later, after four Congressional terms, he was again sent to the
House of Burgesses in Virginia, where he stayed as Speaker until he
was elected Governor in 1782.

With such an elite background, it would be thought impossible to
picture William Henry as a rough and simple man of the prairies,
earnest but crude. If there were First Families in Virginia, his was
one. It was true that he had spent most of his life in the Western
country; but he had been a military man and a colonial official. He had
a country place near Cincinnati; but it was an estate, not a farm. At
the time of his nomination he held a local office because his long public
service had left him poor; but, on the whole, he was as far from being
a product of struggle with the forest and unbroken grasslands as it is
possible to imagine.

---

[3] *Ibid.*

When his father had died while William Henry was a young man Robert Morris had become his guardian. He had gone to Hampden-Sydney College, where he had studied the classics—whence those allusions in the inaugural address so amusing to Webster. From there he had gone to Philadelphia and begun the study of medicine. But what was happening out on the frontier stirred his imagination and, in spite of Morris' objections, he asked Washington for a commission and got it. He was made an officer of artillery in 1791 and joined his corps at Fort Washington on the Ohio. He saw active service with St. Clair and Wayne, rose to be a Captain, and, at twenty-one, married the daughter of John Cleves Symmes, founder of the Miami settlements in Ohio.

Then his career as a colonial official began. He was appointed first to be Secretary of the Northwest Territory but resigned when he was elected a delegate to the Congress. But in 1800, when Indiana Territory was organized, he was its first Governor. His Governorship was a troubled one. There was constant conflict with the Indians as the white men moved into their lands, and it fell to him to negotiate the treaties legitimizing doubtful "purchases" and proscriptions. He made a certain reputation for conciliation during the next ten years; but as the invasion of settlers grew, the grievances of the Indians became more acute. Moreover, a leader of ability rose among them. This was Tecumseh, who in 1809 denounced the Treaty of Fort Wayne as a steal.

It soon became obvious that the British were encouraging and assisting the restless tribes, and Harrison foresaw war. Presently it broke out; and when it came, he was the organizer of strategy for the government.

The Battle of Tippecanoe would be regarded later as a small affair. No more than seven or eight hundred men were engaged on each side; but the result was important. The Indians were defeated and the territory made safe for settlement. The decisiveness of Harrison's leadership established his reputation, and from this time on wherever there was border trouble or the British still had ambitions, he was trusted to settle the matter. As was true of so many frontier leaders, his authority was made secure by giving him military rank. Even before General Hull surrendered to him at Detroit, he was appointed to command the Kentucky volunteers, and presently he was made Commander in Chief in the West.

Even with the rank of General, Harrison had no easy time of it. His troops were mostly untrained; he had incredible difficulties with supplies. Also, it was never very clear just what his objectives were supposed to be. Since this was so, he set for himself the recapture of Michigan Territory, then occupied by the British. There were several inconclusive engagements in 1812, after which he built an encampment at Fort Meigs. In the spring of 1813 he was attacked there by British and Indian forces. The battles were again not decisive; but in the fall there occurred the Battle of the Thames, and this was decisively won.

Considering the miserable military showing throughout the War of 1812, a real victory was something to shout about. And the General who had produced it was perhaps lionized beyond his deserts. He was commended by President Madison; and the Congress, passing a resolution of thanks, awarded him a gold medal. All this glory resulted in the usual envy. Secretary Armstrong of the War Department had had little but criticism for his performance during the war, and his jealous coolness so annoyed the General that he forwarded his resignation. The conquering hero had enormous acclaim as he rode toward Washington to meet his detractor; nevertheless, Armstrong accepted his resignation.

His later career can be résuméed very briefly. He was elected to the Congress in 1816 and to the Senate from Ohio in 1825, which shows how popular he was in the West. Then he was appointed in 1828 by President Adams to be Minister to Colombia; but he was hardly in this post long enough to make a mark. He was almost at once recalled in the Jackson house cleaning. Not being a Jacksonian, he had nothing to do but retire to his North Bend estate on the Ohio. Curiously, for one who had been so prominent, he presently had to accept a lowly political appointment. He was poor and his estate did not pay. He became clerk of the Hamilton County Court. And it was from this minor office that he was elected to the Presidency in 1840. His being a court clerk was adduced as evidence that he was a plain man with no false pride. There was not much other evidence to support the log-cabin legend that grew up in that campaign with him as a center. But it proved to be enough.

Truth and reality were not much bothered with in that campaign. Harrison may not have been a man of the people, and he may have been a Virginia gentleman; but he was successfully presented as a rough-and-ready pioneer. He had had a serious and honorable career, but it was not this that was dwelt on. If his open frankness and honest decency had been used as campaign material, the contrast with Van Buren would have been enough. It can be guessed that Thurlow Weed and the other Whig bosses, although they chose to picture him in false face, took great care to determine that there was a man behind the mask who, if exposed, would not be disgraced. His reputation as a popular hero was an earned one. It was only his genteel ancestry, his education, and his culture that they thought must be concealed beneath frontier commonness.

What is there to learn from this? Perhaps it is that one way to the

Presidency is to be made representative of the contemporary electoral stereotype. But of course Harrison was also a hero, and such a man is often useful to political manipulators. Jackson, Harrison, Taylor, Grant, and Eisenhower were widely enough separated to support such a generalization. But they were, aside from being Generals, very different kinds of men. They range from the austere to the folksy, from the log-cabin amateur (even though the log-cabin was mythical) to the West Point professional. Even Washington might not have become President in 1840; he was rich and wellborn, and he would never have allowed himself to be presented as a farmer. That Harrison felt it necessary to lend himself to the masquerade shows how the electorate had changed in half a century.

Washington did not seek office; Harrison was always seeking it; if he could not have one job, he would settle for another. And anyone who had been cheered along the highways as he was when he journeyed to Washington after the Battle of the Thames to have it out with the Secretary of War, and who practically had an apology from the President himself (he was at once asked by Madison to act as Commissioner to settle Indian claims), must have been conscious of his prominence. When in 1836, without much preparation and with little organization, he showed a very considerable voting strength, he became the center of the bosses' attention. It was nearly a quarter century since his military exploits had been so acclaimed. But they had not been forgotten. Besides, he came from the West, by now the best origin for a candidate. The bosses had only to require the region's favorite sons to give way in his favor. Clay was the most reluctant of these. He had been hovering on the Presidential periphery for a generation, but he was still a younger man than Harrison;[4] he came from the West. He was the Jackson type, the same sort of brash and rakish bravo. But one trouble with him—as with Webster—was that he had not been a military hero; another was that everyone knew only too well where he stood. He was not quite so clearly a sectional candidate as Calhoun; but he was still marked and ticketed. Harrison stood only for rugged strength, for capable leadership, for honesty. Beyond innocuous objectives, he had no commitments. Therefore, no one could really be against him. And things had gone so badly for Van Buren that he was a weak opponent.

Van Buren had tried to achieve facelessness too. He was a thorough politician, and he knew the dangers of commitment. But a President must act when crises come; and then his enemies have him. Van Buren's dodging had to end when hard times came; but his measures were weak, and the depression ran on and on. Harrison, the rugged

---

[4] In 1840 he was sixty-three; Harrison was sixty-seven.

patriarch from the West, was in perfect contrast to the small Dutchman. So victory went to the supposed amateur rather than the known professional. Behind the false whiskers there may have been a capable President; but we really have no way of knowing that, and for our purpose here it does not matter. The log-cabin and hard-cider candidate won.

John Tyler
1790–1862

Born in Charles City County, Virginia
Became tenth President by succession in 1841 at 51

HISTORY

1807	Graduated from William and Mary College.
1811	Elected to the Virginia legislature.
1816	Elected to the Congress.
1823	Elected to the Virginia legislature.
1825	Elected Governor.
1827	Elected United States Senator.
1840	Elected Vice-President.
1841	Succeeded to the Presidency on the death of Harrison. Vetoed Clay's bill for a new bank to replace the Bank of the United States, whereupon the entire Cabinet, except Webster, resigned.
1842	Signed the Ashburton Treaty. Wife died.
1843	Webster resigned, making the Whig defection complete.

1844	Married Julia Gardiner. Failed to be nominated for a term of his own in the Presidency.
1861	President of a peace convention in Washington. Elected to the Confederate Congress.
1862	Died at 71.

FOR A STUDENT of the Presidency, there is no more interesting case than that of the tenth President. It is more than interesting, it is ironic, because when they chose John Tyler for the Vice-Presidency the cynical Whig politicians overreached themselves. We have seen why it was done—to placate the Clay forces after their candidate's summary rejection in favor of a man they regarded as an old nonentity, General Harrison. By nominating Tyler, they calculated to keep the loose confederation of Whiggery intact. They got no commitments from Tyler himself and evidently took very lightly the principles he professed. They had no platform themselves because they could not agree on one; but they seem to have assumed that Tyler, like the rest of those who had opposed Van Buren, would oppose everything Democratic.

Nothing could have been plainer, either, than his stubborn consistency. He had been in politics a long time, and if he had not been a brilliant leader he had certainly been a solid second-rank stand-by. It is true that, like Clay, he was disillusioned about Van Buren and that this was so strong a feeling as momentarily to shake his Democratic affiliation; but there was no reason to have thought that it had changed his principles. It is possible to judge that he took the nomination under the false pretense of having become a Whig in thought as well as alliance; if so, it is another illustration of the sacrifice required sometimes to approach the Presidency. If it was bad faith on his part, we can at least credit him, when he succeeded Harrison, with not changing his attitudes to gain a term of his own. The difficulty with yielding him this credit is that he may very well have hoped to get it from the Democrats, thus betraying the Whigs. This, however, is purely conjecture.

Tyler's retrospective claim was that the Whigs had betrayed him, not he the Whigs. Since he was President after Harrison had died he was the titular leader of the party. If the bosses insisted on passing legislation (the charter for a new national bank) against his wishes, they could expect a veto; that, anyway, is what they got.

The division among the politicians is at least partly traceable to the negative nature of the whole Whig movement. It was directed against Van Buren, but not on principle. There was no principle. Still, if the Whigs had not been able to produce a platform, the Democrats had. And in spite of Van Buren's instinct for weaseling in such matters, it was definite about the issues uppermost in people's minds. It stood for strict construction first and foremost; and thus it implied that the Federal government might not carry out internal improvements, might not foster one kind of industry as against another (and therefore, no

124

protective tariff), might not charter a national bank, and might not "interfere with or control the domestic institutions of the several states," such states being the "sole and proper judges of everything appertaining to their own affairs not prohibited by the Constitution. . . ."

What the Democratic platform went on to say about the slavery issue was that

> all efforts of the abolitionists or others made to induce Congress to interfere with questions of slavery, or to take incipient steps in relation thereto, are calculated to lead to the most alarming and dangerous consequences . . .

The Democratic party was very rapidly, from its strict constructionist attitude, being drawn into a commitment to defend slavery as well as to an extreme version of states' rights. This would very easily become the justification first for nullification and then for secession. Before getting anywhere near this extreme, Jackson had balked and publicly chastised the South Carolinian agitators. But Van Buren, his successor, was not a man to put up his back and fight for what he believed. Anyway, he probably did not know what he believed, or held his beliefs so lightly that they could comport with Southern prejudices. As can be seen, the Southerners, in spite of such setbacks as Jackson's expressed displeasure, were becoming bolder and more intransigent. They were determined to bend the nation to their will. Nothing less than acknowledgment of the right to maintain their "peculiar institution," without interference or even criticism, would satisfy them. It was becoming evident that presently they would demand complete submission. Lacking it, they would always threaten secession. Whether they would actually secede, even they themselves did not know.

Tyler had never made any secret of being one of these Southerners. He was a follower of Clay, who was a moderate; and when the Whigs nominated him, it was generally assumed, however baselessly, that his belief's were the same as Clay's—that is to say, that he was a loose constructionist; and loose construction, in this context, would imply support for Federal public improvements, a national bank, a protective tariff, and generally a strong central government. This was certainly the Clay policy; and since Tyler had been so ardent a supporter, it is understandable that he should have been expected to accept all of Clay's attitudes. That he had a record of his own, a long and definite one, which contradicted any such assumption, was either overlooked or ignored.

At any rate, for our purpose we may leave the puzzle as a piece of carelessness on the part of bosses who were momentarily softened by their victory over Clay and disposed to placate his wing of the party by honoring his best-known colleague.

From Tyler's point of view—that is, from the point of view of a hopeful politician—the Vice-Presidency was a suddenly offered opportunity such as seldom occurs. It can easily be understood how a lifetime professional would react when he understood what was within his reach. For Harrison was a man older than his years; and, as has often been remarked, the Vice-President is never more than a heartbeat from the Presidency.

Tyler's accession, it will be seen, can be interpreted as an instance of a man arriving at the Presidency through mutual agreement—between himself and all those who were active in actually forwarding him—to ignore a fatal incompatibility. In spite of the realism, amounting almost to cynicism, characteristic of professional politicians, they are subject to acute attacks of belief in miracles. Their whole lives may seem to be characterized by a disillusioned appraisal of men and affairs and a complete immunity to sentiment. Yet, at particularly critical junctures, they will sometimes shut their eyes and ears to the plainest evidence of disagreement. And the resultant discord may defeat the ends they have hitherto sought with such admirable single-minded determination.

If the candidate allows himself to be carried along into the resultant situation, he too will suffer the penalty involved in inevitable conflict. Tyler may have become thus progressively involved. The developing situation was complex. A holder of various legislative and executive offices between 1811—when at twenty-one he became a member of the Virginia House of Delegates—and 1841—when at fifty-one he became Vice-President—must necessarily have had to make decisions concerning issues he may not have thought through carefully. He was a strict constructionist, true; but *how* strict? Was he stricter than Jackson, for instance? As for Federal payment for public improvements, Jackson, in principle, was opposed. But when national security was involved, he came down decisively on the other side. When Tyler had been a Senator, the New Englander, Adams, had been President, and he had gone into opposition. When Jackson succeeded, he had supported him in the disestablishment of the Bank. But Jackson was not sound enough on the tariff to suit him; and when Calhoun developed his nullification thesis, Tyler went with Calhoun even though it enraged Jackson. What he said was that Jackson had abandoned the principles of Jefferson. And he was naturally and bitterly opposed to the coercion of South Carolina. So in Jackson's second term he was generally against the Administration and particularly against the President.

Did mere opposition to Jackson make him a Whig? At any rate, when he was elected President pro tempore of the Senate in 1835,

Whig votes were joined to those of the states'-righters in support of him. Confusion and cross-purpose had begun.

In the next year he resigned his Senate seat. This came about because he had got himself into a dilemma. It concerned a political issue puzzling to better minds than John Tyler's and never really settled. It was the question whether an elected "representative" could decide for himself how to vote in the Congress or whether he was obligated to vote according to the wishes of his constituents. All through American and British history this has remained a doubtful matter. Every once in a while a legislator has asserted his right to think for himself. But about as often other lawmakers have loudly proclaimed their virtuous determination to find and follow the voters' wishes.

Recurrently, state legislatures during the first century of the Constitution "instructed" the Washington legislators as though they were mere delegates. Somewhat earlier, we noticed Clay ignoring one of these instructions concerning support for Jackson. As a long-time state official and as a convinced states'-righter as well, Tyler had easily taken the position that such instruction was a necessary adjunct of democracy. Now that he was a United States Senator, he may not have been so sure. But he had talked very definitely about this, as about other items of the strict constructionist doctrine. When as a Senator he was "instructed" to vote for a resolution expunging from the record a resolution censoring Jackson, he found the directed action to be unconstitutional, or so he said; and he resigned. He had also resigned from the House at one time. It is hard to escape the suspicion that, with Tyler, resignation was a way of escaping from unpleasant choices.

Tyler's resignations however, did not give the impression of escaping from a dilemma he had got into from careless acceptance of a popular view so much as being a man of principle who would not compromise. On the occasion of his resignation from the Senate, the mistaken acclaim was so generous as to augur future reward. He was presently "nominated" for the Vice-Presidency by the Maryland legislature and received 47 electoral votes in 1836.

He had not run for the Senate as a Whig in 1836; but his late resignation and his determined opposition to Jackson and Van Buren seemed to obscure his long-fixed position as a strict constructionist. But then the Whigs, as has been noted, were not yet a party of positive principle but only one of opposition. And although the party orientation was upper-class and anti-Democratic, it was stretched to include Clay and even Calhoun. Strict constructionists like Calhoun and Tyler were somehow supposed to favor a national bank because they had opposed Jackson, who was intent on destroying the Bank. They even became Whigs to oppose him. They were, then, involved with people who were determined to do everything they disapproved, including the re-establishment of the Bank.

This was a confusing and delicate situation. Tyler had been retired for several years when he was elected a Virginia delegate to the Whig convention in Harrisburg, and perhaps his views were not well known. He went there to assist in nominating Clay. Clay was equivocal enough to satisfy the Southerners, and he had opposed the Jacksonians. But the Northern Whigs knew he was not really one of them, and Thurlow Weed's distrust was fortified by the belief that he could not be elected. This was when the border candidate, Harrison, was thrust into the picture. And Tyler was the unexpectedly willing gift to the Clay people.

It was fortunate for Tyler's intentions that he had just been in retirement for four years, so that his former commitments were somewhat obscured by his general reputation as a man of delicate sensitivity. His resignation was recalled, but not what had caused it. This cannot possibly have fooled Weed and the other Whig professionals. They must simply have become for the moment convinced, because it was important for them to find a complaisant Southerner, that facts were not facts but foggy obstructions, which would dissolve at their wish. Either that, or they believed Tyler to have made a choice he could not possibly have made to go against his strict constructionism. It was wrong of him, he must have known, to accept preferment from the Whigs; it would be inconceivably corrupt for him to have accepted the principles to which they would adhere when they had to formulate any—that is, if they should win and have to govern.

Yet Tyler became President when Harrison died; and Whig preferences began to make themselves felt. When it came to legislation, the first item on the Whig agenda was the rechartering of the Bank. Tyler then found himself in one of his familiar dilemmas again, and this time he could not escape. He had to make a choice.

When the student of Tyler's behavior has to ask himself why Tyler the Democrat held himself out to be a Whig, he is forced to examine the possibility, obvious in the circumstances, that his Whiggism was assumed because it was the way to preferment. Van Buren was a failure. The Democrats were steadily losing elections in all the years preceding 1840. When the House of Representatives met in December 1839, there were 118 opposing members to 119 Democrats; and five from New Jersey who were Whigs were contesting.[1] No one could miss the preliminary signs. The Whigs were going to win in 1840. And

---

[1] It was on this occasion that ex-President Adams, now a member of the House, saved the situation by asking for order and proposing himself as temporary chairman.

since what was forming was a coalition of dissidents anyway, many of them Democrats, why not join the movement?

This was the background which makes it seem unlikely that Tyler was as innocent in the affair as he later made himself appear. When he had to decide at Harrisburg whether he would now go the whole distance and accept preferment from the Whigs instead of doing what he had come there to do—see that Clay, the half-Southerner, should be the Presidential candidate—he accepted a political obligation. The plain fact is that as President he went back on an implied pledge. He had fooled the party; and they had a right to the indignation they ultimately expressed in an extraordinary statement withdrawing their support. But nevertheless, it has to be said that his compromising at the convention got for him the Vice-Presidency and so the position from which to succeed to the Presidency itself.

When President Harrison died, Tyler was at home in Virginia. He arrived in Washington two days later and was met by Harrison's Cabinet, whom he asked to continue in office. After the funeral he issued a statement amounting to an inaugural address, which was at least not frightening to the Whigs. He confirmed a call, previously issued, for a special session of the Congress. His appointments were those recommended to him by party members. It seemed to the elders that they might after all assume a complaisance in the new President that they had not been certain of. And there was no trouble until a bill for rechartering the Bank was presented for his signature. His veto of this bill was a shock. It had originated with Secretary of the Treasury Ewing and had been supposed to have the President's approval. The majority leaders in the Senate were disconcerted. This was the one measure on which they thought agreement had been complete, and the veto was at once recognized as a threat to the precarious coalition. In the accompanying message, however, suggestions were made for changes. He favored, Tyler said, an institution without discounting powers and limited to dealing in bills of national exchange. Such a bill was promptly passed; but this also was vetoed, and now the Whigs were furious and the Democrats exultant.

The Whig members of the Congress met and appointed a committee of Senators and Representatives to prepare an address to the nation. It gave notice that all relations between the party and the President were at an end. Simultaneously, all members of the Cabinet resigned, with one exception. This was Webster, the Secretary of State, who stayed on to complete negotiations for what became the Webster-Ashburton Treaty settling the outstanding differences with Britain about the Northeastern frontier. The Whigs seemed to have abandoned Tyler. Yet a protective tariff, to which he had always been opposed, had been enacted and he had signed it. And his new appointees to the Cabinet were not Democrats, as had been anticipated, but Whigs; and the Senate confirmed them.

Whatever Tyler expected, he was not taken back into the inner circle. He was treated as a renegade. And although the Democrats praised his "independence," it was with tongue in cheek. They showed no desire to adopt him. From 1842 on he was really a President without a party.

It can be imagined that not much was done in the way of legislating for the rest of Tyler's term. The Congressional elections of 1842 resulted in a decisive Democratic majority in the House; but the Senate remained Whig. There were further Cabinet changes; two Secretaries were killed in a tragic explosion aboard the U.S.S. *Princeton* and had to be replaced, and these were not the last; in one, especially, Calhoun became Secretary of State.

Calhoun's contribution was to negotiate a treaty for the annexation of Texas. It was rejected by the Senate; but it was obvious that Tyler, even after his disturbed administration, hoped that its pro-slavery implications would persuade the Democrats to nominate him. The Whigs were now wholly alienated. As it turned out, they nominated Clay this time as they should have done in 1840. And the Democrats turned again to Van Buren. But Jackson and Van Buren's two-thirds rule returned to torment Little Van. His majority was not large enough; and in the end the convention chose the first of the dark-horse candidates, James K. Polk of Tennessee (with George M. Dallas of Pennsylvania for Vice-President).

It had seemed, until then, that any incumbent President could have himself renominated if he wished. His influence, by patronage and through leadership of the party, was thought to be irresistible. But Tyler by now had no such reserves. He had supporters—the office-holders who owed their positions to him and who would lose them if he went out. But they were cold-shouldered at the convention. The Democrats were not impressed by a Tyler-sponsored meeting concurrent with theirs. They went on to choose Polk. In August, Tyler withdrew from his hopeless candidacy and announced that he would support Polk.

Tyler was heard of again years later. He presided over the fruitless Peace Congress in Washington in 1861; and he was elected to the Confederate Congress. He died at the beginning of 1862, still an enigma to friends and enemies. But he had become President, even if he had had to invent a new way—that of being on both sides at once.

James Knox Polk
1795–1849

Born in Mecklenburg County, North Carolina
Became eleventh President in 1845 at 49

HISTORY

1806	_ Moved to Tennessee.
1818	Graduated from the University of North Carolina.
1820	Admitted to the bar.
1821	Appointed Chief Clerk, Tennessee Senate.
1823	Elected to the Tennessee House of Representatives.
1824	Married Sarah Childress.
1825	Elected to the United States House of Representatives.
1835	Elected Speaker of the House.
1839	Elected Governor of Tennessee.
1841	Defeated for re-election.
1843	Defeated again.
1844	Nominated by the Democrats and elected to the Presidency (Vice-President, George Mifflin Dallas); opponent, Clay with Frelingheusen.

131

1846	Settled the dispute with Britain over the Oregon Territory.
1846–47	Mexican War.
1848	Peace with the acquisition of more than a half million square miles of territory.
1848	Declined to be renominated for the Presidency.
1849	Died in Nashville.

When James K. Polk is spoken of by his biographers as having "ridden into office on Jackson's coat-tails," all politicians and their familiars follow the allusion. So, perhaps, in this instance do most outsiders. But metaphorical language sometimes becomes so esoteric as to escape common understanding. And even phrases that are much used have rich connotations outsiders cannot share. In this instance Polk's indebtedness to Jackson was understated until Newton Cannon, an opponent in the Governorship campaign of 1839, said acidly—Polk being present on the platform—that "*he* had never clung to Jackson's coat-tails, and, as soon as danger threatened, *jumped into his pocket.*"

This rather picturesquely—in the language of politics—described just what Polk had done. But it probably did not seem offensive to the voters. And as for Jackson and Polk—Jackson had a loyal substitute for Van Buren when Little Van was no longer useful, and Polk achieved the Democratic nomination on Jackson's recommendation. He called himself "Young Hickory" and was not repudiated. It was as a result of Jackson's word, sent to the Democratic faithful, that he became the first "dark horse"—which is another expressive locution from the vocabulary of politics.[1] He was trotted out under the Jackson colors and eventually accepted by the professionals with whom the old man still had enormous prestige in spite of having burdened them with Van Buren, who was now being got rid of.

Since the Whigs had been demoralized by Tyler's defection, the Democrats were in a good position to win. No one knew this better than Van Buren; but it was too late for him to reingratiate himself with Jackson. And as the balloting proceeded, Polk, emerging from the ruck, passed Little Van and became the convention's choice. The progression was as follows (omitting a few scattered votes for others):

Ballots:	1	2	3	4	5	6	7	8	9
Van Buren (N.Y.)	146	127	121	111	103	101	99	104	0
Cass (Mich.)	83	94	92	105	107	116	123	114	0
Johnson (Ky.)	24	33	38	32	29	23	21		
Buchanan (Pa.)	4	9	11	17	26	25	22		
Polk (Tenn.)								44	272

[1] Says a dictionary of "dark horse": "a political phrase common in the United States, drawn from racing cant, referring to a little-known competitor who comes to the fore unexpectedly." It seems to have been borrowed from a respectable source. It occurs in *The Young Duke*, Book I, Chapter V (1831): "A dark horse which had never been thought of, and which the careless St. James had never even observed in the list, rushed past the grandstand in sweeping triumph."

This table pictures the beginning of an important political procedure —that of becoming a party candidate through the elimination of the leading contenders. In this case, it will be noted, Van Buren had a majority (but not of two-thirds) on the first ballot, and for four ballots had the most votes. Then Cass of Michigan gained the votes lost by Van Buren and kept the lead (but not a majority) through the next four ballots. It was then that the factional leaders got together and, being practical men, decided on a compromise candidate. They settled on Polk, who would, after all, be a better vote-getter than Van Buren or Cass, if Jackson spoke for him and really allowed him to be called "Young Hickory." A Jackson recommendation would still be magical with the voters.

What kind of man was it who was preferred in such circumstances? What had Polk been doing to have become so suddenly available in his party's emergency? There must be a long preparation behind the unexpected appearance.

First, just briefly, we may dismiss his more serious rivals—Van Buren and Cass. But it must be said that no more than a few weeks before the convention Van Buren had seemed certain to be the nominee. He had at least a majority of instructed delegates. What changed matters was that President Tyler in April, with the convention meeting in May, sent to the Senate for ratification a treaty for the annexation of Texas. Since Mexico had by no means acknowledged the legitimacy of the Texans' claims to be independent, annexation would involve a commitment to break with Mexico. A war would then be risked to establish (Northerners said) a new area for slavery. The submission of the treaty at once polarized the whole nation; and at the beginning of May, letters were published from both Clay (who was certain, this time, to be the Whig candidate) and Van Buren in which both answered questions about their views on annexation at some length. Clay's statement was not forthright. For him, weaseling was usual and he held out an indefinite hope of later annexation. But Van Buren answered with, for him, strange directness. Why, after having evaded for so long every question he was not forced to answer, he should have departed from his rule on this occasion is not too clear. It cost him the nomination and perhaps another election to the Presidency. At any rate, he did oppose annexation. And almost at once many delegates instructed for him announced that they would not obey; others said that they knew their constituents would not have voted as they had if they had known Van Buren's opinions. The result was apparent in his fading vote after the first ballot.

As for Cass, the trouble with him was that he had incurred Jackson's displeasure. He was a native of Ohio who was now a Michigander; but most of his support was Southern. It was afterward guessed that if the

Ohio votes had gone to him on the second ballot he might have won. But there were Jackson men in that delegation who objected strongly, and his support faded away.

It should also be said of Polk, as we turn briefly to follow his career, that he had been slated for the *Vice-Presidential* nomination by most of the leaders. This was when it was expected that Van Buren would be the nominee, and it seemed expedient to have a Southwestern man for second place. Polk filled that bill. He was a politician of long experience, and he had made sacrifices for the party. No one had thought of him as a first-rater, but he was the ideal second man. In the emergency he was graded upward for expedient reasons, important among them the value of Jackson's support.

Jackson took the view, about Texas, that annexation was necessary because so empty an independent territory contiguous to the United States was sure to be seized or dominated by some foreign power, probably Britain; and this was clearly something the nation could not afford. He was not concerned about slavery. Neither was Polk, following him; and Polk had spoken out for annexation at once. This nationalistic appeal, together with the realization that this was Jackson's view as well, captured the convention majority.

The election was a clear decision for expansion. Clay was beaten; Polk won.[2] The new nation was asserting itself; and Polk, even if unexpectedly, was the man to direct the aggression. He looked at once beyond Texas to California and Oregon; and the largeness of his views was somehow understood by the voters.

It is always revealing, in trying to grasp the particular reason why an individual has emerged from a crowd of starters and has become a singular success, to look for signs of ability and ambition, ones that were not noticed before. Polk's case is peculiarly one of this sort. We have seen other Presidents who, superficially, seemed to lack many or most of the qualities necessary to success. Neither of the Adamses, for instance, had any political flair. But neither did "Little Jeemy" Madison, who was equally unprepossessing. We have to look deeper than personal attractiveness. All these had long public careers, crowned by the Presidency. And Polk was another.

---

[2] It is supposed that Clay and Van Buren, regarded as sure to have the respective nominations of their parties, concerted their open letters opposing annexation, thus intending to remove the issue from the campaign. Both were old-timers; but both underestimated Jackson and the nationalist appeal, and they overestimated the anti-slavery sentiment. There is a story about Clay that his son brought him the news of the Democratic nomination and asked him first to guess who his opponent was to be. Clay first guessed Van Buren, then Cass, but then was at a loss. When his son said the nominee was Polk, Clay is supposed to have exclaimed: "Beat again, by God." His practical mind at once grasped Jackson's strategy and saw that his own would fail.

He was pale and often sickly; as a schoolboy, he had a precise rather than an expansive mind; he had as little social life as a person could have, and apparently he wanted none; he regularly overdid his studying and neglected his health. Looking at him casually, an observer would have been likely to predict that he would be a scholar, a civil lawyer, or perhaps an accountant or engineer. He excelled in mathematics and the classics, but he seemed to have no imagination whatever and to be deficient in human sympathy. When farm work was too much for him and his father arranged for a job with a merchant, he rebelled. He wanted an education. When he was allowed to begin it seriously, he devoured its offerings as though he were starved for them. At the University of North Carolina he was always, beyond comparison, the best student in every class; and he consumed lawbooks with the same voracity. Less than two years after graduating, he was admitted to the bar—which was not unusual; but he was rated at once one of the best lawyers in Tennessee—which was.

His abilities and qualities—his energetic application and his desire to accumulate knowledge—were unique among colleagues who were better in the courtroom than in preparing careful briefs; and he at once found himself with a lucrative practice. He thus became, almost in spite of himself, a legal light in Columbia; and his light was soon shining over a considerably wider area.

What does not appear, except on close scrutiny, is that this sickly, solitary boy and youth was being impelled to feats of scholarship and pre-eminence at the bar by a driving political ambition. He fiercely wanted preferment; and he wanted it awarded as a matter of right, because he was superior to alternative contenders. He was resentful of his eternal inferiority in social matters; and his achievements in intellectual ones were not a satisfactory substitute. But it was evident that he would have to use them to get what his ambition demanded. The fire burning in his vitals forced him to make more and more comprehensive demands, both on himself and on all those around him. He was never satisfied. But he was never really a leader, gathering around himself a group of supporters; he was never able to acquire the graces he would have liked to possess; and altogether it would have been judged that he was most unlikely political material.

When he began to think of a political career, he used what resources he had to good effect. He always knew more than anyone else about whatever subject was under discussion. He was, for this reason, more useful to such a slapdash statesman as Jackson than anyone of Jackson's own sort could possibly be. His reputation as an effective assistant, a man who could buttress and defend policies, did, however, threaten to keep him out of the higher reaches of office. To rise in spite of his reputation as a useful second-rater required a tour de force.

Just as he had moved out of brief-writing seclusion into an active practice, he used his abilities as an analyst and expositor to create a situation favorable for advancing in politics. When he had been made Speaker of the House as a reward for long service, and so having got as far in the Congress as was possible, he deliberately chose to put the party leaders in his debt by giving up his position and going home to hold the line in a wavering state. Then, when Whig fortunes were rising, he made himself a Democratic martyr by opposing it in two hopeless campaigns. By 1844, no one in the party deserved better of it than Polk, something the convention delegates all recognized when he was slated for the Vice-Presidential nomination. Then, as a deadlock developed, it was not too strange that they should substitute him for Van Buren—who, they felt, had taken much and given little.

There is this to learn from Polk: it is not the superficial equipment of an aspirant that counts; it is the use he makes of the talents he does have, however unorthodox they may be. There is also this: a willingness to build up party credit patiently may pay off. None of those who have fought and succeeded have been more carefully self-managed than Polk. He had extremely intractable material to work with in himself; but what he did with it offers a clear lesson in the overcoming of handicaps and, indeed, in transforming them into advantages.

Polk surprised everyone when he reached the Presidency. Before his term was over, he would have seen more territory added to the United States than any other President except Jefferson. That this amazed his contemporaries, and still seems remarkable to historians, is Polk's revenge for many humiliations. But it does have to be said that the qualities he was noted for until his accession were the reverse of the originality and brilliance he at once displayed as President; and it was not these that led to his being chosen. He had been regarded as willing to take orders and loyal in executing them. He was a good parliamentarian, and his speeches supporting the Jacksonian policies were exceptionally well prepared. He took great pains to assemble his data; and in a House not noted for erudition in matters under discussion, he could be relied on to possess a complete mastery of the facts. Jackson needed such a helper; he leaned on him all through his Presidency, saw that he achieved the Speakership, and encouraged his ambitions afterward.

When in 1838 and later it became apparent that there was a swing toward the Whigs and Polk responded to the call to come home, Jackson was again impressed. The campaign was a trying one. The Whig candidate for Governor was an exasperating clown who never discussed an issue and who reduced the process of canvassing to the lowest level of demagoguery. Furthermore, according to custom, the two candidates must travel together for weeks, appearing on the same platform and even, on occasion, sharing the same bed. Considering that Tennessee was still mostly forest interspersed with small settlements or farmsteads and that transportation and accommodation were primitive, Polk's sacrifice emerges as heroic. It was the more appreciated because he was far from robust and had rejected several opportunities for an easier life—as a Cabinet member and as a Senator. When the time came, the old General held the party to full payment for all this faithful service, and the leaders acknowledged their debt.

If in the list of Presidents the student looks for the dedicated professional politician—not the back-room boss, but the official sort—he will find him in Polk. Even Lincoln would sometimes waver and evade the worst ordeals. Polk never did. Politics was his career; he followed it intelligently and with diligence. He always remained matter-of-fact, humorless, and unsocial. Being calculating and persistent, however, he never lost sight of his objective and never let down. His arriving there may have surprised others; but as for him, he had figured to succeed. And it was done in the way he had figured.

The voters in the Presidential campaign of 1844 had the choice of two startlingly different candidates, and the actual contrast was exaggerated by the partisan orators in the inflamed press. Political language was becoming more and more specialized. Clay, it was recalled, was a gambler, a heavy drinker, a rake, and a duelist. But Jackson had been the same sort; and these had been the failings of a whole class of Westerners in that generation. To listen to the Democrats, however, it might have been thought that they were immoralities indulged in by no one else. More justly it was said of the tariffs he had sponsored that they taxed mostly the necessities of the poor and not the luxuries of the rich. The Whigs used the same tactics. They said of Polk that he was tyrannical in a petty way, a lickspittle, and a coward. He was accused of having evaded a duel under provocation which no gentleman would have borne. He was also said to be a fake Colonel of militia and, more seriously, to be an infidel—always a dangerous allegation in American campaigns. This last accusation rested on Polk's not being a member of any church and on the undoubted heathenism of a free-thinking grandfather.

Clay to his followers was "Prince Hal"; Polk to his was "Young Hickory." There were attempts on either side to make something of the ownership of slaves; but since both were equally involved, the credit on this issue went to a third candidate, James G. Birney, running on an abolitionist ticket. Birney attracted only 62,300 votes out of more than two and a half million, all of them from the North; but he helped Polk to victory. In a few states, New York notably, the abolitionists held a kind of balance. And Birney, running hopelessly, freely advised his followers to vote for Polk. Clay, it seemed, had made the mistake of soliciting the abolitionist vote in an obviously insincere way, since he did own slaves of his own. In fact, Clay notoriously "talked out of both sides of his mouth" on several issues. He was too well known to do this successfully; and when the Democrats pinned him down, he visibly squirmed. Polk, being less familiar, could evade the issue of slavery; but he was supposed to favor it, and the abolitionists preferred a known opposition to a slippery, half-consenting advocate. Or so they said.

It was ironical that so cautious a man as Polk should have got a reputation for being more forthright than Clay; but there it was. The appellation "Young Hickory" carried the implication of courage and devil-may-care challenge to opponents. It was, on the whole, a campaign less given to claptrap than that of 1840, but not much less. Both sides had their slogans and songs; but none had the swing of "Tippecanoe and Tyler too." The Whigs seemed to have lost their inventiveness. They encouraged their local followers to erect ash poles in the village squares with due ceremony (the reference being to Clay's Ashland estate); but the Democrats had the better of the exchange when they cut hickory trees from the woods and reset them in rival positions. It shows something of the then state of political exchange that this exhibition did really take place in nearly every village where hardwoods were obtainable.

The Whigs had started out well. It looked at first as though they had thought of a devastating slogan, "Who the hell is Polk?" There were very few outside Tennessee who did recall who Polk was. He had been away from Washington for five years and thus had had no national publicity. But when it got around that he was Jackson's choice, the slogan lost its force. It probably did no harm.

The ballyhoo on both sides was less effective than that of 1840 because now there were real issues. Even the Whigs, who had never done it before, felt compelled to adopt a platform. They approved a protective tariff, restriction of the executive veto, distribution among the states of the proceeds from sales of public land, governmental economy, and a one-term limit for the Presidency. All these positions, except the last, were by now familiar. They were, however, mostly meant to blur the sensitive issue of strict or loose construction—states' rights. Only the proposal for a protective tariff represented a firm stand and was clearly provocative to Southerners. But of course Clay and Polk were both from the same region even if very different in temperament. Actually, the election of neither seemed to presage any great change. There was only one real difference—whether Texas should be annexed. Into this one issue the bitterness of the rising sectional conflict was poured. Yet it too tended to blur; for Jackson and Polk approved annexation, not on slavery grounds, but on high national ones; and Clay was against it for reasons which were vague and perhaps even temporary.

The Whig proposal for a one-term President was a more serious matter in the long run, although it did not become much of an issue. It was a response to the leveling sentiment of the moment that people should feel, and politicians should accept, such a prohibition. Within a short time this would seem a dangerous aberration; and it would presently disappear, but only gradually, and with recurrent spasms. That it was consonant with the spoils system and the whole Jacksonian nonsense about government cannot be denied. It was given prominence at this time because it had enough popular appeal to become a platform plank.

On this, Polk was ahead of the Whigs. Years before the campaign, he had publicly favored a one-term limitation, and now in his acceptance speech he said that he would not be a candidate for a second term. No one then pointed out how crippling his limitation might be to Presidential leadership; and Polk would retire as promised. But the precedent did not become a tradition.[3]

The Democrats, in their platform, declared that the Congress ought not to interfere with the powers of the states and referred specifically to the "dangerous" abolition movement. Logically, also, it upheld the other strict constructionist attitudes—against the tariff, the Bank, and the distribution of Federal funds. It called for the immediate annexation, not only of Texas, but also of Oregon.

It might have been guessed that the election of Polk would establish Southern supremacy and that Federal powers would, under Democratic management, be seriously attenuated. But that guess would have

---

[3] The argument used by those who advocated the "one-term principle" as an important reform was clearly stated by Thurlow Weed:

> Let it be firmly established that the Presidency, for *one term* is the "be all and end all" of human ambition in America, and we shall soon experience the good effects of such a change. Men would continue to struggle for the Presidency; devices and arts and stratagems would still be resorted to, during the canvass; but when the elections were over, and the prize obtained, the motive for misrule ceases. A President who knows that he has only *one term* of service, instead of perverting and prostituting his power and his patronage, to purchase a re-election, would aim to administer the Government honestly, that he might live respected in his retirement, and leave his name untarnished to posterity. . . .

This elevated argument was made by Weed in 1845 as Tyler was retiring (in his *Letters from Europe and the West Indies* [Albany, 1866], 389-90). Of poor Tyler, for whom he was largely responsible, Weed said now:

> Even John Tyler, the poor, miserable, despised imbecile, who now goes from the Presidential chair scorned of all parties, but for his profligate and disgraceful, though impotent efforts for a re-election, would have passed at least decently through his official course.

been wrong. The Presidency did to Polk what it so often does to incumbents—it transformed him into the leader and protector of all the people, deeply conscious of the national obligation centered in him. It could not change his nature; but it did make him, within his limitations, a defender of national interests.

It is not known, of course, whether he could have had a second term. Most estimates run against the likelihood. But the imponderable in this is that a self-imposed limitation hampered the organization of support. So the historical guesses are not to be taken too seriously. What is fact, however, is that after Polk the Democrats lost and the Whigs won. It is uncertain whether they lost because Polk had been a bold and determined leader whose policies were disapproved, whether the Democrats could not produce another Polk, or whether the Democrats were inevitably due to split on sectional issues.

Let us see what Polk's policies were. We begin with the notorious case of Texas, inherited from Tyler as he retired. As time went on both foreign and domestic policies were affected by the Texas issue. It was a tempting thought to the British that an independent state could be wedged between the United States and Latin America. But the abolition of slavery was a popular cause in Britain, and there was hesitation to see whether Texas could not be persuaded to abolish the institution before recognition was granted. This possibility made the Southerners frantic. They saw an escape from their multiplying economic difficulties being shut off—there had already been some movement of planters with their slaves into Texas. And they saw their one chance to redress the balance with the North about to be taken away. Texas might even have become not one but three or four slave states.

The Missouri Compromise of 1820, balancing slave against free states among new admissions, had not worked well for the South. There were by now more free than slave territories on the verge of statehood.[4] The Southerners wanted Texas and they wanted it with slavery. This was Polk's policy, and he moved to implement it by bringing on the Mexican War and eventually by annexation. But it was a policy Northern Democrats could not accept. By the time Polk's term was up, there were several dissident groups within the party with enough members to hold something like a separate convention. It was obvious that if the Whigs were clever they could exploit this split. It was made worse by the proposed "Wilmot Proviso." This would have prohibited slavery in territory acquired from Mexico in the future. The argument about this in the Congress spread to the whole country. By election time, slavery was the hottest issue of the campaign.

---

[4] In the election of 1848, there would be thirty states, the new ones being Florida, Texas, Iowa, and Wisconsin.

There was no general satisfaction, either, with Polk's settlement of the Oregon boundary issues. Britain claimed territory south to California; the United States claimed it north to Alaska. The joint occupation was becoming unworkable and obviously the time for action had come. "Fifty-four forty or fight" was a slogan used by Polk's people, which seemed rather inflated when ultimately a compromise settled on a boundary along the 49th parallel. Earlier claims obscured the real achievement of getting the old and bothersome issue settled.

There were differences also about the financial policy and about the tariff. These were not differences with the Whigs only. There were many Democrats who could not accept Polk's policy. Some of the difficulties were old—the Bank and tariffs, for instance. But the Mexican War was easily interpreted as a conflict to extend slavery rather than to acquire territory. Had the fighting been for such a purpose? The suggestion was deeply disturbing in the North. At any rate, Polk's management of affairs made 1848 a difficult year for the Democrats and an easy one for their opponents. The Whigs had only to find the right man, to mute all issues likely to cause party trouble, and allow the Democrats to defeat themselves. This was how they had won in 1840 with Harrison. Was there another General in sight?

Zachary Taylor
1784–1850

Born in Orange County, Virginia;
moved to Kentucky in infancy
Became twelfth President in 1849 at 64

HISTORY

1808	Appointed a Lieutenant in the regular army by Madison, who was a cousin, in spite of complete lack of education.
1810	Married Margaret Mackall Smith. Promoted to Captain.
1812	Fought Indians in Indiana; successfully defended Fort Harrison.
1815–30	Gradually promoted; performed various frontier and recruiting duties. Came to regard the South as a favorite living place and acquired land and slaves in Mississippi and Louisiana.
1832–38	Fought in the Black Hawk War and in the Seminole War; finally appointed Brevet Brigadier General.
1840–46	Appointed to command the Department of the Southwest.
1846	First Battles of the Mexican War at Palo Alto and Resaca de la Palma.

143

1847	Emerged a hero from the Battle of Buena Vista. Returned to Louisiana; discovered a desire to be President, after first rejecting the suggestion.
1848	Nominated for President by the Whigs and elected (Vice-President, Fillmore); principal opponent, Cass.
1849	Opposed extension of slavery in the West.
1850	Joined in the national debate about expansion and slavery with Senators Douglas, Foote, Clay, Benton, Davis, Calhoun, Webster, and Seward. Died in office at the height of the controversy about the admission of California as a free state.

I T HAS NEVER TAKEN much of a war to produce a General-aspirant for the Presidency, and the Mexican War was no exception. It is a curious paradox that wars often cause the defeat of the party in power. The General-hero is apt to be elected by the other party.

Zachary Taylor,[1] in the line from Washington to Eisenhower, rivals William Henry Harrison and Ulysses S. Grant as an illustration of American fondness for this sort of leader. There have been Generals with determined pretensions who did not succeed in being elected. The Civil War would produce these in quantity, beginning with McClellan, whose imagination ran to the displacing of Lincoln in 1864. And the Mexican War produced General Winfield Scott as well as Taylor.

Scott might have been nominated instead of Taylor, but he was identified in people's minds with Polk and Marcy (Secretary of War), who had little credit from the war. And although Scott had commanded the army that landed at Vera Cruz and had besieged and taken Mexico City, there was never any considerable fervor about his candidacy. It was generally felt that he had stolen Taylor's troops for his own expedition and compelled that commander to fight the tough battle of Buena Vista with undependable volunteers. When Taylor nevertheless defeated Santa Anna (the Napoleon of America), who commanded an army several times as large as his own, a glow of satisfaction spread throughout the country. One hero at a time is enough; and nothing could stop the movement to make Taylor a Presidential candidate. Scott had been outshone.

So all Generals, even famous ones, may not become President, as the case of Scott shows.[2] But some of them may, if the situation is right, as the case of Taylor demonstrates; and he does not have to have been the commanding General. Taylor's success in politics was due to the undoubted fact that he was as providential for the Whigs in 1848 as Harrison had been in 1840. Nevertheless, we must recognize that he succeeded. And we must try to understand how and why.

A veteran politician, now seventy-one, still waited in Kentucky to come on the stage again as the Whig nominee; Taylor was an interloper. Clay was not only the party's head by reason of having been its last candidate, but beyond that was really its originator and entitled to appropriate respect. But Thurlow Weed, the Albany boss, who had

---

[1] It may be noted that the election of 1848 was the first held on a common day throughout the nation.

[2] In 1852 he would get the Whig nomination but be defeated by Pierce, a Democrat.

maneuvered Clay out of the nomination in 1840, still distrusted him
as a candidate, a skepticism that had been confirmed by the defeat of
1844. It begins to seem repetitious, but Weed had still another General
in mind, and had had since 1846. This was Taylor. And the popular
fame gained by his selectee between 1846 and 1848 must have made him
feel that he was favored by Providence or gifted with foresight.

It was in June of 1846 that Weed, who, besides being a potent
boss, was editor of the *Albany Evening Journal*, suggested that
Taylor might be the next President. That was after the battles of
Palo Alto and Resaca de la Palma (May 8–9, 1846), but before the
capture of Monterrey (September 20–25, 1846) and before Buena
Vista (February 22–23, 1847).[3]

In those early days, the United States Army was plagued by incompetent leadership; its officers were mostly political appointees,
and many had only the experience of small-scale Indian fighting or
of service in lonely posts on the Western plains. The soldiers were
militia or volunteers with little or no training and with only a few
regulars to supply experience. Their performance, especially when
they met better-trained troops, seldom gave the American public anything to brag about; and bragging was a weakness of the slowly
maturing democracy.

Support for the measures necessary to professional competence,
however, was consistently refused. When "General Zack," who, in
spite of long service, was inexperienced in battle and whose troops had
only a slight infusion of professionals, won several notable victories,
the nation whooped with joy. The parsimony of past years had not
involved the penalty of defeat it deserved. Training and study were
not necessary. Amateurs were as good as professionals. Neglect of
national defense was justified if "springing to arms overnight" sufficed
and if anyone could become a successful General.

The man who supplied the material for this euphoria quickly became a hero. Legislatures resolved that he was, and one of them went
so far as to present him with an expensive jeweled sword. But there
is every evidence that Polk, Marcy, and the Democratic legislators
were annoyed. They showed it rather meanly by causing the attachment of a disparaging proviso to the Congressional resolution of con-
gratulations. The higher command showed it by practically bringing

---

[3] This has remained one of the memorable battles of our history, not because it
was decisive—neither was the Battle of New Orleans—but because it made a
General available as President, and because several notable later leaders were
involved in minor roles. These included Jefferson Davis, who was Taylor's son-
in-law, as a Colonel of Mississippi Rifles; and the later Generals Braxton Bragg
and George Gordon Meade, who were present as young officers. More important
still, both Lee and Grant served with Taylor—and learned from him, as both
would testify.

Taylor's operations to a stop and allowing Scott, in the Vera Cruz-Mexico City area, to proceed with his plans. Scott did well, enough, but Taylor had caught the national fancy, and no other could displace him. He was affectionately called "Old Rough and Ready," a way of showing satisfaction with his unmilitary behavior and justifying the prejudice against organization and preparation.

It must have been galling for the professionals to have a field commander who looked and acted like a farmer turn in such a brilliant performance that he at once became the center of national attention. And it was worse to have him suddenly conceive opinions on larger issues than the conduct of campaigns—such matters, for instance, as the pacification of Mexico and the organization of the Western lands. His Washington superiors had had rather a contemptuous view of his strictly military ability until their disparagements were overwhelmed in the flood of popular approval after Resaca de la Palma. President Polk had confided to his diary early in September 1846 some detailed doubts concerning Taylor's competence even in merely moving and provisioning his troops, to say nothing about fighting:

> I find it impossible to give much attention to the details in conducting the war, and still it is necessary that I should give some attention to them. There is entirely too much delay and too much want of energy . . . General Taylor, I fear, is not the man for the command of the army. He is brave but he does not seem to have resources or grasp of mind enough to conduct such a campaign . . .[4]

Polk was right in a way. Except in battle, Taylor was an indifferent commander. And that the battles themselves were won still seems remarkable to the critics. Evidently, we must conclude that a General need not be respected by superiors to become famous or to be considered eligible for the Presidency.[5] It is more important to act courageously and wisely, to give an army confidence, and, anyway, to have the knack of winning. Victory achieved, all else is forgotten. After Buena Vista, no one would listen to suggestions that Taylor had been in many ways incompetent. His victories implied all other virtues. Detractors might as well have withheld comment; better, perhaps, because they were set down as jealous carpers.

The military historians say of Taylor that the journey from New Orleans to Corpus Christi and then the march south, during which the encounters at Palo Alto and Resaca de la Palma took place, were bungled badly. None of the difficulties was anticipated; transportation

---

[4] *Polk, The Diary of a President*, ed. Allan Nevins (New York, 1929), 144.
[5] This will be more evident when we come to consider Pierce.

was lacking, supplies were short, and there was no intelligence work. This last was evidently a serious shortcoming. Taylor seems never to have known the size, location, or probable movements of his enemy. Battles happened to him. When he found himself engaged, he took charge and got through somehow; but it was an improvised affair. He succeeded because nothing could scare him, because he never lost his head, and because he had a reserve of common sense.[6]

What did the United States want? Only Polk himself knew the answer to this question. He was, to an extent, improvising, seeing how far he could go. When he had a start, he would determine how comprehensive the objective could be. It is probable that the annexation of Mexico, as well as Texas, was in his mind. He was a man of grand designs, and the expansion of slave territory had taken hold of his imagination. But anyway, the objective was strategic and to be gained as much by political as by military means. To have attention centered on a General, and to have him begin defining objectives himself, was intolerable. And, it soon appeared, Taylor was a Whig.

After his first battle, Taylor had been given command in northern Mexico; but Polk was never willing to be clear about this commitment. Monterrey was, however, the center for the whole area. And if there was an objective, its minimum must be to guard against any threat to Texas. But to take one city was not quite enough, as Taylor saw when he actually had Monterrey. Some fifty miles west lay Saltillo over an easy pass. And in those days the road to Mexico City —if it could be called a road—lay through that city.

The Buena Vista battlefield lay out of Saltillo to the south. Taylor was inching down this road rather cautiously, when he became aware of Santa Anna beyond his front with an army that was supposed to be so well trained as to be professional, something that frightened others but that Taylor ignored.[7] It was only at the earnest entreaty of his subordinates that he drew back to the favorable position across the road leading south which became the battlefield. His sizing up of the Mexicans was an almost disastrous underestimation. If he had given battle where he wanted to, defeat would have been almost certain. As it was, the prolonged series of engagements, first on one side and then the other, in and out of gullies, on hilltops and plateaus, was

---

[6] A story illustrating this was afterward told by Robert E. Lee when he had reason to believe that a report being made to him was exaggerated. Just before Buena Vista, it seems, a young officer excitedly said that he had seen 20,000 Mexicans approaching with 250 guns. General Taylor said to him: "Captain, if you say you saw it, of course I must believe you; but I would not have believed it if I had seen it myself."

[7] Santa Anna had been passed through the American blockade of Vera Cruz at Presidential orders. Polk seems to have thought that Santa Anna would stabilize the Mexican government and treat with the United States.

notable for ingenuity and for bravery, but not for tactical skill. Several times it appeared lost, especially when the American left was turned and the Mexicans came clear through to the rear. Quick movement and determined resistance saved the situation after some of the volunteers had turned and run.

When Santa Anna withdrew in the night, Taylor could not follow. His resources were exhausted. This battle, in fact, was the end of his Mexican fighting, but it was a glorious end. He stayed in Mexico nine more months, continually under fire from the War Department. During this time, Scott captured Vera Cruz and marched to Mexico City. Presently Taylor asked for leave and went back to Baton Rouge, Louisiana, where he had established a home.

The Whig politicians by now had the bit in their teeth, and preparations were being made to make Taylor their candidate. Such insiders as Senators Crittenden, Stephens, Toombs, and local bosses, among whom was that same Weed who had managed Harrison's nomination in 1840, wasted no time. Taylor was a gift of fortune.

Nevertheless, his self-appointed managers had a good deal of trouble with him. He seemed almost as determined to lose the Presidency as he had been to lose his battles—that is, before they were upon him and he was really roused. He said everything he should not have said, and said it loudly and often. He was seized with the conviction that he had become a statesman; he also felt that he ought to be considered to be above party. The politicians finally organized a rescue device of sorts, which has collectively come to be known as "the Allison letters." They are worth a further word.

Taylor had a brother, Colonel Joseph P. Taylor, who could be used as an intermediary. He carried the politicians' warning about loose talk to his elder brother, the General, as he had earlier carried the first intimations that the Presidency was possible.

Thurlow Weed, in his *Autobiography*, has told how the Allison letters originated:

> The canvass was progressing favorably until several letters, written by General Taylor in reply to letters asking his opinion upon various subjects, appeared in different parts of the country . . . some of them were written with no thought of their publication, and all unconscious of the facility with which they could be misconstrued and perverted. I hastily prepared a letter to General Taylor apprising him of the use our opponents were making of his letters, and suggesting the form of one which I thought would disembarrass us. Mr. Fillmore (the Vice Presidential nominee) adopted this letter as his own. General Taylor replied promptly, thanking Mr. Fillmore for his suggestions, adding

that he would immediately write a final letter to his kinsman Captain
Allison, in which he would review his political correspondence. . . .[8]

The politicians thus talked plainly to the General, and he conformed. From their point of view, he had been behaving very badly
indeed. He had, for instance, intimated that he was contemptuous of
political processes, that he must be regarded as independent, and that
he belonged to the nation, not to any party. He expressed a hope that
he would be nominated by various groups, including Democrats, and
said that, in any case, if elected, he would be President of all the people.
This he coupled with equivocal statements about policy which displayed a naïveté, and an ignorance of current issues, which was
positively frightening. Numbers of minor Whig leaders turned against
him and threatened to sabotage the election. This was the reason for
Weed's drastic attempt to repair the damage. Weed, being experienced
in such matters, thought Taylor's military reputation would pull him
through. But he also knew well enough that Taylor's instincts were
mostly Whig in the sense of being strong on rule by the wellborn and
well-situated. This was a thoroughly typical army attitude. But when
the inexperienced General was asked about issues he was apt to be
irrational and inconsistent. He reacted without thinking. And not all
his expressed sentiments conformed to Whig doctrine.

Whether or not the Allison letters helped, the election went well
enough; Weed was proved to be right. But the canvass was more difficult than had been anticipated. Taylor was under wraps. He was
taking the high position that an active campaign was beneath his
dignity and was staying quietly in Baton Rouge. But the split in the
party was very deep. There were still those who had wanted Clay,
and the Clayites threatened to take New York.

More important was the irrepressible issue now coming into the
open everywhere. The abolitionists held a "Free-Soil" convention and
nominated Van Buren, who had been rejected by the Democrats in
favor of Cass. It was believed that the Free-Soilers might take votes
from Whigs, many of whom resented the nomination of a plantation owner and slaveholder. The New Englanders, especially,
might be offended, and New York and Ohio could well be lost. The
Free-Soilers added to their attractions the nomination of Charles
Francis Adams—a name much respected in the North. Taylor's glamor
faded fast, but not fast enough, and the opposition did not gather
enough strength to defeat him.

So the second of the Whig Generals became President. It was clear
that he was elected at least partly because of three cleverly publicized

---

[8] *The Autobiography of Thurlow Weed* (Boston, 1883), 578-9.

battles—Resaca de la Palma, Monterrey, and Buena Vista—just as Harrison's two—Tippecanoe and the Battle of the Thames—had been. Neither of these Generals turned politician lived long enough in office for a fair appraisal of their capacities as President to be made. Both were succeeded by Vice-Presidents chosen to "balance the ticket" —Tyler in 1841 and Fillmore in 1850. Both turned out disastrously for the Whigs, as was perhaps only just. If the politicians were betrayed, it was because they had first betrayed the electorate.

An interesting light is thrown on the bosses' choosing of candidates by certain passages in the Weed *Autobiography*. They have to do with the preliminaries. Weed, "with an ear to the ground," made up his mind that "those only who were blinded by their zeal in favor of other candidates" failed to "see" Taylor's popular appeal. If the Whigs did not capture him the Democrats would; "nothing being known of his political sentiments or sympathies, rank and file Democrats as well as Whigs hoped for his election." "Thus impressed," says Weed, "I went zealously but quietly to work, first through the metropolitan and rural Whig press to incline the public mind toward Taylor, and next to secure a delegation to the National Convention in favor of his nomination."

All this was strongly reminiscent of what had taken place eight years before when the way was being prepared for Harrison. Again, Clay and Webster were the leading candidates; as before, Weed had the problem of substituting for them a military hero who was a political innocent. He had succeeded in nominating Harrison; but would the same trick, on the same people, work again? He used the threat he had used before—the loss of New York; Clay, he argued, could not win. But, as he admits, the New England Whigs could not be persuaded that a native of Virginia, a resident of Louisiana, and a slaveholder[9] could be relied on in an emergency, which would determine whether slavery should be extended into the territory devoted to freedom by the Missouri Compromise and whether California should be admitted as a free state. But by a combination of threats and persuasion, the nomination was accomplished. It came on the fourth ballot, when Webster, Clay, General Scott, and John M. Clayton had all failed to demonstrate the strength needed to win.

There followed the same sort of situation that had troubled Weed and his fellow bosses in 1840 and had led to Tyler's choice for the Vice-Presidential nomination. It was settled as before, after protracted negotiation, but not, this time, by accepting a satellite of Clay or Webster; the choice now fell on a politician from New York who had

---

[9] During his leaves, Taylor had acquired two plantations and owned several hundred slaves.

nothing much to recommend him except that he was likely to carry the Empire State.[10]

We see in all this the operation of a well-developed procedure. The bosses had learned the kind of man they needed and could use—although they had not learned their lesson about the second place on the ticket. Their candidate must be possessed of an adventitious glamor but must have no strong convictions adverse to the interests of those who were expected to finance the campaign. He must not have a vulnerable record of marital infidelity, of devotion to the bottle, or of irregularity in religion. He must be amenable to direction, so that the established statesmen of the party could shape administration policy. Beyond this, he might have almost any peculiarity. Taylor, for instance, was a shambling, fattish, and shabby figure, given to the sloth developed in thirty years of army-post life; he was loud, profane, and common. But he had a large family and was fond of them, he was compassionate to his enemies, and he could be roused to determination and forcefulness in crisis. Altogether, he was as good a candidate as Harrison, and if he had lived he might have served the Whigs' purpose very well.

General Scott, who was certainly an alternative to Taylor, was, in a way, a more attractive figure, and he was much more certainly a Whig. Perhaps it should be mentioned that there was still another General in the picture. This was William O. Butler, who had participated in the Mexican victory as Scott's second-in-command and had succeeded him as Commander in Chief. This General, however, was a Democrat. That he was made their Vice-Presidential candidate shows that the Democrats had learned the same lesson as the Whigs. Butler was second to Lewis Cass, a General too, but of an earlier vintage. Cass had served with credit, but not much flair, in the War of 1812. True, he had participated with Harrison in the Battle of the Thames; but by now, in comparison with Buena Vista, that was a faded victory. He had, of course, been Secretary of War in Jackson's reorganized Cabinet during the Black Hawk War, but after a short time he had become Minister to France. He had been talked of for the nomination of 1844 but had given way to Polk. Now, teamed with a new General, he was pitted against Taylor and Fillmore. The one item of romantic interest in his career, of use in the campaign, was that he had broken his sword rather than surrender it when taken prisoner outside Detroit on the occasion of Hull's inglorious capitulation to the British.

But the election of 1848 was determined by something other than the greater glitter of one General as contrasted with another. In fact,

---

[10] Fillmore turned on Weed when he succeeded Taylor and was as much of a disappointment to him as Tyler had been—more so, because Fillmore was Weed's own discovery.

it seemed that glamor was one thing, glitter quite another. Taylor had one; Scott the other. Taylor was called "Old Rough and Ready"; Scott, "Old Fuss and Feathers." Taylor, even on the battlefield, wore the comfortable old clothes of a farmer; Scott was notorious for his fancy uniforms.[11]

But as even the political tyro notices, nomination is one thing and election is quite another. For the one, it is only the insiders who have to be suited; for the other, it is the people's fancy. That fancy is the ultimate puzzle of the politician's life. Capture of it is his goal and vindication. In the instance before us, as in so many others in our history, there were some determining elements not comprehended in a comparison of personal attractions. One of these proved to hold the balance in 1848. This was the Free-Soil vote. The Free-Soilers— the abolitionists—were satisfied with neither Cass nor Taylor. They held a convention and made a nomination of their own—our old acquaintance Van Buren again, still hopeful. They attracted some 300,000 votes in New York, Massachusetts, Ohio, and Pennsylvania. These came mostly from the Democrats, thus giving the Whigs a popular plurality in New York; and this carried with it the entire electoral vote. The Free-Soilers thus helped to elect Taylor and Fillmore without achieving for themselves a single electoral vote. The extremists had been true to a principle. What they held against Cass was what they had held against Clay in 1844—he was not a fanatic on the slavery issue. Cass they called a "doughface" in consequence and would have none of him.

The campaign called up some of the paraphernalia of the Harrison-Van Buren contest of 1840. "Tippecanoe and Tyler too" was matched by hurrahs for "Old Zach" and even for his horse, "Old Whitey." This annoyed the Democrats, who said that "Old Whitey" should have been the nominee: he knew as much about national issues as his rider. Taylor's running mate, Fillmore, was pictured in the South as an abolitionist. It was true that he had shown signs of anti-slavery sentiment in former years; after all, he came from Buffalo in upstate New York. But he had been questioned on the subject in 1836 by the Anti-Slavery Society and had refused a categorical answer. He had said

---

[11] Grant himself commented on Taylor's appearance. He "never wore uniforms, but dressed himself entirely for comfort. He moved about the field in which he was operating to see through his own eyes . . . He was very much given to sit his horse side-ways—with both feet on one side particularly on the battle-field."

He must have seemed hardly acceptable as a regular army General to the overdecorated Scott—or to Santa Anna. His easy dress, according to other commentators, included a straw hat, a checked gingham coat, and a pair of blue trousers. But it may well have been his paternal appearance which gave the volunteer soldiers of his day confidence in him.

several things of some importance, however, about the subject. One was that he opposed the annexation of Texas so long as slavery was legal there, and another that interstate slave trade should be extinguished. But Fillmore, caught, like others, in the embarrassment of formerly expressed views, trimmed his commitment. He was, he said, no abolitionist.

When Taylor and Fillmore were elected, it did seem to be a clear Southern victory. Not only was Taylor a slave owner from Louisiana, but it had become clearer that his principles were those the Southern Whigs approved. Fillmore, as a hostage presiding over the Senate, could do no harm.

Millard Fillmore
1800–1874

Born in Cayuga County, New York
Became thirteenth President in 1850 at 50

HISTORY

1800–13	Raised in poor circumstances without schooling; apprenticed to a fuller and clothier; was mistreated and ran away; was re-apprenticed but bought himself off.
1819	Began to study law.
1820	Made his living by teaching school and working in a post office while continuing his studies.
1823	Admitted to bar and began to practice law in East Aurora, New York.
1826	Married Abigail Powers.
1828	Elected to the New York Assembly.
1830	Moved to Buffalo.
1832	Elected to the United States House of Representatives.
1844	Defeated for the New York Governorship.
1847	Elected Comptroller of New York State.

1848   Elected to the Vice-Presidency (with Taylor).

1850   Succeeded to the Presidency.

1850   Signed the Compromise Bill of 1850.

1853   Retired. Wife died.

1856   Defeated as American or Know-Nothing candidate for the Presidency, endorsed also by remnant of the Whigs.

1858   Married Mrs. Caroline C. McIntosh.

1874   Died at Buffalo, having been for 18 years in retirement, the city's most prominent citizen.

THE CONDITIONS favoring the Whigs in 1848 were drastically changed by 1852. General Taylor, who had been more hero than Whig, and no credit to his sponsors anyway, was dead; and his successor in the Presidency had consented to the Compromise of 1850. At the hot center of this was the Fugitive Slave Law; and it was Fillmore's approval of this measure that began what rapidly became a political disaster. The Whigs would never win another campaign. It is true that the Republicans, soon to succeed them as a party, would inherit many of their ideas and after a certain conditioning would be enormously successful, but that would be when a new generation had displaced the old.

When Taylor died, Fillmore was so taken by surprise that he was some time in finding a policy. When he did, it was one which would contribute to his defeat for a term of his own in the White House. Except for those who died in office, he became the first less-than-a-full-term President.

There is a double problem in the case of Fillmore, as in that of some others (the Adamses, Van Buren, etc.), of understanding not only how he achieved the office but why he was unable to continue in it. It is harder to account for failure than success in bids for continuation in office. The President normally controls a mighty party machine; it ought to secure his nomination if not his election.

Fillmore was a relatively young man when he reached the end of his term in 1853, and by the political rules he ought to have gone on. If he felt that he should have been nominated almost automatically, he was disappointed.

The suggestion has been made that in taking the action he decided on in the matter of the Compromise of 1850 Fillmore deliberately risked his chance for an elected term of his own. And this is now often considered to have been an act of high patriotism. It is said to have postponed the Civil War for ten years and very nearly to have avoided it. If Fillmore had not consented, the argument goes, secession would have begun at once and could not have succeeded. That he did consent resulted in the alienation of the strong anti-slavery Whigs of the North. This not only made him unacceptable as a candidate in 1852 but allowed the issue to run on to a fierce phase when no conciliation was possible.

Thinking for the moment not of the maneuvers preliminary to a nomination, but of a policy for the nation, Fillmore evidently agreed strongly with Clay, Webster, and indeed with Lincoln, that slavery was not the real issue of his time. What had to be thought of first was the nation's expansion. There was a vast work to be done in exploring, appropriating, and beginning to govern the West and in bringing its various regions into statehood. The fierce heat generated by slavery concerned a secondary—almost, they would have said, a false—issue. Slavery was a way of producing cotton and tobacco. Whether there was slavery or not, the nation's essential task of stretching out to the Pacific was exactly the same. It was destined. Any compromise calculated to stifle the irrelevant quarrel about slavery was acceptable because it let the great work go on.

The fanatical anti-slavery forces, however, would not accept this view any more than the fanatical slave owners would. The abolitionists would rather not have Texas, New Mexico, and California than to have them as slave territories. With Jackson, as with Lincoln later, however, union was the sacred symbol. For the nation, united, whole, and strong, they would stand implacably, sacrificing all else. To the abolitionists, liberty for all was more precious than union.

The Southerners who were makers of policy used almost the same words; but the liberty they meant was not that meant by the New Englanders. The Southerners' liberty was for themselves. It involved the right of the states whose governments they controlled to determine the institutions they preferred; and coercion from outside, they said, was tyrannical. That there was at its heart the denial of freedom to a whole race was something they would not permit to be examined.

They offered justification only because they were under pressure. They themselves had no doubts. The abolitionists pretended to stand on the moral height of absolute freedom. Would they plead for the same freedom for animals? the Southerners asked, because after all Negroes were not quite human, and it would be ridiculous and dangerous to treat them like whites. They would run wild; they could not support themselves; they must have the oversight of their betters. Incredible as it seems, Southerners were willing to die to establish this as unquestionable dogma.

There was no end to this argument; not even war could end it altogether. It appalled any politician who considered its effect on his own or his party's interests. And this was not only because it stirred emotions no one could gauge, and so had unpredictable potentialities, but even more because it threatened the integrity of the nation itself. When extremists on both sides began to consider union secondary to liberty, politicians and statesmen of those years felt fully justified in seeking compromise. An agreement to shunt aside the slavery question and center on expansion seemed to them essential to the national interest—as well as politically expedient.

The South had a curious advantage in the bargaining of those years. Because it was so plain that the slaves must sooner or later be freed, and because this was a thought slave owners refused even to entertain, the dialogue between North and South could find no rational basis. Southerners would not discuss the matter without initial concessions that were contrary to the firmly held principles of the abolitionists.

Henry Clay pointed out that, so far as advantages to be had by controlling political institutions went, the South was ahead. Southerners had an equal vote in the Senate and a majority on the Supreme Court. Now that Taylor was President they had a Southerner in the White House and a predominantly Southern Cabinet. But also they had low tariffs. And the prospects for the extension of slavery were good if it could be shown to be economically feasible. There were still areas in Louisiana, Texas, and perhaps elsewhere (Cuba, for instance, and the rest of Mexico) where extension was possible. The abolitionists, in their exasperation at Southern blackmail, had now gone to the extreme of advocating secession too. Let us have a nation, they said, not marked with this evil. Let the South go its separate way!

But this infuriated the Southerners even more than abolitionist agitation. What they must have was an impossible, a mythical, assurance of security for their peculiar institution. It seemed to them to be threatened everywhere and by everyone. What they resented most of all was that they should be so widely disapproved. Their arguments had centered for years now on the moral superiority of slavery over freedom; and this claim was everywhere being rejected. There was abolition in Britain, in the British colonies, in Mexico, and of course in the American North. All this seemed to put the South more and more in the wrong. It was intolerable. It could not be accepted. The only way to meet the outrage of abolitionism was to set up a Southern republic, stretching from the Potomac to the Rio Grande, where slavery as an institution would not only be permitted but would be recognized as a benevolent and necessary arrangement. Southerners would then be a sovereign power, even if not approved by anyone else; and they could defy fanatic opinion in the North.

Trouble in California precipitated the near-war of 1850–51 and caused Fillmore to make the choice responsible for his failure to be nominated in 1852. But it cannot be doubted that compromise did for the time still the rising conflict. The extremists on either side felt an immediate falling away of their support as the moderates lost interest; and it seemed for a time as though economic sense and loyalty to the Union might together avert actual hostilities. The truce was short; but that, perhaps, was because the great compromisers, Clay and Webster, were withdrawing from politics and being succeeded by others who had more regard for their section and their philosophy than for the nation as a whole. Only the victory of one over the other would satisfy the sectional extremists. Curiously enough, the Whigs would suffer most from the compromise, although their leaders, Clay and Webster, had worked it out and Fillmore had signed it into law. Many Northern Whigs would not accept it; the Democrats, on the other hand, would unite as a Southern party.

Fillmore, who was so fatally caught between the sectional hatreds, was poorly prepared for his ordeal. Let us see why. To begin with, he had been another log-cabin boy, advanced by his own efforts to prominence in western New York. It was a familiar route upward, the Horatio Alger way. The young lawyer-politician had cultivated all the right people; he had been careful of what he said and did; he was, moreover, of tall and handsome build. Later in life he would become the very picture of Presidential Presence; only Washington, McKinley, and Harding, of all the line, presented so fatherly and benevolent an appearance. He seemed to embody judgment, wisdom, and human sympathy.

The question, in Fillmore's case, was whether he could rise to occasions greater than those of local moment. Certainly no one, even when he had been nominated for the Vice-Presidency, regarded him as marked by ability for the direction of national affairs. Most of his familiars knew him as a solemn, handsome mediocrity, a man who would do no wrong and not very much right. He would always be correct; he was temperate, phlegmatic, and an unquestioning religious believer of an easy sort; but he was not a leader, not a man of ideas.

Among his political associates, his majestic carriage caused him to be known familiarly as "Father Fillmore"; but this did not signify filial respect; nor did his public think of him, as they have of some Presidents, especially the handsome ones, as a father figure. He was described by one contemporary as having, when he approached the Presidency, a countenance that was open and bland, hair that was thick and graying, a chest that was full, and an eye that was clear and blue. He was not an orator, but he spoke well before committees and smaller gatherings. He had a grasp of detail and an unusual understanding, for a politician, of public finance. The position he was best fitted for was perhaps the one he had reached when Thurlow Weed picked him for the Vice-Presidency—that of Comptroller of the State of New York. He was always earnest and courteous and never domineering. He was, in all things, moderate. That this is the perfect picture of a Vice-President, it must be admitted; but of a President? Not, at least, in troubled times!

What we know of him as a lawyer in Buffalo and as a young worker in the community explains quite satisfactorily why he should have got along well as a local politician. With him it was an avocation, not a profession. But he made it pay. It channeled into his law offices more and more lucrative cases. At quite an early age he was reckoned as well off; and it was obvious that he could expect to accumulate a modest fortune.[1]

No President has moved more gracefully into and through the Presidency to an elegant retirement. More often than not, Presidents have given up reluctantly at the last minute, as they saw power slipping away and an old age without occupation, and sometimes without income, arriving. Fillmore's effort, if determined was singularly ineffective. At the time he probably felt that he had done all he could. But he was not a man of imagination, and he thought of nothing dramatic. He would make later attempts and be nominated once again by the Know-Nothings. The Whigs endorsed him; but they, like the Federalists, were destined to die out for sheer lack of members.

One of the strangest anomalies of America's mid-century years, as we look back, is the mediocrity of the line of President in such a time of activity and expansion. Everywhere there was intense activity, vast schemes being conceived and, moreover, carried out; miracles of invention and administration were being achieved. And all this was presided over—if Polk is excepted—by men of small ability. There had already been Harrison, Tyler, and Taylor; and after Fillmore there were Pierce and Buchanan to come.

These were the years when the magnetic telegraph was spreading, the railroads were being built, factories were rising everywhere, and inventions of all sorts were finding their way into use. Population was increasing and moving wave-like onto the prairies, and the prairies were yielding vast volumes of food. Gold and other metals were being brought out of the ground and processed. And the clipper ship was taking its brief command of the sea lanes. There was talk of shortening the way to California by digging a canal across Central America; and beyond California was the wide Pacific, already known to East Coast sailors.

East, West, South, there were reaches of land and sea to be exploited, perhaps to be brought under the flag. There was no limit to Americans' ambition. But there was one thing they could not decide among themselves. They could not agree about slavery. And periodically the imperial plans and brilliant schemes were submerged in bitter quarrels, becoming more frequent, about this one question.

Fillmore had gone along easily in New York State, serving several terms in the legislature, being marked by Thurlow Weed, the boss, and made a friend by him too. He had gone to the Congress in 1832 and stayed there until the early forties, becoming, as was to be ex-

---

[1] Actually, on retirement he was able to buy a mansion on Niagara Square which had once belonged to John Hollister, one of Buffalo's tycoons, who conveniently succumbed in the panic of 1858. That he married a wealthy widow was much in character.

pected of so magisterial a man, Chairman of the Ways and Means Committee and Leader of the House. In 1844 he was nominated for the Governorship but unhappily defeated by Silas Wright.

Fillmore's law practice, at least, did not suffer from his being a defeated candidate. He was very quickly reaching that position of wealth and prominence he would occupy for the rest of his life. He became Chancellor of the University of Buffalo, an honorary postion he would occupy until death; he was chairman of civic committees, the leader in charitable affairs, and at the top of the social list on Delaware Avenue.

When in 1847 he consented to run for the State Comptrollership and was elected, the victory could not have elated him notably; the salary was $2500, insignificant in comparison with his legal earnings at the other end of the state. But he was Comptroller only one year. In 1848 he was nominated to run as Vice-President with General Taylor.

Thurlow Weed, in his *Autobiography*, tells about his discovery and sponsorship of Fillmore:

> I first met Millard Fillmore at Buffalo in 1828. He had then been recently admitted to the Bar. Although passing but a few hours with him, I was so favorably impressed as in the following year to suggest his nomination for the Assembly. In 1830, while serving with him in the Assembly my favorable impressions of his ability and fitness for public life were much strengthened, and we became warm personal and political friends. In 1832 he was elected to the Congress, where he soon acquired the reputation he enjoyed in our State legislature of being able in debate, wise in council, and inflexible in his political sentiments. . . . He was our candidate for Governor in 1844 and would have been elected but for the unfortunate letter that Mr. Clay wrote to a friend in Alabama. . . . Until the appearance of Mr. Clay's letter, in which he remarked that he did not consider it a matter of any consequence whether Texas came into the Union as a State with or without slavery, the abolitionists had intended to vote for Fillmore. In 1847 he was elected State Comptroller. During these twenty years my intimacy with and friendship with Mr. Fillmore was . . . constantly strengthening.

The friendship lasted through the campaign. Weed anticipated the usual—but no more than the usual—differences about patronage in the state. Seward, his other protégé, was now in the United States Senate. With a Vice-President and a Senator in his stable he had only to think of equitable distribution. But Fillmore now began to have other ideas. To avoid trouble he had begun to suspect was coming, Weed entertained Seward and Fillmore at his home in Albany as they were about to leave for Washington. "Everything" he says, "was pleasantly arranged." But soon after this:

in the hope of serving two meritorious political friends I went to Washington. I met the Vice President at Willard's Hotel. My reception was more courteous than cordial. It was soon apparent that Mr. Fillmore's feelings toward me had undergone a strange and unaccountable change . . .

Seward soon told him that all the New York appointments were being claimed by Fillmore, and indeed this was so. Weed knew why. Fillmore was now "aspiring to the Presidency and saw in Seward a formidable rival, and assuming that he could not rely on me as against the Senator, severed ties which I had supposed would never be broken." Weed sadly continues that this was but the first of a series of such betrayals, not only of "old and cherished friends, but older and even more devotedly cherished principles."

Fillmore had, in other words, come down with the Presidential fever; and for one with this disease the sacrifice of political friendships is often necessary. Whether the Presidency would have come to him through his own nomination if Taylor had lived, we cannot tell. Taylor, by dying, left it to him after only sixteen months.

Weed goes on to speak of Fillmore as President. He was, says Weed, so anxious for a term of his own that he compromised too much. California's admission, with a constitution forbidding slavery, had stirred the South to bitter protests. Taylor, before his death, had said he would approve the admission. But Clay and Webster, frightened by Southern threats, conceived that Taylor had been too harsh; and between them they devised the Compromise Measures of 1850 intended once for all to put slavery in the background and remove it from partisan battle. The measures included, among others, a strengthened Fugitive Slave Law. It was this that split the Whigs and caused Fillmore's political death. Emerson, the gentle transcendentalist philosopher, was moved to write of it in his journal: "This filthy enactment was made in the nineteenth century by people who could read and write: I will not obey it, by God . . ." Emerson's outrage was widely shared.

Why did Webster, Clay, and Fillmore, patriots all, and old experienced hands, make such a political error? The answer is that they underestimated the intensity of feeling on both sides. They could never understand a fanaticism so strong as to subordinate all other issues to its demands. Consequently they could not believe that it would be allowed to disrupt the Union and actually lead to civil war. Nor did they anticipate that Pierce and Buchanan—or other "doughfaces" of their sort—would succeed to the Presidency. They judged, moreover, that if the compromise was found unacceptable to either party it would be the Democrats and not the Whigs. It was the Southerners, they thought, who were the fanatics. The Whigs were a club of well-to-do members with common interests. They were moderate. They would hold together.

These were misjudgments. The statesmen underestimated the abhorrence slavery had aroused in the North. Men who had never broken a law in their lives at once began a conspiracy to forward escaped slaves to Canada. To have sponsored a measure which allowed these unfortunates to be hunted through the streets of Northern towns and returned in irons to their owners in the South was to offend every sense of decency. The indignation was so hot that incidents arising from the law were enlarged and exaggerated. It was not long before Fillmore was a pariah for having signed it. It was an added count against him by the New York politicians who were already disaffected by his patronage policies. Thurlow Weed, usually so urbane in his judgments, was fiercely denunciatory. He could hardly restrain his indignation even when writing about it many years later.

At the convention of 1856 Fillmore had no more chance of being nominated than Van Buren or Tyler, in somewhat similar circumstances before him; and about this problem of a second term nomination, for a President who has succeeded to the office from the Vice-Presidency as Tyler and Fillmore had done, we can by now make certain general observations.

To begin with, successors must recognize that they have the handicap of having been chosen for peculiar party reasons. They have offered a convenient contrast or supplement to the principal in the case, so lending strength to the ticket. Tyler had been nominated because Harrison had been named for the Presidency and Clay's followers had to be placated.[2] So with Fillmore. The head of his ticket was from Louisiana, and he was from New York. He had always been against slavery, as were most New Yorkers, even if he was not an outright abolitionist; Taylor owned several hundred slaves. Fillmore was a confirmed Whig; he belonged to the party machine and was put forward by its boss; Taylor was only doubtfully a party man and was, indeed, chosen because he could not be said to be one—although he was thought to be tractable.

Evidently this contrast, if it is useful for healing party rifts, has its dangers. When a Vice-President chosen in this way succeeds to the Presidency, the troubles ensuing may be complex and disrupting. If he follows the policies he has been identified with up to now in his career,

---

[2] If we examine the defeated tickets during this same period we discover the same rule being followed. The Vice-Presidential nominations went to geographically contrasting candidates or to those from another wing of the party. In the cases of the defeated candidates, it did not matter; but among those who were elected in the same period—Johnson, Tyler, Dallas, Fillmore, King, and Breckinridge—two disrupted their party and the others might have disrupted theirs if they had succeeded to the Presidency by death.

they will contrast startlingly with those his predecessor has stood for— or at least some of these policies will; there are always some agreements, as well as some differences; but they may not be the deciding ones. The Whigs everywhere stood for government by the better people, the wealthy, the leaders in the community. Southern and Northern party members had this in common. It was a heritage from Federalism. But it was the Whigs who in the North were closest to abolitionism. This was not close enough to suit the extremists; and these, as we have seen, were inclined to form third parties more to their liking. But most Whigs were clearly against slavery even if they were not fanatics.[3] It was the fierceness of the California fight that led Webster and Clay to formulate the compromise laws. And Fillmore was naturally inclined to accept them gratefully. He was not shrewd enough to see that when the fugitive Slave Law was included it was more than was tolerable to northerners.

Fillmore was unlucky. The passions of his day were difficult to cope with. But his is only an exaggerated instance of the rule that a successor from the Vice-Presidency must quickly find reliable support, make his peace with those who can and will be his partisans, and cling to them with fidelity. Fillmore alienated Weed and the others who had sponsored him; he now offended the other Northern Whigs. When the Convention met in 1856, he had only office holders to rely on; and they were not enough.

His bid for the nomination was a determined one. On the first ballot he had the most votes (133), but Scott had nearly as many (131), and Webster had a few (29). It was forty-nine ballots later before there was any substantial change. Fillmore's vote never increased; Scott's rose only to 139. But on the next three votes Scott drew ahead and was chosen. Fillmore was thus retired by his party and by the nation. But since the candidate substituted for him was not elected, he might not have been elected either. Losing the nomination probably spared him that defeat.

---

[3] The Whig division in the North was between the "Cotton Whigs," whose business relations with the Southern plantation owners influenced their views of slavery, and the "Conscience Whigs," to whom slavery was abhorrent. The split in New York, especially, but in other states as well, determined the Whig defeat in several prewar elections.

Franklin Pierce
1804–1869

Born in Hillsborough, New Hampshire
Became fourteenth President in 1853 at 48

HISTORY

1824	Graduated from Bowdoin College.
1827	Admitted to the bar and began practice in Hillsborough.
1829	Elected to the New Hampshire House of Representatives.
1831	Elected to the Speakership.
1833	Elected to the United States House of Representatives.
1834	Married Jane Means Appleton.
1836–42	Elected to the United States Senate. Resigned before the end of his term to practice law at Concord. Declined the nomination for Governor and the Attorney Generalship in Polk's Cabinet, but did accept appointment as the Federal District Attorney for New Hampshire.
1846	Enlisted as a private (at 42) at the outbreak of the Mexican War.

1847	Became Colonel of the 9th Regiment, which joined Scott at Puebla in August. Became Brigadier General of Volunteers. Thrown from horse and injured at the Battle of Contreras.
1848	Resigned and returned to Concord.
1850	President of the convention to revise the New Hampshire Constitution.
1852	Nominated by the Democrats for the Presidency and elected, (Vice-President, King); opponent, Scott.
1856	Defeated for renomination and retired.
1869	Died in Concord.

W E HAVE NOT SEEN one President among the twelve since Washington who did not actively covet the office. Of two we could say they were startled to be told of their eligibility—Taylor and Harrison; and of others we could say that they got it in spite of, rather than because of, their efforts—John Adams, Tyler, and Fillmore, for example. But this was not true of the fourteenth President.

Franklin Pierce is usually listed as a dark horse, and in one sense he was. He did not appear among those put forward at the convention of 1852 until the thirty-fifth ballot; and he was not nominated until the forty-ninth. There were contenders who were more prominent—notably Cass, Buchanan, Marcy, Douglas, Love, and Houston—but it was obvious that the split among the Whigs presented an opportunity if a Democrat could be found who could draw votes from both South and North. No Southern candidate would do, and no Northerner either if he was known as an abolitionist or anything like it, or even one who was a loose constructionist.

So clear was the desirability of finding the right man that Pierce, who seemed to his political friends just the kind of person needed, was put forward sometime before the convention. Even though he had been a soldier he was not, like Taylor, surprised to be considered eligible. He was no neophyte, and the nomination surprised others more than it did him.

The Democratic strategy on the slavery quesiton was superior to that of the Whigs. The Democrats had only to cling to the old doctrine of states' rights. If every state could settle the issue for itself, the South need not worry about the abolitionists; and new territories could be admitted with some confidence that the issue would be favorably settled. Pierce was a states'-righter; Scott, his opponent, more doubtfully so. Scott was by origin a Virginian but he had Northern views; Pierce was another of those Northern men with Southern principles so much in demand by the Democrats.

There was no clear choice offered by the party platforms of 1852 as to support for the Compromise of 1850. The Whigs could not refuse to be bound to their own measures.[1] And the Democrats were well enough satisfied with them so that their platform statement could be unequivocal. The party, it said,

---

[1] Their President had signed it; and it had originated in the compromising minds of their elder statesmen, Clay and Webster. But these were now reaching the end of their days; both would die in 1852. Webster's last magniloquent speech was the famous one he made in support of the Compromise bills. Calhoun, that other influential figure, had already died in 1850. The new men in the Senate now were those who were to be prominent in the nation's coming debate: Davis, Douglas, Seward, and Chase.

will abide by, and adhere to, a faithful execution of the acts known as the "compromise" measures—the act for reclaiming fugitive slaves . . . included.

The Whigs, acquiescing, said that

the series of acts of the thirty-second Congress, the act known as the Fugitive Slave Law included, are received and acquiesced in by the Whig party . . . and we deprecate all further agitation of the question thus settled.

The only alternative for the abolitionists was furnished by the Free-Soilers as a third party. They nominated Pierce's enemy, John P. Hale of New Hampshire (with G. W. Julian of Indiana), and adopted a platform which spoke of the Fugitive Slave Law as "unjust, oppressive and unconstitutional." Theirs was an appeal to those who opposed any compromise on the slavery issue.

Nevertheless, the Whigs would not nominate Fillmore; and although he never went below 122 convention votes in the first forty-nine ballots, it was clear from the first that he could not accumulate any more. But Scott, when nominated, was only sullenly accepted by many Whigs. It was different with the Democrats. At their convention the move to Pierce, once begun, was swift; and party members received him with enthusiasm. When the election came Scott got only 42 electoral votes of a total of 296. The Whigs had gone the way of the Federalists, whose attitudes and principles they had inherited.

But it was striking that the Free-Soilers did very badly and that the Compromise Measures were proved acceptable. Out of more than three million votes cast, Hale, the Free-Soil candidate, got only about 156,000—which brought him no electoral votes whatever.

Why Pierce? Mostly because the Southerners could trust him. They were thus confident because they knew his origin, his training, and his apprenticeship. It all went back to his father, Benjamin Pierce.

The old General had been a revolutionary of the true color. He said of his initiation:

I was ploughing in the field when the news first came that the British had fired upon the Americans at Lexington and killed eight men. I stepped between the cattle, dropped the chains from the plough, and without any further ceremony, shouldered my uncle's fowling piece, swung the bullet-pouch and powder-horn and hastened to the place where the first blood had been spilled . . .[2]

---

[2] Quoted from his own account of his life in Professor R. F. Nichols' *Franklin Pierce; Young Hickory of the Granite Hills* (Philadelphia, 1931), 3.

He was too late; the British had retired. But next morning he enlisted; and he kept on re-enlisting until the armies were disbanded. Like others, he then went back to clearing land and farming, gradually rising in the community until he became, among other things, a Brigadier General of the militia. But also he became a legislator, a member of a Constitutional Commission, and Sheriff of his county. Eventually he was elected Governor of New Hampshire.

But he was still the same tough and uncompromising Jeffersonian and militiaman. And it was in his household, and very much under his influence, that young Franklin grew up. His father would not even allow him to go to Dartmouth College because of its Tory tinge; he went instead to Bowdoin, in Maine. He was delivered carefully there by father and mother and safely settled under good conservative auspices.

When Franklin grew up he became as Jacksonian as his father had been Jeffersonian—a natural sequence, and one approved by the Governor, by now a Jacksonian too. In the meantime the Adams-Clay Democratic-Republicans had mostly become Whigs, it being necessary for the better people to have a party of their own. The old Republicans, who were now officially the Democrats, had never wavered. They had not sought the adherence of the Tories under any name. They were detested as heartily under the Whig label as when they were doubtfully Republicans. Franklin Pierce could not have believed in abolitionism or have become a Conscience Whig, because he could not become a Whig at all. He believed in states' rights as he believed in militias. He did, indeed, have many virtues that recommended him to the South.

When Pierce went to Concord from Hillsborough for his first legislative session he was only twenty-four years old. This was in 1829, when Jackson was taking over the President's House in Washington and his own father was assuming the Governorship. Democracy was triumphant. He served for two terms, then went on to the Congress in Washington. Meanwhile, to his delight, he had been appointed an aide to Governor Dinsmoor, who succeeded his father. This carried with it the rank of Colonel, something he was to use as leverage when later he wanted an army commission during the Mexican War.

He was a Congressman-elect when Jackson, entering on his second term, came to Concord in the course of a triumphal journey. During this visitation Pierce became acquainted with the President and with Van Buren. When he went on to Washington it was as an administration supporter. This left him free to speak of abolitionists as "reckless fanatics" and to defend Northern Democrats who had been accused of dodging the slavery issue. Throughout, he seemed more anxious to reassure the Southerners than to please the Northerners—something which was always to be characteristic.

This particular speech got him into a worrisome controversy with a New Hampshire editor. For this and personal reasons 1836 was a time of peculiar anxiety. His newborn son died, his wife became almost an invalid, and he himself had a long illness. One month of this winter seemed to his biographer to have affected all his later career. The conjunction of strains, according to Professor Nichols,

> accounts largely for the intensity of his feeling on the slavery question and his hatred of abolitionism . . . a man of Pierce's emotional and irrational character could never analyze the causes of his complexes. It never occurred to him . . . that the chief reason for the deepseated convictions which were to color his future career was this month of *"sturm und drang,"* with its feverish anxiety to justify himself before Calhoun and the southern leaders.[3]

His father's influence, his dependence on the leadership of older Democrats, the most respectable of them being Southern, set him in the way he would always go. It was quite in character that late in that same session he should have made a vehement attack on the United States Military Academy at West Point. The son of the old militia General still carried his prejudices.

Presently, because he was so docile a Democrat, he was thought of for advancement. Nothing seemed to come of it at first; but before long he was elected to the United States Senate. He was sworn in as Van Buren was inaugurated. He stayed there until 1842. He resigned then, intending to practice law seriously and to keep out of office. But no one with such a strong instinct for public attention could leave politics alone. He was always in demand for party chores. He became Democratic State Chairman and something of a boss; and when Polk succeeded Tyler in 1845 he became the Federal District Attorney for New Hampshire.

Eighteen forty-six was a crucial year for him. The opposition elected a Governor and sent John P. Hale to the Senate. This was the result of a union of right and left—Whigs and Free-Soilers. The Democrats regarded this as an unpatriotic alliance and said so in a convention resolution written by Pierce. The resolution was emphatic that the states and territories must be free to make their own decisions about slavery without outside interference, thus foreshadowing the doctrine of "squatter sovereignty."

That summer Polk offered Pierce the Attorney Generalship of the United States; he was solid now in Democratic counsels, just the man

---

[3] *Ibid.,* 87.

the Southerners needed for their purposes. He refused the legal position; but when the Mexican imbroglio began and the regular army was expanded, he was happy to become a Colonel. He had always dreamed of a military career; even at college he had organized a militia company. From Colonel he soon moved up to Brigadier General. He was delayed in recruiting a regiment; but about the time Scott arrived in Puebla, Pierce was landing at Vera Cruz with his first contingent.

Puebla was on the high plain about fifty miles from the steamy coast, and Pierce had first to wait for the rest of his men, then somehow get them through a jungle infested with guerrillas and onto the uplands where Scott waited, cut off from his supplies and impatient to resume his campaign. Almost at once about half Pierce's 3500 assembled mules stampeded and were lost; he had to find more and see that they were broken. The difficulties of the waiting period and of the harassed march to Puebla seem to have been surmounted by Pierce with some credit.

He was present at the battles for possession of Mexico City, but only barely so. A frightened horse threw him against his saddle horn and injured his testicles so that he fainted and had to be carried to his tent. Next day the heat and dehydration overcame him again. The battle was won, but not because of Pierce's leadership. After a few weeks he went home. He was received as a hero. Heroes were scarce just then in New England.

The years after the peace, until 1852, may have been the happiest of his life. He was a respected citizen of middle years. He had held public office, had volunteered and fought, and was now at the head of his profession. While the Whigs—Taylor and then Fillmore—prepared the way for Democratic victory in 1852, the man who was to be chosen to head the Democratic ticket was becoming more than ever a party elder. Although he refused nominations to office, he became known as something of a local dictator. But New England had never been a happy spot for Democrats with national ambitions; and Pierce had no reason to anticipate preferment.

Nevertheless, as the convention approached, there was some talk of his availability. Especially some of the other political Generals began organizing efforts. But his views had to be made doubly certain if the Southerners were to accept him. This accounts for the letter, labeled by his biographer "the most important of his life," written to a friend but provoked by questions from a Richmond editor. It is a typical statement, the same sort he would still be making when the Civil War had come and, for that matter, when it was over:

> I believe there will be no disposition on the part of the South to press
> resolutions unnecessarily offensive to the sentiments of the North. But

can we say as much on our side? Will the North come cheerfully up to the mark of constitutional right? . . . If the compromise measures are not to be substantially and firmly maintained, the plain rights secured by the constitution will be trampled in the dust.[4]

So a man of mediocre talents, with a flighty mind, a defective education, and schooled to the toadying demanded by the Southerners, was put in the way of becoming President. But the means he used to place himself in position to be chosen were well enough calculated. It would have been easier to go along with New England sentiments. He could even have remained a Democrat and done so. Others did. But this would have prevented his rise in a party whose rewards went to those who, in the fierce sectionalism of those years, carefully cultivated the good opinion of the slave oligarchy.

For our purpose here we have to pursue the inquiry further. Why was he unable to capture the nomination for a second term? Why did the party discard him for the less attractive Buchanan in 1856? Someone has said that "Pierce died of Davis and Cushing." And that statement is as true as the one accounting for his choice in 1852. He did die of Davis and Cushing; and he was there to die because he was a Doughface.

When Pierce became President he naturally chose for his Cabinet those who, like himself, were sympathetic with Southern views or who were actually Southerners. This anomalous situation had evolved in a rather curious way. States' rights had become identified with the liberty made so much of by the Jeffersonians and Jacksonians. It was easy to confuse individual freedom with state freedom. When Northerners voted Democratic they were voting for everything contained in the democracy package and embodied in the Bill of Rights. They were also voting against the rich and wellborn, who were now Whigs as they had formerly been Federalists.

That the support of liberty should have become the means of supporting slavery was thus the result of popular confusion, a failure to see the reality behind the slogans.

The election of 1852 was a ratification of compromise. Pierce felt that he had a mandate to forget slavery and turn to other tasks. The issue did not long stay buried, even though his efforts to divert public attention were strenuous. It came into the center of discussion again through two pressures. One was the agitation and the legislative efforts of Senator Douglas to pass the Kansas-Nebraska bill. The other was the unwillingness of the slave interests, now in power at Washington, to let the issue die. They must look for new slave areas—in Central America, in Cuba, in Mexico.

Douglas was a small, energetic, and opinionated man who was not

---

[4] Quoted in Nichols, *op. cit.*, 201–2.

always able to distinguish between his own and the nation's interests. This was a time when the railroads were stretching across the newly acquired West, and the Senator had invested heavily in land along some most likely rights of way. There were several possibilities—North, Central, and South. He had plumped for the Central. Much of his effort to organize the prairie territories seems to have been motivated by his desire to stabilize the country through which the railroad would run.

Jefferson Davis, Secretary of War, had had surveys made by the army engineers. In spite of his fanatical adherence to states' rights, he was willing to have a Pacific railroad built by the Federal government. And in Pierce's message to the Congress in 1853 the project was endorsed as of interest to national defense. What he meant was national expansion; but what Davis meant was the expansion of slavery.

Douglas, as chairman of the Senate Committee on Territories, proposed, in 1854, that the northern reaches of the Louisiana Purchase—the prairies—should be organized as the Territory of Nebraska. Douglas' bill would have reopened the whole area to slavery by adopting the principle of local determination. So far as Douglas was concerned, it was an attempt to get Southern votes in support of his railroad project.

Implicit in the proposal was the repeal of the Missouri Compromise of 1820. But in the immediately resulting uproar, the Southerners demanded an explicit repeal. There could then be no doubt that the territory would be open to slavery. This aroused the anti-slavery men, led by Senator Charles Sumner; and they furiously attacked the administration. It was Pierce himself who decided finally the form of the bill for organizing the territory—he would have it open to slavery. He was pressed hard by Douglas; but he was also urged by Davis and Cushing in his own Cabinet, stronger men than he, who knew what they wanted. Patronage was used freely, and the bill was passed in 1854.

Why Pierce should have done something so clearly calculated to make his further ambitions futile can be understood only as further subordination to the Southerners. But also involved in it was his attempt to divert interest to an expansive foreign policy. This last was something the nation was prepared for. The revolutions of 1848 in Europe had inflated the pride of Americans, who had the original revolution in their past; and they felt called on to give advice. This brashness was made known as far away as Turkey and Sicily; but closer home in neighboring countries it amounted to a rather irritating self-righteousness.

Naturally the nearest nations were interfered with most often. Mexico and Cuba, as well as others around the Caribbean, were conscious that this sea was now considered to be an American lake. The designs on Mexican, Cuban, and Nicaraguan territory were complex and numerous. That they came to nothing was due to growing preoccupation with an internal struggle. But the interest in expansion was not all adventurous or diversionary. The slave interests had an eye on Cuban plantations and Mexican haciendas; and for Pierce and others interested in blanketing the slavery issue, the turning outward of people's eyes was highly desirable. But at the same time there was a kind of earnest missionary impulse behind it. There could be no institutions so right as those of the United States; they would be equally right for others.

Then there was the expansionism which had grown to be a kind of habit. There was a natural border on the east and west. But this was not true on the north or south. We have seen Canada swimming in and out of expansionists' dreams. If Hull had been a better General, the War of 1812 might have ended in conquest. It was not a dream that died with this frustration. Theodore Roosevelt was muttering about it more than half a century later. Mexico had been ravaged. Considering all that was taken from her, it is a miracle that anything remained when the Civil War usurped attention. And Cuba was always considered a logical appendage whose status would someday —when the slavery issue died down—be regularized.

This is not the place to discuss the schemes of the Pierce circle. They were many and various. Caleb Cushing had lived much abroad and had recently gone around the world. He seems to have regarded it as an American oyster. His initiative opened China definitely to American trade and sponsored the Perry expedition to Japan. The clipper ship was better known just then than any other all across the Pacific. Then there were the various Isthmian schemes. To get to California quickly was an earnest desire among all the adventurers who were drawn there by gold, free for the taking. The clipper ship was one means, but some crossing of the narrow ridge connecting the continents would be better. For this there were competing schemes, as there were competing transcontinental railway routes; and their advocates caused almost as much trouble. An Isthmian railway was built at enormous cost in lives, and a canal was projected which would not eventuate until Theodore Roosevelt's time. Mexican and Colombian life was confused for years by the intrigues of those who had some interest in the crossing.

A hundred years later there were still the hulks of sailing ships at San Francisco docks, abandoned by passengers and crew alike as they rushed for the gold fields. And the bones of starved and exhausted draft animals littered the wagon trails from Kansas westward. The trek was developing its full volume in Pierce's time.

But it was only the surplus of energy and capital that looked abroad. Most of it was finding an outlet on the nearer plains. There were those who saw that, with the new machinery—plows with steel mold-boards, harrows, harvesters, and rakes—the rich prairie soils could be as great a bonanza as California gold. The railways were not only to open up a continental crossing; they were also to bring wheat and pork to the lake and river ports and even to the Gulf and the Atlantic.

Douglas' proposal concerning the Kansas-Nebraska country stirred up a controversy that seems to have been just ready to explode. It spoiled the plans of both parties to damp down the slavery issue. In a matter of days, the compromising efforts of years were ruined. Thurlow Weed, in May 1854, wrote:

> The crime is committed. The work of Monroe, Madison, and Jefferson is undone. The wall they erected to guard the domain of liberty is flung down by the hands of the American Congress, and slavery crawls like a slimy reptile over the ruins . . .

It was this sort of revulsion that created the Republican party—and that ruined Pierce as a politician. It must be said for him that the principle behind the Kansas-Nebraska Act accorded with his lifetime loyalty to strict construction. Douglas called it popular sovereignty. Pierce thought it such good Democratic doctrine that it might carry him on to a renominaton in 1856. It did unite all the Southerners, but rather in opposition to the North than in support of Pierce, whose immediate unpopularity they ungratefully did nothing to combat.

The Kansas controversy soon took on most of the aspects of a local war. The Emigrant Aid Society of Massachusetts assisted Free-Soilers who were willing to take land and defend it from other emigrants moving out from the South. Organized bands, some of them little better than bandits, ranged over the area. Pitched battles on a small scale were frequent. A pro-slavery band of this sort looted the town of Lawrence, and a retaliation was carried out at Pottawatomie Creek that was spoken of as a massacre. This was John Brown's contribution. Soon there occurred the battles at Osawatomie and Black Jack. "Bleeding Kansas" was no exaggeration. A preview of the Civil War was on exhibit.

It was as a kind of echo in the United States Senate that Charles Sumner made an impassioned speech denouncing "the crime against Kansas" and a few days later was beaten unconscious as he sat in his seat by a Congressman (Preston Brooks) who was a nephew of Senator Butler of South Carolina. Butler had been on the receiving end of Sumner's invective.

Not only in the Congress but all through the nation the controversy raged for months. Pierce defended the validity of the Act. He laid the responsibility for violence on the anti-slavery men. The Northerners, according to him, were the breakers of peace, the aggressors. Writing his last annual message in 1856, he claimed that tranquillity had been restored. But it was a military peace. The armed bands ranging over the countryside had been suppressed, but nothing could still the Northern resentment. There were few Northern Democrats left by 1856, and what there were had had enough of Pierce.

The party struggle was much more complicated than can be indicated in any short statement, of course; but what has to be said is that Pierce handled his problem badly. In his anxiety to placate the Southern politicos, he alienated others; and since he was no longer useful, they looked for another man. They found him in Buchanan. And again, as in 1852, a majority confused democracy with Democracy. But the party had lived as long as it could on misrepresentation. Its last victory until a terrible break in our history had been repaired would be this one. After this the Southern recourse would be to violence.

James Buchanan
1791–1868

Born in Franklin County, Pennsylvania
Elected fifteenth President in 1856 at 65

HISTORY

1809	Graduated from Dickinson College.
1812	Admitted to the bar.
1814	Elected to the lower house of the state legislature.
1820	Elected to the United States House of Representatives.
1832	Minister to Russia.
1834	Elected to the United States Senate.
1845–49	Secretary of State in Polk's Cabinet.
1849–53	Private practice.
1853–56	Minister to Great Britain.
1854	Joined in issuing the Ostend Manifesto, gaining favor with Southerners.
1856	Returned home; nominated by the Democrats as a compromise candidate and elected (Vice-President, Breckinridge); opponent, Fremont with Dayton.

178

1861   Retired.
1868   Died at Lancaster, Pennsylvania.

JAMES BUCHANAN, as we shall see, was something less than a solid man, but it was from a solid enough base that he moved to assault the Presidency. This base was the lushly prosperous country of the Pennsylvania Dutch. He belonged to it. It was not until the fourth try that he succeeded—when he was sixty-five years old, and when, as he himself said, he had given up any hope of capturing the prize.[1] Even then it would have to be said that he owed success as much to luck as to good judgment—he happened to be out of the country while Pierce was alienating the party leaders. But perhaps his being abroad was not altogether accidental.

Buchanan would prove to be one of those who could become President but could not win a second term. The list of these is lengthening: the two Adamses, Van Buren, Polk, Fillmore, and Pierce; out of fifteen—counting Buchanan—six.

But it begins to appear that the withholding of second nominations may be because incumbents have found a new dedication rather than because they have not. Their seizure with the public interest may very well have displeased those who had renomination at their disposal. The first-term President may have put the duties called for in a Chief of State above those useful to the party chiefs—and this may have been fatal.

This cannot be said of Buchanan. Nor is it true, as is sometimes said, that his failure to be renominated was owed only to age and infirmities. By 1860 he was sixty-nine years old; but he did not die until eight years later; and for most of those years he was about as capable as he had been during his term. If he had been a success and had held the party together, nothing could have prevented a second nomination. It was part of his failure that a fatal breakup occurred. His situation in 1860 was like that of a person who has been in a disaster he helped to cause and then walks away from the wreckage.

As for getting the nomination in the first instance, he offers another illustration of a persistence which, in the end, prevailed. In the conventions of 1844, 1848, and 1852, he was around, representing his Pennsylvania machine, offering himself, getting insufficient support, withdrawing rather than cause party trouble, but always expectant. In 1856, at Cincinnati, the circumstances arranged themselves and the nomination came to him. Of those who influenced the arranging in 1856, there seem to have been four who were most important—all Senators: John Slidell of Louisiana; Judah P. Benjamin, also of Louisi-

---

[1] "My aspirations for the Presidency had all died four years ago . . ." Buchanan to Hon. J. C. Dobbin, August 20, 1856. Quoted in G. T. Curtis, *Life of Buchanan* (New York, 1883), 179.

ana; Jesse D. Bright of Indiana; and James A. Bayard of Delaware. All were old and experienced insiders. At a time when passions were easily aroused and opportunities for troublemaking were many, they were hard, amoral, practical operators. None of them ever considered so remote a matter as the national good. But they did consider the Southern interest. All were from the South—even Bright was from *lower* Indiana, his home within sight of the Ohio River; all were defecting from Pierce, each with his own reason; all were determined to find another Northerner who would accept Southern direction; and all knew beforehand who that man was. It was Buchanan, and they intended to nominate him.[2]

There were two other possibilities besides President Pierce, who was to be discarded. These were Cass and Douglas. But Cass was old and obese, far past his prime; he had been passed over in 1852 for Pierce and was no longer politically potent. And then there was Senator Douglas. Douglas was such a sturdy small man—he was called the "Little Giant"—and had such a following that he had to be considered. He had advocated "squatter sovereignty," and this once had pleased the Southerners; but it was no longer enough; they were plotting now to make slavery compulsory rather than voluntary. Then there was another objection to Douglas—he was set on grasping active leadership of the party. He had initiated the Kansas-Nebraska policy and had refused to yield the center of the stage to any of his Senatorial colleagues; and they had no intention of trying to direct a dynamo. Douglas generated ideas and influenced people. They wanted the traditional molded man who would be a front for their machinations.

It can be understood why no one in sight suited them as well as Buchanan. He was a Pennsylvanian, and his hold on the electorate in that important state carried over into several others. He was a portly, urbane, rather handsome man who fitted the popular conception of a statesman almost as well as Fillmore. He had held office for forty-two years—as Representative, as Senator, as Jackson's Minister to Russia, as Polk's Secretary of State, and as Pierce's Minister to Great Britain. But he had never exhibited any eccentric impulses, and such policy commitments as he had made had been those central to party doctrine. Even his age might be in his favor; it made him seem safe and judicial.

Professor Nichols, looking closer, has come to certain interesting conclusions concerning him; and they help to explain much that is otherwise mysterious. The well-padded, well-dressed statesman figure was not what he seemed. He might appear to radiate confidence; he might be the very picture of stable assurance; but actually he was

---

[2] In Curtis' *Life, op. cit.*, 170 ff., there is quoted a memorandum by S. M. Barlow of New York, who tells of taking a house in Cincinnati to be the headquarters of this group.

timid, frustrated, and negative. The large, florid, confident exterior concealed a fearsome spirit, a suspicious temperament and a dull mind.

A rather significant facet of his early life has been bowdlerized to the extent of reversing its meaning. He has been pictured as remaining a bachelor because of having lost a boyhood sweetheart. A more realistic suggestion is that he lost her because she found him frigid and unresponsive. His long continued pose as a sorrowing lover may have been a protection from further involvement with the other sex. He was always pleasant to women—and always distant. It is apparent that a whole area of human experience was closed to him.

His successful projection of a false portrait of himself was general. His inability to grasp and deal with the forces that closed in on him as President, the way he fumbled and temporized and finally left to Lincoln a situation grown impossible to resolve short of force, shows this. The exposure of his incompetence, when it came, was tragic. But what has now to be said is that political processes landed him in a situation he could not control. This had happened before, and sometimes it had been serious for the nation—as when Madison fumbled the War of 1812. On this occasion it was more than serious; it was nearly fatal.

It is strange that a personality of Buchanan's sort should have been combined with one of the persistent and gnawing ambitions we have by now become familiar with. The implacable forces of his time were destined to reach a climax during his Presidency; and when their heat burned away his protective dignity, he was inevitably revealed as a hopeless ditherer. The vigilance to protect the central weakness that usually characterizes such persons failed him. It could not operate in the pitiless pressure of great office.

If those who resurrected Buchanan's ambitions foresaw his ordeal, there is no evidence of it. They were intent on forwarding their own immediate interests. They seem not to have given the slightest consideration to the consequences. In this they were not different, of course, from the run of insiders who become so immersed in party affairs and in recurrent campaigns that the purpose of the machinery they operate is irrelevant.

They would have given anyone who suggested the public interest as a criterion the treatment such people have usually had from the professionals. "Amateur," "theorist," "radical"—these are the epithets they would have used. In this instance there was no need. Buchanan was one of themselves. Except for his imposing appearance, he was indistinguishable from the rest. Slidell was crafty and ratty, Benjamin oily and sly, Bright vulgar and intolerant. Only Bayard had the finish of breeding. He came of an old Delaware family. But crafty, vulgar, sly, or aristocratic—all were operators at their work. When they got down to it and determined that they could have their way, they put forward the man they were certain would give them no trouble.

Buchanan, in his time, had taken part in similar operations, with the same motives. He had labored at innumerable conventions, state and national, arranging slates, making trades, sizing up possibilities. He had helped to rig legislatures and delegations, and he had been an inner-group Senator. He was integrated with the Pennsylvania machine. And far outside the state his machine had long-cultivated allies. For years he himself had written prolix letters to a widely scattered acquaintance in the party. Thousands have survived—shrewd about party business, but evasive or indeterminate about public issues.

The convention of 1856 was the first to meet beyond the Alleghenies. The Democrats had always before met in Baltimore. But they had finally recognized their Western orientation and gone to Cincinnati. If they thought this might influence the Ohio vote, they were disappointed. All twenty-three Ohio electors would go to the first Republican candidate—Frémont.

It was steaming hot that June, as it usually is in the Ohio Valley, and the fetid atmosphere of the meeting hall was almost unbearable. The discomfort of the delegates made them easier for the leaders to manage. After a day or two of dissipation, sweating, and listening to windy oratory, any compromise that would bring the proceedings to an end seemed acceptable. And Buchanan was the compromise the Senatorial quartet had to offer. Pierce had supporters; so did Douglas. On the first fourteen ballots neither had a majority; indeed, Buchanan had more than either; his total rose from 135½ on the first ballot to 168 on the sixteenth; on the seventeenth he had two-thirds and was nominated. The danger, in the early balloting, had been that Pierce and Douglas would unite on a dark horse. But Indiana, supposedly a Douglas delegation, defected to Buchanan. Then the four Senators went to work. To the Douglas people they promised a later nomination. Douglas, after all, they said, was only forty-three; and they promised that Buchanan would not run again. Eighteen-sixty would be Douglas' year. Pierce, they argued, could not possibly be elected, and neither could any dark horse. Republicanism was rising rapidly and what the Democrats needed to win was an organization man. This argument prevailed; Douglas' name was withdrawn and Buchanan was promptly nominated.

Buchanan was at his Wheatland seat—near Lancaster—while these matters were being arranged in Cincinnati. He was just back from abroad; and, beyond reiterating that he was for "squatter sovereignty" in the territories, he had had nothing to say. It appeared, however, that matters were not going to be so simple for him. There was a growing movement of uneasy dissidents—Know-Nothings—for the old party professionals to worry about.[3] And some annoyed Democrats were defecting and calling themselves North Americans; but obviously the worst threat was the young Republican party. That there was a real place for a Whig revival was apparent from the amazing growth of this new organization. Its beginning had been in 1854 at a small meeting in Ripon. But in 1855, twenty-three states were represented at a convention in Pittsburgh. When it met in Philadelphia in 1856 it was still inchoate; the states sent large or small delegations as they chose; and it had no more clarity about policy than the Whigs had had. It was opposed to Democrats in general and to Buchanan in particular; but it had radical and conservative wings, and they could not agree on anything. It was, however, growing rapidly.

Its chosen candidate—Frémont—was picked because, although he was politically neutral, he had a certain glamor from his exploits as an explorer and from his part in bringing California into the Union. The Californians themselves did not particularly like him. A. K. McClure, who was one of them, quoted a colleague as saying that Frémont was "a millionaire without a dollar, a soldier who never fought a battle, and a statesman who never made a speech."[4] The Republicans were following Whig precedent in looking for manly charm contained in a large and impressive package which, however, held no surprises and could be counted on to behave as directed. Harrison, Taylor, Fillmore, and Scott were precedents.

Frémont was distrusted by the right-wingers. They suspected he might be radical. The large package might conceal surprises.

McClure later described his feelings:

> I was a delegate to the first Republican National Convention . . . I went . . . hoping to aid in the nomination of Judge McLean, who was sufficiently conservative to command both the Whig and American votes, and I had no faith whatever in the success of a distinctive Republican candidate and party. I was surprised to find the Republicans of New England and of New York who were attending the convention,

---

[3] The Know-Nothing movement began as one of those frightening hysterias that sometimes beset the United States. It had an anti-foreign and anti-Catholic motivation arising from the irritations incident to the rapid increase of immigration, which was largely Catholic. Protestant antipathy to Catholicism ran very deep. It went back to the Reformation and occasionally welled up, as it did in the 1840's and 1850's. The Know-Nothings were joined by many Whigs, of the more conservative and intolerant sort. The first manifestation was a secret society, the Order of the Star-Spangled Banner, whose members, when asked, answered, "I know nothing." When it emerged into the open it was as the American party. Its slogan was "Americans for America." It would not be the last phenomenon of this sort politicians would have to cope with.

[4] *Our Presidents and How We Make Them* (New York, 1900), 137–38.

in favor of a radical policy, and I was so much dissatisfied with the
evident outcome . . . that I did not enroll as a delegate.

I had no faith in Frémont, either as a candidate or as a President. I
shared the general conservative Whig sentiment of Pennsylvania that
the convention in nominating Frémont on a square-toed Republican
platform was altogether too "wild and woolley" in flavor to win.

Nevertheless, there was no other group for conservative Whigs to
join, and McClure, like others, felt forced to support a man he did
not really trust. He reported on a visit some of them made to Frémont
in mid-campaign:

> Frémont made his home during the contest in New York under the
> strictest orders not to discuss any political question, either orally or by
> letter, with any outside of those in charge of the campaign. Along with
> several others, I called upon him at his home some time before the elec-
> tion, simply to pay our respects to the man we were supporting for
> President, and he was so extremely cautious that he evaded the most
> ordinary expressions relating to the conduct and prospects of the
> battle . . .

There did seem to be a touch of the bizarre about the Republican
candidate, and the Democrats enlarged on this during the campaign,
doing their best to extrapolate his explorations into a dangerous predilection for adventure; besides, he might be an abolitionist. There
could of course, be no doubt about Buchanan's solidity and conservatism but his supporters had the difficult task of proving to the South
that he was friendly to its interests, and at the same time of convincing
the North that he was not pledged to serve the slave owners. The
immigrant-labor vote, becoming important now, was wooed by the
Democrats with some success. The party of Jefferson and Jackson
was still the little man's refuge, they said; and the new Republicans
were either Know-Nothings or very near it, out to establish Protestant,
upper-class superiority.

The contest was a hot one. But, as in many elections, the excitement
was mostly in a few closely contested states. Pennsylvania, in this
case, was the one most fought for. It was decided in the end by only
a little more than a thousand votes, and this was accounted for by the
refusal of older conservative Whigs to support the Republicans.

That the Pennsylvania result was so close was a clear indication
for the future. The results were barely decisive, also, in Indiana and
Illinois; and New York and Ohio were lost.

It was remarkable how rapidly from small local beginnings a national Republican party had developed. This was not altogether be-

cause an issue waited for exploitation or because a political vacuum (caused by the Whig disappearance) waited to be filled. It was at least partly because the leadership was competent and the organization carried out with energy and efficiency. Professor Nichols has remarked of it that the party seemed to have been born with a sense of organization.[5]

The Democratic managers by 1857 or 1858 could see that unless something happened to stop the apparent trend the Republicans would win in 1860. Buchanan could not stop them; he had become a prisoner of the South. But to professionals an election in the hand is always better than two in a prospective bush. Something, they always feel, may turn up. Politics being so uncertain, problems in the future, even a few years away, are quite likely to be someone else's. Since Buchanan was committed to being a one-termer, there would by 1860 be a whole new line-up.

It was the North which was fed up and drifting toward sectional solidification. When that had gone far enough, Northern votes would be sufficient to elect a President. Such a candidate would have to be a Free-Soiler who had abandoned compromise, who was dedicated to the destruction of Southern power, and who was a hard unionist. It would be better if he came from the Midwest, since New England had a radical taint, New York was a capitalist center, and the newly made states in the Far West would hesitate to accept an Easterner. If Buchanan followed his indicated course, the stage would be set for a new man with new policies. It seems incredible that the Democratic leaders missed all the signs.

As for Buchanan's motives, we have the Nichols view, which suggests that Buchanan's political ambitions had about them a strong tinge of compensation. This is new in our list. We have seen men who undertook the Presidency as a duty (Washington) or as a challenge (Jackson) or as an opportunity to use talents in the national service (J. Q. Adams). We have seen others who were, if not puppets, then so innocent of political experience and so anxious for honors that they lent themselves to the machinations of stronger, more sophisticated men (Harrison, Taylor, and Fillmore). We have seen one clever and complicated man (Jefferson), several who were intelligent but inept (the Adamses and Madison). But we have not before encountered a complete incompetent who lived in constant fear of deflation and who had risen, stage by stage, to an altitude he could not possibly sustain.

The Whigs were right about the future, but they were wrong about the present. They could not work the Old General racket with Scott,

---

[5] For an account of early Republican history, see Moos, *The Republicans* (New York, 1956).

and people were not convinced yet in 1852 that slavery had to be exterminated and the Southerners deprived of their privileged position in Washington. Abolitionists were often regarded as a nuisance in the North as well as in the South. Their meetings were frequently mobbed and their speakers stoned in New Hampshire and other places. They were thought of as radicals and fanatics. But the events out on the plains during the Kansas-Nebraska battles changed all this. By 1856 the new Republican coalition had a policy the Whigs never had dared develop. They stood for something; and what they stood for was what was coming.

Buchanan was a survival. But there was one more victory in compromise—compromise between North and South—and the Democrats intended to exploit it. For this purpose Buchanan was made to order. He was a trimmer of exaggerated degree. He was always for making a deal—especially if it favored the South.

Mr. Nichols' theory would suggest that he was that way because of the need for visible success to compensate for hidden deficiencies. This led him to aspire beyond his competence and to protect himself from exposure by an eternal effort to escape decision. Those who selected him did not want a man; they wanted a tool. But it would require a man to meet the issues of the next few years—a man who could persuade his party to be wise rather than expedient.

It is hard to work up any sympathy for Buchanan. He must have been aware of his unfitness and must have jeopardized the national security deliberately. That in the end he retreated to Wheatland a beaten old man is true. But he went on protesting that his policies had been justified, that he had done all he could, and that the debacle was one he could not have avoided. What made the Civil War unavoidable was that Buchanan would not—or could not—moderate the Southern arrogance. This could have been done only by a Democrat. When a Republican national victory became clearly foreshadowed in the Congressional election of 1858, the South had either to retreat in humiliation or resort to disruption and force.

Abraham Lincoln

1809–1865

Born in Hardin County, Kentucky
Became sixteenth President in 1861 at 52

HISTORY

1816–30	Grew up as a farm boy, with an indigent father and stepmother, and struck out for himself as a hired laborer.
1833	Appointed postmaster and deputy land surveyor in New Salem, Illinois.
1834	Elected to the state legislature.
1836	Re-elected.
1837	Moved to Springfield and opened law office.
1840	Campaigned for Harrison.
1842	Married Mary Todd.
1846	Nominated as a Whig for the House of Representatives, after several disappointments, and elected; but was not a candidate for renomination.
1854	Made Peoria Speech.
1856	Received 110 votes for the Vice-Presidency in Republican convention. Campaigned for Fremont and Dayton.

1858	Debated with Douglas during campaign for the Senatorship from Illinois.
1859	Legislature declared him to be the state's candidate for the Presidency.
1860	Made Cooper Union speech; nominated by Republicans and elected (Vice-President, Hamlin); opponents, Northern Democrats, Douglas with Johnson, Southern Democrats, Breckenridge with Lane, constitutional Unionists, Bell with Everett.
1861	Civil War began.
1864	Renominated and re-elected (Vice-President, Andrew Johnson); opponent, McClellan with Pendleton.
1865	Victory and assassination.

A MONG THE PRESIDENTS we have so far encountered, Jefferson and Jackson were notable for political finesse. We may now learn new lessons from Lincoln. His is a life in which the most trivial incidents have been recorded. Practically all his days have been accounted for. All his attitudes and his decisions have been analyzed. He has been watched at work and in meditation; in failure and in success. Yet he is a never-ending challenge to those who are fascinated by his final emergence at the highest levels of statesmanship. Some of the attempts to account for his success have been good tries; but in every explanation there is an area of mystery his biographers do not penetrate.

It was certainly a very narrow gate that Lincoln passed through on his way to the White House. In the years immediately preceding his election, he said a number of times—and seems to have meant it—that he was not suited for the Presidency. When the prospect brightened, he overcame these doubts as others have done; but he had them.[1]

His experience shows that even a most unlikely-seeming individual's talents can be really well suited to the circumstances and persons he has to deal with as President. His emergence was from an environment that smothered most of his fellows and reduced them to clods. His was a totally unexpected flowering in the weed patch of Illinois politics.

Still it was not all accidental. He quite certainly gave the most earnest and exhaustive study to every move he made. His calculations were pondered and tried in anticipation; he consulted everyone who could give him help; he never neglected a possibility; he worked and strained and, if necessary, bargained and begged for every gain. His eyes, his ears, and all his well-tuned perceptions were constantly absorbing the knowledge available to him—in print to be read, in the experiences of others to be heard about, in the social and political developments around him.

He may have spoken of himself as lacking qualifications for the Presidency, but when the remarks were made he was obviously in hard training for some political position beyond those he had already held. He was still aiming at a Senatorship in 1858—Douglas' seat—and he may very well have told himself until almost the last moment not to set his hopes too high; but as we look back along his pre-Presidential years the preparation seems more appropriate than can be explained as accidental.

Of course apparent unsuitability has often been changed to suitability overnight. We have seen this happen to Generals Harrison and

---

[1] Cf. *The First Lincoln Campaign* by R. H. Luthin (Harvard University Press, 1944). Mr. Luthin cites (p. 72) at least three occasions in 1859 when Lincoln spoke of himself as unqualified.

190

Taylor, who won spectacular battles; to Tyler, who was made Vice-President when the Clayites had to be conciliated, and, to mention no others, to Pierce, a Democrat in Republican New England, a "Northern man with Southern principles" when compromise was widely longed for and appeasement of the South was popular. Lincoln became "available" in the same way, even if he did think himself "unsuitable." He was precisely the man to embody the indignations of those who elected him.

It is interesting to see how accounts differ about his preparation. Take, for instance, his self-education. There are stories of his avid study as a boy by the light of pine knots in the winter evenings, and later, when he was a lawyer riding the circuit, of his carrying books in his saddlebags and mastering their contents on long rides and during enforced delays in lodgings. Yet his irritated partner, Herndon, was annoyed because nothing Lincoln read was of a sort he approved. He said, in fact, that Abe was no reader.

We know that Lincoln really digested a few classics and made a late project of Euclid; but what he really attacked with gusto and appreciation was a newspaper. Herndon did not think newspapers educational. Lincoln read them constantly, aloud if anyone would listen; he tore out pieces to show to others; he never got enough.

There is something here: Jefferson had the same habit; and both F. D. Roosevelt and Kennedy felt for four or five papers as soon as their eyes opened in the morning. Daily happenings had meanings to be put away in well-stocked memories. So perhaps anyone who aspires to democratic preferment must absorb from the atmosphere around him the materials for his strategy.

There can be no doubt that from early in his life Lincoln wanted to be a Representative and experimented in ways to persuade crowds that he was reliable. So he became a raw state legislator, learning on the job to be a party man; then he went to the House of Representatives and later tried to become a Senator. We see him learning his lessons: how to dicker and compromise and logroll; how to evade hot issues until the time came when there was profit in taking a position; how his party organization could be committed to his advancement—by appropriate sacrifice if necessary; how to seem conservative in a radical environment; how to put together and hold a coalition. These and other political lessons were learned, not from formal study of rules, not even from listening to advisers, but from talk with folk along his way, from the hints and small facts he found in the papers, from shrewd selection of alternatives, and sometimes by making mistakes and being embarrassed.

Somehow, by a process we cannot follow, he came out in the end, on the issues most difficult for all politicians of his time, at solutions

not only expedient but right—so right that, once started, they seemed
to have the persuasive power of the simplest axiom. These, of course,
were slavery and union. It was these that Lincoln approached again
and again, worrying them, chewing them over in public, cautiously
suggesting new approaches, going far off the track once or twice but
coming back to the moral problem at the center of slavery and the
political problem of union, stated simply and powerfully and with
conviction. In his Cooper Union speech in February 1860, so clear and
right was his reasoning, and so appealing was his awkward honesty,
that he carried with him not only his hearers but the sophisticated
press. He was a marked man from then on—a man who spoke the
mind and conscience of those who had so long been troubled.

It would not be far wrong to say that Lincoln drove his way to the
Presidency through these issues. He was no agitator, and for his
country's sake as well as his own, because he feared it, he would have
been glad to see the slavery issue settled by the peaceable process of
argument and attrition. But others would not let it rest. It was always
breaking out in this place or that and being violently argued first with
words and then with arms. There was trouble in Kansas during the
Taylor-Fillmore Presidency when he was out of office after having
been a Congressman; it was temporarily stilled by the Clay-Webster
Compromise of 1850. Lincoln seems to have hoped with others that
the cessation of hostilities was more than temporary. But the debates
he had listened to silently during the last months of Polk's regime had
frightened him to the depths—slavery and disunion, he saw, were
locked in a dangerous logical embrace. This was when Calhoun and
the other militant Southerners caucused to organize against "Northern
aggression." Slavery, they maintained, was a positive good, a blessing
both to master and servant. Those who opposed it were "bigots."

Secession from then on became a looming danger, freely talked about
by those who would impose their will on the nation. Slaves were
property and Congress had the obligation to protect their owners and
to see to it that owners' rights were enforced everywhere in the nation.
And it was at this time that Lincoln, his habitual melancholy overcoming him, may well have wrestled most agonizingly with his conscience. He was relieved when the issue retreated a little from prominence and seemed to be finding a solution in compromise until Stephen
A. Douglas, Democratic Senator from Lincoln's own Illinois, moved
to repeal the slavery restrictions in the Missouri Compromise, and all
the bitterness boiled up again.

This was in January 1854. From then on there was no halt as the
disaster of civil war rushed upon the nation. It was during the next
few years that Lincoln became the symbol of a people searching for a

way to avert the inevitable, one they could accept with good conscience.

At what moment it became apparent to him that the slavery issue was the one he must use for his further rise it is not possible to say; but he knew it soon. He re-entered politics in 1854 and was first defeated in 1855 when he sought the Whig nomination for the Senate. Soon after this and after much hesitation, he became a Republican and was soon the best-known one in Illinois. Then when in 1858 he was nominated and ran against Douglas for the Senate, he had reached his full powers. The debates of that year did not win him a Senate seat, but they identified him as a potential President. Then his years of ceaseless worry and struggle to find some solution for the nation's division had their reward in a mind finally clear and determined. And Douglas was a perfect foil. For Douglas saw the problem very differently from Lincoln in one respect. He did not think slavery wrong; he thought it merely inexpedient. Lincoln was far past that stopping place. It was immoral; and he knew that others had traveled the same way too and had arrived at the same end. And there were yet more who were half persuaded.

This was the vital issue; but there were others. There was the tariff, a perennial source of division. The manufacturing regions—mostly in the North and East—wanted protection; the agrarian South wanted free trade. Lincoln was a moderate protectionist; but this was enough to win the support of Pennsylvania and New England business interests. These same interests were pleased, too, with his rather casual views on the rising labor-capital dispute. He thought workers, as things were, had the most precious of all rights—the right to rise. Moreover, they had the opportunity to do so; and for proof of this he could cite himself. He thought, as employers of that time did not, that workers' privileges as free men included that of striking. But he had no occasion to be very specific, and he was generally regarded as conservatively inclined.

Perhaps next in importance to slavery was the free-land or homestead issue. It can be imagined how a growing and expanding nation, being fed by increasing numbers of European immigrants, would regard the vast open spaces of the West. The Southerners were against easy access to the land; free farming was competition for their plantation system. But Easterners with sons to provide for and peasant immigrants hungry for land wanted homesteads, open to all who would occupy them. The government had the land; the people who voted wanted it. Southern opposition kept the agitation for a homestead law in check during the fifties. Buchanan, still responsive to their wishes, vetoed a bill in 1858. And this presented Lincoln and the new Republicans with just the issue they needed to win over the fathers of large families in the East as well as the Germans and other immigrants. It was fatal for the Democrats to accept the Southern planters' views.

Lincoln, being a Illinoisan, was naturally on the popular side of this issue. It would have been difficult for him to have been otherwise. As boy and man he had seen virgin prairies brought under cultivation by a pioneering folk; he had more recently ridden circuit from town to town across the vacant spaces that still existed even in Illinois. Their occupation was natural; to have them lie unused was a waste. It cost nothing to give away government land; and Lincoln was in on several giveaways—to railroads, not to immigrants—that later generations would have questioned. The Homestead Act of his Presidency would be so carelessly conceived as to be incredibly abused. But for his purpose in the preparatory years it gave him a powerful appeal.

There were other issues; but these were the most useful ones—slavery, union, the tariff, industrial relations, and homesteading. None of them was for Lincoln difficult except the fierce quarrel over slavery and disunion. On this he had to find his way by severe thought and careful experiment, tempering his convictions to popular acceptance, never going beyond what he judged the majority view, and never risking his reputation as a conservative.

It must be recalled that Lincoln was born in Kentucky and that sometimes, even in the fifties, he spoke of it as "his" state. He had married into a prominent Kentucky family. And he and all his relations were typical of the poor whites who in racial feeling traditionally echoed their betters. He came slowly and reluctantly to think of Negroes as having the same rights as whites. And he never thought of them as equals. So if he was not an anti-slavery man at first and was never an abolitionist, as those terms were used in his day, it was quite in character. And if he struggled both in private and in public to come to a conclusion his conscience would accept, and one that would also be "practical" for a politician, it was not strange. Many another man was struggling too. Lincoln and the electorate of 1860 made the transition together, and the participating Northern majority ended up about where he did—a long way short of the New England abolitionist position, but still accepting Negroes as people, and people with rights. White men did not have to go further—to accept them socially, much less approve intermingling—and Lincoln never did go further. But to have made the transition, slowly and with such obvious pain, with argument and hesitation, was to do exactly what the political requirements called for.

Joseph Medill, proprietor of the influential *Chicago Tribune*, said of him, as the campaign came on, that he had excited no hates anywhere. "He has," he said, "made no record to be defended or explained."[2]

Later Americans are sometimes shocked to hear that the man who presided over their worst national schism was favored by important people for much the same reason as, for instance, Zachary Taylor or William H. Harrison: because no one could object to his opinions, since he had none.

This was Medill's estimate; and for the purpose Medill had in mind it may have been useful. But it was not true. On several questions Lincoln was quite firm. He was against the extension of slavery, although he would not interfere with it where it existed. He was known as an anti-Nebraska Whig, and this meant that he opposed Douglas' scheme for allowing the white settlers in the territories to say whether or not there should be slavery. This, he said, was not a local matter. If slavery was wrong, then every American had an interest in preventing its spread. It would not be right simply because Nebraskans wanted to establish it.

This matter of national integrity was something far deeper than any other issue. It did not so often appear on the surface of discussion, but it was stirring men's emotions. Andrew Jackson has stature in our eyes, and we forgive him the harm he did, because when the Union was threatened he saved it. Some of his successors allowed those who made threats again not only to escape punishment but to dictate policies certain to make disruption easier. At the very time when Lincoln was approaching the Presidency, some members of Buchanan's Cabinet were using their powers to weaken the Federal government and make it more difficult to suppress an easily predictable rebellion. Buchanan failed in other respects; but worst of all was his tolerance of officials who were undermining the Federal power and strengthening its challengers.

Lincoln was identified with union; and it was the foundation of the Republicans' strength that their party was unionist. Other issues might appeal to certain groups of voters—the tariff to Pennsylvanians, anti-slavery to abolitionists, free homesteads to potential emigrants. But union went deep down to the American cleavage. On both sides there were those who would die to defend their beliefs—as would be so tragically proved. It is not surprising that it divided their votes.

We begin to see that what is to be learned about Lincoln as an aspirant is that becoming the embodiment of a deeply felt emotion is the most certain of all ways to the Presidency. We see further that it must be a general emotion; also that there is a nice calculation of

---

[2] This was said in the *Press and Tribune* on March 6, 1860. All during March and on into spring Medill was developing the same theme.

time, because emotions of this sort come to a climax; the potential leader must judge his moment precisely, be ready for it, and seize instruments calculated to consolidate the potential majority. In the Lincoln instance there were also enemies such as a candidate must have. His were fanatic ones whose first loyalty was to the states they lived in. This sentiment was outraged, as they believed, by others' unwillingness to accept the principle that slavery was a matter for states and not the Federal government to decide. If Lincoln denied that he thought abolition should be enforced throughout the Union, he did not deny that he thought slavery wrong and that it ought not only to be prevented from spreading but put in the way of disappearing. This was final for the Southerners; they knew him for an enemy.

Until the Lincoln-Douglas debates, there was no complete polarization of the nation on the issue of union. Some Southerners were loyal, and some Northerners talked of separation from the "slaveocracy." Many who later fought so fiercely for the principle had not yet felt its force. While minds were being made up Lincoln very carefully preserved his moderate position. He hoped the Southern unionists would not be entirely disaffected and that the extreme anti-slavery people in the North would agree to keeping it within its present confines. The vast expansion of agriculture in the West and of manufacturing in the East would keep everyone busy enough if the fires of controversy could be damped down. Slavery might not then lead to secession.

But by the time of the campaign, the carefully conservative Lincoln had become, in spite of himself, the symbol of abolition. It was obvious that the division forecast by the election of 1856 and again in 1858 was to be completed in 1860.

So Joseph Medill was wrong to say that Lincoln had made no record. What he should have said, and what he may really have meant, was that Lincoln's record was acceptably Republican and was consistent with the views of enough people to elect him. This turned out to be the fact. But it was fact only because the intransigent Southerners split the Democratic party; in the whole nation there were still more Democrats than Republicans.

Lincoln's extraordinary caution, also, did not satisfy Northern extremists. They put a ticket in the field too. So both parties were split; but the Democratic disaffection was the more serious. Lincoln's was a minority victory, seriously so; but because the vote was distributed as it was, his electoral majority was large.[3]

---

[3] The popular vote was Lincoln, 1,866,452; Douglas, 1,375,157; Breckinridge, 847,953; and Bell, 589,581. This left Lincoln nearly a million votes behind. But in the electoral vote he had 180 to 123 for all his opponents. There were thus no grounds for objection, and the maneuvering which had gone on for some months

Accounts of the Democratic convention in Charleston[4] in April 1860 agree that hard-core Southern intransigency broke up the meeting. The South Carolinians may have been bluffing and have gone too far. But at any rate they tried the tempers of the others present beyond any possible tolerance. They would no longer settle for a sympathetic Northern candidate as they had before; they demanded that Northerners accept one of theirs. Back of this demand was the long, sad deterioration in sectional relations and the increasing extremism on both sides. This finally defeated the efforts of the far more numerous moderates of either view who would have settled for a middle course. They were always prevented by rabble-rousers in the Congress and outside. In Charleston, center of agitation for secession since Jackson's day, the fanatics had an ideal setting. It was as important that the Democrats met there as that the Republicans met in Chicago.[5]

The differences in 1860 between the sectional Democrats went on being irreconcilable; and there did result two candidates—Breckinridge, the Charleston choice (who was Buchanan's Vice-President), and Douglas, who was nominated at a later meeting in Baltimore. To complicate matters still further, another ticket was put in the field. John Bell of Tennessee and Edward Everett of Massachusetts were nominated by the Constitutional Unionists a few days before the Republicans met at Chicago. These were moderates who sought to occupy the policy position Lincoln had now lost.[6]

---

to control the election if it was thrown into the House was useless. Several prominent politicians had wasted their foresight, and the Southerners had lost another—the last—round in their battle for Washington.

[4] Cf. *The Presidential Campaign of 1860* by E. D. Fite (New York, 1911), as well as Luthin's *The First Lincoln Campaign*, already referred to. But the conventions are also described in other less specialized historical works.

[5] Where the galleries seating at least 9,000 could be filled with Lincoln supporters and the delegates kept constantly aware, by continued blasts of shouting and cheering, of his strength with Midwesterners. The Chicago selection was effectively argued by Norman Judd, National Committeeman from Illinois. He defeated the supporters of Seward and others at a crucial meeting of the committee. His plea that Chicago was "neutral ground" was a disingenuous one; but it must be recalled that in December of 1859 Seward was the leading candidate, with Salmon P. Chase, Justice McLean, Edward Bates, and perhaps others more prominently discussed than Lincoln for the nomination. Illinoisans were thinking of Lincoln for President, but to others he did not yet seem a formidable contender.

[6] None of the candidates was nominated by a full convention representing all states. After the Democratic disruption at Charleston, the Baltimore meeting was dominated by Douglas men, but there were six states not represented at all. The convention was responsible for excluding two of these; and this caused a second secession, in which delegates from twenty states participated, none with full delegations. This group nominated Breckinridge and Lane, an action ratified by other secessionists from the Charleston convention, meeting in Richmond, who had refused to come to Baltimore. In the Republican convention only six slave states were represented at all, and the delegates from these had only a shadow of authorization, there being practically no Republican voters. The Constitutional

So the parties were split, and so the issues were focused, at the beginning of the campaign. The conventions at which the candidates were chosen were none of them satisfactory. They were no more than makeshift ways of placing nominees in a position to ask for votes. It could be seen at once that the Democratic split was likely to be fatal; and, since the Constitutional Unionists were only a minor threat to the Republicans, Lincoln was likely to be elected. This prospect confirmed the Southerners in their determination not to acquiesce in the electoral decision. Secession moving at once from threat to imminent reality, the whole campaign was overhung by the potential consequences of irrevocable decision. Perhaps this accounts for the unusual quiet noted with wonder by so many observers. There were fewer of the gaudy and noisy accompaniments of Presidential canvasses than there had been since the second election of Monroe. The Republican Wide-Awakes—youthful marching clubs—are noted in all accounts. Then there was Douglas' violation of tradition to make an active speech-making tour.[7] But an atmosphere of seriousness seems to have prevailed all that autumn. The drift toward war was sensibly heavy in the autumn air. Lincoln stayed quietly at home in Springfield. He was elected without further appeal to the electorate than he had already made.

That appeal had, however, been eloquent and, on the main issues, so complete that others could speak cogently and confidently in his behalf —which even Seward, his disappointed rival, consented to do.

Seward was the party magnifico who ought, he considered, to have had the nomination; his support of the party ticket produced an incident that revealed a good deal about himself and about Lincoln. To Seward, Lincoln was a backwoods upstart, and speaking for him was a duty. But he went out in full panoply, almost in Douglas style, to exhort voters in Northwestern states. His returning train stopped in Springfield and he received the local politicians in his special car. They came in numbers to pay their respects and lined up to shake the great man's hand. Among them was the candidate himself, who came into the Senatorial presence with others, was recognized in a casual way, and went out without any special recognition.

That Lincoln did not then or later acknowledge this affront helps to establish the kind of man he was as he approached his Presidential responsibilities. He doubtless charitably understood the roweling of

Union convention could make little claim to being national. It centered in Kentucky, Tennessee, and Virginia, and other sections were not greatly interested. It gathered in the more conservative of the old American party, which never appeared again on the national scene. It was this group to which Benjamin Harrison, son of one President and father of another, belonged. But he was not followed by his son.

[7] A precedent not to be repeated until Bryan's first campaign.

Seward's soul involved in the likelihood of a Republican victory with another man as the beneficiary. That Lincoln did understand would be shown by his later relations with the same man as Secretary of State. That he should have pretended not to notice shows not only an extraordinary compassion but an unusual discipline of self. Under the rough exterior there were qualities of tolerance and understanding the nation would be grateful for.

They had, in fact, always been present. Many incidents of his youth and of his professional career illustrating the same sublime indifference to indignity, the same half-humorous modesty, are told by his biographers. There is a description, with the same connotations, of his behavior during the campaign of 1858 for the Senatorship when he was running against Douglas.

> Douglas travelled in a private car, gaily decorated with banners and signs. Accompanying him were his beautiful wife, his secretaries, stenographers, and an ever-changing retinue of henchmen. Coupled to his train was a flatcar mounting a brass cannon served by two young men in semi-military dress; and as the train approached the prairie towns the gun crashed out to inform the local citizenry that Douglas was on his way. Often travelling on the same train that drew the Little Giant's private car sat Lincoln, riding as an ordinary passenger.[8]

It sometimes seems that politicians' confidence in their own abilities is proportional to their modesty. This is no doubt partly because they recognize the resentment readily aroused in lesser men by an exhibition of superiority, as well as because they really have a monumental confidence in themselves. Lincoln certainly did nothing to emphasize his improved status as he rose in the world. He was almost as ugly, awkward, and ill-dressed when he ran for the Presidency in 1860 as when he ran for the Illinois legislature in 1834. During that time farms had covered the prairies, roads had been improved, railroads had been built, and Springfield and Chicago had become cities. Lincoln himself no longer argued five-dollar cases in local courts. But he seems to have looked about the same before Federal judges as when he had been riding horseback to country courts.

The conclusion is inescapable that the uncouthness of his younger years was later cultivated. Two of the characteristics that impressed many contemporaries were the unexpectedness of his logic and the incongruous literary beauty of his expression. But it was an artful mastery. Not until they had thought it over did they realize the enduring quality of the argument they had heard or the message they had read. When he spoke, he stood stooped and awkward on the

---

[8] *Abraham Lincoln* by Benjamin P. Thomas (New York, 1952), 184.

platform; he used his whole body for emphasis, throwing out his long arms and rising on his toes; his voice was shrill and unpleasant until his hearers got used to it. But what he said carried conviction. He was always simple, showing that he had earnestly considered what he was saying. He often used parables, and they were always exquisitely relevant; but also they were homely and suited to his audience. No one who heard him, apparently, was ever offended by overemphasis, insistence, belligerence, or floridity.

The concealing of cultivation, intelligence, and sophistication in a rustic shell was not new in American politics. We have seen Jefferson affecting simplicity too. He had a touch of Lincoln's dishevelment and he too was tall and awkward. But his Virginia gentility was quite obvious. He put on democratic manners with exaggerated emphasis. If this was catering to popular weakness, it was catering which was evidently thought by the shrewdest politicians to be necessary. Harrison, of the Virginia-planter gentry, descended from a signer, and himself a Governor, became the original log-cabin and hard-cider candidate. Lincoln was another of those; and he would not be the last. But on none of the others, except perhaps "Old Zach" Taylor, did the manner sit so well. Lincoln carried his origin in every word and gesture.

It is to be supposed that his rusticity assisted in that extraordinary merging of people's minds in his which was symbolized by their speaking of him as "Father Abraham." And of course its effectiveness enraged his opponents. The campaign of villification intended to belittle his person, his abilities, and his intentions, begun during the campaign, was intensified during the following years. He was pictured as a monster, a gorilla, savage and vindictive; and, when the war was on, as a butcher glorying in blood. These attacks, so useful to an office seeker when they have the right emphasis, got out of hand in Lincoln's case. It might well have lost him the campaign of 1864 when his Generals were fighting the costly and apparently futile battles of that year. An awful slaughter was going on that spring and summer. Fortunately, before the election Sherman took Atlanta and Sheridan was victorious in the Shenandoah Valley. But for a while the continued fighting did seem to be getting nowhere. And Lincoln's detractors were having some success in asking whether a gentleman like McClellan might not be a better President.

Lincoln's long self-conceived public role was exquisitely suited to the circumstances of his years. The people to whom he appealed for votes considered him to be one of themselves. That his appearance was congruent with that conception was of assistance as a first appeal. But it also helped him as a mentor and leader that he was so delicately tuned to the minds he was trying to reach. That he was able to sustain a role another man might have faltered in is a measure of his determination to rise in political life, a determination amazing in its strength and persistence. It was this which enabled him to overcome—or rather to make a virtue of—all his handicaps, his ignorance, his poverty, his lack of connections, his frontier surroundings. The flame never died, though it was often cherished in secret.

Consider just the bare facts of his rise. Shortly after his birth in Kentucky in 1809 his parents moved into Indiana and then into Illinois. His mother died and his father married again. This stepmother gave him some of the affection otherwise notably lacking in his life; he had no close feeling for his father; and they moved too often for any lasting friendships to be formed. And anyway, the isolated nature of pioneer farming and the struggle just to live filled the days from dawn to dark with heavy labor. There was no remission in the demands of existence, no time for education, and little leisure. Then, as soon as he was partly grown, he went off on his own, a laborer, a clerk, a handyman. As he grew he discovered bit by bit that the thoughts of other men could be useful. He taught himself to read from what had been written down.

Neither literature nor the other arts had much significance for him. He had a flair for storytelling from the first and practiced it. But his stories usually illustrated a point he wanted to make—this was the talent for parable so distinctive in his oratory. His intellectual life was pointed in one direction—political preferment. He became a lawyer, but not until after he had gone to the legislature, and more as a means of going further—and incidentally earning a living—than as a career of choice. Lawyers were also politicians. Lincoln the politician was also a lawyer.

That he went to the legislature at twenty-five was made possible by his naturally disputatious bent. His compulsion to discuss public affairs rapidly progressed from local to national subjects. About his own views he appeared to be diffident; but this was caution rather than concession. A man who wanted votes, he learned early, has to keep his commitments within bounds. From the very first he was considered a canny, calculating fellow, moderate, and easy on the opposition. Even when he was outraged, as he was by the Mexican War, he was slow to react. He came to the point concerning that imbroglio—because he was then serving his one term in the Congress and because he was a Whig—of sponsoring a resolution deploring the whole affair; but he voted for the appropriations necessary to its conduct.

Subsequently he supported General Taylor for the Presidency and, when Old Zach had been elected, demanded a Federal job. He wanted to become Commissioner of the General Land Office; and the political connotations of that request at a time when the West was opening up can hardly be missed. He was refused, and then himself rejected the offer of the Governorship of Oregon Territory; the way upward from Oregon was hard to see. He spoke for Scott, the Whig candidate, in 1852, but without much enthusiasm. The Whigs were due for defeat, and it came overwhelmingly. The party was evidently at the end of its usefulness. That the decline of his party made a difficulty for Lincoln can be imagined. But the issues surrounding the opening of new territories and the extension of slavery were splitting both parties. Lincoln was not sure for some time whether the Democrats were not worse off and he clung to his old affiliation.

When Douglas, the Illinois Senator, offered the Kansas-Nebraska bill in 1854 and attached to it the explicit repeal of the Missouri Compromise, the Whigs thought they saw a chance for revival; but it did not go far; the abolitionists and Free-Soilers would not join with them. But it was not until 1856 that Lincoln gave in to the inevitable and became a Republican. As his partner, Herndon, said of him, "He was not a speculative-minded man; he was, like Washington, severely practical; he never ran in advance of his age." Herndon was right. Several times Lincoln very nearly got left behind.

Frémont in 1856 was defeated—and defeated badly in Illinois— largely because Fillmore drew a large conservative vote. Lincoln by then had made up his mind about slavery; but he kept his decision to himself for the next two years, allowing his conclusions to emerge only after his nomination for the Senate in 1858, when he ran against Douglas. That nomination was owed to his moderation and to his absolute party regularity. He managed to make his change from Whig to Republican seem a conservative one; and he had the reputation of being willing to spend any amount of time and take any necessary trouble in party affairs. He joined, and kept, a kind of pact with other old Whigs to divide up offices. He had had a term in the House of Representatives and then retired. But he wanted to be a Senator, and in 1858 his turn came.

It is well known that Senators seldom consider themselves ineligible for the Presidency; and it cannot be said that this sense of appointment comes upon them after election to the Senate. It has already been remarked that it is difficult to say, about most Presidents, precisely when they began to turn a calculating look on their chances. Most probably it became a hard decision in Lincoln's mind when he was debating Douglas in 1858; but almost certainly it had been developing for some time.

He was the sort to have a long gestation period for such an idea. He would have allowed it to grow in his mind only a little at a time, entertaining it tentatively and without any outward sign. As one of his biographers said:

Notwithstanding Lincoln's easy ways and his genial camaraderie, he had a certain remoteness that repelled familiarity. Most persons addressed him as Mr. Lincoln or Lincoln; not even his best friends called him Abe. He had personal magnetism, a quality of open friendliness that attracted people and impelled them to confide in him, and yet he was a close-mouthed man himself and seldom revealed his plans or purposes to anyone. His closest friends were baffled by his reticence; there were things about him they would have liked to learn but never did. They confessed they never fully understood him.

But there are even more revealing conclusions. Lincoln was not only taciturn, he was also self-confident:

> He was simple yet complex—natural, unostentatious, humble, but at the same time self-reliant and self-assured. Keen-minded, analytical, and practical, still he was something of a visionary . . . By nature conservative and cautious, he never took unnecessary risks. . . .[9]

We see now that no combination of traits could have been more useful. An unshakable confidence in his own considered judgment was the finishing addendum. If he had not had that, his long progress upward could not have been successful. His speeches and actions would have lacked conviction, as somehow Seward's did—and before him Webster's, Clay's, and Scott's, and after him Blaine's, Greeley's, Sherman's, and Bryan's. Confidence, linked to persistent and driving ambition, goes a long way to explain political success.

Here again a man who turned up and was available at the historic moment must be suspected of having put himself in the way of being chosen. Such a suspicion is not always justified. It would not be in the case of the Generals. But recall how Van Buren managed to be right for the succession to Jackson; and how, for that matter, Jackson happened to be just the man to head the frontier conquest of the Presidency.

One lesson to be learned from Lincoln is a hard one. It is that unremitting work, cautious governing of public commitments, careful cultivation of party connections, and ceaseless advertisement of one's personal virtues are necessary to success. In the last round of the bout with those who will decide his fate, a person needs supporters. Also, of course, he needs to have landed himself on the popular side of the day's issues—whatever they may be. And finally he needs enemies who are easily recognized as the enemies also of an electoral majority.

---

[9] Benjamin P. Thomas. His *Lincoln*, referred to before, was the result of many years' study and represented the compression into one volume of many more discursive accounts. The quotations are from p. 134.

Lincoln had even these, although not by his own choice so much as because the South insisted on opposition. But he had the final luck that was indispensable: the Democratic majority was hopelessly split. That most difficult of all maneuvers he accomplished—he became President *without* a majority. Nothing in politics seems impossible after Lincoln's performance. But no one in his right senses would deliberately maneuver himself into such a situation.

Having become President with a safe Electoral College vote, even if with a popular minority, Lincoln had to face the logical consequence. This was sectional strife likely to turn into war. He had won in his own state of Illinois and the neighboring ones of Indiana, Iowa, Wisconsin, Minnesota, Michigan, and Ohio. Somewhat surprisingly, Pennsylvania, Buchanan's home state, had also gone for him. So had New York and New England. But that was all. The South went against him, even Kentucky; and in nine states he had no recorded votes at all. It was understood—and freely spoken of even before the election— that his election would provoke secession.

One of the tortured dramas of our history was played out in the months following. Lincoln, who had never in his life had a weightier responsibility than that of being one Congressman among many, and one subservient to party discipline, then accepted the burden of such choices as had hardly ever before fallen to even the most experienced of his predecessors. The seemingly still uncouth and awkward provincial lawyer suddenly had to match his wits and his wisdom against the hard, sharp, and accustomed politicians of the South; then too, he had to knit together his own loose coalition of former Whigs, Know-Nothings, Abolitionists, and Free-Soilers. Added to this, he had to begin at once that long series of temporizing moves intended to hold the border states in coalition with the North. The necessity infuriated the Republican Radicals; and it was sometimes a question whether, in spite of his reluctance, he would not have to choose between the extremes he was trying to hold in check.

As late as 1864, when the strategy for the second-term campaign had to be fixed, he still had the border very much on his mind; and it was this that determined his choice of Andrew Johnson of Tennessee, already Military Governor of the state, as his running mate. By that time he was reaching out toward a reknitting of the Union. This was why he insisted that the party be renamed. It became Unionist, not Republican. He hoped that this, along with some military luck, would give him a majority in the states still voting. He had moments of despair. There was one in August 1864 when he wrote the message confided to Secretary Welles saying that to save the Union he meant to "co-operate" with his successor. Like other Presidents before him, he had been enlarged by responsibility and purged of self-interest.

Politician into statesman is a transformation the Presidency—and only the Presidency—brings about in most of the men who attain it. We see it so clearly in Lincoln because of the grave exigency in which he operated.

Any aspirant to the office, making up his mind, must prepare for this test of fortitude. It is a supreme one that not infrequently brings political ruin in the midst of victory and personal disaster through vilification. Being seized of the Presidency is indeed one of the supreme ordeals of human experience. Perhaps this is why men are drawn to it so irresistibly.

Andrew Johnson
1808–1875

Born in Raleigh, North Carolina
Became seventeenth President in 1865 at 56

HISTORY

1822–27	Apprenticed to a tailor without ever having attended school. Moved to Greeneville, Tennessee, opened a shop, and married Eliza McCardle, who taught him to read and write.
1828	Elected an Alderman of Greeneville.
1830	Elected Mayor of Greeneville; served three terms.
1835	Elected to the Tennessee legislature; defeated for re-election in 1837.
1841	Elected to the State Senate.
1843	Elected to the United States House of Representatives.
1853	Elected Governor of Tennessee; re-elected in 1855.
1857	Elected to the United States Senate.
1862	Appointed Military Governor of Tennessee with the rank of Brigadier General.

ANDREW JOHNSON

1864	Elected Vice-President (with Lincoln) and succeeded to the Presidency when Lincoln was assassinated.
1868	Impeached, tried, and acquitted by one vote; unsuccessfully sought the Democratic nomination.
1869	Unsuccessful candidate for the United States Senate.
1872	Unsuccessful candidate for the House of Representatives.
1874	Elected to the United States Senate.
1875	Died in Tennessee.

ANDREW JOHNSON is one of four Presidents (Tyler, Fillmore, and Arthur being the others) who were never elected to the office. He was not only never elected, he was never nominated. He (and the three others) illustrate the hazards of rising by the route of succession. On the other hand, there have been four—T. Roosevelt, Coolidge, Truman, and L. B. Johnson—who were elected on their own.

Johnson's failure should not be taken as meaning more than it really does. He was not a first-order politician, perhaps; but he was also far from being an incompetent. He rose from obscurity and stayed at the upper levels of the profession for many years; and, as must never be forgotten, he actually did become President.

Naturally there are other lessons to be learned from Johnson's, as there are from every successful experience. He furnishes, for instance, another illustration of the traditional American rise from humble beginnings in spite of many handicaps; also, the importance of managing to be on the popular side of the one irrepressible issue of the time; and he is an excellent example of success through everlasting devotion to getting ahead. He had fire in his vitals.

This fire, we must by now acknowledge, is almost indispensable. There have been few Presidents—and those mostly the Generals—who were not driven by ambition. This has had the effect of dedicating them without reserve, and almost without conscious consent, to the pursuit, through all vicissitudes and in spite of all obstacles, of preferment. Among the Generals there do seem to be exceptions; but most of the others pursued the prize over a long period of time and with every resource they could muster. In the Generals' case the time was usually shorter because the objective was visualized only after hero status was attained. Those who succeeded through death offer special problems. A few others, Lincoln among them, aiming at a lesser office, suddenly saw the Presidency within reach. Once the Presidency was seen, however, the subsequent activities show a remarkable resemblance to those of others whose planning was longer.

Johnson furnishes another instance of this sort. He sought fiercely the highest offices available to him and clung to his gains; he cannot have expected the Presidency when it came to him, but when, rather late, his position proved to be precisely that required, he behaved in the same way as others.

We are now familiar with self-made careerists dependent from early boyhood on their own earnings with a mother to look out for. The variation in Johnson's case is that he was apprenticed to a hard-driving tailor who never allowed him even one day of formal schooling. But all this had its peculiar usefulness in politics. He was always so much more than he could be expected to be that the tendency was to credit him beyond his deserts.

Many a voter had a fellow-feeling for him because of his handicaps. His occupation, however, had about as little glamor as could be thought of; it was not to be compared at all with splitting rails, river-boating, or even farming—occupations such as predecessors had boasted about. Tailoring, somehow, called up a picture of confined, sedentary, and rather subservient toil; the others of virile contests with nature and with other men. In a day when men were valued for their ability to become mighty hunters or pioneers, the operation of a tailor shop in a small Tennessee town offered a very minimum of attraction.

But there were certain advantages in that occupation and the shop where it was carried on. They made possible the circle of village philosophers and politicians who promoted his political beginnings. They also allowed him to go on with his trade while his wife taught him to read and write.

Eliza McCardle was unusually devoted and intelligent, and when she undertook his elementary education she made a good job of it. What might be called his higher education was owed to the discussion group whose meeting place was the tailor shop. Johnson was the leader in those discussions and was soon airing opinions on all the issues of the day. These so impressed his intimates that they began to advertise him in the community as a young man of unusual intelligence. This started him on his long climb.

The offices he talked himself into did not at first amount to much; but a beginning at the very bottom was valued by party men. Those who enter at higher levels are seldom really respected by the authentic professionals who operate machines. Johnson showed at once a willingness to work and take orders; so he moved from one job to the next and always a little higher.

But the fairly trivial exchanges with his neighborhood companions seem to have gone on too long. Johnson did not widen his appeal as he should have. He emerged onto the national scene with a set of standardized ideas that were notably parochial and unsuited to an expanding country. They were the same ideas that he had expounded in his shop, and some time was required for him to discover how irrelevant they were to wider needs.

His most displayed opinions centered on demagogic opposition to expanded governmental activity of any kind. He was always pleading for parsimony and against expenditure. He put this continual carping partly on the ground of opposition to tax increases and partly on the ground that government ought to do very little anyway because when it did it interfered with citizens' liberties. In his ideal state bureaucrats played a very small role. He proclaimed over and over, with every

possible variation in exposition, the popular rubric of the frontier that
that government was best which governed least. That this was a very
popular line of argument his early success encouraged him to believe.
It had served others too, as Johnson very well knew. It had been the
core of the Jefferson-Jackson policy. In its advocacy, however, their
successor very nearly ran it into the ground.

The niggardly, obstructionist role for which Johnson cast himself
carried him a long way before it failed him; but it did eventually lose
its attractiveness.

It ought to be noted in all fairness that certain virtues combined
with this attitude rather naturally, and that he always clung to these as
well. They can be described shortly as personal frugality and hard
work. He never neglected an assignment, never shirked unpleasant
jobs, and never asked others to do what he would not do himself. He
may have been unpleasantly ostentatious about this—in fact, he was—
but it led to his becoming the hero of the workers and small farmers in
Greeneville and thereabouts. Combined with his generally anti-
government diatribes, it translated very easily into a kind of class warfare. He became the political representative of those who got too little
pay for much hard work and was the scornful detractor of the more
fortunate.

The "others" for whom he had only bitter denunciation included
all those who would naturally be envied by a boy who had grown up
in poverty, and the specificity of his attacks gave them a reality that
hurt. He meant what he said. But it can be seen in retrospect how
conscious he was that his class grudge had political value. It was
cheered; and cheers stimulated him. He was led on to extremism; and
in the end it was difficult for him to gain acceptance as a responsible
statesman. His obsession followed him even into the White House; it
colored his Presidential behavior and showed in his policies. He always
felt sorry for himself and was always striking out against his "betters."

So persistent was the development of this strain that it became
inseparable from his personality. In a way it makes him easier to understand. It is a common and, however unfortunately, a normal motive
even in many persons who subdue or conceal it. But it is also a powerful one and, when given way to, furnishes a drive less savage impulses
lack. Almost inevitably it leads to overreaching; it is certain to make
enmities; and they may multiply beyond control, thus interfering with
that calculating discrimination a politician must exercise. These faults
almost caused Johnson's official disgrace, and they have certainly
deposited him in one of the lower niches of Presidential reputation.

Johnson's early successes—his first elections as Alderman and as
Mayor—can be accounted for very simply. He confirmed his neighbors in their worst impulses, their most ignorant and self-seeking views

of community government. He made prejudice appear to be reason, and his habitual malice was excused as a plea for reform. The choice in elections was often between himself and other candidates who could be pilloried as "gentlemen," and there were on that frontier many more of Johnson's breed than of the others. They gave him their votes.

There were two conspicuous leaders in Tennessee then—Hugh L. White, the well-known judge, and the famous Andrew Jackson. White was a contender for the Presidency in 1836 when Jackson was promoting Van Buren as his successor.[1] Johnson chose to support Jackson, which was lucky. But until then he had clung closely to both statesmen as mentors. They made a congenial pattern for him to follow. For both were arrant individualists, both inclined to deplore governmental interferences of any sort in social or economic affairs, and both were belligerent states'-righters.

It had been shortly after Johnson was elected Alderman that Jackson had assumed the Presidency. And it was not long before the President let it be known that the rights of the states stopped a good way short of the right to secede. This was confusing for Johnson. He tended to waver.

Tennessee voted against Jackson in 1832; it voted against his choice to succeed himself, Van Buren, in 1840; and it rejected the Democratic candidate, James K. Polk, in 1844. In spite of having nurtured Jackson, Tennessee seemed to have a Federalist-Whig majority. Nevertheless, Johnson, after prayerful consideration, kept a grip on Jackson's coattails. He judged this to be the best affiliation for his purpose.

This can be explained only by recalling Tennessee geography. The eastern part of the state where Johnson had settled was as different from the western part as can well be imagined. The east was broken and hilly country, populated by small farmers and villagers; the west was an area of large holdings with the traditional plantation economy. In the one there were few slaves and many poor whites; in the other, slaves were depended on for agricultural operations. There were few gentlemen in Johnson's part of the state; they were dominant in the west. But it was the west that controlled the state—its economy and its politics. The planters and their satellites had the wealth and the influence. Johnson, the self-conscious proletarian, was challenging his betters. But the votes were there to be marshaled by the right leader.

He had only one setback in his program, and that was not caused by his loyalty to Jackson or to his everlasting insistence that he was only a poor workingman himself, but by his objecting, once too often, to

---

[1] White was a strict constructionist. Jackson, during his second term, pretty well lost control of his own state to White, who was then a Senator.

internal improvements. Even the poor farmers wanted improved roads; nothing, in fact, was more important to them, not even reduced taxes; and when Johnson would not vote for roads in the legislature, they refused him re-election. This was in 1837. Two years later he had learned discretion and was re-elected. By 1841 he was such an enthusiast for public improvements that he was elected to the State Senate as their proponent. He claimed, of course, that his plan was a more economical one than those he had so long been opposing; and perhaps his constituents believed him. Or perhaps they were merely satisfied to have converted him.

This was his last campaign for the state legislature. In 1843, after some rapid and clever maneuvering in which he made good use of his tailor-shop coterie, he was nominated for the Congress and was elected. Four re-elections followed.

The years in the House were important ones. There were fateful issues being debated, and the debate was being carried on by colorful statesmen. Johnson, who still insisted that he was only a poor tailor from Greeneville, took no very creative part in the argument; he merely echoed the Jackson line, advertising himself as "Young Hickory"[2] and in every way he could contrive picturing himself as Jackson's favored inheritor.

It must be said, however, that as a politician he succeeded for a number of reasons other than his following of Jackson. He did put himself in a position to be chosen very largely because he had so long been ardent in his imitation; but it was the part of Jacksonism that fitted him best that he always emphasized. This was a reiterated advocacy of economy and low taxes; and, of course, strict construction and all it implied.

But also, somewhat inconsistently—as Jackson was similarly inconsistent—he was a firm, almost fierce, unionist. This became in his case—as again in Jackson's—a genuine patriotic fervor. For this one cause, among all the others, he was willing to sacrifice, even, if need be, to suffer. Luckily it was the one service, the one attitude, needed by Lincoln, who was searching for a border politician with wide appeal. He wanted to demonstrate that the unionist cause was not sectional and not one of class or race. Johnson had the qualifications. Lincoln adopted him with genuine relief.

Of course Johnson's rise had been powered by appeal to motives Lincoln must have mistrusted even if he understood them. In an age of westward movement and the conquest of new territories, Johnson had gone on opposing every progressive or expansionist proposal. He

---

[2] He was one of several to do this—we have already seen Polk doing it—which shows how potent the influence of the original Old Hickory must have been.

had always been excessively suspicious of executives when he was a legislator, and an equally reluctant administrator when he was an executive.

It happened, however, that this general regressiveness did have one positive and expansionist phase. This was paradoxical but actual. It was the homestead movement. Men and their families in those days simply picked up their goods and moved West to vacant land. They then expected to be confirmed in the title. For several generations politicians made free homesteading part of their appeal for votes, Lincoln among them; and Johnson joined the popular program. Giving away government land involved no expense, and so no taxes. And it opened up the kinds of opportunities for small farmers and their numerous children which would perpetuate their kind. It was passionately advocated even by those who had no intention of migrating.

Johnson had had a familiar model in Jackson and had learned his lesson well. Through all the stresses of border warfare he maintained his enmity for the plantocracy and their associates in the commercial and professional community. By joining Lincoln, he felt no strain in his old affiliation. He could even go along with opposition to slavery. Hill farmers and the artisans were opposed to slavery, and so to the secession that would secure it. The old Whigs and men of wealth generally supported the principle of property and were vigilant to repulse any threats to it. Slaves were property; slavery was therefore so carefully fostered that it became almost sacred. Johnson's positions in the vast struggle were made for him by his earlier commitments.

One of Lincoln's problems was involved in this, one that he at first temporized with and approached with the utmost care but which afterward may be seen to have bulked very large in his calculations. He hoped to establish the border states, from Maryland to Missouri, as a buffer across the deeper South. If somehow he could accomplish this, the secessionist centers could be closed in on slowly but certainly. In this scheme Tennessee was the strategic hinge; controlling it was vital. That in the end it worked out as Lincoln hoped was due to the events that occurred in that state, with Johnson playing an important part.

Sherman could not have marched to Atlanta and thence to the sea if Grant had not taken and held Forts Donelson and Henry and if Chattanooga had not fallen. And without Johnson's advice and hard-willed administration, the border forces could not have kept the Confederate forces in check. More of the Civil War was fought in Tennessee than in any other state, except possibly Virginia, and it was the Tennessee battles that broke the Confederate center and ruined the finest of the Southern armies. Johnson, throughout, was an unshaken unionist.

Convenient enemies are especially necessary to an individual intending to get on by successive electoral appeals. And they are vitally important to political careerists who are unwilling to become the subservient instruments of party, advancing only as the bosses' favors are gained. The party, to such a man, is all very well for use when a mutual arrangement comes easily. But frequently it is necessary to be noticed as other than a party man.

The Democrats in Johnson's part of Tennessee in the prewar days accepted his alignment with the little fellows; but many Democrats elsewhere in the state were not disposed to do so. The advocates of slavery had nowhere to go but to the Democrats. But when the Democrats changed and aligned themselves with the plantocracy, Johnson did not go with them. The party had been good to him; but if it could no longer elect him and if, within it, the dominant individuals were hostile, then it would have to be abandoned. Lincoln made this somewhat easier for him, as well as for all others like him, by renaming the Republican party Unionist. Naturally, this suited Johnson. The enemies now were the *dis*unionists. Fortunately they were also the "gentlemen" he had always fought.

So it is relatively easy to understand how Johnson became the marked man Lincoln needed, conspicuously on the right side at the right time. It can be seen that his progression was normal for a representative democracy. The first stage—the local period—lasted twelve years. Following this, he was for ten years in the Congress. Thus, after twenty-one years in office, eastern Tennessee was still peculiarly his home territory.

When he was fifty-two and a United States Senator, Johnson was established in a respectable way. He had good reason to be pleased with a career which had taken him such a distance. With him, as with others at a similar stage, it is hard to say whether he anticipated anything more. We can only say that afterward it looked as though he must have.

We see the future President, then, on the eve of his great opportunity, a short, stout, irascible fellow, the father of five, living in a good house in the center of Greeneville. His two older boys, pleasant enough young men, were neither of them developing well and were showing the signs of that alcoholism which would be the end of both; but his two daughters were married to well-off husbands who had country places nearby. The good home had only recently been acquired, but it was in every way suitable to a man who had risen in the world but who was still the hero of the workers and farmers round about—substantial but not extravagant.

If Lincoln inquired closely he must have been informed that his chosen Vice-President was not a very pleasing person. His oratory,

unlike Lincoln's, was of the screeching and arm-swinging kind. Physi-
cally, he must have resembled a good deal the contemporary Democrat, Douglas. Both were short and stout; both were a good deal more
attractive in public than in private. But both generated endless energy.
And—what most impresses the student of their careers—both had that
insatiable appetite for power which is so characteristic, in varying
degrees, of politicians who have risen to the higher levels.

Like Lincoln just before him and like others to come, Johnson
might have withheld his expressed ambition, if not his secret one, from
the very pinnacle of political preferment. There are, after all, more
chances to become a Senator than to become a President. And so
enormous an ego as a successful candidate must have will also have
ways of protecting itself. Many a man who has just missed the Presidency must have said to himself and to others that he never really
wanted or expected to achieve it anyway. Lincoln never did get to be
a Senator; if he had defeated Douglas in their contest in 1858, he might
never have become President, and the protective mechanisms might
have prevented him from taking the risk. After all, what he would
have attained would have met his most exaggerated expectations—or
so he might have said.

An individual's various qualities affect each other, supplementing or
canceling as the case may be. In the case of Johnson, if a disagreeable
personality could have disqualified him it would certainly have done
so. Naturally, it could not have helped; but it was outweighed by other
qualities. It was important that he was a Tennessee unionist at a time
when Lincoln needed one; but he had another claim: he had repeatedly
been elected to office. Something about him had attracted majorities
again and again. This was not because he was handsome and had
presence; it was not because he was anything of a statesman; it was not,
in sum, because he was qualified in any way for any of the offices he
ever held. When he was first elected Alderman, Mayor, Congressman,
or Senator he had weaker claims to office than his opponent in nearly
every instance. Actually, he was neither very wise nor very foresighted. He had almost none of the qualifications a representative
democracy ought to look for in its leaders.

He is, nevertheless, one of a line of individuals who are conspicuous
in retrospect for uniform success; and if we ask why this was so when
by all the rules he ought to have been a failure, we see that the answer
lies in an almost perfect rapport with his constituency. This overcame
obvious deficiencies—in their eyes. He was able to persuade a majority
of them that he was what they wanted, and he could do it over and
over again. The exception is that he was never called on to test this
persuasiveness on the whole American electorate, only on Tennesseans.

If he was niggardly and withholding in expansive times, so were the craftsmen and farmers who were conscious of sharing but little in the profits of expansion and who resented the more fortunate speculators who did. If, as a perennial candidate, he was a man filled with envy, mistrust, and malice, so were the Tennessee voters who elected him. There was set up between him and them, no matter what was said, a perfect understanding. He was to punish the fortunate, or at least to denounce them, and he was to praise and, if possible, bring benefits to the disadvantaged. They were to applaud and he was to be rewarded by continuance in office. It was a mutual arrangement that worked.

Johnson thus climbed to a high place on very low impulses. And he is not the only one of the Presidents who used such methods. It is necessary for a political careerist to be something of an exhibitionist, as we know; a colossal egotist, and a shrewd calculator, as we also know. And we can see from his example that one who will not hesitate to reach very far down into human nature for support can be successful because, when evoked, hatred will carry him to his objective.

When Lincoln called home twenty thousand soldiers to vote in 1864—and said that they were "to vote the way they shoot"—it was not an act that a purist would care to defend; but as a local politician he had never hesitated to use such methods. He did it simply because he judged that the election of McClellan would be a national disaster; this seemed to him ample justification.

We do not approve such resorts by lesser politicians in times that are calmer. But the difference is not a moral one. Johnson, who was certainly lesser, even if not as a political success, was a man who habitually resorted to demagoguery, trickery, election rigging, and all the other devices of the unscrupulous. But others have done the same, some even more unreservedly. This sort of thing is indeed quite normal. It has the advantage of being extremely simple and almost foolproof. It takes no skill to develop it, and its victims are usually defenseless. Johnson may be criticized for lack of imagination; he hardly ever found any other way to fight his battles; but he cannot be said to have been morally inferior to his colleagues.

His combination of energy and pugnacity in using political devices —combined with a foresight it is hard to estimate—were sufficient to land him in the Senate. When Lincoln needed a border man, it can be seen why Johnson was exactly right. But, as so often, he seems not to have considered what the situation would be if Johnson should succeed him in the Presidency.

Like Tyler, Johnson did not belong to the party in power—which was Republican in spite of its temporary Unionist label. And that he succeeded Lincoln within five weeks of their joint inauguration was such a shortening of time that no one was prepared for such an accident. The whole country stood aghast at what it had done to itself. In these circumstances Johnson's luck ran out. Conceivably, if he had had a more authentic genius for politics, he might have organized behind himself a majority in the Congress and have ridden out the storm of postwar fury that was blowing up when Lincoln was assassinated. But the turnabout required was too complete. He had been too long identified with the artisans and farmers; he could not now knuckle under to a Congressional group that represented the business interests he had so conspicuously opposed throughout his career. His opponents were able, ruthless, and determined. They had no respect whatever for the integrity of government and were willing to prostitute to their purpose any institution they could make use of. Moreover, although there were still more voters who were of Johnson's general belief, they were blinded at the moment by fanatic fervor for humiliating a recent enemy; moreover, there were many voters who were disqualified in the 1866 elections. The Southern states were still outside the Union.

So Johnson was caught in a kind of double squeeze, and he was no longer agile enough—or perhaps was unwilling—to escape its pressures. His commitment to the traditional "little fellows" of democratic canvasses and to states' rights ran against both the desire of the victorious North to punish the rebels and of the propertied who were seriously alarmed by an increasing hostility to their management of affairs. Many businesses had greatly expanded during the war boom and were spreading widely regardless of state boundaries. It was annoying to have state legislatures impose taxes and restrictions in response to rural and small-business influences. The industrial captains felt much safer with a Federal Congress—especially, of course, a Senate which was in fact a kind of club for the wealthy and influential.

The so-called Radicals who were in revolt against Lincoln, and who were to restrain and humiliate Johnson, were actually conservatives. They had a double purpose in the maneuvers against Johnson—they meant to punish the South and keep its Representatives out of the Congress for a long time to come; and they meant, by doing this, to serve the commercial class they represented. Before the war Southern domination of the Congress had kept tariffs low, encouraged the independence of the states, and stood against the expansion of industry and the public improvements it needed.

Since a different policy could be maintained in a Congress purged of Southerners, businessmen had no intention of consenting to the readmission of their enemies; only their own stooges—the carpetbaggers—would be recognized as officials in the South. The conciliatory policy instituted by Lincoln and sought to be continued by Johnson, of bringing back into the Union the defeated states as fast as they could be pacified and organized, might well result in renewed opposition to Northern policies. This struggle very quickly—and even before Lincoln's death—became one between the Congress and the President.

In this way a large issue became intermixed with a constitutional contest, and not a new one. Strong Presidents are apt to have their way, especially in times of crisis, and weak ones succumb to legislative aggression. There had never been more than a truce in this conflict after the first few months of any administration. It was the misfortune of Johnson to inherit this chronic quarrel at a time when it was exacerbated by characteristic postwar emotionalism and by the emergence of a powerful economic interest centering in the Senate. It must also be added that the activist Radicals who led the fight for Johnson's impeachment were singularly reckless and piratical.

It does not seem strange that Johnson, not a man of breadth or extraordinary intelligence, was unable to assess and conciliate the forces opposed to him; and yet it was inevitable that if he challenged them—as he did—he would be defeated. He missed being found guilty in his impeachment trial by only one vote, and that cast by a man who discovered the necessary courage only at the last moment. Although Johnson thus missed the ultimate humiliation, he was for the remainder of his term completely frustrated. If the fanatical reactionaries did not quite succeed in turning him out of office and installing one of their own number—Wade, who as President pro tempore of the Senate was next in succession and who, incidentally, although he had this direct interest in the result, did not scruple to vote in the impeachment proceedings—they did set up, in a series of smothering actions, a legislative hold on the Executive that reduced the Presidency to futility. Johnson, when the Congress had finished with him, had only such powers remaining as he could hold by force.

And then force failed him when Grant betrayed his Commander in Chief. Perhaps the worst of all the Congressional raids on the Executive was represented by the Tenure of Office Act. This was passed to prevent Johnson from removing Stanton, the Secretary of War he had inherited from Lincoln and who was in league with the Congressional faction bent on suppressing all efforts to rehabilitate the South. Johnson issued orders to Grant—when the situation became plain to him, and he had removed Stanton—not to allow the discharged Secretary to occupy his office. Grant disobeyed and allowed Stanton to return. The resulting quarrel earned Grant the approbation of the Congressional radicals, and so Presidential nomination; but it was the finish of Johnson even though impeachment failed.

He had found a way to gain the Presidency but not a way to keep it.

Ulysses S. Grant
1822–1885

CULVER PICTURES, INC.

Born at Point Pleasant, Ohio
Became eighteenth President in 1869 at 46

HISTORY

1843   Graduated from West Point.

1846–47   Served with Taylor in the Mexican War after having tours of duty at several western posts. Was present at Palo Alto and Monterrey; served with Scott in the battles for Vera Cruz and Mexico City.

1852–54   Sent to California, then to Fort Vancouver in Oregon; loneliness and boredom encouraged an alcoholism which became serious; resigned to escape dismissal.

1854–60   Lived in poverty for six years, finally working in a Galena business belonging to his brothers.

1861   Appointed Colonel of Volunteers by the Governor of Illinois. Promoted to Brigadier General by Lincoln.

1862   Nominated Major General of Volunteers because of successes in the field.

1863–64   Won Battle of Vicksburg; made Major General, regular army; promoted to Lieutenant General and given supreme command.
1865   Accepted Lee's surrender.
1866   Made full General; refused to obey and support President Johnson.
1867   Made Secretary of War while Stanton was under suspension.
1868   Nominated for the Presidency by the Republican party and elected (Vice-President, Colfax); opponent, Seymour with Blair.
1872   Renominated and re-elected (Vice-President, Wilson); opponent, Greeley with Brown.
1880   Movement for his renomination failed after many ballots.
1885   Died at Mount McGregor near Saratoga, New York.

THE NINE GENERALS who have become President are so considerable a percentage of the whole number as to suggest strongly that this is an effective way of reaching the office. To the list of successful ones, moreover, several have to be added who got so far as to be nominated (Scott, Frémont, and Hancock) by a major party but were defeated for election.

This does not tell the student anything about becoming a General, a process with difficulties of its own. It merely indicates that, for a General, a Presidential nomination is much more likely than it is for any other citizen of comparable status, except perhaps Governors of states.[1] But the peculiar difference here is that Governors are almost invariably professional politicians and so are aiming at the Presidency. Generals, presumably, are trying to reach the top of their military profession.

Taken in another way, the percentage of Generals who have attained the White House is not very high (though it is much higher even than the percentage of lawyers). There are, after all, many Generals who have ended a long way from high political office. As a class they are hardly justified in looking expectant.

But the American people do have a propensity for electing military leaders in certain circumstances, and there are some observations that can be made about it.[2]

For instance, it can be said that most of the successful Generals have had supreme, or at least separate, commands—Washington, Jackson, Harrison, Taylor, Grant, and Eisenhower are examples; and those who did not—Hayes, Garfield, and Pierce, for instance—were not chosen because they were military men, although having been in the army undoubtedly helped. They were civilians, basically, and politicians of a familiar sort.

But the preference for Generals also points to a democratic failing. Although there is complete reliance on political processes, there is also an ineradicable distrust of politicians. One of the surest appeals a

---

[1] The following formidable list of elected Governors have become President: Jefferson, Monroe, Tyler, Polk, Johnson, Hayes, Cleveland, McKinley, T. Roosevelt, Wilson, Coolidge, and F. D. Roosevelt. In addition, two appointed territorial Governors may be added: W. H. Harrison and Taft. Also two other Presidents had been defeated as gubernatorial candidates: B. Harrison and Harding.

[2] It is curious that no Admiral has ever been nominated or elected. Why the army more than the navy should make an individual eligible, it is hard to say. Perhaps naval officers are thought of more as professionals. In most wars they have served as subordinates to army commanders; and this may have kept them from political prominence. Still there have been naval heroes and it is strange that none has had the requisite political attraction to become a Presidential candidate.

candidate can make is to protest that he is non-political. And a General can usually make the best showing of this sort. He is a leader of men, used to great affairs, the organizer of vast efforts—uniformly victorious ones; but he is not a politician, or if he is he can claim that he is not and will usually be believed.

Another uniformity is that postwar disturbances have often produced a General-President. The exceptions have been the periods succeeding the Spanish-American War and World War I. Observers were almost ready by 1950 to conclude that this predilection had been overcome. The advent of Eisenhower in 1952 showed that this was premature. But the road to the Presidency by way of military advancement is clearly not open except in the aftermath of war, and then only for those who have had a conspicuous role in victory. This is partly because the following years are ones of severe readjustment, usually accompanied by inflation and all the bitterness incident to deciding who shall pay the bills. There is disillusion because the objectives sought by the use of force have proved unattainable, because the defeated enemy is often in a better situation than the victorious nation—which seems unjust—and because war always produces prosperity, at least temporarily, and its ending introduces a period of reduced activity, at least until readjustment has been made. These are distresses and disturbances politicians are not qualified to deal with.

It is in these circumstances that a General, especially one with a reputation for being masterful and silent (at least on civilian matters), has an overwhelming attraction. Democrats who have been claiming all the privileges involved in blaming each other for the existing difficulties suddenly realize that recrimination is after all not constructive. What is needed is what the army had—single-minded, disinterested, and determined direction. The privileges of democracy are all very well, but they are luxuries. They can be given up if necessary to secure a cessation of civilian disorder.

To the diffused malaise of such times there is added the influence of the returned soldiers. When there are mass armies, these may be a very large proportion of the electorate, and not only large but politically potent. Veterans' organizations are in themselves political machines. Their leaders are conservative, and the weight of their influence can be used to boost General-candidates without much difficulty. The officers of the veterans' organizations support the General; he does favors for them and perhaps also for the veterans themselves; and civilians go along because they want the nation's affairs straightened out.

The United States can count itself lucky that this system has not resulted in dictatorship as it has elsewhere. Washington might have become a King; and Jackson, Taylor, or Grant could have abrogated more civil liberties than they did. The adulation of Generals has been called a father-desire; and this does express something of the relationship between soldiers and their commanders. They are to obey when he commands. Similarly, a confused people want to be directed. It has nothing to do with the General's qualifications as President—his experience, his wisdom, or his faithfulness to democracy. Indeed, it rests on a thoroughly false analogy between the ordering about of armies and the leading of peoples. But it is a sense of security that is wanted, not foresightedness, capability, or the preservation of rights. There are terrible possibilities in this propensity of democracies to embrace dictatorship.[3] Some of them were realized when, in the troubled years after the Civil War, people turned to the man who had taken Lee's surrender.

The people who elected Grant thought they had a father who would stop the family bickering; what they got was a hapless puppet for the Congressional Radicals—and these, in turn, were the representatives of the rising powers of business and finance. Some historians of a later day would be inclined to argue that Grant was the worst President the United States ever had. This is perhaps exaggerated; but there is no doubt that the claim is a strong one. If Grant could have ridden over a hill and disappeared as he left the meeting at Appomattox, he would have had an unassailable place among the nation's heroes; as it is, he is remembered as an incompetent and slovenly Chief Executive who tolerated corruption all around him and allowed himself to be managed by those who thought of the nation as the source of revenge or of loot.

All the Presidents who were in office during the nation's most critical time, before and after Lincoln, were failures in office. None of them ought to have been chosen either for the country's sake or for their own. In the instances of two, better men were available. Frémont would certainly have been more capable than Buchanan. He might just possibly have avoided or postponed the Civil War by a firmer policy. Johnson, of course, succeeded Lincoln unexpectedly. His ordeal was partly due to the carelessness with which Vice-Presidents are chosen, partly to Lincoln's need of the moment. But Seymour, the alternative to Grant, was one of the most competent candidates ever nominated. His election might have resulted in a more humane reconstruction and an administration less likely to allow the debauching of the government.

But when blame for historic mistakes is being assessed in a democracy, no individual can be too much condemned. After all, he might

---

[3] As France and Germany, for instance, have reason to know.

have been rejected. He reached the Presidency by the prescribed processes and with the allowable appeals. Both Buchanan and Grant were decisively elected, Grant more than once. Perhaps they ought to have had the sense not to undertake the responsibility; but also the voters ought to have had the sense not to elect them.

So far as Grant's early difficulties are concerned, the facts are well known. He was born and raised in the border country of the Midwest. He was an indifferent West Point student; but he graduated and became a junior officer in time to serve through the Mexican War. Like a good many other professionals, he was compelled to suffer the command of amateurs in that war. He was brave enough, but undistinguished, perhaps because his superiors also were. And his experience seems not to have counted for much either in furthering his career or in contributing to his later Generalship.

He married Julia Dent and was a happy and faithful husband. No man ever had a more helpful wife. But when he was sent to posts as distant as Oregon without her, moods of depression grew on him. His drinking gradually became known to his superiors and because of it he was sent home. There followed a period of continual poverty and distress. He failed at everything he undertook and was reduced finally to working for his younger brothers in a leather business. When the war began he offered his services but was ignored by the professionals. He was finally put to work at filling out forms by the harassed Governor of Illinois, who had the responsibility, after the then fashion, for raising armies and putting them in the field. More or less in desperation, the Governor later assigned him to train a new regiment in the same way—not because the military approved, but because there was desperate need for someone who could at least begin the training of recruits.

The Civil War volunteers were like those who had served in the Mexican War—not soldiers but civilians, temporarily enlisted. They were stubbornly unamenable to discipline and they had no wish whatever to be instructed in the military arts. Grant had some success with them. And he began to have a confidence he had at first lacked that he could manage a regiment even in battle.

His progress during the next two years was phenomenal, although he had more than his share of bad luck—most of it attributable to superiors who neither knew their business nor would allow him to manage his part of it. The confusion and incompetence of the suddenly enlarged high command is almost inconceivable. All through it Grant patiently, and with silent doggedness, came to entirely correct strategic conclusions and acted on them promptly. This resulted in notable successes at Forts Henry and Donelson; then, after the impressive victory at Vicksburg, Lincoln sent for him to bring order out

of chaos in the general direction of the war. He harmonized the operations in all the theaters, set out to destroy armies rather than capture
cities, and ultimately brought Lee to bay and forced his surrender.

Victory made him a national hero. He had only recently been
"butcher Grant." This was while the battles of the Wilderness, of
Spotsylvania, and of Cold Harbor were succeeding each other with
little apparent effect except terrible slaughter. Richmond was not
taken; and this was the popular measure of success. But Lee was bottled
up there while Sherman chased Johnston's armies into the South, and in
good time Grant revealed his final plan. Then it could be seen that the
Confederacy had been ruined on those battlefields of the year before
whose inconclusive casualties almost lost Lincoln the election of 1864.
Grant was the man who developed the strategic concept and executed
it.

As he rose in the army he had many bad times when jealous superiors seemed about to stop his progress. Halleck once actually relieved
him of command and once reduced his authority to such a shadow
that he resigned. At another time he had to circumvent Lincoln, who
appointed the utterly incompetent politician General McClernand to
carry out a campaign against Vicksburg in competition with him. And
even after Vicksburg he was not allowed to execute the final stage of
his large plan, which was to march to Mobile on the Gulf, thus taking
the Confederates in the rear and compelling Lee to meet him in the
West. He had at that time to watch his victorious army dispersed. The
fighting of 1864 might never have been necessary if his conception
had been entertained. But even Lincoln was too fearful of danger to
Washington and too set on taking Richmond—neither place of any
but psychological importance—to allow Grant his way.

Lincoln's slowness to recognize his talent was partly because he was
such an enigma; he never elaborated his full plans or made much of his
victories. Besides, he was no military stylist. He was a slouching, disheveled figure, seldom in the uniform of his rank, who neglected the
military amenities so dear to the amateurs. What did he feel; how did
he decide; what were his principles? Even his own staff could not say.
The faithful and competent Rawlins, who was his constant companion, protected him as well as he could during his bouts of drunkenness
and sometimes prevented them by exhortation. But even Rawlins really
knew very little about the inner Grant.

Actually, of course, there was not much that could be found out.
His genius was instinctive. When he sensed at Donelson that the
enemy which had driven in his right and demoralized his besieging
army was really not victorious at all but was trying to escape, it was
an ability to outguess the other General that was responsible. This
happened elsewhere too. All the way through he was more an instinc-

tive than a calculating commander. Perhaps because of this he sometimes made costly mistakes. He made one at Shiloh and recovered only by relying on his own reserves of courage and persistence—and by calling for the same virtues in his army. He did not expect to retreat and did not prepare for it. He drove at the enemy with the single intent of destroying their ability to fight; he never cared to capture anything but opposing forces. It was not clever or brilliant. It had no order or neatness. Like his person, Grant's campaigns were messy; but they were irresistible and they accomplished the result.

When the Confederates surrendered, this undersized, impassive, cigar-chewing General took hold of the popular imagination as he had failed to do before. Now the very contrasts between his achievement and his appearance seemed significant to a democratic nation. The suggestion of further honors came quickly when Lincoln was assassinated. Grant at first rejected them as Taylor had. He did it unthinkingly. A soldier's business was not to govern but to fight the nation's battles. This was a simple maxim; it seemed to him unarguable; but presently he was able to turn it around and make it serve as a justification for accepting the Presidency.

It was this same simplicity that gave him his literal interpretation of the President's constitutional position when he judged Johnson and, it must be said, when he himself held the office. The Congress was to make laws; the President was to execute them. And until the end he never understood the fatal fallacy involved in this literalism. The discovery that he held this view was joyfully accepted by the Radicals in the Congress. Said Thaddeus Stevens when Grant surrendered the War Department to Stanton: "Now we can take him into the church." They had him, and they kept him. They had him because he was simple and, in civil affairs, innocent. They kept him because, no matter what happened, he could not escape from the trap. He was prevented by the same stubbornness that had seen him through his battles, no matter how costly they might be. He never departed from a line, once he had adopted it as correct, until the contest was over.

Why did a mature man who was so obviously lacking in all the political arts, who had difficulty in communicating even with his staff, who, on occasions when McClernand or Logan made passionate explanatory speeches to the volunteers, stood passive, unimpressive, and embarrassed, succeed as leader of a vast democratic army? When he assumed command of his first regiment—the 21st Illinois—and Logan made a stirring speech, then turned and introduced Grant, all the new commander said to the expectant men was "Go to your quarters." During the war there were very few manifestos from his headquarters, and those mostly came from more voluble subordinates and were allowed by Grant to go out over his name without enthusiasm. Yet he never had trouble from distrust or disaffection among his men.

His genius was for action in carrying out a concept of his own, evolved in lonely meditation, but held to through all discouragement. Out of his meditations and his apparently careless and casual study of his situation, at the right moment there would issue a command to be argued about by his staff but in the end, because of his stubbornness, to be accepted. It set vast forces in motion. It might seem the hardest and costliest way; it might not even be militarily acceptable, but in the end Grant would see it done in the field. And his armies had confidence that his decisions would be right.

How ill these methods and attitudes comport with the view that the Congress was to make policy and the President was to execute it, he never seemed to see. Did he really believe that his design for victory as a General had not been a policy matter? To believe this, he would have had to work it out that he was told to win the war and that everything else was up to him. But he must have seen that the Congress even then was interfering in operations and was by no means confining itself to policy. He must many times—as he did before Vicksburg—have taken measures to circumvent intervention from outsiders, and he must have cursed politicians as every General since Caesar had done. And if he ever read the Constitution he knew that his Commander in Chief was the President.

When the quarrels between Johnson and the Congress were at their crisis, the heart of the matter was that the Congress was determined to dictate the manner of pacification and was not content to see the return to civil order as an objective. The President was not given latitude to carry out a general directive; the Congress must control every action. Until elected Southern Representatives were refused seats in the House, civil governments had been resuming their functions and order had been returning all through the South. But this was not savage enough for the Radicals; they wanted to punish.

So Grant knew—he must have known—that his elementary interpretation of the Constitution was untenable and that a President must be a legislative leader as well as an Executive. But he saw this no more than he saw the President as Commander in Chief. He refused to follow Johnson in a conception of duties which an instant's consideration, it would be thought, must have shown him was necessary to the maintenance of Federal power. Yet he was still holding stubbornly to the same view when, as late as 1874, after years in the Presidency, he querulously blamed the Congress for not having reformed the Civil Service. He had suggested it, but he had not insisted on it, and when he was ignored he did not protest or try to persuade.

It is true that the relevant events of 1866–67 were complicated and, for an inexperienced and unlearned man like Grant, difficult to sort out. When it came right down to it he had to choose between loyalty to the President and loyalty to the Radicals in the Congress who had passed the Tenure of Office Act and demanded that he enforce it even against the President, who was his superior officer. When he looked at the penalties in the Act for not complying with its terms, he caved in. His own *Memoirs* end at about this point; they explain neither this joining with the Radicals to squeeze Johnson nor his acceptance, quite against his professed principles, of the Presidential nomination.

The kindest interpretation to be made of his behavior in the pull-and-haul of this year is that he was confused. The other, perhaps more realistic, interpretation is that he sensed Johnson's approaching ruin and the triumph of the Radicals. He sided with those who were going to dispose of the Federal power in the immediate future. Whether at the time he thought they might make him President, we do not know. But we must guess that he did, although perhaps by some involved process he concealed even from himself what actually was taking place.

In March of 1862, when he had been severely criticized as a General, he wrote:

> So long as I hold a commission in the army I have no views of my own to carry out. Whatever may be the orders of my superiors and law I will execute. . . .

There is the confusion in this that was to appear later. He went over his superior's head, and when he did this he was interpreting the law. The effect of this was to undercut the President and advance his own fortunes. The rocklike maxim was not so rocklike when it had to be applied in circumstances of interest to himself.

Grant is not the first—nor the last—Presidential aspirant to assert a fealty to generally approved principles and then abandon them when they turn out not to be convenient. Nor is he the first to assert that he did not depart from them although he obviously did. The question is whether any penalty was exacted for this dereliction. And of course there was not only no penalty, there was praise. The Presidency ought not, perhaps, to be the reward of faithlessness. Grant presumably did not consider himself faithless; but he was. No other interpretation is admissible. Also, it has to be said that his duplicity made a direct contribution to his advancement. Without it he would not have been considered eligible by the Radicals. In spite of his momentary adulation by the public, he could not have had the Republican nomination if he had not been adopted as one of their own by Johnson's furious enemies.

The nomination, once the way was prepared, was unanimous. This was the kind of situation Taylor had interpreted as a call from the people, beyond party or faction. And Grant came around to the same conclusion. He had never been a Republican; he had voted Democratic in 1860, and even in 1864 Lincoln had been suspicious of his party feeling—a suspicion Grant tried to clear up by saying that a General ought not to take part in politics and by congratulating Lincoln after he had won.[4]

The unanimous nomination, following months of unprecedented popular acclaim, during which he was praised and feted and sent many costly gifts, must not only have set him apart in his own mind from other men but must have buried under the avalanche of approval any shame he may have had about his behavior toward Johnson. Popularity can very easily become a justification for means used to win it.

It is interesting to speculate on his abandonment of the creed he had professed to live by so recently—that a soldier took orders and carried them out and that he avoided politics. Washington, Taylor, and Harrison before him had reversed themselves in the same abrupt and unequivocal way. For all of them there was the excuse that they did it by popular demand. But there have been soldiers who would not be so beguiled. Some of them were Grant's contemporaries. And one, at least, made himself famous by his rejection of suggested political preferment.

But Grant, like others before him and others who would follow, preferred to believe that so many people could not be wrong. He must have concluded, after consideration, that his own appraisal of himself had been mistaken and that the soldier's creed was inappropriate in an emergency from which only he could rescue the country. It must be that he was—as he was told—the man for the Presidency.

His increasing disapproval of Johnson's behavior made it easier to stifle his sense of duty. For Johnson was an intemperate man, grown more so in late years. He hated his detractors and demanded from all those about him unquestioned approval. Grant began by feeling that this extremism was unseemly. He progressed to doubting whether Johnson was justified in his bitter war with the Congress— the repeated vetoes and the repeated refusals to accept the laws passed over his vetoes.

It is thus easy to understand the stages by which he arrived at outright disloyalty to his Commander in Chief. And if we imagine this strong feeling to be mixed with the perception that if he defected it

---

[4] Doubts about Grant were responsible for Lincoln's asking Meade rather than Grant to send soldiers home to vote when the election seemed in doubt. Grant was never an outgoing man and his relations with Lincoln when he was in supreme command suggest a reticence that may have had its origin in a latent sense of rivalry.

would be to the stronger side where a wonderful climax to his career was possible, we have an entirely adequate explanation of what occurred. Grant's ordeal may hardly have seemed that to him. It may have seemed a completely justified, perhaps inevitable, development.

At any rate he did not resist. We know in retrospect that, although Grant's appearance and behavior indicated a humble and unassuming personality, these were deceptive signs. There was iron behind the quizzicality, and it is a fair guess that he was possessed by an urge to power all the more demanding for the frustrations of his civilian interlude after dismissal from the army.

His opponent in the campaign was Horatio Seymour, Governor of New York. Seymour was an able man and would have made an infinitely better President than he. But Seymour lacked that complete professional dedication to politics he would have needed to defeat so popular a candidate. And actually the campaign was a hero's progress. Grant got 214 electoral votes to Seymour's 80; and Seymour retired, not too unhappily, to his fabulous New York State farms. Grant went to the White House much as he had gone into his campaign—without much idea of what would be required, but with complete confidence that he would find something to do and then would do it with that strange, inexhaustible energy that always welled up from somewhere within his muddy mind.

When Grant drifted into office on the vast wave of popular approval, he was quite convinced that it was he, not the party, not the Radicals, and not their policies, to whom the election had gone. We see here again the operation of the curious political principle spoken of before—that the preferred political leader is often one who can claim with some verisimilitude not to be a politician. This is so potent an attraction to disillusioned electorates that even practicing full-time professionals often make the absurd claim that they are nonpolitical. This sometimes has the more plausible variation that they are a *different kind* of politician—the good kind—in the business only to defeat the bad kind. When the claim is genuine it is all the more irresistible. Grant could make it as convincingly as Taylor had and it was just as effective. But this has an effect on the candidates themselves. They are convinced that as President they can be above politics. Both Grant and Taylor tried it—with what results we know.

The politicians soon realized that they had a problem President to deal with and began the cutting of their hero down to size. In much the same way he had made his army decisions, Grant, without consulting anyone or following any theory, made up his own mind who his Cabinet associates should be and who would be his White House helpers. The politicians were ignored. His choices were purely personal; his staff was carried over from the army—Badeau, Porter, Babcock, and Dent.[5] But Grant soon found that after all he would have to conform to the party spoils system. Throughout his two terms, it was administered with a certain unpredictability, however; and this enraged the regulars. It was because of this that they set up in each state a patronage dispenser. Grant conformed most of the time; but it was not unusual even for the chosen dispenser of patronage to find that an appointment had been made within his territory without his knowledge or approval. Nepotism had been known before, but it had not been such an abuse as it now became. And not only nepotism but amicism became so prevalent as to be a joke among commentators.

The picture of Grant among his strangely assorted Cabinet members is much the same as the one we have of him silent and quizzical among the Generals at his wartime headquarters. They talked over his head while he sat abstractedly, seeming not even to listen. At any rate, he came to conclusions with little apparent relation to the discussion. He dredged up orders out of his subconscious and expected them to be obeyed. It was not the political way. But it was what Grant did.

This alien President achieved a second term, in the confusion of the reconstruction period, largely because the opposition was not yet organized and because the South could not yet vote. His political ineptitude did create an opposition, however, and during his second term it became so formidable that the Republicans were badly defeated in the off-year elections of 1874. Grant circumspectly and reluctantly decided that after all he would not be a third-term candidate. This was not out of respect for the two-term tradition, because he afterward did consider running again; it was because the time for reform, after the scandals and inefficiencies of his administration, had all too obviously arrived.[6] His successor, Hayes, was presented as a reform candidate. The party thus escaped the exile it deserved. For Grantism—as it came to be called—was not a phenomenon peculiar to the White House clique; it was a corruption of the whole society. Grant probably bears more than his share of the odium, although his share is deservedly large. For this was a time when speculation with

---

[5] These names have a certain place in the American record, along with such others as Buchanan's Forney, Jackson's Blair, Harding's Daugherty, and Truman's several influence sellers. Eisenhower had to let Adams go and Johnson was plagued by one Bobby Baker. Men around the President help to administer a power whose pressures open fissures in all but the most solid characters.

[6] Grant wrote a letter to General Harry White of Pennsylvania discussing at some length the third-term question but failing to say whether or not he would seek one. When the Pennsylvania state convention, presided over by General White, resolved against "the election to the Presidency of any person for a third term," Grant's only response was that he did not want a third term any more than he had wanted the first, adding that the Constitution put no restriction on the period a President might serve. Republicans generally in 1876 were much disturbed by the fear that Grant would demand another nomination.

other people's money, faithlessness to any kind of trust, and cynical exploitation of the weak by the powerful were not only allowed but approved. The moral sickness of the postwar years came to a kind of climax in the panic of 1873.

The nation was slow to disapprove; but, almost from the first, Grant's behavior offended many of his hopeful supporters. By 1872 his most effective opposition was coming not from the Democrats, who were in a minority (with much of the South still under carpetbagger administration), but from a new party made up mostly of disaffected Republicans. The Liberal Republicans, as they called themselves, would not outlast this election. But they represented a reaction from Grantism that would carry over to 1876 and give Tilden, the Democratic candidate, a popular majority. But actually in 1872 Grant was re-elected without much difficulty.[7]

That Grant was given a second term illustrates the superiority that an incumbent President has in a contest with a challenger. Lacking any such tremendous issue as had made a second term for Pierce impractical or such a popular challenger as defeated Martin Van Buren in his contest with Harrison, a President has an enormous advantage. For getting the nomination he has control of a whole administration whose members also want to stay in office; and for winning the election he has the party machinery built up during a four-year control of patronage and favors. There is besides a strong relationship between President and people, they looking to him as their advocate and defender, and he to them for support against those who would challenge him. This is a power much feared by would-be rivals in the Congress and tends to discipline them most particularly as elections approach.

Grant conducted himself badly both in his party relations and in keeping the good will of his first entry into office. He was a popular hero then; before very long he was much less a hero and much more the friend of the rich and powerful than of the people generally. He had no program with popular appeal and he developed no enemies who would confirm his leadership. That he was re-elected at all seems to have been due more to inertia in troubled times than to any enthusiasm on anyone's part for keeping him in office.

Grant's example is an encouraging one for ambitious military men. It is encouraging, also, to those who lack the culture, the dignity, and even the minimum mental equipment necessary for the job. Almost anyone, it seems, can become President if the times are troubled.

---

[7] It appears overwhelming in the electoral vote because of the many disputes and quibbles following the death of his opponent, Horace Greeley, before the College met, an event which left many electors uncertain of their position.

Rutherford Birchard Hayes
1822–1893

Born in Delaware, Ohio
Became nineteenth President in 1877 at 54

HISTORY

1842–45	After a boyhood in Lower Sandusky (now Fremont), Ohio, graduated from Kenyon College; was admitted to the bar after study at Harvard and in the office of Thomas Sparrow of Columbus.
1849	Moved to Cincinnati.
1852	Married to Lucy Ware Webb, daughter of a distinguished family.
1858	Chosen City Solicitor.
1861–64	Served in the field; promoted for gallantry; wounded at South Mountain. Campaigned with Crook. Promoted to Brigadier General. Elected to the United States Congress.
1865	Resigned commission and returned to Ohio.
1866–67	In full sympathy with Radical reconstruction group but not influential among them and made no speeches. In 1866 was re-nominated and re-elected to the Congress.

233

1867–69	Elected to the Governorship and re-elected.
1870	Nominated for the Congress but defeated.
1875	Elected Governor for a third term.
1876	Nominated for the Presidency and elected (Vice-President, Wheeler); opponent, Tilden with Hendericks.
1880	Was so unpopular with many elements of his own party, after four years in the Presidency, that he asked not to be renominated.
1881	Retired to Ohio.
1893	Died at his Spiegel's Grove Estate.

T HAT the post-Civil War years were disturbed and uneasy was some excuse for the way Grant had allowed his office to be corrupted; but the excuse was less and less acceptable as the war retreated in time. At the end of his first term there had formed a group of "Liberal Republicans" who had reacted in disgust to the behavior of his close associates; but his prestige with the veterans had enabled the "Stalwarts" to re-elect him and to go on into four more years of even more slovenly administration and more flagrant misuse of governmental power.

Grant would have liked to run again, and the best hope of the spoilsmen was to keep him in office. But public disaffection had made it imperative to have a new front for their machinations. They would have preferred either Blaine or Conkling; both were of the same easy virtue as Grant; both were powerful members of the cabal that had ruled the Senate since the war, dictating policies and appointments, reducing Presidential prerogatives, and protecting their machines from exposure. They were deep in the muddy affairs of the occupied states of the South where the outrageous carpetbagger governments were still supported by military force. But Blaine and Conkling hated each other. Moreover, each had a record that would embarrass a candidate under the scrutiny inevitable in a Presidential contest. The dissidents wanted an entire change—a Republican who was everything Grant was not, one who would clear out the corruptionists and bring the party back to respectability.

There was also the complication that if a reformer was really wanted who would gloss over the past, the obvious one to choose was Benjamin H. Bristow, the Secretary of the Treasury who had exposed the Whiskey Ring. Involved in this had been General Orville B. Babcock, Grant's private secretary; but Bristow had not been deterred from investigating and had been forced to resign by Grant. There had been other scandals. The Postmaster General had been dismissed because he objected; so had several lesser officials whose consciences had bothered them. The situation in the Department of the Interior was notorious, and it was also suspected that similar affairs had been going on in the Navy Department. But Bristow had remained a symbol of rectitude.

Grant had been completely subdued by the Senate cabal; and not only had its members dictated matters of policy, it was at this time that Chief Executives began to accept the rule that only those appointees could be confirmed who had been "suggested" in the first place by the Senators themselves. At the moment they had to recognize the public

235

demand for reform; but they wanted as little of it as they could contrive. So even though Bristow was the logical man, he was too devoted
to the public interest; he would not serve the purposes of the insiders.

This was the background of the convention of 1876. After discovering that Blaine and Conkling had made each other ineligible, and
agreeing instinctively that Bristow was too reformist, the bosses turned
to Hayes of Ohio, whose record was not clouded by the prevailing
miasma of corruption. He was just barely acceptable to the spoilsmen,
whose machinations he had at least never denounced; and the Liberal
Republicans hoped that if he would do no spectacular house cleaning,
he might at least rescue the party from its unhappy reputation. He was
an upright man.

Hayes was no longer the dashing Colonel of the western Virginia
campaigns; he had grown heavy and dull with the passing years. It
was hard now to recall that he had once been a brilliant commander.
He was reserved and conservative, slow to accept suggestions for
change and apparently content with the restricted powers of the
Ohio Governorship in those days.

Lucy, his wife, had fattened too and turned into a termagant; she
now regulated his life and set the tone of his behavior. She was
bigotedly strict and forbade card-playing, dancing, and the other
pleasures held by Protestant sects to be sinful; but all this was at the
moment good. It made her husband eligible.

In religion Hayes seems to have been somewhat the way he was
with Republican Radicalism. He never joined the church himself; but
he went to its service every Sunday and contributed to its funds. He
later became famous for being a teetotaler even in the White House. It
might be thought that this was rather a mark of irregularity or fanaticism than orthodoxy. But the fact is that there were far more temperance advocates than devotees of the bottle, and especially among the
solid Protestant citizenry who went regularly to the polls.

Hayes tried to be pleasant; but he was never very easy, and he had
none of that tobacco-chewing, whiskey-drinking bonhomie which was
very common among the mid-century politicians. His disapproval of
the Grant circle must have been very strong. He never let it be known
except by his own contrasting behavior, but it was useful at a time
when there was revulsion from looseness and public exhibitions of
indiscipline. The calculation involved in being available when such an
organization as the mid-century Republican party needed a man of
impeccable conduct was quite comparable with others we have seen
in our review of successful careers.

That it was not accidental we can understand by analyzing the
choices made by Hayes at various junctures. His careful management
of each succeeding phase of his life began, as we have seen it begin

with others, very early; and it persisted down to final nomination and election. Why it did not last long enough to capture nomination for a second term, when, as we already know, it is almost impossible to prevent an incumbent President from being nominated, we shall have to see.

Perhaps the student should be reminded again at this point that the same sort of calculations as those made by Hayes must have been made by many a politician who made a mistake here and there and who consequently missed the connection he must have made for success. Many who had the same intention, and just slightly less ability, foresight, and good fortune, have been lost at one or another stage in obscurity. The shadows hiding them are so impenetrable before very long that the student has enormous difficulty in finding the material he needs to study failure as he may study success.

Numerous reformers offered themselves for preferment as the reaction to Grantism mounted. But Hayes, who was conspicuous neither as a politician nor as a reformer, was easily chosen over the others. They might have fitted the indicated role with some forcing; he was perfection itself. He justified the calculation of those who saw in him the signs of righteousness rather than of those who hoped that he would show a respectable front but actually furnish no serious opposition to their machinations.

There are very severe and searching examinations preceding a party's final choice of its candidate. At some stage those tough insiders who can prevent most men's further advance always ask the question: How will his performance affect us? But they must also ask whether his record will be approved by the voters.

What the electorate will not approve involves a wide spectrum. Sexual entanglements or doubtful financial deals are only two of many possible causes for veto. From these the examination may reach outward to much less defined conduct. The shadow of unorthodoxy must have jeopardized the future of many an able man who would otherwise have risen to prominence; it must have made numerous candidates ineligible for party nomination.

Being even remotely likely to be called a Southern sympathizer in the period we are now considering was very nearly fatal. This disqualified any Democrat from acceptance by the vast veterans' organization. In 1872 the Democrats were so uneasy that they accepted the Liberal Republican nominee; and although their courage returned in 1876, when they had so good a candidate as Tilden, and when Grant had reduced the Republicans to a weak defense of his record, they were still apologetic and would be until they found Cleveland in 1884. There is reason to think that they were the majority party all through;

but for twenty-four years they were not able to land their man in the White House.

Perhaps this should be put another way by saying that no individual so shortsighted as to have Democratic affiliations was able to become President. There were some—John A. Logan was one—who changed parties with this in mind. Logan had been a Democratic Congressman before the war. He became a Republican Congressman after it, as well as a candidate for the Vice-Presidency on the ticket with Blaine in 1884.[1]

Either something was wrong with every Democrat, in the estimation of the voters, or the Republicans managed to prevent enough Democratic votes from being counted to elect their own candidates. This last sort of finagling went on with amazing boldness during the reconstruction. The most flagrant instance was the one involving Hayes. The truth is that Hayes was not really elected at all but was maneuvered into office by fraud and force. This reduces the value of his lesson for us. Nevertheless, we do learn from it that a cautious, calculating, and purist approach can seem acceptable to the professionals who possess the final veto. Also, we can learn that it may appeal to the electorate. He did not lose in the popular vote by a very considerable margin; and he did, after all, become President, even if with a clouded title.

Then it has to be noted that Hayes had some other qualifications besides the negative one of a clean record. For instance, he had been a General; and the voters were not yet through with Civil War Generals in spite of Grant's deplorable civilian performance. After Hayes there would be two more still to come. The reputation of neither rested wholly on his General's stars as Grant's had; but both found them useful. Nor was this Hayes's only other qualification. His being Governor of Ohio placed him in a favored preliminary position. To enhance this particular attraction, he was a three-time Governor who had defeated formidable Democratic rivals. He had thus demonstrated his durability.

When it is considered how many political attractions Hayes did possess, it is hardly possible to attach any quantitative weight to the one that stands out as unique. Still, when all the reservations have been made, there is a residue of importance. It must be allowed a place in the cumulative record of the Presidents. To have been virtuous, even if mediocre and lacking in leadership, without clear ideas about policy

---

[1] Logan even had a respectable support for the first place on the ticket. This came mostly from Illinois servicemen, who rounded up 63 votes for him on the first ballot at the Chicago convention. There are other instances. Grant himself voted Democratic before the war; and Andrew Johnson was never a Republican; but then, of course, Andrew Johnson was never elected to the Presidency.

and without commitment beyond the position of the party, was to have a strong qualification.

If we are to understand why it had to be Hayes rather than Blaine or Conkling or Bristow who was chosen at Cincinnati in 1876 by the Republicans, it is useful to recall that he was a fatherless boy, a posthumous child, the darling of his mother and an elder sister. He was provided for and watched over by an uncle who was wealthy and had no other younger relatives to look out for. He was therefore not pressed by circumstances. His going to Kenyon College in Ohio rather than a New England educational institution was a curious departure from the course that seemed normally indicated. He had his earlier schooling in Connecticut, and his ancestry was New Englandish. He seemed as much a Yankee as though he had never lived outside a Northeastern state. This, of course, was not unusual among the higher-income families in the Middle West. Generations of young people yet unborn would be sent to New England schools and colleges. But the Yankees took on a special kind of character in Ohio and Indiana. They kept much of their narrowness and thrift, their shrewdness and pride, and were able to feel themselves superior to other emigrants.

But it was fortunate for a politician to be able to point to an Ohio rather than an Eastern education. It added a little, even if only a little, to Hayes's acceptability. No one knows why it happened, and it cannot be said that this first of many shrewd choices was made with preferment in view. But it was not made for reasons of economy or because Kenyon was considered even a passable educational institution. So there is a certain presumption of plan. Going on to Harvard to study law was different—a professional preparation, not an education.

As a college boy and law-school student, Hayes was a conforming and well-favored member of his group. There was nothing very notable about him or about what he did. He was sufficiently intelligent and ordinarily diligent. He got into no scrapes and sowed no wild oats. He made friends, and he graduated in regular course. But when he returned to Lower Sandusky after a year at Harvard and entered on a career at the bar, he began to be tormented by restlessness. His ambitions, he found, reached beyond the routines of a small-town practice; moreover, he seems to have felt generally confined. This unhappiness was, however, rather easily dissipated by a trip to the Southwest and eventual relocation in Cincinnati. The excuse was ill-health; but this was not very real; his health, all his life, was as equable as his temperament. Within a year he was back and setting up a law office of his own.

It was naturally some time before his practice amounted to much.

But the time was well spent. He made many friends; he achieved a
reputation as a respectable and dependable young man; he found
appropriate social circles—one of them a literary club—to which he
was devoted. And by faithful keeping of a diary he developed a very
adequate, if somewhat self-conscious, ability to express his thoughts.
These were not profound, but they were sensible. He did such public
speaking, also, as he was asked to do; and it is probable that this interest in the temperance movement came partly from the opportunity
it gave him for public attention. He spoke of this in his *Diary* for
November 1850:

> I am a sincere but not extreme or violent friend of the temperance
> cause. I mean to prepare myself to speak on this subject by accumulat-
> ing and arranging in my memory as many interesting facts, arguments,
> and statistics as I can; also by jotting down my own ideas on the sub-
> ject as they occur to me. The learning to speak as well as the notoriety
> (not to speak of the good I may do) are objects worthy of the pains.

He joined the Odd Fellows too and, as his biographer says in somewhat the same genre as Hayes's own account, was "in frequent req-
uisition for lectures before its various lodges."[2]

The picture we have of him as a rising young man in his thirties
is one of a deepening and broadening success. He was intent on self-
improvement; he was equally intent on getting ahead; and in both he
had reason for satisfaction. The self-improvement was advanced by
a formidable and long-continued course of "heavy" reading; the progress came through the cultivation of important people and the seizure
of every opportunity to display his speaking talents.

He was often puzzled. Emerson, who came to Cincinnati on one of
his lecture tours in 1850, became the subject of long passages in the
Diary. The New England philosophy seems, he said, to have "some
misty notions on religion resembling the German philosophy." But he
was not satisfied that he quite understood. He was equally puzzled
after repeated reading of Locke:

> I do not know what opinion to form about his doctrine of innate
> ideas. If I had heard nothing against it, I should adopt it. I cannot dis-
> cover its weak points. His remarks about the idea of God are certainly
> correct. What two persons have the same notion of the Supreme Being?

For a busy young man of rather ordinary abilities, the solemnity
and persistence of his pursuit of knowledge for its own sake approach

---

[2] *The Life of Rutherford Birchard Hayes* by Charles Richard Williams, 2 vols.
(The Ohio State Archaeological and Historical Society, 1928), I, 60.

the incredible—at least as it was set down in his *Diary*. One day in 1851 (when he was twenty-nine) he said to himself:

> I feel that I have read too much light reading, too little that is useful, instructive, solid, of late. I must give up my mental habits; become more energetic by tough reading. Let my lightest for a time be biographies and miscellanies such as the statesmen of Cromwell's time.

This, it must be remembered, was when he was systematically reading law as well as a miscellany of philosophy, history, and literary classics! Ten years after his arrival in Cincinnati he could write in his diary:

> Without any extraordinary success, without that sort of success which makes men giddy sometimes, I have nevertheless found what I sought—a respectable place. Good!

One of the reasons he eventually arrived at the summit was undoubtedly this ability to see exactly where he stood. He was commonplace; but part of being commonplace is the possession of a certain realism.

Before the Civil War broke out he had become a locally prominent member of the bar who took an active interest in politics—always on the conservative side—and was in demand in every contest. His *Diary* is full of comments on all the issues leading up to the war. He supported General Scott in 1852, not because he had much admiration for him, but because he was a Whig. When he was speaking only to his *Diary* he was a good deal less than enthusiastic; and when he commented on the election afterward he said of the candidate that he was

> a good man, a kind man, a brave man, a true patriot, but an exceedingly vain, weak man in many points [who] no doubt deserved defeat if weakness and undue anxiety to be elected can be said to deserve such treatment.

He had more enthusiasm for Frémont in 1856 and easily became a Republican. He had no doubts on the slavery question and from the first felt that it was a dangerous issue that must somehow be resolved. He hoped it might be settled peaceably. But in 1858 he was elected by the City Council of Cincinnati to be City Solicitor, and this rather removed him for a time from contact with the larger issues then coming to a crisis. It was a demanding office and he attended earnestly to its duties. His election was the first demonstration of his ability to win in close contests against strong rivals.

When the war came, he was out of office. The Democrats and the

Know-Nothings had carried the city, and Hayes had gone back to the practice of law. But by the middle of May in 1861 he was resolved that what was about to occur was a "holy war" and that he must serve. It was then that he wrote:

> I would prefer to go into it if I knew I was to die or be killed in the course of it, than to live through and after it without taking any part in it.

It was a time when aspiring politicians all over the North were seeing that war service would be necessary to any postwar advancement, and all of them were seeking commissions of as high rank as possible. Many of them were to lose their reputations in the trials that were to come. Those who became officers were to be rapidly weeded out as the war became real; but some did surprisingly well, and Hayes was one of these. From being City Solicitor he became in a matter of months an active field commander in charge of a regiment. He had natural abilities, heretofore not called on, for managing men. But, more important, he had a kind of verve and enthusiasm for life in the field and for leadership in military expeditions of the sort his campaigning in the mountains of West Virginia called for.

When he went into the army he was thirty-eight. He was mustered out in 1865 when he was forty-two. Those four years were really glorious ones for him. His *Diary* is one long reflection of his joy in the life of a soldier; he seldom had a complaint to register. And this satisfaction was evident in his military record. He was wounded several times; his promotions were earned by genuine bravery and ability; he was very popular with those in his command, and he was trusted by his superiors.

The North was not fortunate in its Generals; but those under whom Hayes served were among the better ones—Crook, Rosecrans, and Sheridan, for instance. In age Hayes must have had great satisfaction in his memories both of camp life and of the battles in which he commanded men. He had a good regiment which was unusually steady under fire; and in this Hayes's firm leadership was given a good deal of credit. The 23rd Ohio was present at Second Manassas, fought at South Mountain, took part in the Antietam campaign of 1862, and was back in western Virginia when Burnside met disaster at Fredericksburg. At South Mountain, Hayes was wounded on a day when the 23rd made three bayonet charges.

The prevailing note of all the *Diary* entries continued to be a buoyant optimism even when his regiment was undergoing real hardships from rapid marching, failure of supplies, and the rigors of mountain weather in winter. Even the hardships were to him somehow agreeable. His complaints were not substantial; he seldom brought himself to any sharp criticisms of his superiors, and he had no self-doubts whatever. He always did his best, and that best was very good.

During his absence in the field he was elected to the Congress; but he continued in the army until mustered out after Appomattox. Then he took his seat.

A categorical statement that Hayes's subsequent advancement in politics depended on the decisions he made in the 39th Congress would be thoroughly justified. The difficulty is that they were hardly decisions at all. He simply acted as he would go on acting all the rest of his life. Then and later—until he was President—he conformed. He did not please the extremist Thaddeus Stevens; but then very few Representatives did. Stevens was a raging fanatic, and Hayes was not. But he supported the Radicals in their war on President Johnson. He did this because he thought the rebel states should be required to acknowledge error and should give some kind of guarantee for the future before being readmitted to the Union. He had no thought of the injury being done to the Presidency.

Garfield, who had left the army to take his seat in the 38th Congress and so had preceded Hayes by one term, said of his Ohio colleague that he had entered the House "resolved not to make the mistake of talking too much." Garfield also remarked that "when it was known that he advocated the passage of a bill, it was pretty sure to pass." But it seems out of character, somehow, for a man who was wounded in action four times and had four horses shot out from under him to have been willing to serve industriously on the library committee; it must have been a powerful ambition that changed Hayes the soldier into Hayes the politician.

He was renominated by acclamation and re-elected in 1866, although the signs of dissent from Republican policy were evident in Ohio. The attempt to omit any mention of the newly submitted Fourteenth Amendment from the party platform was fiercely debated. In these exchanges Hayes said a good deal more than he ever said in the Congress, all of it defensive. He was a party man.

Throughout the last session of the 39th and the first session of the 40th Congress, Hayes went his equable way in the midst of tension and recrimination, voting with the majority and behaving circumspectly. Then, in reward, he was nominated for the Governorship.

Altogether he was elected to this office three times in the next few years. The last election was in 1875, and this term was interrupted by his nomination for the Presidency in 1876. Meanwhile he was defeated in a try for the Congress after his first two terms as Governor; but he ran ahead of his ticket, so that even in defeat he demonstrated real political strength. During all this time Grant's fumbling administration in Washington was a constant embarrassment to those who, like Hayes, were contending for local offices; and this was complicated in Ohio by a considerable opposition to the reconstruction policies of the Radicals. It is interesting to see how Hayes, in the party interest, valiantly defended policies and people he must have despised. Countless speeches were devoted to making the best of a bad business all round for Republicans. In public he never criticized Grant and his circle. It is only in his *Diary* that we can see how well he understood the nature of the Federal regime.

He did, however, gradually develop two cautious tentatives of his own—improvement of the civil service and suggestions for ending the "occupation" of the Southern states. These were shadowy and unemphatic; it was possible to believe that he was not too serious about either.

He cannot exactly be described as a dark horse at the time of his nomination. He was spoken of as a possibility from the time of his first election to the Governorship. But he was certainly less prominent than the four who were supposed to be the leading contenders—Conkling, Blaine, Bristow, and Morton—and it would not have been predicted a year in advance that he would be chosen. Yet, looking back, it is obvious that his way upward had been smooth and certain. Nothing could be more ordinary and regular than his rise.

It is true that he was favored by Grant's failure. If Grant had been the success anticipated by the Republicans, they would have risked a campaign with Conkling, the administration's choice, or with Blaine, who had wide popular support. Morton was an invalid and Bristow was a reformer. In the serious discussions of the professionals both had to be discarded. Neither Conkling nor Blaine conformed to the picture of the earnest and trustworthy father-figure needed to offset the disgust so widely felt by the voters at the recent goings-on in Washington. That they should turn to the solemn, bearded man who had been a gallant fighter, a steady Governor, and a conforming party member was not at all strange. They would have lost if they had turned to any of the others. They very nearly lost anyway.

There was a good deal of acrimonious discussion at the time, still continued in the history books, about the election of 1876. It turned on the delivery of electoral votes by the puppet governments in a few Southern states. Hayes's Democratic opponent, Tilden, was a moderate man who would not subject the country to the dissension involved in a determined controversy about the peculiar methods resorted to by Republicans determined to stay in office at any cost. But the fact is that Tilden was elected and Hayes was not. Hayes had neither a popular majority nor an electoral one. Even the rigging in Louisiana and Florida produced only a majority of one. Nevertheless, Hayes was inaugurated and served. The shadow of fraud hung over his administration for all his four years and contributed, perhaps, to his colorless policy. But what was responsible for his being passed over for a second nomination was not this. He did very little; but what he did do incensed the politicians. They were so offended that they very nearly broke off relations with him altogether, as the Whigs had done with Tyler. He first enraged the Radicals by withdrawing the military occupations in the rebel states, and then he insisted on reform of the civil service. This last made him intolerable to the professionals, who regarded public offices as legitimate spoils. They were glad to see the end of his four years.

Involved in Hayes's attempt at reform was the old quarrel between the Legislative and Executive Branches. During Grant's regime especially, although for years the trouble had been deepening, the Senate cabal had ridden high. The Radicals had interfered with the conduct of the war and had, indeed, helped to precipitate it. They had tried to impeach Johnson because he would not conform to their vindictive policies toward the beaten South. And in Grant they had found a tool they could use as they liked. They had not only begun to control policy, they had begun to interfere in administration, the most extreme evidence of which was the Tenure of Office Act.

What this group of strong-willed men had against Hayes was that he meant to install a merit system. Clearly this would prevent them from maintaining political machines at government expense. He even went so far as to remove Chester A. Arthur from the Collectorship of the Port of New York. Arthur was a henchman of Senator Conkling, and this was a flagrant defiance of the established convention that this was a Senatorial preserve. That this same Arthur should, in Hayes's lifetime become an occupant of the White House instead of the New York Customhouse is one of the ironies of American politics. If Hayes had foreseen this embarrassment to the Republican party he might have thought twice about the summary removal; but all he knew at the moment was that his investigation had shown an intolerable situation. Hardly any of the employees were fitted for their duties, and many of them never appeared to perform what duties they might be assumed to have. But to hear the ravings and bellows of the outraged Conkling in the Senate following the dismissal, it would have been thought that the nation itself was in danger of dissolution. So the most commonplace of Presidents, the most conforming of men, earned for himself the reward of political humiliation. He was hardly spoken of at all for the nomination of 1880, and he fell back on his earlier statement that he had never wanted it.

Hayes's protests that he did not want the successive offices that were thrust upon him belonged to the tradition of political hypocrisy. The office was supposed to seek the man. In those days the Presidential candidate made no canvass. All the voters were allowed to know about him was the record he had already made and the figure he presented as a potential chief magistrate. This did not mean that canvasses were not strenuous; they were; more so than in later years; but the candidate's activities were confined to private consulting with party leaders and to assuming the posture appropriate to a national statesman.

This role seemed to fit Hayes at the age of fifty-four. The vigorous soldier and eager public speaker had become the slow and cautious public figure. That was the kind of candidate the Republicans needed; and he gave it to them. But when their effigy came to life and developed a mind of his own in the White House they found it intolerable. Since he had said from the first that he would serve only one term, it seemed to be part of his conception of the Presidential role. No one believed that if he had been pressed he would have refused, but his declaration made it easier to accept the party's repudiation; and he could retire to his estate. For thirteen years he was a kind of living monument to respectability; and he died full of years and without regrets, but, like most retired Presidents, fully believing that he had been badly used.

James A. Garfield
1831–1881

CULVER PICTURES, INC.

Born in Cuyahoga County, Ohio
Became twentieth President in 1881 at 49

HISTORY

1856   Graduated from Williams College after a long struggle for education. Father died when Garfield was two and the family very poor. He went to work early at varied jobs including school teaching and became a lay preacher in the Disciples of Christ Church. When he returned to Ohio he became a teacher as well as a preacher.

1857   Became Principal of the Eclectic Institute at Hiram.

1858   Married Lucretia Randolph.

1859   Elected to the Ohio Senate.

1860   Admitted to the bar.

1861   Commissioned Lieutenant Colonel through political influence. After recruiting, studying military practice, and beginning to campaign, was made a Brigadier General; later became a brevet Major General.

247

1862	Elected to the Congress.
1863	Resigned his commission.
1880	After serving continuously in the House from 1863, was elected to the United States Senate but did not take his seat because of being nominated for the Presidency. Elected (Vice-President, Arthur); opponent, Hancock.
1881	Shot on July 2, by a disappointed job seeker who was inflamed over the struggle between the liberal and "stalwart" factions of the party, and died September 19.

IT IS ALMOST IMPOSSIBLE to imagine how a man could have risen to the Presidency and have contributed less of value to political history than did James A. Garfield. He was a demagogue of the conservative faction; he had no original thoughts; he made the gestures of a leader but had nothing important to say concerning the important issues of his lifetime; he consented to what was orthodox but what was also shortsighted; and he was chosen for preferment time after time on his way to the Presidency because his superficial gloss could be traded on.

He was handsome and virile; he was a voluble and attractive speaker; and when the time came, his pursuit of perfection in the oratorical arts was crowned by nomination for the Presidency on the thirty-sixth ballot of a convention (in 1880) which had, until then, been struggling to resolve the claims of two more likely candidates—ex-President Grant and James G. Blaine. Grant, in politics, was almost always being manipulated by someone else, and this time it was Roscoe Conkling of New York, who had a double interest in the matter—to regain his power over the Presidency and to defeat his old party enemy, Blaine. Blaine felt himself entitled to the nomination not only because of his party position but because of his immense popularity.

The two giants killed each other off. Garfield, already noticed at the convention as a ready speaker, rose to offer a compromise candidate—John Sherman, Secretary of the Treasury in Hayes's Cabinet. This eulogy did not improve Sherman's chances; but it called attention to Garfield himself. He became the only President ever to be present at his own nomination.[1]

The background of this—to Garfield—all-important speech has its own interest. It could not have been made if Garfield had not practiced on a thousand platforms, learned from many teachers, and analyzed the techniques of all the contemporary masters. His skill as a political orator was the result of working with the ardor any successful practitioner gives to an art. Many people learn to speak well as an adjunct to other endeavors of some sort. The student of Garfield's career is tempted to say that he was an orator first and that his preaching, his teaching, his membership at the bar—all were secondary.

He was certainly devoted to perfecting the spoken word. It is doubtful whether even the political spellbinders of the classic period,

---

[1] Of this speech, the historian E. P. Oberholtzer said in an exquisite paragraph that it had been "a really splendid *tour de force* in political eloquence which was in every hearer's mind at a momentous hour, when, despairing of an harmonious issue, the convention sought a way out of a stalemate . . ." *A History of the United States Since the Civil War* (New York, 1931), 73. It was notable for its free classical allusions and its bursts of elocutional passages so much admired in his time.

Clay, Calhoun, Webster, Sumner—any of them—equaled him for sheer eloquence. In all the annals of campaigning, he had only two or three rivals. Ingersoll, Blaine, and Bryan were noted in their day; but none was so immersed in the art. Others—Wilson and Franklin D. Roosevelt, for instance—stirred millions, not so much by the spell of their voices and the grace of their allusions as by what they had to say. Garfield was remarkable because he said so little at such length and because it was done so purely with a view to its emotional effect. It poured out, apparently unprepared, at extended length. He drew men's admiration and made himself glow with eloquence, not particularly to benefit anyone or any cause—although there was always an excuse, religious, moral, or political—but just for the exercise. It was, in a very real sense, pure vocalization.[2]

There were noted preachers whose names were as familiar in most households as the noted politicians'; and Garfield had a long start toward being one of these before he turned to politics. Preaching for him had its limitations because he belonged to a small Protestant sect, the Disciples of Christ, and was closely identified with its missionary and educational efforts. Being vigorous and well read, he was soon drafted for organization work. For this he found he had little liking; politics was in all respects more congenial. He took to it with enthusiasm, and his success was the direct product of his forensic self-training. He could always get a hearing; he could usually rouse an audience to an emotional pitch on any subject; and it seemed not to matter what the composition of the audience was. Later on he was as effective in the House of Representatives as he had been in the pulpit, in school assemblies, or on the hustings in Cuyahoga County.

His career had a curious parallelism with that of Hayes. Both were fatherless boys, although the one had a rich uncle and the other fought his way upward in poverty. But in many ways Garfield's church took the place of Hayes's uncle. It furnished support and a warm and intimate refuge from the world. This, however, did not begin until he was nineteen. Until then he had a hard time, trying first to help his mother run a hardscrabble farm, then doing odd jobs as a laborer at miserable wages. But he kept on going back to school in one or

---

[2] The scene at the convention when, a few days after his speech for Sherman, Garfield was nominated is thus described by Oberholtzer (*op. cit.*, 74): "The noise, both on the floor and in the galleries, was terrific. Garfield went to Bateman with apparent emotion, when he saw what impended, to assure Sherman's principal agent that he had had nothing to do with it—he would 'rather be shot to death by the inch than to furnish his friends any just ground for suspicion of unfaithfulness.' It was 'the escape of a tired convention.' The banners of the states were brought up to surround Garfield who sat motionless, onlookers have said, dazed, in his seat. The crowd sang 'Rally 'Round the Flag' to the music of the band while, outside, cannon fired salutes." This is a perfect picture of its sort.

another place—all in northern Ohio—and managed to progress far enough at his academy to qualify as an elementary teacher. Only by courtesy could his training be called adequate; but it did enable him to hire out at district schools, and this set him on his way to an ultimate degree from Williams College. Hayes had stayed at a college in Ohio; Garfield's New England years might have caused criticism in Ohio. He escaped, perhaps, because he had already studied at a Midwestern school and returned there as teacher and head after finishing at Williams.

The Eclectic (the Western Reserve Eclectic Institute) was a church school, established by the Disciples in the town of Hiram in Portage County in 1849, and had been in existence only a year when Garfield first went there as a student. It was rural and crude, the teachers were dependent on meager fees for their pay, and there was only one red brick building in a cornfield. But Garfield's ardor was by then of the consuming, voracious kind. He attacked education by main strength. He strove to master everything. Here the parallel with Hayes breaks down. Hayes never had that fierce ambition to excel. He was much more easy, restrained, and well mannered. Garfield was a country boy who had to acquire style as well as clothes. He had no restraint at all and recognized no limit to his ambitions. These ran in orthodox channels, however, as Hayes's did. There was never any complaint that either one leaned toward doubtful beliefs—unless the Disciples, being a small company, could be said to have been unorthodox.

Hayes had fancied himself as a littérateur; so did Garfield. Throughout his educational period there was a steady gush from his pen of verse, of apostrophes to his diary, of essays, and of addresses. All were in high-flown, polysyllabic language of the kind so much admired by rural audiences and readers. But it had a kind of power, as though it came from an inexhaustible source and could perhaps be diverted but not by any means stopped. He himself said of it many years later (in 1874, when he was a Congressman and still keeping watch on himself): "I was a very pulpy boy 'til I was at least twenty-two years old. But with all the rudeness and crudeness of those times, I was dead in earnest and was working with the best light I had." He was pulpy far beyond the age of twenty-two; but, for that matter, so was Hayes. If they had not been they would not have commanded the political support needed for a career in the Ohio of their day. Gush was as necessary as gumption for what they had in mind.

It is, of course, another parallel that they were both Ohioans. All Republican Presidential nominees from 1876 to 1920 would be from Ohio, except Harrison from neighboring Indiana (who had been born in Ohio) and Theodore Roosevelt, who succeeded to the Presidency when an Ohioan (McKinley) was assassinated in office. After Roosevelt, there were two Ohioans (Taft and Harding). Even before Hayes, the shift from the Middle Border to the upper Middle West had been fixed by the war. Lincoln and Grant were Illinoisans. But then Republicanism itself was a Midwest phenomenon in origin and in continuing strength. It is not strange that so many of its candidates should have lived in its most populous state.[3]

Very much as the Democrats before the war had looked for Northern men with Southern principles, the Republicans now looked for Western men with Eastern principles. It was a conservative businessmen's and prosperous farmers' party. It attracted financial men because of its conservatism; and, because they financed it, they controlled it and demanded to be satisfied with its candidates. But to win elections, verbal concessions had to be made to the farmers who were in their debt and to the smaller businessmen whom the Easterners exploited. One of the most remarkable phenomena in American political history is the persistence with which the farmers and small businessmen held to their Republican affiliation. They persisted in voting for sound money and high tariffs, which the Democrats argued were against all reason. But these were the policies favored by their larger and richer party brothers, the ones expounded and defended by their nominees for the Presidency. And because for a long time Republicans stayed in office, there were no alternative policies put into effect for contrast. The Democrat, Cleveland, would be as "sound" in money matters, very nearly, as the Republicans before and after him; and this was one reason why he could win elections when no other Democrats could. The Republicans had trouble from time to time with dissenters. The Liberal Republicans abhorred Grantism and made a party row which almost defeated Hayes. And later there were to be Progressives who would give even more trouble. But the Republican success was remarkable until they split so badly that Wilson could win—still a long way in the future.

Garfield would have it easier in this respect than Hayes. There was no criticism of Republican conduct in office in 1880 as there had been in 1876. The Hayes administration had been clean, if not vigorous, and the populist demands for inflation that accompanied the depression of 1873 were considerably eased by returning prosperity; and the surge of progress, again under way, proved to the voters that conservatism paid. The Republicans claimed credit for it. Sound money and high tariffs were safe for some time to come.

But, as we have seen, availability does not depend on location alone; and nomination does not altogether depend on availability. Garfield was not the only Republican politician in the Midwest who might

---

[3] *The Republicans* by Malcolm Moos (New York, 1956).

have been chosen; he was not even the only handsome war veteran with the proper background and acceptable views. He succeeded where the others did not because he had the combination of qualities in the right place and at the right time. As with his predecessors, we must judge that it was more than just accidental.

Garfield worked hard. To those who do other kinds of work, political endeavors may not seem to be very demanding. Nevertheless, they are. A rising politician must take infinite pains with the management of matters necessary to the establishment and maintenance of good opinion among those who count; he must contrive also to be widely known and favorably regarded among the people to whom he is appealing. This involves not only an infinite number of personal contacts carefully calculated to leave a pleasant memory, but also the assuming of popular attitudes on public questions. On most of these last, if he does it skillfully, he may avoid commitment; but he must know when this is inappropriate, and he must be ready to stand for policies he will be respected for defending and against those it may be just as well not to defend. The clever politician will know that many seemingly unpopular causes will presently become popular. He must in this way anticipate opinions not yet formed. In selected instances he may become a leader, urging that his own view be accepted. But he must be very confident that the soundness of his judgment will be vindicated and that due credit will be awarded.

This is illustrated by the difficulties Hayes, Garfield, and other Republicans in these middle years had with the money question. There could be no wavering on this; it was sternly held as a matter of principle among financiers that inflation was wicked. But there were many dissenters, and they had to be persuaded. The Republican candidates always had to oppose Democrats who appealed to the Populists. And very often Republican victories were slim. Garfield was more fortunate than Hayes, who did not have a popular majority and whose claims to the Presidency were doubtful. But his own majority was not so large as to be safe. He was frightened during his campaign. Still, however risky it might be, there was nothing a Republican could do but accept the party line.

Garfield, like Hayes, had been a Republican from the time of the party's beginning. Further back, he had been a Whig. It had seemed at the end of Grant's administration as though the Republicans' time might have run out. The victory in 1876 was not actually a popular one, and that in 1880 was close. Still the White House was captured.

If Garfield had been a Democrat, he would not have become President. Perhaps he knew that from his first venture into politics, for we cannot find any other reason why he was and remained a Republican. It seems to have been something he accepted and grew into. There was no conversion of the sort he experienced in religion. In his part of Ohio, Republicanism was orthodox and, although his nominations occasionally came hard, his Congressional elections—from 1862 to 1878—were easily won. Closest to being an exception was 1872, when Grantism was an issue and the Democrats gained spectacularly. But even in this year Garfield won his seat against two opponents by a plurality of several thousand. He was solid with his people.

He spanned the Civil War as a young state legislator and new Congressman; he became Majority Leader in the House, the representative there of the Hayes administration, and by the time of his Presidential nomination at forty-eight he had had eighteen years of legislative experience. He had acquiesced in the reconstruction policy, the cause of so much bitterness. He had been a sound-money man all through and had studied public finance to some effect, much as, in earlier days, he had become an expert in matters he was to debate. He was not so extreme a protectionist as his manufacturing supporters would have liked, but still he gave them little uneasiness. He was also party-minded and, although he said little about it, he regarded Hayes' civil service reform ideas as impractical. But he was upright, and when the breath of some of the prevalent scandals touched him it was lightly; his involvement was not serious. In the campaign of 1874 he was directly challenged and the threat was repulsed. The voters were not impressed by the allegations of his enemies.[4]

Apart from President Grant, the more spectacular contemporary Republicans were Blaine and Conkling, not to mention the other Stalwarts of the Congressional cabal who had harassed Lincoln, ruined Johnson, and opposed Hayes. They were arrogant and domineering. Especially, of course, they could not tolerate the least independence on the part of a President.

These years from 1876 to 1884 should not have been Republican. The people had many grievances, just as they had had in Jackson's time. Normally they would have raised up a leader—a Democrat, another Jackson—to redress their wrongs. But, as so often happens in a democracy, extraneous issues interfered. The Republicans benefited from the Civil War, and they went on benefiting for decades afterward. Their every effort went to fostering the notion that Democrats were unpatriotic, and there were millions of voters who disliked the current policies but would not accept the alternative of voting Democratic for this reason. The Liberal Republican movement, begun after Grant's incompetence began to be evident, was an alternative for some, but the third party it seemed about to offer was abortive. The

---

[4] This matter is explored in Chap. 15 of Garfield's *Life and Letters* by T. C. Smith (New Haven, 1925).

Liberal and Stalwart difference ran on for some time; but the split did not quite enable the Democrats to capture the Presidency.

It seemed certain that the party split and the attractive personality of Tilden would defeat the Republicans in 1876. Hayes was no stirring leader, and Tilden was. But this ended in a virtual theft of the office and in Hayes's seating. He proved to be a passive President, satisfactory to the business and financial interests. But when he offended the Congressional politicians by developing a conscience about the public service, they made his life miserable. He was undoubtedly glad that he had already committed himself to a single term. Garfield, proposing to follow him, had to satisfy the overbearing politicos that he would not be another reformer. He did so in most abject fashion, but he was well paid.

He was presented as a war hero. The Democrats, although they also had a General candidate (Hancock), were still pictured as the party of secession. With plenty of business money and with Garfield's long record of legislative caution in which nothing offensive could be turned up, the Republicans won easily. They would have won with a dummy in that year.

Garfield might accurately be described as a puppet. This would be to use the word as it might be used to describe the whole succession of Presidents from Hayes to Theodore Roosevelt. They represented the rising and burgeoning business interests of the country, they accepted the views of the financiers, and they were little more than ceremonial heads of the nation. Occasionally the Congressional politicians went too far and their encroachments on the Executive were repulsed; but succeeding administrations weakened the Presidency more and more and strengthened the Congressional power. There were one or two Presidential assertions that the separation of powers provided in the Constitution must be respected—as when Hayes refused to appoint Conkling's followers to Federal offices—but this was a long way from the position of the "strong" Presidents in our history.

When the deadlocked Republican convention of 1880 had to consider what compromise candidate would be best, Garfield was almost incredibly right for the choice. He was not only superficially attractive but, when he was examined more closely as a possibility, it seemed that he might have been trained for this moment throughout his life.

The politicians found that he conformed to the log-cabin preference attributed to the electorate; that he had gone to college but was far from being an intellectual; that he was capable of expounding orthodox views in what seemed like a diverting and even original manner; that he uniformly won his political contests the hard way—by campaigning strenuously; that he came from the pivotal state of Ohio; that he had served in the war and become a General; that his Republican services were many and worthy; that he was the right age (forty-eight); that he had no domestic troubles and no bad habits; that he was properly religious; and that he rated as one of the best exponents of Republican doctrine on the several issues of the time. It was overwhelming.

He and William McKinley, who was before long to succeed him— and also to suffer assassination in office—were perhaps the most perfect candidates the Republicans ever found. Hayes had far less popular appeal, and the crust of dignity he had been accumulating for some time almost removed him from the world of politics entirely by the time he became a candidate. Harrison was very difficult to picture as a suitable occupant of the White House in spite of his distinguished ancestry: he had no thoughts on any question that carried conviction, and he peculiarly lacked warmth and attractiveness. But McKinley again would be perfect, as Garfield had been, if in a somewhat different manner.

It seems unlikely, but it has to be recognized as true, that for so long a time in our history candidates could be found who would be attractive enough to be elected and yet who were profoundly unsuited to the responsibility; and ones, also, whose intention it was to make the Congress supreme and their own office subordinate. It will not do to state this too categorically. No one of them would have admitted that this was his intention. Grant, being the most naïve, came closest to saying it outright, and he was the most conforming because the most fearful of the aggressive and powerful legislators who had made him, watching suspiciously from Capitol Hill. It is a matter of more or less. A President can cease being a President just by keeping quiet and abandoning the continuous and wearing struggle he must always keep up with the Congress if he is to be what the Constitution clearly contemplates. And this Republican succession on the whole, each to a different degree and each in a different way, did just that.

This matter of principle makes even more interesting their dedication to politics and the determination of each to succeed. It might be thought that the minimizing of the Presidential office would diminish the enthusiasm of its potential occupants. This has never been so. Republican careerists have been every bit as concentrated on rising as have Democratic ones. And, among all of them, none was more fiery than Garfield. There seems to have been one period when he contemplated leaving politics for the practice of law. This was between 1872 and 1876. But this was when he was being attacked for such connections as he had had with the Crédit Mobilier scandals and when a viciously determined small group of enemies—without any apparent motivation—turned up in his home district and worked strenuously to discredit him. He was momentarily distressed and discouraged; but that he seriously considered giving up politics is doubtful. And if he did, Hayes's pleas for him to assume the majority leadership in the House changed his mind.[5]

At this time Garfield might have had the Senatorial nomination. This is supposed to have been one of his ambitions. Hayes thought he would be more useful in the House. It was intended that he would be Speaker, but the Democrats were in control throughout the administration and he was never more than Minority Leader. It is true that he had already been elected to the Senate when he was nominated for the Presidency; but he had not taken his seat. He was therefore one of the few Presidents who came to the office from a career as Congressman. Long service in Washington of any sort has always made the attainment of the Presidency difficult, and continuous service in the House has made it impossible—except for Garfield. Only two other Presidents had long House careers—Polk and McKinley—and both were later Governors of their states and better known for this service.

Garfield's career ran contrary to expectation in several ways. That he got to the Presidency anyway shows that errors are relative and can be overcome by other circumstances. Garfield ought not to have gone East to be educated; he ought not to have left the army to take his seat in the Congress in the middle of the war; he ought not to have passed up chances to run for the Governorship; he ought not to have run for the Senate; and he ought not to have offended both the powerful party chieftains—Conkling and Blaine. He was able to climb in spite of these mistakes because he was so amenable. He was essentially a weak man; and the tougher politicians around him always recognized this.[6] They found him useful. So, even for the Presidency, he was not chosen because he had any qualifications for the office beyond this. He was still to be useful. His fine figure and his speechmaking facility were to be a front for a return to power of the Stalwart Republicans after their frustration by Hayes. The assassin who killed him because he was anathema to Conkling was mistaken; he would have given the Stalwarts no real trouble. He would not have insisted that the Presidential prerogative was an exclusive one. Legislators would have been "consulted" on appointments in the Executive establishment; they might even have been happier with Garfield than they were with his successor, Arthur. That New York ally of the corruptionists would

---

[5] Smith, *op. cit.*, Chap. 22.

[6] Hayes, who was stiff and narrow but was much more of a man than Garfield, was one of those who recognized Garfield's weakness. He said of him at his maturity that he "was a smooth, ruddy, pleasant man; not very strong." This appraisal was confided to Hayes's *Diary* after attending the first caucus of the Ohio delegation to the 39th Congress in December 1865. Hayes had just taken his seat; Garfield was beginning his second term. Hayes had served out the war in the field; Garfield had resigned his commission and taken his seat.

turn out to have a tougher make-up than seemed possible in one with his past.

Garfield, like Grant, Hayes, Harrison, and McKinley, was nominated not because he was a leader himself, one who determined policy and devised ways of getting it adopted. He was chosen precisely because he did not do that. Like the others, he was a stooge for the real bosses. It is curious that all four of these Republican Presidents were remarkably similar in appearance, in record, and in character. They have differences. Garfield was the most attractive; McKinley had the most authentic stance as a statesman—he seemed intended for statue-making; Hayes was the most rigid moralist; Harrison had the safest family cachet. But these seem in retrospect superficial differences. They were much more alike than they were different, in the essential qualities needed by the party bosses. They were safe. They sold this virtue very cleverly in a rising market.

Chester Alan Arthur
1830–1886

Born at Fairfield, Vermont, son of a Baptist minister
Became twenty-first President in 1881 at 51

HISTORY

1848	Graduated from Union College.
1853–54	After teaching school and studying privately, began work in the firm of Culver & Parker, New York City, and was admitted to the bar.
1859	Married Ellen Lewis Herndon.
1860	As a lesser lieutenant in the Republican organization in New York City, helped elect Edwin D. Morgan Governor and was appointed to his ornamental military staff as Engineer in Chief.
1861	Appointed Assistant Quartermaster General of New York, later promoted to General, and took part in organizing new regiments and forwarding them to the South; resigned when Democratic Governor Seymour took office in 1863; returned to law practice.
1866	Helped to elect Roscoe Conkling to the United States Senate.

1867–68   Became a member of City Executive Committee of the 18th Assembly District and Chairman of the Central Grant Club of New York.

1871   Helped Conkling win control of state convention from Greeley and Weed forces. When Thomas Murphy was forced to resign as Collector of the Port of New York, Arthur took his place as a Conkling-Grant man.

1878   Suspended, along with two colleagues, from the Collectorship after investigation by Hayes.

1879   Dismissed after making a careful defense.

1880   Nominated for the Vice-Presidency (with Garfield) as a convention move to conciliate Conkling.

1881   Succeeded Garfield in September after the President's assassination and served out the term.

1886   Died in New York.

GEORGE F. HOWE, writing about President Arthur,[1] realized when he finished that his book was more an account of an era than a biography, and he added the subtitle "A Quarter Century of Machine Politics." He felt that he had been dealing with an organization—a political organization—in which Arthur, as an individual, was hardly distinguishable. It was a New York machine, but New York was a big city; it loomed large in the calculations of national leaders, and it was, of course, Democratic; Tammany saw to that. But it seldom controlled the state legislature. That body, because of upstate weighting, maintained a Republican majority and, in those days, it elected United States Senators. This, in turn, made it possible for those Senators to fill the Federal jobs in the city as well as in the state. They never won a city election; but they were in a position to bargain sturdily with the Democrats and there was a kind of compact respected by both.

The boss of this organization for a whole generation was Senator Roscoe Conkling. He was a man who is described for us as one who spoke with authority in the Senate and ruled his machine as a dictator but who was nevertheless self-serving, ungrateful, and hated by his associates. How he kept the loyalty of so many men of genuine ability is still a matter of wonder. He came finally to the humiliation he had long asked for; but it was long delayed and meanwhile he enjoyed the perquisites of a vast influence.

Such a leader as Conkling must have lieutenants. They must be in touch with henchmen, keep a live roll of those who are deserving and those who are doubtful, maintain a trading position with the other party's representatives, and, generally, carry out the laborious tasks of organization. The chief of Conkling's lieutenants was Chester A. Arthur, a lawyer and ward worker who had risen by sheer ability to a position of usefulness. When he had reached first rank Conkling placed him in the Collectorship of Customs for the Port of New York. This was the largest patronage pool in the country, and Arthur managed it in the interest of the machine with an efficiency worthy of a better cause.

Long before he arrived at this political eminence, however, Arthur's talents had been recognized. His father had been a Baptist minister who moved from one small community to another in upstate New York, a pastorate that ended in Albany in 1863. Before that it had included Schenectady, and this was where Chester had gone first to the Lyceum Academy and then to Union College. He entered Union at fifteen in 1845 and graduated in 1848, having pursued the traditional classical course. He was obliged to earn most of his living in any way

---

[1] New York, 1934.

he could, mostly by odd jobs. He was a good student, evidently, because at graduation he was elected to Phi Beta Kappa. About his college activities one negative fact and one positive one are of some importance. In spite of the attention given to debating at that time, he was not a debater. He did become a member of one of the early national fraternities—Psi Upsilon.[2] His not being a debater indicated an unusual preparation for a political career; but it followed from his temperament and talents. He was always diffident about public speaking and avoided it whenever he could and, when he did speak, made a poor job of it. But he was a member of many organizations and was always within the inner circle. This was his lifelong role in politics. Others were assigned to exhortation and debate. He seldom was noticed; but he manipulated the machinery. He did it smoothly and effectively, making many friends and few enemies. He became, in the end, indispensable. It was his situation as the second man—not the first—in the New York organization that brought him the nomination for the Vice-Presidency in 1880 and the succession to the Presidency when Garfield died of an assassin's attack.

Nothing is known of why he chose law as a career when he graduated from college; but there seems to have been no doubt or hesitation about it. He spent a few months in a local law school at Ballston Spa, then began to teach school for a living, meanwhile continuing to study. It was not until 1853 that he considered himself well enough prepared to make an actual start. In that year he was taken into the office of his father's friend, Erastus D. Culver, in New York City. In May of 1854 his employer, after the manner of that time, certified that he had studied for more than a year and was of good moral character. He was thereupon admitted to the bar and made a partner.

In 1855, with Henry D. Gardiner, he established a new partnership with offices on Nassau Street. At the same time he moved in from Williamsburg, where he had been living, and took rooms at the Bancroft House in Manhattan's mid-section, at once becoming a working member of the Young Republican political organization.

Why was he a Republican and not a Democrat? Because, it seems, he had from the first been "of a Whiggish cast"—that is to say, a conservative and a Clay supporter. But he was also, as his father had been, a strong anti-slavery man. It was not until 1856, actually, that New Yorkers had an opportunity to vote for Republican candidates. Arthur had had some part in the preliminary switching over from Whig to Republican, and that fall he worked for Frémont's election. He was,

---

[2] Union was the place of origin of the national college fraternity, followed closely in point of time by Williams and Amherst. By the time Arthur became a student, several had chapters on the campus.

characteristically, on the Executive Committee of the Eighteenth Ward Young Men's Frémont Vigilance Committee. At election time he was an inspector at the polls. He was well begun as an organization politician.

Nearly all of those who have reached the Presidency in somewhat unlikely ways seem, when their previous careers are examined, to have calculated their moves with that end in view. There stretches out in retrospect a series of events exactly suited to the purpose. They may not have had the Presidency in mind—some of them cannot have had it in mind—yet the preparation appears to have been deliberate. We have seen this sort of thing in the case of Tyler, of Polk, even of Lincoln. Arthur seems less likely as a contender than any of the others—and seemed unlikely to his contemporaries. In fact, there was a general feeling of shock when it was realized that he was to succeed Garfield. Men are said to have turned to each other and said, "Good God! Not Chet Arthur!" But they had also said, "Who the hell is Polk?" And he had been elected. Neither of these turned out so badly as their apprehensive contemporaries expected.

When Arthur was a young lawyer in New York before the Civil War, his worst embarrassment was the one many young lawyers have —he had to get business. He was not a spectacular performer in courtrooms. He was an office man. And he had no family connections in the city, nor a wide acquaintance. He set out to make friends. One way to do this was through hard political service; another was to join organizations and help in the tedious job of running them. As it turned out, one of these gave him exactly what he would need when the time came—some sort of relationship to the military. For nearly forty years after the war, no one but Cleveland would get to the White House without a military record. Even McKinley liked to be called Major, and his perennial opponent, Bryan, could claim a colonelcy. Until after Garfield it was necessary to have been a General to be endorsed by the most potent political force of that half century—the Grand Army of the Republic. Arthur became a General. He was not exactly a General of the line; he was, in fact, a Quartermaster General in New York. But he was familiarly called by the title as he operated his machine from the Collector's office during the seventies. It helped.

This fortunate circumstance came about in a natural way. As a young lawyer needing connections, he joined the militia. He became Judge Advocate General of the 2nd Brigade in New York. Then, when he had assisted in the election in 1860 of a Republican Governor, he was picked to take a decorative stance in elaborate uniform when the Governor made public appearances. His title was the curious one of Engineer in Chief. And that was his office when the war broke out. The purely honorary officer was now made Assistant Quartermaster

General. Soon he was performing most of the unexpectedly arduous duties of the office, and presently he succeeded his Chief. During the war, and particularly its early stages, troops were raised locally and the state was responsible for their training and forwarding. The opportunities for graft in such a situation were quite apparent to Arthur. Everything was done in a hurry and on a large scale. But under his control matters moved with exemplary speed and without the least suggestion of corruption.

The Republican Governor, Morgan, was succeeded by a Democratic one, Seymour, in 1863, and Arthur naturally resigned. But he was by now well known and much admired for the energy he had displayed and the honesty of his performance. When he returned to the practice of law he immediately became much sought after, and he was soon very prosperous. The poor boy from upstate, now a handsome man, moved in good society. He seems to have been considered something of an intellectual—his habit of wide and constant reading was often spoken of—and he was elected to that most exclusive of New York clubs, the Century Association.

But his new position in the city did not keep him from going on with his political work. He enjoyed shaping and controlling the organization and was now, naturally, a member of its innermost circle. When, after complicated factional struggles involving the aging boss Thurlow Weed, the editor Horace Greeley, and other rival leaders, Conkling was elected United States Senator in 1866, Arthur's part in it was recognized. He was now the leading member of the 18th Assembly District Executive Committee, and in 1868 was Chairman of the Central Grant Club of New York.

When Grant became President, Arthur's position was an inner one. He was one of the four or five most powerful party leaders in the state. When further factional fighting ended in the victory of the Conkling forces in the state convention of 1869, Arthur was credited with a large share of the devising. And when Thomas Murphy, a political hack, was advanced to a job completely beyond his competence and got into trouble as Collector of the Port, the Grant machine turned to Arthur. It was recalled how well he had conducted himself in the difficult circumstances of 1861. He proved to be exactly what it had been hoped he would be—an honest and competent administrator but also a thoroughly political one. He used the office as it had traditionally been used, as a reservoir of jobs for the politically faithful. He expected them to carry out their duties, but also he expected them to behave as faithful members of the party. As time went on, there was bound to be criticism. His subordinates often gave more service to the machine than to the Collector's office and he found trouble in disciplining them.

The Grant administration came under suspicion at first and then under violent criticism for corruption. But the General, supported by the G.A.R., was nevertheless re-elected, and Arthur was reappointed to a second term as Collector in 1875. By this time the state had gone Democratic again, and there was a strong reform movement even within the Republican party. In spite of this, Conkling determined to try for the Presidential nomination—with Arthur as his manager. He was disappointed. The reformers were strong enough to arrange the nomination of Rutherford B. Hayes to run against Tilden, the Democratic candidate.

In the end, when Hayes was seated in the White House, New York State had not contributed to the victory. It had gone for Tilden. This, and the strong promises of reform made by Hayes after the weaknesses of the Grant administration, led to trouble for Arthur as well as for his chief, Conkling. Hayes's Secretary of the Treasury, John Sherman, appointed a commission, headed by John Jay, to look into the operations of the Collector's office. The result, in the prevailing circumstances, was inevitable. In 1878 Arthur was suspended, along with two colleagues. The public may have thought this the result of a sincere intention on the part of Hayes to reform the civil service; but professional politicians regarded it as punishment for the Conkling machine and expected no considerable changes.

In spite of displeasure in Washington, Conkling was re-elected Senator in 1879 and was therefore gloweringly present in the United States Senate when the confirming of Arthur's successor came up. Arthur did not accept the condemnation of the reformers without resistance. He met the charges of the Jay group with detailed answers and he could show that there were some errors and misinterpretations. Still, it was incontestably true that his management had been first of all political and that, so long as he remained in office, the President's claim to be a reformer would be an empty one. For Hayes the discharge of Arthur was an act of necessity. It had to be done against the violent outcries of Conkling in the Senate; there was no other way.

The President won, but not until Conkling, in desperation, had made one of his most bitter, personal, and intemperate tirades. The successors to Arthur and his subordinates were confirmed and the Customhouse was lost to Conkling. Arthur, as New York City boss, was still powerful, however; and he set about showing the Washington administration that this was the fact. Alonzo Cornell, who had been removed with Arthur, was elected to the Governorship. Nevertheless, Conkling and Arthur were on the defensive and their only chance of staying in power was to work for changes in Washington. It was this that lay behind their determined drive to return Grant to the White House for a third term. If that could be done, the Hayes-Sherman attritions in

New York could be wiped out and the machine re-established in its old position.

The Republican alternatives were few in 1880; among them only Sherman showed strength. At the convention Conkling made the effort expected of him; Arthur controlled the New York delegation and Conkling made the nominating speech for Grant. It was, in an age of oratory, a notable production. But, as was so often the case with Conkling, it was more vituperative than eulogistic. It gained no adherents and possibly lost some. Another speech, very different in tone and effect, putting Sherman into nomination, was made by Garfield. Its moderation and persuasiveness, after Conkling's heated demagoguery, caused the delegates to recall that the speaker himself was available. When the deadlock between Grant and Sherman remained unbroken through twenty-eight ballots, the delegates turned to Garfield. Conkling was furious; another Midwestern President would ruin his machine, and every regular knew it.

There would not be much chance of a Garfield victory over General Hancock, the Democratic nominee, unless Conkling could be conciliated. While Conkling sulked, the other New York delegates behaved as politicians might be expected to—they resolved to get as much out of the situation as they could. When the Garfield managers offered them the choice of a Vice-Presidential candidate, therefore, they determined on Arthur, who, after Conkling, was their premier man.

Arthur, when he saw what was coming, recognized it as the big chance of his career. All the backbreaking work in the committees and conventions, all the long management of a political machine dependent on patronage controlled by himself, and, further, the humiliation visited on him by the Hayes-Sherman administration, now going out of power—all this could be converted into acceptance of his services, even the honorable post of Vice-President in Washington. He would accept.

Conkling, however, was angry at what he regarded as Arthur's defection. The meeting between the two, before Arthur gave his answer to the waiting delegates, is told about in a reporter's recollections. The two met in the press room, deserted except for the one reporter and Conkling, who, in rage, was pacing up and down the floor. Arthur met Conkling in the middle of the room:

> "I have been hunting everywhere for you, Senator," said Mr. Arthur.
> "Well, sir," replied Conkling . . . There was a moment of hesitation under the uncompromising attitude of the Senator. Finally, Mr. Arthur said:

"The Ohio men have offered me the Vice-Presidency."

The Senator's voice rang out in indignant tones: "Well, sir, you should drop it as you would a red-hot shoe from the forge."

There was a flash of resentment in the eyes of Arthur as he replied:

"I sought you to consult, not . . ."

Conkling broke in on him:

"What is there to consult about? This trickster of Mentor will be defeated before the country."

"There is something else to be said," remarked Arthur.

"What, sir, you're thinking of accepting?" fairly shouted Conkling.

Arthur hesitated a moment, and said slowly, but with emphasis:

"The office of Vice-President is a greater honor than I ever dreamed of attaining. A barren nomination would be a great honor. In a calmer moment, you will look at this differently."

"If you wish for my favor and my respect, you will contemptuously decline it."

Arthur looked Conkling straight in the eye, and said:

"Senator Conkling, I shall accept the nomination, and I shall carry with me the majority of the delegation."

The Senator looked at him for a brief moment, and then in a towering rage, turned and walked away. For another moment, Arthur looked after him regretfully.[3]

So Arthur made his decision. Conkling continued to sulk. Even when Garfield made an undignified journey to New York in an effort to stir his party loyalty, Conkling expressed his displeasure with the nominee by refusing even to meet with him.[4]

It was Arthur who held things together, and New York, as well as the country, finally went Republican. But it was close: in New York, 555,544 to 534,511; in the country, 4,454,416 for Garfield and Arthur to 4,444,952 for Hancock and English. Arthur characteristically did not campaign but worked through the organization. Garfield, being a compulsive speaker, made some twenty speeches at whistle stops between Buffalo and New York on the pilgrimage to Conkling, although he did not make campaign trips on the later model. This was something of a portent. The precedent would be followed by Bryan and would eventually place something of a premium on candidates with oratorical gifts.

Garfield was not only an impressive figure and a florid speaker, he had a kind of bearded dignity. There was considerable criticism of a

---

[3] Howe, *Arthur, op. cit.*, 109.

[4] He did finally make a speech in Warren, Ohio, and made a brief visit to Garfield at Mentor. But it was a late and reluctant performance.

ticket with Arthur on it, but the uneasiness was stilled by the comforting reflection that, being so vigorous, Garfield was certain to serve
out his term and a Vice-President could do no harm.[5]

The Republicans, however narrow the margin, did win. And then
Arthur's scene of operations moved to Washington. During the pre-
inaugural period there were complicated maneuvers. Garfield chose
James G. Blaine to be his Secretary of State, something calculated to
further infuriate Blaine's rival, Conkling. Conkling wanted Levi P.
Morton to be named Secretary of the Treasury, but Garfield did not
agree. And when Morton was offered only the Secretaryship of the
Navy, the Stalwarts were more than ever annoyed. Their machine was
going to pieces; and their situation was made even worse by losing the
Senatorship. This office in the end went to Platt, in spite of all Arthur's
efforts for an organization man named Crowley. These efforts were
considered to be most undignified in a Vice-President-elect. And when
the new administration actually began, Arthur's position was that of a
discredited politician shunted aside into an office of little consequence
who, moreover, had behaved in unseemly fashion in the attempt to
keep his organization in a position of influence.

After inauguration the situation was made worse by another quarrel
over the Collectorship. This resulted in the resignation of both Platt
and Conkling. They would, they said, appeal to the New York legislature for re-election and so a decision. Arthur again went to Albany
and did his best for Conkling; but this proved to be the Senator's death
struggle. The contest went on for weeks and was disastrous for the
machine. True, at the end of it Arthur was still Vice-President, but his
activities had discredited him still further.

When Garfield was seriously wounded there followed one of those
interludes so embarrassing when a President is incapacitated but when
there is no one to make it official and so no one to take his place.
When Arthur did finally take office on September 19, there had been
several months when the public business had been neglected and leadership was badly needed. He did supply it, but everyone was surprised
that he should.

Even if he had got there by an unusual series of maneuvers and was
not much respected when he came to office, he was President just the
same, with all the perquisites of his most reputable predecessors. And
that the route to the White House was not so important as the actual

---

[5] About this, a passage from *The Nation* of June 17, 1880, is often quoted:
". . . there is no place where his [Arthur's] powers of mischief will be so small
as in the Vice-Presidency, and it will remove him for a great part of the year
from his own field of activity. It is true General Garfield, if elected, may die
during his term of office, but this is too unlikely a contingency to be worth
making an extraordinary provision for."

arrival was soon demonstrated by his full use of the Presidential power for the good of the country.

If there is a lesson in Arthur's success, it is that one way to retain availability is to work faithfully for an organization with genuine weight in the national party. It was the wish of the New York delegates that Arthur should be the Conkling man named to the Vice-Presidential candidacy; and this was because he was their acknowledged leader. Even more than Conkling himself, he represented the machine. There was a large element of chance in the actual choice, but there nearly always is. If the nomination had gone to Sherman instead of to Garfield, Arthur's co-candidacy would have been unthinkable. And if, at any number of crises in his career, Arthur had followed a different course, he would not have been available. He had chosen to be, steadily and cheerfully, the one dependable organization man in the Conkling machine.

His nomination represents a kind of thing that was becoming usual in American politics—the compulsion in the two-party system for each party to stop quarreling and confront the other with closed ranks. Each has its contenders for power, each its various factions, each its differences about policy and patronage, and sometimes these conflicts become openly violent. But if a national campaign is to be won, they must be stifled. It was the unwillingness of Conkling to follow the rule of compromise that eventually lost him the leadership. Arthur behaved according to rule, and his professional correctness was recognized by his colleagues.

But Arthur was unable to maintain factional peace in New York even from the White House. He had hoped that his policy of moderation would draw most of the Republicans there to his support. This did not happen. In the Congressional elections of 1882, New York went overwhelmingly Democratic; and this made it very doubtful whether it could be recovered for the Republicans in 1884, especially since no leader was left, now that Arthur and Conkling were gone. When the convention of 1884 assembled, the President, it was realized, had only the second largest following. The first belonged to James G. Blaine of Maine. Blaine, of course, was nominated. Arthur would be dead in two years, but there was no sign of weakness yet. He should have been able to grasp the nomination for himself; it was perhaps because he did not try hard enough that he failed. At any rate, he became one of the few Presidents who would have liked to continue in office and was unable to achieve it.

Grover Cleveland
1837–1908

UNDERWOOD & UNDERWOOD

Born at Caldwell, New Jersey, son of a minister
Became twenty-second President in 1885 at 48

HISTORY

1855	After interrupted and inadequate schooling became an unpaid student-clerk in the office of a Buffalo law firm.
1859	Admitted to the bar.
1862	Elected Ward Supervisor, having worked in the local Democratic organization for some years.
1863	Became Assistant District Attorney of Erie County.
1871	Elected Sheriff of Erie County (until 1873).
1881	Elected Mayor of Buffalo.
1882	Elected Governor of New York State.
1884	Elected to the Presidency (Vice-President, Hendricks); opponent, Blaine with Logan.
1888	Renominated for the Presidency; defeated by B. Harrison.
1889	Returned to law practice, this time in New York City.

1892	Nominated for the Presidency, a third time, and elected (Vice-President, Stevenson); opponent, Harrison with Reid.
1907	Retired to Princeton, New Jersey. Elected a Trustee of Princeton University.
1908	Died at Princeton.

A PART FROM those Presidents who have come to office through the death of a predecessor, a few others have appeared so suddenly as to take everyone by surprise—except, perhaps, themselves. And of these Cleveland was the most surprising of all. In 1882 he was Mayor of Buffalo, in 1883 he became Governor of New York, and in 1884 he was elected to the Presidency. Two years from Mayor to President does seem almost miraculous. How did the electorate come to choose a man so little known?

It just happened that Buffalo was in urgent need of reform in 1882 and that the state was in similar need in 1883; also that the city and the state were in no worse situation than the nation in 1884. Twenty years of weak or incompetent Executives had disgusted the electorate with Republicanism. Cleveland had cleaned up the Sheriff's office in Erie County so thoroughly that his designation for Mayor was clearly indicated; he had also given both city and state the sort of going-over the nation clearly needed. The voters had no difficulty in seeing that this was so.

No Democrat had quite succeeded in becoming President since the Civil War; and Cleveland had the supposedly fatal handicap of not having been a soldier. But the war was now fading into the past, and a change was long overdue. Perhaps Cleveland could furnish the leadership the Republicans did not believe in. His handicaps were overlooked. One of the worst—besides his lack of military record—was that he was not a family man. Only Buchanan, among his predecessors, had been a bachelor. This was made worse by the revelation during the campaign that he was the father of an illegitimate child. But those who thought this fatal had something to learn about politics. He frankly acknowledged it and was elected just the same.

There did seem to be several good reasons why he would be a vulnerable candidate in the rough conflict of campaigns in the eighties. But like so many others, he helped to prove that traditional qualifications are not a reliable guide. They can be ignored if some overriding appeal can be made. The stronger one this time was that Cleveland was impeccably honest. So industrious and capable an Executive could be trusted to restore to the Presidency the respect it had lost in the postwar years. True, Hayes had been honest too, and Arthur had had an unexpectedly seemly presence; but the Grant corruptions had given the Republicans a bad name, and Blaine, their present candidate, would have to defend a very doubtful record.

Blaine, of the State of Maine, was in a way a good deal like Conkling of New York. Neither could be called a statesman, yet both had con-

272

siderable followings and commanded votes. They acquired and kept their influence by oratorical arts, by shrewd encouragement of local machines, and by belonging, in consequence, to the ruling inner circle of the party. Neither had an entirely defensible private life and neither was scrupulous about the public service as Cleveland was. It was their sort who made the Senate a club for politicians of their own grade. They supported each other except when they got into internecine quarrels, and ordinarily they kept a strong hold on the Presidency itself. Grant had been supine before this powerful and unscrupulous clique. He had felt that he owed them his office, and his one or two gestures of independence were feebly undertaken and soon abandoned. Of all this group, Blaine was the most powerful, rivaled only by Conkling, who had now disappeared.

As a candidate, Blaine was indeed a perfect foil for the Cleveland who had suppressed corruption in Buffalo and gone on to show New York State how a Governor behaved who regarded his office as a public trust. In an age of lax standards, when political offices were generally regarded as havens for incompetents or as sources of private enrichment, Cleveland was a conspicuous example of public virtue. Buffalo was not enormous, and its government was of no considerable interest generally; but it was known to be sunk in the same mire of corruption as most other cities. What the "rings" in these municipalities did not realize was that they had presumed too much, grown too careless. Their disposal of public contracts, their selling of favors, their protection of lawbreakers for regular fees had all become notorious. And everywhere there were developing small cores of citizens who were deeply offended at the subversion of government. This would issue presently in the muckraking literature of the turn of the century and in leagues of reformers.

These were already in process of formation. Such a group in Buffalo was determined on a thorough purge. What was going on there was typical, no better and no worse than the situation elsewhere. In time other cities would find champions too—Tom Johnson in Cleveland, Henry Hunt in Cincinnati, Brand Whitlock and Golden Rule Jones in Toledo, as well as others all the way from New York to San Francisco. In Buffalo it was to Grover Cleveland that the offended men of influence turned. It is interesting to see why they relied on this particular man—interesting because it was for the same reasons that reformers everywhere turned to him when he was offered as the Democratic candidate for the Presidency so short a time later.

Young Cleveland had been a familiar of the politicians. They had no secrets from him. And when his brief-writing habit required him to specify what the practices were that the politicians were so slyly concealing, he could make brutally plain that he knew what he was talking about. It took only a few such exposures to teach the Buffalo politicos that the Mayor could neither be fooled nor kept quiet.

They might have known what they were up against. Years before—beginning in 1871—when he had become Sheriff, he had shown in the official jungle of that office how an honest man could behave among crooks. But it had not been for long; and the lesson must have been unconvincing, because when he became Mayor every trick of the trade was tried. All of them were countered by massive exposures from which the spoilers retreated unreformed but beaten and frustrated.

How he dealt with his recalcitrant Council is explained in one biographer's account of this period:

> Each bill presented to him received his patient study, and not one veto was ever issued unadvisedly. His carefully written arguments were constructive . . . aiming at the creation of a system which would stop the abuses . . . Over and over again they contain fundamental discussions of public morality. He spoke not as a Mayor dealing with the comparatively insignificant interests of a small city, but as a statesman enunciating the great principles on which free government rests.[1]

And it was this reputation that spread rapidly throughout the country and stood in contrast to the corruption of the machines.

When he was approached by the Buffalo reformers and asked to accept the Democratic nomination for Mayor, he was becoming wealthy from a large corporate practice. Besides, he was of lethargic habit. He still had not entirely given up his old custom of spending evenings in favorite saloons, playing cards and drinking beer; and he had become very corpulent. He was beyond the adventures of politics, or so he thought. And he said to the petitioning committee that they had only to look at his desk and files to see what weighty trusts he had undertaken and how reluctant he would be to relinquish their guardianship. When pressed, he declined outright, and it took a stalled convention awaiting his answer to bring him around. Even then he made what would ordinarily have been an impossible condition—that the name of John C. Sheehan, as candidate for Comptroller, be removed from the ticket.

Sheehan was the undisputed boss of the convention, so this arbitrary demand might have been expected to end any consideration of Cleveland. But Sheehan was one of those devious politicians who sometimes

---

[1] *Grover Cleveland: The Man and Statesman* by Robert McElroy (New York, 1923), 32.

outsmart themselves. He felt that he had to give way to the reformers temporarily. If they had their way and Cleveland should be nominated, the result would be defeat at the election. This should re-establish the bipartisan ring in its old position.

Politicians were always inclined to underestimate Cleveland, partly because he resembled so little the popular figure of the demagogue and partly because they could not understand the wide appeal, especially at that time, of a reputation for sheer integrity. In none of his four trials did the professionals really expect him to win. And to an unusual extent his victories were due to the picture he himself managed to project without campaigning. It was so in the Mayoralty election. He had the largest majority ever given a candidate for the office. In his letter of acceptance—constituting most of his campaign—he used the phrase later most identified with his career. "Public officials," he said, "are the trustees of the people." And this was his sole appeal.

This phrase still identified him when he began to be talked about for the Governorship—this and some passages in his many veto messages emphasizing what such a public trustee felt compelled to do in practice. At first he had thought of himself as a sort of interim city official; he would set things right and go back to his law office. It was only when the Republicans of the state nominated Charles J. Folger for the Governorship that the urging of his respectable friends began to engage his interest. For, although Folger was himself a worthy figure, it was clear enough that he was intended to be no more than a front for hidden interests Cleveland had come to distrust.[2]

Cleveland had taken so little note of his own possible advancement that he had stayed for a prolonged time with his ailing mother in New Jersey during the summer before the election. When he did come back to Buffalo he was only very slowly persuaded that he must agree to run. He felt and said that if any public office could attract him it would be a judgeship, not a Governorship. Still, he did after a while become convinced, and late in the summer he took active charge. That was when "the hickory-grove conclave" began to meet in the large back-yard garden of one of Buffalo's most earnest reformers, George Urban. In that retreat, around the beer keg of German-American tradition, Cleveland's friends—and Cleveland himself—planned their pre-convention moves.

These moves were successful beyond their most optimistic expectations. The Tammany leader at the state convention was John

---

[2] The most notorious was Jay Gould, who always had favors to ask in Albany. But the Arthur machine was involved too; it was to build up Folger that he had been appointed Secretary of the Treasury before being offered for the Governorship. The intention was to renominate Arthur for a term of his own.

Kelly; the anti-Tammany organizer was Daniel Manning. There was a question about the seating of his delegates, and Kelly had to waste a good deal of effort on this. To succeed he had to—and did—convince both factions that he was on their side. The two candidates with the most votes were General Slocum, the aging Tilden's choice, and Roswell P. Flower, ex-Congressman and ex-Chairman of the State Executive Committee. Each claimed 158 votes out of a 384 total. This left 72 uncommitted. It was on these that the Cleveland people hoped to build.

In spite of the conviction of both the Slocum and Flower forces that they controlled the Tammany vote, neither could assemble a majority on the first two ballots. And on the third, the whole Tammany delegation unexpectedly voted for Cleveland. This started a landslide. Kelly left the convention thinking that he had named the candidate and that, in due course, he would be able to claim the customary reward in patronage and favors. But something had happened he did not know about. Cleveland had been in town on a late evening and had conferred with Manning. No one knows what was said or done on that occasion; but Manning was always afterward a devoted Cleveland man. The inference is that Manning must have been well satisfied. He must also have been made happy by Cleveland's acceptance letter. It was another declaration of principle—in favor of civil service reform and of honest elections.

Cleveland's majority in this state election of 1882 could not be accounted for on party grounds: 535,318 out of a total of 915,539 indicated that many Republicans had deserted to him. There were many, also, who must have stayed at home rather than vote for his opponent.

An account of his candidacies as Mayor and Governor is important because these established a pattern for his Presidential assaults—three of them. It is important also to note that, although his appeal was novel for his time, he did not neglect to cultivate any party leaders who were possible allies. Bosses are not moved by the same considerations that move voters; they have their own interests in view. They are sometimes quite content to lose an election. What they are tender about is the welfare of their organizations; and this can be as well served by defeat as by victory if the defeat brings into power a friendly enemy and success would bring into office an unfriendly reformer. This concern of the professionals is a weakness. Time after time in our history it has allowed outsiders, often sheer amateurs, to succeed in nominating a candidate and occasionally in electing one. They know, when the bosses will not or cannot see it, that the electorate will accept a change.

It was not long before Kelly discovered that the Governor he had helped to nominate and elect was not amenable to influence. His man in the State Senate, Thomas F. Grady, proceeded to apply pressure by opposing Cleveland's favorite legislative projects for reform. This, in turn, led later to Cleveland's opposing Grady's renomination. He did this in a letter to Kelly, and letters are hazardous in politics. Kelly, when the time was appropriate, made the letter public, saying that the Governor had attempted to interfere in the New York legislative election—as he had. But Cleveland was justified when Grady was defeated. Rules are sometimes best broken.

A good many other Democrats were also defeated. In fact, the whole state went Republican. This party loss might have been serious for Cleveland except that everyone was aware by now that he had the enmity of Tammany, a considerable advantage for a Presidential candidate.

It was apparent by 1883 that Cleveland was likely to get the Democratic nomination purely on his record. He had made no attempt until then to organize support; he had merely gone on working hard as usual, performing his duties. But these offered the same sort of opportunity that the Mayoralty had. His characteristic thoroughness and industry enabled him to veto many bills favoring special interests; and these veto messages began to constitute a commitment concerning public policy. In his message to the legislature in January 1884 he reviewed and summarized his previous statements. He also spoke of the accomplishments of his administration. The address was confined strictly to state affairs; but the whole country was listening. He spoke of civil service reform, of honest elections, of efforts to improve industrial relations, of the protection of forests and waterways, of efficiency in the care of public property, of regulating insurance companies, of new courts of claims. Then he went on to discuss the control of corporate practices in terms that must have shocked the big businessmen, who felt themselves immune to any sort of control.

It was in effect a platform for his candidacy. And it was enough. That he would probably be opposed by Blaine, the orotund Republican professional, made it all the more appealing. The resulting contest is known to historians as the Mugwump campaign—the derisory name referring to the Republican deserters. Such men as Carl Schurz and George William Curtis could not stand being on the side of a man whose personal life was certain to be exposed during the campaign and whose public conduct made it unlikely that he would become a worthy President. There was not only the Crédit Mobilier scandal in the background but also the Whiskey Ring, the Navy Department's corruption, the Post Office Star Route incidents, and many others.

This sort of thing ran back to Grant's tolerance. Blaine had risen to prominence in an era of plunder. He had, in fact, been one of the bosses responsible. He had been Arthur's Secretary of State and, if anyone did, he personified the whole postwar attitude that government was a source of profit.

By this time a gifted newspaperman had resolved Cleveland's many heavy approaches to the trusteeship theme into one of the most effective political slogans ever invented: "Public Office is a Public Trust." The shortening rather annoyed Cleveland, who accepted its use by his supporters but would never adopt it himself. His own style was dull, conventional, and discursive. He used long words and sentences wherever he felt they conveyed a little more than shorter ones would. But this too may have been good in the circumstances. His appeal was that of a weighty, almost indomitable, judge-like figure, not to be moved from his convictions and capable of subduing any opposition to what he believed right.

It was this phrase, endlessly repeated, that overcame his opposition. Tammany undercut him in every way possible in New York; but in the end he carried the state, thus coming to the Presidency a complete independent. And the Democrats had many troubles even worse than the defection of Tammany. They were still being forced to carry the responsibility for the rebellion of 1860. They were the party—in Republican speeches—of treason and even of slavery. The Grand Army of the Republic was practically a branch of the Republican party.

But Cleveland and the Democrats had some advantages and some of the luck. There was, for instance, the Burchard incident. This was the sort of thing that gives political managers sleepless nights. They are almost impossible to foresee or prevent because they are precipitated so naïvely and extemporaneously. This incident would not have been serious except for the size of the Irish Catholic vote in New York City. This was mostly controlled by Tammany, and since Tammany was betraying Cleveland and backing Blaine, it seemed doubtful that the Democrats would win the state. If they did not and New York's electors went to Blaine, he would almost certainly win. To make matters worse, Cleveland was the son of a Protestant minister, and Blaine, if not himself a Catholic, had a Catholic mother.

Blaine had been advised that the West was safely Republican; but being, nevertheless, a compulsive campaigner, he had made a strenuous trip through the Plains country. He arrived in New York tired, and rather absently received a delegation of clergymen who had refused to follow their Mugwump partisans into the Cleveland camp. Burchard, their spokesman, outdid himself in eloquent affirmations of party loyalty. He ended on the sentence: "We are Republicans, and don't propose to leave our party and identify ourselves with the party whose antecedents have been rum, Romanism, and rebellion."

This was much resented by the Irish, who were being urged to vote for Blaine. It swept through the city and is suspected of having influenced enough voters to make at least some difference in the New York result. This was very close indeed. Cleveland won by only 1,149 votes, a conclusion that was not certain for some ten days. And New York did determine the election.

He still had ahead of him two more Presidential contests, both close, both against a Midwestern Republican with the historic name of Harrison who was the last of the Civil War General candidates. He lost the first of these in spite of being an incumbent President—which is unusual; and he won the second in spite of being out of office and having been once defeated—which is unique.

The campaign of 1888 was rancorous with villification. This sort of thing had happened before; in fact, it was getting to be almost customary for the personal life of candidates to be talked about by opponents in scandalous terms. Usually these stories were manufactured for the purpose; only occasionally did they have some foundation in fact. But obviously it was believed by the professionals that they had some effect on the voters. This was expected to come mostly through the clergy. In Cleveland's first campaign Buffalo ministers had attacked him over and over as a grossly immoral and unfit person to become President.[3]

At this sort of thing an organization like Tammany was very efficient. Stories could be passed from one voter to another without ever being made definite or proof being needed. In this instance, unlike that in 1884, the whispering campaign seems to have had an effect. At any rate, Cleveland lost New York, a loss made more striking by the victory for the Governorship of the Democrat, David B. Hill. However, there were two other issues, besides Cleveland's character, that may have contributed. Just before the campaign—in his December 1887 message to the Congress—he upset his followers and pleased his opponents by devoting his entire argument to the tariff problem. This had long been recognized as politically dangerous. Democrats professed to be low-tariff believers; but they were much happier not to have the issue raised. Ever since the Civil War, import duties had been creeping higher and higher, and the number of influential interests favored by protective schedules had multiplied. A Treasury surplus made a tariff for revenue absurd. It was purely for the protection of their supporters that the Congress always found it inexpedient to make any downward changes.

---

[3] Cleveland ignored these attacks at the time, but the extent of his resentment could be understood when he refused, after his retirement, to make his home in Buffalo, where he felt he had been so unfairly treated.

It was characteristic of Cleveland that study convinced him of the deep corruption involved in this. It was not a matter he had known much about before he became President. He had not known much about any national problem; but about this complex subject he felt compelled to educate himself thoroughly. The more he considered, the more his conscience drove him to protest. The message was an effective brief. There was no logical answer, but that made matters worse for the politicians who were forced to take sides. Manufacturers who were protected shared their profits with legislators in one or another way, whether they were Democrats or Republicans. It was biting the hand that fed them to accept Cleveland's definition of the paramount issue for that campaign.

Still he was nominated. This was partly because he had no outstanding rival, but also because his conduct in office had been so admirable. To have repudiated him would have been to admit that integrity was unacceptable. There was not much enthusiasm, however, and Tammany, although Kelly was by now dead, was openly hostile.

Not only was there an attempt to persuade the voters of New York and New England that lowered tariffs would favor British manufacturers—something calculated to infuriate the Irish—but a similar controversy arose about American fishing in Canadian waters. Instead of dealing with this issue as a politician might, creating xenophobic furor, Cleveland met it by appointing a commission to draw up a treaty. This done, the Congress rejected the proposal and even refused to allow its supposedly objectionable features to be revised. Cleveland, in spite of efforts to meet Congressional objections, was labeled "the confessed ally of England."

Then, to make matters complete in this respect, the British Minister, fifteen days before the election, was trapped into making the sort of pronouncement that diplomats seldom allow themselves to make. In response to an inquiry as to his preference, he said in a letter that he appreciated the friendly disposition of the Democratic party toward Britain. This letter was the cause of excitement hard to explain in any other circumstances than those of a late-nineteenth-century American political contest. Even Cleveland's judgment seems to have been impaired. After getting no satisfactory action from the British government, he asked for the Minister's recall.

So it was an ugly and unhappy contest. It is more realistic to say that Cleveland lost than that Harrison won. Cleveland was made out to be "The Beast of Buffalo" who drank to excess, beat his wife, and generally behaved in ways no decent man could condone. This was the stranger because he was so circumspect as to be almost ponderous, so honest as to be almost self-righteous, and so gentle as almost to dissolve, sometimes, in sentiment. It must be noted, however, that although he got only 168 electoral votes and Harrison 233, his popular vote was almost 100,000 more than that of Harrison—another instance of the exaggeration characteristic of the electoral college.

That he had had that popular majority apparently encouraged Cleveland to feel that only an unfortunate distribution of votes had kept him from being re-elected and that the continuation to which he was entitled would come in the next contest. So, although he retreated to New York City and the elegant law office of Banks, Stetson, Tracy, & MacVeagh, he began almost at once to think about strategy for vindication.

On the few occasions when it became possible in very favorable circumstances, he delivered carefully considered addresses; and these became campaign documents. They defended the reforms he had always stood for, reiterated the ideal of faithfulness to the public interest, and were generally models of conservative but forthright expression. They were heavy still and must have been painful to listen to; but they were perfect representations of the man. The whole country learned to expect from him this sort of stolid reiteration of his position. The detractions of the past campaign were forgotten. It was ridiculous to go on saying that this model of uprightness could ever have been guilty of the excesses Tammany attributed to him.

The choice he had to make in the year before 1892 was not easy. His party was becoming convinced that the gold standard would have to be abandoned and that the coinage of silver would have to be accepted. This was part of the whole revolt of the West against the East, of the farmers against their creditors; and Wall Street was about to become the foil of rural orators. There was, in that year, a free-silver bill before the Senate. It seemed abhorrent to Cleveland, who was as reactionary in economic and financial matters as the most convinced Republican, and he refused to let expediency govern his action. He denounced the bill as a reckless attempt to favor one class over others. It would, he said, undermine the whole financial structure. The party politicians shuddered and agreed at once that this was the end of Cleveland as a candidate. Even Hill, Governor of New York, who was a hopeful alternative, gave in to the demand from the West, but Cleveland was unmoved. When asked to reconsider, he reiterated his position even more emphatically. He was loudly denounced by the silver advocates, who were, of course, encouraged by Tammany and the rest of his detractors.

The Tammanyites—and Governor Hill, more and more hopeful— prepared a coup at the beginning of 1892 calculated to eliminate Cleveland for good. The national convention had been set for June; but a call was sent out for a state convention to be held in February.

This famous "snap convention" had the bad luck, however, to be reported in the newspapers at the same time as an address by Cleveland at Ann Arbor.

For once the Clevelandites, although despairing about Tammany's control of New York and Cleveland's unpopular stand on free silver, staged an effective appearance. Instead of going quietly to Michigan, as had been his habit during the past few years, he was persuaded to permit a public show. A special train was engaged, every important Cleveland man along the route was invited on board, and the whole affair was planned to bring out the vast latent support Cleveland's friends were certain existed. It emerged in such volume that, beginning then, it began to be clear that nothing could stop his nomination. The public demanded it.

He was nominated on the first ballot, and his victory in the election was very satisfactory: the electoral vote 277, and the popular vote 5,556,543—more than he had received in either of his other contests. He had not campaigned, and he had not given pledges. The Tammany men asked for them, but what they got was a profane refusal. He stood as a symbol of righteousness. It was enough.

Speaking of the Presidency, Cleveland represents a transition from one period of administration to another. His predecessors, all the way back to Jackson, had a conception of the office and its responsibilities entirely different from his. For them it represented the climax of a political career; to have a majority of votes was quite enough to prove their right to the surpree office and, in fact, to justify acting as though they owned it. They were not less patriotic, less democratic, less interested in the national welfare, but office to them was a kind of payment for having popular views and for party regularity. They were not much concerned with administration—although the Grant scandals had immensely strengthened an incipient movement away from the pervasive spoils system toward civil service reform. It had become fashionable to advocate appointments for qualification and promotions for merit in the Executive establishment. But actual accomplishments were not likely to be extensive in spite of the small beginning represented by the Pendleton Bill of 1882. The Senate was scornful of such idealistic nonsense.

Cleveland, on the other hand, meant literally—he was always literal, even though he could be florid in his literalness—the phrase about public office being a trust. As Mayor, as Governor, and as President he saw that the government's business was carried out with fidelity and honesty. He was overinclined to do everything himself. He had no skill in delegation, an art any first-rate Executive must know. And so he sometimes failed in great things because he was involved in lesser ones.[4] But he stood, as President, in the most startling contrast to his immediate predecessors. He often rejected the advice or protests of his supporters and took positions he was warned would be unpopular. Some of them were accepted with despair by those around him, and some did actually cause the disaster about which he had been warned. This was the case when in 1887 he sent the Congress his message about lowering the tariffs. It lost him the election in 1888—it would seem, since the tariff was the main issue.

That he could gain the Presidency once might have been because unusual circumstances favored an outsider. Such things happen when events adjust themselves properly—when, for instance, a depression occurs or an unpopular war has to be brought to a close. But he gained at least a popular plurality three times—without joining in the excitements of the canvass, by simply stating his beliefs in such a fashion that there could be no doubt where he stood, and then by standing solidly on those statements. There was, of course, more than that. There was, above all, his acceptance of a trusteeship everyone knew would never, even in the most extreme circumstances, be betrayed.

No President since Washington had owed his accession to sheer character in this same way. He had invented—or, shall we say, he represented—a new way of achieving the Presidency. He was not the product of a machine; he was no one's appointed successor; he was not supported by any powerful interest; he made no emotional appeals by oratory or by making of promises; he was no military hero; he was not a man with physical attraction or one magically endowed with personality. He was simply a large, solid, honest public servant, a lawyer known to be able, a man of sense and judgment.

To recommend to an aspirant that he seek the Presidency in the Cleveland way would be to ask him to have a character and a history it would be too late for him to develop. Cleveland was a self-made man —in a way peculiarly his own. If anyone else attempted to read law in a Buffalo office, spend his leisure hours doing ward work and playing cards in the back rooms of saloons with the sort of men who customarily hang out in such places, he would gain a reputation, without doubt, just the reverse of Cleveland's. It was because he was known to have had these associations and not to have had his character eroded by them that he was judged to be so practical, as well as honest. He knew the score. No one could fool him. But he would not compromise, he would not be blackmailed, and he would not give or receive any favors.

---

[4] As when he let his Attorney General, Olney, involve him in the railroad strike in Chicago in 1894, during his second term, by which time he should have learned how to control subordinates.

In the end, even if from such different beginnings, it comes out as Washingtonian. It is no doubt the best way to become President. Having attained the office, the incumbent then has complete freedom. He can become as great a man as he is capable of becoming. But it is not a way open to one whom circumstances do not favor and whose struggles involve compromise and promises.

Benjamin Harrison
1833–1901

FROM THE COLLECTIONS OF THE LIBRARY OF CONGRESS

Born at North Bend, Ohio
Became twenty-third President in 1889 at 55

HISTORY

1853	Admitted to the bar in Cincinnati after graduating from Miami University and reading law.
1854	Moved to Indiana.
1860	State Supreme Court reporter.
1862	Appointed Second Lieutenant of Indiana Volunteers; made Captain, then Colonel.
1865	Breveted Brigadier General; honorably discharged.
1876	Unsuccessful candidate for the Governorship.
1879	Member of the Mississippi River Commission.
1881	Elected United States Senator.
1888	Elected to the Presidency (Vice-President, Morton); opponent, Cleveland with Thurman.
1892	Defeated for re-election by Cleveland.
1893	Returned to the practice of law in Indianapolis.
1901	Died in Indianapolis.

How DID IT HAPPEN that a Republican conservative from Indiana who was hopelessly dull and negative could displace so solid and successful a President as Cleveland? One suggestion already made is that Cleveland went a long way toward defeating himself and that Harrison happened to be the alternative. For it is never easy to displace an incumbent. In spite of several examples of the opposite sort—Adams, Van Buren, and Pierce—the momentum of office, resulting from earnest work of officeholders and party workers as well as the hold the President may have gained on the affection of the people, is a powerful help in re-election. He almost has to defeat himself in order not to have a second term.

But there was, from the beginning of Cleveland's campaign, something lacking. His conduct in office had been strict and high-minded, and this had not suited the insiders, who had felt that after twenty-four years of Republicanism they were entitled to many more of the spoils of victory than they got. So far as he could, Cleveland had repelled them. He had not succeeded in this as well as he would have liked. Most of the jobs that became available had gone to Democrats, but there had been some conspicuous rejections. Partisan claimants had naturally resented their lack of influence, and consequently there was a withholding of effort throughout the party organization. The alienation was not sufficient to deny him nomination, but it was enough to damp down the hard work in the local districts necessary to election.

Cleveland's rather plodding mind occupied itself best in negative acts. When floods of private bills favoring individuals came to him from the Congress he studied them patiently—and vetoed hundreds of them. Then, too, the Civil War veterans, now so used to governmental favors, were indignant. Any hope the Democrats had of being forgiven for having been "the party of treason" was lost by the President's veto of a bill that would have provided pensions for dependents even when disability had no relation to service during the war. The Grand Army went into the campaign of 1888 roaring for vengeance. They revived the story that Cleveland had bought a substitute instead of serving himself—he was a slacker and had all a slacker's vindictiveness toward braver men, they said. Harrison, in contrast, had been a hero. He would have the veterans' interests at heart.

It was undoubtedly Cleveland's tariff message, just before the campaign opened, that furnished the Republicans an issue of real importance. The anguish of the Democratic leaders was fearful. They had come to depend almost as much as the Republicans on the wealthy industrialists for their financing. They were never treated so generously, because they were never quite trusted to serve business faithfully, but still it was their one dependable source of revenue. And businessmen wanted high tariffs. So the campaign was not only conducted slackly by the bosses but was poorly supported by its usual backers. It developed into a Republican year.

The Indianan as a candidate had some advantages. There was the Harrison name—a great-grandfather who had been a signer of the Declaration, a grandfather who had been President, and a father who had been a Congressman. There was also the Indiana home—Indiana and New York being the recognized states of decision in that year. He had, as well, a most complete respectability—respectability that went so far as to become a colorless chill. Nevertheless, it was invulnerable to reprisals for the kind of attack the Republicans intended to make on Cleveland—the old story of the illegitimate child, new inventions about drunkenness, wife-beating, and unbecoming conduct in the White House. Harrison could be above all this—a symbol of impeccability.

Harrison had the services, too, of a remarkable newcomer to politics—Marcus Hanna, the businessman of whom more would be heard later—who "helped out" delegates to the Republican convention and "arranged for" votes in the election. The convention delegates did not in the end choose the man he preferred (Sherman of Ohio), but the money he commanded helped tremendously in the election. For the industrialists were genuinely frightened by the prospect of lowered tarriffs, and Hanna found it easy to "fry out the fat" they had accumulated in the Republican climate. This made a campaign fund of unprecedented size.

Cleveland, of course, had not advocated the repeal of all tariffs; but it suited the Republican purpose to say so. They "worked the free-trade racket" for all it was worth. Workers were frightened by predictions of unemployment and low wages; farmers were persuaded, somehow, that protection kept up their prices and increased their markets; and of course businessmen of all sorts were already convinced that the Democrats meant to ruin them.

What with the whispering campaign about Cleveland and the horror stories about free trade, as well as their success in convincing the Irish voters that the Democrats were favoring the British—the incident of the British Minister, Sackville-West, has been mentioned before—the Republicans staged so effective a contest that they won.

In Harrison they had a President who was perfect for their purposes. He had been a member of the party since its earliest days—had campaigned as a very young man for Frémont, their first candidate. He had been faithful and industrious in party work. He had a clear but fixed view of public questions, one that was orthodox among businessmen. There was no danger that he would depart from the faith.

His nomination had come about in a convention that was unusually confused. The moneyed men of the party found it difficult to give up their long concentration on James G. Blaine, beaten in 1884 by Cleveland, but not too badly. They preferred to think that, with the tariff as the main issue, they could win with him in 1888. But Blaine was by now discouraged and indifferent. At the time of the convention he was in Europe, traveling northward toward Scotland in luxurious style as the guest of Andrew Carnegie, the controlling member of the powerful Iron and Steel Association and one of the richest Americans. When Blaine arrived at Carnegie's castle, he cabled a renunciation. This may have been taken more seriously than he intended, although it was the last of several such messages; but at any rate most of the Blaine delegates at once switched to Harrison.

They might have preferred Senator Sherman, for it certainly could not be said that Harrison was a better Republican than Sherman; but Blaine's two sons were at the convention and they would not forgive Sherman his long opposition to their father. They and some of their friends thought of supporting McKinley, and they did give him a few votes in early ballots. But they soon saw that Harrison was a more likely favorite and turned to him. After having had only 80 votes on the first ballot, 31 less than Judge Gresham of his own state,[1] Harrison was nominated on the eighth. Between the first and the eighth there was one of those weekends of trading and maneuvering so common in uncertain conventions. The Sherman and Blaine delegates were stubborn; neither would give in to the other, and so the way was opened for the safe little man from Indiana with the historic name and the Brigadier General's record. No one had wanted him; but he would do.

So climaxed a career begun when, in 1857, Harrison had accepted election as City Attorney in Indianapolis, thus cutting himself off from a promising law practice for a salary of $400 a year. Why should he have taken a position of this sort, one that traditionally went to a political hack? His biographer, H. J. Sievers, is quite clear about this; it was

> precisely that which, a year later, would force him to choose between a candidacy for the legislature and the secretaryship of the State Republican Central Committee. There is no question that at this time of his life he aspired to political prominence . . .[2]

That this decision revealed the direction of his ambitions is shown by earlier exchanges between himself and his father when he was

---

[1] Who had been a member of Arthur's Cabinet. He later became a Mugwump and supported Cleveland in 1892.

[2] *Benjamin Harrison: Hoosier Warrior 1833–1865* (Chicago, 1952), 127.

twenty-three years old. He had the utmost respect for the elder man
who was a Congressman; yet he would not follow him into the Constitutional Union party as the divisions and realignments of 1856
occurred. He believed the new Republican party had a good chance
to dominate Indiana. He would grow with it, be part of it, be so
closely identified, in fact, that his name would be synonymous with
Republicanism. His father capitulated to his judgment and wrote, when
the son became City Attorney, that he "looked forward to a period
in the future when Benjamin would occupy a high position among
the political men of Indiana."

Having recognized reality, as far as his son was concerned if not
for himself, his father watched with paternal interest the further
development of the young man's career. He even offered some political advice:

> If I were in your place, I would content myself with a general endorse-
> ment of the doctrines of the Republican party, and would not be *too
> ardent* in my support of all these (so called *Republican Principles*) or
> you may find some of them are fallacious and will not stand the test
> of true patriotism . . . and therefore you will not long be popular with
> the American people . . .[3]

When, in the following year, Benjamin had to choose between running for the legislature and becoming Secretary of the State Committee, this warning had to be considered. It was finally disregarded,
but only after some hesitation.

Twenty-eight years later there were issues to be fought over which
were, naturally, entirely different, and Harrison had no need to be
cautious. But he might have difficulty in finding a winning line.
Slavery had been abolished; the Union was intact; but the Republicans
at last were finding it difficult to stand on their reputation for having
saved the nation and freed the slaves, ignoring completely all newer
problems. They tried, and were now to save the businessmen—and,
as well, the workers—they said, from the same party that had once
threatened the nation's very existence. This meant keeping government from doing much of anything.

Harrison, as a United States Senator from 1881 to 1887, had behaved
in seemly Republican fashion. Although he had lost his Senatorship
the year before, he was now being launched among the political men
of the nation—not, as his father had hoped, among those of Indiana
alone. Cleveland probably knew Harrison well, since any President
must deal with opposition Senators as well as those of his own party.
But if he did not, George Hoadly, a lawyer friend of his who had

---

[3] *Ibid.*, 131.

been intimately connected with both Benjamin and his father, described for the President what his opponent was like:

> . . . an honest gentleman of high private character, without any sense of humor at all, rather disposed to be narrow and bigoted than wide and open to new thought, but very sincere and true in all his relations, public and private.[4]

Harrison by now, being fifty-five, was thick as well as short—he was about five feet six—and wore the beard Grant had made fashionable. Behind that convenient facial covering there appeared to be little interest in whatever was going on. He resisted meeting people, could not remember names, and spoke in dry and reserved tones. When his record was reviewed it was recalled that he was no civil service reformer. As a Senator he had demanded numerous jobs for Indianans regardless of their qualifications. Blaine, who had been Secretary of State during his Senatorship, complained that Harrison had asked for thirteen more diplomatic appointments than there were on the whole Department list. But then Blaine was in a way a rival and notoriously careless with facts.

Neither candidate campaigned, but both received and spoke to delegations. If it had not been for the frantic activities of the press and political managers, it would have been one of the dullest canvasses in election annals. Neither Cleveland nor Harrison was capable of inspiring workers, and neither had anything thrilling to say. The tariff might frighten certain people, but it was at best a forbidding subject. When Harrison had accused Cleveland of wanting to undermine the protective system built up by the Republicans and Cleveland had pointed out the iniquities that hid behind the tariff schedules, about all that could be of any interest had been said. Yet all historians agree that the fanaticism exhibited on both sides was extreme. The Republicans were more outrageous because they had such enormous funds to spend; but the Democrats did their poverty-stricken best.

> The Republican journals, led by the *Tribune* in New York and the *Press* in Philadelphia, whose editors held the intelligence of their readers in so little esteem, daily scattered their stories about the "rebels" of the South and about England—about the high wages which were inseparable from a high tariff, about the poverty and starvation which would afflict the country at the mere mention of free trade. Men who had passed through colleges and were numbered among the higher intellectual classes of the people shouted in print and on the stump

---

[4] E. P. Oberholtzer, *op. cit.*, V, 35.

sentiments which they must have thought of with wonder after the
ardor of this year had cooled . . .[5]

In the midst of the frenzy, the two candidates repeated the sentiments to visitors that everyone knew them to hold; and neither recorded any recognition, any more than did their loud supporters, of
the disruptive forces working in the economy—the agrarian revolt
fomenting in the West, the anguished protest of long-suffering
workers, and, behind these phenomena, the upheaval caused by the
economic and social changes of an agrarian nation transforming itself
into an industrial one.

Those who looked at Harrison's history had to conclude that he
had not changed his conception of society since his war service more
than twenty years before. His participation in that struggle had exhausted all the adventure in his system. He had returned from the
field to resume the practice of law and the political hack work he had
begun before it had interrupted his career. When Lincoln's call for
volunteers in 1862 had failed to stir even the Midwest, which until
then had been most responsive to such calls, Governor Morton, la-
menting it, had at once accepted Harrison's offer to raise a regiment.
To Harrison's embarrassment, after having organized it as a Lieutenant
he was made its Colonel by the harassed Governor. But his ability
to master the most intricate subjects, in bouts of concentrated study,
enabled the youthful officer to become a respectable tactician; and
his reserved and chilly manner—perhaps enhanced by a new beard—
established the discipline so hard to enforce in the Midwestern regi-
ments. Like Hayes and Garfield, he had become a Brevet Brigadier
General in due time and had performed creditably in the field. Many
others had not. Only those who combined the ability to concentrate with
a respect for authority had succeeded; but for those, especially those
with political ambitions, such a record of success was a precious asset
for the rest of their lives. They became the darlings of the Grand
Army.

His services to the party and to the veterans carried him to the
Senate in proper sequence. It was the same faithfulness that caused
the politicians of Indiana, when the test came, to favor him over
Judge Gresham, a worthy man and much more attractive, but not
one who had a famous name, a brilliant war record, and a history of
complete trustworthiness.

It is not possible to say of Harrison at exactly what time he saw
himself as a potential President and began to shape his course accordingly. This involves discovering when a general aim to claw a way
upward becomes a specific ambition for the summit—quite a difficult

---

[5] *Ibid.*, 50.

matter. But there is this: he must have been aware for a long time that he was so situated as to be among the very small number of those most eligible. Indiana was a likely state to produce a postwar candidate. The political Brigadiers were a prime source of material— and there were not so many of these remaining after Hayes and Garfield had had their turn. Also, having become a Senator, he was one of a select club, none of whom considered himself excluded from the list of Presidential hopefuls and none of whom believed that there could be better candidates.

Harrison, therefore, must have been conscious of his eligibility at least ten years before the convention of 1888; and during that time every move he made must have been fully considered for its effect on his ambition.

It remains to be said that the country was not happy either with Republicanism or with Harrison as President, and when it came to another test in 1892, Cleveland, not taking any extraordinary pains, defeated the man who had beaten him in 1888. Curiously enough, Harrison, in comparison with Cleveland, had to defend the charge that he was a spender. This was because of his weakness for favoring the veterans. There were scandals in the pension office too. And now the Republicans had to defend themselves on the very issues they had advocated in 1888—the tariff, for instance. Wages, prices, and employment were not what the Republicans had claimed they would be under the protective system. And the bloody Homestead strike had embittered the workers. This, moreover, was not an isolated incident. In Idaho at the Coeur d'Alene mines, in Tennessee iron mills, and on New York railroads there were disturbances involving such violence that troops had to be used to suppress them.

Perhaps a student at this distance may be allowed an interpretation of the facts and events of the Harrison career that seems to explain, even if it makes some assumptions, the rise to the Presidency of an individual fitted out with so few political characteristics.

The strain in Harrison of ancestral pride should be emphasized. By Benjamin's generation, this had become very strong. It had been repugnant for the descendant of such distinguished forebears to be dependent on the good will of the Indianapolis merchants and the courthouse hangers-on for the start of his law practice. It had galled him to ask for support when he ran for offices below the dignity and capabilities of a Miami University graduate who also came from an aristocratic family.

There were explanations, not hard to find, for the development of the inconsistent behavior—the split personality—which all Harrison's biographers speak of.[6]

---

[6] William Allen White's essay on Harrison in *Masks in a Pageant* (New York, 1928) comes closest to a sympathetic interpretation.

When he attained the Presidency and felt able to behave more as he pleased than as others expected him to, he became an aloof and uncommunicative representative of the upper class, the elite he belonged to by birth. There had been signs of this all along, but they had been confused by his determined conformance to the customs and habits of Indiana in the seventies and eighties. He was, however, utterly unable to become an alert and ingratiating politician, and this was what was looked for in a leader. Blaine, for instance, the idol of a generation of Republicans, was the very model of the political man; there had been, in 1884, almost enough votes to elect him. Except for the accident of the Burchard incident—the "rum, Romanism, and rebellion" statement—he might have defeated Cleveland. Yet, although that marvelous mover of men, Robert Ingersoll, spoke of him as a "plumed knight," Blaine represented all too fairly the strain of deliquescence in the political life of his time. Perhaps the voters had just had enough of his sort.

Republicans on many occasions have had to make choices that were repugnant to them. The party bosses at such times cannot choose the candidate they prefer because they know he cannot win. So they hesitated over Blaine three times and nominated him only once in a rush of enthusiastic irresponsibility. The insiders in 1888 had to think of a campaign against Cleveland, whose monumental integrity contrasted so vividly with the Blaines and Conklings and Grants of their own party—men who were so close to the big businessmen that for a long time their affiliation had been commonly known. Their oratory was ready and florid; they could elicit cheers from party rallies; but they could not win. None of those the politicians preferred—Blaine, Sherman, or Chauncey M. Depew—would serve to counter the Cleveland image. There were also others who appeared in the early votes, among them William McKinley. He might have had a better chance, but he refused; anyway, they were not yet sure of him.

In a way Harrison presents himself to us now as a man who led a tragic life. He was always forced to associate with characters he despised but who must be conciliated. He was compelled to behave in ways he could not defend to himself—except that they would lead him to places of power. Along the way somewhere he must have discovered how permanent a prisoner he was of this compulsion to succeed. A Harrison must be an important figure—a judge, a Senator, even a President—so he must do the things necessary to each next step along the way. But was there never a time when he might be excused from the humiliations of politics?

When he finally reached the Presidency he felt that at last he had emerged into a situation where he could act as a Harrison should. But there was a penalty even for this, and in the spring of 1891 he discovered what it was. The professionals were so enraged by his independence and hoity-toity airs that, although they dared not deny him renomination, they slacked in the campaign and succumbed to Cleveland and a revivified Democracy. Harrison had been President somewhat longer than his grandfather; but this was not so important as that he had vindicated the family honor. Through degradation and unhappy experiences he had come through to the very top. His last days in Indianapolis, when he was the respected citizen, the elder statesman living in dignity and retirement, were certainly the happiest ones of his life.

It may be guessed that he would have said, being honest, that if what he had had to suffer—the indignities, the associations with men he despised, the compromises with politicians—was the only way to the Presidency, the office was not worth what it cost a gentleman— at least not for one term.

William McKinley
1843–1901

Born in Niles, Ohio
Became twenty-fourth President in 1897 at 54

HISTORY

1861	After attending public school and Allegheny College, and teaching school in Poland, Ohio, enlisted as a volunteer in the Union Army.
1862–64	Promoted to Sergeant; commissioned Second Lieutenant and soon rose to be Captain.
1865	Breveted Major of Volunteers.
1865–66	Read law.
1867	Admitted to the bar and began practice in Canton County.
1869	Prosecuting Attorney, Stark County.
1876	Elected to the House of Representatives, where he would serve until 1891 with an interruption of one term.
1888	Received two votes in Republican convention for the Presidential nomination.
1890	Defeated for the House of Representatives.

1891	Elected Governor of Ohio.
1892	Received 182 Republican-convention votes for the nomination.
1896	Nominated and elected to the Presidency (Vice-President, Hobart); opponent, Bryan with Stevenson.
1900	Re-elected to the Presidency (Vice-President, T. Roosevelt); opponent, Bryan with Stevenson.
1901	Assassinated in Buffalo.

W E COME NOW to a true professional who earned the Presidency in the most orthodox way—if there can be said to be one—stretching the pure political method to its limits. It cannot be denied that his opponents assisted in his final victory, but he had carefully put himself in the way of benefiting from mistakes and divisions of this sort. It would hardly be just to withhold credit because of this assistance. He is one of a very small number of inner professionals who were risked in a campaign and who won.

In two Republican conventions before the one that nominated him, he had had some votes. This shows where he stood in the party, although he had refused to let supporters proceed. In 1888 this had been because of his loyalty to Senator Sherman, for whom he had been working; in 1892 it was because he had felt that a President was normally entitled to renomination. In this he may have been influenced by the private conviction that 1892 was not a Republican year. But four years later circumstances were different: he came to the convention an admitted contender for the nomination; he won it on the first ballot and was elected with a good margin.

No Presidential candidate has seemed to a large majority a more satisfactory embodiment of the Presidential image. He commanded widespread affection as well as support. This was evident from the beginning of the campaign and continued to be true after his election. He looked the part; he talked, too, as it was felt he should, in carefully considered phrases calculated not to disturb but to reassure. He was always calm and unsurprising.

It can be seen at a distance how hollow a figure he was, how unfitted for the great office he assumed; but it could not be seen in 1896, and not by many during the whole of his Presidency. He was handsome, portly, and sleek. He wore a frock coat and a spotless white vest and seemed never to lose the carefully stuffed look. If, in fact, he had an inner uncertainty because of ignorance concerning public issues, he did have a remarkable talent for ingratiation which saved him from exposure.

It was never any purpose of his to discover the nation's needs or to persuade the electorate of the policies it ought to follow. He had become, as he matured, one of the ruling group in the party, but not a forceful one. It had been his habit to find out which way opinion was turning and join the movement before it was too late. He had an acute sense of what was popular. When a few times he avoided guidance by the stronger characters around him, it was because he was certain they were mistaken about public opinion. His feeling for the popular pulse was his most trusted guide.

It was so even after he became President. When, for instance, he resisted agitation for war against Spain, he soon gave in to the whipped-up furor of the Hearst and Pulitzer newspapers and to the xenophobes in the Congress; and he would not listen to the conservative Republicans, who knew war to be unnecessary and feared that it would result in uncontrollable disturbances. Historians deplore McKinley's weakening, but it was enthusiastically supported at the time. He had followed the course he instinctively knew to be popular.

From his early days he was an arranger, a compromiser, especially in those matters Americans were so divided about just then—the tariff and the money question. If his Republican colleagues could convince the public that hard money and protectionism were desirable, he was willing to be an advocate too—a moderate one. These were the core tenets of Republicanism and he was inclined to feel this way and to give in as he must. If he had no strong convictions of his own, he suspected that a majority did not support the extreme position of businessmen.

He was incautious once about protection. It was when he was a Congressman and Chairman of the Ways and Means Committee. He sponsored a high-tariff bill that he thought would make him famous, but hard times in succeeding years were widely attributed to it and he could have done without the kind of fame it brought him. The McKinley Tariff was something Republicans had to defend against sardonic Democrats in 1892. But by 1896, when the country, with the Democrats in office, seemed to have come apart in panic and could not be put together again, the Republicans were in a position to blame the Democrats. There was unemployment, low farm prices, and consequent protest. The last Cleveland years were uneasy ones for the whole country. But McKinley could contend that the tariff was not to blame. The Democrats had not lowered it much, but it could be made to appear that they had.

This weakness was one Bryan acknowledged by trying to ignore it in 1896. But the Republicans made much of it, and whenever the issue was mentioned, there stood McKinley. Protection was now the road back to prosperity.

As it turned out, this was a good thing, because on the currency issue McKinley's position was much less clear. Ohio, his home base, was neither wholly rural nor wholly urban and, trying to follow majority opinion, he had several times made statements favorable to cheap money. He hoped he could satisfy the desire of the rural debtors to find a way of paying debts incurred during the postwar expansion. Gold had grown scarce. Its production expanded less rapidly than that of other goods, and as its value rose the values of other things declined correspondingly. A man who was owed money could buy a good deal more wheat or cotton with it when the debt was paid than he could have done when he had lent it. Commodity prices fell and thousands of debtors were enraged. National politics tended to become a line-up of debtors against creditors. This meant West and South against East—because East was where the moneylenders were.

The agrarian drive of the nineties failed; but it frightened the financiers mightily. This fright gave McKinley's angel—Mark Hanna —his opportunity. He seized it with vigor, amassing such unprecedented campaign funds, and using them with such efficiency, that he eventually saw his chosen candidate seated in the White House. McKinley actually won with nearly a million majority over William Jennings Bryan, the thirty-six-year-old hero of the Western Democrats. But there never had been such demoralization among the conservatives. It amounted to panic. And the relief at McKinley's victory, expressed by a one-sided press, was so glowing that a foreign observer would have thought the nation barely rescued from complete ruin. Actually no candidate with Populist support would ever win; but a decade or two later it could be seen that many of the policies they had fought for had made their way into legislation sponsored sometimes by one and sometimes by the other of the dominant parties.

When the incidents of McKinley's career are enumerated—especially those having to do with the successive offices he held—his rise in the party hierarchy, his selection as Presidential candidate, and then his election are seen as a steady progression. It is no more certain with him than with others at precisely what time he saw himself as a potential President and began to direct all his activities to that end. It is even harder with McKinley than with some others because he was always so pliant a worker in the party ranks. This was perhaps because he recognized his own weakness of mind. He must select those he would accept as his mentors and follow their lead. He perceived that if he did this and used his talent for ingratiation he would be safe. In time he would be trusted by stronger principals, and this might carry a young politician from Ohio very far—as it had done with Hayes and Garfield.

He might not have had a trustworthy intelligence, but he did have certain advantages—the same ones that Hayes and Garfield had had. He was handsome. He was a dignified, even an impressive, figure; he had never been tempted to irregularities of a moral sort; and he had a war record to be proud of.

What it was that attracted Mark Hanna to McKinley is not at once apparent. Their acquaintance had begun as far back as 1876, when McKinley had appeared as attorney for a miners' union in a suit against one of Hanna's companies; but their co-operation began only in 1888, when both were enlisted in the effort to win the Republican nomination for Senator John Sherman. Their defeat in this purpose gave them a common interest. The initiative even then, however, was almost wholly Hanna's. It was so vigorous that in 1892, at the succeeding convention—of which McKinley (then Governor of Ohio) was the permanent chairman—Hanna offered to support him instead of Harrison. The attempt might have succeeded. Harrison was not a popular President, and by now Hanna was a power in the party, turning more and more to politics and away from his business interests in Cleveland. He had, in fact, become dominant among the professionals. But McKinley was too regular. He would not make the effort.

Hanna's fondness was a curiously one-sided affair. He gave everything and got very little in return—not even intimacy. It cannot be said, actually, that McKinley was Hanna's friend at all. Perhaps he might have been if there had ever been a real McKinley; but there was none; and friendship presupposes contacts between men who trust and like one another and between whom there are no serious reservations.

Almost at once, when young McKinley returned from the Civil War, he became a public figure. He seems to have recognized early the need to conduct himself always as though he were being watched by a critical audience. He carefully composed his features, his words, and his actions, and never allowed himself to be caught unaware. It can be guessed now that this was protective. But it did in time become for the people of northeastern Ohio a reliable stereotype. He never exhibited other than proper emotions—such, for instance, as his long and often expressed sorrow that his war comrades were so neglected. The Grand Army came to view him as a trusted advocate. Harrison had been a disappointment to them in spite of his Brigadier status and his earnest efforts. McKinley they supported with the enthusiasm the prospect of increased benefits invariably engenders. But other ordinary folk approved him too. They trusted his composed imperturbability.

Hanna was rough and practical; anyone talking to him for five minutes could be certain that he knew Hanna's intentions. Indeed, he never made any secret of what he proposed and how he meant to effect it. Yet he was much misunderstood in his lifetime, partly because of Democratic distortions, deliberately created. He was pictured in cartoons as a moneybags, a ferocious figure whose formal clothes were plastered with dollar signs. It was true that he was the principal "fat-fryer" for the Republicans and that he amassed unheard-of funds to be spent in doubtful if not actually illegal ways. But he made no secret of anything he did, and it was generally acknowledged that he got results commensurate with his resources. He ran his campaigns— he had managed McKinley's campaign for the Governorship and he was made Chairman of the National Committee immediately after McKinley was nominated for the Presidency—with an efficiency hitherto unknown. He applied the talents with which he had succeeded in the tough competitive business world of the seventies and eighties. He had become a man of wealth and influence in Cleveland. The city now served as a base for larger operations.

He adored McKinley and was as tender with him as if he were a child. He served him faithfully until the President's last hour. He was in the room when the President died some days after being wounded by an assassin in 1901. It is perhaps not necessary to conclude, as historians sometimes have, that because of these services McKinley was Hanna's puppet. There were others who had some say about party policies, but most of their views did come to McKinley through Hanna. This was less true after the Presidency had been won, and it became less true year by year. But while the image was being created, Hanna was enormously helpful. He understood how to make the best public presentation and he arranged the background, the stage setting, for the actor. It was a consistent performance, not only on McKinley's part, but on Hanna's. The front-porch technique they evolved was exactly suited to the pleasantly bland statesman-figure.

These arrangements were costly. Even in the nineties private trains and the appropriate entourages came high, in spite of the deep interest of railroad managers and other businessmen in McKinley's success. And in 1895, when Hanna had made up his mind to go all out for the next year's nomination and his business affairs had been given over to his brother, he had no hesitation in borrowing large sums for the winter program he had in mind. There were two hundred Southern delegates who could be "bought" in one way or another. None of them had any hope of being on the winning side in their states, and none would be of any use in the election, but each would have a certain importance at the nominating convention—as delegates or as members of state committees and so on.

Hanna arranged a luxurious safari to an estate he had rented and staffed in Georgia. There the politicians were received by McKinley and made to feel important; then they were taken aside by Hanna for a practical talk. McKinley was going to be nominated, he told them; it would be well if they could claim to have had some part in the process. What did they want in return? They wanted patronage, favors, contributions to their organizations, an assurance of continuing place in party councils. Hanna could make credible promises and he had funds. In the course of this interlude he tied up nearly all the two hundred delegates, so that when the other bosses, such as had not yet admitted Hanna's right to dictate, got around to looking for specific support among the Southern crowd, it was too late. Joseph

Foraker from southern Ohio, an old-time rival of Hanna's, who had beaten him a time or two in earlier days; Thomas B. Reed of Maine, the mighty Speaker of the House and a very possible rival for the nomination; Matt Quay of Pennsylvania, who ran his state as a baron would run his fief; Tom Platt of New York, who was at the height of his power; and others—such as Levi P. Morton of New York and Senator Allison of Iowa—recognized that they were beaten before the contest had really started. McKinley was nominated almost without a contest.

Then when Hanna had become National Chairman he was in a position to do what, as an experienced business administrator, he had all along been intending. He reduced the regional bosses to subordinate positions. The party, for his time, ceased to be a federation of jealous rivals, each contending for the good of a local organization. It became for the first time a truly national organization. The bosses were recognized, but they were not allowed disruptive powers. Blackmail of the candidate for future jobs and for contributions was no longer in order. For one thing, Hanna had the money and it was he who distributed campaign funds. It was he who organized the relationships between the governing interests of the business world and the party so that there was no doubt where anyone stood. Business supported the party, and the party served business. This was what Hanna believed in.

The candidate himself had no part in these arrangements. He was shielded from the doubtful details, and when Hanna spoke of them to him he was careful to do it in such a way that they appeared to be merely the recognition of reciprocal interests, voluntary and friendly. At times McKinley even warned Hanna that if he became President it must be without any commitments having been made. Hanna agreed. His deals were merely part of recognized political methodology. He could not conceive that McKinley would stop being a politician when he became President, and of course he did not.

By the time the climax of his career had been reached, McKinley's debt to Hanna was larger than could ever be paid. He must often have recalled the one time—although so far as is known it was never mentioned, and he tried to put it entirely out of his memory—when he had slipped. It had not been an unworthy slip, more one that any carelessly overaccommodating man might easily have made. He had countersigned the notes of an acquaintance in Youngstown who intended to manufacture tin plate. This enterprise had gone bankrupt, leaving him liable for some $130,000. This had been at the time when, having just been triumphantly re-elected Governor of Ohio, he was looking forward to the nomination for the Presidency. For a faltering moment it seemed that, in the character of an honorable gentleman, he might have to leave politics, return to the law, and earn the wherewithal to pay the debt. Hanna stopped this. He gathered contributions from a number of prominent people who had the same interest in a safe President that he had himself, and together they paid what was owed. McKinley was not expected to acknowledge the considerable favor or even to know who the donors were. Hanna went on with his plans.[1]

This incident, like the momentary interruption of Harrison's career, might easily have stopped progress toward the Presidency. Otherwise, looked back on, that career, again like Harrison's, seems to have been inevitably upward. Whether in some unrecorded conversation Hanna spoke plainly to McKinley about his soft-headedness does not appear. Probably not.

At any rate, McKinley's discretion failed very rarely. He became a kind of inscrutable Buddha in whose promotion huge sums and vast energies had been invested. He had already learned, as Chairman of the Ways and Means Committee of the House, how to deal with complicated subjects—such as the tariff—when his ignorance might all too easily be exposed. As a master of double talk, his equal had never really appeared on the political scene. He left sharper and more determined men confused at the end even of long discussions of highly technical questions.

This tendency to ponderous evasiveness was cultivated. His speeches during the front-porch campaign of 1896 were affirmations of belief in generally acceptable attitudes, but they went no further. The only definite commitments were to a moderate protectionism and, in response to the prodding of his more powerful supporters, to sound money. Here there had been invented an evasive formula. It was called international bimetallism. It promised to "do something for silver" when other nations could be induced to join the United States for the purpose. This was intended to placate the Western silver producers, who had a different interest in the metal from that of the Populists, who wanted cheaper money. The producers wanted a better market. But there were not many of these, and Bryan was sure to carry Colorado anyway (as he did), so the main emphasis was on soundness. This turned up an electoral vote of 271 for McKinley to 176 for Bryan.

The agrarian challenge had been repulsed, and the consolidation by Hanna of political and business interests in the national Republican party had been successful. Also, it proved to be durable.

---

[1] Among those who contributed were Andrew Carnegie, Myron T. Herrick, H. H. Kohlsaat, H. C. Frick, Philander Knox, John Hay, W. R. Day, A. A. Pope, and Hanna himself. Among these are names that appeared in Republican annals again and again during McKinley's Presidency. They must have felt their investment to have been a good one.

McKinley's part in this grand maneuver seems in retrospect almost that of a bystander. He was the beneficiary, not the creator, of the strategy, nor was he its administrator. He stayed at home in Canton radiating cheerful and reserved confidence. This seemed to please visiting voters; and if it sickened practical bosses like Quay and Platt, it was nevertheless accepted as a device. It even wrung from them a grudging admiration. The front-porch technique was perfectly suited to the candidate and the circumstances. It stands unique in recent political history—the contribution of an otherwise unimaginative man.

The old-fashioned residence in Canton inevitably suggested prosperous small-town living, quiet, reverent, conformist; its owner could hardly be other than a good citizen with an affectionate family and friendly neighbors. The lawn was spacious, and there was an air of retirement but not withdrawal. Hanna understood how complete the contrast was between this model of dignified and fatherly thoughtfulness and Bryan, who was staging the first of his hectic campaigns, careening about the country, speaking many times a day to crowds of all sizes wherever there was a platform and people before it. As campaign manager, Hanna made the most of it.

There were some technical considerations here of interest to professionals. Bryan had a most remarkable voice. It was a carrying one. He could reach an incredible number of hearers even when he had to speak outdoors to a crowd gathered for sociability as well as politics, with small children dodging through it and restless individuals coming and going. It might be hot or cold; the wind might be blowing; a storm might come up. To all this he adapted himself. And even when he spoke indoors it was usually in a hall or auditorium built with little consideration for its acoustical qualities and without adequate ventilation.

Bryan's argument, it must be said, was not much more rational than that of McKinley's supporters. But it was apparent that he was on the side of the debtors, the underprivileged, the dissatisfied. It was this that he emphasized. He made only one unsuccessful appearance. He invaded New York City and was so intimidated by a huge, and probably hostile, metropolitan crowd that he chose to read a two-hour address, something he had never been known to do before. Its tediousness, together with the unhappy accident of a cruel heatwave, resulted in a disastrous failure—made much of by the press. The fakir, the mountebank they had been picturing to their readers, had accommodated them with a long and senseless disquisition on the currency question. They dwelt happily on his shallowness. Bryan went on to more natural performances in his best oratorical vein in New England and even back in New York; but he never recovered. Or perhaps he did not gain what he had never had but hoped for—majorities in the Eastern states.

Meanwhile the frock-coated McKinley had continued quietly at home, comfortably greeting from his porch pilgrims shepherded by Hanna's men. They came by the trainload and were accommodated on a lawn worn by thousands of feet. There they heard a few mellifluous sentences, were blessed by a fatherly smile, were perhaps awarded a handshake; then they picnicked and were entertained by lesser politicos until their special trains departed. Church groups, fraternal organizations, veterans' posts, even many delegations of labor unions, came one after another and went away with a feeling of having received a benison.

Actually the front-porch campaign was only a better-organized version of a familiar method. Visitors in Springfield had been similarly received in 1860; and Hayes and Garfield in other small towns of this same state of Ohio had made themselves, in a staid and sober way, available to visitors. It took Hanna's energy and executive ability to see that the shepherding was done on schedule, that there were no embarrassments. And of course it took McKinley to do so superbly the honors on the porch.

The credit awarded Hanna and McKinley for the success of the 1896 campaign may be exaggerated. Without Hanna to scare the conservative businessmen and the workers, it is possible that Bryan's diatribes, so extravagantly publicized by a press almost completely devoted to picturing him as an irresponsible demagogue, might have been enough. So perhaps McKinley might have stayed quietly in his parlor instead of making graceful appearances on his porch. But certainly nothing done by the candidate or the Chairman of the National Committee reduced the likelihood of victory. They went along with the drift, took advantage of the situation created for them, and missed no opportunity to enlarge their chances. Bryan, too, did what he had to do. He was the challenger. By invading the Democratic convention and making it his own with his "Cross of Gold" speech, he had committed himself and his followers—there were some defectors—to the overthrow of many existing institutions deeply embedded in American life. His campaign had to be a rampaging one, calculated to arouse such emotion as would overcome both inertia and rational argument.

Observers of long experience have been known to contend that no campaign changes the outcome of the election process. When all the excitement has died down and all the money has been spent, they say, the situation is no different than it would have been if all the effort had been spared. Is it true that candidates, following Bryan's example, needlessly wear themselves out traveling many exhausting miles and making hundreds of repetitive speeches? And that all the ringing of doorbells, the distributing of literature, and the organizing of the faithful for months of work are unnecessary?

There may have been campaigns of which this is true, and that of 1896 could well be one of them. Others will come to anyone's mind who knows our political history. But it would be hard to convince professionals that the really close contests would have had the same outcome if the contestants had stayed at home, making only nominal appearances, and if the campaign workers had not labored through summer and early fall in makeshift headquarters and meeting halls. It is hard to believe that Henry Clay could have won, no matter how frantic the effort; but it is also hard to believe that Cleveland's campaigns were not affected by campaign incidents, at least the first two, or that with a little more effort Tilden might not have become President in 1876. Time after time it is possible to figure how a few more votes or a few less in certain states might have made the difference between victory and defeat in the electoral count.

It is these few voters, in what are spoken of as the *key* places, that the professionals are always after. They use the utmost ingenuity to determine where these states and districts are and concentrate their forces there. But they can never be certain that it is safe to neglect many others. Consequently they harry the candidate to expend the last energy he can summon up in covering every doubtful area, and they can always use any amount of money they can raise for the campaign. It is true that certain contests hardly seem worth the effort. Grant was certain to best his opponents, Seymour and Greeley; Jackson was irresistible; and Lincoln could not have lost in 1860 with the Democrats split as they were.

It is the possibility that the last expenditure of energy, the one more speech, the final dollar, may persuade the few voters necessary to determine the result of a close election—and some have been amazingly close—that, after Bryan showed the way, set the pattern of frantic and prolonged canvassing.

The McKinley example, then, was simply not available to his successor candidates. At any later time it could be made a custom only by mutual agreement among the parties or, what would probably be easier and more likely, statutory regulation of the whole campaigning procedure.

It still remains true that McKinley's approach to actual candidacy is well worth study and, possibly, imitation. To be regular, to be labeled conservative but not hidebound, to be genial and co-operative, to be accessible and helpful—these are the characteristics he cultivated. They became so habitual that they appeared to be inseparable from his personality. It was what was wanted when reliability was at a premium. He was turned to so generally that he was nominated on a first ballot. What candidate could expect greater success—except to be elected, as McKinley was, so decisively that no doubt could exist about his hold on the electorate?

Theodore Roosevelt

1858–1919

CULVER PICTURES, INC.

Born in New York City
Became twenty-fifth President in 1901 at 43

HISTORY

1880	Graduated from Harvard, after a mostly tutorial preparation during a sickly childhood. Began the study of law at Columbia, but did not graduate.
1882	Elected to the New York State Assembly.
1884	Turned to ranching in North Dakota.
1886	Unsuccessful candidate for the Mayoralty in New York City.
1889	Appointed by President Harrison to the Civil Service Commission.
1895	Appointed President of New York City's Board of Police Commissioners.
1897	Appointed by McKinley Assistant Secretary of the Navy.
1898	Resigned to organize a regiment of Volunteer Cavalry (Rough Riders); commissioned as Colonel; mustered out in the same year.
1898	Elected to the Governorship of New York.

1900	Elected to the Vice-Presidency.
1901	Succeeded to the Presidency on McKinley's death.
1904	Elected to the Presidency (Vice-President, Fairbanks); opponent, Parker with Davis.
1910	Went on a big-game hunting expedition in Africa and toured European countries.
1912	Unsuccessful candidate for the Presidency as a Progressive, after failing to displace Taft as the Republican candidate.
1916	Refused a second Progressive nomination; turned to writing.
1917	Offer to serve in the armed forces refused by Wilson.
1919	Died at his home in Oyster Bay, New York.

I T LOOKED for a long time as though Theodore Roosevelt would never make it. It was not that he did not try. On the contrary, he worked, schemed, traded, compromised, and, when he had to, even humbled himself and came close to denying the deepest beliefs he held. But there was so much against him!

At the beginning, for instance, he was a dude in rough company; and as a candidate for his first offices, he could never hope to reach a large number of voters and expect them to support him, since he hardly spoke their language. Then, when he began to fight his way upward toward preferment, he still lacked political appeal. His physique had been improved by strenuous measures, but it was still not impressive; his voice was shrill, his eyes were weak, and his legs were short. Worst of all, however, he had nothing to offer as a program, nothing to stand on or hold to. He simply believed that he ought to be in public office.

But there was a flame in him. He regarded his handicaps as merely obstacles to be overcome. He was determined that nothing should stop him. His whole career is an illustration of the possibilities in politics for a man of vitality and determination who has something to distinguish him from the run of his contemporaries, even if it is only a willingness to show off. He must, of course, have—and Roosevelt did have—supreme confidence in himself. He was personally virtuous by his own standards, and he never hesitated to judge others by the same measures. He had a similar attitude about the views he somehow came by. Because they were his, they must be right, and it was a kind of apostasy to question them. So he became a teacher, an exhorter, and an exemplar. This was his stock in trade. But he had no difficulty in justifying departure from his norms if it involved his own advancement. He regarded this necessity as a quite sufficient excuse. If he did not attain office, how could he exert the influence and set the example he talked about?

His causes, apart from the effort to make Americans more moral, were simple. They included honest government, faithful work in the public interest, resistance to those who would exploit public agencies for their own advantage, and what he called a "square deal" for all individuals, high or low, rich or poor—so far as was practical. This might be thought to be a more suitable program for a churchman than a politician. But he always had difficulty in understanding economic issues and disliked the complication of many social ones. Only about morality was he perfectly certain. He made a career of it. And it was an amazing success.

One of the illuminating incidents at the very start of Roosevelt's political experience was his affiliation with the Jake Hess Republican Club. This was in the Diamond Back (21st Assembly) District of New York.[1]

The name would suggest that it was something of a silk-stocking neighborhood; but there was nothing effete or refined about Jake Hess or the habitués of the club. The part of the district they came from might have been miles from Madison or Fifth Avenue. It did have enough conservatives, however, so that, together with Jake's voters, it could be kept Republican. Arrangements with the Democrats allowed the organization to get along well enough; and then there was Federal patronage, seldom lacking after the Civil War, since both nation and state were usually Republican. Altogether, the organization did very well and it was a good place to start a career.

The club had the usual disorderly rooms over a saloon at 59th Street and Fifth Avenue. Roosevelt discovered it and came to understand its importance to democracy while studying law at Columbia. In joining it, he chose to associate with the work horses of politics, the ward heelers, the shyster lawyers, the hangers-on of all sorts who make contact with voters and hold them by a system of favors and handouts. His older friends regarded the club as a hangout for bums. But these, he told them—finding one of those phrases so useful to him throughout his life—were "the governing class," and he proposed to belong to it. This was a telling retort to those who regarded politics as a low trade, not to be engaged in by the rich and wellborn.

Roosevelt was twenty-two and recently married when he began to frequent the club. He was also about to enter the second year of his law course. But this he gave up. He saw a chance to begin the career he was now attracted to and was willing to sacrifice education for experience. It was a peculiar circumstance that made so early a start possible. It happened that Jake Hess was annoyed because President Arthur, from whom he had expected better treatment—he being a New Yorker and former head of the Republican organization—decided to follow the policies of his predecessor, Garfield, with respect to the merit system in the public service; and this meant that there were lean days ahead for the organization.

Jake talked of rebellion and of using the votes under his control in subversive ways. This in turn offended some of the club members, and especially one Joe Murray, an Irishman of natural political ability. Joe determined to teach Jake a lesson, and his way of doing it was to create a situation in which the absurd young Roosevelt could be substituted in the Assembly for one of Jake's men—Richard J. Trimble,

---

[1] It was called Diamond Back because of the popular notion that its inhabitants dined nightly on terrapin, a symbol of lavish living.

the then incumbent. Why Murray chose this method and why he chose young Roosevelt as his instrument are not questions that can be answered with any certainty; but he carried out the scheme skill-fully, so much so that at the district meeting held in the clubrooms in October, Jake recognized that he had been outmaneuvered and acceded to the substitution. Murray ran the Roosevelt campaign effi-ciently. After allowing his candidate to make a few trial speeches, he thought it best to confine his canvassing to the precincts over on the East Side. He then gathered in votes by the usual methods and carried the election quite comfortably.

So on January 1, 1882, Theodore Roosevelt became a member of the state legislature. For him, life had suddenly taken on meaning. This was what he had been meant to do. He was inevitably regarded at first as an exotic member of the machine-run Assembly, whose mem-bers were hardly gentlemen. But he was so genuinely anxious to learn, to make himself one of the boys, that they soon began to forget, or at least to ignore, his Harvard accent, his naïveté, and his obvious ambition. He managed not too badly, and when the time came was re-elected.

There followed about fifteen years of public service in various jobs of some importance. They were not, however, important enough to make him happy. He served in the Assembly for three years. Then he ran spectacularly, but unsuccessfully, for Mayor of New York in 1886. He made himself so conspicuous that he was compensated for defeat by an appointment to the Civil Service Commission. President Harrison was following his predecessors in enlarging the number of merit appointments. There were interludes during this time when Roosevelt wavered in his determination to follow politics as a career. He had shown signs while still at Harvard of longing for a strenuous and primitive life not to be had in bureaucratic offices or legislative halls. He went off to the Maine woods, looking for remote places. Then, after his first wife died and he was lost in sorrow, he went West to Dakota and turned rancher. There he roughed it with pioneering individuals of the sort he always loved to cultivate. But there were drawbacks. Ranching was risky as a business and was not so adventur-ous as he had supposed. The attractions of political life soon began to draw him again, and he came back to the appointive jobs he was to hold until 1898.

This phase of his career gave him experience in Washington for several years; then in 1895 he was made President of the New York City Police Board—a job he probably enjoyed more than any other before he became President. He sleuthed about in the city streets at night; he bucked up the police and tried to keep them honest. But finally, in 1897, when McKinley was elected, he was taken into the sub-Cabinet as Assistant Secretary of the Navy. It was a good time to become second man in the Department, although he would have preferred to be the first. He had little respect for his superior and was quite certain that he could do a better job than he. But anyway, it did take him for the first time into the policy-making range of Federal affairs, and he made the most of it.

The imminence of trouble with Spain over the Cuban situation, where rebellion had been endemic for years and where the methods of suppressing it, even when not exaggerated, were too horrible to be tolerated, exactly suited his temperament. War was inevitable, and for him it was the opportunity he had so long awaited. He did not propose to have conciliation rob him of his chance. His chief, Secretary Long, and President McKinley were not belligerent men; and he chafed under their policy of inaction. But he was certain it would not last long; the press was howling for intervention, the public temper was rising, and the Congress was strong for action. In these circumstances, the Assistant Secretary took advantage of a lengthy absence of the Secretary to order Admiral Dewey and his fleet into position at Hong Kong for a move to Manila when it should become feasible.

This deployment of the fleet proved to be a strategic success. When war was declared, the first American engagement was at Manila Bay; and this resulted in control of the Philippines. A long conflict, mostly with Filipinos who wanted independence rather than a new occupation, followed, with incidents hardly more defensible than those in Cuba, so loudly denounced by the Hearst and Pulitzer correspondents. But this was later, and Roosevelt was not directly involved. He had by then become a favorite American volunteer, a hero.

For at once, when war had been declared, Roosevelt had resigned his civilian post to become the Colonel of a cavalry regiment to be raised by himself, soon given the name—the correspondents of those days were gifted public relations men—of Rough Riders. This collection of hardy horsemen from the Plains captured everyone's imagination; and their service in Cuba was given such publicity as an American force had never enjoyed before and has never enjoyed since. It was a question whether the Cuban campaign was won by General Shafter or Colonel Roosevelt; but it was clear that it could not have been won without Theodore's services.[2]

But Roosevelt was not aiming to be an army officer. He knew what to do with his fame. And as quickly as he could, he resigned his commission and looked around for the most likely elective opportunity.

---

[2] The Roosevelt publicity led Finley Peter Dunne—Mr. Dooley—to remark that if Roosevelt got around to writing his memoirs, as he surely would, an appropriate title would be "Alone in Cubia."

The obvious office was the Governorship of New York. When he was still in process of being discharged at Montauk, he was approached by a reform group in New York—former Mugwumps and Cleveland Republicans—who saw the possibility of forming a new group for political action, dedicated to the causes he had so often expounded and with him as its spokesman. These independents had some reservations about their man. He had on several occasions, while posing as a reformer and discoursing on the evils of machine politics, made some compromises that could hardly be reconciled with the principles he professed. Yet they felt their best chance of advancing the cause of good government in New York might be through him.

Roosevelt was delighted. He agreed to head the movement. While still in Cuba, he had heard from his friend Henry Cabot Lodge that there was much talk of his running for Governor or Congressman. And he himself had written that the good people of New York "seemed crazy about me." It was Lodge's opinion that he could have pretty much anything he wanted. A crusade such as the reformers pictured was just the thing for the returning Colonel of Volunteers. He saw himself as a reformer.[3]

While he was dealing with the delegation at Montauk, he had no intimation that certain ideas concerning himself were evolving in the mind of sly old Boss Platt sitting in the Amen Corner of the Fifth Avenue Hotel. The "easy boss" had no liking for unreliable individuals with independent ambitions; and Roosevelt quite evidently had a fancy for publicity. Quite possibly he thought of himself as a rising popular leader. On the other hand, such a hero as he had become might be more of a nuisance in opposition, carrying on a crusade against machine politics, than as a protégé, however reluctant, of a boss who could put him in office and keep him there. Pondering whether he could make the young man (he was now forty) useful, he decided to send an emissary to find out what there was to the rumor that he had accepted the proposal of the reformers. If the deal had not gone too far, he might be persuaded that his ambitions could better be satisfied as the candidate of the regular organization. He could be told that he would only be wasting his energy, at this opportune time for himself, by entering on a hopeless crusade. With the organization behind him, however, he could almost certainly become Governor—and Governors of New York, he did not need to be told, were in a strategic position for still further advances.

Platt, cynical as he was from long experience in party affairs, must

---

[3] *Selections from the Correspondence of Theodore Roosevelt and Henry Cabot Lodge, 1884–1918* (New York, 1925), I, 334; Henry F. Pringle, *Theodore Roosevelt* (New York, 1931), Chap. XV; and Matthew Josephson, *The President Makers* (New York, 1940), 139 ff.

have been somewhat surprised by the immediacy and completeness of
Roosevelt's acceptance of his proposal. He not only consented to be
the regular Republican candidate, but actually signed an agreement to
accept Platt's direction. The conditions imposed were that Roosevelt
"must acknowledge and respect" Platt's position as head of the New
York organization and "consult" with Platt fully and freely; also, he
would "adopt no line of policy and make no important nominations
without previous consultation."

When Roosevelt made public his acceptance of the Republican
suggestion, it dismayed and angered the reformers to whom he had
made pledges. John Jay Chapman, speaking for them, said that it made
the movement they had been planning quite impossible, and he accused
Roosevelt of being "a trimmer, a brokenbacked half-man." This embarrassed Roosevelt, but he did not give in. Chapman said afterward
that during his session of many hours with him "the Colonel broke
down and cried like a baby." Nevertheless, his letter to the press was
not withdrawn.

It would be amazing if any individual could make a decision of this
kind, denounced as a double cross by so many earnest citizens of
unimpeachable character, without looking for rationalizations to
explain his action; and Roosevelt did. Turning on his accusers, he
indicted them for being soft-headed and impractical. The truth was,
his political sense had told him that Platt could indeed make him
Governor, and the reformers could only make him a martyred leader
without an office.

It is interesting that the disappointed good-government people who
turned against him at this time did *not* include two who would remain
close to him for many years—John Hay and Henry Cabot Lodge—the
latter often spoken of as his evil angel. They were practical men. They
accepted the necessity of winning and the ethic that anything contributing to it was justified.

Roosevelt at first was satisfactory to his sponsor. He came to Sunday
breakfasts with Platt and there was instructed in the realities of
politics. He knew quite well that Platt was getting payments from
business interests and was delivering, in return, appointments, legislative acts, and gubernatorial easements. The funds thus received were
distributed downward to local captains and lieutenants and finally to
the actual workers in the precincts who kept the votes lined up. Each
of these was expected to deduct an understood percentage. So the
system was fueled, and so it ran on year after year. And by inter-
party arrangement, it made no considerable difference what party
actually won elections; the boss's power continued to be recognized
and the system continued to function.

Roosevelt knew all about this; as Governor, he consented to be part of it. Occasionally he made an effort to modify the worst directives. He objected to appointing scandalously unworthy candidates for office; he held back on proposals for laws that too flagrantly ran against the public interest; and he refused, when aroused, to protect the thieves who were looting the treasury. But it was mostly done with discretion. He did not care to be cut off from the organization that could hinder or advance his further ambitions. He had chosen his method; he must go on with it. There might come a time when there would be a break and he could muster enough independent strength to defy Platt and the organization and gather into his own hands the power they now held. But that time was not yet, not nearly yet.

Runnning strenuously for the Governorship, he had a feeling of imminent fulfillment. He began to build up the public personality that might become too important for Platt to contain. Campaigns, with the gathering-in facilities of the organization, were made to order for this purpose. This had caused Platt's initial hesitation. Bosses are fearful of burgeoning personalities. He continued to hold the document of submission Roosevelt had signed; but in spite of this, he was uneasy. There was altogether too much appeal in the progress across the state of the returned hero. He would have to be watched carefully. After all, he had double-crossed the reformers. It might be something he would do again.

Writing of him at this time, his biographers are captivated by an emerging flair for noise and movement, for blown-up causes, for sheer exhibitionism. These were as well displayed in this campaign as in his later appearances when contending for greater offices. It was a time when the Republicans were on the defensive. They had presided over a useless war still dragging itself out in the jungles of the Philippines. The natives there, McKinley had convinced himself, needed Christianizing, and it was the duty of Americans to see that it was done. But Americans were strangely reluctant, at least those in New York; and the Filipinos were even more so.

The tag end of wars are always dangerous for parties in power; and this indecent subduing of guerrillas was particularly repugnant. Public reaction was all too plain. Yet Roosevelt refused to accept what he regarded as a shameful retreat from duty. His campaign was as robustious as brass bands, waving flags, and a clattering escort of Rough Riders could make it (those Rough Riders would turn up at hundreds of Roosevelt rallies in the future). It was too bad he could not win more decisively; but he went stubbornly on his belligerent way.

The "easy boss" had, for his sins, an Executive with whom he was far from easy. And the new Governor had time to consider now the problem of further advancement. Had he been too precipitate? Bad timing in politics can be as fatal a mistake as any other. And it did seem as though the way ahead was becoming clouded.

His larger ambition could be attained in one of two ways: he could continue to accept orders from Platt and trust the organization to back him when the time came for promotion, or he could stage a public and spectacular rebellion, seeking to establish such rapport with the electorate that the boss would be forced to compromise with him. As he considered his course, he backed and filled, not satisfying himself and not keeping Platt happy either. He longed for action, for further acclaim, for power of his own. Platt, watching and listening, saw the signs. He had made a mistake; he must get out of it as best he could. But he was deeply involved and he could hardly refuse his Governor renomination; such a refusal would cause an explosion damaging to the whole organization. Roosevelt was quite capable of becoming completely irresponsible and appealing for power on his own.

Happily, before the issue became an open quarrel, he saw a way out. It was furnished by the convenient death of Vice-President Hobart. Here was a position exactly suited for the taming of an unruly amateur. He recalled the old Catholic saying that a troublesome priest should be made a bishop. The Vice-Presidency would be a promotion, an honor, a fitting advance; it would also be a smothering pocket. The Senators would know how to take care of a presiding officer who got above himself.

Platt made the suggestion to his inner-circle colleagues and at once found allies in the Pennsylvania camp of Penrose and Quay; but Hanna, McKinley's mentor, still Chairman of the National Committee, was reluctant. When he thought it over he became positively balky. But an unexpected occurrence modified even his determined opposition. Roosevelt made a sort of preliminary testing tour into the far Southwest, and the enthusiasm accompanying it furnished a warning to the bosses. Here was a burgeoning figure who must be taken seriously.

Roosevelt was unhappy about his situation. He had been forced to adopt a split public personality. Matthew Josephson has commented on this:

> Attractive as was the picture that Governor Roosevelt made before the public (the mythical Rough Rider in politics, with his mask of furious energy, of "pure act," as Henry Adams described it), there was in him a more troubled, inward self known to only a few intimate friends, such as Cabot Lodge and Brooks Adams. It was that of an upper-class intellectual of uncertain convictions and limited knowledge, now facing the deeper questions of his time, in more responsible office,

while endeavoring to push himself toward the further goal of his over-whelming ambitions.[4]

For the student, there are several special things to remember about Roosevelt's gaining of the Governorship and his advancement from there to the Presidency. The first of these is that he had chosen immediately after his adoption by Platt to play patriot for all it might be worth; and now he would go on, in the most newsworthy manner possible, to impress himself on the public as a roaring expansionist. He was also, he began to say, a champion of fair play. This did not mean that he was a reformer except in a limited moral sense. He did not advocate changing anything in the economic system; he was hostile to organized labor and on the slightest provocation used the militia to "keep order" during strikes. He did not propose any stringent regulation of business, although businessmen who broke the law had to be punished. He talked often about honest government, about equality for all, and about some special instances of governmental change that he regarded as necessary.

The war theme was emphasized from the first. Pringle has described briefly his very first address; it was at Carnegie Hall and the topic was "The Duties of a Great Nation."

> A dozen Rough Riders were escorted to the platform. The meeting opened with cheers for San Juan and for its hero. The hall was smoth-ered in flags. The candidate for Governor—that he was not running for the Presidency was difficult to learn from his speech—began with generalities on integrity in government. He said not a word about the canal steal (a current scandal in New York), and was soon in the midst of an appeal for the new imperialism. "The guns of our warships have awakened us to the knowledge of new duties," he said. "Our flag is a proud flag, and it stands for liberty and civilization." Then he praised the army and navy . . .[5]

This sort of appeal was blunted by the widespread suspicion that the Republicans had bungled the war, and even that it had been unnecessary. Also, he did not wholly escape newspaper criticism for evading practically all state issues. He was attacked by such old-time Mugwumps as Carl Schurz for his inflated imperialism. He won by the very small margin of 17,000 votes.

He then had the problem of getting on to the Presidency in spite of not having any clear issues—except his exaggerated patriotism, quickly

[4] *Op. cit.*, 96.
[5] *Theodore Roosevelt* (New York, 1931), 205.

declining in popularity—and in spite of not having demonstrated any considerable support in his own state. Besides, there was McKinley, who would certainly be renominated by the Republicans. There was no chance of replacing him in 1900; and to look forward to succeeding him in 1904 meant re-election in New York State twice, and even then there would be a two-year interval before the national election. And Platt was already obviously unhappy in their liaison.

There appeared to be only two other alternatives; one was to become Secretary of War—no other Cabinet post was thinkable—under McKinley, and the other was to become Vice-President. His friend Lodge favored the Secretaryship of War; but this post soon went to Elihu Root (after the incompetent Alger was induced to resign), and so disappeared from among the possibilities. There remained the Vice-Presidency. This he did not like—he was afraid of being "buried"—but he gradually came to see that it was the only real chance. He knew well enough that his hold on the New York electorate was, as he admitted, "entirely ephemeral." And two re-elections were quite unlikely.

The difficulty Roosevelt found himself in was not uncommon. The Vice-Presidency was traditionally a dead end. There were a half dozen past occupants of the office whose names would not even be recognized in any company of educated Americans. Some who had been associated with the most famous Presidents were completely forgotten —Hamlin, for instance, who had been elected with Lincoln. One of this same sort underlined the nature of the office by dying almost unnoticed in November of 1899, when Roosevelt was most worried; but at the same time, the death did open the way to what now seemed the only possible opportunity to continue within striking distance of the Presidency. To this extent, his own and Platt's reasoning ran parallel. He would have to take what comfort he could in the thought that some Vice-Presidents had become Presidents, the last being Arthur, who had served out most of Garfield's term. He did not like the other thought associated with the office: no Vice-President since Van Buren had been elected to the Presidency. But he would have to take the risk.

A good deal has been made of the arrangement among the bosses to get Roosevelt out of New York and into the Vice-Presidency. And there was certainly a complex contest. Platt's problem was made worse when McKinley himself, in his gentle way, let it be known that Roosevelt could hardly be considered a suitable running mate. But when the Pennsylvania bosses lent themselves to Platt's conspiracy, and when Roosevelt's growing appeal among certain of the voters was made apparent, his selection gradually became inevitable.

His popularity had been apparent since his testing journey to the

Rough Rider Convention in New Mexico. He had been received everywhere in the West with whooping enthusiasm—exactly, he exulted, as though he had been a Presidential candidate. This surprised the Easterners, but it was genuine and they recognized it. He was even obliged rather slyly to disavow any immediate Presidential ambition. After all, a direct challenge to McKinley was unthinkable. Still, everywhere he went, there did seem to be a revival of enthusiasm for martial affairs and for himself as paramount patriot. The Rough Riders were acclaimed; and exhortations, such as he depended on, aroused the crowds.

At the convention in 1900, McKinley's nomination came on the first ballot, and Roosevelt's followed immediately. There was no contest.

The problem, for the moment, was solved. But there still remained the even more difficult one he had been dreading. How could he move into the Presidency from the lesser office? Accident, as we know, made this easy; but he must have been considering what to do if normal events occurred and McKinley simply lived on to retire in 1905.

Obviously, he must convince the regulars all across the country that he was a regular too. For the most considerable obstacle to be overcome would be resistance to his nomination—both because he was thought of as unreliable and quite capable of appealing, over the heads of the bosses, to the people, and because, as Vice-President, he would not be thought eligible for the Presidential nomination. The higher opportunity was more likely to go to a Governor who could deliver the votes of a large state—such as Ohio, Illinois, or his own New York. He would have no great following in New York when he was no longer Governor, and he had never been too popular there anyway.

His method called for impressing his personality on the crowds who could be got out for campaign meetings. He had a superb talent for platform oratory. He had no such organ-toned voice as Bryan possessed; but his flamboyant gestures, his swelling neck as he made his points and castigated the enemy, and his flair for phrases of telling sharpness made him quite as effective as Bryan ever had been. He campaigned tirelessly, day after day, all across the country, seizing every opportunity to reach an audience. He had very little of substance to say; he had to preach McKinleyism, which was gallingly dull; but he did have the flag to wrap himself in, and a patriotic contingent of the Rough Riders was always on hand.

It sufficed. He caught the imagination of the electorate and partially won over the regulars. The result was that he earned the right to be considered, after McKinley, as first among the Republicans. If there existed in the hearts of the professionals any gratitude at all for services rendered, he would be high on the list of those available for the nomination in 1904.[6]

The assassination of McKinley in 1901 and Roosevelt's fortuitous accession to the Presidency made all this elaborate preparation unnecessary. But if the McKinley tragedy had not occurred, he would probably not have been nominated. He had put himself in the strongest position he could have contrived, yet he had no real machine and so no delegates.

Having come to office by accident, with a background that aroused suspicion among the regulars, he had a difficult technical problem for an interloper to work out. It was not a foregone conclusion that he would be chosen. Others who had succeeded to the Presidency in this way had not. He would have to demonstrate that he was as safe as McKinley and as attractive to the electorate.

It was another disappointment for the Mugwumps that immediately on taking the oath of office in Buffalo, where McKinley died, he issued a conservative statement, saying that he intended to carry on his predecessor's policies faithfully; also, that he would make no changes in the Cabinet. But after all, he could not have done otherwise. It was McKinley who had been elected, and presumably his policies were approved ones. Any changes would have to be approached with suitable preparation. But aside from his feeling that they were commonplace and uninspiring, he had no alternatives to offer. About tariffs, currency, and economic policies in general, he was as innocent as a child. Only about expansionism—called imperialism by the Democrats—was he certain. He meant to make the power of the United States felt in the world.

But even about this he was cautious. Above all, he wanted to reassure the Republican professionals; and they were moderate in all things, even their newly developed outward look. Actually, for more than a year McKinley might have been in the White House. But time was on Roosevelt's side. He had three years; and in that time he meant to give people the feel of a new personality, a fresh and vigorous leadership, and new policies. Some of the old bosses would lose their prestige or die, and new ones would succeed; these he could win over with patronage, with favors, and with blandishments. Within two years it was clear that a new wind was blowing. Instead of the solemn, fat, and uninteresting figure, for whom, to be sure, they had had a

---

[6] There is a curious parallel to this behavior all the way through the later Roosevelt's career, as we shall see. Coming out of the obscurity of second place in the Navy Department, F.D.R. campaigned so hard as the Vice-Presidential candidate (with Cox) in the hopeless electoral contest of 1920, after another war, that he earned the gratitude of his party. When the time came, they recalled this service.

genuine affection, the people had an opportunity to see a vigorous leader at the head of a lively corps of younger men, restless, clever, and anxious to make their own impression. They saw in him a man who loved to hunt, to play games, to tumble on the floor with his children, to get about the country and meet people. He entertained his electorate. There was something new every day.

He bothered the Congress very little. They went their way and he went his; and so the powers there had few complaints, even if many suspicions. There was no reason for not nominating him in 1904. He was safe enough, if somewhat bizarre; and he undoubtedly had a hold on the voters. He was chosen on the first ballot, and he had one of the largest majorities any candidate had ever had. Bryan had already been ditched as the Democrats went back to conservative Cleveland ways; in the campaign, Roosevelt had to face one of the weakest opponents in all Presidential history. Alton B. Parker could not conceivably have been elected, and he did not get even a respectable vote—about five million to Roosevelt's seven and a half. Even Roosevelt was astounded; for his circumstances and with his talents, he had done precisely the right things.

Perhaps the most important thing to be said about this success story is that Roosevelt could never have attained the Presidency if he had not been Vice-President when the President died. But it was also important that he accepted and developed the one line of policy he was best fitted to exemplify—that of national power and prestige appealing to American pride.

William Howard Taft
1857–1930

Born in Cincinnati, Ohio, son of a lawyer who had been Secretary of War
Became twenty-sixth President in 1909 at 51

HISTORY

1878	Graduated from Yale University, after attending Woodward High School in Cincinnati.
1880	Graduated from Cincinnati Law School and admitted to the bar.
1880	Law reporter for Cincinnati newspapers.
1881–82	Appointed Assistant Prosecuting Attorney for Hamilton County, then Collector of Internal Revenue for the First District.
1885–87	Appointed Assistant County Solicitor, then Judge of the Superior Court of Cincinnati.
1890	Appointed Solicitor General of the United States.
1892	Appointed Judge of the Federal Circuit Court.
1896	Appointed Dean of the Cincinnati Law School.
1900	Appointed President of the Philippine Commission and then Governor General of the Philippines.

323

1904	Appointed Secretary of War by T. Roosevelt.
1905–7	Sent on missions to the Philippines, Panama, and Cuba.
1908	Nominated by the Republican party and elected to the Presidency (Vice-President, Sherman); opponent, Bryan with Kern.
1912	Renominated in a contest with Roosevelt, who felt that he had turned reactionary, and received fewer votes than Wilson or Roosevelt.
1913	Appointed Kent Professor of Law, Yale University.
1921	Appointed Chief Justice of the United States.
1930	Died in Washington.

FOLLOWING THEODORE ROOSEVELT, William Howard Taft became President as a protégé of the retiring President. Roosevelt had sufficient power in the party to dictate Taft's nomination on the first ballot and sufficient prestige with the electorate to get him elected. Since his opponent in the campaign was Bryan, running for the third time on a series of rather outworn issues—or, as he said, ones that had been stolen by Roosevelt—the competition was weak. The Midwest revolt had worn itself out and the country generally was convinced that Republican policies, modified by a few mild reforms, were what was needed. This was in spite of a serious depression in 1907 and a lingering and agonizing recovery during which absolutely nothing was done to relieve the distress of farmers, unemployed workers, or businessmen. The time had not yet come—although it soon would—when the Federal government was expected to ensure the welfare of its citizens.

In spite of many signs indicating that something was terribly wrong with the economic system, and in spite of the campaigning that had been carried on by the Populists and their allies, Roosevelt had been a popular President. This enthusiasm was largely personal. He talked in a way people liked. He threatened those they distrusted—the "malefactors of great wealth." And he offered the first example in a long time of Presidential activity in the manner of Jackson. In fact, he put on a continuous show. There was no doubt that the center and focus of American affairs was in the White House; and this was approved among the growing number of middle-income Protestant folk. By 1908 they were ready to believe that if he thought Taft the proper successor for himself he must be right.

That Roosevelt did think so was evidenced not only by his official actions favoring Taft but by many private expressions of confidence. But he had a problem. If a candidate was wanted who would without doubt be elected, Roosevelt himself was the one. But he had spoken about retiring and had conceived an ideal picture of himself as elder statesman giving sage advice to a compliant successor. He used all his advantages as President to make certain that his preference was accepted. When it was done, he said of Taft from the White House:

> He is not only fearless, absolutely disinterested and upright, but he has the widest acquaintance with the nation's needs, without and within, and the broadest sympathies with all our citizens. He would be as emphatically President of the plain people as Lincoln, yet not Lincoln himself would be freer of the least taint of demagogy, the least tendency to arouse, or appeal to, class hatred of any kind.[1]

---

[1] The *New York World*, June 19, 1908. Quoted in H. F. Pringle, *Theodore Roosevelt*, 502.

It is one of the curiosities of American political history that Roosevelt so misread the mind and intentions of the man he forced on the Republicans—and on the electorate—to succeed himself. It was done, he said, to carry on the work he had begun. But the almost inexplicable truth is that he was an entirely different individual from the one Roosevelt thought him. He was conservative, judicial, without political gifts, and if not lacking in that sympathy "with all our citizens" spoken of in Roosevelt's statement, certainly unwilling to see it implemented in any effective way. He would be anything but President of the "plain people"; he would, on the contrary, be President of an elite. He thoroughly believed in the superiority of his social class. This misunderstanding—if it was a misunderstanding—had a result famous in political history. In retirement Roosevelt convinced himself that Taft had betrayed the policies he had been chosen to defend. And in 1912 he decided to do what he had refused to do in 1908: run again for the Presidency himself.[2]

Some friend of Taft's ought to have warned him of what lay ahead. He would not be what Roosevelt expected him to be; and he would be a woefully unsuccessful Chief Executive by any standard.

Years later, in lectures at Columbia, he would criticize Roosevelt for holding that Presidents possessed the "residual powers" temptingly open to claim because the Constitution was so vague about their ownership. This, Taft said, was "unsafe"; and certainly his administration, in contrast to Roosevelt's, had been one of withdrawal and renunciation rather than leadership and decisiveness. But this provided opportunities for those who had not been democratically chosen to seize the levers of state. The country was run by the rich and wellborn.

Taft in the White House behaved very much the way a Judge would behave in his court. The making of policy for the nation, at a most unfortunate time, was done by those who knew what they wanted of the Federal government but who were shortsighted even in their own interest and had only a secondary concern for the public good; that is to say, they believed that what was good for them must be good for the nation. So a decent man passed into history as one of the worst failures in office in the whole Presidential list.

---

[2] There was question whether this would be a third term. It will be recalled that Roosevelt succeeded to the Presidency on McKinley's death and had actually been elected only once. There was no prohibition against a third term but only a strong tradition going back to Washington's renunciation. But Roosevelt chose at first to make the gesture of interpreting his tenure as having been substantially two terms; a gesture he repudiated in 1912. This matter of terms of service was cleared up in the Twenty-second Amendment, which defined the time a successor would need to have served to have it counted as a full term, even if he had not been elected to it.

Looking back on his reluctance to be a candidate, it can be guessed that he had a premonition of what might happen. He is, in fact, one of the Presidents who actually did not want the office—Washington, of course, being the first. But he was chosen by the ebullient Roosevelt, pushed by his wife, and supported by a wealthy brother. And characteristically he let it happen without too much resistance. He was lethargic by habit and, except when intrigued by a legal problem and writing an opinion about it, he was very much the jolly fat man of tradition.

This corpulence was characteristic. He had been that way since boyhood and as an undergraduate at Yale had weighed 225 pounds. This rose rapidly to well over 300 by the time he became a Federal official. Sitting high on a bench as he presided at trials, his size was not so grotesque as when he was an active official. But even then it may have had its uses, because mostly what he had to do in the years just preceding his nomination was conciliatory—for instance, persuading political enemies in the Philippines and Cuba to co-operate and to accept reasonable solutions to their problems. But it became increasingly difficult for him to get about, and good resolutions about diet never lasted long. He was a fat President as he had been a fat young man at Yale.

What Taft really wanted when he was old enough and prominent enough to be a Presidential candidate was to be a Supreme Court Justice, and eventually he became one. It has to be said that this represented a sound appraisal on his part. His dislike of political activity was complete. He considered that Judges and Administrators were above the sort of thing politicians did. And he had been one or the other all his life. But he was intensely interested in government and all its operations and had been since his youth.

At Yale, Taft stood high in his class. He was genuinely intelligent. He was also incorrigibly honest, something that stood in the way of a number of later preferments he might have wanted.[3] But, along with his honesty, he also had a sense of privacy. He considered that his personal beliefs and relationships were no one's business but his own. This proved to be a good thing when he was pushed into the final political campaign he dreaded. His liberal religion, as well as other of

---

[3] About religion, for instance. It was suggested to him in 1899 that he might be elected to the Presidency of Yale if he would accept. He answered that he did not believe in the Congregational faith, and he was afraid this would make difficulties. He said frankly: "I am a Unitarian. I believe in God. I do not believe in the Divinity of Christ, and there are many other postulates of the orthodox creed to which I cannot subscribe." As Pringle in his *Life and Times of William Howard Taft* (New York, 1939) remarked, this single sentence would have been more than enough to send Bryan to the White House in 1908. But it did not come to light during the campaign.

his beliefs, would undoubtedly have been held against him. It was no crime to be a Unitarian, and neither Jefferson nor Lincoln had been orthodox; but both had obviously been devout in the deepest sense. Taft's departures from orthodoxy were not political. In Cincinnati he followed his father's lead and never wavered in his Republicanism, something that in those years was often difficult for a man of self-respect.

To understand his unlikely progress in a career he professed to feel degrading and was always trying to escape, it is necessary to go back to the very beginning. From 1881, when he became Assistant Prosecutor of Hamilton County, until 1913, when he left the White House, he was continuously in the public service and always by political preferment. This anomalous characteristic of his career is one it would be difficult to match. But he had a politically prominent father, and he lived in the turbulent circumstances of Cincinnati and the state of Ohio in the years from 1880 on. Other sons of such fathers have not always succeeded so well, however, and other disturbed political situations have not proved to be ones in which progress upward was easy for an intellectual. There must also have been something unique about the man himself.

One clue is that, in spite of his dislike for physical exercise and even for legal work which did not engage his interest, he always did his jobs well. The first of these he was appointed to because two politicians of the city fell into a squabble and Taft was of assistance to one of them. He was rewarded with a post which gave him some experience of courtroom work in minor criminal cases; but that he did not like it was shown by his quick acceptance of the next appointment offered. This was the Collectorship of Internal Revenue. It was no more a job for a serious lawyer than the work as a reporter he had been doing immediately after his graduation from law school. In fact, the general character of his early career shows a certain indecisiveness. Was he, or was he not, really going to be a lawyer? The answer seems to be that he was if he could find an easier way than through the drudgery of practice.

William Allen White, studying him, was puzzled by this. When nomination by the Republicans seemed certain, White undertook to write a sketch of his life. There was an exchange of letters. White's inquiry was in his best light manner:

> I went to see your brother this evening in the hope that he might tell me how you got these jobs at so young an age . . . I find . . . that you were given these appointments chiefly because you were an angel of light, and the offices were chasing you around in your youth without reference to the rules of the political game . . .

> I admire your brother's fraternal admiration and doubt not that he is
> perfectly sincere in believing that in those young days you were a
> Lovely Character to whom offices were drawn as to a magnet, but
> someway politics as I know it makes me think that you were active,
> forceful and not entirely a negligible force in Cincinnati politics, or
> that you had powerful friends who pushed you . . .

Taft answered candidly, and what he said explains a good deal.
Some of it seems inconsistent with his character and his preferences;
but it cannot be thought to be anything but the simple truth:

> Like every well-trained Ohio man I always had my plate right side
> up when offices were falling . . . I got my political pull through my
> father's prominence; then through the fact that I was hail-fellow-well-
> met with all of the political people of the city convention-going type.
> I also worked in my ward.

The picture begins to focus. The large young man who was lazy
but good-natured stirred himself when it became necessary to please
the Republicans who were his father's associates. He worked in the
elder Taft's unsuccessful campaign for the Republican nomination as
Governor (in 1879); and his acquaintance was enormously enlarged
by his work as a law reporter, more so than it would have been by
active practice. Very few people—none of record—had occasion to be
annoyed with young Will any more than they would be with old Will
in after years. He continued, in his letter to White, something of an
account, as he recalled it, of those days:

> I worked in my ward and sometimes succeeded in defeating the
> regular gang candidate by hustling around among good people . . . I
> didn't hesitate to attack the gang methods but I always kept on good
> terms with all of them so far as was consistent in attacking them . . .

But Pringle is inclined to feel that there was a little more to it. He
cites what he calls "a scrap of evidence" to show that Taft was sometimes regular at the expense of principle:

> In March, 1885, some voters in Cincinnati's Eighteenth Ward re-
> belled against Boss Cox's selection of delegates to a city convention at
> which a municipal ticket would be chosen. So they named, instead,
> delegates of their own. Cox was defiant. "The Credentials Committee
> of the convention will take good care of the matter," he said. It was an

excellent prophecy. The machine delegates were seated the next day—and William H. Taft was chairman of the Credentials Committee.[4]

In 1885 he was appointed Assistant County Solicitor. This gave him a fixed, if small, salary, welcome because of his impending marriage. There was not much work, and there was a good deal of mixing in city and county politics. The life he lived in these years can almost be taken as a model for young men expecting to have a political career. He went out frequently in the most respectable society of the city; he was a member of the Unity Club of the Unitarian Church, performed well in its amateur theatricals, wrote papers for its serious discussions, and had a large circle of friends. His fiancée, soon to be his wife, was a much-respected young lady, quite his equal intellectually. She would always be an asset, the only difficulty being that she was more ambitious than he—or in a different way; she liked the excitement of administrative life. A number of the succeeding adventures in his career would never have been undertaken if she had not objected when he sought retreat to the bench. But he had his way in a few instances. In 1891, when he was thirty-four, he had a choice. One alternative would have kept him in the Federal circle among the ambitious Republicans—Roosevelt, Henry Cabot Lodge, and their contemporaries. The other was an appointment to a United States Circuit Court. He chose the judicial offer.

He had already been Solicitor General of the United States, an office more active than that of a Judge and one he had not liked; he was a poor speaker and the work was heavy. He had owed his appointment to Joseph Foraker, a force in Ohio politics for many years, not always a decent one. But characteristically he had been supported by numerous other friends as well, some of them already in positions of responsibility. Still it was Foraker, at the moment Governor, who chose to think his own prestige would be enhanced by the appointment of Taft. He first tried to get him a Supreme Court appointment, but this President Harrison thought hardly necessary; and the petitioners had to settle for the Solicitor Generalship. This seems to have been expedited by Taft's assurance to Foraker, who was running for re-election, that he was now an ardent supporter, news that was welcome since Taft's crowd had theretofore not been admirers of the devious Governor. In this he was compromising beyond what was permissible. It was another instance of inability to break with affiliates even when there were ghastly facts to be overlooked. It was better to have a Republican in office, even of the Foraker sort, than to see preference given to a Democrat. What part in decisions of this kind ambitions played, it is not possible to say.

---

[4] These quotations are from Pringle, *op. cit.,* 57 ff.

They would naturally not appear in any record. But the recurrent conjunction is obvious. It must be concluded that this partisanship was somehow held apart from the moral structure adhered to by an otherwise upright man.

But the Federal Judgeship came to him in 1892 from a different source. This time Senator Sherman, an altogether more admirable character than Foraker, but still a member of the reactionary wing of the party, was his sponsor. It was a post he was to occupy for eight years. These were for him, if not for his wife, agreeable times. His seat was in Cincinnati; he was among his old friends; his participation in politics was that of one who, standing somewhat apart, was still warmly concerned that the party should remain in power. Nationally, during this time, Harrison lost to Cleveland and was retired for good. Then, after Cleveland, had come McKinley. And presently the Spanish-American War had begun and run its course, leaving in its wake troubles of many sorts. If during this time Taft had anticipations, they were that a Supreme Court vacancy would occur and that he would be moved up to occupy it. He was in every way eligible.

When in 1900 he was summoned to Washington by McKinley, he supposed that, although there was no such vacancy at the moment, one might be in prospect. But what happened was that the President asked him to become a member of a Philippine Commission he was about to appoint. Taft was frank. The whole Philippine policy had developed in a way he found it hard to accept. He was opposed to taking the islands. Still, he did feel, as he told the President and the Secretaries of War and the Navy, who were gathered to persuade him, that a commitment had been made and it ought to be carried out honorably. A new administration must be set up which would be adapted to the needs of the Filipinos and would lead to self-government.

But he protested that he was not the man for the job. He knew no Spanish, for one thing; but for another he was not willing to abandon his judicial career. To this Secretary Root made a characteristic reply, one calculated to be a challenge. He said to Taft that so far he had had an easy time of it, holding office since he was twenty-four. Now his country needed him. It was a kind of parting of the ways. He could continue sitting on the bench in a humdrum, mediocre way or he could do something that would be a real test, requiring effort and struggle.

Taft was impressed, but he asked for a week to consider. He also asked for assurance that acceptance would not mean the end of his judicial career. This McKinley gave him, saying that if he himself lasted, he would see that Taft did not suffer. It ended by Taft's saying that he would accept only if he were made head of the Commission.

But the kind of decision he had had to make was revealed by the letter he wrote to his brother Horace asking for advice:

> The question is am I willing to give up my present position for what is offered in *praesenti* and *futuro*. The opportunity to do good and help along in a critical stage in the country's history is very great. Root especially urges this view. I am still young as men go and I am not afraid to go back to the practice though I confess I love my present position. Ought I to allow this to deter me from accepting an opportunity thrust on me to accomplish more important and more venturesome tasks with a possible greater reward?[5]

This was the question of a man who sensed that the decision was more than a temporary one. It expressed the reluctance of a natural Judge to undertake less agreeable duties of a sort he might very well not perform well. And he was right to think that for him it was a fateful choice. If he had not made it he might sometime have become a Supreme Court Justice, but he would not have become President. If he had had it to do over, after twenty years, he might have refused. But we must understand that it was for Taft the opening of a final stage in his approach to the Presidency.

Such a choice comes to most rising politicians in one or another way and at one or another time. In the case of Taft, who belonged to the small Republican elite, first by birth and, after his years of office-holding, by obligation, who came from Ohio, and who was agreeable if not so hearty as could be wished in political company, the idea that he might rise to the very top was always present. It was talked of among family and friends almost before his career began and recurred occasionally whenever one of his numerous new opportunities opened up. He himself might resist, but not actively. For what he had to be and do to rise in the Judiciary was not very different from what he had to be and do to rise in the Executive line. And, actually, however nonpartisan he might be in court, there was never any doubt about his Republicanism.

He was called on, when necessary, for services—such as we have noted—and he never refused. It cannot be said that he gave in to the prospect of being President rather than a Justice until his final assignment as Provisional Governor in Cuba in 1906. His success there determined that he would be Roosevelt's—and the Republicans'—choice. This was only two years before the convention nominated him to succeed Roosevelt. Until then he had kept on saying that he hoped only to go on with his judicial work. But what had happened in the interval—between 1900, when he was first sent to the Philippines,

---

[5] *Ibid.,* 161.

and his Cuban mission—really made him the inevitable choice. Still, in the American tradition, this was strange.

No other career of the sort he entered on when he became Governor General of the Philippines, following a year of Commission rule, had ended for an American politician in the Presidency. The sequence most similar was that of John Quincy Adams, now far back in our history and at a time when Secretaries of State often succeeded to the White House. In later years, Secretaryships had been terminal positions. Cabinet members were so overshadowed by the President, and usually so far along in life by the time their chief was through, that they retired quietly with no suggestion of succeeding. There is another feature of this to be noted. Secretaries had a good many of the trappings of power and they felt themselves to be at the head of such formidable groups—agricultural, commercial, financial, and the like—that at one or another time they were apt to present some appearance of rivalry for the President. This he could not tolerate; and he either subdued them or got rid of them in more or less delicate ways. But he always saw to it that they were not eligible to be successors, especially if he was in his first term.

It was as an exception to this rule that Roosevelt built up Taft and designated him as a preferred successor.

When he sent Taft to the Philippines he was worried. McKinley's philanthropic intentions all seemed to be defeated. American businessmen were making a good thing out of the new connection; but the Filipinos, or a good part of them, were fighting as bitterly against their liberators as they formerly had against the Spanish. From Taft's Commission he hoped he might get recommendations that would result in a better future for the Filipino people. The Commission, of course, produced only a report, and after that a new start had to be made. It was done by making Taft Governor General, and he was inaugurated on the Fourth of July in 1891. Presently McKinley was assassinated and was succeeded by Roosevelt. And there then began the association that ended seven years later in Taft's election.

Meanwhile he was a successful Governor, partly because of his liberal policies, so much in contrast to those of General MacArthur, who had been Military Governor, and partly because the revolt was wearing itself out. He was made ill by the heat and his gross eating habits, together with various tropical disorders, and had to take leave; but he returned and worked earnestly at finding a better way of governing than through an appointed Viceroy. And the Filipinos understood that this was the intention, so that there grew up a genuine fondness for the large, friendly man who represented the American government. His popularity, even so far away, made agreeable hearing at home, where very little good was usually heard about emissaries.

A tapering off of imperialist enthusiasm was noticeable in the States as the Spanish war passed into history. Roosevelt, sensing this even if not liking it, gave the people much else to think about; and it was clear almost from his first accession that the Republican nomination in 1904 would go to him. Taft's acquaintances had spoken of his success overseas in a difficult assignment as making him more than ever eligible. But Roosevelt's charm ended that hope. And Taft was not disappointed. He went on and in 1903, with some acclaim, made the settlement with the Vatican about the friar lands that is always set down as one of his greatest accomplishments. This enabled land reform to go on. But it did not create a utopia in the islands. There continued to be shortages of food, unemployment, and terrible epidemics of disease. Then there was an apparently ineradicable corruption in the government. The Governor General found himself presiding over a people ravished by many troubles. Before they were resolved he received the long-hoped-for summons from Roosevelt to come home and become a Supreme Court Justice.

This was a hard offer to refuse. It not only represented his own secret ambition, it would take him out of the impossible job he was now struggling to master. But he knew well enough that he must stay until he could at least begin to see improvement in economic conditions and the beginning of a better government. Then it occurred to him that the Roosevelt offer might have been made to relieve him as Governor. It might have got about that he was not a success. This would not be surprising, considering the situation as it must appear in Washington; and he was worried. But this was not at all Roosevelt's reason. He was having a difficult time finding Justices who would not oppose his policies.

The same thing happened several times. Nevertheless Taft stayed on in the East until in 1904 Roosevelt appointed him Secretary of War to succeed Root. This offer he could not refuse. But when the activities of succeeding years while Roosevelt was President are surveyed, it appears that Taft hardly functioned as Secretary of War at all, so frequently was he on special assignment. His reputation by now was a great, if special, one. Frederick Palmer, a reputed newspaper correspondent, for instance, spoke of him as primarily "the proconsul of good faith to fractious islands; an ambassador to stubborn tasks at far corners of the earth."[6]

He was sent to many places where there was trouble and always seemed to have a good effect on the situation. The last of these missions, in 1906, was to pacify a rebellious and rioting Cuba. The aftermath of war was as bad as in the Philippines and, because it was

---

[6] *Collier's Weekly*, April 13, 1907.

closer home and because commitment had been made to independence, potentially more embarrassing. The then President (Palma) had been elected under doubtful circumstances and the corruption of his regime had caused revolts to break out all over the island. There was no real leader in sight, and the self-determination conferred by act of the Congress seemed a mockery. But people in the United States were in no mood for further undertakings in far places; and this made a problem for Roosevelt, with the Congressional elections of 1906 impending. There was no doubt in his mind that he had an obligation to maintain order and to give the Cubans a decent government, and under the Platt Amendment the legal situation was clear. But there was political reality to deal with. What Taft was sent to do was to restore normal conditions without using force, a task that seemed impossible, and was. On the scene he soon discovered that intervention, however obnoxious, would have to be resorted to, and he had to tell Roosevelt so.

For Taft this was a crisis. He received from Roosevelt a stream of messages telling him that intervention must not occur, then that the word itself must be avoided in any necessary proclamations, then finally that, whatever was done must be done "in as gentle a way as possible." Taft knew well enough what Roosevelt's problem was; but he was in Havana, and he knew what the administrative problem was too. Whatever he did appeared certain to be wrong.

By now, two years from the end of Roosevelt's tenure, it had become plain to Taft what his fate was to be, and, whatever his feeling about the prospect, he had no desire to have it blighted by failure in a mission of this sort. The painful situation prolonged itself for some time. It was the worst in his whole career. Writing to his sister Helen after he had advised Roosevelt that immediate intervention was inescapable, he said of the day just past that it had been

> the most unpleasant of my life. I am in a condition of mind where I can hardly do anything with sequence . . . I wake up in the morning at three and four o'clock and do not go to sleep any more. My appetite ceases to be sharp . . . I don't know what they are saying in the United States, but I feel as if I was going to have a great fall from the height to which the compliments of the press have raised me.[7]

But everything came out better than he had anticipated. He was named Provisional Governor but passed on the office to a successor in a matter of weeks and was able to withdraw from the situation with the customary credit. Somehow, in such emergencies, he inspired everyone with confidence in his good intentions and his wisdom. Even

---

[7] Pringle, *op. cit.*, 309.

the unruly Cubans allowed him to soothe their rebellious habit. Demagogues shouting that the United States was about to annex the island
were no longer credited; insurgents began to turn in their arms; and
when Taft promised that new elections would be held, Cubans
believed that under American auspices they would be honest.

All that he promised was not completed until after he became
President. But what was important to Roosevelt was that the whole
matter receded from public attention. With Taft in charge, all was
done in the quietest way.

This, for Taft, worrying in the heat of Havana's September, was
the final ordeal. Instead of falling from that great height he had
spoken of to his sister, he was raised to an even greater one. There
was no longer any doubt of his acceptance by the Republicans—if
Roosevelt actually withdrew.

For whatever reasons Roosevelt allowed himself to drift into a situation in which he could not run again without embarrassment; it was
apparent by 1905–6 that it was a final decision. He had said too
much; and there was no crisis to justify a later reversal. He must have
regretted it. He enjoyed the office as no other President had, and felt
himself more competent for its duties than any other person could
possibly be. For a man of fifty, active and popular, to give way to
another seemed unnecessarily deferential to the American tradition of
sharing offices. But Taft finally recognized that it was going to be done
and that he was all but certain to succeed. From this time on, he
regarded himself as an active candidate and measured all that he did
by its effect on his prospects.

He must sometimes have wondered why Roosevelt had made up his
mind that there was no other available successor. Possibly he thought
that because Filipinos and Cubans liked and trusted Taft he must be
a good politician. But he was not effective in the Rooseveltian way;
and as for their agreement on fundamentals, it may have been that it
was Roosevelt, rather than Taft, who changed after the succession;
and the indignation that led to charges of betrayal and to the fatal
split of 1912 may have been more synthetic than real. Perhaps Roosevelt merely could not stand to see someone else in the White House.
This is what a biographer of both statesmen believed; and his contention seems a reasonable one.[8]

At any rate, for two years before the matter was consummated, Taft
was a candidate and Roosevelt was his manager. Presidents about to
leave office may not have much influence with the state leaders who
dominate the nominating conventions. But a President who deliberately
sets himself to rig the machinery years in advance has many oppor-

---

[8] *Ibid.*, 337 ff.

tunities to establish a situation in which all will be done as he wants it done. And Roosevelt made full use of every opportunity.

Bryan's strategy in the campaign was to claim that he was more to be trusted in carrying out the Roosevelt policies than was Taft. Sensing the temper of the voters, however, he sought to picture himself as more conservative than his reputation promised. For instance, he repudiated public ownership, which had so long been an item on the Populist—and his own—agenda. But Taft had a strategy of his own too, and it proved to be an effective counter to Bryan. This was to suggest that, without giving up the Roosevelt policies, he would administer them more equally, without so much disturbance to business; so he said:

> The chief function of the next administration, in my judgment, is distinct from, and a progressive development of, that which has been performed by President Roosevelt . . . to complete and perfect the machinery . . . by which lawbreakers may be promptly restrained . . . but which will operate with sufficient accuracy and dispatch to interfere with legitimate business as little as possible.

This was just the sort of thing the business community liked to hear; they yielded generously to appeals for funds; and the campaign was smoothly and efficiently handled by the party.

But Taft did travel and speak. His temperament may have favored the McKinley method—the front-porch campaign—but Roosevelt would have been outraged, and Bryan, as usual, was rampaging up and down the country. The fashion had been fixed. Candidates thereafter would be condemned to the terrible ordeal of active campaigning.

It remains to be noted that Taft would be numbered among those few Presidents who were refused election for a second term even when renominated. This had occurred first to John Adams, who was beaten by Jefferson and carried with him into oblivion the party of Washington, Hamilton, and Jay. It would happen again to Hoover, who would be overwhelmed by the visitation on himself of old Republican sins, much as Blaine had been when Cleveland had run against him in 1884. In the one case Republican corruption through several administrations, and in the other failure to check wild business excesses through the Harding and Coolidge regimes, lost the party public confidence.

This was not the case with Taft. In spite of Roosevelt, who now castigated him as a reactionary and who finally, in enraged frustration, ran against him as a third-party candidate, he was renominated for a second term. He was not elected; he ran third to his two opponents. But, if it had not been for the humiliation, he probably would not have cared much. He became first a professor of law at Yale and then

Chief Justice of the United States; and this was what he had really wanted all along.

He offers an interesting illustration of one way to attain the Presidency: by having the blessing of a retiring popular leader—much as Van Buren had done. And if neither instance is very encouraging, considering the ordeal both underwent in office, still it is a way to get there. Staying there, of course, is another matter.

Woodrow Wilson
1856–1924

Born at Staunton, Virginia, son of a Presbyterian minister
Became twenty-seventh President in 1913 at 56

HISTORY

1879	Graduated from Princeton University.
1882	Admitted to the bar after attending the University of Virginia Law School. Practiced law in Atlanta, Georgia.
1885	Married Ellen Louise Axson. Taught history at Bryn Mawr College.
1886	Received Ph.D. in political science at the Johns Hopkins University.
1888	Began teaching history and political science at Wesleyan University.
1890	Became professor of jurisprudence and political economy at Princeton.
1902	Elected to the presidency of Princeton.
1910	Elected Governor of New Jersey.

1912	Elected to the Presidency (Marshall, Vice-President); opponents, Theodore Roosevelt with Johnson, Progressive, and Taft with Sherman, Republican.
1915	After death of first wife, married Edith Bolling Galt of Washington.
1916	Re-elected (Vice-President, Marshall); opponent, Hughes with Fairbanks.
1917	World War I.
1919	After attending the Paris Peace Conference, signed the treaty for the United States. Undertook speaking trip to force ratification of the peace treaty by the Senate; suffered a stroke in Pueblo, Colorado, after which he was incapacitated for many months.
1920	Awarded Nobel Peace Prize.
1921	Retired and resided in Washington.
1924	Died in Washington.

No INSTANCE of approach to the Presidency is more instructive than that of Wilson. It was planned and carried out with ruthless energy and was completely successful.

In September 1910 he was nominated for the Governorship of New Jersey—being at the time President of Princeton University—and a little more than two years later he was elected to the Presidency. At the time of his nomination he had never held public office of any kind, had never attended a political convention, and had taken no interest in local politics. Very often he had not taken the trouble to vote even in Presidential elections. He had not voted in 1909, the year preceding his induction into politics.

This approach stands in the most complete contrast to that of his immediate predecessor, Taft, whose father was a politician and who himself was a political worker from youth. The contrast is the more striking, also, in another way. Taft was, until almost the last, a reluctant candidate. Wilson was a ferociously ambitious one, with the Presidency clearly in mind and with no distracting ambitions of any sort. The intensity of his desire for the office is explained, at least partly, by two circumstances. He had reached the pinnacle of the academic profession at forty-six, had occupied the presidency of Princeton for eight years, and would probably have been forced to resign very soon because of hostility within the university's governing board. He was too young to retire and was bitterly resentful that his situation had become so untenable. It was imperative for his self-respect that he move upward.

The other circumstance was his academic standing. He was the best-known political theorist in the country. One of his books had had an amazingly wide circulation for a technical discussion of government (*Congressional Government*, 1885). And a later volume (*Constitutional Government*, 1908) had been almost as well received.

One curious thing about his academic progress is that on the subject he was supposed to know most about he reversed his views. In *Congressional Government*, he proposed that since the American Presidency had been completely subordinated to the Congress, the Legislative Branch should be obliged to accept the accompanying responsibility. This amounted to a plea for adopting the Parliamentary system. It was published at a time when there was widespread disillusion with the line of Republican Presidents from Grant to Arthur, and his views were seriously discussed throughout the academic world.

His later *Constitutional Government*, however, took the opposite view—that the Presidential system was quite capable of furnishing the initiative and leadership so necessary in a democracy. The trouble had been with the Presidents, he now said, not with the Presidency.

It is suspected by some students of his career that the Columbia University lectures which became this later book were made at a time when it had already begun to appear, at least to himself, that an advantageous situation might develop. The prospect of the Presidency, however dim at first, is suspected of generating gradually a specific ambition; and it probably governed his every action from that time on. He could hardly advocate a revolution in the system he expected to exploit.

His reversal may be, however, and usually is, explained in another way. It is said that the performance of Cleveland was what convinced him that all the office needed was a strong man to occupy it. But there is at least a similarity in another reversal. Until he became an acknowledged candidate for the Presidency and was already Governor of New Jersey, he was conservative, almost a reactionary. In a very short time he became an outspoken progressive, almost a radical. It is possible that his acute political perceptions were at work. They may have told him that majority political orientation during the coming years would be strongly progressive. He may have seen that the powerful movement stirred up by Bryan and the Populist leaders was by no means exhausted and that it needed only a more responsible formulation and a more respected leader to carry the country. At any rate, he had been a contemptuous critic of Bryan in the earlier phase and, in the later one, took considerable pains to show his admiration. No retreat ever paid more dividends. Bryan was to fight like a lion for the Wilson cause in the Baltimore convention of 1912; to him, more than to anyone else, Wilson would owe his victory in that terrific battle.

As his abrupt changes of attitude in public affairs would indicate, there are some mysteries to penetrate if Wilson's conquest of the Presidency is to be fully understood. The reversals themselves offer one of the worst difficulties. They were so drastic and so fundamental that their acceptance by his supporters, to say nothing of the voters, is in itself hard to explain. The Princeton president was not an obscure academician who had confined his views to books and articles in learned journals. He had traveled over the country for years, lecturing sometimes to collegiate groups, but often to all sorts of other audiences, and so what he thought and how he felt had become known among large numbers of people.

His conservative bias was largely responsible for his adoption by the New Jersey bosses, notably James Smith and James R. Nugent, who accepted the word of Colonel George Harvey, editor of *Harper's Weekly* and the first and most persistent advocate of Wilson for President, that from the man he proposed for the Governorship there would be no expressions businessmen could take exception to. And Harvey had every reason to believe what he said.

Wilson had been publicly deploring even woman suffrage and had said that regulation of utilities by the state or Federal government had its justification in a theory "compounded of confused thinking and impossible principles of law." And when the panic of 1907 was in full course, he had offered the peculiar suggestion that it could be attributed to "the aggressive attitude of legislation toward the railroads." In another speech during the same month, he had argued that it was impracticable to give entire publicity to everything done by corporations, going on to characterize the "rough and ready reasoning of the reformers" as socialistic.

It was a time also when labor unions were struggling with their early organizing problems. Workers were still at a disadvantage in bargaining and had none of the protections they would later win. Wilson had no hesitation in condemning the whole movement. As late as 1909 he had spoken of himself as "a fierce partisan of the Open Shop and of everything that makes for individual liberty and I should like to contribute anything it might be possible for me to contribute to the clarification of thinking and the formation of right purposes in matters of this kind." There are echoes of the nineteenth-century British economists in some of his anti-labor pronouncements. He felt, he said, that labor in America was rapidly becoming unprofitable under the regulation of those who had determined to reduce output to a minimum.[1]

There was too much of this sort of thing to be explained as the unthinking pronouncements of a popular lecturer; it was a deliberate and cultivated conservatism, owed not only, as we must suspect, to his respectable Southern associations but to attitudes he had arrived at by study and thought. This was not the McKinley era, when to hold progressive opinions was to be allied with the fanatic Populists. Bryan had done his work well, and La Follette had supplemented it with his painstaking campaigns for reform. The muckrakers had abandoned their crusade, but they had left businessmen with a bad conscience. Matters had gone so far that Wilson was conspicuous as one of the few remaining defenders of contemporary commercial practices. He had persisted so long and been so consistent over the whole field of proposed change that Colonel Harvey cannot be blamed for vouching

---

[1] More of this precampaign attitude of Wilson will be found in *The Political Education of Woodrow Wilson* by James Kerney (New York, 1926). The author was at the time editor of the *Trenton Evening Times* and was thus a close neighbor of Wilson for many years. He was also in the confidence of many New Jersey politicians, including those responsible for Wilson's selection. His is one of the most realistic and rational essays in American political history. Quotations following are from his account.

that he was "safe," nor can so troubled a boss as Smith of New Jersey for accepting the assurance. Smith himself was under something more than suspicion at the moment for using his political influence to favor his own enterprises. He was cautious. But he accepted Wilson.

Practically no one among the New Jersey politicians, except Smith, wanted Wilson. He was unknown to them, they not being either intellectuals or attendants at popular lectures. He had shown no interest in their affairs. He had never even discussed, in his many speeches, any specific New Jersey issue. At the state convention that nominated Wilson there were among the delegates from Mercer County, in which both Trenton and Princeton are located, none who favored him. But Smith, from Essex County, outweighed all the rest. He was "The Big Fellow." But even for Smith, it was not easy. What went on is related by Kerney, who was there:

> During the evening preceding the convention, Harvey went by automobile to visit Wilson at Princeton, and when he returned to Trenton he found Smith almost a wreck in his effort to hold the votes in line. Altogether it was a bad night for Smith and Harvey . . . and the busiest night of Smith's political life. Not only did he have Nugent actively at work on the firing line, but old timers like William J. Thompson, "Duke of Gloucester," of race-track notoriety, Thomas Flynn, starter at the track, and other handy workers . . . It was a tough job. In that convention there were no hearts aching for the salvation of the world. The impelling and unadulterated motive was the desire to pick a man who could carry the election. Uncontrolled delegates, as well as many party chieftains, felt that Wilson was not the man . . . Nugent told me as he entered the hall that there was no sentiment whatever for Wilson . . . In order to make it appear that Essex, Smith's home County, was solidly with Wilson, it was necessary to throw out a large flock of delegates who had been chosen in opposition to Wilson . . .
>
> John W. Wescott, who subsequently nominated Wilson for President at both Baltimore and St. Louis, made a vigorous attack on high-handed methods being employed by the old line bosses . . . There was considerable disorder. Wescott hammered away at Wilson . . . "We want a candidate whose wisdom is derived from experience and not from dreams," was one shot . . . Wescott, glowering at Smith, added, "The sun of demoralizing commercialism in politics is set."
>
> When William K. Devereux, reading off a list of the candidates, announced "Woodrow Wilson of Mercer" there was a lusty demand from the Mercer delegates that Wilson should not be listed from their County, and a wag in the gallery shouted, "Accredit him to Virginia."

Nevertheless, Smith had his way and doubtless felt it to have been a good night's work, even if exhausting. And there was not the least doubt in anyone's mind that Wilson stood for the policies so long and openly expounded by Smith.

But immediately after his nomination he began to campaign with quite different pronouncements. From a conservative he became almost overnight a progressive. It is obvious that he had taken thought and become convinced that he must give the electorate what was wanted. Progressivism was in the air. And he was not interested in becoming merely Governor of New Jersey. Having got a start, it was instantly apparent that he was running for the Presidency. The Governorship was just a stop on the way where a useful record could be made.

It was another Jerseyite who won Wilson to Progressivism, or perhaps finished a conversion that was already working in an uneasy mind—for Wilson cannot have been ignorant of the massive demand for reform in his generation. George L. Record was the instructor who brought him into direct contact with Progressive thought and with its most prominent national leaders. Among these were William S. U'Ren and Senator Jonathan Bourne of Oregon, who, along with the La Follettes of Wisconsin, originated so many reformist measures. Wilson, under this influence, was soon elaborating a defense of direct primaries and even of the initiative, referendum, and recall. His conversion did not stop there; he was soon thinking that a corrupt-practices act was necessary, and there must be some such regulation of public utilities as the one Governor Hughes was sponsoring in New York. Another borrowing from New York was an employer's liability act. Taken together, these were a large part of the contemporary Progressive agenda, and even some of Wilson's new radical friends thought it too much for New Jersey; but he had all the enthusiasm now of a convert, and he determined to push for the whole package.

Before very long he was among the three or four leaders of the national movement and an avowed colleague of the Oregonians, of La Follette—and even of Bryan, of whom he had recently been so scornful. Record, who converted Wilson, had been active in New Jersey for ten years before Wilson came in contact with him. He had been an associate of Mayor Fagan of Jersey City, who was a contemporary of the municipal reformers in the Midwest and, like them, the subject of a characteristic treatment by Lincoln Steffens.[2] He had been, more than anyone else, responsible for rescuing New Jersey from what Wilson's biographer, Arthur S. Link, has spoken of as a "state in bondage." It had been "ruled by an oligarchical alliance of

---

[2] "A Servant of God and the People. The Story of Mark Fagan, Mayor of Jersey City," *McClure's Magazine*, January 1906.

corporations and politicians and completely dominated by big business and bossism." It was "one of the last strongholds of an industrial-feudal order that was the object of violent attack by progressive leaders throughout the country."[3]

Although Wilson was at Princeton, first as professor and then as president, during the whole of the period when the reformers had been struggling to free the state from oligarchical control, he had shown no sympathy with their ordeal. He had not only failed to offer any assistance but, whenever he had an opportunity, had spoken disparagingly of those who were active in the fight. It was not until 1910, in October, when he was already campaigning for the Governorship, that he first came into contact with Record. It happened because Wilson, in a confident mood, challenged any responsible Republican to debate with him, and Record, running for the Congress, accepted. Actually there never was a public debate; but an acknowledgment of conversion to Progressivism did result from Record's correspondence with him.[4]

This took the form of an arranged reply to certain questions asked of him by Record. It was so lucidly and sincerely stated that it convinced Progressives of his conversion. This frightened his conservative supporters; and there was soon a break with Smith which furnished Wilson with the extremely useful foil any candidate needs. And in time Harvey withdrew his support.

One of the fortunate results of the conversion was the consent of Joseph P. Tumulty to become Wilson's secretary. Tumulty, who had been elected to the legislature in 1907 as a rebel, had fought strenuously at the state convention to prevent Wilson's nomination, believing him to be a tool of the bosses. Tumulty would be a devoted assistant throughout his Presidency.

Wilson knew how to make use of his new orientation. And when he became Governor he knew how to make use of his position in striking for the Democratic nomination. He was aware that now he must expect his support to come not from the machine politicians but from the Progressives. He must appeal directly to the people if he expected to go to the Presidential convention with convincing support. If the delegates believed him more likely to be elected than other candidates, they might nominate him in spite of the older bosses who were certain to oppose him. The question was whether he had esti-

---

[3] *Wilson: The Road to the White House* (Princeton, 1947), 135. In 1926, when James Kerney was writing about the political education of Wilson, he spoke of "addresses and papers, carefully edited by friendly hands," and referred to his subject as "an enigma." Professor Link, more than two decades later, went a long way toward explaining the enigma by careful examination of original papers, letters, and other evidences of Wilson's day-to-day attitudes and actions.

[4] An account of this significant exchange will be found in Link, *op. cit.*, 189 ff.

mated correctly the temper of the country. Was it turning Progressive in a massive way?

In a strenuous first year, he persuaded the legislature to enact a series of long-delayed reform measures, and then, with this record to talk about, set out to convince the country that he alone met the demands of the times. Early in 1911 an organization to manage various phases of the coming campaign began operations. William F. McCombs opened a headquarters in New York to take care of political correspondence and to raise funds. Speaking trips were planned by Frank Parker Stockbridge and were so managed that Wilson spoke only to civic organizations without party affiliation. This was to avoid entanglement in factional disputes. All those associated in this work were known insurgents and reformers.

There was immediate and voluminous response. The newspapers and magazines gave him full coverage, and money began to come in. What was also of special significance, he finally succeeded in convincing Bryan that his former disparaging remarks ought to be forgotten. This was not easy. Wilson's aspersions, made so short a time ago as 1907, had been downright contemptuous and could not have been forgiven easily; but Bryan reciprocated in a most generous way.[5] And the result was seen in the Baltimore convention. All a hopeful candidate's plans and all his arduous labors must finally come to their test in this meeting; and even with Bryan conciliated, Wilson's supporters were not too hopeful. Most of the party's power and money was still available to rival candidates.

There is no doubt, after Professor Link's research, that in spite of Wilson's delayed discovery of Progressivism he had had the Presidency in mind, now vaguely as a mere dream, now actively as one with expectations, since 1902. To a person of Wilson's sort, this meant an even stricter dedication than it might have meant to a practicing politician. It became the center of his most earnest thoughts. It is not too much to say that his Columbia lectures were an academician's rationalization of ambition. These were made in 1907, and by that time the anticipation was real. He must not leave it on the record that he favored such a revision of government as would make the Presidency an arm of the legislature. This was three years before he repudiated his conservative economic views. He was getting ready.

In a way, this was characteristic. It was a familiar complaint of the

---

[5] Link, *op. cit.*, 352 ff. Wilson some time before had written to a railroad president, who had made an anti-Bryan speech, that he wished something could be done "to knock Mr. Bryan once for all into a cocked hat." This letter from a previous year was published by the *New York Sun* in the January before the Baltimore convention, thus threatening to undo all Wilson's belated cultivation of the veteran Democrat.

professionals, who saw his appeal becoming more formidable throughout the country, that he had taken no part whatever in active politics; that, in fact, he knew nothing about the machinery of democracy. They did not mention it, but this aloofness went further. He was also ignorant about current economic and social happenings. This did not mean that he was unintelligent. It simply meant that his interest was selective. He had a distaste for mixing in political operations; but he had no liking either for the stream of comment and discussion to be found in newspapers and magazines. He was not up on things and had no desire to be. This is why he failed to note the rise of the Progressives.

And it is one of the curiosities of political history that he could so effectively use a reputation gained in the earnest exposition of one set of views to persuade his public that an entirely new set must be reasonable.

Throughout the years when his reputation as an intellectual leader was being established, his approach to government had been purely academic. When he commented on Progressivism in a supercilious way, he was measuring it by the standards he had accepted as a graduate student and had gone on expounding as a teacher. These criteria had been arrived at by political theorists he most admired—such, for instance, as Walter Bagehot, the author of *Physics and Politics*. He knew a good deal more about English writers of Gladstone's generation than he did about his contemporaries.

This might annoy the professional politicians, of all views, who sometimes had the impression that he did not know what they were talking about, but it turned out to be advantageous in furthering his ambition. If the Presidency came to him, it would be because he was a man of thought and principle, one who was above the questionable affairs of everyday politics.

It was also an advantage that he had always held to the strictest faith in religion. His father had been a Presbyterian minister, and he was as dogmatic and intolerant as his father had been. Altogether, his reputation as one who guided his life by standards of immutable rectitude was one he most carefully guarded. His pleasures were not literary ones, not sporting ones, and not social ones; his leisure was given to meditation, mild exercise, and conversation. He had three adoring daughters and a wife who devoted herself to his comfort, and he leaned on the female cousins who could be counted on to admire and sustain him. He seems to have avoided risking the abrasiveness of male company; and his opinions were seldom challenged. This is perhaps why they gradually fell out of tune with contemporary movements.

When he spoke to the audiences he so carefully cultivated, it was as a preacher, instructing them from fundamental and righteous positions. By long practice, he had become an eloquent speaker in the ministerial manner, handing down wisdom, marking out guides to conduct, using parables. He practically always spoke without manuscript or notes and allowed no question periods. His often-used phrases and paragraphs could be repeated if they proved useful—it was before the day of radio—and he had no fear of repetition. The people in his sort of audience seem to have appreciated him as a gentleman and a scholar dealing with puzzling affairs in a confident and summary way. What he had to say agreed with their own preconceptions and disturbed no prejudices.

The president of Princeton was naturally assumed to speak with authority. But actually he had long since abandoned scholarly labors; he was now an oracle, further and further separated from investigation and original generalization. He went on writing and had a large and profitable audience for his books. But some of the later ones were deplorable productions. His five-volume *History of the American People,* published in 1902, the year he became president of Princeton, was hastily written, marred by errors of fact and interpretation, and extremely partisan. It is best described as a Tory document. When the rising tide of his popularity threatened to carry him to nomination in the Democratic convention, his *History* was used by his detractors to show the emptiness of his claim to authority. His supporters indignantly rejected these criticisms, but Professor Link thinks them justified:

> Unfortunately for Wilson, the attack . . . was all the more devastating because most of what they said was true. Wilson had written American history from the conservative point of view; he had castigated the agrarian radicals, praised Cleveland's attack upon Debs and the railway strikers in 1894, ridiculed Coxey's Army, in short, had written history he would not have written if he had known he was some day to become a presidential candidate.[6]

His oratorical gift could not be held against him. It had gained him the reputation of being a popular instructor, wise about national policy because of investigation and long study. But his writings were available to be read. They could not be explained away by the newly converted crusader for all the things he had once ridiculed. Fortunately, the attack came from the Hearst papers; and Hearst could be shrugged off as a yellow journalist who had no scruples about distortions and misinterpretations. Wilson himself took this line. If he had changed his opinions it was for good reasons. Fortunately, in his new progressive role, he had the support of organized labor. But he had

---

[6] *Op. cit.,* 381.

at last been forced to get down in the dust with other Democrats. When he abandoned his lofty stance he fell back on the defense that the attacks he suffered were unfair. Nevertheless, his familiar pronouncements made him vulnerable, and spells of self-pity were frequent. Not long before the convention, he wrote to a woman friend:

> Not that I actually lose heart. I find I am of too firm a fibre, and of too firm a faith, for that; but the world grows sometimes to seem so brutal, so naked of beauty, so devoid of chivalrous sentiment and all sense of fair play, that one's own spirit hardens and is in danger of losing its fineness. I fight on, in the spirit of Kipling's "If," but that is oftentimes a very arid air.[7]

But there were many embarrassing passages yet to come before he could occupy the rare air of the White House and withdraw again from undignified contacts with detractors. By the spring of 1912 his nomination had become a cause with many dedicated supporters, who worked in his behalf through the days and into the nights. There were discouraging intervals as the opposing forces mounted their successive attacks. Wilson, staying above the battle, alternately suffered euphoria and dismay. His self-pity had, in any case, to be hidden.

Every individual who approaches the Presidency as Wilson did, not by succession, not because of being a military hero, and not because of being a member of the upper-level political club, must pass through these ordeals. Two of them are familiar to all candidates but are much worse for the self-created statesman. The fight for nomination and the campaign for election itself are exhausting stretches. By Wilson's time they were becoming longer and more intense. For one thing, Bryan and Theodore Roosevelt between them had made it impossible for McKinley's front-porch technique to be used again. Even Taft, who was fairly certain of election in 1908, hauled his 300 pounds of avoirdupois around the country, scheduled by the party managers, making so poor a showing against Bryan that his uncomfortable campaigning could not possibly have done other than lose votes. Still, he was not excused. The Republicans, not Taft, won in that year.

But Wilson would not have cared to be exempted from this particular duty. He was at his best on the hustings. He prepared most of his own speeches in the preconvention campaign; they were usually delivered, as he had made his public addresses, with no more than a few notes before him—or perhaps no notes at all. He went on this way during the campaign as well. Audiences inspired him, especially those

---

[7] *Ibid.*, 390.

gathered by party workers. This was almost the last time such freedom for a candidate in speaking would be considered allowable. Too much might be lost by an inadvertent reference; also, it was becoming difficult for a traveling candidate even to keep track of where he was. The era of ghost writers was at hand. The possibility of making a gaffe became a nightmare as the airplane age came on and it was possible to appear anywhere in the country within a few hours of having appeared anywhere else. With Coolidge the radio would appear, and after that speeches could not be repeated.

During the winter and spring of 1912 the Governorship of New Jersey got very little attention. Wilson was on tour most of the time. And as the convention approached in June he was a man distracted. This was the worse because he was assumed by the gathering professionals to be conversant with political procedures. But he was not. They had to be explained to him in the most elementary terms. And not all of what went on was explained to him at all. Where the money came from that was paying the considerable bills; what promises were being made in the frantic effort of his supporters to reach the convention with a majority of the delegates; what arrangements were being made to make sure of a friendly gallery; what interpretations were being made of his pronouncements—he was incredibly ignorant of all this.

As the opening day approached, it seemed certain that Champ Clark, who had become Wilson's most alarming opponent, would have a majority on the first ballot. He had won several state primaries, some of them by surprising votes (Illinois), and was the favorite of the conservatives. It was to be a test of progressive sentiment. It would soon be shown whether Wilson had been right to put himself at the head of the movement. It was certain that the contest would be close; and how they could gain a decisive advantage for Wilson, his managers could not see. It was an old convention custom to accept the candidate who reached and passed a majority even though the two-thirds rule still stood. It was not invariable, but it was usual. It had not been ignored since 1844.

When the first ballot did come, after frantic rounding up of delegates by the opposing forces and after the first all-night session, Clark lacked a majority; but it was known to all that New York's votes—all 90 of them under the unit rule—would go to Clark on a later ballot. That, it was expected, would start a landslide. The switch did come on the tenth ballot, and it did give Clark a majority. But the expected landslide did not start. There were about a hundred votes controlled by the Underwood managers, and these would have increased the Clark vote almost to two-thirds. But the Underwood people held firm and refused to trade even for the Vice-Presidency.

Why the opposition to Clark was so solid is not clear. It is thought that Underwood may have supposed the two leading contenders would kill each other off and that he would have become a dark horse. This had happened before. At any rate, as the balloting went on, it gradually became apparent that Clark had reached his peak. Meanwhile, Wilson himself and McCombs, his representative, had decided that he could not win. McCombs was instructed to withdraw his name. Others—McAdoo among them—were unwilling and persuaded Wilson to rescind his instructions. The fight went on as one ballot followed another in the steaming, turbulent hall and its environs. Then the Wilsonites turned to Bryan, the old mentor of the party. On the fourteenth ballot, Bryan rose, when Nebraska was called, and said that his state's delegation had been instructed for Clark but that it had been with the understanding that he was to be a progressive candidate. That unspoken agreement had been violated. He himself, and the delegates who were with him, would vote for no candidate supported by Tammany and the Wall Street crowd.

The Wilson people hoped this declaration of Bryan's would bring enough others around to make a majority. But actually, even on the twenty-sixth ballot, Wilson was still considerably behind Clark; the break did not come until the forty-third, after a weekend of bargaining. McCombs, McAdoo, Daniels, and others finally persuaded Kentucky, West Virginia, Maryland, and Virginia to come over. On the forty-sixth ballot, the Underwood votes were cast for Wilson and it was done. Wilson, at Sea Girt, and Champ Clark, in Washington, had suffered through the week of uncertainty at the end of long-distance telephones, each in turn alternately hoping and despairing. It had been a cruel ordeal for both.

As Link remarks, it was ironical that Wilson should finally have owed his nomination not to his new friends but to old-line Democratic bosses in the most conservative states, people who had been his bitterest antagonists. He goes on to summarize:

> It is a long story from Harvey's Lotus Club speech in 1906 to the Baltimore convention. Wilson's own political activities brought him first into the public consciousness; the labors of the little group of men in the headquarters at 42 Broadway in New York furthered his presidential movement; the important work of state politicians and editors won him support among the people; Bryan's fight at Baltimore emphasized the progressive character of Wilson's leadership and generated widespread popular agitation for his nomination; the Underwood delegates helped prevent Clark's nomination at a critical time and, later during the balloting, definitely turned the tide in Wilson's

favor; and, finally, the support of the machine politicians brought over the votes without which Wilson could never have been nominated.[8]

If it is wondered why this should have been so much more furious a struggle than others, the answer is that the nomination in 1912 was so much more valuable than any since the Civil War. The nominee would in all likelihood win the election. This was because of the Republican split, preparing for several years and now obviously fatal. This was a time—one of the rare times—when the club of insiders might have dared go to the people with one of their own, not with an outsider. That they turned down Clark and took Wilson was, as we have seen, a last-minute surrender, and one they made with the utmost reluctance.

When Wilson began to make his determined leadership felt, it was gradually borne in on the party leaders that Bryan's long dominance had been handed over to Wilson. The new regime was of a kind hardly recognized by the professionals. Wilson owed his power not to the party, and not to any faction or class, but to his own position. In spite of being an aloof intellectual, he held himself to be a people's man. He had arrived after a hard struggle of a new sort, and it remained to be seen whether he could capture the election as he had the nomination. There were more Republicans than Democrats by several millions; but here he had luck.

In August, about the time Wilson was being officially notified of his nomination, Theodore Roosevelt was accepting the Progressive nomination and leaving the Republicans decimated. It was a contest then between two progressives. Taft actually was nowhere, and in the end did run a bad third. But Roosevelt could not find enough progressives in the Republican party willing to sever their old ties, and although he was strenuous and noisy, he succeeded only in making Wilson's election certain.

If it had not been for Roosevelt's attempt, Wilson would not have been elected. Between them, the Republicans and Progressives had seven and a half million votes. Wilson had more than a million less than this. He was not the first minority President, but he was the one who was most decidedly in the minority.[9]

In the campaign Wilson fumbled badly at first, hardly knowing what to settle on as a theme. Should he make an outright progressive appeal? And, if he did, how should he distinguish his own policies from those of Roosevelt, who seemed to cover the whole field, having

---

[8] *Ibid.*, 465.

[9] It is worth noting, however, that he had more than 80 per cent of the electoral votes. The exaggeration of popular victories by the electoral system was never more conspicuous.

gathered up the entire unfinished agenda of the progressive movement
and loudly proclaimed it to be his own? He maintained that he "stood
at Armageddon and battled for the Lord." And this made for a hard
contest. So Wilson wavered.

It was Louis D. Brandeis who rescued him from his difficulty. That
astute lawyer had made himself the best-known advocate of a policy
that almost amounted to a movement. He sharply defined a progressivism that before had been simply a series of political reforms. He
advised Wilson to become a trust-buster, an advocate of littleness, a
believer in free enterprise. If he preached the restoration of competition as a public policy wherever it had been stifled through consolidation, said Brandeis, he would carry the West and South. He convinced
Wilson that this was feasible on an August day at Sea Girt, the
Governor's summer home, in a long luncheon and post-luncheon conversation. It was this that was to emerge as Wilson's New Freedom
—compulsory free enterprise, something for everyone, not too much
for anyone—and to dominate his domestic policy as President.

This gave him the alternative to Roosevelt he so badly needed, for
Roosevelt proposed to regulate and control big business but not
actually to break up and destroy it. This was the theme of the campaign, and it sufficed. If Wilson never really knew what he was talking about, Brandeis did; and that wily enemy of big business had now
what he had always wanted, a mouthpiece for the philosophy he had
for years been trying to propagate. Again and again, Wilson asked
Brandeis for further elucidation. He himself was making eloquent
speeches, but it was painfully evident that they had no very solid content. As he went along, Brandeis' tutoring gradually shaped his appeal.

But naturally, the politicians were at work too. Before long the
demands of the local leaders had become so exhausting that the candidate felt himself able to go on only by sheer nerve. He complained;
but he did go on, as every candidate after him would have to. He was
buoyed up by the practical certainty after the middle of August that
he would be elected. He had only to show himself, stick to his atomis-
tic appeal, make no mistakes of a sort that would offend large minorities, and await the result.

When it came he could feel that the Presbyterian Providence he
believed in so devoutly had guided the affair. He was appointed to
win. And he would be the kind of President who was certain that this
was so—confident in the righteousness of his policies, ruthless to use
the power of his office and become the leader of his people.

When the next test came in 1916, his certainty of judgment had led
the country through several crises, but not yet into the war that
seemed clearly to be coming. His hold on the electorate was no more
overwhelming than it had been in 1912. He again became a minority

President, thus establishing a record. The Progressives returned to the
Republican party, and although Wilson had three million more votes
than he had had four years earlier, the Republicans and the minor
parties together had still more. But they were in the wrong places.
This time the Democratic electoral majority was only a little more
than 52 per cent. But it was enough. Wilson was a two-term President,
not a repudiated one-termer.

Warren Gamaliel Harding
1865–1923

FROM THE COLLECTIONS OF THE LIBRARY OF CONGRESS

Born at Corsica, Ohio
Became twenty-eighth President in 1921 at 55

HISTORY

1882	Attended Ohio Central College.
1884	After studying law, teaching school, and having been an insurance agent, purchased the *Marion Star* (with two partners).
1895	Appointed County Auditor.
1898	Elected to the Ohio Senate (served until 1903).
1903	Elected Lieutenant Governor of Ohio.
1910	Unsuccessful Republican candidate for Governor.
1914	Elected to the United States Senate (served until 1921).
1920	Nominated by the Republican convention and elected (Vice-President, Coolidge); opponent, Cox with F. D. Roosevelt.
1923	Died in San Francisco.

356

W<small>E COME NOW</small> to the third of the reluctant Presidents. Washington would rather have cultivated his estates at Mount Vernon, Taft wanted to be a Supreme Court Justice, and Harding knew he ought to stay in the United States Senate, where his duties were within his powers and the life was congenial. Nineteen-twenty was, however, one of those election years when it was quite clear which party would win. The Wilson administration had tailed off into the dismal aftermath of war. There was no elation about victory in Europe; there was only disillusion following the afflatus of the crusade to make the world safe for democracy. Wilson had been so ill as to be almost incompetent for two years, and the Presidency had hardly functioned during that period. Opposition Senators had prevented approval of the Treaty of Versailles, and there was as yet no formal peace. The Democrats were demoralized and the Republicans had a clear prospect of victory.

When it was considered that Wilson himself had twice been a minority President, which meant that there were probably fewer Democrats than Republicans, and certainly fewer Democrats than Republicans, Progressives, and insurgents taken together, it was as probable as anything can be in politics that whoever was nominated by the Republicans would be elected. It is this certainty that occasionally gives the party insiders the opportunity they always hope for but seldom have. When it occurs, their choice will be one of their own, one who belongs to the inner circle, who will not change but will remain faithful and docile. If, besides, one can be found who is a skilled compromiser, so that internecine quarrels can be damped down, that is good. And if, still further, he has—or can be made to have—the public appeal that draws votes, he will be the perfect professional's candidate.

Harding not only had all these attractions for his hard headed colleagues but also one other; and this was decisive. Without having an aristocratic, or even a genteel, background, he had the appearance *par excellence* of a statesman. No one could look at the Senator from Ohio and believe that he would be other than a thoughtful, serious, and careful guardian of the Presidential office. He was large, handsome, virile, and well dressed; he had that elusive quality of presence, and he had demonstrated on a thousand platforms his ability to speak extensively without making dangerous commitments. He called this "bloviating"[1] and regarded it as a gift. It had helped immensely in his long

---

[1] "Bloviate," as a contribution to Americana, probably explains itself, but its political origin and connotations should be emphasized. Harding has not been its only practitioner, although no other can have been more skilled. It describes the orating of one who seeks to project a favorable picture of himself and his cause

political career in Ohio. Along with his other qualities, it had brought him to the United States Senate; it had been turned to the uses of his smarter colleagues who had interests to be served, and they saw the prospect of further uses.

The drawback was that Harding was everything he appeared not to be and nothing that he did appear to be. He was good-natured to the point of never being able to make a decision. His father is said to have told him once that it was a good thing he was not a girl, because he could never say no. But he was really congenial only with the sort of friends who would drink and play poker with him the night through and who could be trusted never to devil him with conversation. Non-questioning acceptance of party dictates had led him, time after time, into confusion—for, after all, there was sometimes need for interpretation. And, almost worst of all, he had a personal history of slack living, careless habits, and sporting associations. He was as nearly an empty shell of a man as could have been found. He was not, after all, the perfect candidate the professionals thought him to be—not if he should ever be put under pressure.

It is quite apparent that all this was at least suspected, if not known; and only overconfidence led the leaders to put forward so doubtful a character as their candidate. It was done by fifteen men in a room in the Blackstone Hotel in Chicago. This was what afterward came to be a characteristic political allusion; never, after 1920, would anyone misinterpret the meaning of a choice made "in a smoke-filled room."[2] It would always mean that a Harding had been picked, with all the consequences that must follow.

Even after the leaders' minds had met, they had a moment of doubt. They called in the Senator and put him to the question. What actually was the form of words on this occasion can only be guessed; there are numerous versions. Apparently, those trusted with the interrogation were the same Colonel George Harvey, now an inside Republican, who had been such an early promoter of Wilson's candidacy, and Senator Brandegee, one of the Old Guard. The version accepted by reporter Mark Sullivan is as follows:

We think you may be nominated tomorrow; before acting finally, we think you should tell us, on your conscience and before God,

---

but at the same time seeks to avoid taking a stand he may later regret. He finds safe objects for praise: home, home town, family, mother, nation, party, and the like; and he denounces, sometimes passionately, immoralities, foreigners, bureaucrats, high taxes, and all the paraphernalia of a complex civilization so much resented by simple folk. To go on at this for hours, as Harding could do, is to "bloviate." To such practiced users it becomes second nature.

[2] Wesley M. Bagby, "The 'Smoke-Filled Room' and the Nomination of Warren G. Harding," *Mississippi Valley Historical Review*, XLI (March 1955), 657–74.

whether there is anything that might be brought against you that would embarrass the party, any impediment that might disqualify you or make you inexpedient, either as candidate or as President.[3]

Harding was stunned, Sullivan reports, and asked for time to think it over. He was shut into a room by himself; but he emerged in about ten minutes to say that there was "nothing; no obstacle."

He must have convinced himself that all the old stories associated with his small-town sporting proclivities were not likely to be repeated now, or at least that they could not be substantiated. It also meant, however, that a certain Nan Britton, who was at that moment in Chicago and with whom he had carried on a liaison for some five years was "taken care of." True, she had a child, and the affair was by no means over; but he had been generous, and she had been discreet. She could be trusted. So he said that there was no obstacle. The contrast with Cleveland in similar circumstances is inevitable; but Cleveland had already been nominated, and Harding might not have been if he had made full disclosure.[4]

This raises the question of Harding's desire for the Presidency. At this late stage he was willing to risk a scandal, almost certain to involve further exposures, and this would seem to indicate that he had a consuming ambition for the office. But all the biographical studies of the man clearly indicate that he had not. He was happy in the Senate and knew that the Presidency would be beyond his mental and moral capacities. His forebodings of this sort had led him to discourage such mention of his name as had from time to time been made. And these withdrawings were sincere.

But there was one person who, years earlier, had determined that Harding should be President and had ever since been maneuvering to place him in his present position of availability. For Harry M. Daugherty, this was to be a sort of compensation. He himself was an abler man than Harding, smarter politically, and more capable in the management of affairs; but he lacked the charm, the ability to conciliate, the talent for "bloviating" that Harding had. He had conceived the unlikely plan of pushing the juvenile figure ahead of him and becoming, himself, the man behind the throne.

---

[3] *Our Times* (New York, various volumes), VI.

[4] Forty-four years later (1964) one of those trunks, long forgotten in that attic so ardently hoped for by historical researchers, yielded a bundle of letters that told the tale of still another involvement. Nan Britton was not the only mistress with a claim on Harding. The remarkable loyalty of these—and possibly other—ladies frustrated the critics until it was too late for any effect on his career to be registered. Still, a President so vulnerable must have felt his hold on respectability to have been tenuous. It seems probable that Harding was always a worried man; and if his cronies knew of his adventures, they were in a position to do about as they liked. And, of course, they did.

Unfortunately, Daugherty was not only incapable of attracting votes but had no more than a rudimentary sense of decency and no public conscience whatever. He had been, back in 1895, an unsuccessful candidate for Attorney General of Ohio; he had several times tried for the gubernatorial nomination; and he had twice been defeated in tries for the Congress. Finally he had been badly defeated for the Senatorial nomination in 1916. The best he had been able to do was to win a seat in the state legislature. Even in 1920, when he had his finest hour in the smoke-filled room of the Blackstone Hotel, he had not succeeded in becoming a delegate to the convention; he was present as a private citizen. But if he could not win anything for himself, he could adopt Harding and make something of him. Contemporaries often spoke of the Senator as "Daugherty's meal ticket."

Daugherty had other affiliations; but he was shrewd, and there always seemed to be more smoke than fire in the scandalous stories about him. Some passages in Samuel Hopkins Adams' *Incredible Era* are devoted to outlining his career. One runs as follows:

> No just estimate of Daughtery can fail to give him credit for courage, capacity, and loyalty, keen comprehension of his own special brand of politics, and consistency in pursuit of his principles, such as they were. With his mental equipment, he might have been an able lawyer. His tastes did not lie in that direction. First, last, and all the time, he was the political manipulator, the adroit fixer.

The comparison of Daugherty with Hanna is inevitable. McKinley, as we have seen, was another weak individual who would never have become President if he had not been promoted by a more forceful second; but McKinley, who was certainly negative and flabby, was nevertheless a man of conscience who sometimes balked at taking orders. Besides, Hanna was a man of wealth and status, not, like Daugherty, a frequenter of doubtful company, a seller of favors, and manager of a center for small-time crooks. If Daugherty had had some of Hanna's connections with the world of big business, he might have done better. As it was, his operations were carried out by hangers-on who operated in the back streets of politics, making little deals for small sums, dividing them up, and spending the proceeds in attempts to impress the world of gamblers, intriguers, and dealers in corruption whence they had emerged. They were certain to be exposed. Eventually they were.

They were called, after they descended on Washington, "the Ohio Ring." And their operations from "the little house on K Street" became notorious. But long before that, they had carried on their trade in Ohio. Harding was their front and Daugherty their protector. It was beyond their furthest ambitions that they should have the Presidency to exploit. But it was not beyond Daugherty's. He had it in mind for years before the opportunity he was waiting for really opened.

If Warren Harding lacked the fierce and driving ambition that so many Presidents can be seen to have had, he had another kind of ambition with the qualities necessary to satisfy it. He did want to join the company of politicians. He wanted to live among them, be part of the kind of life they lived, and enjoy the indulgences characteristic of their profession. To satisfy this longing, he had the requisite temperament. He was easygoing, amoral, and attractive; and people were inclined to do him favors. Also, he soon uncovered a talent for making the bloviating kind of speech. When he got to the legislature, a reporter said he was the most popular man in that body:

> He had the inestimable gift of never forgetting a man's face or name. He was a regular he-man . . . a great poker player, and not at all averse to putting a foot on the brass rail.[5]

He soon became the legislature's favorite conciliator, the expert in "oiling the party machinery."

It is because Harding was so empty a vessel himself that it is necessary to explain the stronger personalities who advanced him. The Republican party in Ohio was then almost the private domain of two strong leaders. One, of course, was Mark Hanna; the other was Joseph B. Foraker. The one we have seen managing McKinley; the other, from the lower end of the state, playing an important part in the fortunes of Taft. Between them, although sometimes with epic differences, they ran the Ohio party. A lowly legislator had only to follow the orders that came down to him from one or the other or both. Harding was happy, for the most part, to do so and was always available to smooth things over; and, because he was so good-natured, he often succeeded.

> Popularity was his stock-in-trade. Who could help but like a fellow member so smooth, so amenable, deft at playing the game, and assiduous in doing small favors for adherent or opponent? He was rich in eulogy, sparing in denunciation . . . To the hand of his superiors he was a fit tool. No prickly principles hindered him. Theories of good government, of public service, those stumbling blocks to party progress, were not permitted to interfere with his carrying out of

---

[5] "Harding" by George McAdam, *World's Work*, September 1920. Quoted in *The Incredible Era*, 51.

orders . . . He worked with and for the corruptionists. But there was no talk of dirty money sticking to his fingers . . .[6]

In 1903, after having been a legislator for four years, he was nominated for the Lieutenant Governorship. This came about in a characteristic way. Since Harding came from Foraker territory and was identified with the southern branch of the party, he might have been offensive to the northern—or Hanna—branch; but actually his talent for compromise made him acceptable. When Hanna succeeded in getting control of the Republican nomination for Governor with Myron T. Herrick as his candidate, the Foraker forces demanded compensation. There was not too much reluctance among the victors when Harding was suggested as Herrick's running mate. So "Herrick, Harding, and Harmony" became the winning slogan of that year.

The next state convention threatened to become a bitter battle between factions, both ready for a fight to the finish. Harding undertook to soothe the rising passions and succeeded against all probability. The *Cleveland Plain Dealer* reported it:

> The man who stepped into the breach today was Lieutenant Governor Harding . . . By the use of a rare flow of words he for the moment made the delegates believe that the word harmony had been written with indelible ink. Roused from a condition of lethargy produced by the previous monotony the delegates vociferously cheered the name of each one of the men who will constitute the Republican Big Four, and at the end poured forth approval on Harding himself. If the enthusiasm of the afternoon is any criterion, Lieutenant Governor Harding is destined to figure to an increasing extent in the future counsels of the party.[7]

But it did not happen that way. He was not renominated that year; in fact, he was not renominated at all. He withdrew voluntarily; and he was not heard of again as a candidate for four years—until 1909. Why he did this, no one knows. The party did not win that election, and he may have foreseen defeat. Or he may have felt that he had gone as far as he ought to go in public life. Some commentators thought so. He did have an active sense of his own insufficiency, was uncomfortable in his confusion whenever decisions had to be made, and was unhappy in any serious discussion. Then, too, his newspaper in Marion was prospering, and being its editor gave him a position in the community he had never enjoyed as a younger man. Besides his political success, he now had a certain income. From a boy of rather

---

[6] Adams, *op. cit.*, 55.
[7] October 1, 1903. Adams, *op. cit.*, 59.

doubtful family, raised in a poor home, and having for connections none of the more respectable citizens, he had now become perhaps the best-known individual in town. And if his habits had not changed much, his position was so different that they could be overlooked.

The former Lieutenant Governor may have seemed to be out of politics, but actually he was not. He never could be. His contacts were many and his friends numerous. He traveled a good deal and kept in touch with most of the local leaders. Then, as the fatal Republican split of 1912 began to approach, there were repercussions in Ohio, and a person with his talents was needed. In the beginning, there was question about Taft, who had been picked by Roosevelt as his successor. This did not suit Foraker, who had ambitions of his own and who succeeded in getting the Ohio Republican League to endorse him. And the endorsement had been drafted by Harding.

Now there occurred one of those incidents so characteristic of political careers but so difficult to reconcile with the view of themselves politicians like to encourage. They do not usually pretend to serious virtues, to industriousness, or to competence; but they do ask credit for faithfulness to each other. If they have one honored principle, it is loyalty. That even this is not always allowed to stand in the way of advancement, however, we have seen before; and it appears again in the Harding history. Not long after having written the resolution of support for Foraker, his long-time sponsor, Harding published in his Marion newspaper a repudiation of the old boss and a declaration of support for Taft. The burden of the prominently displayed editorial was that Foraker was already, in effect, defeated and that Ohio was for Taft:

> This is not a band-wagon climb; it is the calm recording of the trend in Ohio politics . . . The contest for Presidential preference is at an end . . . Senator Foraker may keep up the semblance of a fight for district delegates but it will make no difference . . . Licked is the laconic way to put it and in political honor his followers are prisoners of war and will have to be good . . .

This was a determinative switch in Harding's career. If he had not made it, he would not have been nominated for the Governorship. He was defeated in this campaign, in spite of most strenuous efforts to knit the Republican factions. But he had established preferred consideration for the Senate nomination of 1914. If he had earned it by a betrayal, still he had earned it.

In the 1912 national convention he was given the singular honor of making the nominating speech for Taft. This was going well until he inadvertently broke a rule of such performances and, considerably before his peroration, mentioned the candidate's name, thus setting off the set demonstration called for in the circumstances. After that the rest of his speech was anticlimactic. But still, as he said later, it had been the most valued honor of his life. Then, too, in 1916 he was made temporary chairman of the convention that nominated Hughes for the Presidency. He first wrote his own speech and liked it; but his colleagues got hold of it and rewrote it as they preferred it to be. He sadly asquiesced, and it was, as he said, "rotten; my friends in the Senate made me put things in—the tariff, reciprocity, public lands, pensions, and God knows what—and now, it's a rag carpet."[8]

But Daugherty felt that his plan was unfolding. Many of the delegates to this convention would also be delegates to that of 1920. They would recall the handsome chairman of 1916.

The honor involved in presiding over a convention can be appreciated only by understanding that he was a professional, for whom appearing as the central figure at the supreme working occasion of the party's machinery is a moving experience. Even if it does not contribute to the satisfying of an ambition, it enhances him among those who stand highest in his regard. But for Harding, there was another reason. And to understand that, we shall have to look backward briefly to his younger years.

Harding's father was a homeopathic physician with a small and unprofitable practice. There were eight children, and they were always crowded into a small, ramshackle house in a run-down neighborhood. His mother had no formal education, but she practiced midwifery; and it appears that the children raised themselves as best they could. Warren, who was the oldest, seems to have felt none of the classic family responsibility. He was neither industrious nor, apparently, ambitious. He got along from day to day, doing a little casual work if it was not too hard. It was at fourteen that he went to Iberia and entered the institution called Ohio Central College. That institution has long since disappeared without leaving records; and Harding did not stay long. Then he tried schoolteaching, but he found the life too exacting; he quit after one term.

By this time his foot-loose family had moved to Marion. He followed and, to make a living, tried various jobs, the most agreeable of which was selling insurance. But even this became too arduous. Next he tried reporting but was soon fired, because, it seems, he spent too much time hanging around the local Republican headquarters. In view of what happened afterward, this seems prophetic. But it would scarcely seem to qualify him for ownership of a newspaper. Yet presently, with two other young fellows, one of whom had a couple

---

[8] Finley Peter Dunne, *The Saturday Evening Post*, September 12, 1936. Dunne reported that the speech was "dismally unsuccessful."

of hundred dollars, he did buy the *Star*, a paper that "was destitute of both circulation and reputation." It was an afternoon publication of four pages printed on an antique press and filled with boiler-plate material. One partner acted as newsman, and Warren was only a general helper. But in this enterprise he seems to have found himself. This and politics were his lifelong interests. And before very long the *Star* responded to the partners' hard work. It became profitable and influential in Marion.

Still, Warren had the handicap of being a village sport, of coming from a shabby home and a family that did not mix with the better people. He did a good deal of pool-playing; he was known as an avid poker player; he still liked to frequent political headquarters. He had no respectable attachments—church or other organizations—and he was as casual in his lecheries as might be expected. He always drank a good deal; but it was sociable and not habitual drinking. After several years his remaining partner—the third, who had furnished the initial funds, had left almost at once—dropped out. They had differed over the installation of a telephone in the offices.

The newspaper business was one that could be pursued without much change of habit, and Harding seems never to have changed his. He pursued the same amusements; he had the same sort of friends. And he was regarded as a pleasant but hardly respectable young man.

Then he met and married Florence Kling.

In contrast to Warren Harding, Florence Kling was born to one of the better families of Marion. Her father was a businessman and a strict Mennonite. It was a constant irritation to him that his daughter was defiantly nonconformist. She had what, for that time, was a good schooling, ending with a course at the Cincinnati Conservatory of Music. But she would not obey the rules he laid down. She liked to dance and to roller-skate; and she preferred that these amusements should be in the company of young men her father distrusted. Father and daughter were in constant conflict, and sometimes he locked her out of the house overnight.

She was never a pretty girl and, as she grew up, became even less attractive. But she had vigor and drive, and her initiative substituted for her rivals' more placid beauty. At nineteen she caught a husband who seemed to share her preferences; he was of good family too; but he turned out to be incompetent. Presently he abandoned her and disappeared, leaving her with a small child. She refused to appeal to her father and, with the help of friends, set herself up as a music teacher. She divorced this first husband, and before long he died. When she married Warren Harding ten years after her first marriage, she was quite free. With the passing of time, she had grown into a hard, managing woman. She was five years older than Harding; but the instant she saw him, she made up her mind that he was what she wanted. Her infatuation enraged her father even more than her former entanglement. His furious opposition became common gossip and even appeared in print in the rival paper, the *Mirror*. But she persisted, and Harding's capitulation was foregone. He could not resist any strong character who wanted anything of him.

This was the first time that the long-continued story concerning the Harding ancestry actually became public, although it had long been circulating in Marion. There was supposed to have been a Negro in the family some two generations back, and this, in the lower Ohio of the eighties, was regarded with horror. It was used in Amos Kling's onslaught on his daughter's intended; it failed then, but it went on and on underground, until it emerged again when Harding was a Presidential candidate. The contribution it made to the Harding reputation among the prejudiced purists was considerable, and his own well-known shiftlessness and mental incapacity were often attributed to it.

But her father's opposition was no more than an added incentive to his daughter, and the rumors about her intended were offset by his handsome and easy carriage. For so popular and promiscuous a young man, the match was a strange one, to be explained only by the determination of the lady. Her innate ability showed itself not only in her capture of another husband but in the capture of his business almost at once afterward. Warren was seized with a debility, probably connected with laziness, and when he began to stay away from his office to rest, Florence simply went down and took his place. But if he thought the rest of his life could be spent in the relaxations he was used to, he was mistaken. He had married a driver.

There is an amusing account of the subsequent situation, written, in response to a question, by Norman Thomas,[9] who as a boy worked at the *Star:*

> Mrs. Harding in those days ran the show. She was a woman of very narrow mentality and range of interest or understanding, but a strong will and, within a certain area, of genuine kindness. She got along well with newsboys of all sorts and kinds, in whom she took a genuine interest. It was her energy and business sense which made the *Star*. She was, for years, pretty nearly the whole show on the business side; —advertising manager, circulation manager and what have you. Even when the paper was strong enough for her to get help, she kept a close eye on those to whom she delegated various tasks.

---

[9] This is the same Norman Thomas who grew up to be a Presbyterian minister and, for almost a generation, the perennial Socialist candidate for President. It is recorded that, in spite of their political differences, the Hardings kept a lifelong affection for this—as for other—of their "boys" on the *Star*. This, it will be recognized, is in the best tradition of old-fashioned American small enterprise.

Her husband was the front. He was, as you know, very affable; very much of a joiner and personally popular. He was a fine small-town or city booster and wrote editorials telling how Marion, Ohio, had more miles of Berea sandstone sidewalks than any town of its size in the United States. Nay, he ventured to say, in the whole world. This was his best line.

In the days of my youth, Mrs. Harding and his tailor had not discovered how well Warren could be dressed up. He used to loaf around his office in shirt-sleeves and, if memory serves me, often with a chew of tobacco in his mouth. He was always personally more popular than his wife, but I am quite sure that most folks up to the end of the nineteenth century who lived in Marion would have told you that it was she who was the real driving power in the success that the *Marion Star* was unquestionably making in its community.[10]

It is generally agreed that without his energetic and ambitious wife Warren Harding would, in all likelihood, have remained a newspaperman. The paper, growing with the town, was a real political influence, and the Hardings discovered that it could be useful in other ways as well. New enterprises starting out in the area could procure good will rather easily by cutting in the Hardings on stock issues. These became valuable only as the businesses prospered, and the *Star* could help in their expansion. It was a good arrangement all around—rather doubtful, according to later newspaper ethics—but it has been said before that such considerations were never known to trouble Harding; and Florence was a practical businesswoman.

Florence Harding and Harry Daugherty made a team. They had no affection for each other, but they had a common ambition, and it proved to be a sufficient binder. They worked together at first in a peculiar way. Florence surrendered Warren's political management to Daugherty, and she stayed at home in Marion to run the *Star*, only to show up when needed to prod her husband when he dropped off into lethargy.

Harding's first political essay was a failure. Amos Kling controlled the local Republican machine and knifed him when he ran for County Auditor. But even if he lost then, he discovered his oratorical fluency. And since his wife was running the *Star*, he often went off to speak at rallies, specializing in praise of Ohio, of the nation, of the Republican party (by then the G.O.P.), and of the Grand Army of the Republic. He never denigrated or criticized; he had a common humor; and audiences liked him.

At one of these country meetings (in Richwood), Harry Daugherty noticed him. And this beginning led to all that followed—one political

---

[10] The original letter appears in *The Incredible Era*, 25–26.

incident after another, some successful, some not, but all contributing
finally to success in storming the citadel of the Republican convention
in 1920.

Charles Willis Thompson recorded, after hearing the speech of 1916
and watching the then Senator preside over the national convention,
that during his years in the Senate, Harding had come more and more
to "grate on him, with his perpetual smile and his meaningless geni-
ality." It seemed to him, he said, that there was something humorous
in the attempted launching of a Presidential boom by the Hamilton
Club of Cincinnati in the winter of 1916. Then, when in June the
convention performance occurred, Thompson was overcome with
distaste:

> There was nothing in the man himself to arouse such a feeling; it
> was only the incongruity between himself and his pretensions. If I had
> known him as a traveling salesman, a vaudeville actor, a night club
> entertainer, or a restaurant keeper, I should have liked him very much,
> I know, for I have had a strong liking for many men just like Harding
> who held those positions. But if one of these hash-twirling or ribbon-
> selling or banjo-playing friends of mine had undertaken the role of
> public teacher and President of the United States, and had tried to
> instruct me from a "rostrum," I should have felt toward him just as I
> did toward Harding. "The bungalow mind," ex-President Wilson said
> once when he was talking of his successor . . .

Still, there it was; he was moving toward the Presidency, and such
an incongruous progress needed explanation:

> . . . He did not take himself too seriously, and was really surprised to
> find himself a Presidential candidate. He knew himself pretty well, and
> neither expected to be President nor very much wished to be. Left to
> himself, he would not have tried. But for the persistent insistence of
> Harry M. Daugherty he would not have kept on trying. Often he used
> to tell Daugherty that he was no statesman and that it was time to
> stop the nonsense and close the show. Daugherty always told him he
> was wrong about himself, and at last, as events seemed to confirm
> everything Daugherty said, he began rather dubiously to believe.[11]

It remains to be said that although Daugherty had no feeling except
one of triumph after an arduous campaign, persisted in for many years,
Harding's pushing wife had last-minute qualms. The Presidency was
a demanding job, requiring austerity, industry, sense of obligation—
all that. She recognized that her husband had none of these. As Presi-

---

[11] Charles Willis Thompson, *Presidents I've Known* (Indianapolis, 1929), 333–34.

dent, he would be a tragic failure. She said so, and tried to hold back when it was too late.[12]

By then, of course, Harding had allowed himself to be convinced that all would be well if his friends were available to guide him—especially Daugherty, who would be Attorney General. This was, in itself, a monstrous conception, as soon appeared. But Harding did go on into the inevitable disgrace. He was the worst President in the succession; but he was the choice of his colleagues in the profession.

As a statesman once remarked in such a circumstance, "Some profession!"

Still, if our political processes sometimes produce such regrettable results, they are still results, and our regrets do not allow us to ignore them. For the student of ways to the White House, there are lessons of value in the Harding conquest—if it can be called that. They may be summarized as follows:

1. Equivocation and perpetual avoidance of commitment (in political language, "trimming,") will contribute to availability, or at least will not reduce its probability.

2. Party regularity and faithful service will also contribute, if the circumstances prove to be right (if a regular can win).

3. Personal irregularities will have to be carefully concealed. They may appear unexpectedly and do damage.

4. Recognized incompetence may not be a handicap to a candidate, even if it is fatal to him as a President.

5. It is necessary, if personal drive is lacking, to have a guide, sponsor, and energizer.

---

[12] She is so quoted in Thompson, *op. cit.*, 334.

John Calvin Coolidge
1872–1933

Born at Plymouth, Vermont
Became twenty-ninth President in 1923 at 51

HISTORY

1895	Graduated from Amherst College after attending Academies at Black River and St. Johnsbury.
1897	Admitted to the bar; began practice in Northampton, Massachusetts.
1898	Elected to the City Council.
1899	Elected City Solicitor (served one year).
1904	Clerk of the courts, Hampshire County (served six months).
1906	Elected to the General Court of Massachusetts.
1909	Elected Mayor of Northampton.
1911	Elected to the Massachusetts Senate.
1914	Elected President of the Senate.
1915	Elected Lieutenant Governor.
1918	Elected Governor.

370

1920	Nominated by the Republican convention and elected to the Vice-Presidency of the United States (with Harding).
1923	In August succeeded to the Presidency on Harding's death.
1924	Elected to the Presidency (Vice-President, Dawes); opponent, Davis with C. W. Bryan.
1928	Refused the nomination for another term.
1929	After retirement to Northampton, accepted various honorary positions, wrote a syndicated newspaper column, and published an *Autobiography*.
1933	Died in Northampton.

No other President represents so typically as Coolidge the escalator method of attaining the office. He simply and with quiet caution always looked for a way upward, and, having found it, schemed and worked indefatigably to place himself so that elevation would be very natural and easy. It was essential that he should be regular beyond any doubt and that he should not develop ideas of his own or any attitudes likely to offend party leaders. To this rule he conformed rigidly.

He always lived well within his means, was abstemious, unostentatious, and careful. He seemed almost to be invisible; yet he always came into sight when a man of his sort was needed. And one often was needed during his lifetime. The Republicans were not innovators; they were the party of those who wanted the government run quietly and with economy. They were strong for peace and order; but they wanted it to come cheap so that taxes could be low. That was what Coolidge was always saying they were entitled to and that he would help them get.

At the same time, the man from the tiny Vermont village who had settled in western Massachusetts could be seen, when looked at closely, to be a personality with sharply individual characteristics. It might be thought that so common and colorless a person as the Coolidge of his early years would be hard to distinguish, and certainly that it would be hard to find in him such rich material for amusement that he could become the darling of cartoonists and political commentators. But he did finally become the ideal conformist the Republicans needed so badly; and when he was needed he was ready and available. What was even more remarkable, his sharp differentiation from anything ever before known in national political life seemed to offend no one's sense of the dignity appropriate to the White House. Coming after the Harding regime and its affronts to propriety, he was such a relief that he quickly became a Republican idol. If he seemed a comic figure to intellectuals, ordinary people thought it almost indecent to satirize his solemnity, his laconic speech, and his Yankee idiosyncrasy. It was said of him that he pronounced "cow" in three syllables, but that he never pronounced it at all unless there was a compelling reason.

It was eventually discovered—when he came on the national scene—that he was not so unique as had been thought. He was descended of a long line of dry, hard, suspicious farmers and small-town people and he was the apotheosis they had been breeding toward. He was harder and drier and more suspicious than any of them; but these were not strange characteristics. They were those of interior New England and were considered quite normal there. A different sort lived on the coast from that on the rocky farms of the mountain valleys—in Vermont, New Hampshire, and western Massachusetts. Adventurers could be found around the seaports, men with expansive ideas, innovators, capitalists. But in the Coolidge country the note was one of parsimony, industry, gingerly acceptance of change, and shrewdness.

The Coolidge character was shaped in the simple surroundings of the home and store where his father carried on his small but sufficiently profitable affairs. Curious travelers who began coming to Plymouth as soon as Calvin had reached the Presidency found even then that they were totally unfamiliar with the kind of existence he must have lived as a boy. He had been born and, during his early years, had lived in an earlier century! His home was a plain farmhouse without any of the conveniences Americans have come to accept as natural to their culture. There was no running water, no electricity, no communication with other towns (when he was Vice-President and visited in Plymouth he had to use the telephone in a nearby inn; and when he was notified of Harding's death, it was belatedly for the same reason), and when the Coolidges traveled they had to begin their journeys on the kind of dirt road that was maintained by farmers working out their taxes.

It was a boy's duty to bring in wood for the kitchen stove and often to chop it, care for the poultry, and keep the yard in order. He was to accept from his otherwise uncommunicative father directions for other tasks judged to be properly his responsibility. These, in Calvin's case, were various because his father was a horse trader and something of a politician as well as a storekeeper. He served in such positions of local trust as selectman, road commissioner, constable, and tax collector; and he was elected to three terms in the Vermont House of Representatives and one in the State Senate. It was not farfetched to describe him, as newspapermen later were apt to do, as a David Harum.

Growing up in a household where the mother, and then the stepmother, kept to the tasks of the household and the father earned his living by making deals and doing his own outside work, Calvin had ground into his character the caution, the practicality, the industriousness that enabled the Coolidges to establish themselves, even in their village circumstances, as what was often described as "a leading family."

The 250 registered voters of Plymouth seem to have been divided into pro- and anti-Coolidgeites, so that his father could maintain his position against competitors only by constant watchfulness and the careful cultivation of his neighbors. He was never able to sit back and let things drift. The Coolidge supremacy was disputed every year in the March town meeting; and young Calvin saw his father operate with a shrewdness that shaped the plan of his own career.

There might be differences in the village about keeping the elder Coolidge in one or another office, but there were few about national party affiliation; Plymouth was nine-tenths Republican. And this, too, was something Calvin absorbed. He would no more have thought, ever, of supporting a Democrat than of turning sinful in any of the ways he heard about in the long Congregational sermons he listened to. If there was ever a youth and man who could confidently be said never to have been irregular in any respect, but especially in politics, it was he.

Part of his father's view of a boy's duty was that he should get himself an education with the utmost economy. But if he was to go to college and prepare to be a lawyer—his father never had, and he had drawn many a will and many a more complicated legal paper, but times were changing—he could not do it at Plymouth; so when he was thirteen he went away to the Black River Academy in Ludlow, twelve miles distant. He was there at Ludlow during term for four years, living in boardinghouses and keeping very much to himself. He was no athlete and not much of a mixer; but neither was he much of a student. When he went to Amherst first to take the entrance examinations, he failed and had to go back home for a year. The latter part of that year he spent at the St. Johnsbury Academy, and there he achieved a certificate admitting him to Amherst without further examination. This was an easier way to get in.

At Amherst he faded into the crowd so completely that when he afterward became famous it was nearly impossible to reconstruct his activities. But in the year he entered there were fewer than four hundred students all told and only thirty faculty members, and it was difficult for him to become quite invisible. As far as that was possible, however, he managed it. He always went to class, did his homework, and passed his examinations. He ate and lived at student boarding-houses—he was used to them by now—and succeeded in graduating inconspicuously in four years. He was not taken into a fraternity, something significant at Amherst, where most of the students became members, until his senior year, when a new one was looking for recruits; and he made no close friends. The fuss made over him by Amherst people in later years must have been viewed by him with sardonic amusement. They had paid as little attention to him as could well have been managed while he had been on the campus.

His inconspicuousness was made easier by his appearance. He was pale and his hair was thin and dusty-blond; he was undersized and thinnish. His face was hatchet-shaped and sourish-looking, and he gave every evidence of disapproving much that his light-colored eyes took in. He seldom smiled, never joked, and was capable of sitting for hours quite immobile while other lads were exercising their muscles. The quick, shrewdish wit that began to appear when he came to be studied closely was hardly noticed in the boisterous company of undergraduates. And he left Amherst to go on to Northampton with no reputation of any sort.

Of all the people in the Amherst company, he would have been the very last to have been picked as possible Presidential timber. But the only other conspicuously successful member of his class was another rather retiring student with whom he sometimes shared eating places— the cheapest ones in town. This was Dwight W. Morrow, destined to be a Morgan partner. The one neglected student ultimately was able to appoint the other Ambassador to Mexico.

Of Coolidge's start as a lawyer it must be sufficient here to say that he was taken into the office of a Northampton firm, where he was to "sit at a desk and read." This is just about what he did. After twenty months of reading and learning to draw ordinary instruments, he was examined by a committee of the county bar and duly admitted to practice. This was in 1897, when he was twenty-five. But even before that he had had his initiation into local politics.

This first experience was a modest one. He handed out leaflets and did other menial jobs when one of the partners of the firm he was reading with ran for Mayor; then he was named an alternate delegate to a convention called to nominate a state Senator. After the excitement of the campaign in 1896, which, to New Englanders had more than a tinge of moral indignation, with Bryan as the devil, the young man was named to the Republican Committee for Ward 2. All this was before his admission to the bar. He obviously intended to make politics as well as law his career.

Two years later he was elected City Solicitor, a job that was within the gift of the City Council. It had light duties and carried a salary of $600. Explaining why he took the position, he said that he felt "it would make him a better lawyer." This statement introduces a rule he followed in all his successive appointments and elections. These finally ran to an amazing count, and the number is partially explained by the rule. He explained to his father repeatedly, when the older Coolidge was worried about his running for office, that he would be "as well off if he lost as if he won." What he meant was that he would be set forward even if he lost—as a lawyer, as a deserving servant of the party, as a figure who stood for righteousness even when defeated. Whether his father was convinced, we do not know.

But of his other rules—party regularity, careful assessment of chances, cultivation of the sources of strength—protected him from defeat so well that these electoral tests were mostly theoretical. In fact, he lost only two, and one of these was when he failed to be chosen for a third term as City Solicitor; but this, it will be noticed, was not a popular election. And his defeat was wholly due to the principle of rotation. He was asking for more than his share. He never again made that mistake. The other loss was just after his marriage in 1905. He ran for election as Northampton School Committeeman without taking his usual careful look at the possibilities and found, when he could no longer withdraw, that another Republican had already taken out nomination papers. They split what would have been a majority for one, and the Democrat got in. This too was a lesson he never forgot.

His next venture was in 1906, when he was elected to the lower branch of the Massachusetts General Court—the legislature. It is worth noting how cautiously this matter was approached. His biographer quotes the "feeler" paragraph in the *Daily Hampshire Gazette:*

> But seven days remain in which candidates for the Republican nomination for representative can file their petitions . . . Calvin Coolidge has shed the most light on the situation by saying that he would consider the nomination. He says that he would like to go to the legislature sometime. At present, he thinks, because of business conditions, he would prefer to wait, but adds that probably there always will be something of the kind, so that now might be as favorable for him as any time. He says he does not care enough to fight for the nomination and that if some prominent party man . . . wants it he would gladly stay out and put his shoulder to the wheel. And even then . . . he adds he cannot now say whether he would accept . . .[1]

Everything that Coolidge was is now before us for consideration. He would go on from this campaign to others, presently becoming Mayor of Northampton, a member of the State Senate and then its President, and rising to become Lieutenant Governor and Governor— all without the slightest change of method or habit. In each instance he accepted party discipline, allowed the normal sequences to happen, subordinated himself when it was appropriate (as when he was Lieutenant Governor), said nothing startling, and was floated upward at regular intervals. But, as has been suggested, this did not mean that he was a wholly uninteresting personality. Colleagues from other sections of the state and reporters looking for color and angles discovered him to be an amusing conversation piece and a ready source of copy. He might not give anything away; but his evasion or denial

---

[1] This revealing statement is quoted from *Calvin Coolidge* by Claude M. Fuess (Boston, 1940), 95. This is among the better Presidential biographies, even if somewhat official and defensive. But there exists a corrective in William Allen White's *Puritan in Babylon* (New York, 1938).

was likely to be voiced in Yankee phrases, so economical as to contrast vividly with the usual political verbiage. This is illustrated by an incident of his first legislative term:

> . . . a Representative made a very long and wearisome speech in the course of which he began many successive paragraphs with "Mr. Speaker, it is . . ." After he sat down, Coolidge drew himself out of his chair and said, "Mr. Speaker, it is not!" Everybody laughed and the measure was killed.[2]

Later, when he was Governor, he still practiced the same art of economical communication:

> . . . he was once approached by three prominent persons who wished him to increase an appropriation . . . One of them delivered an oration on the subject. The Governor asked, "Anybody else got anything to say?" A second presented the same viewpoint at even greater length. Coolidge then said, "I understand you all agree on what you want." The three said, "Yes," almost simultaneously. "Can't be done," replied Coolidge. "Good-bye."

This kind of dry, sharp remark became almost a legend in Massachusetts years before it did in the nation as a whole. It seemed more a cause of admiring humor than offense. There was disappointment when it was not forthcoming. Newsmen often tried to provoke it and it was seldom withheld. But there is a strange contrast that commentators, and especially his biographers, have preferred to ignore. The fact is that there can hardly have been any individual in the history of our politics who made so many speeches of such length in the effort to keep his name known. The volume of his utterances was enormous. This garrulity in an individual whose stereotype was laconicism is striking. It illustrates the falsity of the image-making process. Coolidge cultivated Yankee mannerisms. He realized that they were the outward signs of the character most useful in the circumstances of his rise. He undeviatingly pretended to be the silent, reliable, ascetic, economical public servant. His talkativeness was public; but it was low-keyed and seldom widely reported. It was dull, and uttered in a manner that highlighted its orthodoxy. It convinced his hearers that he was the Massachusetts opposite of Boston's ebullient Irish politicians. He went on talking for years while his reputation for silence spread.

In 1919 he was Governor of a small state, with no national reputation whatever—his abnormal outpouring of verbiage was so far con-

---

[2] Fuess, *op. cit.*, 102.

fined to New England—and not likely to attain one. He would never do anything exciting; such a performance would run against his rule. There would be nothing spectacular about his further political behavior. He would be re-elected; but that would be because the Republicans were in the ascendancy and because he had drifted to the top; then, in regular course, he would retire to his two-family house in Northampton and resume the practice of law, a staid citizen and a trusted attorney, more respected and entitled to higher fees because he had occupied such prominent posts.

Anyone who suggested that this pale, unexciting Governor had any future whatever in politics, except possibly in the United States Senate, would have been thought to be suffering delusions. He had never moved his family to the capital; he had continued to occupy a room in the Adams House; he was known to save money on his meager salary; he had no other desire than to be regular; and, if he was impeccably honest, he had also no desire to appear as a reformer. He walked a narrow path, took little notice of affairs beyond the borders of Massachusetts, and certainly never commented on them. So far as anyone knew, he had no further expectations.

But it is not farfetched to suspect that he had still unfulfilled ambitions. He was always so close-mouthed, so unrewarding to talk to, that no one penetrated his thoughts. But he was as shrewd and sharp as he had been when, as a young lawyer, he had run for City Solicitor with a view to bettering himself whether he gained the office or not.

He had acquired one priceless asset which he may or may not have valued at its true worth. This was a friend and booster, a strangely devoted and capable man of affairs—also of some wealth—who saw in him virtues invisible to everyone else and who conceived it his privilege and duty to push forward into the most responsible posts the darling of his limited imagination.

Frank W. Stearns first met Coolidge in 1915 when Coolidge was a Senator and when Stearns was already nearly sixty—a fattish, merchant type, kindly, philanthropic, and phlegmatic. He was an Amherst Trustee among other public affiliations; and at a meeting Dwight W. Morrow said to him rather casually that a classmate of his in Boston had turned out to be "quite a fellow" and asked if Stearns had met him. Stearns hadn't, but at a dinner shortly afterward he made an opportunity to speak to the Senator. All he got was what most people got, a limp handshake and an indifferent "howdy-do." But after dinner Coolidge came by his chair, leaned over and said, "Ever anything you want up on the hill, come see me." Stearns did. Coolidge sat him on the rostrum beside himself and allowed him to watch the proceedings. He was impressed by Coolidge's quiet control of the session and wrote afterward to say so. This was the beginning. It was much like falling

in love for the elderly man. The object of his affection was unresponsive; yet from time to time he made some slight gesture of appreciation. He allowed no intimacies and he limited very strictly the favors
he would accept; but a kind of identification nevertheless arose—
something like a long and cool company-keeping. They were going
together.

Stearns never quite learned the unspoken rules of this association.
He was always offering favors Coolidge would not accept, such as
free accommodations and even gifts of money. But within what was
allowed to him, he became a practical, self-effacing, indefatigable
promoter of the Coolidge fortunes. He also gave advice, reams of it in
naïve communications. Some of it Coolidge paid attention to, but most
of it he ignored. It came in such obviously well-intentioned letters,
however, that he could not take offense. Stearns, it will be seen, was no
Hanna; and Coolidge, for that matter, was no McKinley. But the two
sets of relationships are nevertheless comparable. There was devotion
on one side and cautious acceptance on the other. There was selfless-
ness, and there was willingness to be glorified. The differences were
that Coolidge was a watchful and suspicious Yankee and McKinley
an open and expectant Ohio climber; that Stearns was a simple,
sincere, self-conscious, and lumpish man and that Hanna was a roaring
enterpriser, turned to national politics for another kind of excitement.
Conceivably Coolidge might have become President without Stearns
as McKinley never could have without Hanna. But Coolidge, very
little less than McKinley, was fortunate in having the adoration and
constant industrious support of an admiring man of affairs. It
smoothed his way. It made his coming apotheosis easier to take
advantage of. And he had to pay nothing, absolutely nothing, for it,
even in gratitude.

If an individual was thus added to Coolidge's assets, an event was
even more fortunate. It was a most unlikely one; but it lifted the plain,
wry, sharp-nosed Governor of Massachusetts, cautious subordinate in
Senator Crane's machine, out of the undistinguished ruck and made
him a national hero. No one ever resembled so slightly a man of courage, yet to a national majority he would presently seem exactly that;
bold, determined, forceful, a foundation stone for law and order.

To understand the Coolidge miracle, it has to be recalled at what
time it occurred and what state the country was in when it was
shouted in headlines from Massachusetts to California—ones just as
large in remote states as in the place of origin. It was 1919. World
War I was just over. Readjustment was causing unemployment,
deflation, and unrest. There were more labor disturbances, and of a
more disillusioned nature, than the country had ever known. The
nation seemed to be disintegrating. The hot loyalties of wartime had

cooled and been replaced by the resentments of a society that could not settle into peace. The appearance of class war was more real then than it would ever be again in the United States.

It was against this background that the drama of the Boston police strike took place. Aside from its tragic consequence for the thousand misguided policemen who lost their jobs, the strike was most notable for its effect on the Coolidge prospects. It can almost literally be said that it made him President—more accurately, that if it had not happened he would not have been nominated for Vice-President and so would not have succeeded Harding in 1923.

It could not have occurred as it did if there had not been one of those peculiar administrative arrangements in Boston so typical of the years when escape from municipal corruption was the objective of local reform movements. The Police Commissioner was an appointee of the Governor, not of the Mayor, and could be removed only for cause. Still, he was administratively responsible to the Mayor and was supposed to be under his direction.

The Mayor was a Democrat, the Commissioner a Republican. Both were decent people; but both were politicians too, and their affiliations made some difference when the police decided that they had grievances only to be redressed by striking. There was notice, there were hearings, there were attempts on the part of the Commissioner and of the Mayor to conciliate and to meet the petitioners' demands. But the men's mood was ugly and they were supported by the rest of the labor movement. In fact, it was their determination to form a local and to affiliate with the American Federation of Labor that precipitated the first of several succeeding crises. When application for an A.F.L. charter was made, the Commissioner told the organizers that he could not allow it, and presently he promulgated a prohibitory rule. But they went ahead and organized their local; furthermore, the Central Labor Union of Boston, as tension rose, resolved that they should have "every atom of support" that organized labor could mobilize.

When it came to last-instant conferences the Mayor was in favor of compromise; but the Commissioner had passed that point and would not yield. The policemen, he said, must withdraw from outside affiliation. They met and voted overwhelmingly to leave their duties. On the Tuesday when posts were to be abandoned, the Mayor persuaded the Commissioner to meet him in Coolidge's office. After listening, the Governor said that he would accept the Commissioner's assurance of ability to control the situation. He would not call out the Guard since he had no power to interfere unless there was imminent threat of disorder.

The Commissioner had overestimated his influence with the policemen. They did leave their posts and the city was left open to the boiling up of vicious trouble. There was violence. It occurred almost spontaneously as hoodlums discovered they were out of check. And it occurred nearly everywhere. Before many hours the city seethed with lawlessness. It was a frightening evidence of urban tension.

The next day was spent in organizing volunteer police, and before the next night was over the worst had passed. But the frightened citizenry, represented by an impassioned press, at once began looking for someone who could be blamed. The Mayor and Coolidge were by now in controversy. The Mayor alleged that his citizen's committees had had no co-operation from the Police Commissioner or from the Governor. Coolidge's response was an executive order taking over the duty of re-establishing order. The militia was called out, the Commissioner was given orders by Coolidge, the strikers were told they were permanently discharged, and the crisis declined toward an uneasy truce.

Samuel Gompers, protesting from New York as head of the A.F.L., gave Coolidge, at this stage, the opening he needed to make himself the defender of citizens abandoned to hoodlum rule. "The Lord," says his biographer, "had delivered his opponent into his hands." With the whole country listening nervously, Coolidge sent his reply to Gompers; it contained these sentences:

> The right of the police of Boston to affiliate has always been questioned, never granted, is now prohibited . . . Your assertion that the Commissioner was wrong cannot justify the wrong of leaving the city unguarded. That furnished the opportunity; the criminal element furnished the action. There is no right to strike against the public safety by anybody, anywhere, any time.[3]

There was more; but the rest of it merely said that the authority of the state over all its officers would be maintained. Gompers knew when to stop; he never replied; he ought never to have provided the opening.

There was such a tidal response to these words as occurs only once in a long while. What came through to the public was an embattled Governor standing like a rock against the threat of civic disintegration. He might be small and sourish, cold and unimpressive. For one moment he was tremendous. And for the purpose it was enough.

So enlarged was the reputation of the slight man from Massachusetts after a year of worshipful praise by the press that the convention of 1920, after allowing itself to be bossed into the nomination of Harding, escaped completely from control in its later hours and went

---

[3] *Ibid.*, 225.

for Coolidge in a storm of enthusiasm. The bosses' candidate for Vice-President, another of the Senators—Lenroot—was swept into the shadows when an unauthorized delegate stood on a chair and shouted the name of Coolidge.

The surge of support for Coolidge was hard for the patrician Senator Lodge to accept. He was one of the inner circle and he regarded Coolidge not only with contempt because he lived in a two-family house in Northampton, but enmity because his own machine and Crane's were at war in Massachusetts—more than ever just now, because the League of Nations issue had become an obsession with Lodge. He was the leader of the "willful men" who had been castigated by Wilson; more than any other individual, he had been responsible for rejecting the Treaty of Versailles. Crane, on the other hand, had succeeded in having the League actually endorsed by the Massachusetts convention of that year, an affront Lodge would never forget. To have a Crane man and a common fellow like Coolidge gain preferment was for him a ruinous blow. But arrival at the top by the way of the Vice-Presidency was quite agreeable to Coolidge. He had always served in subordinate positions, almost unnoticed, while he studied the current scene and made up his mind how best to take advantage of its opportunities. When his study was complete, he considered what came next. This is what he was about to do in the large arena he was being transported to from his small one in Massachusetts.

Now for two years as Vice-President he contained himself almost precisely as he had as Lieutenant Governor of his state. He sat and watched. He made innocuous speeches; he went to innumerable dinners where he played cranky Yankee until it threatened to become monotonous; he amused himself as he had always done by sitting immobile for hours on end. Harding asked him to attend Cabinet meetings, and he did; but he made no contribution. He must have known that Harding's affairs were reaching some sort of hopeless entanglement; but following his rule, he continued to speak well of his superior and gave no sign of discomfort in the company of Secretaries Fall and Denby or of Attorney General Daugherty. The Vice-President simply was. He watched and must have seen, but neither then nor later did anyone blame him for his acquiescence in what went on.

When in 1923 Harding died and Coolidge became President, he accepted the situation as calmly as it is possible to imagine anyone doing in such circumstances. There was the usual stir of adjustment around him as the seekers and dispensers made their moves. But he accepted the whole Cabinet, including Fall and Daugherty, until they themselves resigned with Senatorial investigators nipping at their heels. Still he heard nothing, saw nothing, and recognized nothing wrong.

He spoke soothing words to the country, allowed matters to move in natural course, and, because business was good and everyone reasonably content, except the farmers and some unruly laborers, he gradually accumulated the odor of sanctity usually awarded Republican figureheads. He moved toward a nomination of his own in 1924 as he had moved toward the Governorship in Massachusetts after having been Lieutenant Governor. He allowed it to happen. There was no dissent to speak of, except that heard from the Progressives in the Midwest. The Democrats had one of their worst quarrels at the New York convention, when Smith and McAdoo held their followers through a hundred bitterly monotonous ballots and John W. Davis was finally nominated on the 103rd. He was not a formidable opponent; if the country wanted a conservative—as the Democrats by then should have known—it would not choose a Democratic one. La Follette did remarkably well with his third party; but after all, four million votes out of nearly thirty million amounted only to a rather strong protest. Coolidge had almost sixteen million, and Davis a little more than eight.

This was a remarkable performance. Taken together with the quiet rise from City Solicitor and County Delegate in western Massachusetts to the Governorship, it was nearly miraculous.[4]

When Coolidge had the Presidency by right of election, he was no more adventurous than when it had been his by inheritance. On the contrary, he seemed to feel confirmed in his passive policy. But it did become clearer as time went on what a peculiar dilemma he had got into by his acceptance of finance and speculative business at the value put on it by its expositors in the Chamber of Commerce headquarters across Lafayette Square from the White House; the representative little man became the oracle of the big ones in the encouragement of excess. Whenever there was the slightest hesitation in the climb of security prices, Coolidge could be called on for reassurance that started the surge upward again. The accumulation of private debt began to outweigh the decline in government debt during the second Coolidge term; the market reached a fantastic level by 1927, and as 1928 opened there was a chorus of funereal warnings from economists. To make worse the potential disaster at home, capital had been exported in large volume, and the prohibitive tariffs made repayment next to impossible. A time was coming when the vast burden of debt obviously could never be discharged. Repudiation was inevitable. But even after this had become clear to everyone in his senses, the market

---

[4] For an account of Coolidge's careful maneuvers which caused nomination to be so smoothly accomplished, see White, *op. cit.*; reading Coolidge's *Autobiography* will not be very enlightening—as indeed it is not about any phase of his career. He was laconic even then.

continued to rise as more amateurs were encouraged to believe they could get rich quick by gambling in securities.

During the summer of 1927 Coolidge vacationed in the Black Hills. One day in August he issued a statement, consisting of a single sentence. It read, "I do not choose to run for President in 1928." The reporters were by now fairly familiar with Vermont language; but this was beyond their ability to interpret. The President refused any elaboration, then or afterward. Hardly ever has there been a Presidential announcement so speculated about. To the whole country it seemed cryptic. Did it mean that he actually would not run? That he would rather not run? Or that he wanted to be urged? When the convention assembled in 1928, even his closest associates still did not know. It has since been accepted, from rather uncertain evidence, that he was bitterly disappointed because he was not renominated in spite of his statement. He could have been if he had made the least effort. The business world had found him ideal; the hectic advance in the markets was still going on; taxes had been reduced; regulation was as light as it could be without being lifted entirely. True, there were sinister signs of trouble to come; but many even of those who read them were taken in by the prevalent talk of "a new era." The old rules were no longer valid, it was said; prosperity had come to stay, the enormous volume of speculation was a mere discounting of the future.

Coolidge himself, as he grew older, withdrew more and more from contacts with other than politicians and businessmen. His shrewd handling of the situation in 1924 had revealed how masterly he could be. The Crane faction in Massachusetts which he had joined as a young man and which had raised him to the Governorship was by then dominant. Its representative, William M. Butler, had managed the Coolidge pre-convention campaign and Butler had afterward been made Chairman of the Republican National Committee. He and his group were in complete control in 1927, and if Coolidge had given them a hint, his renomination would have been certain. To be sure, there was another contender. But Herbert Hoover would have got nowhere, as he well knew, if he had had to appear as a Coolidge rival. It was known that Coolidge disliked him; but this was not a publicly declared distaste, and Hoover could ignore it. He must in some way have heard what Coolidge remarked to his Secretary of Agriculture in a conversation that spring. "That man," said Coolidge, "has offered me unsolicited advice for six years, all of it bad!" Secretary Jardine was certain then that Coolidge was counting on a deadlock in the convention and a final turning to himself. But it must be unsolicited. He would not ask for it.

When the Hoover movement resulted in nomination, and Coolidge had had only a decent minimum of applause for his long service to the party, he was made ill by the disappointment, or so his intimates said. He himself said nothing. He merely sulked. If he had wanted to go on, he had chosen the wrong way. The Presidency seldom calls; it has to be fought for. There is the further question, in view of all that happened so soon afterward, as the result of his uncritical support of speculative business, whether he did not have some intimations of disaster and was getting out in time. It did seem later that fate had missed a chance to exact a personal penalty for antique Vermont simplicity in a vast and complex modern economy. But that was an afterthought. As a political practitioner of the orthodox sort, Coolidge had been superbly successful. It had been done so cleverly that it had appeared to be easy. But this would confuse only an amateur! A professional would recognize its masterly quality.

ꞓ𝒽𝑒𝓇𝒷𝑒𝓇𝓉 𝒞𝓁𝒶𝓇𝓀 ꞓ𝒽𝑜𝑜𝓋𝑒𝓇

1874–1964

BROWN BROTHERS

Born at West Branch, Iowa
Became thirtieth President in 1929 at 54

HISTORY

1884	Moved to Oregon as a boy, after the death of his parents.
1895	Graduated from Stanford University as a mining engineer after a public school education. Began to work for a San Francisco consultant.
1899	Married and went to China as a manager, promoter, and consultant.
1900	Involved in the defense of Tientsin during the Boxer Rebellion.
1914	Served as Chairman of the American Relief Committee in London; gradually closed out all business interests; became Chairman of the Commission for Relief in Belgium.
1917	Appointed United States Food Administrator.
1919	Chairman of the Supreme Economic Council in Paris.
1920	Chairman of the European Relief Council.

386

1921	Appointed Secretary of Commerce by Harding (continuing with Coolidge).
1928	Nominated for the Presidency by the Republicans and elected (Vice-President, Curtis); opponent, Smith with Robinson.
1932	Renominated but defeated by F. D. Roosevelt.
1946	Appointed by President Truman Coordinator of the European Food Program.
1947	Appointed Chairman of Commission on Organization of the Executive Branch.
1955	Appointed Chairman of Commission on Administrative Reform.
1964	Died in New York City.

W HEN HERBERT HOOVER moved up to the Presidency from his position in the Commerce Department, it was unusual; and it was even more a novelty because his predecessor, Coolidge, refused to give him the least praise—was, indeed, known to dislike him intensely. There must have been some strong reason for believing he would appeal to the voters. He was even nominated on the first ballot without any considerable struggle in the convention. How had he arrived at a position to claim the honor so decisively?

It has to be recalled that this was 1928 and that Coolidge had been regarded as a most satisfactory President. He had governed in Republican times—that is to say, when prosperity, at least for promoters and speculators, was mounting from one incredible level to another. After the decisive victory of 1924 and the confirmed dominance of the Old Guard in the party, it might have been supposed either that Coolidge would have been drafted to run again or that some really representative politician would have been chosen. The prospect was for a Republican year. The country was prosperous; and the Democrats seemed certain to nominate Smith, who ought not to be a formidable candidate. Why should Hoover, who was hardly regarded as a Republican at all, have been chosen rather than one of their own? It is true that the embarrassing memory of Harding still lingered. After his discreditable performance, the inner circle could hardly pretend to appealing virtues or even to competence. They themselves were trying to forget, but they knew well enough that the voters still remembered. It was in being respectable and efficient that Hoover was especially notable. It was also thought that he would appeal to the Progressives, who, although Coolidge had been elected, had made an impressive showing in 1924; indeed, if they had joined with the Democrats, the combination would have won 27 states. This had to be considered. It was obviously no time to chance a genuine reactionary like Curtis, who was the insiders' first choice, or some other member of the inner circle.

Curtis was almost another Harding. That is to say, he was a member of the long-seated Senate club, was a deeply committed reactionary, and had no observable abilities except those of a strictly political nature. But there were others with reputations for competence in government as well as in large affairs—notably Governor Frank O. Lowden of Illinois, whose deadlock with General Wood in 1920 had prepared the way for the Harding nomination. Then there was Charles Gates Dawes, whose Vice-Presidency had been colorful, at least, and whose work in organizing the Bureau of the Budget had been approved by all good-government people. But Dawes had long been a Lowden supporter and disclaimed any ambition for himself. Lowden was extremely popular in the farm states, where depression had gradually been getting worse ever since 1921, when farm prices had fallen so precipitously; but he was unpopular with Easterners, where most of the campaign money came from.

All during the preconvention year businessmen were relying on the development of a draft-Coolidge movement. They were sure that at the right moment he would announce his availability. Hoover, who by then was openly eager, feared it too; and although, being an able administrator, he had established a formidable organization and was making the widest possible appeal for support, he knew that if Coolidge should even hint at consent, his own chances would evaporate instantly.

The others who had influence—Andrew Mellon, for instance, the millionaire who was regarded so respectfully as a party resource—were paralyzed by the dead silence from the White House. It was the Hoover strategy to pose as the administration candidate. He could not actually say so, but his organization let it be known that he was favored to succeed. This annoyed Coolidge, who would undoubtedly rather have seen anyone else nominated and seems to have preferred Borah if he himself was not drafted. But in his sulky mood, as he waited for a swelling demand that never came, he refused any comment at all.

Hoover and his followers spent large sums and built up a considerable machine; but until the convention opened, they had no reason whatever to think that he might have the Coolidge blessing. True, he was the one available candidate who was of undoubted integrity and had a history of useful works. He was, indeed, already pictured as "The Great Engineer." But the regulars dreaded his nomination. They said he was no real Republican; he was too cold and reserved to be imagined as a party leader; and they wondered, in fact, how they happened to have so strange an animal in their own yard.

To understand how, in spite of the forces indifferent or actually opposed to him, Hoover won the nomination and was elected we have to understand how his power was accumulated and brought to bear in such a way as to be irresistible.

Going a long way back, to his boyhood even, we can see how ideal his preparation was. If he was not born in a log cabin, the home was, anyway, a simple one in the village of West Branch, Iowa. The place of his birth gave him an advantage no other candidate had ever had: he was the first from west of the Mississippi, and by then that was where the pioneer country was. Also, the life he lived as a boy conformed in almost startling fashion to the stereotype of poverty and self-reliance so long preferred by Republicans in their candidates.

It was a long road, and a tortuous one, from West Branch to the White House. But, unlikely as it appears, nearly every step taken on it by Hoover counted for what he had in view. Not that the boy doing chores and odd jobs in Iowa and, a little later, in Oregon imagined himself as President. That probably began only when he had become a world figure, almost an independent nation in himself as he operated between and among the belligerents during World War I on his gigantic tasks of mercy. He must then have seen himself as the equal of any statesman on the world scene, perhaps as the superior of most. He was first the savior of ten million Belgians, then Food Administrator in his own country, and, to climax his series of missions, he had averted starvation for millions of East Europeans in the postwar chaos. No one compared with him; no one approached his size or his dedication. He was still unique in 1928. He was then serving in a bizarre job for an aspiring politician but one not strange for an administrative genius who had been an engineer to begin with. The Secretaryship of Commerce was a post he could utilize to display all his talents. And he had done so.

His father and mother had died when he was still small and he had begun to be farmed out among relatives. There was no difficulty about this. The family were Friends and close in feeling even if widely separated in space. So during his teens he was sent out to Oregon, where he lived with a country doctor, another relative, also a Quaker. He was not coddled; none of the relatives was affluent; but he did not suffer and he was warmly welcomed. His Quaker faith settled deeply into his nature, and his Swiss-German inheritance made him sturdy. He was as industrious in his way as Coolidge had been; and he was more on his own after a certain age. That age came when he decided to go to Stanford University—a place of learning not yet actually in existence but one with a powerful appeal when, by accident, he heard about its founding.

He had been busy helping to earn his keep and had taken his responsibility more seriously as he had grown, so that at eighteen he was not at all prepared to enter a university. Besides, he wanted to be an engineer, and this required a knowledge of mathematics. He had already discovered that this range of subject matter came easily; but his progress in it had not gone nearly far enough. Still, a visiting friend who was acquainted with the Stanford prospectus encouraged him. He went to work on the problem and presently was admitted. He was happy to have a part in the university's first venture and seems to have contributed his full share to undergraduate activities even though he had to earn his own way. He did the usual odd jobs during term and in summer went out with his teachers on surveying parties. Even hard work seems to have been a pleasure; he was that sort.

In 1895, however, the whole world was wallowing in the wake of depression, and the mining industry was depressed. It was not a favorable time for the beginning of a career. Young Hoover, after trying several possibilities, did a characteristic thing—he went to work as a miner. Doing this for a year gave him a workman's practicality, so when in 1896 he gathered up courage to ask Louis Janin, the most prominent consulting engineer in the West, for a job, he had behind him something more than a diploma. But there were a good many young men in the same situation, and actually the consultant's office had no use for him.

But an interview was granted. When Janin asked what he had to offer he could say "a degree from Stanford, a summer with the Arkansas Geological Survey, three with the United States Survey, and some work at Nevada City." It may well have been this last that had most interest, for although Janin had no job, he said he could hang around the office, making himself useful, in the hope that something might turn up, but without pay. Hoover accepted. He wrote letters, ran errands, waited on others. His savings had about run out when the chance came that he knew how to make the most of.

It does sound like a Horatio Alger story, or perhaps the Alger stories of the day sounded like things that actually happened. At any rate, when Hoover was rather casually asked to make a report of the facts involved in a mining suit, he did it so rapidly and put it in such good order that Janin was impressed. And prospective hunger was at least postponed by a salary. The young engineer began almost at once to do the sort of thing, in a small way, that he would before very long be doing in a large way. He was sent out to evaluate possible new fields, to suggest how others could be made profitable, to solve problems having to do with water and transportation—all the matters consultants of Janin's standing were asked about. Then came the young man's big chance. A British firm asked for a report on the prospect for profitable gold mining in Australia, and Hoover was sent.

This was the beginning of something that went on from 1897 until 1914. At the end of that time, when Europe was breaking up in war, Hoover was a more prestigious consultant than Janin ever had been. He was much more than an engineer. He had first been an organizer of field jobs, one after another, in remote places, then a promoter and financier, and finally the head of a London firm with offices all over the globe. Also, he had become a wealthy man with income flowing into his office from fees, royalties, profits, and speculative gains. He had found time to marry Lou Henry, a girl he had known at Stanford, and had led a life of almost continuous excitement and change. He had penetrated far into the interior of China, had worked in the back-lands of Australia; had, in fact, been everywhere his profession reached, and that was wherever metals were to be found in the earth.

It is an interesting and probably a revealing thing about Hoover that his adventurous experiences intrigued him only as logistical problems. If he had to get deep into the Altai Mountains or had to cross the Gobi Desert, he made the most efficient arrangements possible and then regarded the interlude until he arrived as delay to be suffered impatiently. What happened along the way was hardly even noted. But his ventures required a reliable constitution, good fortune, and singular ability to get ahead with any job he had to do. These he had, and they were gradually discovered by his associates. If he had been distracted by adventure, entranced by primitive customs, or tempted by wild and unknown scenery, his single-minded search for what he had gone to find would certainly have been reported in less laconic terms and might have been longer delayed.

During these years we have a picture of a round-faced, stocky, un-communicative man with a lot on his mind. He had a talent for going to the heart of problems and an even more notable one for creating organizations to carry on the operations he thought necessary. He had a spectacular, even if specialized, talent for organizing large enter-prises. The operations he conceived and carried out from his office in London were quite comparable with the development of mergers and trusts in the United States. In 1912, only thirty-eight years old, he was able to consider quitting altogether and going into something "of public service." He may not have meant it, but very possibly he did. He had two sons to be educated in the American West. He had con-ceived a bitter distaste for everything European. He had income enough. The profession that had served him so well might graduate him into something of public importance. What can easily be sus-pected is that his Quaker upbringing was influencing his decision. At any rate, from his accidental first contact with a relief organization he went on to devote the rest of his life to public work.

It is interesting to note that he felt it a point of honor never to accept pay for his further labors. This may have given him satisfaction as a Friend, but it was a doubtful precedent for others who had no such income as his. He did not make a great matter of it, but it was something often spoken of, and the inescapable inference was that somehow it made him more virtuous than others. Many of his associ-ates in later volunteer work with refugee and relief organizations made the same gesture. He apparently encouraged it, feeling, perhaps, that it made them immune to criticism. He must have been aware that public service cannot be manned by unpaid volunteers. But it was an impulse he could indulge and he took pride in it. Later it did count as a political credit.

The opening into this career came in an unexpected way. Hoover happened to be in London, his headquarters for many years, when war broke out in the summer of 1914. There were more than two hundred thousand Americans scattered throughout the various nations who were immobilized. Borders were closed, transportation was halted, currencies were frozen. In a few weeks Hoover, working at top pressure and using his intimate knowledge of the governments he had been dealing with for years, got together the means for getting the refugees home. This was an amazing feat of initiative and innovation. It led directly to his next assignment.

Belgians soon became a helpless people shut off by belligerents on both sides. Nothing was allowed to pass through the lines. A population of ten million whose food was more than 80 per cent supplied from outside was quickly reduced to a starvation diet. Certain diplomats, and some others, who saw what was happening, tried, in a series of frantic conferences, to open ways into the little nation for essential supplies. The belligerents refused absolutely: the military were in control. Hoover sat in on some of the discussions and finally was given complete charge.

He succeeded in doing what had seemed impossible. It involved, in the first place, persuasion of the busy war leaders, indifferent to any interest but military advantage, then the procurement of supplies and shipping, then finding the funds to pay for them. It was clear from the outset that the job would require more than a shipment or two got together in emergency fashion. The operation would have to go on month after month, indefinitely, until normal exchanges were restored. The supplies would have to come from North America; they would have to cross blockades; they would have to be devoted, clearly and exclusively, to feeding civilians; and they would therefore have to be distributed under the close supervision of an organization trusted by both sides. Somehow, Hoover found ways to do it. The devoted people who worked with him through that enterprise in good will were always afterward a kind of alumni society. And they were not finished when Belgium had been taken care of. The occupied area of northern France was in the same situation. And the German Generals were similarly reluctant to allow relief for the people there.

All the persuading, the bargaining, and the maneuvering were done either by Hoover or under his close supervision. He learned then much that he had not found out in his dealings with top-level people during his consulting career. And the work, once organized, brought him further responsibilities of a similar sort. For no sooner had the

United States begun to approach a declaration of war than the Europeans told Wilson's Council of National Defense that their joint needs would be food and troops—and food came first. They sent for Hoover. He left London, having for two and a half years fed the people of Belgium and northern France under incredible difficulties. He had become, in doing it, one of the best-known men in the world.

He had then to organize the furnishing of food for the coming effort. The United States Food Administration was the result. Its success enlarged his now prodigious reputation as an organizer. When the armistice came in 1918 he warned President Wilson of the chaos likely to follow all over Europe. Supplies were exhausted, winter was coming, and even in spring there would be no seed for planting. Obviously, if wholesale disaster was not to happen, relief must be furnished on a scale never before contemplated. It was known that Belgium and France had no stores for the winter; but the shortage reached into Germany and across Eastern Europe—and, beyond, there were the immensities of Russia where starvation was already spreading.

These works of good will were of a kind and size never before attempted. In the feeding of Belgium, the first of them on a really big scale, when there were not even any funds, everything had to be done under the hostile eyes of occupying forces. Later jobs were easier in one respect: he did not have to beg for private help. He did often have to convince indifferent or hostile bureaucrats that starving German children were not proper hostages for favorable Allied peace terms. Clemenceau, together with most of the Generals, were unmoved by suffering of any degree beyond the battle lines. They had to be overruled.

Only Hoover's prestige, together with his record as a pure missionary of human decency, served to break down this resistance. But he accomplished it. And his reputation, when it was over, was something no man had ever had before. It would have been foolish for the Republicans—who, somewhat doubtfully, claimed him—not to take advantage of such an asset. Among the sincere admirers was Harding; and when in 1920 he became President, he insisted that some Cabinet position be reserved for Hoover even if he had lately been serving under Woodrow Wilson. The inner circle objected. But Harding, in this matter, had developed a rare stubbornness.

Together with Charles E. Hughes, who was made Secretary of State, Hoover went a long way toward making even the Harding administration respectable. Hughes organized a bold and successful naval disarmament conference;[1] and Hoover operated with similar

---

[1] The only time in history when arms were actually scrapped and limitation effectively imposed.

startling boldness from his unlikely position as Secretary of Commerce. His performance gained him friends among businessmen as well as among intellectuals; it became one of the wonders of the decade. It was this, as much as the recollection of his labors during the war, that gave him confidence in striking for the Presidency.

Some idea of Hoover's standing when war ended can be gathered from his virtual ultimatum when Harding asked him to join the Cabinet. He was somewhat surprised at the invitation—not because he undervalued himself, but because he fitted so badly the developing character of the Harding regime. He felt himself superior to the whole lot of them, including the President-elect, and, thinking it over, decided to lend them his prestige only on his own terms.

In explaining afterward why he was asked at all, he said that Harding had told him he was traded for Andrew Mellon, who was so badly wanted in the Treasury by Senators Penrose and Lodge—and others of the Senate group who were responsible for the President's selection. This was not really an explanation of Harding's motive; but it had its own interest. He went on to relate one of the most amazing ultimatums in political annals:

> Mr. Harding formally tendered me the appointment on February 24, 1921. I told him there were some ideas in my mind that he should consider before the matter was finally settled. I stated I was interested in the job of reconstruction and development in front of us; that for the Department to be of real service, I must have a voice on all important economic policies of the Administration. I stated this would involve business, agriculture, labor, finance, and foreign affairs so far as they related to these problems. I stated that if I accepted I wanted it made clear to the other departments from the very beginning. He said that this was what he wanted and he would make it clear to all the other Cabinet members. He subsequently informed me he had done so except to Mr. Hughes, who was to be the Secretary of State. He said he did not know how Mr. Hughes would take to this idea. He seemed a little afraid of his stiff Secretary of State. I replied I would see Mr. Hughes about it myself. Mr. Hughes was enthusiastic over both the idea and my entry into the government.[2]

What Hoover asked for, he got. This was a general commission to direct reconstruction in the wake of the war and to see that American business was given every opportunity for expansion. Hoover's conception of the way this should be done was to eliminate waste and wasteful competition, to enlarge markets at home and abroad, to en-

---

[2] *Memoirs: The Cabinet and the Presidency* (New York, 1952), 36.

courage research, and to avoid depression. This seemed a practically impossible undertaking, but he believed it could be accomplished.

He began by appointing an advisory committee made up of twenty-five leaders in business, labor, and agriculture. He meant everything to be done voluntarily but still concertedly. He summoned this group to his office and suggested that, later in the year, there should be a national conference, but only after committees had made adequate preparation. The businessmen were delighted to have this recognition, and even more delighted when three hundred others were invited to the later meeting. By then the crisis had deepened, and emergency measures were discussed:

> The unemployment had increased over the summer to more than 5,000,000. Under the committee on unemployment, we set up a vigorous organization with headquarters in the Department. I gave it personal direction. We expanded the conference committee by establishing a branch in each state where there was serious unemployment, and the state branches in turn created subcommittees in cities or counties. They had the responsibility to look after the destitute, and we undertook national and local drives for money for their use. We developed co-operation between the Federal, state and municipal governments to increase public works. We persuaded employers to divide time among their employees so that as many as possible would have some income. We organized the industries to undertake renovation, repair, and, where possible, expansion of construction.[3]

It sufficed for that crisis. But 1921 was not a true depression. It was merely a period of readjustment and proved to be a prelude to the most startling increases in productivity ever made by industry. The advances in technique made during the war were now available. Soon there were labor shortages rather than surpluses.

While Harding and his friends, and then Coolidge, were occupying the White House, all unknowing, immense, almost revolutionary activities were being carried out in the Department of Commerce. Such prestige as these administrations had was due mostly to Hoover. He and Hughes, whose initiative gained for him enormous respect, got along well—felt themselves to be in strange company, but were given enough freedom so that the doubtful behavior in other departments could be ignored. Hughes had most cause to be proud of the naval disarmament conference; but he gave steady and competent direction to traditional foreign policies. Hoover's scope, as he had anticipated, was wider. He not only set up an economic foreign

---

3 *Ibid.*, 46.

service and enlarged facilities for domestic commerce, but presided, also, and most happily, over repeated conferences among businessmen. These resulted in a multitude of improvements. Wastes were spotted and eliminated, "scientific" studies were introduced, standardizations were suggested and accepted. After Hoover, machine parts were always reliably the same, measurements were reduced to understandable terms, trade designations were made intelligible, and, generally, confusion and duplication were reduced.

When Hoover was campaigning for the Presidency in 1928, he made a speech full of pride in these accomplishments; but one paragraph was obviously more prideful than the others:

> One of the oldest and perhaps the noblest of human aspirations has been the abolition of poverty. By poverty I mean the grinding by under-nourishment, cold, ignorance, and fear of old age by those who have the will to work. We in America are nearer to the final triumph over poverty than ever before in the history of any land . . . We have not yet reached the goal, but, given a chance to go forward with the policies of the last eight years, we shall with the help of God be in sight of the day when poverty will be banished from the nation . . .

This would return to haunt him during his Presidency when the dismal results of the Republican years would be registered in stagnation, suffering beyond anything before known, and inability to recover from the consequences of the rugged individualism the party was so proud of. But that time was not yet.

Hoover's assault on the Presidency might have been made in 1920. There was talk of it. Even the Democrats, some of them, wondered whether he might not be their candidate. He had, after all, been one of Wilson's administrators. He had kept so clear of political affiliations in the interest first of his relief work and then of his Food Administration that his party preference was not known, even to some associates —such, for instance, as Franklin D. Roosevelt, who guessed he knew Hoover well. Roosevelt, then Assistant Secretary of the Navy, thought it not at all bizarre to suggest that Hoover might succeed Wilson— and perhaps that he himself might be his Vice-Presidential associate. However, when Hoover entered a Republican Cabinet, all was made clear.

The delay until 1928 allowed the Old Guard their turn. Meanwhile Hoover waited in the wings to come on stage. Hoover and Hughes might be an uneasy part, but they were still a part, of the Harding-Coolidge regime. They sat at the Cabinet table with Fall, Denby, and Daugherty. But when those characters disappeared in a cloud of scandal, it no more reflected on Hoover and Hughes than it did on

Coolidge; as President, he may not have enjoyed the prestige of his two Cabinet members, so much superior to his own, but it would have been politically unwise for him to have let them go. At any rate, both kept the unusual freedom of their Harding service. This was partly because Coolidge was a President without a policy—or rather with only one policy, the uncritical support of business. Hughes did not interfere with this, and Hoover contributed to it. Hoover was something of a businessman's darling, and Coolidge's jealousy merely seethed under the surface.

The passages of Hoover's *Memoirs* devoted to his service in the Cabinet record a solemn pride, fully shared by the American people. The Department of Commerce was his own choice. Harding offered him either Commerce or Interior. But he understood something still obscure to most politicians. This was that the American system of production and distribution had been thrust into a new stage by the demands and freedoms of the war. There had been a vast need then for goods of all sorts, and the restrictions of a long trust-busting period had been swept aside. There was such a burst of productivity as had never before been experienced, and much of it was obviously due to consolidations and the techniques of central management. These could and would be used for private restriction and for price-fixing if there should be no public interference; but, also, they were necessary to the gains. It was an anomalous fact that even though immense contributions had been made to European Allies, and although large armies had been withdrawn from the labor force and supported, the war years had raised the civilian levels of living by much larger percentages than had ever before been known.

Ultimately, all the organizing work he had done as Secretary of Commerce was forgotten. He was no longer credited with having stimulated gains in productivity. He was only blamed because they had been made the excuse for wild speculation. He was a great engineer, but he was not a foresighted economist. He saw how to make the industrial machine work more smoothly, but not how to make it run for the public benefit. And it is in this that the student of his career finds the most puzzling contradictions.

The most admired benefactor the distressed masses of the world had ever known made up his mechanical mind sometime and somewhere that people's characters would be jeopardized by governmental interference in their favor. The curious combination of Quaker individualism and engineer's faith in social mechanisms somehow worked to prevent him from seeing that, unless the income existed to take the product of the factories, the factories would have to restrict their operations for want of customers.

But the fatal showdown had not yet arrived in 1928. He was, at that time, at the very height of his reputation. What he had done seemed entirely praiseworthy. Being no less business-minded than he, most people would have considered hopelessly impractical the measures they would be clamoring for within two years. If Hoover felt then that he was unfairly blamed, that the people had betrayed him rather than he them, there was a certain justification. Only if it is accepted that leaders of a democracy must exhibit a wisdom people generally do not possess can Hoover be blamed for the disfavor—almost disgrace—into which he fell.

The campaign of 1928, after Hoover and Smith had been safely nominated, was never much in doubt. Prosperity was unbeatable. The only real weakness of the Republicans was in the disaffection of the farmers. This Smith tried to exploit. But he was the wrong man for that. The Midwest and South could not be persuaded that the product of New York's East Side could actually offer them more than the man who had been born in Iowa. Smith tried. He took what he believed to be the best advice about agricultural matters from George N. Peek, Hugh Johnson, and other old-timers in the long-drawn-out battle for farm relief. And he had a large target. For it was well known that the favorite measures of the farm bloc of those years, the so-called McNary-Haugen bills, had been vetoed by Coolidge in messages prepared for him by Hoover.

This issue loomed large and would continue to loom large for years to come. It arose because farmers had been encouraged to expand production so grossly when they had had to feed half of Europe as well as the Allied armies. When the war ended and European farmers demanded protection from the flood of American products—and got it —the surpluses of corn, pork, cotton, and wheat soon backed up on the farms. Prices fell disastrously; farmers who had gone into debt for land and machinery lacked incomes large enough to meet their debts; and it was not long before foreclosures and repossessions became a national issue.

Hoover refused to accept the responsibility for having precipitated the farm crisis. And following his strong instinct against governmental interference in favor of private individuals, he refused to agree that farmers were entitled to special consideration. In desperation, after he became President, he was forced to accept the necessity for a Farm Board, charged with the duty of stabilization. But this, by then, was a small finger in the dike. The floods of surplus products overwhelmed his Board.

But this is to anticipate. During Coolidge's Presidency he interfered again and again to prevent any remedial action. This infuriated the then Secretary of Agriculture, Henry C. Wallace (father of Roosevelt's Secretary); but Wallace was helpless against Hoover and

Coolidge, who believed that the general prosperity would spread to farmers too, and that if subsidies were once begun they would never end. It was a position supported generally by industrial interests—so the Hoover-Coolidge vetoes stood. And agriculture's plight got worse and worse until the disaster of 1929 struck all the commercial world and an already depressed agriculture hardest of all.

This was an issue that did not help the Democrats in 1928. Smith did not carry a single agricultural state. But the effort remained in the record for another candidate to use in the next campaign. For the first time then, since the years of Populism, the Democrats would carry the Midwest. Naturally, it counted against Hoover in his maneuvering for the nomination in 1928. But it was not sufficient to stop the demand.

This demand was much more widespread and went much deeper than is usually thought. As we have seen, what appears to be a popular movement may have been contrived by an ambitious politician working with a coterie. And if that coterie has as an organizer a Hanna or a Stearns or, more luckily still, a President (Roosevelt for Taft, or Jackson for Van Buren), the nomination goes more smoothly. In Hoover's case, he obviously hoped that Coolidge would decide to indicate that he was a chosen successor. He was as puzzled as anyone else by the cryptic "I do not choose to run" statement and several times—he admits to three—tried to get an elaboration. After his coterie had been working for some time,[4] with considerable success, he went to Coolidge and told him that his friends had 400 pledged delegates but that if he, Coolidge, intended to run again the whole thing could be called off. Coolidge was skeptical, but what he said was: "If you have 400 delegates, you better keep them." And, says Hoover, "I could get no more out of him."

The other possibilities were Governor Lowden, who was generally considered the candidate who should have been nominated instead of Harding in 1920 and was still available, and Senator Willis, who filed as a favorite son from Ohio in the spring primaries. But Lowden was making no campaign this time, and Willis was almost as unfit for the Presidency as Curtis. When the Willis name was filed, Hoover went again to Coolidge and told him of the suggestion that he should enter the primary too, but that he did not care to do so in opposition to the President he was serving under. Was Coolidge intending to let his

---

[4] Its more prominent members were James Good, former Congressman from Iowa; Congressman Burton of Ohio; Secretary of the Interior Hubert Work; Ogden Mills, Ruth Pratt, Edward Anthony, Edgar Rickard, and Alan Fox of New York; Claudius Huston of Tennessee; Governor Goodrich of Indiana; Walter F. Brown of Ohio; Ferry Heath of Michigan; Mark Requa and Milton Esberg of California. Cf. *Memoirs: The Cabinet and the Presidency*, 191. These were all able men, committed to Hoover for various reasons; but none could say that he was a manager or anything of the sort.

name be entered? Coolidge said, "No." The question then was, should Hoover enter? Coolidge answered, "Why not?"

In all the turmoil of the spring, Hoover was tormented by the obvious desire of the Senate to repeat the coup of 1920. The White House had been under Senate control for two terms now, and the inner circle liked it that way. Why not one of their own number again? The Harding disgrace had had for them no lesson at all; it was a mere accident. What was important was that the Presidency should not become independent.[5]

Their constant attacks, usually indirect, on Hoover were clumsy. They attempted to investigate the expenditures of his campaign committee. But the committee had been wary enough not to organize formally. And Hoover had not publicly recognized its activities. It had spent large sums to good effect, but not in ways that could be objected to. The investigation, conducted by Senator Steiwer, who himself was hopeful, faded out. The opposition fell back on belittlement. Stories began to circulate that would torment Hoover for years. These were based on his long absences from the country. He was not even a citizen, it was said. He was more English than American. And it became fashionable in the Senate to speak of him as Sir Herbert.

This sort of thing can be dangerous; and Hoover's friends recognized it. Their answer was to deluge the country with accounts of his service as director of various relief agencies. The potential danger from the farm belt, because of his refusal to recognize the farmer's special disabilities, was averted by a mistake the Old Guard made. They were aware that in the House there was a strong Hoover movement, partly supported by jealousy; the Congressmen had no desire to see the Senate cabal nominate a President and dominate Executive affairs during another administration. But there was the possibility that the farm problem might split the Representatives. So the Senators had a speech written to be delivered by a House member denouncing Hoover's policies as Food Administrator. Unfortunately, Hoover had in his files a fulsome letter from the same Congressman praising those policies. It had evidently been forgotten. It was so embarrassing when made public that this attack was promptly abandoned.

In fact, every device failed and Hoover went on gaining strength and delegates. When the convention opened, he had at least 450 delegates; and the only remaining question was whether Coolidge at the last moment would say the one word that would change everything. But he did not. It was a horrible few days for Hoover. However, the

---

[5] Among those who would have been acceptable to the Senators were Watson, Curtis, Goff, Steiwer, and Willis. Then, of course, there was Vice-President Dawes, although he was less popular, being more independent.

first ballot gave him 837 out of 1089 votes. It was one of the most popular choices the Republicans had ever made. It seemed certain not only to carry this election but to perpetuate the party in the White House indefinitely. What could stop them now?

And, of course, Hoover did defeat Smith by a majority of more than five million popular votes. The electoral vote was 444 (forty states) to 87 (eight states). This made a Democratic revival at any time soon seem beyond all likelihood.

Franklin Delano Roosevelt
1882–1945

ACME

Born at Hyde Park, New York
Became thirty-first President in 1933 at 51

HISTORY

1907	Admitted to the bar, after school at Groton, college at Harvard, and law school at Columbia. Began practice in New York as a clerk.
1910	Ran as a Democrat for the State Senate in Dutchess County and was elected.
1912	Re-elected.
1913	Appointed by Wilson to be Assistant Secretary of the Navy on the recommendation of Josephus Daniels.
1914	Defeated in a primary for nomination to the United States Senate.
1920	Nominated for the Vice-Presidency (with Cox) but was defeated; then became vice-president of the Fidelity and Deposit Company in New York.
1921	Stricken with infantile paralysis, underwent a long and difficult convalescence.

403

1924   First visited Warm Springs, Georgia, for treatment of dam-
        aged tissues. Formed the law firm of Roosevelt and O'Connor.
        Worked for Smith's nomination; made the "Happy Warrior"
        speech.

1928   Nominated for the Governorship of New York at Smith's
        insistence. Put Smith in nomination for the Presidency.
        Elected to the Governorship even though Smith was defeated.

1930   Re-elected to the Governorship by an impressive majority.

1932   Nominated for the Presidency and elected (Vice-President,
        Garner); opponent, Hoover with Curtis.

1936   Re-elected (Vice-President, Garner); opponent, Landon with
        Knox.

1940   Re-elected for the first third term in United States history
        (Vice-President, Wallace); opponent, Willkie with McNary.

1944   Re-elected for a fourth term in the midst of World War II
        (Vice-President, Truman); opponent, Dewey with Bricker.

1945   Died at Warm Springs in April, just as the war was coming
        to an end.

THERE is no clearer case of a single-minded political pursuit, ending in complete success, than that of Franklin D. Roosevelt. As a young man, he determined that the Presidency was for him the most desirable objective in life; he judged that attaining it was possible; and he thereafter schemed incessantly, worked unrestingly, and sacrificed unsparingly to accomplish what he had in mind. He arrived at the White House at about the time he had set for himself, and he stayed there more than twelve years.

His career has the interest for students that an inspiring example must always have. For those with a similar ambition, it offers the possibility of planning a lifetime endeavor. They must, however, if they are to copy closely the Roosevelt pattern, have similar circumstances to operate in; and they must see, as far ahead as he, what the general political climate will be. And there is also the matter of talent. For his kind of pursuit, Roosevelt had unusual abilities. The meaning of this may be that such a gift is essential.

Still, those whose ambitions demand the effort may take courage, as they assess their own differences from Roosevelt, from an analysis of his striking departures from the accepted stereotype. He was not born in a log cabin; far from it, he was the son of wealthy—and aristocratic —parents. He did not have a democratic upbringing; he played as a child on a Hudson Valley estate, was started off by governesses and tutors, and was continued in an upper-class education at Groton and Harvard. It was impossible to regard the product of this cultural experience as a common fellow.

One of the most interesting phases of Roosevelt study has to do with an irritatingly superior manner that gradually turned into an aggressively friendly one. By the time he had become Vice-Presidential candidate at thirty-eight, it was very rare for any individual to see him a second time without being addressed by his first name; and his smile and his handshake were already legends. None of this was something he knew how to do when he began; he learned it as part of self-imposed discipline. But he did it so well that even the most suspicious of his detractors failed to see the art behind the act. In time, the acting became habitual.

One early question must recur to any student studying Roosevelt. He has to ask why a young man, wealthy, handsome, active, with many interests, should set himself to the long and hard task of becoming President. And even if he cannot answer this question, he must accept the obviously powerful compulsion as a fact. Only if he does this will he be able to follow the Roosevelt progress with any understanding. It would have been easy for the young and dilettante lawyer

405

to practice fashionably and not too arduously, mostly looking after the large estate; to travel; to exploit his hobbies; to cultivate his interesting family. Yet he chose to run for office, suffer humiliations, learn difficult methods of appealing to politicians, voters, and legislative colleagues, neglect his house and his relatives, and overcome a distressing disablement. And the learning was not always easy or immediately successful. He made mistakes, but he profited by them; and none proved to be fatal. He gradually became eligible personally; and, by unremitting care, he managed to put himself in position for preferment when there were possibilities to be exploited. He arrived at the summit, not quickly, but decisively. It was done thoroughly and persistently, a genuinely professional job.

The first note to make is one that originated with a colleague in the New York law office. Grenville Clark has testified that one day when a number of young men were sitting around talking in the big room where they had their desks Roosevelt declared himself. As for him, he said, he wasn't going to practice law forever; he intended to run for office at the first opportunity; he wanted to be, and thought he had a very real chance to be, President.[1]

He was evidently more serious about this declaration than he was given credit for being at the time. At any rate, he was offered, and accepted, the nomination to the State Senate in 1910, something he regarded as a preliminary. This, in itself, was a fairly brash thing to do, seeing that he was a young man of twenty-eight and that Dutchess County had never been known to elect a Democrat. But this may have been the only kind of nomination he could have got—one that was considered desperate. The professionals are said to have expected generous campaign contributions from himself and his friends, but not a winning campaign. He fooled them. This was the year Theodore Roosevelt first began to split the Republican party in his disillusionment with Taft. And the younger Roosevelt profited.

It is the general testimony, however, that his first campaign was not won by any attractions he displayed as a politician. He toured the country in an open red car, scaring the farmers' horses, made speeches in a broad Groton-Harvard accent, and was generally condescending to the voters. The politicians were aghast. But he did win; and, incidentally, he won again in 1912; but this time it may have been fortunate that he was kept off the platform by typhoid fever and that events were allowed to decide. It happened to be a heavily Democratic year and he was elected.

His second victory was not so decisive that he could have much

---

[1] *Harvard Alumni Bulletin*, 47, 452. Cf. also my *Democratic Roosevelt* (New York, 1957), 69–70.

confidence in his hold on the electorate of his district; and besides, he had mortally offended Charles F. Murphy, Tammany's Grand Sachem, by organizing resistance to his candidate for the United States Senate. Murphy had a debt to pay, and he was very annoyed by this check. It made the Roosevelt future in New York politics more than doubtful. So when Wilson became President he was very glad indeed to be offered the Assistant Secretaryship of the Navy and removed to Washington.

But even before these events, he had made the most important general decision of his career. While he was a state legislator and the Republican party was having internal troubles, he had made up his mind that the image he must project was that of a progressive. No one can say why this was, unless it was a remarkable forecast of political trends during the next decades. His father had been a Cleveland Democrat—which meant a conservative one—but the experience of the party with Parker in 1904 (who had lost disastrously) may have shown him that if the electorate wanted a conservative it would choose a Republican one. Then, too, he may have been influenced by Theodore, who was suddenly a professed Progressive. But if so, it did not result in his leaving the Democrats to become a Bull Mooser. On the contrary, when he saw Wilson's fortunes advancing, he visited him in Trenton—Wilson was then Governor of New Jersey—and, in effect, enlisted as a supporter. This cannot have impressed Wilson as being a very important accession. Nevertheless, he brought a party of upstate New Yorkers to the Baltimore convention in 1912, all unasked, took headquarters in a conspicuous place, and whooped it up for Wilson all through a hot and hectic week. If Wilson did not note his activities, one of Wilson's supporters did. This was Josephus Daniels of North Carolina. And when Daniels became Secretary of the Navy, he recommended that Wilson appoint the boisterous young man Assistant Secretary.

Roosevelt soon discovered that he had escaped from an impasse in New York State, only to get himself into a confining box in Washington. An Assistant Secretary is not high enough in official ranking to be given much patronage or even much responsibility, and his opportunities to call attention to himself are limited. He can settle down and perform his executive duties industriously; but that is not usual and the permanent bureaucracy is not likely to be friendly. During the first few of his seven years in the Department, Roosevelt made several efforts to escape. They were unsuccessful. But he went on calculating what could be done to open out a more attractive future. One of his first efforts was made in 1914, only a year after his appointment. He attempted, on this occasion, to capture the nomination for the United States Senate without asking the collaboration of Tammany.

He was defeated so decisively that he was made to understand the value of support from the organization.

One of his difficulties in Washington, especially at first, was that in an effort to make himself better known he had allied himself with the big-navy group in and out of the Congress. Lodge, Gardiner, and others of this persuasion welcomed a recruit from within the pacific and neutralist Wilson administration. The conservative civilians approved such views as Roosevelt expressed; but also the Admirals in the Department, for whom his admiration was considerably more evident than any Assistant Secretary's ought to be, were pleased with this unexpected ally. They were always in favor of increases and expansion.

But his speeches demanding more and bigger ships so popular with the patriots were noted with distinct displeasure by Wilson and Daniels. They felt that if there was an administration policy it ought to be honored by inferior officials who owed their appointments to the party. And the Wilson line was neutrality, not belligerence. As a result of this, Wilson conceived a dislike for Roosevelt which persisted throughout his administration. Daniels was considerably more understanding. He had reason enough for disciplining his subordinate; but he let the occasions go with mild advice and even defended Roosevelt to Wilson and perhaps kept him from dismissal. It is one of the less creditable things in the Roosevelt history that he failed to appreciate either this remarkable forbearance or the ability of the plain old politician who displayed it.

This difference with his superiors was prevented from coming to an actual climax by Daniels' mildness and was erased, of course, when the war came closer and a defense build-up did become a Wilson policy. It was something of a lesson to Roosevelt that the North Carolinian who wore string ties, elastic-sided boots, and a broad-brimmed Quaker's hat was much more effective in actually getting appropriations than all the excited pro-British agitators. The Congressmen liked and trusted Daniels and were inclined to accept his suggestions.

It was during this trying period, when he was suffering from his superiors' disapproval, that Roosevelt worked out a sort of peace with his old Tammany enemies in New York. They, being professionals, were not likely to hold it against him too strongly that he had taken a young man's way to get himself talked about in Albany, even if it had been at their expense. And they saw the advantage of friendly relations with a navy official who also came from upstate New York. But since the war was coming on, this new relationship did not result in immediate support for a Senatorship from New York. Roosevelt pictured himself as a naval officer, both for political and personal reasons, and hoped soon to enter the service. He put off trying for elective office until after the war.

Politicians, during wars, had better manage to get into the armed services or they will have explaining to do afterward. Besides, the navy was, in Roosevelt's estimation, the career he would have liked to follow if it had not been for the death of his father and his being thus made the head of the family while still in college.

Suddenly, now, as the navy expanded, he was needed in the job he had begun, and he entered on several years of really hard and devoted work. He made occasional attempts to escape and become a uniformed officer; but Daniels and Wilson vetoed each of them, and the last was frustrated by the advice that an armistice was imminent.

After the war, the Wilson regime dragged on to an unhappy and harassed conclusion, with the President ill and the Republicans in control of the Congress. Roosevelt stayed on, but only to close out the navy's war effort. He survived investigations by hostile committees and generally stood so well with the party that, when the San Francisco convention of 1920 fell into argument about nominations, Tammany's Murphy himself suggested Roosevelt for second place.

This was the only concession to the President made by that convention. The Presidential nominee, Cox, Governor of Ohio, was chosen largely because he had had nothing whatever to do with the now unpopular expiring administration; Roosevelt's nomination was itself a somewhat cynical gesture. Wilson's official colleagues regarded him with reservation, and he would have been their last choice as a representative official; yet he had been part of the administration, and it could not be said that he was an outsider.

This was a matter of little importance, however, because there was no chance whatever that the Democrats would win, whoever their candidates. Roosevelt knew this well enough, but, being in the profession permanently, he made the best use he could of the opportunity to ingratiate himself with the party leaders all over the country. His barnstorming trips that summer eclipsed those of the Presidential candidate. He traveled in special trains, conferring with local leaders, making numerous speeches, finding out what the regional problems were, and storing up, in his capacious memory, information he hoped to use on later occasions.

The campaign had the effect he had worked for. When it was over and the party had been beaten by Harding and Coolidge (who, unlike Roosevelt, had remained inconspicuous), it was Roosevelt rather than Cox who was the recognized leader of the national party. And he set out to keep himself in this position. This was made possible by Louis M. Howe, a newspaperman who had adopted Roosevelt in Albany, had come to Washington as his secretary, and was now prepared to go on working for him. Howe kept the correspondence going, gathered information about local situations, advised Roosevelt almost daily about political matters, and, above all, kept all the local leaders aware that Roosevelt shared their concerns. He was usually on the payroll of some organization not recognizable as having anything to do with Roosevelt; but actually, his single interest was the furtherance of his hero's political career.

The terrible ordeal of 1921, when he was attacked by infantile paralysis, threatened to end that career. But within a matter of weeks, while Roosevelt was still prostrate, Howe—abetted, it must be said, by Eleanor, Franklin's wife—engaged his patron's mother in a battle concerning his future. The Duchess, as she was called in the family, had never approved of his political activities anyway, and now he was a hopeless cripple. She proposed that he make his home in Hyde Park and for the rest of his life follow the country-gentleman pattern. Howe fiercely opposed this proposal. And he so rallied the sick man that the imperious mother retreated in frustration.

Roosevelt, for the next few years, labored to get back the use of his legs. Not much was actually known either about the disease or about recovery from its crippling effects; and he experimented with various treatments, most of them involving strenuous and persistent exercising. Finally, the effort at rehabilitation, so discouragingly slow and so often disappointing, centered in physical hydrotherapy at Warm Springs, Georgia. There he worked daily in the warm mineralized water and came to love the western Georgia countryside and its people. He presently bought the property around the Springs and made it into a rehabilitation center. While he was doing this, he learned a good many things he had not known before.

He became aware of the hardships in a worn-out country of farmers and villagers, left derelict by economic changes they could not control. Cotton had fallen to six cents a pound and, besides, had been attacked by the boll weevil. It is hardly an exaggeration to say that the New Deal was born in Meriwether County; and it is no exaggeration at all to say that by making western Georgia his second home Roosevelt prepared the way for the later coalition of Southern and Western Democrats that would carry him into the White House.

It could not escape notice that the former aristocratic young man who had designed for himself a career in politics and who had for some time thought himself appointed to hold the party together— for the years from 1920 to 1932 were Republican ones—had become more and more a Democratic spokesman. Howe, working in New York, had kept up an immense correspondence in his name and had kept alive the idea that when Democrats did come back to power they must have a progressive program. The New Era of Harding, Coolidge, and Hoover, so prosperous a time for some, was a time of deepening trouble for many others. Depression for farmers began in 1921, when European markets could no longer absorb the expanded production of the war effort. When prices dropped disastrously, the high-cost areas—such as that in western Georgia—were suddenly not able to produce at all. And there was distress in the countryside long before there was in the cities. Economists had been saying that the one was bound to produce the other; it was only a question of time. For after all, the farmers were customers. If they had no income and could not buy machinery or even food and clothing, the scarcity of buyers would be felt in the factories. Roosevelt came to understand this when he talked to the people around Warm Springs; he was sensitized to their problems. He was one of very few public men who did understand.

It was soon apparent that he would never be able to resume his old active life but would always be a semi-invalid condemned to a wheel chair or to crutches. But he continued to struggle and continued to have hope that some life could yet be brought to his paralyzed legs; and the regime at Warm Springs, especially exercise in the mineralized water, at least kept him in good health. Except for his legs from the hips down, he was exceptionally strong, made so by constant exercise. And he had actually more interests than ever before. Politics fascinated him as much as ever; and with Howe's collaboration he kept on working toward the resumption of his career. But also as he matured and gained in understanding he began to consider what could be done by a successful politician besides winning elections. He had always felt that the trend in the United States, during his lifetime, would be toward the assumption by the government of more economic and social responsibility. What had been left to individuals and families—or to local governments—in earlier times had to be done nationally now. Individuals were out of jobs; families consequently were without income, not for reasons he or they could control, but because of ones originating in the operations of the whole economy. And only some large governmental undertakings could make things better. What he saw in western Georgia aroused a genuine ambition to be of use to these good people who were so hardly used by fate and so indifferently regarded by the Republicans.

He began to see, in the late twenties, as he became Governor of New York and had to formulate policies, that the prosperity so much talked of, which he knew did not reach the farmers, did not reach a good many others either. During the whole decade of feverish speculation, of enormous business profits and increased productivity, real wages did not advance at all. Unemployment grew, movement off the farms to city slums increased, and the nation's health deteriorated.

Local governments could not enlarge their revenues and so could not meet their responsibilities; and this was true of the states as well. But it was Republican doctrine, held to tenaciously, that individualism had not lost its value; that a man must look after his own family; that if he did not have a job it was because he would not work. But further, if there was need of public assistance, it must be provided in the old way, by local authorities or by charitable individuals.

The Democratic candidate in 1924, when the Harding-Coolidge regime was well under way, was a conservative—John W. Davis of West Virginia. He was chosen after a long wrangle in Madison Square Garden between the followers of Al Smith, Governor of New York, and W. G. McAdoo, who had been a member of Wilson's Cabinet and was now resident in California. It was a struggle that left the Democrats so split that Coolidge had no difficulty at all in defeating both the Democrats and La Follette, who that year ran as a Progressive. The vote (four millions) attracted by La Follette showed that Progressivism was still very much alive in the Midwest. It was plain that the Democrats would not win again soon unless they could offer the clear alternative to Republicanism that Bryan and Wilson had represented.

It seemed to Roosevelt, now part businessman and part invalid, but having time for meditation, that Al Smith most nearly met the need. He was a notable Governor of New York. His welfare measures were well in advance of those enacted in most states; and, although he had apparently given no attention to the larger questions of national policy, he had brought the agencies of his own state to the assistance of those individuals most in need of protection and support in the hard and complex modern world of industry. So it was Roosevelt, advancing to the Madison Square rostrum on his crutches, who made what was afterward called the "Happy Warrior" speech, putting Smith in nomination. It denounced Republican individualism, it praised Smith for his accomplishments, and it was a notable attack on bigotry—necessary because Smith was Catholic and much of the McAdoo support came from an outright anti-Catholic bloc.

That speech did more for Roosevelt in the long run than it did for Smith, who, having lost the nomination, went on being Governor; but Roosevelt so enlarged his reputation as a leading Democratic spokesman, that his position was more and more widely recognized. And when in 1928, at the Houston convention, he repeated the performance and Smith was actually nominated, his position was again enhanced. It was natural that when Smith began to campaign and realized how small his chance of election was he should press Roosevelt to run for the Governorship of New York. This would at least strengthen the ticket and might even carry the state. Smith reluctantly realized that he might not win even in the state he had carried so many times in contests for the Governorship; but he was a shrewd politician, and he appraised the situation realistically. He was already in a bad way after some weeks of strenuous travel, but some weeks, too, before the November election.

When the state convention met, Roosevelt was in Warm Springs. He had had hints, and he dreaded the decision he must make. For he was a shrewd judge too, and he knew that Smith would lose. There was no chance, he felt, that even New York could be carried. The long Republican run must come to an end before long; but he was convinced that the first feasible Democratic year would be 1936. Hoover, already nominated by the Republicans, would almost certainly win and would almost as certainly be re-elected in 1932. In these circumstances, Roosevelt was far better off as a former Vice-Presidential candidate, and a prominent party worker ever since, than as a defeated candidate for the Governorship of New York. Since 1920 he had been on the national scene; he was already eligible for the Presidency; and he had long been waiting for a Democratic year. Louis Howe was frantic with fear that defeat would return Roosevelt to obscurity and sent messages from New York saying so. Roosevelt wished he could simply disappear temporarily from political view; but this was impossible, as he knew well enough. But he did stay away from the Springs, on a political trip, quite out of touch, while the state convention deliberated. He hoped they might decide on someone else.

Smith, however, was not to be denied. He persuaded the convention to recess until Roosevelt could be reached. Then he and the other leaders made it quite clear that theirs was a party call. If he ever wanted any further consideration, they told Roosevelt plainly, his behavior in this instance would be the test. There was nothing to be done but accept. It was done with the gravest foreboding.

Fear, however, did not prevent him from making a typical campaign —a vigorous one, much resembling his Vice-Presidential effort eight years earlier. He went everywhere in the state, made many informal talks and some lengthy ones, cheered on the party workers, exhibited himself to show that his paralysis did not reach his head, and even occasionally spoke about this, something he disliked intensely to do.

A delicate situation resulted when he won by a small majority and Smith lost not only the Presidency but the vote of the state. New and unexpected prospects now opened out. The first thing Roosevelt did was to make it clear that Smith was no longer to be regarded as the state's leader, to say nothing of the nation's. He had lost; he was through. He was not even to be consulted about new appointments or policies. Smith took this very badly. He had been Governor so long and had so definitely considered Roosevelt a protégé that this show of independence infuriated him. But Roosevelt went on to organize his own administration quite independently; and Smith soon retired to a job in New York that promised a good living.

There was no certainty that Roosevelt would be re-elected two years later. It was not even clear that he would be renominated. This was when the test would come of his actual drawing power. Smith was still a powerful figure in Tammany, if not in upstate New York. Would he prevent Roosevelt from going any further? What his intentions were, Roosevelt could guess; but his own political organization had had two years to work on the state Democracy from the Governor's seat in Albany; and he was nominated on the first ballot. Smith could only concur. And to everyone's amazement, including his own, Roosevelt in the election of 1930 carried the state by the largest majority any candidate had ever had.

By then his personal timetable had been accelerated. The target year was now 1932 instead of 1936. The depression had come on. Hoover had lost his reputation as a great engineer-statesman. He had inherited all the troubles of the Republican years and had not been able to extricate himself. As the economy went to pieces, his chance of re-election went to pieces too. And Roosevelt, Governor of New York, old-time progressive, believer in governmental responsibility, was now in position to strike for the Presidency. He could be glad now that he had been forced, against his will, to take that gubernatorial nomination in 1928. He conducted his affairs in New York for the rest of his term with the skill appropriate to his expectations. He gave evidence of concern for the condition of the nation, as well as of New York. He favored such legislation as a state could enact to help farmers, he organized a system of unemployment relief, and his welfare measures were a continuation of those sponsored by Smith. Also, he began to show that he owed nothing to Tammany.

But before 1932, Smith, who had told Farley that he would not be a candidate, began to understand how valuable the nomination of that year would be. Hoover would certainly lose; and even the Catholic East Sider who had proved so unpopular in the South and West could hardly lose in 1932. Besides, as the sacrificial candidate of 1928, he was entitled to the better opportunity of 1932. There were others, as well, who knew the value of that nomination. Roosevelt was, of course, in the first position; by late spring of 1932, Howe and Farley had amassed a majority of instructed delegates, an excellent beginning, but one with its own dangers. The possibilities, besides Smith, were Ritchie, Governor of Maryland, Newton D. Baker, who had been Wilson's Secretary of War, and, in his own estimation, Harry F. Byrd of Virginia. All these were conservatives, and none was acceptable to the progressives. Their only chance was to form an alliance, prevent the Roosevelt delegates from becoming a two-thirds majority, and then combine on one.

There were complications. Hearst in California, with McAdoo as his agent, was pushing Garner of Texas, Speaker of the House, without having much chance of consideration except as a gambit for bargaining; and it was certain that Hearst would not agree to any candidate favored by Smith. They were old and bitter enemies. The opportunity was obvious. If Farley, speaking for Roosevelt, could make a deal with the Hearst-McAdoo-Garner crowd, the nomination would be assured. But before doing this, Farley made a tactical error. He tried to get the two-thirds rule abrogated. It had governed Democratic conventions since 1832, and a loud complaint of unfairness was made, especially by the Southern delegates, who still valued its veto potential. Roosevelt was quick to see what the reaction was likely to be and from Albany repudiated Farley's effort. It required only a few hours of negotiation thereafter to make the winning deal. Hearst and McAdoo were offered the Vice-Presidential nomination for Garner in exchange for their support of Roosevelt; and the necessary two-thirds was achieved.

The campaign of 1932 need not have been a strenuous one. As Howe remarked, the Democrats could have won with a Chinaman. But Roosevelt already had larger things in mind than four or even eight years in the White House. He meant to capture the party, initiate and carry through a program that would complete the progressive agenda, and, in fact, transform the party into a permanently progressive one. In order to do this, he had first to weld together a working alliance between the West and the South—something Democratic candidates had historically hoped to do but had generally failed to accomplish. He hoped to hold the South from his "second home" in Georgia—counting on a certain sentiment.

But the Midwest was apt to be more difficult. The voters there, after spells of Populism, usually reverted to their basic Republicanism, and high-tariff Republicanism at that. They could not be counted on for long. But there was an emergency now, one that had lasted for nearly a decade. During all these years Hoover had frustrated repeated attempts of the farm bloc to find any relief. It was, by now, one of his most vulnerable policies. By playing on the Hoover negativism, Roosevelt could appeal to the rural areas and win them to himself, at least this time. The future could be calculated from the White House. It was successful. He did not put forward any clear proposal of his own; but he did say that if the farm leaders would get together and agree on something he would see it through. This was such a change from the

treatment they had been getting that even the most reactionary farmers' organization—the Grange—was persuaded.

As for other issues, he was conciliatory and willing to compromise,
the sensible thing to do from the professional point of view. The only
exception was a certain castigation of speculators and financiers. If he
was certain to win anyway because of disillusion with Hoover, it was
much better to be careful. Mistakes, as he was well aware, had lost
many votes and even some elections, such as that in 1884, when Blaine
was the victim. So he excoriated Republican apathy in a nation disintegrating from paralysis, said that he would activate the government in economic matters and would stop abuses in Wall Street. This
was safe. For the rest, he cultivated the local leaders and waited for
Hoover to lose. It was quite all right by 1932 to attack big businessmen; but even about this he was selective. As a result of his caution,
the victory came according to expectations.

It is a fair question whether this kind of campaign loses more than
it gains. It does succeed in winning; but it succeeeds without any commitment to a program; and this may make it more difficult to get
measures enacted by the Congress or accepted by the people. And
Roosevelt had in mind a very extensive program indeed. The circumstances of 1933 and 1934 proved to be special. In March of 1933, when
inauguration ceremonies were in progress, a nationwide banking crisis
had finally emerged as the climax of the long-continued depression;
and the Congress was reduced to the complete submission it manifests
when only Executive energy can save a dangerous situation. In what
is now called "the Hundred Days"—the three months after inauguration—several emergency acts were passed that promised to help the
farmers, reduce unemployment, provide relief for those who continued to be out of work, and rationalize industry so that many competitive abuses would be ended. This last was the result, largely, of the
general education furnished by Hoover's many studies and conferences. In fact, Hoover's own small approaches to the ills of the economy were simply enlarged to make up what was now called the New
Deal. There were some additions devised by those who were suddenly
encouraged to think creatively about social and economic matters. But
the body of the program was already accepted in principle before
Roosevelt's time.

This was even true of the Social Security system proposed for adoption in 1934. This was a program long in use in other countries, in
some of them for generations. And when Roosevelt announced his
intention to propose it, the feeling was that it had been long overdue.
But for the Congressional election of 1934, it made an effective
appeal; it climaxed the humanitarian measures of the preceding year.
The businessmen were ruining the National Recovery Administration

by using it to fix prices, divide markets, and generally exploit consumers. And Roosevelt, although he professed indignation, was glad when the Supreme Court declared the Act invalid. Social Security diverted attention from some serious failures.

Altogether, he went into the election campaign of 1936, after being nominated by a roar of approval in the convention, with such evident popularity that Farley predicted victory in every state but Maine and Vermont. There was some surprise when his estimate proved to be correct; but not from those who had followed events closely. In four years the progressive program had been almost fully enacted. Even Wall Street had been disciplined and financiers put under restraint. Roosevelt had not even proposed the nationalizing of public utilities, something the early Progressives had wanted but that had gradually been given up as an objective in order to hold onto the conservative farmers. But the Tennessee Valley Authority was a sort of substitute. It enabled Roosevelt to show himself favorable to experiments of this sort, and it drew the Republicans into claims that it was socialistic— both of which were politically desirable.

It was gradually realized as the years passed that the measures taken may have filled out the progressive program but that they had not rehabilitated the economy. There was still a dangerously high level of unemployment, kept from furnishing more crises only by enormous public expenditures for relief and relief works, which badly unbalanced the budget and induced inflation. And when an attempt was made to reduce expenditures so that the budget could be brought into balance, a severe sinking spell at once occurred. In 1937 there had almost to be a re-enactment of the early New Deal measures in order to get things going again.

It was not long after this, however, that war began in Europe and measures to stiffen the military posture of the United States were passed. This caused nearly everyone to forget the long-unbalanced budget, and consent was general to larger and larger appropriations for the army and navy. This solved the unemployment problem. The spending was at last sufficient to give everyone the income needed to become an effective customer. And the standard of living had never risen so rapidly as it did during the years when immense efforts were going into preparations for the war; the national productive equipment not only turned out immense quantities of materials of this sort, but enough consumer goods to give everyone more food, shelter, and clothing than had been available before. This paradox was at least a lesson, even if it was accomplished through an inflation that made many inequities and, in fact, substantially diminished the benefits of the Social Security system.

As a presidential politician, Roosevelt has to be set down as the most successful of the line. No other, for instance, succeeded in having more than two terms.[2] Roosevelt judged that by 1940 the old tradition —having no legal basis—was not strong enough in the voters' minds to prevent his re-election. He judged correctly; and Farley, by then alienated and replaced by Flynn as National Chairman, and Garner, who had finally outlived his usefulness as Vice-President, both of whom counted on prejudice against third terms as being decisive, were proved to be wrong. Both were retired to private occupations.

But it was not only the two-term tradition that gave Roosevelt trouble in his later campaigns. He was forced to change his base of support. He was no longer even the hero of all the progressives. Such important ones as Wheeler of Montana and Johnson of California, and even the younger La Follette of Wisconsin, were alienated. The gratitude of the farmers had long since evaporated. Returning prosperity had, as usual, meant returning Republicanism too; and the strongest opposition to the New Deal farm program was now coming from the farm organizations themselves. They were eloquent in denouncing the measures they had wept for a few years earlier. And the South was no longer Roosevelt territory. Its inherent conservatism had reasserted itself. The New Deal suddenly seemed socialistic; and this was important, because it was the Southern Congressmen who had the seniority to demand committee chairmanships and hold them.

The President, after 1936, had to bargain in Congress for every measure he advocated; and often these bargains were disastrous. The New Deal began to melt away as the urgency of defense measures that had to be bought at a high price began to give the conservative Southerners an even stronger position. The alliance between the West and the South that had served to nominate and elect him no longer held together.

The new Roosevelt territory was one he had not been able to count on at all in 1932. It had gradually come over to his side because of his favors to labor, his welfare measures, and his policy of relieving unemployment through public works. Along with the popular sentiment in the urban areas had gone an alliance with the city and labor bosses. They had by now replaced the old Roosevelt intimates. Flynn from the Bronx in New York, Kelly in Chicago, and Hague in Jersey City were the big bosses; but the machines in the other cities were on his

---

[2] In fact, only eight were able to have two—that is, to be re-elected as well as elected, and to serve out the second. Several died in office; and these might have had two terms. But, as we have seen, there was a long period when the two-term tradition was shortened to one term, under the influence of the party demand for rotation. This had been broken after Hayes. Harrison tried to have a second term, and both Cleveland and McKinley were re-elected. But only Grant had made tentative efforts to be renominated for a third term.

side too. They nominated and re-elected him in 1940. And in 1944 they did it again.

But in this last campaign there were special factors. The war was in its last stages, almost far enough along for the customary reaction to set in—such as had been so tragic for Andrew Johnson and Woodrow Wilson. The adjuration not to change horses in the middle of the stream was only partly effective.

The city bosses had persuaded Roosevelt that his current Vice-President, Henry A. Wallace, who was of Iowa origin and a former Republican, was a serious handicap, and that the candidate to run with him ought to come out of the strongest center of his current support. Harry S. Truman was the product, and was still a faithful member, of the Pendergast machine in Missouri. He was now a Senator. His record there was ordinary, but good. He would be recognized for what he was. With him on the ticket, the urban vote might be expected to more than overcome the losses suffered through the years of attrition.

It worked. The new Democratic party was based on the city vote. And when Roosevelt died a few months later and Truman became his successor, the ownership was confirmed. Roosevelt's deal with the bosses had completely changed the national line-up. And for nearly eight years—for Truman would be re-elected—the orientation of the Democratic party would be urban and Northern rather than Southern and rural. The Southerners—the solid South—could not be expected to like this. They had not liked it when Roosevelt was bringing it about; it was their intransigence that had given him his worst political problems. Even as early as 1938, he had broken the very strong Presidential rule against interference in local contests and attempted a purge of conservatives in the Congressional elections of that year. One of his targets had been Senator George of Georgia. In this contest he pitted his long cultivation of the South against George's machine; and he lost. From then on he knew he could not count on the South for backing. This confirmed his judgment that he must change base.[3]

This was only six years after his first success in 1932; and only two years after his tremendous victory—unprecedented because a winning party usually loses at least part of its majority in a second-term contest. There followed what he knew would happen—a working coalition between Southern conservatives and Republicans. It had, in fact, already happened, which was why he had made the attempt to defeat Senator George. And he never again could count on a safe majority in the Congress. For his last six or seven years he accomplished nothing

---

[3] The break with the South was made more decisive by the rescinding of the two-thirds rule in the Convention of 1936. The southerners, after this, no longer had a virtual veto in the convention proceedings.

he could not persuade the most reactionary members of the Congress to approve—and this was very little.

Still, the maneuver of substituting an entirely new and formerly hostile base for the one he had lost was an operation that could have been conceived and carried out only by a master strategist. This base, moreover, held through a fourth campaign in the midst of war.

The pattern established during the campaign of 1932 was somewhat changed in later battles. He still depended on personal appearances, making direct appeals to the voters; and some speeches were carefully prepared by a staff.[4] Others were short, personal, and informal. But during the later campaigns, television had made considerable difference. It was now impossible to repeat; each speech had to be new. Also, there was less need to travel, since television reached into so many homes, no matter where the speaker was. But Roosevelt never gave up his belief in the actual appearance of the candidate. In 1944, when he was reported to be in failing health, he made one of his most strenuous trips to show that he was still vigorous. The value of this had been known to him since his appearances in New York State when he had felt compelled to demonstrate that the infantile paralysis that had made his legs useless had not actually impaired his ability to carry out a public official's duties.

Then, too, he always sought, and always found, some tremendous and moving support outside himself and quite beyond party influence. Recurrent crises were his best campaign material. In each of them he could simply present himself as the needed man for their management. In 1932 it was the depression still awaiting action; in 1936 it was the new welfare legislation and the relief of drought in the West; in 1940 it was the approaching struggle against Hitler and Mussolini—the nation's defense; in 1944 it was the war itself and the arrangements that must be made for a settlement.

In 1936 his opponent was Alfred Landon, Governor of Kansas, who was no match for the President who had brought relief to the Dust Bowl, who had set up a system of Social Security, and who had reduced Wall Street to proper humility. In 1940 Wendell Willkie, chosen to run by the desperate Republicans, made a valiant fight against the man he himself called "the old champ." But Willkie agreed too well with Roosevelt's policies, and his only real argument was that they were being badly executed. The voters, however, were in no

---

[4] A process described by Samuel I. Rosenman in *Working with Roosevelt* (New York, 1956). Rosenman was the oldest such assistant. He had first been lent to Roosevelt by Al Smith when Smith persuaded Roosevelt to run for the Governorship of New York. After a few years on the Supreme Court in New York, he came to Washington and stayed with the President until his death. He also edited the thirteen-volume collection of the President's *Papers*.

mood to entrust their gains to Republicans. In 1944 Thomas E. Dewey, Governor of New York, was not exactly a regular Republican of the old breed either, and he was suitably aggressive. His castigations of the war's management were those of an experienced prosecutor, and they hurt. Roosevelt thought Dewey unscrupulous and perhaps dangerous. He had intended to ignore him, but took the advice of the new party managers and made a last effort. It won, but by a smaller margin than in any of his others. The Republican party that seemed almost to be disappearing in 1936 could now be seen to be rehabilitated. Its chance would come in the aftermath of war. But that would be when Roosevelt was gone.

The re-elections of Roosevelt were reduced in significance, for our instruction here, by the adoption a few years later of the Twenty-second Amendment to the Constitution, making the limit of two terms mandatory. That Roosevelt's long political mastery should have had this result was a tragedy for the Presidency that would show its results in future years. Second terms had been futile enough when the limitation was only a tradition that any President could threaten to break. When it was absolute, there was certainty that the power of the office would rapidly attenuate after re-election. No great national project, it could be predicted, would originate in any future second term.

These later campaigns for re-election did, however, demonstrate something new in American politics—how a leader could change base while in office and find a support he had almost altogether lacked in his first bid. The city bosses and the labor movement had opposed him for the nomination and had worked reluctantly for him during the campaign. It was only the urgency of demand for a change that had defeated Hoover. It was Roosevelt's strategy, after election, to find a more secure backing than that of Hoover's critics; this would certainly evaporate. He found it in the greatly strengthened labor movement, in the beneficiaries of relief and welfare measures, and in the old Progressives. And when this meant the sloughing off of the former party high command, including the Chairman, James A. Farley, he did not hesitate. He had become the supreme boss, to whom all the others must defer. Many of them did it grudgingly—John L. Lewis of the Mine Workers leading the objectors—but the fact was that they could not lead their union men away from Roosevelt. And the same thing was true of the city bosses; they were helpless.

When Roosevelt led the forces that created a Social Security system, he took away from the old political machines their most effective appeal. They were no longer the only source of small favors in the crowded precincts of the cities. When unemployment compensation came from a systematized organization, when old age no longer made men and women helpless and despairing, it was no longer the city boss who dispensed aid and asked for votes in return. It was Roosevelt the voters looked to.

The political tour de force of becoming the hero of the workers, of the country's dependents, and of all those in trouble was one of the greatest political coups in American political history—comparable with similar ones of Jefferson and Jackson. But it was one that cannot be repeated, not only because of the two-term limitation, but because the work of creation and organization has been done. Social Security can, of course, be threatened; and if so it can be defended.

The suspicion that Goldwater threatened it was enough to defeat him in 1964—even if there had been nothing else against him.

Roosevelt was a remarkable strategist, whose shadow would lie over elections into an indefinite future. His coattails were even longer than those of Jefferson or Jackson.

Harry S. Truman
1884–

BROWN BROTHERS

Born in Lamar, Missouri
Became thirty-second President in 1945 at 60

HISTORY

1890	Moved to Independence, Missouri, after working with his father as a farmer.
1901	Graduated from high school and went to work; held various jobs until 1906.
1906	Began working again as a partner on his father's farm.
1917	Helped organize 2nd. Missouri Field Artillery, National Guard; commissioned First Lieutenant.
1918	Went to France, attended various training schools, served until the Armistice.
1919	Discharged as a Major; organized a haberdashery business in Kansas City.
1921	Business failed, leaving heavy debts.
1922	Elected Judge, County Court, Jackson County (supervisory position, not judicial).

1924	Unsuccessful candidate for re-election.
1926	Elected Presiding Judge, County Court.
1934	Elected to the United States Senate.
1941	Chairman, Special Committee to Investigate the National Defense Program.
1944	Nominated for the Vice-Presidency; elected with Roosevelt.
1945	Succeeded Roosevelt as President.
1948	Nominated for the Presidency and elected (Vice-President, Barkley); opponent, Dewey with Warren.
1953	Retired to Independence.

WHEN HARRY S. TRUMAN succeeded the second Roosevelt in 1945 it was in a familiar pattern. The President had died. There was no longer any doubt that the Vice-President became the President in such circumstances (and not simply Acting President); there had not been since Tyler's assumption of the office. And Truman at once had to accept the serious responsibilities of a Chief Executive and Commander in Chief in wartime. Within a few months, hostilities would come to an end, the peace settlements would have to be negotiated among the Allies, and the nation would have to accommodate itself again to the ways of peace. How difficult this would be was already evident from the revolt in the Congress against the disciplines of emergency. There was already contention, for instance, about price controls.

It was with Roosevelt as it had been with Lincoln: death released him from the inevitable letdown after hostilities were over. This is always a time when old domestic quarrels are renewed after the unity of common enmity. The worst of these is that between the President and the Congress. These involve wartime restrictions but also any arrangements he may make with other powers. He has had his way as Commander in Chief for the duration of hostilities; and all the pent-up resentments of his political adversaries and of the Legislative Branch in opposition to the Executive are released. Fortunately for President Truman, he did not have to face an election for almost four years—Roosevelt had died only a few months after his fourth inauguration; but unfortunately for him he would have to deal with a Republican majority in the Congress. Resentments would have full play.[1]

These difficulties were made worse by Truman's lack of executive experience and by his schooling in the Legislative Branch—he had been a Senator from Missouri for ten years before becoming Vice-President. This is quite long enough for a Senator to become a member of the inner circle if he happens to be a professional politician and is modest; and Truman appeared to be both. He followed the Senate tradition of watching silently for an appropriate period, accepting minor committee assignments, and deferring to the party leaders. Only twice had he displeased them; once he had voted for the passage of a bonus bill over the President's veto, something excusable because of his weakness for fellow veterans; and in another instance he had refused to comply with Roosevelt's wishes about a change in the majority leader-

---

[1] A running account of his Presidency with numerous documents was published by President Truman himself after his retirement in *Memoirs* (New York, 1955, 1956).

ship. This was in 1937, when Senator Robinson had died in the midst of the Supreme Court struggle. The President wanted Senator Barkley to succeed him. But this conflicted with one of Truman's principles, one he regarded as involving his politician's honor. Following the rule of seniority, so sacred in the Senate, he had promised to support Pat Harrison. Roosevelt felt that the reactionary Harrison could not meet his requirements and asked the Senate to elect Barkley.

A count revealed the need of a single vote; and the White House manipulators thought they knew how to get Truman's. They appealed to Boss Pendergast of Kansas City, who was Truman's sponsor and whose orders he was supposed to take. But Truman told Pendergast that he was committed to Harrison and that he would not give in even for the President. Pendergast did not insist. And although the needed vote was found, it was not Truman's. This appeal to Pendergast annoyed Truman, who by then was feeling neglected anyway. He considered that he had served Roosevelt well but that he had never had the recognition he ought to have had; he had hardly seen the President in all his years of service. Even now, to express his indignation at not having been spoken to directly and at having been supposed to be so completely under the boss's orders, he protested to a Presidential secretary—Stephen Early—not to the President himself. With Roosevelt, Truman was distantly respectful. As for Truman, Roosevelt hardly knew he existed.

This small incident was, however, a rough passage in what was for the most part a quiet Senatorial career. And in this instance he had the sympathy of his fellow Senators. From 1937 until the beginning of the war he continued to be retiring and amenable. But during the war he did become well known in a modest way by his conduct of the investigations entrusted to a special committee. It will be recalled how the Committee of the Conduct of the War had embarrassed Lincoln by its repeated interferences with his functions, even attempting, for political reasons, to discredit certain Generals and force the promotion of others. It was part of the early apparatus of the Radicals, who would show their worst intentions when Lincoln was succeeded by Johnson.

Truman took pride in his knowledge of American history, and he was well aware of the embarrassments caused by the Civil War committee. There were Senators who would have established the same sort of oversight; but he sought and got the chairmanship and turned its attention to investigations of profiteering and wastes rather than to military performance. It was a most useful service. It assisted rather than hampered the President, and he was suitably grateful.

When therefore it was proposed that Truman should displace Wallace as the Vice-Presidential candidate in 1944, there was a disposition in Roosevelt's mind to accept him as trustworthy, perhaps even as statesmanlike.

The man who had thus come out of the Senatorial anonymity he had so modestly accepted as his proper role for many years was the product of peculiar circumstances, ones not quite like those of anyone who had previously been nominated by one of the major parties. He was a farm boy who had lived in the city with his family for a few years, then gone back to running a farm with his father.

In an interesting miscellany, partly written by Truman himself, but edited and annotated by William Hillman, there is offered a certain amount of information about his earlier years.[2] From these notes we learn that having been born in Lamar, Missouri, of old, mostly English, stock, he spent his boyhood in and around an ordinary farmstead. None of his ancestors had prospered. Mostly they had been farmers as his father was when Harry was born. They lived very simply, he says, on land that required the usual dawn-to-dark devotion and in a house with no more of the amenities than other farmhouses had in the eighties. But when he was six the family moved to Independence; and most of the President's nostalgic early memories were centered there. They lived in several different houses, one of them described as "nice"; and young Harry went through the grades and the high school while his father worked at one place and another as a laborer. Then he made a try for Annapolis and West Point. He failed, he says, because his sight was defective. Indeed his eyes had been a problem since early childhood, unrecognized for some time; and he describes rather movingly how encouraging it was to be fitted with glasses and for the first time be able to see normally.

His experience in school was nothing remarkable. He has only praise for his teachers. And he seems to have contracted the reading habit then, confined, however, almost exclusively to American history. In all his later life he missed no chance to deliver little historical homilies to whoever would listen. These were mostly incidents in the past that in his view illuminated some current problem.

After failing to get an appointment to either West Point or Annapolis, he went to work. No mention is made of any ambition to go any further with education; it seemed impossible in the circumstances of the family. He worked for a contractor and for a bank; but then in 1906 the family moved back to the farm. He, his father, and his brother, as partners, did all the work on the six-hundred-acre place for

---

[2] *Mr. President* (New York, 1952). The quotations following are from Part IV, 151 ff., titled "Forebears and Biographical Notes." These were written by the President himself in a reminiscent mood, and were published as written.

eight years. But, as he says, they never did catch up with their debts. They always owed the bank something—sometimes more, sometimes less, but always something.

Then, as for so many of his generation, everything changed. The war began in Europe and it became obvious that the United States would be drawn in. When his father died, after his brother had moved away and was operating a farm of his own, he gave in to an old call. He rejoined the National Guard—to which he had belonged earlier in Independence—and went on active service. This was in 1917. He became a First Lieutenant, then a Captain, and in the spring of 1918 landed in France in command of a field artillery battery. He was a competent officer, and his service record was a good one. But by 1919 he was back home and being mustered out. His soldiering had taken two years of his life and he was no further along. One thing he knew. Farming was no longer worth while; the work was hard and confining and the living it yielded was meager.

It was at this time that, together with an army friend, he organized the unfortunate merchandising venture his political opponents would make so much of in all his future campaigns. For the business failed miserably, leaving him with debts he was still paying years later out of what savings he could salvage from his public jobs. This was disaster compounded. He was now thirty-eight years old and had recently married a girl he had known for many years. She was used to better things than he could now give her. She stood by loyally, but he had a fierce desire to be a decent provider in the American tradition. He was nearly desperate.

It was then that he turned to politics; county politics. He owed his first preferment to his friends in the army, who, when appealed to, recommended him to Boss Pendergast. These friends, and those of his wife, went on supporting him; and the boss learned that he was a valuable asset—bright, trustworthy, honest, but not inclined to look beyond his own jurisdiction. And in matters having to do with the life of a machine, he gave no trouble. He himself, making notes when he was President, became ambiguous when telling about his early connection with Pendergast. Of his choice for his first job he said merely that it "was decided," and went on to explain—what puzzles nearly everyone—how the job happened to be called a judgeship. For he was not a lawyer,[3] and the office had nothing to do with legal matters:

> It is an administrative body. Taxes are levied by the court, and
> expenditures for roads, homes for the aged, schools for delinquent

---

[3] He did study law at the Kansas City Law School for two years, mostly at night, but he neither graduated nor took examinations for the bar.

children, and the insane in state institutions are supported by orders
of the Court on the County Treasurer. The only really judicial act
the Court performs is to make a finding of insanity when such finding
is recommended by two reputable physicians.

His first campaign was a hot one and he worked tirelessly, marshaling all his friends and rallying the Pendergast faithful. He won
both in the primary and in the election, as all the Pendergast candidates
did. But, having won an easy victory, they began to quarrel about
the spoils. What followed in the next election, he described with some
disgust:

> . . . in 1924 the Rabbits bolted the ticket and the two District Judges
> were beaten. My only child was born that year and I was broke and
> out of a job. But I had a lot of friends and pulled through until 1926
> when I was elected Presiding Judge of the County Court of Jackson
> County by a majority of 16,000 votes. That was the beginning of a
> fantastic political career that ended in the White House. It does not
> seem possible that it could happen. It could not happen anywhere but in
> the United States.

Years later he was still proud of the way he had "run the county."
He had seen that roads were built, put the institutions into better
shape, refinanced the debt, and generally brought affairs to a state of
efficiency never known before. And in 1930 he was re-elected by a
large majority. Then, as he says, he "was maneuvered into running for
the Senate in the primary, just as I had been in the primary in the
county in 1922 . . . The election was a walkaway." So he landed in
Washington, Pendergast's man in the capital.

If it seems a long jump from a County Judgeship of the sort he
describes to the United States Senate, that is because it was a long
jump. He does not say that his political success, after such a dismal
start in business, was owed to anyone else. But, when asked, he
readily gave credit to Tom Pendergast, and did it without shame. He
behaved as a completely loyal henchman should behave—except that
he seems never to have been asked for any payment beyond the usual
support provided by such machines. No one ever claimed, or even
suggested, that Truman was corrupt or that his behavior was in any
way improper. He was one of those machine members who are
useful precisely because of their rectitude. They are a necessary cover.
Truman's indignation at any suggestion of wrongness in his connection with the boss was apt to be choleric. But when he got to

the White House he expressed immense satisfaction in being able to fire the prosecutor—one Milligan—who had convicted Pendergast and sent him to jail after years of trying; and until the boss was actually behind bars Truman never lost an opportunity to protest that his sponsor was a man sadly misunderstood by the public and persecuted by political enemies. This blindness is of course too convenient to be explained as entirely sincere. Truman was not stupid; on the contrary, he was brighter than most of his associates. So his compulsive loyalty has to be put down to protective blindness—that and an acceptance of machine methods as usual and necessary in political life.

Until his middle thirties, Truman was lonely; but his lack of friends had the advantage of giving him time to read. And when he became a "Judge" he centered much more intensively on his job than political appointees usually do.

His disinterest in public affairs had been caused partly by his myopia; but it was also a natural turn of mind. He liked facts and regarded historical writings as literal accounts of past events. His world was extremely circumscribed, even if his intelligence was sharp. This is inevitably reminiscent of Coolidge, who was provincial in the same way and throughout early life almost as inclined to avoid notice. He was especially suspicious of widened governmental activity and felt that Federal expansion had become dangerous. He once explained to a correspondent that he was a Democrat because it was the party that held most closely to states' rights and local controls in contrast to the Republicans, who believed in centralization. This was when he had become a Senator. But he was obviously a puzzled statesman at that time. The Democrats were not conforming to his standard for the party. During the Roosevelt administration, he confessed, the situation seemed to be "somewhat reversed," adding wistfully that "it was because of the emergency . . ." But, he asserted, "the general principles of the Democratic party are for as little government as possible."[4]

Quite obviously he had not yet accommodated himself to the new world and the policies of President Roosevelt. The county official from Missouri who, until he got to Washington, had never lifted his gaze beyond Jackson County was bewildered by the swirl of New Deal events. Apart from doing his small administrative job, he had served creditably in his artillery outfit; but he had had no occasion to think of anything beyond doing a good job with his company; and outside

---

[4] Quoted in Allen and Shannon, *The Truman Merry-Go-Round* (New York, 1950), 10. The letter was written in 1936, when he had been in the Senate for one year.

of his political work, his time had been given to Masonry. He had been an earnest lodge member and had gone upward degree by degree. This had involved study and faithful attendance at innumerable meetings and, together with the National Guard, had monopolized his time and his interest. What he knew of larger affairs, such as a United States Senator had to deal with, was as near nothing as can be imagined. His confusion about the New Deal was symptomatic.

But there was one thing he did know. He had to be regular. This meant that he had to vote as he was told and behave generally as a Democrat loyal to his leaders. This was a condition of his service. Pendergast had not picked a convenient rural candidate to run for the Senatorship without being certain that the return in favors would be steady. And, of course, it was. Pendergast, like other city bosses, did very well out of the expanded Federal activity. Relief, public works, and all the other agencies needed local administrators, and they were not appointed from civil service rolls. There were contracts too; and they could be profitable. Truman, voting as he was told and keeping quiet, whatever he thought, was extremely useful as the Washington representative of the machine.

As a Senator, Truman could not join in the New Deal because much of it he did not understand, and most of what he did understand he did not approve; but he did have one interest that seemed to run with those of his new associates. He was against Wall Street. The big fellows in the banks there exploited the little fellows out in Missouri. How they did it, he thought he could perhaps find out by earnest committee work. It happened that Senator Burton K. Wheeler of Montana was investigating railroad finance, and Truman enlisted with him, studying earnestly, reading closely, and becoming something of an expert in the machinations of the financiers who used railroad securities as gambling counters. What he found out confirmed his suspicions. He worked up real indignation about the mistreatment of small businessmen. He now saw, or thought he saw, that his own business failure had been caused by their machinations; he spoke of it, even after he became President, as having been the result of the Harding-Mellon deflationary policies. This conviction gave him a personal reason for digging into the affairs Wheeler introduced him to; and he showed the persistence of a terrier in the work of the committee.

Having landed in the Senate of the United States immediately after having been a county official in Missouri, having had only a high school education, and having been a failure in business, he knew others must feel that he had been projected into a situation far beyond his capacity to fill—as, of course, he had. Perhaps because it was so obvious, he made the admission of his inferiority often and was so obviously impressed with his Senatorial betters that his humility became somewhat tiresome after a while. Senators enjoy praise and swell with pride when admirers follow them about; but Truman for years spoke of himself as a willing subordinate. He seemed destined to serve out his time in the cloakrooms and at the committee tables where he was allowed to listen to and serve more certain leaders.

Even in the affair of the war investigating committee his role was not actually that for which he was given credit. The committee had a brilliant young counsel, Hugh Fulton, who organized the research and wrote the reports. It was Truman's part to preside, to be pleasant, to be helpful, to be fair but severe with those who were exploiting defense contracts. Still, it went a long way toward modifying the self-detraction he had so long been insisting on. He began to feel like a statesman. As one colleague remarked: "Harry must read the newspapers too." He almost never said anything on the Senate floor and especially never put together anything that could be called a speech. He seemed incapable of generalizing what he had learned or of expounding the lessons it held for public policy.

He had not grown appreciably during his ten years in the Senate. He once ventured the opinion that if anyone understood Jackson County, Missouri, they understood the country. But that seemed a hopeful and rather defensive opinion. He probably understood his county very well; he remained still the industrious official who had built roads, repaired courthouses, and taken care of the indigent. This was hardly at a Senatorial level; but this was where he felt most at home.

It is a mistake, however, to suppose that he did not become ambitious for something further as his years in the Senate lengthened. With him, as with others, lack of ability or preparation did not seem an obstacle. He knew that he was honest; he thought he knew politics; and he had at least watched Federal government at work. That made him a qualified aspirant; and the thought came to him, as it does to all Senators, that he might look higher. Especially after he came to national notice by way of the investigating committee, this ambition grew more plausible. But one thing stood in the way—that persistent self-deprecation which had generally been accepted by his colleagues, the more so because it seemed so thoroughly justified.

But when the 1944 campaign was imminent, Robert Hannegan of Kansas City was Chairman of the National Committee and Roosevelt was in the difficult situation of having to depend for re-election almost wholly on the city bosses. He was still immensely popular in the country; but the hard organizing work and the necessary financing must be done by the local machines, helped out by organized labor.

Hannegan was also a protégé of Pendergast. He knew Truman intimately and felt that with him on the ticket the enthusiastic work he must have in order to win could be counted on; he would be recognized by the bosses as one of their own. Henry Wallace, who had become Vice-President in 1940 at Roosevelt's insistence, was distrusted. He was a liberal; this was not so bad; but he had once been an Iowa Republican—which is the worst kind—and he was so independent as to be unpredictable. The professional politicians were worried. Moreover, he had not pleased the Senators over whom he had presided for four years. He had been chilly and unco-operative. He had never joined in their poker games, and he did not enjoy the pleasant relaxation of bourbon and branch water in their gossipy back-office sessions.

One of Truman's attractions was that he had become an accepted member, if a humble one, of the several "Boards of Education," such as that of Garner when he had been Vice-President, and of the Senate Secretary, Leslie Biffle. In these informal gatherings he was a non-aggressive member of the circle, not given to controversial discussion or to irritating inquiry. All he asked of the leaders was how he ought to vote.

Considering his Presidential behavior, he was curiously conservative as a Senator. He was at least as hostile to organized labor as he was to Wall Street. He always stood for economy when he could, although it was hard in Roosevelt days. But on one occasion he did vote to cut appropriations for relief (January 1939), and earlier (in 1936) he had voted against a bill to establish a low-cost housing program. These showed his real preferences; but they were exceptions. For the most part he voted as he was expected to, straight down the party line.

In 1940, when he had had to run again for the Senate, he had been in trouble. Pendergast was now in jail, and this made a problem. But Truman bravely and aggressively used his old tactics. He covered the state as he had once covered the county, talked home-town talk, being folksy, and clinging to the Roosevelt line. And after a narrow primary victory he was elected along with all other Democrats who had been faithful to the administration. The hard work for his re-election was almost wholly done by organized labor, especially the railway unions. They supported him because he had faithfully voted for the New Deal measures favoring labor, and they did not want to lose him. They sent representatives into the state, flooded it with literature, and generally supplied funds and workers he himself did not have. They did not know, or they overlooked, his anti-union sentiments.

It was following this, during his second term, that he had the fortunate idea of presiding over the Committee to Investigate the National Defense Program. In this he could be of such considerable service that he would at last be noticed. And its labors would not take him into those realms of finance and sociology that baffled him. It was the notice he got for this work, also, that enlarged his view of his own abilities and encouraged him to look higher; by 1944 he was prepared for Hannegan's suggestion.

> The story of Truman's nomination for the Vice Presidency has been told many times. One myth connected with it, however, should certainly be dispelled. This is the fiction that he received the nomination with no effort on his part and that, indeed, he took it with considerable reluctance. Actually, he battled for it furiously . . . deep down Truman has always been an extremely ambitious man. This is shown by the way he fought like a tiger to hold any office that anyone ever tried to take away from him . . . When Tom Pendergast offered him the Senatorship in 1934, he could scarcely believe it. Similarly, ten years later, when those delicious rumors began to float around that Roosevelt and the big bosses were considering him for the Vice Presidency, it took him some time to adjust . . . but all the time he knew that with the right breaks it might come to him and his mind raced with wild anticipation.[5]

There is considerable confusion about the events and discussions leading to his nomination for the Vice-Presidency. Roosevelt had to consent; that was the main thing. And it appears to have been Hannegan himself who managed that. It was done by getting Roosevelt to say that he would accept any one of several possibilities, including Truman, and then arranging matters with his big-city colleagues so that all but Truman were excluded. This has sometimes been regarded as ingratitude on Roosevelt's part. Henry Wallace had done nothing to deserve being dismissed. He had been eager and not very tactful, and he was alien to the city scene; but he was of Presidential size, and he had been loyal to Roosevelt in the New Deal vein as well as an energetic prosecutor of the war. But Hannegan evidently told Roosevelt that he would handicap the campaign, perhaps seriously, and since Roosevelt intended to make little or no effort himself, it would be important to have a running mate who was regarded sympathetically by the most important source of votes.

In considering Roosevelt's decision in this matter, it can be recalled how little attention had usually been paid to Vice-Presidential choices,

---

[5] *Op. Cit.*, 13.

or rather how often it had been forgotten that the person selected might become President. As we have had occasion to see, there have been relatively few who would have been considered for the first place on the ticket, relatively few, even, who had appeared importantly in convention voting. Roosevelt, like all powerful leaders, gave little or no thought to succession, except—again like all powerful leaders— to make certain that potential rivals were kept potential.

It is therefore futile to consider whether Roosevelt thought of his running mate in 1944 as a likely successor. Hindsight would make this seem negligent, almost recreant. But in November, Roosevelt had not been told that his life was at hazard. So there was no other sort of consideration given to the choice than had been given on any such occasion in the past.

What happened is a fault of party politics, of the constitutional pattern, perhaps of democracy itself. The case of Truman is not the first instance, and will not be the last, of neglecting the national interest for party advantage. So much had the custom of choosing mediocrities been accepted that first-rate individuals often refused summarily to be candidates; and when energetic ones did accept, it was usually for some special reason. This was the case when Theodore Roosevelt consented to run with McKinley, Charles Gates Dawes with Coolidge, and Henry Wallace with F. D. Roosevelt. But such an able person as Governor Lowden of Illinois had several times withdrawn his name from consideration by the Republicans. He was of Presidential caliber and did not see himself as Vice-President. And this had been true of others.

After that of his choice by Roosevelt as a fellow candidate, the most unaccountable mystery in the Truman history is his re-election in 1948. This was an achievement no one would have predicted from his early performance as President and, as the election approached, had seemed so unlikely as to be wholly unexpected.

His Presidency had gone exactly as would have been predicted. He had acted in character as a county politician. The able executives who had surrounded Roosevelt had been dismissed and their places had been filled with nonentities, sometimes of fantastic inappropriateness. His own considerably enlarged White House staff was even worse. They were best described in Harding terms as cronies. But their capabilities as Presidential assistants when there was a war to be liquidated and a peace to be made were tragically shallow. One, an accidental appointee, Clark Clifford, turned out to have ability; but if it had not been for him and for the holdover from Roosevelt, Judge Samuel I. Rosenman, the work of the White House would have been hopelessly inadequate.

As it was, newspapermen who had had a long schooling in

Roosevelt's mastery of his job were outraged by the new regime. There was something worse than incompetence as the White House assistants began to feather their nests in the tradition of courthouse politics. The scandals were petty compared with those of Harding's day; but they were the more damaging to the Presidency for being so cheap and mean. Several of Truman's most intimate assistants were behaving in ways that would eventually land them in jail; and if he did not know what was going on it must have been because he did not read the newspapers. But it seemed to faze him no more than his earlier association with a boss who went to jail too.

There was another handicap. Having come from ten years in the Senate, where he had enjoyed life among legislators he had learned to respect, Truman held the familiar belief that he could rely on his old colleagues for advice and co-operation. He came very close to saying, as some other Presidents—such as Grant—had, that it was the business of the Congress to legislate and of the President to execute. Senators do not believe in Executive leadership; they will combat or stifle it whenever they can; and if the President will allow them they will appropriate one after another of the powers he ought to reserve to himself. It took Truman nearly two years to get rid of illusions. He gradually discovered at least part of what the Presidency required. But it was a longer and even costlier education than most Presidents need.

By 1948 he seemed so much a failure that professional predicters thought he could not possibly be re-elected; the polls said so; and it was apparent from the general disillusion with his administration. Dewey was running again as he had against Roosevelt; and he was an aggressive campaigner, not at all adverse to digging out White House scandals and Presidential ineptitudes. He had ample ammunition, and he made lethal use of it as the campaign progressed.

Then there was the complication for Truman that Henry Wallace was running on a third-party ticket. He had been nominated by a newly formed Progressive party and early in the preconvention campaign threatened to draw at least as many votes as La Follette had in 1924; and all of them, nearly, would come from the Democrats. As time went on, the Wallace support leaked away. It became evident that he was doing something La Follette never had—accepting support from the Communists—and this drove many liberals away who might otherwise have voted for him. Their disillusion with Truman was abysmal; but they could not support Dewey, and they would not associate with Communists.

But the Wallace threat woke Truman at the last moment. In mid-campaign he turned suddenly liberal. His speech-writing team was augmented by more capable assistants; he went out on whistle-stop trips and on the whole exhibited a wholly new and more aggressive personality. It seemed incredible, but he won. The margin was slim; but he was in fact to be President for four more years. He had succeeded in becoming one of the few successors by death who go on to becoming winning candidates on their own.

Dwight David Eisenhower
1890–

Born in Denison, Texas
Became thirty-third President in 1953 at 62

HISTORY

1909	Graduated from high school in Abilene, Kansas.
1915	Graduated from the United States Military Academy and commissioned Second Lieutenant.
1918	Commanded tank training center at Camp Colt but did not serve overseas.
1920	Promoted to Major.
1922	Executive Officer, Camp Gaillard, Panama Canal Zone.
1925	Sent to the Command and General Staff School, Leavenworth.
1928	Sent to the Army War College.
1929	Assistant executive, Office of Assistant Secretary of War.
1935	Made assistant to General MacArthur, Philippines.
1942	Made Brigadier General (temporary); Chief of Staff, Third Army.

1942   Appointed Chief, War Plans Division, General Staff; appointed Commanding General, European Theater; Lieutenant General (temporary); Commander in Chief, Allied Forces in North Africa.

1943   Made Supreme Commander, Allied Expeditionary Force; full General (temporary).

1944   Promoted to General of the Army (temporary).

1945   Appointed Chief of Staff, United States Army.

1948   Retired from active duty; became president of Columbia University.

1950   Commander NATO forces, Europe, on leave from Columbia University.

1952   Resigned his commission, resigned from Columbia; nominated and elected to the Presidency (Vice-President, Nixon); opponent, Stevenson with Sparkman.

1956   Renominated and re-elected (Vice-President, Nixon); opponent, Stevenson with Kefauver.

1961   Retired.

A T OUR DISTANCE from Zachary Taylor and Ulysses S. Grant, it is difficult to follow the operation of their minds as they were seized with the conviction that they were suitable candidates for the Presidency. This is not so true of Eisenhower. He was watched and analyzed at work and play, and even his meditations were copiously reported. His most casual remarks to friends, often a significant indication of an individual's thoughts about himself, were made the subject of speculative analyses. By early 1952, the year of his nomination and election, this had been going on for several years. The whole country wanted to know how his mind was working and, specifically, whether he would give in to the demand that he be a candidate for the Presidency.

There was a sort of unreal quality about the intense concentration on one man. It was as though, at the moment, the United States had only one figure corresponding to its image of a desirable President. That he was reluctant made no difference. That he was obviously unfitted made even less difference. There was in full operation, after seven years of Truman, the old prejudice against politicians. It was interesting also, and it became widely known, that they were an "abomination" to Eisenhower; he had said so; and this made the popular demand for him all the more insistent. What the country wanted was a President who could keep them in their place, disciplining them if necessary—as they imagined Eisenhower had disciplined his Generals. Such a one would give the nation the security, peace, and isolation it longed for.

How Eisenhower, who in retrospect seems so unlikely an individual to have gathered up a whole nation's hopes and to represent their ideal, came to occupy this place in the American scene is not too hard to understand. He was the symbol of victory; he was a common-seeming man of ordinary habits; he had risen from poverty by his own merit; and what he said he wanted was precisely what millions of Americans wanted: a country quiet and free of restrictions. It was a perfect correspondence. And they intended to have him.[1]

---

[1] What is more difficult to follow is how military men convince themselves that they are indispensable. Political scientists always hope for the kind of material about leaders they actually seldom find. About Taylor and Grant, the two Generals most like Eisenhower in circumstances and in previous experience, they are forced to make many more inferences than they like to do. About Eisenhower, they are fortunate. At the time he was being yearned for most longingly, there were very experienced and sensitive observers. One of the best of these was Marquis Childs, who was moved to write Eisenhower: Captive Hero (New York, 1958). This comes as close to really explaining what had by then become a first-rate puzzle as such an endeavor ever can. Two other interpretive accounts were less useful. One was John Gunther's Eisenhower (New York, 1951), written

It was amazing and gratifying, as Americans began to explore the career of their favorite, that he should so closely conform to an old and accepted stereotype; should, in fact, almost reproduce in his person the familiar qualities. These were looked for most wishfully when people were disillusioned and discouraged and wanted a rest from alarms and when, for a time, they had had a vigorous and demanding leader. The adoption of Taylor and Grant was to be explained in some such way. In neither instance had the result been good; but this was forgotten. In the case of Grant, disillusion with him as a President was not something that reached the electorate generally; it was something discovered by reformers and passed on to historians. It was never admitted by his colleagues in the Grand Army; and he might very well have been elected to a third term if the Republican convention in 1880 had not fallen into dissension and nominated Garfield as a compromise.[2] But lessons of this sort, especially ones from another generation, are not really influential.

Generals are convenient heroes, even when they have done nothing more heroic than other wartime administrators. But the one who has had the most publicity is pretty certain to be the one centered on. General Marshall, Eisenhower's superior, was a more competent strategist and administrator; and General Bradley had survived more severe military tests. But it was Eisenhower who was the darling of the correspondents and remained in American civilian minds the organizer of victory. That he must make a good President was not a question to be examined; it was simply so.

And when it appeared, on investigation, that he had been a poor boy, born in Texas and raised in Kansas, that he had lived on the wrong side of the tracks and had to fight his way out of the ruck of village boys, and that he had got through the Military Academy at West Point with no more difficulty than boys who had come from the best schools, the picture all this made was so gratifying as to seem arranged by a kindly Providence.

Ike, as he was fondly called, had been late in getting to West Point. At his graduation he was nearly twenty-five, and this gave him a discouraging start in a peacetime army whose promotions came with

---

while Eisenhower was making his decision, or rather pondering the best time to make it known. It had much of the character of a campaign biography. The other was Robert J. Donovan's *Eisenhower: The Inside Story* (New York, 1956). This was an account of the first term, unique in having for material many papers of the sort usually not made public during the Presidential term. It was a reporter's notebook, but not a useful interpretation. Even the factual accounts were selected and were calculated to present the President in the best light.

[2] Garfield himself had been a soldier, of course, and even a Brigadier General; but this did not equate him with a Commander in Chief. He, like Hayes, was professionally a politician rather than a soldier.

maddening slowness. And nothing happened to speed up his advancement for some twenty-five monotonous years. Even after promotion during World War I, he reverted to a Captaincy. But he had no serious thought of leaving the army, as so many others did, for more exciting and better-paying civilian jobs. And this is strange, because he was intelligent, attractive, and energetic.

In 1890, when he was born, his father was already a failure, at least in the economic sense; and he never became anything else. To raise six boys on a wage of fifty dollars a month was just next to impossible even in Abilene in the early years of the century. It meant that the boys, as they became able, had to find jobs to help out, and even so, the economies necessary were humiliating. The family was never actually hungry, but it was often reduced to short rations, and it got through the hard prairie winters because Ida Eisenhower, the mother, was a hard-working and provident housewife. She filled the cellar every summer and fall with preserves and root crops raised on the three acres of the home place. Under her discipline, the boys cultivated and harvested the large garden meticulously; she made a factory of her kitchen, and somehow they managed. But there were times when clothing was painfully scarce; and the boys learned to do without many of the amenities their friends took as a matter of course.

At the Academy he did well enough. He was nowhere near the top of his class; but he was popular and well regarded by his instructors, even though his deportment left a good deal to be desired. He showed promise of being a first-rate football player until his knee was so badly injured (and so badly treated) that he never could subject it to the strain of athletics. It would, however, allow him to play golf; and this became a lifetime preoccupation, an outlet for his peculiar need of physical activity. In regular course he became a Second Lieutenant; presently he married Mamie Doud, a popular girl, met in San Antonio when he was posted there; and then, as a family, they began to be moved about in army assignments. He was gradually promoted and had the temporary rank of Lieutenant Colonel during the war; but was still a Major, permanent rank, when he was posted to the Philippines as an aide to General MacArthur, where he stayed from 1935 to 1939. But as the army suddenly became more interesting to politicians with another war looming ahead, he came home and was made Chief of Staff of the Third Army and given the temporary rank of Brigadier.

Until then, his highest anticipation had been that he might become a Colonel. What happened during the next five years was so bewildering that he must sometimes have asked himself if he could be dreaming. For, after serving with General Krueger in realistic war games in Louisiana and doing very well in what was mostly an exhibition of terrifying unpreparedness, he advanced rapidly in staff positions until General Marshall promoted him finally over more than three hundred officers who were his senior. He soon became Commander in Chief, Allied Forces in North Africa, and then went on, by Roosevelt's decision, to become Supreme Commander, Allied Expeditionary Force, and a full General.

Such miracles do not happen to ordinary men. And Eisenhower was no ordinary man. If his career was looked back on, there were several items not paid much attention to except by a person with the responsibility General Marshall had for picking a leader who could meet the awesome needs of a Commander in modern circumstances. One of these unusual credits from the past was that he had stood first in the grueling tests of the course for officers at Fort Leavenworth; another was that he had specialized in tank training and mobile warfare; still another was that hardly anyone had anything critical to say of him. He had a most extraordinary ability to get along with people. In the small and rather isolated society of peacetime army posts, animosities are usual in the competition for promotion, and lifelong feuds are apt to grow up around fancied wrongs or simple jealousies. This did not happen in Ike's case. His outward-turning nature, his interest in the physical aspects of army work, his disposition to like and trust his associates and to be helpful when he could had made him popular. He and his wife were very close to the narrow circle of friends whom they met again and again as they moved from post to post. He had his golf and was an enthusiastic cardplayer. The Eisenhowers were always welcome wherever they went, and these two resources kept them satisfied with their otherwise dull lot.

His charm, his wide smile, his rather homely but open face, his athletic build, his radiant vigor, his simple pleasures, and his serene home life all commended themselves to Marshall. And that harassed General, looking over his list of possibilities, finally decided he was what the circumstances demanded.

The trial in North Africa was a kind of test. The battles there were finally won, even if with more difficulty than ought to have been encountered. And when Roosevelt had to choose the Supreme Commander for the invasion of the Continent, he knew that Eisenhower was no military genius. But he also knew that Eisenhower did have another most important qualification. He had demonstrated that he could organize and manage a mixed command with as little friction as could possibly be expected. This, and Roosevelt's reluctance to spare Marshall, who might otherwise have been designated, determined that Eisenhower should go on. In Africa he had picked a staff of hard-working and sometimes talented British, American, and French officers and made of them a headquarters group that had the morale of a missionary enterprise. Besides, the charm he had shown as a young officer had captivated the public through the press, and this was of importance to the support of such a vast enterprise as Roosevelt and Churchill were heading in their respective democracies.

D-Day came and went, and Eisenhower was credited with doing what neither Napoleon nor Hitler had been able to do—mount a Channel crossing and make it good. And when the thrusts up through France penetrated the German defenses, the elation of victory spread through the whole Allied world. There were other claimants for credit. General Patton was a more picturesque figure; and Montgomery habitually disputed Eisenhower's judgment. But in the American mind the triumph was inevitably associated with the Supreme Commander's direction. The Battle of the Bulge, when it had been thought that the war was practically over, ought not to have taken him by surprise; but it proved to be a last desperate effort without sufficient power to be made good. And by late in spring of 1945, a year after the invasion, German capitulation was being received. And it was Eisenhower who was receiving it. He then became Commander of the occupying forces and presently succeeded Marshall as Chief of Staff.

This last was an anticlimax and certainly the most unpleasant of all Eisenhower's tours of duty. For the army was being disbanded, and it was being done in haste and disorder. Every temporary soldier, now that the war was won, wanted to get back as quickly as possible to finding a job, to his education, or to the occupation he had left; and the Congress put every conceivable pressure on the commanders to get them back home. It was not easy to preside over the disintegration that followed. After having been the most powerful military force in the world, the United States Army was reduced to a feeble remnant of its recent strength.

But Eisenhower again did his best. And there was no diminution of his enormous popularity. The vast number of ex-soldiers became, as the Grand Army had been after the Civil War, the most potent political force in the country; and they wanted Eisenhower as the Grand Army had wanted Grant. The professional politicians fell into a bizarre competition to enlist him.

No one knew to what party he belonged or even which he approved. He had never voted; and he was known to have made disparaging remarks about politics and politicians—the same ones military men usually make. And he had no opinions that anyone knew about concerning public issues. He had merely been a good soldier carrying out orders. He had associated with statesmen in the past few years. Roosevelt and Churchill had necessarily conferred with him often on matters of military management. But the grand strategy of the war had been determined above his echelon; even the African invasion and the cross-Channel expedition were not of his making.

Much of his service in the years preceding his choice by Marshall had been staff work. Even in World War I he had been kept at home in training jobs. And there had been those years when he had served with MacArthur, who, if he offered as much training in dramatics— as Eisenhower once said—as in military procedure, was still a General of genius.

He had made most of his reputation as a paper-work officer. This seems strange again, considering his ineptness in expression when he became President. The same man who then fell into ridicule because of his confused ideas, his mixed-up grammar, and his inability to put anything clearly was thought in his junior years to have been an exceptionally lucid expositor, a clear analyst, and a practical planner. He was even in demand as a ghostwriter for his superiors. But as Commander he had a massive public relations organization, and whenever he had occasion to say anything it was carefully prepared for him. His more informal contacts with the press yielded the impression of modesty and common sense. This was the picture projected to his soldiers as well as to readers back home, and the same impression was made in his service after the armistice.

When he had finished his duties as Chief of Staff, he seemed to face the prospect of retirement. But there were already complications. He was a hero of such glamor as the country had not known since the best days of Grant. The acclaim of 1945, abroad as well as at home, still echoed in many minds, the politicians' most of all. There were those who wanted to use him as politicians had used other Generals; but there were also those who wanted to discredit him so that he would no longer be a threat to their own ambitions. Everything he did and said began to have political overtones. He was naturally bewildered, being innocent in such matters, but he would have been superhuman if he had not accepted the public judgment as being, after all, soundly based.

It is again curious, in view of later events, that at this time he was regarded as a liberal. Vast publicity machinery had pictured him as the embodiment of American idealism. This symbolic role he came to play with ease and grace. And he seems not to have suspected how fierce the suspicion and jealousy of the extreme conservatives could be. Actually, his views of domestic policy—and of foreign relations as well—were naïve; they made no sense, liberal or conservative. But what he believed was what he thought businessmen believed. In an after-dinner conversation in 1947, he said that in the problems involving wages, prices, and the quarrels between workers and employers, what was needed was for everyone to think more about the country and less about himself. This might begin with the employers, as responsible leaders. They might forgo profits for a time and thus take the lead in preventing inflation and the general confusion that was plainly getting out of control. An extreme rightist commentator—Fulton Lewis—was told of these comments and delightedly publicized them; and this made the General seem to be a dangerous radical. This was his first clear notice of the vicious currents that were swirling in the politics of the postwar world. But instead of repelling, they seemed to fascinate him. He believed, it was quite apparent, that they could be resolved by his talent for compromise, the charm he relied on, and the simple principles he constantly appealed to.

He was by now considering the possibility of becoming President. The suggestion was repeatedly being made in the press, and his intimates were pressing him from every side. He was thought to have made a negative decision about this some time since. When he had had his hero's reception in Abilene in 1945, he had said that he had no political ambitions. He had even said that he would go further than General Sherman had on the subject. In the ensuing argument, he himself had marshaled all the reasons why a man who had spent his entire life in the army ought not to become President. He was obviously unfit for a considerable part of the duties. It was an impressive disclaimer; but in repetitions its elaboration became less dogmatic. He was having an argument with himself.

The demand did not lessen; and his indecision grew. He had mentioned Sherman; but after the Abilene statement, he never went so far again. Presently he was even saying that the Sherman statement, at least the second part—that if elected he would not serve—denied a soldier's obligation to serve his country; and if that obligation required him to accept the Presidency, how could he refuse? It was quite obvious to the shrewder observers—and is even more obvious in retrospect—that the argument with himself was already decided. It is a familiar one to us now. We have seen it in Taylor and Grant. Military men begin by being flabbergasted that anyone should think them eligible; but they soon progress through all the states of persuasion to the point of accepting the politicians' assurance that the times call for their unique talents. The country needs them; no other leader will do; it is their duty. They do not resist very long or very obstinately.

In Eisenhower's case, he even came to the point of feeling himself appointed to lead a crusade and began an active fight for the Republican nomination. This was a reversal of his position at Abilene; but it did not happen actually until 1952, and Abilene had been in 1945. During those years, the man who thought it improper, if not absurd, to suggest that a professional soldier should become a candidate convinced himself that those who opposed him were in a sort of conspiracy. He must enter the lists against them. At no time was there clear definition of his differences with these conspirators. He did oppose the withdrawal from world obligations that the extreme reactionaries were advocating. He had not won a war against dictatorships in order to abandon the position forthwith. But it was only in this that he went against the prevailing current of opinion in a country sick of responsibility and anxious only to get back to its private affairs. And actually he was not called on to speak of this in any emphatic way. As Chief of Staff, he had more immediate problems. While he was in office, the struggle over unification of the services took place. The army wanted much more consolidation than the navy. This was an old quarrel; and what the army got was a half measure. Forrestal and the Admirals, together with the Congressmen who were afraid of integration, defeated Eisenhower and Truman. This failure, together with the state of the army by the end of his term as Chief of Staff, left him with a much-diminished military reputation. But this had no effect, so far as could be seen, on his popularity. He was still a valuable political property.

This was made more apparent because of disillusionment with President Truman. As 1948 approached, the Democrats were quite convinced that his re-election was impossible. But there was no alternate in sight who might do better. We have seen how the Roosevelt-Truman victory of 1944 was based on the city vote, marshaled by the machines. No other leader had arisen who could appeal to this electorate. The Democrats had lost the Congressional election of 1946, and Truman had had a hostile Congress to deal with. He had been made to look ineffective. Then, too, he had had to preside over the unhappy disestablishment of the war machine. It was no fault of his that controls had been abandoned; he had fought the Congress' determination with such strength as he had; but, as always happened, it was he who was blamed for the tremendous resulting rise in the cost of living. He was distinctly on the defensive.

Some, seeing that Eisenhower seemed to be out of sympathy with the most powerful leaders of the Republicans—Taft and his friends, most importantly; but MacArthur too, who was known to have political ambitions—thought he might be a Democratic possibility. He was much like Hoover had been for a time in 1920. No one knew for certain that he was a Republican, and he had served Roosevelt intimately. Perhaps he was a possibility; they might make a Democrat of him.

In May of 1948, a Presidential year, Eisenhower found a way back to civilian life on a level consonant with the position he had reached in the army. He became president of Columbia University. The trustees of that institution had offered this opportunity in a strange mood. They were taking advantage of the prestige so renowned a hero had, and they could hope that it would bring the university the support it needed and had not lately been getting. It was bound to lower the university in the regard of the scholarly community. But, like other trustees of other institutions, to Columbia's this was not the first consideration.

It turned out to be a mistake. Eisenhower never really made contact with the faculty; he had no way of meeting them at the level of their own interests. A man who had never read anything but military history and Western adventure fiction could hardly feel at home in so noted an intellectual company. His embarrassment was evident from the first; and his relief at being called back into service as head of NATO in Europe was natural. It extracted him from the only real failure he had ever made.

At his headquarters outside Paris, surrounded by a competent staff, living the pleasant life of top-echelon military men, and able to devote himself to matters he understood, he was again at ease. And it was from this post that he made his decision to head the crusade for his ideals at home corresponding to his crusade in Europe against the dictators.[3]

By now he had lived for some years with the suggestions surging around him continually that he owed his country the benefit of his service as President. If the continual pressure from Republican politicians—those who did not want Taft, the most prominent other contender—had not persuaded him, the upsurge in 1948 of Democratic pleadings that he supplant Truman must have convinced him of his unique position.

The Democratic offers had come to him in spite of a carefully worded letter he had written just as he was leaving Washington to go to Columbia. He had been told by an admiring New Hampshire editor that, unless he objected, a slate of delegates pledged to him would be entered in the state primary. His reply was an even more cogent argument against the participation of military men in politics. Among other things, it said:

> Politics is a profession; a serious, complicated, and, in its true sense, a noble one. In the American scene I see no dearth of men fitted by training, talent and integrity for national leadership. On the other hand, nothing in the international or domestic situation especially qualifies for the most important office in the world a man whose adult years have been spent in the military forces. At least, this is true in my case.[4]

---

[3] His own account of his service was called *Crusade in Europe*. It was published in 1948 while he was Chief of Staff.

[4] Childs, *op. cit.*, 111.

Childs, commenting on this renunciation, and remarking on its doubtful sincerity, points out that an almost irresistible pressure was encountered at once when he arrived at Morningside Heights:

> . . . he had hardly established himself in his spacious office . . . before a procession of politicians, most of them Democrats, lined up outside his door. At least eight Senators and a half-dozen governors made the pilgrimage. They all said more or less the same thing: the times demanded a man of Eisenhower's great stature and prestige, who could rise above ordinary political considerations, and he would therefore have to put aside his personal desires and accept a draft. While they may have received little encouragement, they were for the most part not convinced of the hopelessness of their case.

The Democrats did not enlist him, although they made earnest and sometimes fantastic efforts. Curiously enough, the most impassioned beseechers were the Americans for Democratic Action, who had banded together in an effort to keep the New Deal spirit alive, and the liberals who had reacted strongly against Truman's petty politics and reactionary associates. The most vocal of all was James Roosevelt, the late President's son, who was an impassioned advocate for several months.

As for the Republicans, Dewey had a movement rolling that he had no intention of surrendering to Eisenhower. It was based on his New York State machine and well financed by businessmen. The fight between himself and Taft was a fierce one; and there was a moment when it seemed that a stalemate had been reached, one of those moments when the professionals begin to look for a dark horse on whom all factions can, by compromising, agree for the sake of harmony. Eisenhower was obviously the man; but he refused to talk with the representatives who tried to get in touch with him, and the moment passed. Businessmen were not yet convinced of Eisenhower's safety. It was reported that he had only one interest in the convention —to prevent the nomination of an isolationist. He is even said to have had in mind, if Taft had been nominated, to issue a call to all those who would join him in opposing the effort to take the country back to isolation and unpreparedness. If this had been done after the Republican and before the Democratic convention, he might have overwhelmed the Truman machine and captured the nomination. But he found no considerable objection to Dewey and relaxed when he saw him nominated. His moment was postponed.

Even so, the Democratic demand continued. No one knew for certain, even yet, that the popular General was a Republican; and, if he was, whether he was a serious one. It frightened the Republicans any-

way; and they were moved to threaten reprisals if he joined the Democrats. What these would have been was never made plain; but they
may have had some effect on the General. He was, for the first time,
exposed to a new kind of enemy, an unscrupulous one that struck at
a man's inner defenses—threatened his reputation, his honor, his position. He was vulnerable to this sort of attack—always would be.
Nothing ever made him so furious as the questioning, regarded as so
natural in politics, of his competence and his habits of life. Especially
these last were private, no one's business. He never got used to the
customs of this new profession. He always felt they were somehow
indecent.

When the election was over and Truman asked him to take the
NATO command, he was enormously relieved. He could return to his
favorite surroundings. It was in these, with trusted advisers pouring
into his ears the adulation he now considered his due, that he came to
the conclusion that, after all, he must undertake a new crusade.

It was a curiosity of the Eisenhower progress from this time on that
it took on the almost nauseatingly pious overtones implied by that
word. This served an obvious purpose. It excused the intrusion into
the civilian complex of politics and policy of an uninstructed military
man. He was to rescue the nation from the mistaken, even desperately
dangerous, policies of the politicians. He was to save it from bankruptcy, from socialization, from disarming, from the abandonment of
its historic dedication to moral principles. He expected, as Taylor had
so long ago, that it would raise him out of the muck he had had
glimpses of, set him on a plane well above party and the usual routines
of strife, and allow him to preside benignly over a country whose
contentions were healed and whose well-being was assured.

His participation was to be one of the few instances of the office
seeking the man. The politicians, Lodge, Duff, and others who kept
going to him at his NATO headquarters and urging consent as his
duty, were quite willing to put it on this ground. They knew well
enough that they represented a faction and that there was another
determined one; but this, they told Eisenhower, was the very development he feared. If this group attained power, it would withdraw the
United States from the responsibilities assumed in the war, liquidate
overseas bases, establish a citadel at home, and let the rest of the world
take care of itself. NATO, supplemented by the Marshall Plan, just
getting under way and having the difficulties usual in the first stages
of so broad and complex an effort, furnished a target. The Russians,
with their two hundred and more divisions poised in Eastern Europe,
could obviously overwhelm the smaller forces based in the disorganized
Atlantic nations, with their unsettled economies and restless popula-
tions. It was foolish, Taft was maintaining, for the United States to

risk any considerable number of soldiers and support an expensive establishment that actually was no deterrent at all; was, in fact, not much more than a provocative irritant and would be an instant sacrifice in any crisis. Better get out of Europe and rely on the atom bomb that was an American monopoly.

Eisenhower could always be stirred to indignation by this argument. He instinctively detested socialism and believed in an alternative he called freedom. He regarded these as simple opposites. He was still hopeful that the Russians could be won over by the kind of mediation he had carried on with Zhukov when the two had been the collaborating occupation commanders in Germany. He relied on latent good will. But, at any rate, the United States had a mission that went further than the overthrow of the dictatorship in Germany and Italy. The Allies were owed the support needed to get on their feet again, and defense, moreover, while they made the effort. His dislike of socialism and his internationalism did not seem to him inconsistent. The Marshall Plan administrators were intent on re-establishing business in Europe. The Western world, at least, would turn out to be very much like the United States. It might be difficult to coexist with the Soviet Union, but it ought not to be impossible.

When he left the United States to go to NATO early in 1951, it was a time of discouragement. Russia was powerful, Europe was despondent, and Korea was a bitter disappointment. But things changed rapidly. The Marshall Plan was reaffirmed by the passage of the Mutual Defense Assistance Act, which would not only strengthen military defenses but would pour immediate sums into the effort at economic rehabilitation. And Eisenhower at NATO, who had nothing whatever to do with these gestures and beginnings, was nevertheless their beneficiary.

As optimism returned, he again became the focus of the politicians' hopes. And this time he had a sponsor more experienced and far tougher than any of those who had approached him before. This was Thomas E. Dewey, Governor of New York, who had twice tried for the Presidency and twice lost. It was the consensus that his last defeat had been fortuitous, although there were those who unkindly said it was because he simply could not convince the electorate that he was anything more than a shrewd calculator reaching for power. This is always a devastating impression for the voters to develop; and his cynical public relations machine had done its best to offset the spreading criticism. But Dewey himself by now recognized that he and the American people would never establish a real communion.

When from his seat at Albany, as Eisenhower prepared to leave Columbia for Europe, he proposed the General for the Presidency in 1952, he was abdicating long-held ambitions and retreating to the status of supporter. It had enormous effect. Eisenhower became once more the public figure who had a mission. The word "crusade" appeared again, and European assistance as a whole began to be fathered on him. There were signs no one could miss. In 1951, on a visit to Washington for military talks, he said that his return to duty must not be interpreted as joining the administration; and when asked about the activities of Senator Duff in his behalf he said that he could hardly be expected to stop his friends from activities they were privileged to carry out.

But it was not until January 1952 that decision was precipitated. Senator Lodge announced that Eisenhower would be entered in the New Hampshire primaries in March. Now it was time; and Eisenhower rose finally to the demand. He defined himself as a Republican (somewhat later, in an aside that must have annoyed his Democratic promoters of the past years, he said that "Democrat" had been a bad word out in Kansas where he had been raised) and seized the opportunity—somewhat more gracefully than Taylor had in long-ago 1848—to say that unless there was an overwhelming reason, something transcending his present responsibility, he would continue to devote his full energy to the vital task he was then assigned to do. He also said that he would, under no circumstances, ask for relief from his duties to seek nomination for political office. Only one month afterward, he did precisely what he had said he would not do; but in the mode of politics, no one held the reversal against him.

The following months were among the strangest in the history of Presidential careers. Eisenhower was part candidate and part crusader; and obviously the politicians meant to keep the two intertwined—his politicians, that is. The opposition still had something to say. He had inherited the efficient Dewey machine, and this was a counter to the Taft drive, which was becoming formidable; but he was now down in the ruck with people he despised and was exposed to the unhappy experiences that were always so painful.

What he had to contend with up to and into the convention proceedings was a combination of opposed reactionaries. They depended a good deal on their identification of him with Truman and his policies; and they countered him at one phase with MacArthur, who had been burning for a long time over the neglect both of himself and of his theater in the Pacific in favor of Eisenhower and Europe. And now he had been dismissed by Truman and had come home to participate in an orgy of sympathy for a military martyr shamed by politicians. This was complicated by the Taft contention that Truman—and this implicated Marshall—had been responsible for the loss of China to the Communists. And this, in turn, merged into an implied sympathy for communism put into sharp and unprincipled focus by the McCarthy activities of those years. This was a miasma in public life Americans would later like to forget. But it was real and it was a complication that all politicians recognized. The Taft forces hoped to use it against the internationalists, and among them Eisenhower. They stood for Fortress America, solidly capitalist, shunning foreign entanglements, and going about the business of business.

MacArthur's bitterness toward Marshall, who had determined the strategy of Europe-first, was a hot and unforgiving emotion, and he allied himself with the extreme right wing of the Republicans now. As their authentic representative, he spoke at the convention. The idea was that he might stampede it with his eloquence and become Taft's Vice-Presidential companion. It is said that MacArthur saw it the other way round. But anyway, it did not come off. MacArthur spoke; but there was no response. The Eisenhower legend was overwhelmingly present. The "We like Ike" slogan that thundered through the country wherever the former European Commander went echoed in the convention too. And with Herbert Brownell's manipulation (he had been Dewey's manager and was now presented to Eisenhower) the first ballot was not over before the result became apparent, and the vote was made unanimous.

It could have been guessed what the General would say when he made his appearance to accept the honor done him by the convention. With him as leader, the Republicans were to undertake still another crusade. When the Democrats met, the likely result, whomever they might choose, was all too evident; and their candidate would have a difficult time from the first. Truman, the old pro, knew better than to joust with Eisenhower. He withdrew; and his judgment was vindicated. The hero had only to make appearances; and if he had nothing much to say, so much the better; no one was listening anyway; they were roaring approval before he spoke. His smile, his warm presence, captivated those who had had doubts. His firm stand for the old virtues, and for the antique culture he represented, exasperated his opponents; but at that juncture it had an appeal that was hard to match. The crusade ploy may not have been taken seriously, but the voters did not gag over it as the professionals did.

It was an unequal contest that Governor Adlai Stevenson of Illinois was asked to undertake by the Democrats. He had in his favor that there had been twenty years of Democratic administration and that there was, consequently, a formidable official machine to rely on. Five successive victories must mean that there were more Democrats than there were Republicans; and if this was so—as surveys showed— Stevenson's task was simply that of getting all the Democrats to vote for him. But there was known to be much disaffection. Especially the Korean War, being pictured now as "Truman's war" and so as a

Democratic one, was a sore issue. It had been a most humiliating failure. Vast efforts and vast sacrifices had not resulted in victory. American soldiers had never suffered worse than they had in Korea. It was no sort of image to present to the nations that were relying on American prestige to counter disaffection and Communist pressure. It was the foremost issue and, it would be said afterward, one largely responsible for Eisenhower's victory. For he escaped, after the convention, from implication in Korea. He had been in Europe; he condemned it as a useless conflict and said, at a critical time, that when elected he would go personally and close it out.

Apart from this, he behaved, under Dewey's tutelage, in the worst tradition of Republican candidates. Where now was the honor of a military man, the above-the-battle loftiness? Stevenson might doubt his pretensions; but he himself, even when he stepped off the pedestal, went on talking blandly as though he, being above politics, stood apart from the gutter tactics of his sponsors. And because a hero was necessary, his compromises were overlooked by all but the Democrats —those who stayed with Stevenson; for many of them turned to Eisenhower. He ran, not as a Republican, in their regard, but as the man in the sky they had been wanting after the earthy Truman.

If this aloofness of Eisenhower worried the Republican politicians, as it must, they did not disclose it at once. But when they examined the returns, they could not gloss over the distinction made by the voters. Ike ran far ahead of his ticket; and this was a presage of trouble to come.

The campaign was hard on Stevenson, who was the most worthy candidate the Democrats could have chosen. Speaking of honorable men, this was one; he was also intelligent, eloquent, and competent. He labored and spent himself; looked at now, his political ethics can be said to have been far more admirable than those of the Republicans. They had been long hungry for office; they had a Presidential candidate who was a perfect front for their own practical activities; and they had a Vice-Presidential candidate who had demonstrated his brand of political morality in several campaigns in southern California. In one of these, for a seat in the House, he had defeated Helen Gahagan Douglas with such underhanded tactics that enraged liberals would never forgive him. This campaign may even have lingered in enough minds to have made the slight difference that would defeat him for the Presidency in 1960. But at the moment he was a good supplement for Eisenhower. The General was uneasy with him, he being exactly the sort so despised by dedicated soldiers. But in this, as in all else, Eisenhower went along in a sort of absent-minded way. He was there in the political vortex; but it was not where he belonged, and this was no secret to the electorate.

Being managed by Dewey's professionals was sometimes humiliating, as when he was required to delete from a Wisconsin speech a passage praising General Marshall. He owed Marshall much; but Senator McCarthy demanded it and the Senator had to be conciliated.

His winning was foregone; his crusade was a success; and, never having been much of a churchman, the first thing he did when he was counted in was to join the Presbyterian Church. His first gesture with his selected assistants, just before inauguration, was to pray with them. They could do no wrong, he implied; and this was an even better cover than his own prestige for the usual political take-over in Washington. It was a preview of his administration.

The alliance lasted through four years, in spite of everything. It was impossible to get a hearing for any criticism. And he rode through the campaign of 1956 much as he had the one of 1952. There was, by this time, disillusion about the Republicans he trained with. But he had found it easy and agreeable to go on cultivating the aloof manner that separated him in his eyrie from the low fellows operating the party. He emerged occasionally to bless the workers' efforts; but there was grumbling about his lack of enthusiasm in doing it. And they began at once to lose elections. He had a hostile majority in the Congress from 1954 on; and it grew worse. In 1956, when he was re-elected, again against Stevenson's lucid exposition of issues Eisenhower understood only dimly, his party lost dismally. It was evident that when his term was over the Republicans would be very lucky to elect anyone else—and especially Nixon, who had a lively opposition of his own to contend with. He did what he could to give Nixon opportunities for display; but the fact was that from 1956 on he was a lame duck by reason of the Twenty-second Amendment sponsored and ratified by Republican and Democratic-conservative resentment against Roosevelt's long reign in people's regard. They would allow no popular leader to have so long a tenure in the White House again. It obviously never occurred to them that they might have a President of their own who might be useful for more than two terms. When they lost in 1960 to a new young man, the event made one of the more delicious ironies of political annals.

John Fitzgerald Kennedy
1917–1963

BROWN BROTHERS

Born in Brookline, Massachusetts
Became thirty-fourth President in 1961 at 43

HISTORY

1940	Graduated from Harvard University after preparation at Choate Academy; published *Why England Slept*.
1941	Joined the United States Navy and served with distinction until 1945.
1946	Elected to the United States House of Representatives from Boston.
1952	Elected United States Senator from Massachusetts.
1953	Married Jacqueline Bouvier.
1956	Tried for the Vice-Presidential nomination but was not selected. Published *Profiles in Courage* (Pulitzer Prize).
1960	Elected to the Presidency (Vice-President, Johnson); opponent, Nixon with Lodge.
1963	Assassinated in Dallas, November 22.

A N EERIE SENSE of unreality seems to pervade the progress of John
F. Kennedy toward the Presidency. And it tends to intensify as
his election is approached.

To account for his final success, some supposed rules have to be
modified. But since he freely discarded established precepts and
ignored old political lore as he went along, and since his coup has
made obsolete many of the conclusions usually accepted before his
spectacular success, it would be foolish for any aspirant to ignore his
example.

His approach, through a period of years, was managed by amateurs
with only a little professional help; but all the way through it must be
rated as a highly finished performance. It was all done in the open. Yet
it is still true that what clearly appears can hardly be believed.

When Henry Ford planned to start his own factory to make glass
for his automobiles, he is said to have ruled that no one should be
hired who knew anything about making glass. Kennedy seems to have
had some such idea too. Very few of his associates were experienced
in national politics. Working everything out for themselves, they
adopted some novel devices and methods. But what is certain is that
they succeeded with almost frightening precision.

There were many good reasons why the aggression should not
have succeeded; and evidently his competitors relied on these too
much—which may be why so many mangled remains lay scattered
along his path by 1960, each dispatched with cold and bewildering
efficiency. They had been guided by the accepted rules and had acted
according to the code of fair competition for politicians. The rules he
did not follow; the code he would not acknowledge.

It is easy to see now why his rivals felt that he need not be taken
too seriously. A formidable list of disqualifications was undoubtedly
passed around among them. It would have run something like this:

1. He would be only 43 in 1960. That rivaled T. Roosevelt's youth-
fulness at accession, but Roosevelt had become President because of
McKinley's death. He had not campaigned for the Presidency until
three years later.
2. He was a Senator, and Harding had been the only Senator who
had gone directly to the Presidency since Garfield—not a happy
precedent.
3. He was the wealthy son of a fabulously wealthy father, and he
certainly had not been born in humble circumstances nor made his
way upward by candlelit study.

457

4. He was a Catholic, and the defeat of Smith in 1928 still stood as a warning to prospective candidates.

5. He came from a relatively small state with few electoral votes.

6. He was a maverick among the party professionals, neither one of them nor regarded by them as reliable.

7. He was inclined to proceed strictly on his own and to ignore his party duties.

8. He was reserved, calculating, and studious, rather than open, voluble, and slick, as politicians were supposed to be.

9. He was a product of expensive education and had in exaggerated degree the peculiar mannerisms of private schooling.

10. He was the author of two books, both widely read. This made him an intellectual, the most undesirable of traits for a politician.

11. He was supposed to be dominated by his father, whose attitudes had hardened into isolationist and reactionary patterns after an earlier association with Roosevelt.

This list could be extended. For instance, he made no secret of his ambition; and this attracted the critical attention of rivals, something wise candidates try to avoid. Until almost the last moment there seemed certain to be a coalition that would check his progress. That is what had happened to many others, and it should have happened to him. Then, too, his record as Senator, after his election in 1952, was vulnerable, and this ought to have counted. His absences had been prolonged; his preoccupation with his approach to the Presidency rather than with his Senatorial duties was notorious; and his relations with the party leaders had tended to worsen rather than improve. This was because of his disinclination to accept discipline or to undertake any work that did not contribute to his personal purposes. He came to be regarded as self-seeking, unco-operative, and cold. His colleagues had no reason to look with sympathy on his intentions.

If there was one conclusion that was permissible from all that was known of other such campaigns, it was that an individual must either have irresistible attractions of his own—be a hero, like the Generals, for instance—or be so faithful a servant of the party as to have been selected and supported by a group of insiders.

The Presidents who had not been happily accepted by such an inner circle—T. Roosevelt, Wilson, and a few others—had got there either by accident, such as a predecessor's death (Tyler, Andrew Johnson, Chester A. Arthur, and Theodore Roosevelt), because of a split in the opposition (Lincoln, Wilson), or some other special circumstance (Hayes, whose uprightness curtained off the Grant scandals); but none had ever succeeded who was not wanted by the insiders, who had no country-wide appeal, or who had no emergency to exploit (as F. D. Roosevelt had exploited the depression and dis-illusion with Hoover).

Kennedy's drive for the Presidency was like the badger's savage, instinctive plunge for his victim's jugular—intent, ruthless, and direct. It went on through some fifteen years with undeviating purpose and ended in a breathlessly narrow final victory. He remarked of this that the margin might be narrow but that the responsibility was clear. He was, anyway, President. The kill had been made.

During the campaign he had shown no yearning for affection from the electorate; he had only argued that he was more acceptable than Nixon. What he wanted was the Presidency, and if less than a plurality sufficed, that would do. He would then do what he had done before—build on what he had. He knew quite well that for new Presidents who understand the potentialities of the position it is easy to enlarge and strengthen an originally shaky support. Look, for instance, at F. D. Roosevelt—as Kennedy often did—who had been elected mostly to get rid of Hoover but who had known so well how to use his oppor-tunity that in his next contest he carried every state but two. Ken-nedy, the calculator, might not do as well; but he figured to do well enough.

It has been remarked of other Presidents—most of them—that they relied on their own assessment of the strategy needed, or anyway that they learned little from studying their predecessors. This was partly because, being politicians, they were not serious students of history. But it was also because in politics history never repeats itself. Every problem is novel, or at least novel enough so that experience is not of much use, and might, if closely followed, cause serious miscalculation.

There is truth in this broad generalization even if its implications must not be pursued too far. And it consists in this: no first-rate politician sees his own situation as similar to any other. Time has passed; the circumstances are different; the voters have changed; the issues have shifted; the means of communication are novel, and so on. But most important of all, he himself really resembles none of those others. The way they did it may have been good for them, but it would not do for him.

Kennedy was peculiar in being more independent in this way than any of the others, even Wilson and Roosevelt. Being an analyst, he knew all the lessons; but he also knew enough not to copy. He was above all a realist, and his course was plotted by himself from informa-tion he was certain of. Acting as navigator as well as captain of his assault force, and following his own calculations, he defeated some formidable Democrats for the nomination—Adlai Stevenson, Lyndon Johnson, Hubert Humphrey, Estes Kefauver, and Stuart Symington, not to name others who were eliminated before the final proceedings.

And he won the election over an opponent so popular that he not only gathered in most of the Republican votes but many independent ones as well.

Kennedy demonstrated, let us say, that if politics is an art, not a science, he was its supreme contemporary practitioner. That by the use of his ingenuity he could have overcome so many obstacles and have prevailed against such opposition must stand among the most remarkable of American success stories.

Let us look at the odds. When he first ran for a seat in the House from the Eleventh District in Boston he was twenty-nine. It was a seat being vacated because Boss Curley had decided to make one final try for the Mayoralty; and one of the tough Irish professionals would have suited the district better than a product of Choate and Harvard. It did include the Harvard neighborhood, but gerrymandering had drawn its lines around much more populous tenement areas as well, where low-income workers and their families lived in teeming density. This had been done to preserve the district from the possible onslaught of some intellectual.

The slim, English-tailored young man looked even more alien than he was; and he would have to get the nomination in a primary contest open to all comers. His competitors were of varied sorts. Some were professionals of the Irish tradition, some were Boston Brahmins, and one was a WAC Major who campaigned in her dress uniform. No one had even suggested that he enter; but Kennedy, when in some mysterious way he had made up his mind, began months early and proceeded—as he was to do in his succeeding contests—to use every known device and every one his assistants could think of and, besides, to work, himself, as though his life depended on the result.

In the furious activity of Kennedy campaigning it was possible to detect an analogy with the family's devotion to competitive athletics —particularly touch football and similar games. They liked best the ones they could all play. They competed as though their lives depended on winning, as though some demon drove them. They took risks; there were many injuries, sometimes serious; but whenever they got together, one of these melees began and drew in any visitors who happened to be present. Any of these who did not understand the Kennedy compulsion were soon run over, knocked out, winded, or forced to quit. Any sign of faltering lost them the family's respect.

It was said afterward of this first campaign, as it would be of later ones, that Kennedy won with his father's money. And it would certainly have to be admitted that he could not have won without it, just as he could not have won the Presidency in 1960 without it. Altogether, millions of dollars of the Kennedys' money helped mightily to lift their Jack into the White House. But if he did not have to earn a living, to skimp in advertising by billboard, radio, or newspaper, and if he could hire competent assistants in numbers, that did not account for the competitiveness or the cleverness; these were always his own. And his success showed, if it had not been known before, that the processes of Presidential selection are vulnerable to well-financed and intelligent aggression. This was the way football games were won.

The team of players put together on this first occasion was—like those to come—composed of an inner circle of dependable friends from Choate and Harvard; but this soon widened to include many promising locals. These were young, too, not the old and cynical Irish; not slick and noisy, but businesslike; not disorderly, but precise and rational. They were hard and ruthless players. They were, in fact, of the breed and generation that had already discarded Curley and most of his sort. They were ready to be taught the Kennedy rules.

He instructed them; he made them extensions of himself; but he did not skimp his own contribution. He put in long days and nights on the streets, in and out of poolrooms, barbershops, and stores; he sat down with longshoremen at noon and followed them after work into steamy saloons; he hung out in firehouses; and he sat up all night at wakes. He listened as much as he talked, for one of his qualities was that he knew himself, and he was well aware how incongruous he must appear. He had never associated with people like these. He hardly understood their talk or they his. From his boyhood he had lived in better neighborhoods, moved among educated people, never thought it necessary to associate with those of lesser degree. The Kennedys had been working up, not down.

Moreover, although he was the grandson of both Pat Kennedy and Honey Fitz Fitzgerald, who had once been politicians known to all Boston, that connection had been broken for a generation. He was, in fact, as he was sometimes reminded by his rivals, a carpetbagger. His home might be said to be in New York or Palm Beach or Hyannis Port; but it was not now, and never had been, the Boston he was running in. He knew no more of it than any wealthy Harvard student would have known. His claim to residence was a suite in a hotel.

But he was determined to learn about getting ahead in politics, and considering that up to this age he had shown no interest whatever in its procedures, his sudden complete conversion was startling. True, he had shown no talent for any other occupation. After graduating he had made tentative gestures toward the law but had soon given it up, and he had tried journalism but had not become a serious reporter. His only real effort had been in the navy. To this he had given himself with the dedication it took to become a genuine leader. And all his courage had been called on finally when a Japanese destroyer ran down and sank the PT boat he commanded. He had come out of that experience an authentic hero. But the strain had aggravated an old football injury. His back was lamed and it refused to be cured. Thereafter he had to go in pain most of the time, especially when he stood or walked, or even rode in a car for long stretches. Much of his campaigning involved an agony he could hardly conceal. He ended up on crutches. But it did not slow him down.

That he was willing to endure such physical punishment was proof enough that he had found the career he could give himself to unreservedly. That he was inventive about it, that he was willing to experiment, that he tried every device, proved that this was not just another venture to be abandoned when its novelty had worn off. He was in this thing for good.

He was shrewd enough not to pretend that he was other than he was. He was a Boston Irishman by descent, but he did not ask his voters to believe he was one of them. He had risen and, in doing it, had shown what his—and their—heritage was worth.

There was another indication of his absolute commitment. He had no program. There was nothing he wanted to do if he should be elected—that is to say, he had no cause. He was a Democrat because he belonged in the party by birth and by association, but also because Democrats had a better chance of election. But he had no notion of serving the party any more than he had of serving the people of his district. It was simply a way to office, to a start in the competition for power. In this he was much like some others—the two Roosevelts, for instance, or Nixon, the man he would defeat.

But just to want power was all right in Boston. Candidates made personal appeals, not ideological ones. Very often they did not take sides on large issues, and they never did if they could avoid it. Talking to a gathering in a saloon or a crowd on the docks, he simply said that he was running, that he was a Kennedy, and that he wanted to see what he could do in office. This was what they were used to. It might be said that he carried this practical approach pretty far even for Boston. It came out when the McCarthy issue polarized the whole country somewhat later. Kennedy never said one way or the other what he thought of the Wisconsin hooligan. His Irish-Catholic constituents were strong McCarthyites; his associates and liberal friends were repelled. Avoidance of decision became difficult. His father let everyone know that he was a supporter. This, it might easily be inferred, committed his son. But he avoided saying so. And luckily he was able to hold out until McCarthy was gone.

His father was not only thus illiberal, he was an ideological colleague of Senator Taft and other Republican isolationists. He had been a Roosevelt supporter in 1932, one of several wealthy men who separated themselves from the prevailing hard line of the conservatives; and Roosevelt had rewarded him handsomely by making him Chairman of the new Securities and Exchange Commission—thus setting him to watch his fellow speculators—and by making him Ambassador to Great Britain—a typical bit of Roosevelt impishness. (Sending an Irishman to the Court of St. James's was much like sending Josephus Daniels to Mexico—the man who had directed the capture of Vera Cruz in 1914.)

Daniels captured the Mexicans' affections, but Kennedy annoyed the British by being openly skeptical of their ability to survive their war with the totalitarians. Before the son entered politics the father had made new connections, mostly reactionary, and he was especially hostile to all the Truman policies involving foreign aid.

This was not important in any of the younger Kennedy's three campaigns in the Eleventh District of Boston; but it was a factor when he challenged the incumbent Senator, Henry Cabot Lodge, Jr., in 1952. For Lodge had reversed the position of his grandfather, who had so effectively opposed Wilson's attempt to carry the United States into the League of Nations, and was regarded as the successor to Senator Vandenberg in organizing bipartisan support for the rehabilitation and defense of Europe. And a Senate race was sharply different from one for a House seat. As a Representative, John F. had kept largely to advocacy of benefits for his district. He had favored the Federal programs intended to alleviate the hard conditions of life in the crowded tenement areas—public works, housing, relief, and Social Security. If he could be called liberal at all, a label he said himself he did not accept, it was because of this. No one could have said whether he agreed or did not agree with his father on issues having to do with foreign affairs or domestic policy. Sometimes he did and sometimes he did not. And he equivocated whenever racial issues were under heated discussion.

But whenever he was in a political contest, his father was somewhere close, using influence, commandeering the services of those who owed him something, contributing to auxiliary committees, expressing strong opinions in private. Whether because his son asked it or because he realized it would cause unfavorable reaction, he mostly kept out of sight. This went on right up to 1960, when John F. crawled over back fences to see him while the convention was going on. The old man was in town, corralling the Catholic vote and calling on business friends, spending money, sending the word out along his lines of communication. John F. obviously hoped his father would not be noticed. It could only do him harm.

But having a father who could dispense funds thus lavishly was apparently not regarded as it once had been. Franklin Roosevelt had shown how riches and democracy could go together. And the elder Kennedy, if rich, was no third-generation financier. He had made his money himself. And, if anyone could, he conformed to the stereotype of the self-made American. "Up from the slums" was the contemporary equivalent of the log-cabin tradition.

But his children had no slum experience. One of his preferences for them was that none of them should have to think twice about money —and this included making it. He wanted them to keep entirely away from business. It was an indecent occupation. If they were in it their associates would be—as John F. said, in quoting his father, when as President he clashed with the upper echelon of United States Steel— SOBs. So he proceeded to settle on each of them a million dollars and put them in the way of turning it into more millions while they devoted themselves to good works of public service. There were nine of them, but only four were boys, and one of them, the eldest, nominated by his father to be President someday, was killed in the war. It was this putative nomination that the next younger son inherited. And this was why his father was always pushing and pulling whenever another election impended.

It was a close-knit family. Even the girls gathered for every contest. So did the in-laws; and it may be that the efforts of his female relatives were as influential in his House and Senate victories as his father's money and his brothers' exertions. They organized and managed the social affairs that lent a new cast to campaigning. Kennedys covered the district, and very nearly the state, with their receptions and teas.

There were so many of them and so many voters were reached that it became a dependable device. The candidate himself, with his associates, found the gatherings useful for spotting potential helpers, and they seemed to say to those who were invited that they were part of the Kennedy success; but best of all it served to recall the Kennedy name to indifferent voters. In John F.'s first primary, for instance, there were ten candidates. When he shook hands in a barbershop and said he was Jack Kennedy, running for the Democratic nomination, he was competing for identification with a whole crowd of hopefuls. But when a woman received an engraved invitation to a social affair and was entertained by a mother and several lively daughters and daughters-in-law, and when several handsome sons turned up to shake hands all around, they began to recall that Rose was the daughter of Honey Fitz and that Jack's lineage was authentic Boston. Sometimes they turned in and worked. It was a very efficient operation. The Kennedys knew how to get through several of these affairs in a day.

This device, along with the wealth that supported a large, able, and permanent organization of his own, gave Kennedy complete independence of the seedy Democratic organization. His success in going it alone in this way taught him that competition for party influence could be avoided—perhaps had better be avoided. He used the same method in his Presidential essay, gradually separating himself from the organization or forcing it to accept him by direct appeals to the voters. His mothers and sisters could not entertain all the female voters in the United States. They did reach an amazing number. But by far the most effective device was the primary. No aspirant had ever used it to better effect.

When Kennedy took the party label in his first race, was then elected, and set up his own machine, he simply went on from there in the same way. It enabled him to capture (or to supersede) the whole state organization in 1952. He was confident enough to give up his safe seat in the House to run against a strong opponent—Henry Cabot Lodge, Jr.—and was entirely justified by the result.

In this instance, as was now his custom, he began more than a year ahead to place his own workers in every part of the state. He covered it himself even in the worst weather of winter, coming from Washington on successive weekends, speaking wherever there was a gathering to listen, being driven headlong for incredible distances, seldom having a decent meal or a real night's rest; and he kept this up for months. He was still almost a cripple. His back was an excruciating handicap he tried to ignore and seldom mentioned. It was a real ordeal. That he persisted showed how final a commitment he had made.

What office he was running for during the early months of this campaign, no one could say, because the then Governor, Dever, could have had the Senatorial nomination had he wanted it; and not until that shrewd politician decided it was not a Democratic year and eliminated himself could Kennedy go after it. Just in case, as before, he was making himself known in Massachusetts. He meant to be ready for the first opening, even if it might be a doubtful one.

Dever was right; it was not a Democratic year. And he probably would have lost. But Kennedy was much less a Democrat than a Kennedy. His policy of having a party of his own paid off handsomely. He beat Lodge by 70,000 votes when the national candidate, Stevenson, lost the state to Eisenhower by more than 200,000. His own arduous efforts, his mother's receptions, and his father's support thus made him uncontested political head not only of the family faction but of the party. He now had a solid base he could move from. The House seat had been his school; the Senate would be his college. He would graduate into the Presidency. No one in the clan doubted it—and certainly not he.

Kennedy had not beaten Lodge because any policies he advocated were preferred by the voters. His were hardly distinguishable from Lodge's. Both had been unwilling to follow their leaders' line and had made decisions for themselves. But on matters of importance to Massachusetts voters the records of both were acceptable. Kennedy was even more critical of the Truman administration than Lodge; and if he was not as isolationist as his father, he did contend that the United States was being exploited by the Europeans, something every Irishman was ready to believe, and many other conservatives as well. Lodge was as handsome, well married, and gracious as any man in political life. He did come from the other strain in Massachusetts—the Yankee Brahmins who had fallen into a minority. But he was one of Eisenhower's favorites, and he would command the entire Republican vote.

Kennedy seemed to be taking on more than he could finish successfully. Whether his Irish background was favorable is not certain. Lodge's own accent was not nearly so Boston nor so redolent of Harvard as Kennedy's, and his ties with the Cambridge intellectuals were no closer. Dever said of Kennedy, in wonder, that he was "the first Irish Brahmin." And perhaps the amalgamation was one reason for his success. At any rate, this time, as always, it was as Kennedy, not as a Democrat, that John Fitzgerald got ahead.

And when from the Senate he moved on the Presidency, he made his first maneuvers so far ahead that afterward they were hardly traceable. He began by cultivating the nation as he had the Eleventh District and then later his state. It was the same strategy. His remarkable organization was enlarged. Offices were opened and wide areas felt their influence. Recruits invaded cities and towns, spread literature, made opportunities to do what the regular party workers had become too lazy to do. The old leaders were accepted if they wanted to join; but many of them could not believe what they saw, and only a few of the bosses surrendered until it was late, sometimes too late. Two months before he captured the Presidential nomination on the first ballot—taking it away from such contenders as Humphrey in a crucial primary in West Virginia, and from Lyndon Johnson, the grand panjandrum of the party, in the convention itself—some of them still had not found out that their power had leaked away. Against him would be Truman and all his professionals, who thought they would have the last say in spite of the primaries. And the faithful Stevensonians would be left grieving by the wayside. But some—like Lawrence of Pennsylvania—were harder-headed. They saw that they were beaten and so they joined up.

There were many who seemed to think a miracle had been wrought. But anyone paying close attention might have recognized it as the same one that had been wrought before in a smaller way—by the same man.

Kennedy had had some difficult passages during his Senate service.

There was, for instance, the prolonged sickness. The ailing back finally had to be operated on; there were complications and anxious months. He was so near death once that the rites of the Church were administered. He was a full half year in hospital; and his convalescence seemed interminable. He had no financial worries, of course, but there must have been times when he wondered whether he could go on with his drive for the Presidency. During the seasons at his parents' Palm Beach home, anxieties were relieved somewhat by reading—a wonderful consolation—but still they were very much like those of F. D. Roosevelt's as he struggled with the aftereffects of polio.

Profiles in Courage was one result of his leisure; for Kennedy could write as well as read. This was not a profound political treatise; it was a tribute to certain of his Senatorial predecessors who, the critics were inclined to say, had had more moral courage in their days of decision than Kennedy himself. But indirectly it showed that he did have concern for the responsibilities of public life. He was so fiercely and obviously concentrated on getting ahead that it was hard to believe he gave much thought to what he might do in the office he hoped to attain—a prognostication borne out by his improvisations during his early months in office.

It is quite possible that the critics of *Profiles* neither understood what Kennedy was after nor what he had become during his hard experiences. As we have seen, many Presidents, taken at the stage of near approach—say six to ten years away—with good possibilities to be exploited, have had to choose between being brave in the way their friends would like them to be, and avoiding positions that might count against them in the final hours of choice. At these times, stony-hearted judges weigh public and private records. A single offense may make an aspirant less desirable than a rival—not necessarily unworthy, but unreliable; not lacking ability, but not having presence. And the hard fact is, as Roosevelt once said to his Brains Trust, "none of what you want will get done unless I am elected." So calculating candidates are better off if they are not on the record as being identified with most causes.

Hairbreadth decisions are sometimes made when nominees are being chosen. At such times some one delegate, or a few of them, may call up some trivial or irrelevant vote or speech, some errant behavior. A very small incident, hardly noticed when it happened, may influence a meeting of insiders—if insiders are making the choice, as they often do.

Kennedy was very conscious of these possibilities as he came back from his long convalescence. He was safe in the Senate. He had been more an advocate of economy than generosity, unless his own constituency was involved; and he had refused to support most liberal causes. The Southern-conservative alliance was inclined to support his obvious ambitions. His best audiences in those years were in the South —which amazed a good many observers; he was, after all, a Catholic, and the Bible Belt should not have been so cordial. But the South was still hoping to find Northern men with Southern views. In all this it may be that Kennedy felt he had something to give the country, something none of his competitors had; and that, like Roosevelt, he could give it only if he became President; but if this was so, no one knew it.

In quite another strain his marriage in 1953 should be spoken of. Jacqueline Bouvier was an elegant girl, Catholic too, finished in the best schools. It is certain that she was comforting and ornamental, but not in any sense a partner as the born Kennedys were. She joined in their activities halfheartedly at first, but they both bored and tired her with their endless athletic competitiveness. Their habit of rallying around whenever one of them ran for office was one she was glad to be excused from when they found out how useless she was. She turned out to be a valuable asset as a President's wife, but as a candidate he could not rely on her as he was used to doing with Fitzgeralds and Kennedys. Not much else in his personal life can be sharply separated from the long chase of the pre-Presidential years; but Jacqueline would not bend to political requirements.

It is clear, looking back, that the strategy of the early campaigns was projected into the culminating one. It was to be an individual race, not a party one. This was an immensely bold defiance of tradition. To cut himself loose from, even to defy, the party powers was to undertake the seemingly impossible. It could only have occurred to a Kennedy as practical at all; and only a Kennedy could have put the resources and drive into it that made success even faintly likely.

The wealth made it possible to hire able assistants, pay enormous bills for travel (private plane), and generally to support the drive. But once the re-election campaign for the Senatorship was behind him and he had demonstrated that all of Massachusetts was a safe constituency, he could concentrate even more single-mindedly on the Presidency. It was at this time that he acquired the services of Theodore Sorensen and—as he acknowledged—found him almost a second mind. For Sorensen was a prize among assistants. He could write better than Kennedy; but all ghost writers are better writers than their principals; what was more important, he had also a luminous intelligence. He must have had some qualms from time to time, because he belonged to the Minnesota strain of dissent.

These Scandinavian radicals tend to regard capitalism with skeptical disfavor. Kennedy was no collectivist, and Sorensen must have relied on his calculating intelligence to find a way into the future. Whatever his reasons for joining Kennedy, his continued attachment was a better recommendation to liberals than anything they heard about Kennedy himself.

The other assistants, O'Donnell, O'Brien, and the rest, were carefully enough chosen for particular capabilities. There were, in the inner managing group—not counting Kennedys and their connections—about a dozen. Among them, they worked out an expansible scheme that no expert in administration would believe could be effective, even in politics; but it held up when the tests came.

These were severe. The resolution to by-pass and then to coerce the professional party bosses was incredibly bold and risky. It required that the primary system should be relied on; and the primaries were devices invented by reformers to take the nominating power away from the bosses. They had been adopted in the more progressive states (such as Wisconsin and Oregon) and even in a few others (such as New Hampshire and West Virginia). In a few states they committed the state delegations to a candidate; in most they merely expressed a voter preference to be honored or not as convention-chosen delegates decided. Professionals hated them and advised that they be ignored. Truman, for instance, fumed whenever they were mentioned, and his protégé, Symington, followed his advice in keeping out of them. But this dislike was the sign to Kennedy that they offered a way to beat the insiders. And Truman's man was one of the easiest casualties.

As Kennedy put it to his helpers, if they could win every one of the primaries they entered, it would be more than just evidence that he was wanted; it would make it impossible for the bosses to reject him. They would be forced to take whatever compromise he was willing to offer. He meant to control the convention before it opened; and if he did, the bosses would surrender.

As the year of election approached it promised to have some peculiarities. All the contenders of note were Senators. This in itself was unusual; but it meant that his competitors were likely to follow the rules. They were not outsiders, strange to politics—no Eisenhowers were involved. They would rely on their party service, would avoid primaries, and would round up delegates in the traditional way—by trades among themselves and by deals with state and city leaders, who would be free to support the candidates who offered them the most. This was the way conventions were ordinarily managed.

The exception to this was Adlai Stevenson, who had twice been sacrificed to Eisenhower and was rumored to feel that he deserved a better chance. It might be thought that he could beat Nixon, who would clearly be the Republican choice. But Kennedy sized up Stevenson quite accurately as a gentleman and so not likely to be assertive. He would accept a draft, but he would make no public demand. If he had, it might have succeeded because he had an intensely loyal following; but he behaved as expected. He held himself available, but he had only a volunteer organization and gave no direct encouragement. His followers were hopelessly outclassed in the fierce struggle that developed during the spring and summer of 1960.

Kennedy's strategy of winning primaries—all of them—had results the professionals had not believed could happen. They had tacitly agreed among themselves, following Truman, that only amateurs— like Kefauver in 1956—would go the primary route; and one who did could be taken care of when convention time came. It was not so. For instance, Lyndon Johnson's party position and his reputation as the cleverest of all political manipulators could not stand against Kennedy's demonstration of power in one state after another. The caving in of the state bosses soon made Johnson's claim as empty a one as Symington's.

It was another maverick, who did not believe in the Truman rule, who was Kennedy's really formidable opponent. Those who disliked Hubert Humphrey said he was an empty demagogue, but he was of the same Northwestern lineage as Sorensen. He had intended, for as long a time as Kennedy, to become President; but he had been forced to proceed in a different way. Because he was marked as radical and because he was poor, he could neither count on conservative support nor carry on a massive campaign of direct persuasion. The South was against him; so, generally, were any moneyed interests there might be in the Democratic party. He had been more amenable to Senate discipline, however, and did not have the opposition from other politicians that Kennedy had, perhaps because they did not regard him as formidable. He had been able to call attention to himself in two conventions; and a long Kremlin interview with Khrushchev in the spring of 1960 got him several days of identifying publicity.

Humphrey intended, as Kennedy did, to force the power-dispensers to accept him because of popular demand; and he had a record that had lost him large segments of support. To have any chance at all, he would need what Kennedy had and he did not—freshets of funds to pay for the impression he must make on millions of minds in the primary contests. He was a much more appealing orator; he had a wide following in his own region—where he had risen, as few politicians have, from Mayor to Senator, fighting all the way; and he thought he might win in spite of the odds against him.

Since it was Humphrey that Kennedy had to beat, the method was indicated. Money must be made to count. It was done by saturation appeal, first in Wisconsin, where Humphrey believed himself strong, but then, decisively, in West Virginia. Both these primaries should have gone to Humphrey on form. But money was lacking, and this meant publicity and organization; and Kennedy won.

Of course all the Kennedy cash would not have bought these two victories if it had been awkwardly used. Actually, although much was wasted, none was used so blatantly as to cause any important reaction except the few anguished cries that came from Humphrey as his chances diminished from day to day in the last weeks.

It was a performance of amazing efficiency, considering the circumstances. At the crisis, there were Kennedy headquarters in several cities, and there were representatives in every locality. Doors were being knocked on, voters were being individually exhorted, and radio and television channels were being flooded with propaganda. The candidate himself and, in this instance, Franklin D. Roosevelt, Jr., made dramatic and well-prepared appearances. It took thousands of workers in West Virginia alone, deployed lavishly wherever they seemed to be most needed, to do the job.

It very possibly might not have succeeded if Kennedy had not, for once, showed genuine concern on a public issue. He was shocked by the conditions he belatedly discovered in West Virginia, and his promise to repair some of the damage left from the chronic sickness of the coal industry had the sound of sincerity. Also, he met the most difficult issue of all with a disarming declaration that relieved the minds of many who would like to vote for him but could not bring themselves to accept a Catholic. What he said was that he believed in the separation of church and state and that his religion was spiritual, not secular. His speech was direct and convincing, and it freed many Protestants from bigotry.

The astonishing thing about the West Virginia primary as an organizational accomplishment was that it came only a few weeks after the Wisconsin victory, that Nebraska voted on the same day, and that Maryland would follow later in the same week. In these and all the other primary states there had to have been, years previously, surveys and planning and the framework of organization. In all of them, as the contest approached, new offices had been opened and new personnel installed with amazing rapidity. And as the day of voting approached, there had to be thousands of workers arguing, persuading, swarming in every gathering place. By then, too, the Kennedys and their intimates must have arrived to spread their peculiar charm over the state.

Robert, the younger brother, was the chief organizer during the final year. Ted, still younger, worked too; so did the sisters and brothers-in-law. The mother began to give the familiar teas and receptions; and old Joseph P., who had been co-opting everyone he could reach for months, now organized a furious activity of his own. He remained anonymous, but the rumor of his presence was often reported.

After West Virginia, Humphrey withdrew and, reading the signs, became an ally. Stevenson was unresponsive to his followers' urging that he declare himself available. He found Kennedy and his methods distasteful. It was a kind of competition he would not enter. This was not the reaction of Lyndon Johnson or Stuart Symington. They did not have Stevensonian hesitations and did not pretend that they must be invited. They were frankly candidates. But they were contending with a swelling force they had not allowed for and still did not gauge at its true volume. They continued to expect that the professionals would control the convention.

Kennedy and his father were now applying the pressure, accumulated in the primaries, to these local and state bosses. It had been demonstrated that an electoral campaign of formidable power could be anticipated—on the model of the primaries. It could win. And, they asked the bosses, did they want to win with Kennedy and share in the rich fare to be available after the Republican years? Or did they prefer to go along with the old professionals and see the usual skimpy Democratic campaign come up against the lavish job that would be done for Nixon?

It was a bread-and-butter argument to supplement the pressure. By convention time it had prevailed. Symington had no chance, which so annoyed Truman that he sulked at home (imagine Truman not attending a Democratic convention!). And Lyndon Johnson, after spasms of agonized humiliation, had to settle for second place.

To say that it had been an impressive demonstration is a weak recognition of the Kennedy technique. And it carried over into the campaign. All that the bosses had been promised was delivered. Nixon was not easy to beat, largely because the problem now was to corral the Democratic votes. And it had got around that, in capturing the nomination, all had not been done for the good of the party, to say nothing of the country—that it was a Kennedy hunt and that the Kennedys alone would profit.

The election was won because those Democrats who resented the Kennedy methods, distrusted his promises, and saw him more and more clearly as having gone for the Presidency and won it regardless of his probable competence still could not bring themselves to vote for Nixon. It was indeed a narrow decision, and Kennedy could not feel that he had won because of confidence among the voters that he would make a creditable President. Very few Presidents had taken office in quite such an atmosphere of suspended judgment.

Many voters, looking back at the experience of 1960, wondered whether a better way of selection could not be found. What could be said of institutions vulnerable to such an attack as had been mounted purely to seat a Kennedy in the White House? Was that good enough?

True, there was nothing novel about such an aspiration. The ambitions of other politicians had been as single-minded. But this was a naked, savage conquest, dependent on the use of vast wealth. There was no denying, however, that the effort had been well adapted to the circumstances. It had succeeded.

Lyndon Baines Johnson
1908–

Born in Stonewall, Texas; parents soon moved to Johnson City
Became thirty-fifth President in 1963 at 55

HISTORY

1927	After education in public school, entered Southwest Texas State Teachers College.
1929	Left college for a year to teach school in Cotulla.
1930	Graduated from college and began teaching speech in Sam Houston High School.
1932	Appointed secretary to Congressman Richard Kleberg after working as a solicitor in his campaign.
1934	Married Claudia Taylor of Texas, who soon came into a small inheritance that gradually became a fortune.
1935	Appointed Director, National Youth Administration, for Texas.
1937	Elected to the United States House of Representatives (Tenth District of Texas) and re-elected five times.
1941	Defeated in special election for the United States Senate.

474

1941	As United States Naval Reserve officer, requested active duty; served until members of the Congress were made ineligible for active service; left the service as Commander in 1942.
1948	Elected to the United States Senate after an extremely close primary contest, disputed by his opponent, but validated by the courts.
1949	Elected (by acclamation) deputy to the Minority Leader.
1951	Elected Whip.
1953	Elected Minority Leader of the Senate, 83rd Congress.
1955	Elected Majority Leader, 84th Congress.
1960	Contended for the Presidential nomination but was defeated by J. F. Kennedy; then was nominated for the Vice-Presidency.
1963	Succeeded to the Presidency at Kennedy's death.
1964	Re-elected (Vice-President, Humphrey); opponent, Goldwater with Miller.

I T WAS while most of the world's people halted their business in shock after President Kennedy was assassinated that the Vice-President chosen at Los Angeles in 1960 was inducted.

Citizens of the United States were brought up shorter than others. They had just begun to appreciate the man they had so narrowly chosen over his competitor, Nixon, and since had watched so critically. But even the most withholding watchers now recognized that he would be grievously missed. His cleavage to excellence, his clear and active mind, his mastery of fact seemed suddenly, when it was too late, the virtues and qualities most needed in a national leader. As he was borne back to Washington and buried in heroes' ground, it seemed fantastic to suggest that anyone could take his place.

But Lyndon Johnson had to try; it was his duty. The deed was final, and the responsibility now was his. As days and weeks passed and men (and nations) went on into the future their young President would no longer share, they hesitantly accepted the fact of his replacement. There was some resentment at the change in style. They had discovered, however belatedly, an immense pride in the Kennedy performance. But clinging to the past was impossible; the future was crowding in; and the choice of a man for meeting it had already been made.

If Johnson had been quite incompetent for the duties he now assumed, it would have served the American people right. This was the eighth (of thirty-five) Presidents to die in office and the fourth to be assassinated. Vice-Presidents had thus succeeded in nearly one-quarter of the administrations, and none had been selected because he was judged to be the next best national leader if the one chosen to be first should be removed. Johnson, like all the rest, had been nominated for another reason.

He had been picked because the ticket "needed to be balanced." This was an ambiguous political locution meaning that his selection improved the prospect of victory. Kennedy, facing his campaign, rightly judged that his own strength lay in the North and East. Johnson, from Texas, was to hold the South where there were signs of weakness.

A structural defect encouraged party conventions to take this risk with the nation's security. Successors so chosen were not always poor Presidents, but many of them were. Judged by historical evidence, the risk was considerable. Tyler, Fillmore, Andrew Johnson, and Arthur were unfortunate. Perhaps Truman and Coolidge were more satisfactory; and Theodore Roosevelt was an improvement over McKinley. But by any test there was something like a 50 per cent chance that choices made by the going system would turn out badly, and only one in eight could be said to be a superior selection.

Conscious of this probability, but not conscious enough to have insisted on reform, Americans watched Johnson take office with a trepidation they certainly deserved. There could hardly have been a worse time for leaving national direction to chance. The United States was confronted by implacable enemies, kept from active attack only by convincing evidence that their own losses in such a conflict would be unacceptable. Kennedy had been determined, patient, and effective. It could be hoped that Johnson would show equal firmness and wisdom. But nothing of the sort was guaranteed by his having been Vice-President.

Only a few close students knew that he had always intended to achieve the Presidency, that he had been as dedicated to that ambition as any of the others we have looked at, and that his qualifications were at least the equal of recent Presidents.

Not many recalled now, as they waited for a sign, that he had prepared himself as few emergency successors ever had. And fewer recalled that in his life, as in that, for instance, of the Roosevelts, there had been a time of black discouragement, and that coming through it had not weakened but strengthened his character. Some years after a severe coronary attack, when he had demonstrated that he could go on unaffected, he was described during an interlude in spring. He was lying in a hammock under the trees on his LBJ Ranch; alongside was a portable telephone switchboard connecting him with his many aides in Washington:

> As his butler served cooling drinks, Johnson was briefed on the state of his business operations by his wife Lady Bird; on world news by his Secretary . . . and on the gossip of Stonewall by his cousin Oriole . . . In the distance ranch hands tended his herds of purebred cattle and sheep.
>
> Johnson suddenly said to me, "Would anybody give up all this to run for President of the United States?" Then, without waiting for my answer, he said sadly, "Yes, I guess he would."[1]

But in the crisis of succession, what most Americans recalled about Johnson was his secondary part in the 1960 campaign, and even this was meager. He had made a quite fruitless play for first place. But it had had to be largely from the base he had built in his own state. And that was Texas. He had asked to be thought of as more Western than Southern, but he had not been convincing. Very little support had

---

[1] Cf. articles by B. Davidson, *Look*, August 4, 1959, 38; August 18, 1959, 63.

developed in other regions, and as the convention approached his only chance of being chosen came down to an improbable deadlock that might prevent Kennedy's nomination.

His customary cool judgment deserted him in the false euphoria of competition. He said and did things, even when all was obviously lost, that would have caused a less calculating opponent than Kennedy to erase him from any list of future associates. But that young man was made of ice and iron, and when Johnson spoke insultingly of his relative inexperience and untried ability, Kennedy returned a soft answer. Even an accusation of neglected Senate duties caused no visible wincing.

When Kennedy went on, after taking the nomination on the first ballot, to designate Johnson as his preference for a running mate, it was only one more in a bizarre series of events. When Johnson, after having charged Kennedy with so many political immoralities, immediately consented to run as his second—a situation that would require loyal subordination—even experienced politicians seemed surprised.

True, none of those mentioned for the candidacy, and certainly not Kennedy, had had anything like his record of political success. No Senate leader had ever shown quite the same talent for getting legislative work done in spite of difficulties. His achievements had been cumulating for years, and his reputation had grown correspondingly. Reporters knew a phenomenon when they saw one; and Johnson was extraordinary.

But his legislative work had been that of a specialist, an arranger, whose identifying phrase was "Let us reason together."

He argued that the laws he maneuvered to passage might not be perfect but that they were at least something. And often they were more. Certainly the civil rights legislation of 1957 was remarkable. For nearly a hundred years the constitutional amendments conferring these rights had been in existence without having been implemented. The gain for the Negro race was not tremendous—the compromises were too serious—but to have got any law at all was amazing.

Those progressives who had long since conceded Johnson to the conservatives had second thoughts after this achievement. It might very well be that the young man who had come to the Congress as an ardent follower of Roosevelt had not really changed but had only become more wily and persistent. Perhaps he realized how empty victories can be when they are approved by no more than a small majority—if that. His exhausting persuasion might make gains more permanent than winning by violence.

It was an indication of this appreciation that, when he tried for the Presidential nomination, there had been at least as many liberal supporters on his side as on Kennedy's; and when, after the assassination, he moved into the White House, they were of the opinion that his ability to prevail with the Congress might enable him to succeed where his immediate predecessors had most notoriously failed.

It had to be admitted that Kennedy, for all his precise planning and his lavish Executive lobby, had done no better with legislative programs than Eisenhower, Truman, or Roosevelt (in his later terms). The country was not notably moving again. The tax and other fiscal proposals, the enlargement of Social Security to include medical care for the aged, and most of his measures to relieve poverty and reduce persistent unemployment—all had either been refused or emasculated. Unemployment was, in fact, still rising, and the growth rate of productivity was little if any higher than it had been in the Republican years he had found so deplorable.

Kennedy's hopes had been those of a humane and far-seeing leader. What he asked was demonstrably in the national interest—meant to strengthen the economy, right old racial wrongs, care for the helpless, and make the United States a responsible co-operator with other nations. The proposals were expounded with eloquence and reason. The arguments against them, when any were made, were feeble or mean; but mostly the legislators who opposed them did not commit themselves to replies. They simply looked the other way.

It may have been that Kennedy would have had some successes if he had had more time. But it was unlikely. It was his way to avoid any show of exasperation. He accepted delays and even defeats without protest and took the little he was given with gratitude. But a quiet crisis was developing, and if it continued much further into the future its consequences would be registered in slackened productivity and lowered levels of living; a great people were allowing themselves to be strangled by an irresponsible cabal of reactionary politicians.

Undertaking to reform the system was perhaps beyond reasonable risk for a President whose electoral majority had been as narrow as Kennedy's. If he had gone on to a more secure mandate he might have dared to suggest structural change. But whether he had even identified the mission some President must undertake very soon, there is no way of knowing. He had given no hint. He was, apparently, a loyal alumnus of the Congress.

Johnson had not been involved in Kennedy's failure in this area of his duties, but he had been involved in Eisenhower's. He had made the exhausting effort to get a little when much was essential and had kept at it session after session, apparently content. Not only had he not suggested any change, he had an obvious pride in his unique ability to overcome obstacles. He had a stake in their continuance. How serious the crisis had really become was not known until another Majority Leader had taken over. Johnson, now Vice-President, was not called on for expedition. On the contrary, when he tried, the Senate he had recently found so malleable let him know that interference from him would not be tolerated. He perforce withdrew to his prescribed role of understudy.

Considering his fitness for the Presidency, however, it was recalled that as Vice-President he had traveled widely in a ceremonial way and had got to know the world and its statesmen as he had not known them before. More importantly, he had been admitted to the administration's inner counsels, and he had supervised the Latin-American and space programs. These duties, however, were not much publicized; so that when he became President, he had been in virtual obscurity for three years, and the next election was terrifyingly close. Theodore Roosevelt, Coolidge, and Truman—who had won elections on their own after similar tragedies—had had longer to prepare.

This was important. With an amplitude of time they could turn the nation from sorrow and recollection to a future with themselves as the center of interest. It was not supposed that Johnson could do more than carry out the Kennedy plans. At first he seemed resigned to this confinement. "Let us continue," he said, echoing his predecessor's "Let us begin."

When it was seemly, Johnson's restlessness for the attention necessary to establish his own centrality took charge. There might not be time to accomplish more than Kennedy had laid out—he would see about that; there might at least be changes in emphasis—but it would be done in the Johnson style.

The Texas intonations, muted in the Senate and hardly listened to from the Vice-President, would now be attended to with the concentration Americans always yield their Presidents. Besides, they were anxious for reassurance and ready to confer their loyalty if it should seem deserved. The Congress, of course, was something else—its elders crouched as was customary and waited for the first sign that yet another President needed to be taught the lessons so often administered to presumptuous Executives.

Johnson's conduct during the rites for his fallen predecessor won preliminary approval; all was done with devotional correctness; but almost at once the Texas glitter began to show through the veils of mourning. The Congress had to feel the new power first. The measures stuck there must be torn loose, preceding any show of originality. With the old program behind him he could best offer fresh proposals for a campaign. The Kennedy phase must be closed out.

What the new President heard from his former colleagues was expectable. In the common experience of grief, they said, there ought to be an interval for healing; quarrels ought to be adjourned so that in the national crisis there could be a show of unity. What this came to was that they wanted to go home and leave their unfinished business until another day.

They got the response to this of one who knew that what they really wanted was a pause until they had sized up a new adversary. This he could not accept; he was in a hurry. They had had dilatory months. He let them know it was time to move. He obviously conveyed to them privately what if they did not know they should—that the revival of all the old jokes about Congressional ineffectiveness was fast becoming a national pastime.

He had plenty of support. A leader in the *New York Times* (of December 26, 1963) put the matter clearly:

> At the turn of the century that cynical American observer, Ambrose Bierce, defined Congress as "A body of men who meet to repeal laws." At this time cynical Washington observers could shorten the definition to: "A body of men who meet." The performance of the 88th Congress, which has done little, and taken an unconscionable long time to do even that, proves the point.
>
> There is a built-in malaise in our legislative branch . . . President Johnson has refocussed the nation's eyes directly on the Congress. The scandalous lag . . . is out in the open for all to see.

Beyond this growing disillusion, his fellow Democrats were re-minded of something a politician cannot afford to forget—an election year was opening, and the party had not only lost its leader but had no accomplishments worth mentioning to point to. As things were, how could he ask for supporting votes?

But the old hands, as always, seemed not to hear. They came from states or districts that would return them anyway. There was more risk as far as they were concerned in doing something than in doing nothing. They would not much mind having their majority responsibilities transferred to Republicans who were similarly reactionary, similarly sure of their seats, and therefore similarly immune to Presidential urgings. The interests they most wanted to protect would not be disturbed. What they—and their supporters—did not want, and what they would be vigilant to prevent, was a crusade for new legislation that would change old economic and social arrangements.

Knowledgeable observers watched sharply for revealing signs. Could the Majority Leader, now President, become as effective in his new role as he had been in his old? And if he could, what would be the demands he would make? There was hurried inquiry into the talents, the ambitions, and the complex of ideas that had brought Johnson so far and must be relied on to earn him a term—or two terms—of his own in the White House.

His Texas origin was, of course, noted; but now it did seem Western as well as Southern. Even more significant were the facts that until he was grown he had never seen a city, that he had gone to public schools, and that he had earned his own way when his father had failed him. These might not be the political attractions they once had been, but the ability to succeed in spite of obstacles was still admired. It also offered the same reassurance it always had to others whose circumstances were no better than his had been.

It was noted too that the Johnsons, if poor, were of substantial stock. It was true that Lyndon's father had been permanently impoverished by a spell of hard times; but he had once been prosperous and for twelve years had been a member of the Texas legislature. When he had given up in Stonewall and had moved to a larger town, it had been to Johnson City, named for a pioneer grandfather.

To the west of Austin, Texas is a rolling country, sparsely populated, and so poorly watered that drought seems normal. Its cattle ranges are wide and open; and the Pedernales is one of those mile-wide, inch-deep rivers often found in the short-grass country. If anyone wondered later why Johnson the Congressman was so enthusiastic about conservation, rural electrification, and other projects of use to farm folk, he had only to visit the country Johnson was raised in and where he established his home ranch—the LBJ—when he had the funds.

When young Lyndon had graduated from high school, after having pretty much supported himself by doing snatches of work, and seeing no prospect of bettering himself in Johnson City, he set out for California. But the promise of that golden bourne proved false. He found nothing to do but casual labor he was too young and too stringy to sustain. He came back home, thoroughly whipped and with his future bleaker than ever.

There was not much his parents could do to raise his spirits, but they did urge him to make another effort in a different way. It was arranged that he might borrow enough from the local Masonic Lodge to pay his tuition at Southwest Teachers College in San Marcos. And in 1927 he became a freshman.

It was not much better at Southwest; he still had to find after-class work, and his earnings did not run to room rent. But he discovered a garage on the President's property with an unused attic where he could fix himself a bed. Presently he was given a job in the college office. Things went on for two years in this way. By that time he was qualified, and he had not yet repaid his loan. So he went to teach Mexican children in the small town of Cotulla. This enabled him to pay his debt and accumulate enough to finish at Southwest.

At Cotulla he was moved by the special troubles of the Mexican-

Americans. They seemed always to get the worst of everything. They were the last to be employed and at the lowest wages. They found it hard to borrow and so to own land and homes. And their children came to school in deplorable condition. He almost adopted some of them, and he used more than he could afford of his salary to help them.

Stories of this sort get around. The Mexicans in Texas are a minority, but a sizable one. They would never have anything to repay Johnson with except their votes; but those he had whenever he asked. Years later a Lyndon Johnson Club was organized by his prideful students at Cotulla.

He had the same sort of outreaching feeling for Negroes, although expression of it had to be deferred until he had the disposal of Federal benefits as National Youth Administrator. But a Negro college president testified then that Johnson used to call him and say that there was a little money left over and could he use it.

How did this happen? One suggestion is that in Lyndon's part of Texas there were very few Negroes and that he never developed the prejudice that follows contact and competition. But when his record had grown longer, this seemed inadequate. It was much more reasonable to acknowledge that he was one of those people to whom men are differentiated by what they do, not what they are. Texans generally were violently repressive about both Negroes and Mexicans. It is no wonder they were standoffish about admitting that Johnson was really quite one of them. But if they felt some of the noisy demagogues Johnson ran against in his subsequent campaigns represented them more truly, he always had the Negro and Mexican votes to count on. The Tenth District was after all pretty far West. He had more trouble when the whole state was involved and some compromising was necessary. But the minority people never lost their faith in him.

When he went back to college, his special talents began to be noticed. He was always doing several things at once, and all of them were calculated to put him in charge of whatever was going on. He learned as he went along to conciliate potential enemies and to marshal supporters. He was still short of funds and had to devise ways to make a living, but he managed to become a notable member of the debating team.

It was quite natural that when he graduated he should resume his teaching—this time public speaking in a Houston high school. And it was when he was settled at this that he began his real political career by being assigned a district in a state campaign and working through it from door to door asking for votes. Somewhat later Richard Kleberg, running for a seat in the House of Representatives, assigned him a similar duty. Kleberg was a member of the King Ranch family and a powerful figure in his part of the state. He liked Johnson's work and offered him a job in his Washington office.

This was the world young Lyndon meant to conquer, and he went about it with that concentration to be observed in most first-rate politicians. He lived simply, ignored distractions, took his meals on the run, and before long got himself elected Speaker of the Little Congress, an organization made up of Congressmen's secretaries. His education was widening. He carried it further by resigning to become assistant doorkeeper in the House at a considerably lower salary. He meant to know how the House worked—knowledge he intended to use. But he was not meaning to be a mere political mechanic. To have a law degree would advance his limits, so he began to go to Georgetown Law School at night.

It was during this period that he began to cultivate Sam Rayburn. He asked the older man for advice and, when it was needed, for help. Rayburn had been in the Texas legislature at the same time as Lyndon's father and had sympathized with his financial troubles. He liked the son; and what he could do for him turned out to be a vast deal. There would be many occasions when Rayburn's backing and counsel would be important to one more impulsive and less experienced. His last service would be to organize the Johnson-for-President movement in Texas. His first was to see that he got a valuable appointment in the New Deal family. In 1935 the National Youth Administration was set up, and Johnson was made its Director for Texas. He tackled its organization with the same energy he customarily used; and when, two years later, James P. Buchanan, Congressman from Austin (Tenth District), died suddenly, Lyndon filed his intention to run in the following special election. He was one of ten candidates. He was only twenty-eight, but he had several new admirers who were willing to help. The most effective of these was the owner of the two Austin newspapers. This gave him the communication he needed with the voters, and his own shrewd appraisal of miseries and hopes in the continuing depression gave him his platform: complete and vociferous support for the Roosevelt program. There were politicians who thought this a mistake. It was during the months of the court-packing fight and many conservatives were turning against the New Deal. But he did not waver. Roosevelt, he said, was giving workers security and young people the hope of a career. There were some thirty thousand Texans who, through him, had actually been given a new chance in life by the Youth Administration. He won by a good margin.

President Roosevelt heard about this as he heard about most political events; and when, after a recreational fishing trip in the Gulf, he landed at Galveston to visit his son Elliott's ranch and go on by train to Washington, the newly elected Congressman was among the older greeters. And he was taken into the Presidential car for one of those rides that symbolize political blessing.

Looking at Lyndon, Roosevelt may well have been startled by the younger man's resemblance to himself—a quarter century earlier, say, when he had just become the Assistant Secretary of the Navy. Lyndon, like the Roosevelt of that time, was the tallest one in most crowds, and the thinnest. His sharp features, his mobile face, his eagerness to be noticed and to please—the President must have marked all these with some sympathy. When Roosevelt died in 1945 Lyndon said sadly, "He was the greatest man I ever knew." That translates easily to: "The man I would most like to resemble."

Being a New Dealer then was good politics for a superior technician —one who knew how to go past the defecting businessmen and bosses straight to the people.

It was good then, and in his own district; but when he ran for the Senate in 1941 Texas as a whole went against him as it was going against Roosevelt. But he continued in the House, generally following the New Deal line. However, when Roosevelt was gone and the war had ended, he had to recognize that things were changing. Farmers were better off; and anyway, the state was more industrial and less rural. The helpless, hopeless times were past. He had earned a good deal of credit by working for projects peculiarly favored by his people. He had had as much as any Congressman—except Rayburn—to do with public housing and with rural electrification as well as many water and land-improvement programs. But oil, now, was a big industry, and the cities were growing. The state's new-rich were becoming a legend. Johnson had at least to prevent their power from being used against him; and perhaps he could even get support from some.

When he ran for the Senate again in 1948 it was not as an all-out New Dealer but as one who could bring favors to the state and befriend its businessmen. He still held the vote of the Negroes and Mexicans, who would never forget his compassion; but his way to nomination and election was smoothed by the friendship—and the contributions—of some very rich supporters.

By this time he was a millionaire himself. And this needed explaining. How could a man who had all his life been in public office and had never been known as a businessman have accumulated a fortune? When looked into, it seemed much less a mystery than his enemies liked to believe. It came to him through his wife.

Claudia Taylor was a graduate student at the University of Texas, and he was still secretary to Congressman Kleberg, when they first met. She was a popular girl and at first failed to appreciate the attentions of the tall suitor; but, like most of those who were besieged by Lyndon, she gave in. They were married within a few

months. Presently she inherited some $67,000, and with it she began
a career all her own of speculation and good management that built
the small initial sum into a fortune.

What contributed most was the purchase of a radio and television
station in Austin. It was losing money when she bought it but within
a few years was grossing a half million a year. She and her husband
began dealings in land and city properties that seemed always to yield
rich profits. They had two daughters; she was a busy but loyal wife;
and together they made the career that Lyndon had set his heart on
pursuing.

It was thought curious—but it was nevertheless true—that his rich
supporters in Texas were not the oil people; they were other businessmen, and particularly contractors. The firm of Brown and Root (Root
later died) were intimates, and he was accused by his enemies of
favoring them with government work. There were many who found
it hard to believe that Brown's interest in Johnson was merely
friendly.

He went to the Senate in 1948. There were charges of fraud in the
primary that had to be settled in court. Texas politics was rough; and
investigation might have turned up some things on both sides that
had better be left undisclosed. Lyndon's margin was slim—less than a
hundred votes—and afterward, in the humorous way Americans call
heavyweights or seven-footers "Tiny," he was called "Landslide
Lyndon." But before long his position had been consolidated, and he
had no trouble in his bid for re-election. Texas had begun to be proud
of him; he was the most powerful figure in the Senate; and even
Eisenhower had to deal with him on equal terms.

As Leader of the Majority he had developed several identifying
characteristics. These, together with his fierce ambition, account well
enough for his success. He had a complete command of facts bearing
on proposed legislation; but also he knew its probable effect on the
fortunes or prejudices of his Senators—and many Representatives as
well. This enabled him to keep a magazine of favors in hand as well
as a comparable list of obligations. He could make deliverable promises and demand co-operation. Many a bill was passed or defeated
because he backed a Senator—or several Senators—into a corner and
invoked the exchange rules of politics. These work. They make life
livable in the Senate. They also produce negotiable favors for supporters who may have important influence.

To operate a system of this sort, a Leader cannot rely wholly on
his memory, however reliable and comprehensive. He must have
helpers, many of them, compiling facts, analyzing the interests he must
play on, and keeping up dossiers of all the individuals he may need
to use. Often an induced call from back home will change a vote or

keep one secure when it is most needed. This staff was costly.[2] And the premises it used were so various that no one seems ever to have known about all of them; they were collectively described as "the White House on Capitol Hill."[3] Johnson's command post was

> . . . a newly refurbished suite close by the Senate chamber . . . decorated in the modern manner . . . Here the Senator does most of his work, receives callers, makes dozens of telephone calls, ponders the strategy that he hopes will put the Democratic party on top next year.
>
> Six other Capitol rooms are occupied by the Democratic Policy Committee . . . Its staff is his staff. The latest in inter-office communication systems link all these rooms.
>
> In the Senate Office Building, Senator Johnson has a three-room suite and another staff which attends to the affairs of his Texas constituents. In both buildings other rooms, some of them "hideaways," accommodate additional Johnson forces. Several efforts have been made to add up the total of rooms and of staff men. The numbers change and grow. No definite conclusions have been reached.[4]

Johnson used this machinery to good effect. It enabled him, for instance, to assess the origin, the intention, and the effect of amendments that might be worse than defeat and that are offered, often, without notice. They must be met as they arise, and delay in marshaling a majority to meet them may be fatal. The payment for such support must be economical. The hoard of favors must not be depleted except for valuable return. It will be called on again and perhaps in more urgent circumstances.

Johnson gradually learned that he could often get along without using it at all. To do this, it was necessary to argue, persuade, insist on party obligation, and, most of all, appeal to compassion or decency. The ability to know when a colleague could be influenced in any of these ways was one of the resources he used repeatedly. And it was not in the least affected by his colleagues' knowing exactly what he was up to. In fact, he often made it quite plain that what he was asking ought to be given simply because it was right. The most cantankerous, vain, and prejudiced individuals, reached with precise timing, lent themselves to Johnson's purpose—that of making the legislative machinery work. Those who would delay or stop it to satisfy a whim, punish the President, or insist on recognition ran against the intense Senatorial desire to maintain the peculiar prestige

---

[2] Douglass Cater, *The Reporter*, July 7, 1960.
[3] *The U.S. News & World Report*, February 12, 1959.
[4] *Ibid.*

of their institution; every Senator wants, almost more than a good
name at home among the voters, the regard and respect of his fellows.
Johnson made himself the conscience of recalcitrant members. He
had ways of conveying the idea that he represented a kind of collective rule and that it was violated at the risk of degrading the august
body they must protect.

To see Johnson at this work was the delight of all the professional
reporters who knew the Senate from long service in its halls and
galleries. Their comments dwelt repeatedly on the skill and devotion
they were seeing exhibited. One of them classified his techniques:

> He uses the Face-To-Face Talk (in which he wears another Senator
> down with well-prepared arguments over a period of two or three
> hours); the Bear Hug (in which he will wrap one or both arms around
> a Senator in a public expression of personal comradeship); the Seven
> A.M. Phone Call (in which he will rout a Senator out of bed to express
> undying fealty and appreciation for a job well done); the New-Boy-
> In-School Approach (in which he will go out of his way to befriend
> a lonely, bewildered Senator and personally show him the ropes); and
> the Horse Trade (in which he will say, "You do me a favor and vote
> for this bill, John, and I'll see to it that we schedule the bill for that
> new dam in your state.")[5]

Observers all wondered how he found the energy to pursue day by
day, month by month, for years, the wearing method he had developed. He was early at one or another of his offices; he stayed until
the last useful job was done. He made telephone calls by the hundred
and had dozens of conferences every day, including days of rest.
To master the intricacies of a bill or the statement of a policy, he
sometimes had to seclude himself; but he relied on his staff of researchers, analyzers, memorandum composers, and ghost writers to
minimize these tasks. He was seldom caught without needed information.

This concentration excluded any possibility of general reading, of
developing new ideas by contemplation, or actually going beyond the
idea-pattern he had accepted as a young man. As time passed he
changed very little—in contrast with Kennedy, who paid more
attention to understanding the world and making great choices than
to any present business unless some crisis had to be faced.

There were, in Johnson's leadership period, some traits that caused
grave doubts on the part of observers when he began to be talked
about as a Presidential candidate. His legislative talent was so highly

---

[5] B. Davidson, *Look, op. cit.*

specialized and had so monopolized his mind that another and very different one could hardly be concealed in the same individual. That he could become the head of his party, the shaper of national policies, the guardian of national security, and manage a vast executive establishment seemed inconceivable.

There was another thing. His label could not be read. He was less a notable Democrat than a notable Senator. He was less a progressive or conservative than an expediter of policies he believed to be decent and necessary. What he thought of as decent was largely the agenda of the New Deal that had either never been carried into legislation or had since been attenuated or destroyed. He was always a supporter of extensions for security, for conservation, for mediation of Democracy's disputes, for social improvement and civil rights. But he never showed much interest in, or knowledge of, foreign relations; and equally, he sometimes seemed not to understand the nature of the government he helped to operate.

As for foreign relations, he made almost a fetish of refusing to allow interference with the President's prerogatives. But in Eisenhower's case this meant approving policies that were more those of Secretary Dulles than of the President, and that sometimes approached the dangerously fanatic. When Dulles was playing God and Eisenhower was playing golf, Johnson was usually doing his best to keep his Senators from making protests.

About the government, it was wholly inexplicable why he wanted to amend the Constitution so that the Senate and not the President should have first voice in foreign policy. He had always resisted this sort of encroachment, but he was an active sponsor of the Bricker Amendment.[6]

These and other deficiencies or inconsistencies were laid to his gradually narrowing interests and perhaps inattention to the larger issues of national policy. He read nothing but processed memoranda; the world of art, of literature, and of scholarship was foreign to him, and his circle of acquaintance was not calculated to broaden his outlook.

The way he worked, too, gave rise to doubts about his potential ability to direct and energize the Executive establishment. Keeping track of Senators' caprices and relationships, cajoling, arguing, and demanding in order to get passed an act he had been asked to expedite

---

[6] This proposal for a constitutional amendment was introduced in 1952 by Senator Bricker with 58 Senators as co-sponsors. It would, in effect, have asserted the supremacy of legislation over the provisions of any international treaty, including the United Nations Charter. In 1953 the number of sponsors had risen to 63. There was argument about language, and a version was agreed on; but the decisive vote on submission to the states lacked one of being two-thirds.

were things a President needed to have done for him. They were not things he could afford to do himself if he was to fulfill his whole duty.

For these and similar reasons, there were doubts about his developing ambition to be the Democratic nominee in 1960. This became talked about during the late fifties in a serious way; and Kennedy watched him as the most formidable of his rivals. This was because of his immense prestige as Leader. But Kennedy judged that he would still be thought a Southerner, and so would have worse handicaps than his own to overcome. He was no more a favorite of the elders, either, than Kennedy himself, who had a personal organization that reversed the usual rule and whipped party leaders into line. They hated the humiliation, but they were realists. Being such, they knew they would be no better off with Johnson; and he failed to pressure them with primary victories. True, he was a favorite son and could probably claim the whole South; but he had been too exclusively a Senator to be trusted by state and local leaders.

Until almost the last minute, also, he seemed to be so much aware of his handicaps that he might well not try for the Presidential nomination. He said so repeatedly. But candidates usually did that; and it was something besides his disclaimers that made many watchers take it seriously. He had several special handicaps—his being a Southerner, his ambivalent record, his lack of demonstrated competence for such an exalted position, and especially his history of coronary weakness.

What there was to say about this last had long ago been said, because his heart attack had been in 1955. It had been a serious one and his recovery had been slow, but there had been no recurrence. It had begun to be thought that a coronary recovered from and duly respected guaranteed a healthy future. It might not be so vigorous a one, and certainly not so careless; but learning how to live with a heart that had given warning seemed to be a way to live, too, with all the other organs, including the brain. It was very probable that Johnson was a better risk and a better man for having had his attack. But would it be believed? Several responsible accounts of his recovery and of his probable escape from any further involvement had been published. But there was lingering doubt that he was as sound as he seemed.[7]

But by 1960 all his own doubts and hesitations were resolved. He determined to go against the advice of those friends who thought he ought not to sacrifice his tremendous prestige as Leader for the pos-

---

[7] For a careful account, *Newsweek*, November 7, 1955; and "A Heart Attack Saved His Life," by J. H. Pollack, *Today's Health*, October 1958.

sibility that he either might not be nominated, and might not win, or that he would be the mediocre President they were inclined to anticipate.

He had cast up his chances and somehow had found them possible —they cannot have looked good. Perhaps his worst handicap, when the inner circle asked whether he could be elected, was that his successes in the Senate, communicated to the public, seemed no more than deals and trades, small and slightly questionable givings and takings. He was not a man who stood for something, who had a public reputation, only one who got things done and who was respected, outside of Texas, mostly in Washington.

This was unjust. His long and exhausting effort to bring the issue of civil rights to actual discussion between antagonists who had heretofore not even discussed it was a contribution to the public good and certainly came from deep conviction. But even the minority leaders who knew about it valued more highly the louder claims of Humphrey and Kennedy, who had accomplished exactly nothing.

Then, too, Johnson's being a New Dealer may have seemed old-fashioned now. The Kennedys thought so. Their promise was that they would increase productivity—"get the country moving again." The aging adherents of the New Deal—Acheson, the Brandeis disciples, Justice Douglas, and others—who regarded old wrongs as only half righted, felt that Johnson might complete the agenda; new beginnings could wait until poverty and insecurity had been finally conquered, until big business was brought under control and civil rights had been firmly established.

They went to work in late 1959 and early 1960. But they had no power bases and no way to reach a wide public. And Johnson had no Northern or Western allies who would do for him what Rayburn was doing in Texas. The old Speaker, together with Governor Connally, long a satellite of Johnson, had set up a well-financed local movement that spread throughout the South and into the West. It proceeded by making appearances at every Democratic conclave with spectacular appurtenances peculiar to Texas—whooping orators, cowboy costumes, hillbilly music, and all the rest. But it was doubtful whether they persuaded many delegates who were not already committed.

Johnson himself seemed not to appraise his situation realistically until James Rowe, a Roosevelt operator, now a Washington lawyer, abandoned work he had been doing for Humphrey and undertook Johnson's management. Rowe's analysis must have disclosed just one possibility. There might be a deadlock. The determined Stevenson following might balk at Kennedy; Symington might hold Missouri and a few other states; Humphrey's following would go to anyone rather than Kennedy; and several favorite sons—such as Governor Brown of California—might hold for several ballots. This might be long enough to start a move to some other candidate, and this might be Johnson. All or any of this grew less and less likely; but Johnson and Rowe evidently counted on the accumulation of credits among legislators. These might be cashed in now.

But this hope rested on a typical myopia. Senators tend to think a reputation with other Senators extends beyond the Capitol. Being a realist, Johnson should have known, and probably did come to see, that the structure of national conventions is something peculiar to itself. No one can be a leader there. All he can do is hold out to one after another of the figures who control delegates the rewards that may come to the adherents of the final nominee. And the cold appraisals are not in the least affected by past favors or any except definite promises. Only one general expectation is effective: that with one or another hopeful the chance of winning will be best. This final appraisal had kept many a much-respected leader from being nominated. The Republicans had known they would lose with Taft or with Knowland as they had once lost with Taft's father and, further back, with Blaine. They were forced to think of popular appeal.

The same rule governed the Democratic operations. They had lost a number of times by not observing it—by picking Bryan and Smith, whose appeal was sectional or in some other way special rather than universal. Roosevelt had been the other sort, approved in the West and South, if not so much in the North; but there was no way to make Johnson agreeable to Minnesota or Michigan. His supporters could argue that their man would make a competent President, and they also contended that almost any Democrat could defeat Nixon (their underrating of Eisenhower's heir was a general Democratic weakness). But this line of reasoning was not convincing to a majority. Nixon might be weak, but still there ought to be a candidate with a wide appeal.

Kennedy's popularity had been established in repeated primary successes. Johnson and Symington, sharing Truman's prejudice, had preferred to neglect these contests, only to be faced in the end with an accumulation of Kennedy delegates they could not match. Johnson's only hope, finally, was that Symington's supporters, under Truman's urging, would prevent a Kennedy majority on the first ballot, and that then he might begin to gather in the uncommitted.

But it did not happen. Johnson's last-minute attempt to persuade delegates by argument was no credit to his good sense. But the account of his nomination for the Vice-Presidency represented a return to reason. It was also an example of Kennedy's calculation. Curiously enough, what was the right thing for both hardly anyone expected to happen.

Kennedy could not choose a running mate who would leave any considerable group of Democrats sullen and unco-operative. Johnson could bring him the South; and the big-city bosses joined up when David Lawrence of Pennsylvania, the most respected among them, acknowledged Johnson's potentiality. But there were Stevensonians, and mixed with them the labor bosses. Most of these viewed Johnson with suspicion. They regarded him as a dependent of the Texas millionaire fraternity. He had voted the wrong way a few times, and they knew that his most active friend and financial angel was the toughest and most effective anti-union employer in the United States. One of the most publicized episodes in Johnson's life had occurred at George Brown's Middleburg estate—his heart attack. This had underlined the closeness of the association. Brown was not far away in Texas; he was in a suburb of Washington, and Johnson was a regular visitor.

But the labor leaders, although Walter Reuther dissented violently, had to give in. They had against them the city and state bosses, who were not too happy anyway about the intrusions of unionists. On this occasion they were outspoken in their skepticism about the delivery of the labor vote. Much of it had gone to Eisenhower in the last two races. And, of course, Southerners were furious that labor should oppose their champion. There was actually nothing to do but consent, recalling that Vice-Presidents are much less dangerous than Majority Leaders anyway.

Why did Kennedy turn to Johnson? His close associates expected him to favor either Senator Henry Jackson of Washington or Symington of Missouri.

But there was evidence afterward, not of documented sort, but the only sort available in political exchanges, that Kennedy sometime earlier had hinted to Johnsonite Philip Graham (publisher of the *Washington Post*) that the Vice-Presidency ought logically to be Johnson's. What was said afterward was that Kennedy had always been willing to make the offer if there had been assurance of its acceptance. Since Kennedy certainly could not have won if he had not made the choice, this comports with the careful analysis he always made of his moves. He must have figured that whatever happened in Ohio, California, and such places (neither of which did give him their electoral votes), the Northeast and the South would be enough.

But why would Johnson agree? Everyone he depended on seems to have been against his acceptance—except perhaps his wife, eying the letdown of the more obscure job. But as many famous decisions have been, it was made, after all the hammering at him by friends, in the secrecy of his own counsel.

No one seems to have suggested, as they might, that another reason governed his choice. He would never become President now except by the chance of fate that had brought seven other men to the office. Neither Tyler, Fillmore, Andrew Johnson, Arthur, Theodore Roosevelt, Coolidge, nor Truman could have made it on their own. Succession was not a good way, but it was a way. This must have been an overwhelming consideration as he listened to the first roll call that nominated Kennedy.

And he did reach the office by that tragic chance.

Having become President, with less than a year to go until the next election, his position had become such that the nomination of 1964 would not thinkably be denied him; the question was whether he could offer the country, in the time he had, the picture they would want of a leader vigorous in their interest, safe to entrust the national interest with, and attractive in the glamorous way they like in a President. It was a challenge new to Johnson, a call to work quite different from any he had ever undertaken; yet he knew its rules and requirements. And by now he had traveled widely, had dealt with the world's statesmen, had joined in the counsels of those charged with guarding national security, and had watched Kennedy win over a skeptical public.

Much depended on his competitor, the Republican opponent he had to face. But there was none in sight with his advantages. He advanced into the year 1964 with high confidence, with a style of his own, and with an enormous good will. The people had lost a President they had much admired. He had seemed so capable of absorbing criticism, so determined on an excellence and high-mindedness they resented having to reach with him, that they had not, they suddenly saw, given him his due. He was regretted.

They turned reluctantly to watch the dazzling show Johnson soon began to present, responding with reluctance at first, but then gradually recalling that he was a Rooseveltian, that he was an experienced operator who might actually get them things that Kennedy had failed to get, and that anyway he was interesting, too, a fine figure of a President. They began to be proud of him. A good many of them, watching his performance as President, asked themselves how Kennedy could have defeated him for the nomination in 1960. The answer is that Johnson behaved professionally and that Kennedy disregarded the rules. Energy and money did the rest. Johnson had actually to show his competence before his defeat in people's minds could be overcome; and nothing but death could have accomplished that.

When the campaign was over and Johnson had registered his remarkable victory, it could be seen that it had really been won in those first few weeks after Kennedy's death, when anxiety had been so prevalent. Johnson's quick assumption of responsibility had been convincing. He had presented himself to the nation as a man of resolution and prudence. Steadiness was shown. Fears were relieved. And now, a year later, he was given a slightly larger proportion of all votes cast that even Roosevelt had been given in 1936.[8]

More important, the program that Kennedy had not been able to move through the Congress, Johnson could claim to have moved. For the moment, at least, his prestige with the legislators had held, and using the familiar methods of his Senate leadership he was able to overcome resistance to all his proposals but Medicare. The session ended with that measure still hung up in the House at the will of a Southern committee chairman. Unpassed, this measure could not be counted as a credit; but it was even more useful as an issue than as an accomplishment.

This issue alone was good for millions of votes. The Republicans were no more involved in this than the conservative Democrats; but Johnson's own position was quite clear. It was clear also on the other important issue that only Republicans were wrong about: they still held to the belligerent aggressiveness of John Foster Dulles toward the Communist nations. That it was fatally inappropriate to risk genocide in this way was by now widely seen. Truculence was out of date.

Social Security at home and collective security abroad—these were what Americans wanted. Goldwater, Johnson's opponent, proposed to allow them neither.

This myopia was exploited with enormous effectiveness. Johnson's grand strategy for the campaign was to center on himself such a consensus as few candidates had ever dared try for. He even praised the free enterprise system that businessmen were so anxious to have statesmen accept even while they were exploiting it; and if he did it with tongue in cheek, they did not seem to know it; many of them publicly accepted his offer of cooperation. He had no trouble in consolidating his position with organized labor, now become a middle-income group. He earned the support of the racial minorities so influential in certain of the largest states; and the Negroes were almost unanimously with him after the passage of the Civil Rights Bill.

In trying for consensus, he gave up the device so familiar in past

---

[8] Americans might recall with profit that the third largest percentage was given to Harding in 1920. Since Harding rates as the President with the lowest moral quotient as well as a competence level below any other, approval of his candidacy can at the least be taken to show that the electorate is capable of making unfortunate and even disastrous choices. True, Johnson's victory came after a year of performance in office; but that victory does not result from competence alone is quite clear, and Johnson's did not.

campaigns of singling out an enemy; he spoke of unity and good will. Peace and prosperity were his promises. They were irresistible.

Some time before the national conventions his position was so obviously consolidated that the usual contributors to Republican funds began to lose interest. One after another, big businessmen and financiers declared themselves satisfied with Johnson's performance. This had the peculiar result of allowing a reactionary minority in the Republican party to capture its machinery and nominate a candidate. For a generation this group had been maintaining that elections were being lost because the party offered no real alternative to the continuing expansion of the New Deal. Given the chance, they said, the electorate would support a candidate who promised to diminish government, abolish welfare measures and really set out aggressively to destroy Communism. They showed astonishing energy in organizing the hard core of reaction and bringing it to bear on the capturing of convention delegates.

Moderate Republicans, awakening late, saw the convention slip from their control. Nelson Rockefeller from the Governorship in New York tried earnestly to convince the elders that the course being followed would end in party disaster. He offered himself as a moderate, but he proved unacceptable in several primaries and failed to establish himself as a candidate. Governor Scranton of Pennsylvania made a last minute try of the same sort but found himself blocked; state delegations to nominate Senator Goldwater had already been chosen. The party's managers had been persuaded that the country was ready to accept the "real" Republican they had waited so long to nominate. The moderates got nowhere.

Johnson saw that he was right to go on shaping his potential consensus, say nothing that would alienate anyone, encourage Goldwater to expound his outlandishly unpopular views—and wait for the results to be registered. Trust in him grew as the alternative exposed itself in reckless willingness to use the nuclear arsenal, and in a determination to undo a generation of welfare measures.

What was to be lost by this method was obvious. Johnson, if he won, would have no mandate for going on from where he had already arrived. He had now about exhausted the New Deal agenda and would need a new program. What it was to be he did not say. This may well have been because he could not conceive what it might be—his was not a creative mind—but for the moment his coming to rest at the New Deal apogee was entirely satisfactory. He did speak vaguely of a Great Society that he intended to present for approval, and he did appoint a series of study groups to discover what a Great Society consisted of; but they would not report until after election; and as the campaign progressed he concentrated more and more on presenting himself as the perfect avuncular leader. So long as he was in charge, he told the voters, neither nuclear war nor economic depression need be feared.

There was substantial agreement on Johnson's nomination at the Democratic Convention—except among the Southern delegates who were mortally offended by the platform stand on Civil Rights. The vote actually was by acclamation. When this had been accomplished according to design, there was a momentary delay while he named his choice for the Vice-Presidential nomination. It turned out to be Senator Hubert Humphrey; and in making the announcement Johnson made a point that counted for something in the picture he was painting of responsibility and moderation. He had chosen Humphrey, he said, for no other reason than his belief that he would be a competent President if called on to assume the office. Sharp recollections of Kennedy's assassination underlined the importance of this departure from custom. Johnson himself had not been chosen for such a reason; that he now designated Humphrey made Americans consider their entirely un-earned good fortune that Kennedy's choice had, by accident, yielded a capable successor; and there were many expressions of appreciation for putting the national interest above political opportunism. For Humphrey might well lose more votes than he gained for the ticket— especially in the South—but that he had statesmanlike dimensions there was no widespread doubt. And Humphrey, being an experienced cam-paigner, easily assumed the role assigned to him. Johnson said of him afterward that "he made no mistakes." This was true; he did no more than support his principal and promise "loyalty"; but that was enough.

Circumstances during the campaign months were mostly favorable to the Johnson-Humphrey ticket. There were several new causes for uneasiness. The Chinese exploded their first nuclear device; after Khrushchev was ousted from his posts in the Soviet Union it was not at all clear what policy his successors would follow; and there were changes elsewhere with unpredictable consequences—such as the gov-ernmental overturn in Britain that brought Labor into power with unknown intentions after twelve years in opposition. Caution, compro-mise, and conservatism were paramount virtues for an American Presi-dent—and for a candidate. Goldwater's tendency to bluster and threaten was dangerous; Americans shuddered at the possibility of his controlling the Presidential power.

The year 1964 was one of the few times when foreign relations assumed first place in people's thoughts as an election approached. This was possible because the economy was experiencing a run of prosperity that had lasted longer than any previous one, and domestic policies did not need to be attacked or defended. Even reluctant conservatives had begun to admit that Social Security and anti-poverty programs were furnishing a solid floor for the economy and that other measures so long regarded with suspicion—monetary and fiscal management, including tax manipulation—might just possibly have created an entirely new situation, one of stability. Kennedy had said they would; but it had been Johnson who had persuaded the reluctant legislators to pass the crucial tax reduction measure which was a symbol of acceptance. The country was at last beginning to move, and with every passing month the belief that it would continue to move was growing. So, resting on this as a Democratic accomplishment, Johnson could offer himself as the reliable custodian of America's awful power. Goldwater, of course, was in this the perfect foil.

What counted against Johnson might have been serious in other circumstances for, naturally, his fortune was not wholly good. Some of his household embarrassed him. One was exposed as a dealer in favors, and some of the favors he had sold had been Johnson's. Another, late in the campaign, was caught in deviationist sexual practices and so could be denounced as a security risk because he was subject to blackmail. These weaknesses among Johnson's intimates seemed to the rather primitive extremists around Goldwater properly exploitable as campaign material; and they were used unmercifully. The efforts to show that morality had gone to pieces in the top echelon of the government were not successful; indeed they roused some sympathy for a harassed executive let down by his helpers. If Goldwater's managers had considered only a little of the relevant experience in the past—Cleveland's illegitimate child in 1884, Grant's Cabinet scandals, or those helpers with loose morals who betrayed both Truman and Eisenhower—they would have known that the chief result would be to expose themselves as driven to desperate and unacceptable resorts. Betrayed Presidents get more sympathy than blame.

When, within a few days of each other, the Russians dropped the relatively friendly Khrushchev for unknown successors, and the Chinese achieved a nuclear explosion, Johnson appeared on television to tell the American people that these were not surprises to him, that he and his Administration were unshaken, and that he could be counted on to assess carefully the consequences to American interests. The triviality of Goldwater's attack was heavily underlined. He was likely to get the worst beating any challenger had had since Al Smith had tried to defeat Hoover in 1928. This was apparent to Johnson, of course, and it confirmed again his wisdom in gathering the remarkable consensus now coming together as a result of his political management.

In any but the atmosphere of a campaign, Johnson's complete adaptation to the protector image would have had a dangerously comic appearance. The Texas cowboy disappeared; his dress became severely conservative and his public appearances friendly but solemn. It could be seen that he carried a heavy burden and that he sustained unfair attacks; it was a sacrifice, but it was his duty and he would do it cheerfully. There was no remaining trace of the flailing arms and shrill speech used in his Congressional campaigns. He sometimes reverted to the vernacular ("come to the speakin', folks, and bring the kids"), but for the most part he was ministerial and reserved. He read the words written for him; he was not afraid to be dull. He was, after all, President. He could not be careless even with words.

Johnson cannot really be blamed for not making commitments in the campaign, thus storing up power for further progress. Caution was customary, and it was true to his belief in being professional. Because of his avoidance he would be much less able to get his way when the interests of powerful people were threatened; but it sufficed to yield the electoral approval candidates crave so avidly. As it had been with Roosevelt, so it would be with this younger man; the larger his vote the more it would be resented in the coordinate branch. He might well have been warned by Roosevelt's experience after the enormous outpouring of support in 1936. No more humiliating defeat was ever registered in the Congressional-Presidential war than the one being assimilated by Roosevelt in the Supreme Court matter when Lyndon Johnson met him at the Galveston pier in the spring of 1937. He may have admired the elder man's gallantry through it all, but he cannot have missed the lesson it had to teach. Or is that a lesson Presidential candidates simply cannot learn? It did look like it. Still, he had the politician's answer: the rest is all conjecture, but a landslide is a justifying fact.

He achieved the landslide; what it would mean for himself and the electorate was another matter.

PART TWO

Choosing the Best of the Ways

Rules and Exceptions

Since politics is the art of gaining and using one particular kind of power, it would be expected to have traditions and a methodology. And actually its practitioners do recognize certain techniques and count on their being used. There is, in fact, a sort of morality about this. Not to follow the accepted methods is to be so badly behaved that other professionals are offended; and it may even be that penalties of a special sort will be in order. There is, however, a strange but well-known rule about rules—that politicians who refuse to accept them may be rewarded. Chiselers who, because all their competitors behave according to a code, profit from ignoring it may not be penalized. In politics, as in business, this is thought to be smart; and if it gets them ahead, perhaps it is.

The code of conduct tends to become tenuous whenever there is pressure. The magnanimity of the professionals is so notorious that it is almost true to say that anything an individual gets away with is acceptable.

Even loyalty, supposed to be the firmest of all political virtues, is not universally honored. The author was somewhat startled to have Senator Pat Harrison point this out at a time when a President-elect was surveying the resources of the Democratic party. It was in 1933. F. D. Roosevelt had recently been elected but had not yet been inaugurated. The Democrats had been in the minority in the Senate for the preceding twelve years.

Harrison had for a long time been Minority Leader. He had been called to Warm Springs for a conference and was unhappy about the prospect he was now forced to consider. There was an hour to wait for a delayed train, and he talked as he walked up and down the platform. "Since Wilson went out, we Democrats haven't been thinking about anything but how to make trouble for the Republicans. It's gone on so long we've forgotten how to do anything else. I can tell you I don't look forward to the next few years. I can see that this fellow Roosevelt is going to hold our feet to the fire, and it's not going to be pleasant. Just think of all those committee meetings and all those speeches in the Senate. Charlie McNary [Republican Leader] will have the laugh on me now." Then after a few moments, thoughtfully: "*I'd* be better off if we hadn't won."

Or take an illustration of another sort: Party platforms give candidates instructions; the directives may not be very definite, but they sometimes concern issues that are deeply felt. And the candidate, having been chosen formally, is duty bound to expound them. He may enlarge or even modify them somewhat; but there have been nominees who have given notice that they would not be guided by one or another declaration that they found objectionable.

Smith did this in 1928 when he refused to accept the party position on prohibition, then a much-disputed issue. He gave notice that he meant to campaign for repeal of the Eighteenth Amendment and said that no one who differed should vote for him. The writers of the platform could not disnominate him; but offense was taken; and it was generally considered that he had violated a tacit agreement—that he should not have accepted the nomination if he had not meant to defend its adopted policies. In this case there was a penalty; the disapproval of the regulars certainly had something to do with Smith's defeat in that year. There was a noticeable diminution of enthusiasm among workers; and from the beginning of the campaign it could be seen that he would lose in the states where temperance was strongly believed in.

It was considered the more unfair because Senator Robinson, his running mate, came from Arkansas, as dry a state as could be found; and he was put in a most awkward position. But besides this, Smith's apostasy created a dilemma for those who had nominated him. They could be loyal to their nominee or they could be loyal to the party's platform, but they could not be loyal to both. This sort of dilemma is one that ought not to be imposed on colleagues.

But other sorts of refusals to follow the rules are always turning up, just as people are always sinning and then either being punished or escaping punishment. That they sin does not mean that the rules they break have been abolished, only that they have been violated. And if they escape penalty they may still have disapproval to deal with.

So we do not conclude from the behavior of Theodore Roosevelt, disappointed in his successor and perhaps driven by a renewal of ambition for the power he had once renounced, that his defection from the Republican party was politically moral. He sinned. Besides, on this occasion he did get more votes than Taft; but he enabled the Democrat, Wilson, to win. He thus involved his party and caused it to suffer penalty along with himself. It was his last political appearance.

It is plain that the prospect of their colleagues' displeasure does not sufficiently deter hopeful candidates if they calculate they can win by misbehaving. But on the whole, the experience of such mavericks constitutes a warning. Even Presidents who have departed from party directives have been disciplined. Tyler is a notable example of this; but Andrew Johnson, Fillmore, Hayes, and Arthur are others. They had broken the contract and found themselves in trouble.

But an extraordinary practitioner will sometimes escape punishment. Since the Presidency is the most concentrated position of power in the Republic, it would be expected that competition for it would be fierce and ruthless and that under these pressures, if ever, sharp practice would be resorted to. And in fact it is. The fierceness makes regulations matters of convenience, traditions controversial, and even attenuates the sacredness of bargains. Few Presidents have been saints. And some have got ahead by quite unsaintly behavior.

Still the heat and aggressiveness do not abolish tradition, extinguish rules, or justify betrayals. The recognized ethics still exist, and it always has to be considered what penalty may be exacted for sin. F. D. Roosevelt is not usually thought of as devoted to policies laid down for him by others. But in the months of his first candidacy he was. His departures began when he had got to the place where he could shape things for himself as the party chief. He went very far then, as when he violated the second-term custom; but he was wonderfully dutiful in 1932. He not only said in his acceptance speech that he adhered to the platform "one hundred per cent" but shortly afterward made another address to the nation defending and explaining its provisions—some of which were inexplicable and others of which were indefensible.

Roosevelt understood the rules. He acknowledged his compact with the party. He had asked it to nominate him and, having been accepted, he meant to carry out his part of the bargain. He expected that if he did, however awkward it might be, the party powers would carry out their part. And, being professionals, they did. There were partings later; but the compact kept all factions together for the first assault.

It is interesting that in this case Roosevelt did have some problems of reconciliation. He was not a very convinced wet, but the platform said the candidate must be against prohibition. And he had for a long time been an advocate of adherence to the League of Nations, and this he had to repudiate too. He was caught between the principle of loyalty to the party and loyalty to a policy he had openly avowed. He swallowed hard and made his choice. The requirements of politics are often thus cruel. And its practitioners must accept the fact.

What we have to say is that all such accepted guides, the result of innumerable trials and many mistakes, embody the values of experi-

ence. Departure from them disturbs traditionalists. What is necessary
in each case is to weigh the possible gains against the losses. Only the
best practitioners have succeeded in substituting new guides for old.
And they have waited for propitious times when their influence was
sufficient.

There is sometimes a fine distinction to be made here. A candidate
is clearly under party direction; a President is clearly a policy maker.
But the transition is not always an easy one. As candidate, he may
have reservations about the directives imposed on him; as President,
his leadership may be questioned—especially if he is at all aggressive
in forwarding policies objected to by the older long-time legislators.

But those who have succeeded in establishing reforms are recognized
as the strongest of the Presidents. Think, for instance, of Jackson,
Lincoln, Cleveland, Wilson, and F. D. Roosevelt. Each in some important way asserted his intention to make policy regardless of party
commitment. Starts have been made in a campaign, but not often. It
looked as though F. D. Roosevelt might be taking such a chance when
he made his address at Oglethorpe University advocating national planning; but this was before his nomination, and what he heard from
the elders caused him to retreat. Presently he was tamely defending
laissez-faire as the Chicago platform said he must, and his campaign
pronouncements were as traditional as the most orthodox Senator
could have wished.

When the Presidency has been gained and policy decisions have to
be taken, then departures may be necessary. So Jefferson resorted to
the Rule of Necessity and made the Louisiana Purchase much against
his own and the party's principles; so Jackson faced down the secessionists; Lincoln suspended *habeus corpus* in the interest of national
security; Wilson, after a campaign featuring refusal to go to war, almost at once did go to war; and F. D. Roosevelt went off the gold
standard by Executive Order, to the horror of his more conservative
supporters.

Everything can be different after an electoral victory. Presidents
are popularly regarded, especially when they first assume power, as
specially gifted with a wisdom they would not have been credited
with a short time previously. They are able to break away then from
at least some restrictions. It hardly seems possible that anyone could
attain so glamorous a pinnacle without having been designated by some
higher authority than a mere majority of people's votes. This does
not impress the elders, but it not only gives new Presidents courage,
it actually gives them power. They even have to be reminded that
they have not suddenly become omnipotent, as some of them are apt
to consider that they have. They do not at once recall how narrow

their victory had been and how dependent they are still on party leaders in the Congress for the votes needed to pass legislation.

They soon discover that theirs is a limited power and that what they propose had better be something they can find very wide approval for. But some of the pressure for conformance to orthodoxy is relieved. They can have a say about doctrine. Even in this, however, Presidents are not sole arbiters; they are first among their peers; but there are many peers.

What Is Striven For

PRESIDENTS, if they do not already know it, soon find out how narrow their new freedom is. But the restriction is really on the giving of orders, and there is no limit to achieving the influence that enables them to say and do what they feel they must. No one, no group, no institution, has the sole say about policy; but Presidents who understand the nature of their power will make good their leadership.

When Truman put a sign on his desk saying "The buck stops here," he was not asserting his authority; he was saying that after all the influences, pressures, and contributions had been made he was the one who had to choose among them. He could not originate, but he could select. Also, he knew very well how his decision would fare when the bureaucracy put it into effect or when Congressional committees began work on it. He might not really be the Chief Executive, but he was the final arbiter.

The instance has been cited of Truman bringing his hardly acquired knowledge to bear on his successor's likely lack of sophistication. He will give orders, said Truman, and he will be frustrated when he discovers that nothing happens.

This revealed more about the man who made the observation than about Eisenhower. It showed that he had learned how to be frustrated and still carry on. It had taken a long time—longer than for most Presidents. But that may have been because he came from the legislative branch and had brought with him the characteristic faith such migrants have that they know the secret of conciliation.

There is no such secret. The tension between the branches is inherent in the Constitution and is essential to our plurality. The education of newly inducted Presidents is usually a long and—for the country—dangerous process. It is longest and most dangerous when the new man is slow to learn that he and the Congress are established in opposition. Because he knows its work and understands how it operates, an ex-Senator is likely to think he can find ways to get a co-operation he never yielded when he was a member. He cannot for long.

Truman eventually found this out. But it is evident that he had not found out the nature of a General's power. Eisenhower had not presided over situations in the way the former Captain of artillery evidently thought he had. He had had a bureaucracy, too, and had had a public back home to consider. His giving of orders had been very conditional indeed, and the consensuses he had had to get were quite like those a President must accumulate before he acts.

There is good reason to believe that many Presidential candidates have known much better than Truman did the nature of the office they sought. Many have shaped their campaigns in view of it, something he escaped by succeeding from the Vice-Presidency.

The limiting of initiative begins for the President long before he takes office. He has had to follow very closely the median line of party regularity to get maximum support while he was a nominee as well as afterward, when he must accept the Presidential responsibility. If he departs as Smith did, he must expect to lose some of this support and must calculate whether it is more than can be afforded.

When Eisenhower embraced McCarthy and others of his sort during the campaign of 1952 and allowed them to dictate what he should say, he was perhaps mistaken in identifying the Republican strong men. He was nearer right when he made his compact with Senator Taft. The Taft support was something he really had to have. It hardly comported with the "crusade" he had proclaimed, but it was essential to his progress. He was doing what he must.

Wilson, after having ridiculed Bryan before he was a candidate, publicly retracted and apologized when candidacy became imminent; and if he had not he would neither have been nominated nor elected. Bryan was the Grand Old Man of the party and must be respected. In the same interest Theodore Roosevelt accepted McKinley's principles, and Grant allowed his campaign to be run by the dominant faction of the Republican party.

Presidents, it is quite clear, have very generally understood what they were getting into in running for office and have accepted the conditioned power it offers. The point has been made that not many of them were sensitive to historical tradition. But if they learned from anyone it might well have been Jefferson, who was a consummate politician and who understood Presidential limitations:

> In a government like ours, it is the duty of the Chief Magistrate . . . to endeavor, by all honorable means, to unite in himself the confidence of the whole people. This alone, in any case where the energy of the nation is required, can produce a union of the powers of the whole

and point them in a single direction as if all constituted but one body and one mind . . .[1]

This was early in our national experience. Modern Presidents, faced with the need to act in complex circumstances, and not able to command united support, look at least for a consensus in their official family. An incident in Truman's Presidency illustrates the point.

A furor was caused by the removal of General MacArthur during the war in Korea. There could be no doubt about the right of removal, since Presidents are also Commanders in Chief of the military forces; but MacArthur was popularly supposed to be a gifted strategist, and his removal constituted a rebuke on strategic grounds. Who was Harry Truman to tell MacArthur how to behave in a military situation?

The General came home to an enthusiastic reception. He was greeted everywhere as a hero and was asked to address a joint session of the Congress, where he took leave to dispute the President's wisdom and was loudly applauded. But the President's dismissal stood. He suffered the implied rebuke and withstood the widespread criticism. His view continued to guide policy.

If anyone wondered why the brilliant MacArthur was unable to reverse the Presidential decision when the whole nation seemed to support him, the reason was supplied years later when a secret paper was finally published. It was a report by the National Security Council prescribing the course to be followed in international affairs.[2] Truman's part in its preparation was no more than an initialing when it had been completed. But it furnished the support he relied on. It may have seemed an arbitrary checking of a man of vast knowledge and experience by one who was far inferior. It was nothing of the sort. Truman was an agent of a collective judgment, acting on an agreed consensus.

When those who seek the Presidency are candidates they are agents of the party. When they assume office they become the head and acting administrator for a national consensus. This is what they must try for as aspirants and accommodate themselves to in office. The best of them have understood it from the beginning, as Jefferson, F. D. Roosevelt, and L. B. Johnson did. Others, not understanding, or believing themselves to have transcended such limitations, have had the experience of Andrew Johnson or Theodore Roosevelt or Wilson, leading to frustration and tragedy. Or they have failed as candidates, as Clay, Douglas, and Bryan did.

---

[1] Letter to J. Garland Jefferson, June 25, 1810.
[2] Numbered among Security Council Documents, NSC 68. It was the subject of a story in the *New York Times*, April 13, 1964.

The Uses of Exactitude

IN SEEKING this peculiar Presidential power, a hopeful individual may try to be quite rational in calculating his procedures. But the problems are not easily reduced to the competence of computers. Nomination and election are only the ultimate crises in a long series reaching back to a beginning that can hardly ever be precisely located. Each stage in his rise has compelled some sort of decision, and the factual material necessary to exactitude was either lacking altogether or so incomplete as to be almost useless.

A youngish man confronted with the question whether he should contend for a lesser office as preliminary to a more important one will have uncertain guidance. But his success or failure at this time may begin or end a career. Political history is full of such incidents—Garfield deciding whether he would be convention manager for Sherman in 1880, Theodore Roosevelt torn between running again for Governor of New York or accepting the suggestion that he have second place on the ticket with McKinley, F. D. Roosevelt feeling compelled against his wishes to run for the New York Governorship in 1928 to help out Al Smith—all relied on casually gathered information leading to a decision, and perhaps even then felt compelled to follow a course contrary to their judgment. Theodore Roosevelt dreaded the obscurity of the Vice-Presidency, and F. D. Roosevelt was quite certain that if he ran for the Governorship he would lose and that would end his hope of someday being President. The success of such people could be attributed to good planning only in part; many had to take risks, and many of their choices were involuntary.

Still, although exactitude may have been alien to politics in the past, at least in this sense, it may be more useful in the future. There has indeed been a tremendous increase in the gathering and analyzing of facts to be used in decision-making. There are poll-takers of varying reputation; there is a profession of forecasting; and undoubtedly future candidates will rely on statistical analyses more confidently as they are improved.

Presidential aspirants must never forget the final winning of a majority vote from an enormous electorate. They therefore consider their own talents, the particular circumstances of the moment, the mood of the various voters who must be persuaded, and—very thoughtfully—their opposition. Having made conclusions about these, they then formulate a strategy. This will be determined partly by tradition—their own past record and that of their party. But most important in their minds will be the idea of themselves they have determined to project.

There are, among professional office seekers, and especially successful ones, those who have been actors throughout their public lives. Having marked out a role, they have continued in it, elaborating on it and, in the end, almost incarnating the image they have created. Those who study politicians of first rank find it difficult to discover the real person. Besides, the public stereotype has been so generally accepted that there is resistance when any other account of him is suggested; and this may turn to resentment if a hero is involved—a Jackson, a Grant, or an Eisenhower. Sometimes, of course, the picture is one chosen not by the person himself but by others. There may, indeed, be more than one. There may be contention among competing partisans to project on the one side a benevolent personality and on the other the attributes of an ogre. Consider, for instance, the Radicals' views of Lincoln in contrast to the benevolent Father Abraham of the soldiers.

It is plain that the intention of a political candidate and his organization is different from that of a researcher who seeks to establish some fact or some uniformity. The political aim is to *create* a fact, *to bring about* a conclusion. It is not a reach for truth but a reach for power.

This process may be studied after the concluding event with the most precise analytical methods. Some facts of use to students—or even to candidates—may emerge; but the goal of the campaign as it progresses, whatever methodology is used, is the same as that of a military engagement—victory.

And as the heat of battle increases and confusion is compounded, guesses, estimates, and trials disrupt plans and distort strategy. Exactitude tends to be forgotten in the weeks before an election. This is the time when hunches and hopes take control.

Successes Are Worked For

IT HAS been suggested repeatedly that there is a presumption of deliberate pursuit when the Presidency has actually been achieved. The one solid fact an observer can be certain of is that the individual he is studying was elected. The rest is not so reliable. The life and circumstances of the man are looked into, his early aptitude or lack of it is noted. He is seen assuming office and behaving in such ways as do or do not result in a second term. He had a way of working, perhaps even a strategy that he followed. How can it be uncovered?

The difficulty is that what must be dealt with is imponderable. There are many deeply buried data, hard to exhume in usable condition; involved are devious personalities acting from elusive motives. There are insufficient accounts of many individuals' lives and, far back, of the times they lived in. Recording has not been done for the purpose we have in mind, and there is an apparently irrepressible tendency to bring famous men into stereotyped patterns. Sentiment enters, too, and spreads across the record. Presidents, especially, are elevated and dignified by a kind of compulsion among their biographers; and when a military hero is involved, restraint tends to disappear altogether. He becomes larger than life, he ceases to have the ordinary human vices, and all his virtues are seized with a kind of elephantiasis.

In assuming that all the Presidents, with a very few possible exceptions, have wanted the office and that, wanting it, they have plotted and worked to get it, we can feel fairly safe; but we should be careful not to assume also that their planning was efficient.

All schemes are charts for advancing over a certain kind of political country, not over just any terrain, and not in just any season. Appeals likely to succeed with fellow politicians (the nomination) or with voters (the election) rapidly become obsolete. Every President can be pictured at a moment in his career much as we have seen Generals pictured before their battles. They find themselves in a place commandeered for the purpose, cluttered with maps, charts, memoranda, and estimates; a considerable group of aides is present; and attention is

513

centered on competing schemes for throwing the opposition into disarray and for making a final overwhelming attack.

A proposal will be produced and discussed. There may be competing ones or, in subsequent sessions, ones that have been drastically revised. Out of this conference or series of conferences a plan will emerge and the available forces will be appropriately deployed. It is hoped the tactics of the enemy will not so completely disrupt the proceedings that demoralization will occur on the field; but actual battles do not usually follow an orderly course, and the best schemes allow for revision as events dictate. This is true also of political struggles. It is an unusual one that does not have to be recast when the enemy's intention develops.

Campaign planning is a group or party matter. But back of it, perhaps far back, is a dim, perhaps wholly hidden, occurrence in one man's mind when he conceives a desire to reach the highest office and his energies begin to gather and deploy about this central intention and to create the personality he believes desirable.

If he lacks the gift of understanding public opinion, if he fails to forecast the trend of events, if he adopts a plan of life that voters do not approve, he will never rise far in the political world. And at every stage the requirements become more exacting, the talents to be used more specialized. The chance of being mistaken increases, and the probability of being chosen decreases.

The roll of our Presidents is a list of those who have survived in a long and exhausting competition. Whether or not they proved to be admirable as Presidents, they must be credited with endurance, foresight, and an instinct for behavior proper to their special purpose.

Some Uniformities

W HEN ACCOUNT has been taken of the approach made by each of the thirty-five, it is proper to ask whether any uniformities can be identified and, if so, what they are. Computers might conceivably produce a composite from their histories. Presumably, future Presidents would generally resemble the conglomerate, and an analyst could say what sort of individual might reasonably hope for preferment as well as what sort the party chieftains will look for.

Some early requirements have disappeared, and some that are recent. An indication of these changes can be had by imagining Washington and the first few of his successors—down, say, to J. Q. Adams—confronted with the cold-war and welfare-state problems of Truman, Eisenhower, Kennedy, and Johnson, and with the trials of airplane and television campaigning as well.

Those early Presidents were elected too; but since they had a smaller electorate and presumably a more select one, they had more use for dignity and less for the demagogic arts. It will be recalled that suffrage became fairly universal only in Jackson's time, and even then voters had to be male and white. Negroes were supposed to have gained the franchise by the constitutional amendment in 1868; but a hundred years later (because the states disqualified them) they still could not vote everywhere. The long struggle involved in this had made the contests for nomination and election different than they would otherwise have been. And this was true, too, when the suffrage was widened by the Nineteenth Amendment to include women. Their voting privilege was available at once, but their practical admission to political processes was much longer delayed. Women by 1960 made up more than half the electorate; but in the Cabinet appointed after the election of that year there was no woman, and there was no woman in the next policy-making echelon either. There were a few women Representatives and two Senators, but no Governors. Judging by the record, women had settled into supporting roles. Certainly none seemed likely to be a dangerous challenger for the Presidency within the foreseeable future.

515

There was no Negro in the Kennedy-Johnson Cabinet, any more than there had been in any preceding one; but there were several in the next official rank. There were some in the House, none in the Senate, none in the Governorships—elective offices. But there were several on the Federal bench. Negro men were making faster progress than women of any color, but it would still be unrealistic to suggest that one might become President soon.

These two were the most obvious and certain disabilities. Others were less certain. Still, they must be taken by the computer as they appeared—some, of course, with reservations appropriate to the record.

The question whether an individual who is white, male, and thirty-five years old is justified in considering himself likely Presidential timber will call to mind a number of other qualifications. In the list of those who have succeeded, for instance, there are no alcoholics (except Grant, who had overcome an earlier weakness) and no personalities more unstable than Jackson and Polk. Probably none had peptic ulcers—unless it may have been Polk; most certainly had excellent digestions. This, however, usually induced a portliness, sometimes becoming, as in McKinley; sometimes not, as in the Adamses, who in age became pudgy caricatures of their youthful appearance; and at least twice (in Cleveland and Taft) was grotesque. None is divorced. All are at least third-generation Americans. None is from the Deep South, although there is one from Texas. All at inauguration were forty-two years old or more; but none was more than sixty-eight, the average being about fifty-five.[1] None is of other than western Europe ancestry; and none has a criminal record (unless Jackson's dueling counted).

It might be judged that no one is likely to become President whose ancestry, equipment, and career do not correspond with these norms. But these qualifications include many individuals who cannot possibly be counted as eligible. We shall need to narrow much further the number in any generation who are at all likely to become President.[2]

---

[1] Section I of Article II defining the qualifications is specific only about minimum age and residence:

> "No person except a natural born Citizen, or a Citizen of the United States, at the time of the Adoption of this Constitution, shall be eligible to the Office of the President; neither shall any Person be eligible to that Office who shall not have attained to the Age of thirty-five years, and been fourteen Years a Resident within the United States."

[2] No question has been raised about the definition of "natural born" because no individual born abroad has approached nomination.

Some Handicaps

THERE are some handicaps that only rarely have been surmounted. These range from those a single President has overcome to those that several have successfully contended with—but still only a very few.

For instance, there has been only one cripple of any sort. This was F. D. Roosevelt, who, it will be recalled, lost the use of his legs as the result of poliomyelitis. His attack did not occur until he was thirty-nine years old and after he had been a candidate for the Vice-Presidency. The lateness of his crippling, and his subsequent success in coping with the New York Governorship, softened any objections there may have been. It was, however, something he always had to consider; he took pains to show how vigorous he was except for the uselessness of his legs, and how much exhaustive campaigning he could endure. His disability may even have won more votes than it lost because of sympathy for his cheerful way of ignoring his legs. His success shows that such a difficulty is not an absolute bar to a determined person and may even be turned to advantage.

Only two bachelors have become President; and this is one among other reasons for concluding that those who help to choose candidates look carefully at the family status of those suggested for nomination, and that the happily married have an advantage. Only one divorced candidate (Stevenson) has ever been nominated. He, of course, was not elected; but the divorce is not thought to have lost him many votes, since it was well known how blameless his conduct had always been. This instance, however, should not be taken too seriously, especially if in another case any moral dereliction should be suspected; and anyway, it must be regarded as serious because of Catholic sentiment. At least it would be something to explain, and explanations are not happily undertaken. Again, however, this is relative. In percentage it ranks with membership in the Catholic Church. If among major party candidates only one has been divorced, only two have been Catholics.

None of the more ebullient evangelical sects has contributed a

517

President, and several successful candidates have been religious liberals. Jefferson was what in his time was called a deist; Lincoln was unclassifiable but certainly not a sectarian; Taft was a Unitarian who did not believe in the divinity of Christ, and so were the Adamses and Fillmore. But the larger number have belonged to such Protestant denominations as the Episcopalian (nine), the Presbyterian (six), the Methodist (four), the Baptist, the Disciples of Christ, and the Dutch Reformed (two each), and the Congregationalist and the Society of Friends (one each). President Kennedy was the second Catholic to try for the Presidency as the nominee of a major party. He chose to defy the warning of Smith's disastrous defeat in 1928, usually thought to have been caused, at least in part, by religious prejudice; Kennedy's experience seems to have shown how the electorate can change in such matters. There were several million additional Catholic voters by 1960, and candidates' religion may have counted less anyway; but Kennedy's forthright explanation of his duties as a member of the Church certainly helped.

For reasons peculiar to the nominating process, mostly, members of the Congress and of the Cabinet have seldom been nominated, and the tendency to exclude them seems to have strengthened with the passage of time. Before Kennedy, the only three Senators to become President since Garfield (who had been elected but had not taken his seat) were Benjamin Harrison, Harding and Truman. And the peculiar circumstances of Harding's choice made his case quite special. Truman, too, was so much a boss-chosen candidate that his example is hardly more significant.

Thirteen Presidents before L. B. Johnson had previous experience in the Senate; and seven were members, at one time or another, of both Houses; except for Kennedy, these last, however, were nineteenth-century ones. For instance, those who had been in both Houses were Jackson, W. H. Harrison, Tyler, Pierce, Buchanan, and A. Johnson. But Kennedy contradicted the rule, if rule it was, and so did Johnson, except that he was not nominated for the office but came to it by succession. It is a familiar saying that every Senator thinks himself a potential President. The statistics hardly support the anticipation.

But this may be changing. It ought to be noted that all but one of the prominent Democratic contenders in 1960 were Senators, that several recent Republicans (Vandenberg, Taft, Knowland) were much talked of as candidates, and that the nominee in 1964 was Goldwater. A Senator has the advantage (or disadvantage) of being well known, and if he has been successful in avoiding classification (as Kennedy was), his Senatorship may be favorable; but the circumstances of the campaign have to favor his identifying attitudes if a man long in public life is to succeed.

Senatorship may not be the best situation for an aspirant, but it is not so clearly a dead end as service in the Cabinet. It is true that nine Presidents have been Secretaries in various administrations, but all except Grant, Taft, and Hoover predate the Civil War. Three belong to a period when it seemed natural to advance from the Secretaryship of State to the Presidency. There was one Secretary of War—Taft (Monroe and Grant were also War Secretaries, but only temporarily, and both were better known for other responsibilities)—and Hoover was Secretary of Commerce. If the figures are to be believed, Cabinet membership has become a weaker support than Senatorship for a last leap to the White House.

No one, however, has so good a claim for attention as a Governor who can control a state organization and become a favorite son. He had better be from a large state, and he must have had an acceptable record; but fifteen state or territorial Governors argue strongly for this sort of start.

Some Advantages

IF WE TURN this inquiry around and ask what traits or situations seem to give hopeful individuals an advantage, there are again precedents to examine. Those who look into things when it comes to decide who will be chosen regard one qualification as extremely important. This has various names. In the political vernacular it is often spoken of as "heft," which, translated, means "presence" perhaps, or, less accurately, "dignity." It is something more easily identified than described; but that it is very necessary, and that it can be recognized, cannot be questioned.

Even during the long period from Jackson to McKinley, when there was emphasis on commonness, when birth in a log cabin or its equivalent was considered advantageous—and sometimes essential—there was always a paradoxical preference for men who were clearly *not* common, even though their origins may have been humble. And if the Presidents of that line are looked at, it will be noticed how dignified most of them seem. This may sometimes have been the pomposity of a posturing candidate. But their appearance was as little like farmers or laborers as it is possible to imagine; if they were not personages, they were a good imitation. This may have been made easier by the peculiarly stiff portraiture of the time; candidates' pictures were circulated, even though they themselves were not often visible. But clearly the intention was to emphasize statesmanship or at least to simulate it.

During the whole of the nineteenth century a candidate, once nominated, withdrew to a respectable domicile, assumed an air of solemn composure, and left publicizing to his partisans. Even when he was pictured at home among his family or on his front porch, he was dressed in broadcloth and had handy a tall silk hat. It was much preferred also that he should wear a full beard. Such an outfit on gaunt and ungainly Abraham Lincoln does seem incongruous now; but there are few pictures of him that are not obviously intended to emphasize his respectability rather than his country connections. There is no doubt of its utility in the opinion of the experts.

The contrast here may have been soothing to democratic sentiments. Few voters were in any real sense sophistical. Their acculturization was narrowly provincial. We tend to forget how recent general education is—how many voters were not even literate; also how difficult and slow communications were. It is a characteristic of such a population to believe, or wish to believe, that being wellborn and literate is not necessary to success. If an individual with few advantages and crude manners could still make his way to such a status as required him to dress formally and to carry himself with dignity, it was evidence that any other person could do it too. Rising from a humble origin, symbolized by the log cabin, was far more admirable than being born to fortune and nurtured in an affluent household.

There are remnants of this feeling even in our time. Truman's experiences—having been born on a farm, not having gone to college, and having had to struggle with adversity—were used so freely as campaign material that the shrewd managers who planned his rise must have considered them to be useful. Curiously enough, this sort of appeal has been made even oftener by Whigs and Republicans than by Democrats, and even more effectively. Being conservative and upper-class, and having to attract voters who were neither, they were compelled to make an extraordinary pretense of ordinariness. Indeed it was the Whigs who initiated the style in 1840. The tortured efforts, however ridiculous they may have been, to present General Harrison as a crude fellow who had become a military hero and a territorial Governor from a log-cabin start were considered to have caused his victory.

In fact, this appeal became a Whig-Republican strategy never really copied with equal effect by the Democrats. Whig and Republican candidates were traditionally presented as having originated on hardscrabble farms and having got their start in life as common laborers. Their education in little red schoolhouses preferably ended with the familiar three R's. What else they learned was by candle- or lamplight after hard days of labor in fields or shops. Many of them got to be lawyers, but not by way of law school. They read in some older man's office and also lit fires, swept floors, and ran errands. They became members of the bar on his recommendation rather than by formal training. Their careers thereafter were of their own making, something anyone could achieve if he worked hard and behaved as he should. This was supposed to—and perhaps did—make the voters feel that they themselves might have been candidates if they had had a little more luck. If no General was available, a Lincoln, a Garfield, or a McKinley would have to do—a country boy who had made good.

Jackson had shown the way to this contest of commoners. He was just next to illiterate, as evidenced by his unreliable spelling; his spoken words were salted with frontier profanity; and he was openly scornful of culture. These were characteristics of his supporters, too, and they could be proud of his rise for that reason. Other evidences of lingering crudeness were put down to the reluctance any real Democrat would have about imitating aristocratic manners. But it was the Whigs who really learned the lesson. Zach Taylor did have the appearance, even on battlefields where he was in command, of a farmer inspecting his crops. Lincoln, in his grave habiliments, never seemed to get the prairie mud off his boots. Whig or Republican, they were convincingly common even though favored by conservatives and supported by financiers.

It is noticeable, however, that even Jackson was no ordinary fellow. He had much more distinctively the quality of presence than most of his contemporaries; and his protégé, Van Buren, who was accepted once because Jackson recommended him as his successor, could not win a term of his own, and it was largely because, in spite of lavish endeavors, he never really acquired presence. He was called a popinjay. Polk was another who lacked it; but he was a dark horse—the first—and would not have been renominated even if he had tried (as he did not). These were Democratic failures in this regard. But no Whig or Republican all the way through needed to be afraid of the photographers or journalists who were watching their behavior. Even Clay, Scott, and Frémont, all of whom lost, were presented in the traditional fashion. If they failed it was not because they fell short of this qualification. The trouble was that they had to compete with more impressive characters.

It is hard to say how much of this log-cabin preference has persisted. There are the cases of McKinley, Harding, Coolidge, Hoover, Truman, and Eisenhower, all of whom had humble enough origins but none of whom was self-educated (although Truman did not progress beyond high school). On the other side are both Roosevelts, Taft, Wilson, and Kennedy. Three of these came of wealthy families and one from a clergyman's home. None would be said to have had really humble beginnings, all were very well educated indeed, and three were at least well off in a financial way.

But anyway, the desirability of presence, as a corollary of commonness, becomes more apparent as various campaigns are examined and it is seen how often strenuous attempts have been made to deface the composed picture candidates have sought to present. Democrats have usually been most vulnerable to these attacks. The reader will recall the much-publicized remark, "Who the hell's Polk?" And Greeley, Bryan, and Al Smith suffered even more grievously from similar defamations. But the Republicans have not been immune. Lincoln was cartooned as uncouth and illiterate, Grant as usually disheveled or, even worse, drunk, McKinley as a stuffed shirt, Taft as a puppet,

Hoover as cold and unfeeling, Nixon as an unscrupulous opportunist. Most of these were nevertheless either elected or made close approaches; but the hope that defamation will succeed seems to be a permanent professional trait. It is the same, also, with scandal. Revelations of real turpitude have been few and no known ones have prevented nominations; but such revelations as there have been were not effective in causing the defeat of any nominee—a lesson campaign managers seem never to learn. They were tried again in 1964, in order to smear L. B. Johnson, with the usual result—a backlash.

Discussion of this range of qualities quickly runs over into the consideration of anti-intellectuality. Is it true that intellectuals continue to be ineligible? Professor Hofstadter and others have explored the matter exhaustively—or as exhaustively as is possible. It is as difficult to define this quality as it is to identify the elements of heft. Most arguments seem to identify intellectuality with sophistication and to speak of its opposite as virtual illiteracy. The prototypes often used are Eisenhower and Stevenson, rivals in two campaigns. Eisenhower was not an intellectual, it is said, because he enjoyed none of the pursuits common to the breed—classical music, modern art, advanced theater, theoretical literature, and so on. Stevenson was an intellectual because he had charm, wit, and a cultivated gloss, recognizable whenever he appeared. Eisenhower won because he was more like ordinary individuals. Stevenson was resented because he conveyed the impression of civilized tolerance and willingness to consider before he judged. The trouble with this generalization is that Eisenhower was president of a great university when he was nominated, and Stevenson was Governor of Illinois. These situations do not seem to fit the stereotype.

Hofstadter, studying the Stevenson case, has pointed out how university associations counted against him. He had studied at the Harvard Law School (not to mention Princeton), and he must have associated with erratic characters there. And when a considerable number of the Columbia University faculty published a statement praising him—an obvious repudiation of their own president, Eisenhower—the *New York Daily News* responded with an exposure of what it called "pinko professors." Before the campaign of 1956 ended, this sort of thing had descended to a lower level. The *News* took to calling Stevenson "Adelaide," thus tying together intellectuality and effeminacy. Was this playing to a popular distrust of educated candidates?[1]

There is an obvious difficulty with this illustration—and others: it is virtually impossible to define "intellectual." If it means having writ-

---

[1] Richard Hofstadter, *Anti-Intellectualism in American Life* (New York, 1963).

ten books, Theodore Roosevelt and Wilson ought to have been defeated; and so should Kennedy, but not Stevenson. If it means having been a professor, Wilson and Taft were vulnerable, not Stevenson. If it means being witty and sophisticated, there is Jefferson to consider, and, for that matter, the Roosevelts and Kennedy. Public men have not always been illiterate and philistine.

Possibly the connection here is no more than the lingering of a fading tradition. The feeling that there is merit in having had humble beginnings and having risen in spite of immense handicaps is something to be expected in a nation whose history for a century was dominated by the conquest of vast empty spaces, a conquest that called not for scholarship but for hardiness, not for sophistication but for endurance. If these virtues are still sought in public men, it is not strange. But unless it is a preference that is passing, how account for Wilson, Taft, the Roosevelts, and Kennedy?

Eisenhower, it is true, took himself with portentous seriousness, and clichés were the stuff of his public expressions; his tastes and habits perhaps did mark him as philistine; but he was a war hero too, and this accounts for his victory quite satisfactorily. It is not necessary to conclude that his advantage over Stevenson was a crudeness that contrasted with Stevenson's polish. And what has either of these to do with intellectualism?

Lawyers, Generals, and Businessmen

WHETHER OR NOT it is disadvantageous to be an intellectual, there can be no doubt that belonging to certain professions helps; and among them the most favored is the law.

It is easy enough to understand how this should be. Law and politics are cousins. Most lawyers practice in and around the places of government. The judges before whom they must appear may have been elected; and even if appointed, their party affiliations may have brought about their selection. The courthouses of democracy are political places as well as judicial ones, and a lawyer will be immersed in politics from the beginning of his practice. If he does well, and if he makes himself useful to his party, he will be marked for candidacy when some office falls vacant, either judicial or elective. And potential usefulness to the organization is more often responsible for preferment than professional competence.

It will be recalled that many Presidents started their careers in some such way. Most were not made judges, but some were (Jackson in the frontier style, and Taft, even before he had practiced), and others were pushed into elective offices by older sponsors. It happened to Polk, Pierce, Fillmore, and Buchanan, for instance; and, nearer to our time, Cleveland, McKinley, Taft, and F. D. Roosevelt. All these began by being neophyte lawyers, all were fascinated by politics, all asked help from those further along, and all were able to rise by being useful to their sponsors. Some, like Coolidge, seem to have depended on their legal connections all the way through; some seem to have taken off on flights of their own, once they were fairly launched in the regular way. This was true of F. D. Roosevelt, whose practice was never of much account. And it is at least interesting that, counting backward, six of President Johnson's immediate predecessors were from other occupations. These were Wilson, Harding, Hoover, Truman, Eisenhower, and Kennedy. Only Coolidge was really a lawyer; Wilson and Roosevelt were no more than nominal ones. This may not mark a trend; but it does seem to contrast with Wilson's predecessors, all of

525

whom but two, back to the Civil War, were lawyers—Taft, McKinley, Cleveland, Harrison, Arthur, Garfield, and Hayes. Theodore Roosevelt and Grant were the only exceptions. And back of Andrew Johnson, all were lawyers except the Generals, Taylor, Harrison, and Washington.

The mention of the exceptions, here, suggests the advantage of having been a General. Some were not, perhaps, real Generals—that is to say, they were not professional army men; their chosen calling was law, temporarily abandoned when soldiers were needed. But military records were immensely helpful in the development of all their careers. In the years between the Civil War and the end of the century, only Cleveland had not been in the army. Even McKinley, following him, had been a Major. Some of their losing opponents had been Generals too—McClellan and Hancock, for instance. But the Democrats seem unaccountably obtuse to have chosen Seymour, Greeley, and Tilden to oppose candidates with military records.

The distinction between volunteers and career officers is important. The only Generals who had made the army a career until nominated and had had military education were Grant and Eisenhower. But this leaves out Taylor and W. H. Harrison, who were soldiers so long that, although they were not West Pointers and were landed proprietors, they can be pretty well identified as Generals. And, moreover, their political appeal rested on their military service. They were heroes. Washington was a hero too; but his military identity tends to be lost in that of his statesmanship.

In this connection it seems curious that all candidates from the armed forces who were seriously considered were from the army. No admirals appear in the list (Kennedy and Johnson were junior reserve officers). Some difference must characterize the two services. Perhaps this is because the army is more democratic, or is it because only a few naval victories have been so picturesque or so recognizably essential to national survival as those of Washington, Taylor, Grant, or Eisenhower? Closest to this sort of position in popular regard was Admiral Dewey. The Battle of Manila Bay made him an authentic hero, and he was talked of for a while as a Presidential possibility; but he behaved so foolishly in his civilian role that nothing came of it.

The rebuttal of an annoyed naval person to this implied aspersion can be guessed. Tours of duty in the navy are often on remote stations or at sea. Officers cannot make civilian contacts or attract popular followings. And the nature of ship command is different from that on army posts, more centralized and autocratic. A naval officer gets used to the stiff and aloof behavior customary in his profession. The army is larger, more dependent on leadership as distinct from discipline. So the argument might go; but at any rate, the record does not suggest the emergence of a naval officer as a serious contender for the Presidency.

The one apparent disqualification is to have been in commerce of any sort. No one whose sole occupation has been business has ever become President. Only one has been nominated by a major party. This may seem peculiar in a society that so admires financial success; but evidently businessmen are not wanted for the leadership of those they are accustomed to exploit. They have been members of the Congress (a few) and of the Cabinet (a considerable number), but not Presidential candidates.[1]

---

[1] The possible amendment to this categorical statement is that several Presidents, beginning with Washington, who, as a speculator on a large scale in Western lands and as a planter, had commercial interests; and others have at one time or another had similar connections. Hoover was perhaps as much investor and speculator as engineer until he went into public work. Harding and Cox were newspaper publishers; and Truman was—briefly—a haberdasher. But all were so much better known for other occupations and so much longer engaged in them that it would be an exaggeration to speak of any as a businessman in the usual sense. Even McClellan, who was a railroader, owed his prominence to being a General, and of course he was a graduate of the Military Academy; and Goldwater, who had once had authentic commercial rating, was really retired. He had become a politician some time since. Anyway, the tour de force of his nomination was so emphatically rebuked by the voters that the exception proved the rule—if it proved anything at all.

The Prevalence of Diversity

I F IT IS possible to speak of favored occupations and helpful characteristics, this is about the end of it. Beyond these, we move into a
bewildering maze and are soon lost in diverging paths marked by
betraying signs and confusing landmarks.

Concerning the personal appearance, personalities, temperaments,
sympathies, interests, and varying energies of our thirty-five successes,
only one conclusion is clear—the differences are more striking than the
likenesses. Obviously no model, no composite, is likely to be useful to
one who would conform in order to join the select company; and no
computer could do more than eliminate those of certain origins or
undesirable traits—so long as they were male, white, and of the proper
age. There have been ones who were lethargic and ones who were
restless; lively ones and dull; outgoing ones and inturning; optimistic
ones and pessimistic; intelligent ones and those who were sluggish;
ones who were in their early forties and others who were in their late
sixties; ones who were undersized and others who were of majestic
heights; slender ones and some who were obese.

Some of the contrasts are amazing, the more so because those who
were most popular in their day seem to refute any deduction made
from the characteristics of others who had equally devoted followings.
Consider, for instance, Washington and Jefferson; the General was
reserved, dignified, portly, dull, important in his own regard, practical,
determined and formal; Jefferson was clever, devious, artistic, ingenious, lanky, changeable, charming, flexible, and informal. Or consider Buchanan and his successor, Lincoln; the one was timid, pompous,
fat, unimaginative, lethargic, subservient to pressures, and soft on
secessionists; the other was eccentirc, awkward, sympathetic, abstemious, gaunt, humble, humorous, and fiercely unionist.

There are later contrasts even more relevant because made in the
matrix of a more modern society. Think of the difference between
Theodore Roosevelt and his predecessor, McKinley. The one was
ebullient, mercurial, opinionated, aggressive, loquacious, literary, op-

timistic, and in love with life and the power of his office; the other was fattish in body and mind, the creature of party and associates, pious, passive, and pleasantly evasive.

Or look at the contrast of Eisenhower with Kennedy, his immediate successor. Eisenhower was mature, deferential to the business elite, a philistine in intellectual matters, a believer in weak government, self-satisfied, homely but charming, and clearly in the tradition of the country boy who made good; but Kennedy was young, volatile, cultivated, intellectual, wealthy, restless, aggressive, coldly analytical, eager for power, and with the same expansionist view of his office that the Roosevelts and Wilson had had.

Between these two, the one following the other, there was as marked a difference in every category as that between Washington and Jefferson in early years, or Buchanan and Lincoln in the middle period. And others as striking could be cited: Adams and Jackson, or Polk and Pierce. And of all the contrasts, none seems stranger than that on one day in November 1963 the President should have been the Kennedy of Choate and Harvard, and that on the next he should have been L. B. Johnson, teacher of speech in Sam Houston High School. Intellectualism and reserve were suddenly exchanged for the flamboyant outgoing typical of Texas; and both commanded wide and intense loyalty.

It is true that during the long Republican run from Grant to McKinley one President is hard to distinguish from the others. Hayes, Harrison, and Garfield, especially, seem to have come out of one egg. And Cleveland, the interloping Democrat, appears to have come out of it as well. This would seem to indicate that there are fashions; and it may well be that circumstances make one sort popular at one time and others at different times. There are also disconcerting shifts—such as that from Hoover to Roosevelt or from Eisenhower to Kennedy. But it is evidently not a physical, temperamental, or any other outward characteristic that makes an individual attractive to the electorate or, for that matter, makes him popular after his election.

Both Washington and Jefferson, different as two men could be, are always named when Americans look back to their most remarkable leaders. In his day, Jackson had the fanatical support of a majority; but so did his complete opposite, Lincoln, in *his* day. And what is even more remarkable, the responsive and charming Theodore Roosevelt was no more enthusiastically approved than was the eccentric, cold, pale, and anemic Coolidge a little later—both Republicans. Coolidge, in fact, was regarded as one of the most acceptable of all the Presidents; and considering the disaster that followed his regime, this is something hard indeed to explain. It is true that most of his contemporaries were no more prescient. He was passive and complaisant in the White House while speculative fevers were rising in Wall Street and spreading widely. His contribution was to encourage a headlong progress toward the worst of all domestic disasters. But the Republicans would have kept him if they could. And if he had chosen to run he would undoubtedly have carried the election of 1928. He need not have given way to Hoover.

Americans are proud of the Presidents they regard as the strong ones and are often surprised to learn that in their time they were far less popular than others recognized in retrospect as weak or incompetent. Both Lincoln and Wilson were minority Presidents, Wilson twice; so was Cleveland, twice; and so were J. Q. Adams and Polk.[1]

Certain of these while in office were able to increase their popularity, but not all. Lincoln did, but not until late; and then eleven states were excluded from voting, all of which would have gone overwhelmingly against him. Even so he was very worried about re-election and took the doubtful course of causing large numbers of soldiers who were dependable voters to be sent home for the election. Wilson almost lost to Hughes in his second try, and neither Adams nor Polk was even renominated.

What conclusion is to be reached from the electoral weakness of those who stand so high in historical regard, and from the popularity of the less competent? Is it that strength—that is, aggressiveness, commitment on important issues, insistence on Congressional co-operation —are apt to cause more disaffection than respect? A willful leader, such as Wilson was, could carry the nation through frightening crises, but he could not hold his following for longer than it took to surmount immediate challenges. The electorate tired and would not accept the responsibilities he had contracted for them. F. D. Roosevelt could demand unpopular measures to meet the crisis of depression, but conservatives soon began to rebel against reform. His majorities were slim in 1940 and 1944.

Even Washington left office in a hail of disparagement from Jefferson's Democratic-Republicans. And Lincoln, the embodiment of victory in 1864, might well not have lasted long in that role when the Radicals got to work on his proposals for reconstruction; Johnson, who tried to carry on his policies, was nearly driven from office and was not even considered for a term of his own.

Or taking it the other way around, among the weakest of Presidents, and those a later generation finds so hard to excuse its ancestors for exalting, are Buchanan, Grant, Harding, and Coolidge. But all

---

[1] Fourteen elections have produced minority Presidents. Besides those named, the list includes Taylor, Buchanan, Hayes, Garfield, Benjamin Harrison, Truman, and Kennedy. The reasons were various; usually, however, third parties captured sizable votes.

were enormously popular. Buchanan would have been re-elected if his party had held together. If Grant could have captured the nomination he might almost certainly have been elected to a third term even after having left office in something like disgrace. Harding died after only half a term, with scandals pursuing him; but sorrow throughout the nation was abysmal, and the memorial erected to him in Marion is quite as impressive as Washington's monument and much more so than any memorial to the brilliant Adamses, the stalwart Cleveland, or the inspiring Wilson.

To go on with this wondering recital, Eisenhower lived to help dedicate a museum and library at his boyhood home with the good wishes of his countrymen. He spoke on the day of dedication in funereal terms, fearful of the country's future. Kennedy was pushing and persuading it into movement after eight years of standing stubbornly still. Renewed progress would enlarge the nation's debt, and Eisenhower was full of foreboding. It was a day not of rejoicing in survival but of head-shaking about the future. Kennedy's popularity was as incomprehensible to the General as to ordinary observers. He could not believe that his loyal constituency could have turned so quickly to a young man he disapproved. But he had the satisfaction of being quite sure that only the Twenty-second Amendment had kept him from being renominated in place of Nixon and re-elected in place of Kennedy. His principles had failed to survive, but that was because he was no longer able to defend them.

What he could not understand, and what no one is wise enough to explain, is the undoubted predilection of the electorate for accepting completely contrasting leaders: Eisenhower was not loved less because Kennedy was approved; and Kennedy was not admired less because Eisenhower was trusted. Such things had happened before. They will happen again. The facts we observe in our pluralistic society are not always intelligible. But they are facts; and if their lessons are obscure, they are the only ones there are.

The Attraction of Leadership

DISSERTATIONS on leadership sooner or later deal with something spoken of as "nervous energy" or "drive." A respected author has this to say on the subject:

> Those who rise in any marked way above the mass of men have conspicuously more drive, more sheer endurance, greater vigor of body and mind than the average person. The leader's effectiveness is in the first instance dependent upon his basic constitutional strength and robustness.
>
> The subtle ways in which one person vitalizes another are closely related to the possession of this endowment. Energy seems to be imparted and to be drawn out of others by an effective show of energy. The leader's energy begets energy in the followers. The existence of abounding vigor goes far toward making the leader crave to work for significant purposes, and toward producing that total mobilized zeal we call enthusiasm . . .[1]

This passage would seem to indicate that Tead made a faulty assessment of leadership qualities or that many Presidents—who are supposed to be the nation's supreme leaders—have not possessed the qualifications they should have had. Certain ones could be named who met the Tead tests. Most conspicuously, Jackson, Polk, Cleveland, Wilson, the Roosevelts, Kennedy, and L. B. Johnson. It might have been written to fit Johnson; it does not fit a good many others: Fillmore, Pierce, Buchanan, Grant, Hayes, McKinley, Taft, Harding, Coolidge, or Eisenhower. None of these last, at least when President, was notably vital, aggressive, and able to energize subordinates and supporters.

There have always been those, as we have seen, who would not agree that Presidents ought to be leaders, formulating policies, seeing to their embodiment in legislation, and firmly controlling the Execu-

---

[1] *The Art of Leadership*, by Ordway Tead (New York, 1935), 82–83.

tive Departments. The Federalist-Whig-Republican conception has been that others—outside the government, mostly—possessed the necessary qualities for making decisions; they held high positions in banking or industry, owned the productive facilities, and financed the party organization. It seemed no more than just that the government should allow them the initiative. What they want in a President is illustrated in the candidates they have chosen—Taylor, Harrison, Hayes, McKinley, Taft, Harding, and Eisenhower, to name only ones they succeeded in electing. Many of their losers were of the same sort. None of their selections corresponded with the Tead formula. None was an energizer.

The Presidency has been controlled by those who had this regressive view about half the time. And if we go back to the Jeffersonians, who, although dedicated to public service, conceived the whole Federal government as secondary to the states, it has to be concluded that Americans often favor Presidents who preside over the Federal establishment but do not dominate, try to lead, ask for sacrifices, or fight for issues they believe in. Those who conceive the Presidency to be what Wilson, the Roosevelts, and Kennedy strongly felt it ought to be, and tried to make it, have been on the whole not nearly so pleasing to the Establishment and often not to the people. And this is as true of recent history as of periods further back. The complexities of civilization, with the frightful exigencies of the nuclear age to be met, have apparently made no change in this preference. Beginning at the turn of the century when industrial problems began to force themselves on public attention and to become issues in campaigns, the passive candidates continued to be more numerous than the active ones, and more often elected—McKinley, Taft, Harding, Coolidge, Hoover, and Eisenhower against two Roosevelts, Wilson, Truman, and Kennedy.[2]

Leaders of causes have not often been nominated since the Civil War, nor have strong advocates of any panacea. Bryan tried but did not succeed. Even F. D. Roosevelt, who did offer to cure a depression, said he would do it without pain to anyone except speculators. Honest businessmen—except perhaps bankers of a sort—were not threatened; people generally were to be better off. No one was asked for sacrifices. Progressivism had begun as a radical movement, but by Roosevelt's time it had become mere reform.

It simply is not always, or even nearly always, true that "those who rise in any marked way above the mass of men," as Tead put it, do have "conspicuously more drive" than the average person. What must come to mind, looking back, is Buchanan allowing traitors to infiltrate

---

[2] But were in office fewer years because the terms of McKinley and Harding were cut short, and F. D. Roosevelt served for more than twelve years.

the government, McKinley resisting feebly the drive of the yellow press for war with Spain, Harding confused and evasive as the trials of office pursued him and scandals broke over his head, Coolidge staring from his armchair into space for hours, and Eisenhower deferring to those he ought to have disciplined. And there was no dissatisfaction of a heated sort with any one of these Presidents. On the contrary, all were extremely popular and remained so when in office. Only Hoover, of all the list, suffered when business depression was not arrested.

Is it something quite different from the leadership common to other occupations that Americans look for in their Presidents? Perhaps; yet to say that passivity and a disposition to resign essential power to others are necessary qualifications would be to ignore the examples of a quite different sort. Jackson, Polk, Lincoln, Wilson, and Kennedy did achieve election and did rally such popular support that immense excitement resulted. They were known leaders, even if not agitators, before nomination and they brought on enormous undertakings as Presidents.

We must conclude, unsatisfactory as it must be to one hoping to discover uniformity, that when the electorate is offered a choice of two types, it is not energy, initiative, and leadership that determine. It is some other quality. It is true that most of the inept or withdrawing Presidents professed to have something in mind besides simply being elected when they were candidates. Eisenhower promised that "he would keep the long nose of the Federal government out of the business of the states." He called his campaign a crusade. But what he meant to do—as everyone knew—was to lead his Republican hosts rapidly to the rear—a curious crusade. This may have been a throwback, an exception. But then, as we have seen, all Generals are exceptions. What they *say* makes no difference; they are wanted because people feel safer with them in the White House after a time of disturbance, adventure, and responsibility. And there can be no doubt that the response, at such times, to the suggestion of quiet retirement from world involvements is massive. Anyway, it suffices. Heroes are invincible in their adherence to reaction.

Presidents who are chosen not because they promise to do something, but because they promise not to, offer a refuge from the restless rush of history with its frightening disturbances; but there are other occasions when something must be done, and the man is chosen who promises to act as Roosevelt did in 1932, not radically but vigorously.

This, however, is to introduce another confusion. An analyst ought to make up his mind whether Presidents seem to be chosen for personal qualities or for statesmanlike ones. Unfortunately he cannot honestly do it. There is evidence of both propensities. Democracies are contradictory, inconsistent, irresponsible, unpredictable. They are like the heroines of the romancers—mysterious, irresistibly attractive to suitors, but not always rewarding. One who sets out to woo must take his own chances. As Truman once said, using a homelier expression, "Those who can't stand the heat should stay out of the kitchen." But many feel the possible victory worth the pains, the costs, and the risks of humiliation. They find the heat bearable.

Also, it should be said that although the passive Presidents seem to have been devoted to preventing the government from going forward, this has not been true of themselves. They may always have been conservative and sometimes reactionary, but about getting to the Presidency they have been shrewdly active. When it was called for, they could call on enormous reserves of ambitious energy. Some of them underwent ordeals of campaigning that would have exhausted an athlete, some found ways to create heroic moments, and all had a dogged pertinacity in seizing advantage and outwitting enemies that was completely unlike their later Presidential behavior. Getting there is indeed different from being there.

The Selection Process

THE LACK of clearly identifiable characteristics making for Presidential eligibility, except for a few personal qualities and certain environmental circumstances, raises some serious questions. In the original Constitution the requirements that a candidate must be natural born and at least thirty-five years of age were supplemented by the provision for an Electoral College made up of select citizens who, it was obviously felt, would choose from among the rich and wellborn (as Hamilton called them), after due deliberation, a suitably distinguished Chief of State. Since there were as yet no organized parties and, in the modern sense, no candidates, there would be no appeal to voters, and not even any contest for nomination, except perhaps a genteel one within the College. This was the expectation. The existence of "faction" was repeatedly spoken of by the Framers as a danger they were especially proud to have averted.

Actually the strong differences of attitude between those who were equalizers and those who believed in the supremacy of an elite became furious confrontations when the Constitution had been ratified and the government activated. Washington, Adams, Hamilton, Jay, and others of the Federalists were anguished by Jefferson's equalitarianism; and his Democratic-Republicans were ready to use violence if necessary to unseat the aristocrats. This difference is the deepest and most persistent one among the many that run through the American years. It is responsible for a basic two-party confrontation.[1]

All those who have had any hope of becoming President have had to be nominated by either one or the other. This has eliminated a few able contenders, such, for instance, as Van Buren and Fillmore,

---

[1] There have been third parties representing special departures—Free-Soilers, Greenbackers, Populists, Socialists, Progressives, and so on, but none has seriously threatened the two dominant ones.

Actually there were thirteen with candidates in 1960, but eleven had negligible support. The most formidable challenge to the two dominant parties was that of the Progressives, who twice attracted more than four million votes, in 1912 (Roosevelt) and 1924 (La Follette), but then disappeared.

who were third-party candidates for second terms, Theodore Roosevelt in 1912, La Follette in 1924, and Wallace in 1948. But its most important effect on the Presidency has been to make adherence to a major party one of the leading qualifications for eligibility, the very thing the Framers had taken such pains to avoid.

Concentration on party loyalty has been responsible for choices that could not possibly have been made by the original Electoral College. This is true of all those who became President by succession from the Vice-Presidency—Tyler, Fillmore, A. Johnson, Arthur, T. Roosevelt, Coolidge, Truman, and L. B. Johnson. None would have been chosen even for the lesser office, except to widen the party's appeal or to conciliate a schismatic minority. None would have been considered, either, if the convention delegates were actually selecting a possible President. In spite of the record, the possibility of Presidential death is seldom present in the euphoric atmosphere of conventions. Humphrey is the single exception to the rule of party expediency.

It has to be said, too, that only a few of the elected Presidents might have been chosen under the original rules and before the organization of parties. Jackson would not, certainly, and it is necessary, really, to come all the way down to Eisenhower for a selection that was not party-determined and that might have been made if parties had not appeared. This is not to say that the selections were unworthy. But the conclusion is inescapable that many Presidents have been second-rate members of their generation, even if only prominent politicians are considered. The virtues of desirable alternates are all but lost to us now and we cannot say how ably they would have filled the office; but we know all too well that the man chosen was weak, sometimes so weak that almost any other likely choice would have been as good or better. Think, for instance, of Buchanan, Grant, Hayes, B. Harrison, and Coolidge. Their opponents were Frémont, Seymour, Tilden, Cleveland, and Davis, all better men. And other competent contenders disappeared in the earlier processes of elimination.

Some elections have been so irresponsibly carried out that the resultant President was capable or incapable by sheer chance, and if there was a weight of probability it was on the side of incompetence, if only because of the qualities looked for by the inner circle at the particular time. Garfield emerged from a contest between the supporters of Grant and Blaine, a compromise—a dark horse. The same had been true of Polk; and, among losers, it was true of Davis in 1924. What party leaders wanted in instances of this sort was a harmless, nonirritant, dignified individual with no strong views except ones accepted by undoubted majorities. This required no leadership. And the country got along without it if such an individual became President.

But compromises of this sort are not exclusively responsible for incompetence in candidates. The choice has often been made of persons who were not only so moderate and conservative as to be colorless but who would be amenable to inner-circle direction—who were "safe." This was the case with Pierce, Buchanan, Hayes, Harrison, McKinley, Taft, Truman, and Eisenhower. They were expected to accept directions from fellow professionals and their business associates, and on the whole they did.

The problem of the American democracy in this regard is to devise a process calculated to choose *every time* able and independent individuals for the heads of the tickets, so that, no matter which party wins, the nation will have the Chief Executive it must have in the circumstances of recurrent—almost continuous—crises that seem likely to run on indefinitely into the future. But such an objective seems so incredibly unattainable with the processes in use that the student despairs of suggesting ways to reach it; and an aspirant for the Presidency is fully justified in ignoring the criterion of excellence and assuming that any respectable politician may be acceptable.

Guiding Suggestions

For students of the Presidency—and hopeful individuals who are looking for guidance—the following are suggested as important considerations:

1. A career of faithful party service has resulted in nomination for the Presidency or the Vice-Presidency: Van Buren, Buchanan, Hayes, McKinley, Coolidge, and Truman are examples.

2. Exceptionally able individuals with less faithful records have also been known to succeed; but this has almost always been after reaching a certain elevation in the orthodox way. The instance of F. D. Roosevelt is instructive in this; so are those of Cleveland, Lincoln, and Jackson.

3. Few instances of unfaithfulness to party, or even of irregularity, have resulted well. Willkie in 1940 might be cited as an exception; but he represented a schismatic group in the party; in the same way Dewey and Eisenhower were hardly regulars. The weakness of Robert A. Taft, who was the alternate to Willkie, and of those who might have been chosen instead of Eisenhower (MacArthur or Taft again) was that they obviously could not have been elected. Willkie was not elected either, but he was considered to have come closer than the others would have; and perhaps one reason he lost was that party workers did not really try very hard to elect him.

4. Conspicuous and able men of recent years who were Presidential timber—LaGuardia, Norris, Lowden, Dawes, and Root among Republicans, and Wallace, Jackson, Douglas, and Kefauver among Democrats—were not considered because they were simply not approved by the powerful in the party; although any one of them might have been elected. They had been offensive to those who could stop their progress.

It appears that a hopeful individual ought to make his party affiliation very early, concentrate on becoming trusted, and, after having demonstrated his ability to campaign and to serve in lesser offices, preferably elective, try to become the Governor of a populous state. He will then be extremely eligible.

A Governorship is obviously the best staging base for an attempt on the Presidency; but it ought to be neither a small nor a Southern state. The most favorable locations are not the same for different periods. Virginia once had almost a monopoly, but that was before the South became secessionist territory. And some others have become favored because of growth—California, for instance. California would not have produced a candidate at any time before it began to have a significant number of electors. Its first national candidate was Warren for Vice-President with Dewey in 1948 (unless Frémont is counted, who was really an Easterner); but the signs had been appearing before that. The Democratic convention of 1920 was held in San Francisco. This was some sort of recognition for 13 electoral votes. But these, by 1948, had grown to 25. It is interesting that Warren's nomination did not win California for the Republicans, although that was the obvious hope in nominating him. Ohio, for a time, was the most favored state. From Hayes to Harding, five Presidents came from there. There are others—such as Iowa—where there are fewer voters at every census and so fewer electors with every redistricting. They are poor bases for an attack.

Unfortunately the conditions for attaining a Governorship are even less certain than those for rising further to the Presidency. Faithful party service counts heavily where there are strong parties and no primaries. Only in a state like California, for instance, with its open primaries, may a maverick hope to succeed. But there is this to be said —a Governorship is some sort of trial run for a serious contender. He may demonstrate ability to head a bureaucracy, to dominate a legislative body, and to become influential in, or even to control, a local machine. A Governor, chosen to be a candidate, has a record he can point to; but it is also one he cannot escape. He had better be notable as well as acceptable to the political leaders who will influence the nomination he seeks for the Presidency. He may then come to national conventions as a favorite son and perhaps be favored by the insiders.

But reservations must be made. Being so acceptable a Governor of Ohio that he was twice re-elected against strong opposition counted a good deal in Hayes's favor at the Republican convention of 1876; but it did not guarantee, as might have been hoped, that he would be a popular candidate; and he was really defeated by Tilden. Having been Governor of the same state influenced the selection of Cox by the Democrats in 1920 but did not help him much in the election. In both these instances other considerations outweighed Governorship records. Hayes was needed by the Republicans as an offset to Grantism; and this was the most important reason for choosing him. The choice of Cox was influenced by his complete isolation from Wilson's administration. The leaders knew that the country was ready for a regressive candidate; but, of course, the Republicans had a more regressive one. Or, to take another case, Roosevelt's Gubernatorial successes in New York made him a logical candidate in 1932; but he would have been defeated by the incumbent Hoover if it had not been for the depression.

It happens that Hayes, Cox, and Roosevelt were regarded as satisfactory Governors, and generally such a reputation has been necessary. A failure in office would not be considered. But it is also true that, in the year or two immediately preceding the election he is aiming at, a Governor may spend much of his time making appearances in other parts of the country, in conferring with leaders and making ready for the struggle to come. F. D. Roosevelt, during his last term, 1930–32, was no more than half a governor. The other half was the Presidential candidate. There was some criticism about this, but not much. And if he used the facilities of the Governorship rather freely for his preconvention campaign, it was no more than was expected. Later New York Governors—Dewey, Harriman, and Rockefeller—did the same thing. But Governors who are candidates may be better Governors because of their candidacy. They try to present something of a preview of themselves as President. Both Roosevelts did this; and the second rose to the challenge of the depression and offered a real contrast with Hoover. By helping the unemployed with such relief and public works as a single state could undertake, by formulating a farm program, and by criticizing Hoover, he showed that he would make a vigorous attempt at recovery.

Also, he chose this time to make a break with the Tammany machine. He was given an opportunity to investigate and condemn; and the individuals concerned, including Sheriff Farley and Mayor Walker, could be pilloried and, with national publicity, forced to resign. This infuriated the Sachems, naturally, but it convinced the progressives elsewhere that he was not the creature of the bosses—something necessary for any Democratic Governor of New York to do if he is to gain the confidence of the rest of the country. Cleveland, nearly half a century earlier, had shown the way in this.

By his speeches and his behavior, much publicized because he was the leading contender for the Democratic nomination, Roosevelt used his Governorship expertly to create the impression most useful while his lieutenants were rounding up instructed delegates. The result was that he came to the convention with a lead long enough, with a simple trade involving the Vice-Presidential nomination, to make him the winning candidate.

Devices and Their Uses

A S HAS BEEN SUGGESTED, one of the more serious criticisms to be made of the selection process is that in so many instances it produces Presidents not chosen to be President. Eight have succeeded from Vice-Presidential status: Tyler, Fillmore, Johnson, Arthur, T. Roosevelt, Coolidge, Truman, and another Johnson. And none of these was chosen with his possible succession to the Presidency in mind.

It is a serious indictment to say that for about twenty-three years the office has been filled by men not elected to it—and ones, moreover, who could not have been nominated to be their party's offering.

When Vice-Presidents chosen for such reasons have succeeded they have frequently been problem Presidents. Apart from incompetence, several have precipitated division and quarreling. Tyler and Andrew Johnson are the worst examples of this. But neither Arthur nor Fillmore was representative of a majority even in his own party and so neither could accomplish very much. Something of this sort happening at a time when the nation had desperate need for leadership could be fatal.

In only a few conventions have contests for the Vice-Presidency seriously interested either the delegates or those mentioned for nomination; and there have been a good many instances of refusal to accept. Dawes and Lowden thus rejected bids in 1920. One of the few instances of a contest for the nomination was that in 1956 between Democrats Kefauver and Kennedy. As things turned out, Kefauver, who won, lost the election with Stevenson, and it was fortunate for Kennedy that he was out of it. A defeat in that year would have been conspicuous in his record when it came to his Presidential effort in 1960.

The likelihood that only second-rate, discouraged, or drafted candidates are offered or will accept the second place is explained by recalling that since Jefferson only one has ever subsequently achieved the Presidency except by his predecessor's death; and that one is Van Buren, who was imposed on the party by Jackson. He was elected, but only once. He was renominated in 1840 but was defeated by Harrison.

This behavior of conventions makes it seem very strange indeed that as a device it should have persisted so long without much change. It was invented by professionals with interests to protect; and they usually have no difficulty, except for struggles among themselves, in getting their way. They may be discreet in meeting the probable wishes of the electorate—that is, in choosing candidates with a chance of winning; but still the meeting is best described as a conference of power groups—state bosses, Congressional leaders, and representatives of financing interests. What these few decide in private, the meeting itself is apt to vote in public. The "word is passed"; and when the roll is called the delegations fall in line.

The obvious alternative is the primary. But primaries make it necessary to undertake what amounts to an additional campaign. And there is the possibility that the appeal of an ambitious maverick may make an embarrassing situation. This happened in the case of Kefauver in 1952. There were sixteen states with primary laws, and he made an impressive record in long-drawn-out campaigns; but some were merely preferential, and the states were not the largest ones. But even though he came to the convention with this support the leaders would not take him; and although on the first ballot he had 340 votes, more than Stevenson, who had 273, his strength failed rapidly and Stevenson was nominated on the third ballot.

Kennedy did better with primaries two elections later, in 1960. It was the showing he made in them that convinced the state bosses of his pulling power.

A Wisconsin primary killed off Willkie as a contender in 1944 and established Dewey as the Republican favorite. One in West Virginia ended Humphrey's try for the nomination in 1960. It can be seen from these illustrations why the party powers find the device so objectionable. A situation otherwise more easily kept under control is made uncertain.

Where primaries that are only preferential are in use they are a nuisance to the bosses, but no more than that. The convention's delegates may still be under close control. Such contests are entered only by candidates who feel the need to establish their drawing power and ones who, like Kefauver, are not acceptable to party professionals. Even when the primaries are over, the convention is the place of actual choice, not so free as formerly, perhaps, but still often able to decide matters in small conferences from which "the word" is passed.

The movement to establish primaries was active for a generation.[1]

---

[1] The first state primary law was passed in Wisconsin in 1903.

It has since lost momentum. Some states have given them up after a trial. But those still in use force the candidates to begin their travels—and their expenditures—in early spring and give them no rest until the eve of election. The consequent expenditures grow to fantastic amounts, and the ordeal of working steadily through state after state leaves the contenders numb with fatigue. In the campaign of 1960 the Kennedy wealth had a significant effect, since each state offered a different problem and each required an organization. The resources of other hopeful candidates were hopelessly inadequate for such a campaign. Humphrey, who seemed to be pressing Kennedy most closely, finally lost hope after West Virginia expressed a preference for his rival and withdrew from the contest.

There is no doubt that Kennedy's use of the primary to force recognition of his power caused restudy of the device. For a candidate willing to work exhaustingly as Kennedy did it has possibilities. But it would be as futile as it was in Kefauver's case without enormous financing; and candidates at that juncture do not have party resources to call on. They must find their own finances and put together their own organization. Meanwhile the local bosses are watching skeptically, reluctant to be involved until they can see what strength is developed.

The Reluctant Seldom Succeed

USING SUCH DATA as we possess, it is instructive to speculate on the length and intensity of personal effort made by the thirty-five who have become President. One thing is sure. Active ambition began at an earlier time than has usually been supposed, in some cases much earlier. It is only occasionally that the advent of hope can be located with certainty; but it is somewhat easier to say when expectation arose.

Jefferson, for instance, cannot seriously be said to have helped establish the nation so that he could become its President, but looking back across his career, it almost seems that way. Certainly as soon as there *was* a President (although he did not approve the kinds of powers he was given), he set himself to capture the office. He succeeded speedily and with complete ruthlessness, discrediting the Federalists, including Washington, and consigning John Adams to premature retirement.

Nor can Generals have been seized with the notion that the Presidency was possible for them while they were undistinguished junior officers. This could only have happened after they had become famous, and then only when powerful politicians found that their reputations would make them useful and encouraged them to believe they were indispensable.[1]

Looking back over the list, it is apparent that the first succession of Presidents, down to Jackson, were aware many years ahead that they might be chosen. With Madison and Monroe, as successors to Jefferson, there was some scrabbling about to see who would come first;

---

[1] The data on the beginning and course of Presidential aspiration tend to be unreliable for a number of reasons. Biographers have not looked for it specifically or they may have felt it more seemly for their subjects to have been sought out and urged to become candidates. But the approaches of the Generals are more usually recorded. It is probable that the word "indispensable" as used above is exact. All the Generals believed they were called to power, an arrangement by Providence that excused them from the military avoidance of politics theretofore one of the maxims most honored throughout their careers. They appeared to think, and did not hesitate to say, that their campaigns were crusades.

but having been Secretaries of State and, moreover, intimates of their sponsor, both could have actual expectations. Jackson was offering himself at least eight or ten years before he was elected, and during four of these he was intriguing incessantly to displace J. Q. Adams. In the preceding years he had been maneuvering in the contest Adams won (in 1824). So he came to office with years of anticipation—backed by aggressive plotting—behind him.

Van Buren, using Jackson as a sponsor, and backed by his New York machine, was working definitely for at least eight years, and probably for several more, to rise by the professional route. But after Van Buren, the convention as a nominating device made things somewhat more chancy for candidates with inside backing than the procedures of earlier years. However much a convention might seem to be arranged in advance, there was the possibility of a contest. And if this went far enough an unexpected compromise might have to be accepted. Polk was only the first dark horse; others followed—Garfield, for instance, who in 1880 managed to be elected in spite of his party's acrimonious quarrels; and Davis, in 1924, who did not. Davis was probably surprised by his nomination; Garfield probably was too, in a sense, but only that his preferment should have come in 1880 rather than later. He had worked all his life for some such break in his fortunes.

Buchanan had been trying for twenty years to get attention and had had expectations in at least two conventions before that of 1856. All his personal postures had had the Presidency in view; and his control of the Pennsylvania machine had been with this purpose in mind. Lincoln's was a convention tour de force in which his representatives traded every favor the party might have to dispose of, if he was chosen, in order to secure his nomination. He had been mentioned for the Vice-Presidency four years before; and his debates with Douglas had made him famous, although they had not led to the Senatorship he had hoped for. His speeches during the few years preceding 1860 were calculated to bring him to popular notice; but on most occasions he had followed a conservative line suitable to an old Whig uneasily turning Republican. Only on the slavery issue and on the preservation of the Union was he at all clear, and only on Union was he bold. But that he schemed and worked for party support, there cannot be any doubt. He would have settled for the Senatorship he contested with Douglas, but he doubtless knew that he was better off as a Presidential possibility for having lost that contest in 1858. Did he expect to be President someday? He may not have expected to, but he certainly hoped.

Hayes, Harrison, and McKinley were so regularly Republican, and made such devoted efforts to rise, that their anticipations of eventual success must have come fairly early in their political careers. For each there were probably ten expectant years when every move was calculated. Cleveland had only two years of definite notice that he was eligible; but, being Governor of New York, and the times calling for a man of his caliber, he knew what the probabilities were. His was one of the quickest rises; but he was active in his own interest and in his own way.

The Vice-Presidents after 1900 who were most expectant were T. Roosevelt, Coolidge, and Truman. Neither Roosevelt nor Coolidge had actually anticipated the death that placed them in the White House. But both had been in politics during the whole of their working lives and, having risen so far, naturally had hopes even if ones they were resigned to seeing deferred. Both had cultivated their home precincts, become Governor, thus demonstrating their ability to attract votes, and then come on the Washington scene as possible successors. Both had done so well and were so clearly committed to careers in politics that maneuvering for the next higher post was part of their daily lives. This was easier for Coolidge because he was being eased upward by the inner group as soon as he got to the Vice-Presidency. He belonged to the Crane rather than the Lodge crowd in Massachusetts, and there was antagonism between them that caused him some anxiety; but he was lucky in this as in most else; Lodge was fading as a power in his state, and the Crane faction was growing. There was no trouble about his nomination in 1920.

For T. Roosevelt, everything came harder because the regulars disliked him and resented the popularity that forced them to accept him. He was too independent. They did not like the threat of change, perhaps of reform, that he represented, and they were skeptical of his promise to carry on McKinley's policies. He must have been discouraged by this Old Guard suspicion. Yet it is quite evident that every move he made after his appointment to the Assistant Secretaryship of the Navy in 1897 was calculated to further his ambition. It became obvious when he resigned his civilian post to organize the Rough Riders. From 1898 to 1901 was not a long wait; but it was a grueling one for the impatient Roosevelt. There were many humiliations to be accepted as the price of eventual success; but all of them were undergone without hesitation. These two are not the only ones who took the Vice-Presidency as the only way to the Presidency; L. B. Johnson was another; and all three gambles were winning ones.

As the Presidents come closer to us in time we are able to penetrate reserves about the onset of ambition with somewhat more assurance. Taft was reluctant until two years before his nomination; but Wilson had intimations of the climactic event at least seven years before his nomination in 1912 and definite ones, rising to expectation, by 1909.

From then his movements were steadily and ruthlessly focused—
something that surprised the bosses, who thought he was their creature
since he was their creation. They were resentful; but once he was a
Governor he knew how to proceed from there. Harding, we know,
was a reluctant dragon. He was as much aware of his own weakness as
Taft had been—although they were of a different kind—but he was
unable to resist being conscripted by a cynical group as Taft had been
by an aggressive predecessor. In 1920 the insiders knew the Republicans were certain to win, and they meant for once to select a really
pliant candidate.

Hoover's assault on the Presidency from the Department of Commerce was a steady siege of eight years. But even before his Cabinet
appointment he had been talked about by both Democrats and Republicans as a man of the proper stature, even as the ablest man of
suitable age in public life. The trouble was that no one knew his
political preference, if he had any. And he undoubtedly felt then, and
always, that he was above the political struggle. In a sense he was.
When he had served in both the Harding and Coolidge Cabinets he
was clearly a Republican, but still not one regarded by the party powers as one of themselves. His nomination in 1928 was a decision taken
as reluctantly as any they had made since Hayes had been called on to
make people forget the scandals of Grantism.

We know, about the second Roosevelt, that from a young man he
meant to emulate the first Roosevelt. His career had many disappoint-
ments, as when he found no way out of the Navy Department for
seven long years and ended by failing to match the military exploits
of his Rough Rider relative. Late in the war he did conceive a spectacular adventure with naval guns mounted on railway cars; he knew
well enough that in the political world military service would very
likely be a future condition of election to any office. But his superiors
were reluctant, and before he could invent another scheme the armistice was imminent. Then he was defeated with Cox in 1920 and had to
retire to private business. But worst of all there was the fearful mis-
chance of his polio attack and his subsequent crippling. His achievement in overcoming this—and every other—handicap was, as a political tour de force, superb. But he had luck, too, on occasion. The most
fortunate incident was his unexpected election to the New York Governorship in 1928 when so much else was lost to the Democrats. But
almost as lucky was the disaster of depression that enabled him to
advance his time schedule and replace Hoover four years earlier than
he had thought possible. He always had to be an opportunist; but that
he kept one steady purpose in mind there can be no doubt.

It seems fashionable to avoid mentioning Truman's maneuvers
through the years preceding his displacement of Henry Wallace as

Roosevelt's fourth-term Vice-President. But the way it was done—through a National Democratic Chairman out of the same Pendergast machine—is a giveaway. It requires extraordinary naïveté not to see the calculated intention of the big-city bosses and Truman's own part in being pushed at precisely the right moment.

We have seen that Eisenhower, from his first protestations of military dedication, rapidly came to regard himself as obligated to answer a call that took precedence over his commitment to stay out of politics. He presently found himself resigning from NATO and fighting as savagely as any ambitious politician for the nomination. He protested, of course, that it was a call to duty, undertaken to save the country. But anyway, the people wanted him, and at the end of four years they wanted more of him. He gave them the familiar safe feeling that heroes project.

Kennedy's successful attack was the result of the longest planning and the most competent management since F. D. Roosevelt. Like Roosevelt, Kennedy was an opportunist who managed to turn nearly every supposed handicap into an advantage. He meant to be President from his first campaign for office and he arrived there at the age F. D. Roosevelt had aimed at unsuccessfully. It was the most admirable exhibition of technique in the history of American ascents, not least because much of it was, in old terms, unorthodox.

Kennedy depended on a coldly contrived approach; he allowed no caprice to be followed; he accepted no challenges he did not see as contributory; he joined no cause that would prove unpopular; he kept company he must privately have been ashamed of; and he took fearful chances in using his father's fortune with the constant risk of having it said that he was buying his offices and would presently buy the highest one. He conciliated the Democratic bosses surviving after Eisenhower's regime but reinforced his standing with them by taking on his challengers in all available primaries; and, although he was young and there was reason to believe that he would follow a scheme that would be of advantage to himself and to no one else, the state leaders were so far committed when the convention met that he was nominated on the first ballot.

It is apparent that the myth of the office seeking the man describes very few of the Presidential approaches. Those of the Generals are most like the stereotype, but even all of them except Washington soon abandoned their military reserve and scrambled for the power disclosed to their astonished and eager eyes without much concern for abandoned principles.

No, the Presidency must be said to come most often to those who put aside all other interests and plot to achieve it. But it must be recalled how many have offered themselves and have undergone the ordeal to the fullest and in the end have failed. It did not come to Clay, to Seward, to Seymour, to Bryan, to Lowden, to Robert A. Taft, to Dewey, Kefauver, Stevenson or Nixon. And all, if we judge by their dedication and even by their workmanship, earned it as truly as their successful competitors.

The failures did not see or could not become identified with the dominant drift of events; they made a misstep; they were met by a suddenly stronger or less scrupulous opponent; they were badly financed; or they faltered in the final battles. Then there were those who lost within the party, as Seward did and Kefauver much later.

Sometimes their defeat at the polls is inexplicable, as was that of Nixon, who lost by so small a margin as to make the contest of 1960 practically even. It can only be imagined what agonies the loser must have suffered in recalling this incident or that in the campaign that may have cost the few votes by which he lost. Kennedy going on to dispose of the Presidential powers and he, his rival, forced into complete retirement! Such thoughts must have rankled in an exhausted mind almost beyond bearing. But as Nixon knew, this was a hazard he had risked. It had happened to others. He could, for instance, recall Tilden, who in 1876 had clearly won but still had been maneuvered out of his victory.

There may not be many eligibility rules, at least not many that genius cannot either meet or evade; but one thing is certain—only those who enter the Presidential race with the most exclusive concentration are likely to succeed. They will not survive contests with challengers more earnest and studious than themselves. And if they lose they are likely to lose everything, since no way has been found to make certain that the talents of the defeated will be used. These talents are very special. Only a few remarkable individuals have made themselves useful after defeat or in retirement. Stevenson is so unusual as to constitute a phenomenon. After two defeats his Ambassadorial services were the more valuable for his honorable but hopeless contests with Eisenhower.

Whig-Republicans and Democrats

O NE of the most carefully examined attitudes of a potential candidate is always the way he may use the power of the office. Party
chiefs want to know whether, if elected, he will set himself up as a
policy-maker, demanding legislative concurrence, and, if he does not
get it, use his hold on the electorate to force action, thus compelling,
or trying to compel, the Congress to follow his lead.

The Whigs and Republicans have always looked hard for candidates who will not develop notions of this sort. Their ideal candidate
is a passive one who will not advocate changes or push for them when
elected, who will accept advice and conform to party traditions. The
Democrats have claimed more often, and with more reason, to be a
people's party rather than one run by and for an elite. It has therefore
more often sponsored reform movements and welfare programs. It has
also been more insistent on business regulation and less sympathetic to
financial interests.

It has always had a wing with the same preference for Presidential
weakness and a strong leaning to states' rights; but in crises this
element has accepted reformist leaders often enough to give it a fairly
held reputation as defender of the poor and sustainer of the weak.

This difference is an old one. When the Constitution was being
formulated, the British Ministerial system, giving the legislature the
upper hand, was just coming into operation. It reduced the Executive
to an arm of the Parliament. But such Americans as John Adams, accepting the reasoning of Locke and Montesquieu, believed in separated
and interdependent powers. This required an Executive owing his
powers to the electorate, not to the legislative branch. One of the most
persistent arguments at the convention involved this issue. Again and
again, the viewpoint of those who would have gone the British way
was put forward. Such members as Sherman, Pinckney, Rutledge, and
Randolph were for it; and the convention voted five times to make the
Executive thus subordinate to the legislature before it finally decided
to make him independent.

If either the Virginia or New Jersey plans, introduced at the outset, had been adopted, the Republic would have had what amounted to Parliamentary government. But in the end those who believed that an independent, even a strong, Executive was needed prevailed. The President became responsible not to the Congress but to the people, even if indirectly (through the Electoral College).

Those who prevailed in that argument were more afraid of legislative tyranny than of a powerful Executive. They had watched occurrences in Britain, and they felt—or the more influential did—that the reaction from monarchical dictatorship had gone much too far. Parliament needed checking even more than the King. Then, closer at home, as Madison had said, speaking of the state governments, the legislature was everywhere expanding its sphere of activity "and drawing all power into its impetuous vortex."[1]

The most influential Framers were, in fact, Federalists. They had found the legislatures of the states unsatisfactory to "the commercial, financial, and planting interest of the tidewater."[2] This was because such assemblies were "popular" organs and responded to demands of the "mob." The "perils of democracy" were often talked about; and it was intended that the Federal government should be able to avert them. The model for the Presidency was found in certain of the state constitutions where it seemed to the Framers that these dangers were least in evidence—principally Massachusetts and New York. The New York constitution, especially, gave the Governor wider powers than had been customary in the reaction from colonial executives. This example seemed to the Federalists well suited to the structure they had in mind.

So there began a subterranean struggle, for a long time not too clearly recognized for what it was, even by those who were engaged in it. And it was even less understood by the electorate in general. It has continued ever since.

But a strange reversal took place. The Federalist determination to have a strong Executive because the colonial legislatures had a tinge of demagogy was gradually seen by them to be mistaken. The select few, the prosperous citizens, who believed they ought to manage gov-

---

[1] *The Federalist*, No. 48.

[2] This whole matter is discussed in W. E. Binkley's *President and Congress* (New York, 1947). No one has better understood the conflict fixed in our Constitution between the governmental branches than he, although this book discusses only that between the legislature and the Executive. See also *The Deadlock of Democracy* by J. McG. Burns (New York, 1963); and *Congressional Control of Administration* by J. P. Harris (Brookings Institution, 1964). There is an extensive literature provoked by Charles A. Beard's contention that the Constitution was shaped to protect the economic interests of its Framers. It belongs mostly, however, to a former generation. The economic interpretation is generally accepted now as one influence among many diverse ones.

ernment as well as commerce and the professions, began to find that the President was hard to control. He owed his position to nationwide support, often arising out of protests or demands for change. These sweeping movements were at times almost irresistible, and their leaders, by the time they had become candidates for the Presidency, were so committed that nothing could be done to check them. In these circumstances, the elite found their only recourse in managing the selection of candidates; and they were willing to do it by almost any means. This might result only in heading off the worst "demagogues" and the selection of only half-satisfactory men; but it also might result in the successful search for passive characters who, when in office, would conserve the status quo. If one could be found who was something of a demagogue himself and could persuade the public this was in the general interest, this was ideal. Not many Grants and Hardings have been found. Often the Republicans have had candidates they could not trust. But they never stop looking.

Since this reversal of party yearnings, completed in Jefferson's time, legislatures have been easier to control than the Executive. And the Democrats have become more a Presidential than a Congressional party.

This, for a long time, had part of its reason in the election of United States Senators by the legislatures of the states (changed to popular election by constitutional amendment in 1913). These bodies for many reasons had become notoriously susceptible to influence and were in numerous instances even corrupt. But it was also true that the Federal House of Representatives was normally more conservative and amenable to management by the elite than was the President. Election every two years, the need of Representatives for keeping up a home machine while they were away in Washington, and concern with projects of local interest made it natural—almost necessary—for them to differ from Presidents who had in mind the interests of a national constituency. These so often ran counter to the demands of Congressmen's supporters at home that an unremitting hostility existed from the first.

The division of the parties into what eventually became Democratic and Republican (confused by the earlier nomenclature of Democratic-Republican and Whig) had this background. The Democrats—Jackson being the founder and shaper—had as their tenet that the Executive should be a man with a program, who led, who enhanced the Presidential powers and kept the Congress from encroaching on his prerogatives. The Republicans developed the theory of Congressional government. Their feeling that if power was diffused it could not be brought to bear on powerful private interests with such effect as was possible if it was concentrated in an Executive tended to grow. Therefore the Congress must oppose the President's initiatives and attenuate his powers.

Much of the Republican party's history is to be understood as a double effort to build up the legislative branch and to restrain the enlargement of the executive branch. A perfect President ought to begin his term by announcing that it was the duty of the Congress to make the laws and that of the President to execute them.

This was the way Grant began, and it was the way he went on. Hayes had the same theory; but he had a puritan conscience and he would not condone corruption or even extreme amicism. He resisted Congressional encroachments, so notorious during the Grant regime. Garfield, however, retreated from Hayes's position; he was no crusader even for political righteousness and was giving way to Congressional control of the executive establishment when he was assassinated. It remains to be said that Arthur, Harrison, and McKinley carried on the Republican tradition except in a few isolated instances. And so, of course, did Eisenhower.

Democrats could hardly brag about the pre-Civil War doughfaces; but, apart from Davis in 1924, most of their modern candidates had been genuine leaders. Bryan, Wilson, Smith, F. D. Roosevelt, Kennedy and Johnson—all, in their own way, were enlargers of the Presidency.

On Taking Positions

T HE DIFFERENCE just referred to has an important bearing on the division of authority between the Congress and the President, but almost as important a one on the spheres of the Federal and state governments. In every generation ambitious men have taken positions about Presidential or Congressional supremacy and states' rights in the hope of furthering their careers. Sometimes the assuming of an attitude has proved to be useful, sometimes not. Actually we are able to conclude no more than that the evidence is confusing. Jackson was a unionist, and so was Lincoln. Even the Civil War did not fix Federal-state relations. The states were not allowed to secede; but the extent of their powers continued to be argued in campaigns as well as in the courts.

When Eisenhower said in 1952 that if he was elected he would see to it that the long nose of the Federal government was kept out of the states' business, he may merely have been reading a speech written for him by the Republican publicity office. It is doubtful whether he knew what ghosts he called up from the past. But whoever approved the address must have been certain that such an appeal would attract votes.

Choices on such perennial issues are avoided when avoidance is possible, but sometimes they have to be made; and candidates have to estimate public reaction. Eisenhower was certain that states' rights still had appeal. His successor as Republican candidate, Nixon, was not so sure. But Kennedy the Democrat was not sure either. Neither had made any very definite statements in the past; both had tried, throughout longish careers, to remain silent except on safe issues. As a kind of substitute they presented themselves as vigorous, sane, and able—but conservative—young statesmen, capable of taking over from Eisenhower. They succeeded so well in this that the electorate could hardly make a choice. Kennedy presumably was thought just a little safer and saner.

But in spite of the Kennedy-Nixon equivocation, it may be said that even a determination to be forthright or to dodge is one to be arrived at only by studying the circumstances of particular times and places. Lincoln was finally forthright after years of evasion; others have not been.

No previous experience, remote or contemporary, is really irrelevant. This conclusion is reinforced by simply recalling that even though new issues have arisen and been added to the old ones, those old ones may still be very much alive and may cause division. Washington was chosen as a fatherly figure in 1789; so was Eisenhower in 1952. Neither wittingly made any commitment concerning policies other than those considered to be the policies of a majority. Eisenhower felt safe to uphold states' rights; and Washington supposed that after the Revolution and the Constitutional Convention everyone agreed on union.

When we say that both these Presidents were chosen because they stood in a father relationship to a people tired from years of strain and strife and longing for peace and security, it is undoubtedly true. But it is impossible to conceive of Washington favoring Virginia interests over those of the Union. That Eisenhower, however vague, could be elected when he proclaimed such a principle shows, perhaps, how much more the citizens of 1952 needed refuge from fears than those of 1789; either that or fear of Federal power must have infected a wider public than seems possible. Business interests had been trying to propagate it for several generations; but rescue from the depression by the use of Federal powers could not have been forgotten. Perhaps states' rights had finally been equated with liberty as its proponents wished; it may even be that Eisenhower believed that it was so.

It could be argued that the manner of election in 1789, contrasted with that of 1952, made the difference. If the men of 1789 seem heroic compared with their descendants, it does have to be recalled that early Presidential electors really were expected to exercise their judgments and that those of a later day are not. It was a very few of the better citizens who selected Washington; but more than thirty million voters cast ballots for Eisenhower. There was no demagoguery in the first two choices. Speciousness, irresponsibility, cynical deception, and promises meant to be broken came to be common only later.

If we follow the Eisenhower case it is quite clear that he was mistaken to advocate states' rights. He tried repeatedly to reduce Federal responsibilities, but the Governors he appealed to saw the implications and appeared not to hear his offers. It was the kindest way to rebuff his attempts to give away his powers.

This does not mean that it was a poor plea for campaign purposes. It may or may not have helped elect him; certainly, however, it did not *prevent* his election. It is something to be argued about—an interesting illustration of choice. But future candidates will find in it only the warning that they had better avoid such commitments unless they are heroes and sure of election anyway.[1] Goldwater, in 1964, had no such reticence. He however presented himself in the contradictory role of belligerent withdrawer. The voters very distinctly did not approve; but then, of course, he and his supporters did not approve of *them*.

---

[1] The particular subject Eisenhower made his commitment on was later made the subject of inquiry by a subcommittee of the Senate Government Operations Committee in the early sixties. The results of an elaborate questionnaire sent to local officials of many grades, and some academicians, showed about what would have been expected—that a large middle group accepted present arrangements without much difficulty. A few took the extreme states'-rights position; they amounted to 11 per cent, which would seem to indicate that Eisenhower's speech writer spoke for no more than a small hopeful minority. The general public was indifferent, not indignant. The other extreme—consistent nationalism—commanded, again, only 13 per cent.

The importance of this is its underlining of the danger a candidate runs in taking an extreme position. His best policy is to find the center and stay there on all general issues. Senator Muskie of Maine, chairman of the subcommittee, wrote about the results of the questionnaire in *Saturday Review*, April 18, 1964, 18.

Politics and Ethics

OBSERVING THE BEHAVIOR of politicians often leads to the conclusion that the gaining of office must seem to them to justify any means used to win. It is true that, going about their occupation, they resort to devices abhorrent by the standards of decent individuals. But it must be pointed out that they too profess these same standards and probably, as individuals, conform to them. When they depart from them in politics they are perfectly well aware of the discrepancy. They speak of this conduct as practical, thus setting up a category of behavior measured entirely by its results for them and separated from its results as measured by the code. They imply that they would prefer to behave differently but that circumstances make it impossible.

The virtue attributed by Lincoln Steffens to the bosses he had studied so long was that they recognized their sins. They did not defend them; but they made no pretense that they were being good, simply saying that they did what they had to do to win or to keep their power. Most such bosses did not run for office; they managed others who did. They themselves did not have to make public appearances, and so made no pretense of leadership. Such individuals, staying strictly in the background, need make no secret of the methods they used; but they made no display of their successes either. Steffens thought them more amoral than immoral.

Candidates belong in an ethically lower category than the bosses, said Steffens. They make a show of having no part in the deals and swaps in which the public interest is sacrificed to private ones. But they allow these things to be done for them by the boss and pretend not to know what is going on. The higher they rise in the hierarchy, the more pretense of detachment they make. Finally, they become "statesmen" and not politicians at all.

By this standard a President, because he has risen to the very top, must be the worst hypocrite of all. As a candidate he has presented himself to the electorate in ideal terms; he was sought by the office instead of seeking it; he is free of obligations and can therefore pursue

public aims with detachment; he is controlled by no interests, only by
the desire to be of service. Actually, as we know well enough, he is
almost always a man who has wanted desperately to be President. And
very likely he has had supporters who have contracted obligations to
be discharged when office has been won, and promised favors no
private individual ought to have.

To complicate the moral matter, it has to be recalled that there have
been Presidents who were not politicians in the professional sense at
all. Some, like Harrison, Taylor, and Eisenhower, have been genuine
innocents. They may have been astounded to be mentioned for the
Presidency only a short time before having been nominated. Often,
too, they have not had to make any extensive promises. The bosses
who adopted them relied on their continued innocence. Their role
was to be a complaisant and passive one.

Voters know something about bosses and suspect a good deal more,
wherefore they tend to think their occupation demeaning. The good
citizen prefers to consider that his President has not been contaminated.
He likes to overlook the nature of the office and not to be reminded
that its occupant becomes, ex officio, Chief of Party as well as Chief
of State; or to recognize that to meet his obligations to the nation a
President must accept those of the political organization he must work
through. As President he will become, even if he never has been one
before, and however reluctant he may be, a politician.

That this reaction of the electorate is often catered to is a kind of
confirmation that there are standards even if they are recognized more
by being departed from than by being honored. It is never denied that
the ideal is one of public service. Even the worst offenders would like
to shape their conduct by a code they know about and honor; and to
the extent that they can, they probably do. Their lapses are so frequent and so flagrant that they are not credited with such perceptions;
but these very violations define what should not be done, and so, per
contra, what decent practitioners should be concerned to do.

Steffens was very pleased at discovering this hidden virtue in the
subjects of his study. But it hardly seems to compensate for the harm
done by individuals who, even if they are not hypocritical, still use
the powers they control to exploit the public.

It is possible to rise without compromise of a demeaning sort, and
without accepting support that must be repaid with public favors; but
it has not often been done. The heroes were in a position to do it. But
what shall be said of Grant, who presided over the most scandalous
of all administrations; or Eisenhower, who was defiantly agreeable to
all those who had reason to soften Federal control of their affairs?

And there is the case of Lincoln, who instructed his promoters at

the convention to make no promises, but when the time came met a
long list of them with some of the most odoriferous consents imagin-
able. Even his Cabinet had soon to be cleansed so that he could go on
with the nation's business. The appointments and favors had been a
condition of his nomination.

The Evolution of Instruments

THE INVENTION AND SPREAD of devices appropriate to universal suffrage, well begun by the time of Jackson and Van Buren, made a change from earlier years that amounted almost to revolution. As restrictions on suffrage were removed and there was a much larger number of voters to be reached, devices for mass appeal had to be invented. This was not easy in the then state of communication. Later campaigners, who had first the railroad, then the telegraph, then the telephone to use and, still later, radio and television, could appeal to audiences of millions rather than dozens, hundreds, and thousands.

Jefferson, in his war on the Federalists, was confined to partisan pamphleteers, small argumentative newssheets, correspondence chains, and the oratory of followers before small audiences. Mails were slow, newspaper circulation limited, and party organization correspondingly loose. The Federalists could use the same facilities, but they found it hard to give up the idea that the elite ought to rule. This may have seemed to them self-evident, but it was not something the untrained and unprivileged were likely to admit. And the Jeffersonians' appeals to equality were enormously effective even though they had to be made by clumsy means. Besides, the number of Federalists tended to diminish in proportion to the whole. This was the inevitable result of a widening suffrage. Jefferson probably seems to have been a better politician than he was.

The position of the elite was inherently precarious as soon as those who were neither wellborn nor prosperous were admitted to the suffrage. And the general tactic of the Democratic-Republicans and their Democratic successors was simply to gather in the newly franchised by mass methods. The Whigs, and later the Republicans, were at first baffled. They gradually shifted from the Federalist claim of privilege to mass campaigns on their own. They were able to bear down heavily on the Democratic tendency to corrupt the government and fall into inefficient ways; but their really tremendous discovery was the father-figure, usually a General hero, who would promise the voters rest from disturbances and tensions, and who, with the use of the funds always available to them, could be made even more a hero than he was.

The contributions of Jackson and Van Buren were the convention to replace the Congressional caucus, the recognition of local machines for the maintenance of party strength, and the systemization of spoils. Party organization could not take hard and permanent form until these devices were available. The later Jeffersonians had succeeded each other in orderly fashion and conducted the government in seemly ways. The Jacksonians brought disorder into politics as well as into government, so that even Van Buren, who was co-organizer of the new devices, could not gain re-election with their use. He was a machine technician, but either more was demanded or his opponents had also mastered the technique; and he was beaten at his own game.

The Civil War, so disastrous for the nation, was a gift of fortune for the Republicans. The inner group—the Radicals and their successors—relied on secession for fifty years, first to keep states of the South from participating in elections, and then, when they were finally readmitted, to maintain the reputation of Democrats as disunionists, tending to subversion.

The careers of successful contenders for the Presidency were shaped to the requirements set by these party policies. They were Generals, carefully selected and conditioned to the support of business expansion. Down to the thirties of the twentieth century, when the Civil War had finally faded into the past, the same reputation for respectability and faithfulness to old institutions was carefully cultivated. The free enterprise of the expansionist century became an item of faith, and departure from it was an abandonment of "the American way." Justice Holmes might protest that laissez-faire was not a tenet of the Constitution; but, even as he protested, it was being written into a consistent body of laws. It was, indeed, the dominant orthodoxy. So much so that the Democrats found themselves competing. The Republicans, they said, were for *big* business; they—the Democrats—were the defenders of small business. This was a later version of Jacksonian equalitarianism; and it was often effective. It held its appeal even through the Great Depression and Roosevelt's reforms.

That depression changed the qualifications for the Presidency very little. Roosevelt's long incumbency ran on into a quite different period —that of another world war. And following it the usual reversion to tiredness and disillusion gave the Republicans another chance to elect a General in the pattern of Taylor, Harrison, and Grant.

The form was continuing; the problem of the aspirants and of the political managers was much the same as it had been since Jackson's time.

Finding a Leader

THERE is another persistent pattern to be found among the complexities and confusions of political choice. And this too may be of some use to the hopeful individual and to the student. The joining of vast movements and working up to their leadership account for the success—in very large part—of those Presidents looked back on with most admiration. They seem to have been carried into power on an irresistible wave. These are the strong ones: Washington, Jefferson, Jackson, Polk, the Roosevelts, and Wilson. Each of these became more than a man, more than a President—the representative, almost the embodiment, of something larger than himself, something in the national mind and spirit, moving out of deep places and taking shape, slowly, usually, but inevitably. Such movements create heroes as wars do. They also create opponents who may delay but cannot stop what is happening.

They are easily enough identified afterward. They have been successively these: independence, equality, expansion, union, industrial growth, social security, opposition to aggressors, and organization for peace. Each of these had its phase and its hero, a man who saw what the drift was, who joined it early and rode its ninth wave into power. It does not need to be said that some of these have not yet been completed.

There is a complacent attitude, based on the dangerous conception that when crises arise and wise leaders are desperately needed, they appear; and it is all too prevalent. Like drunken men who are supposed to be the special protégés of Providence, it is assumed that the nation is inevitably destined to survive and even to prosper. This attitude has actually influenced several sorts of policies. William Jennings Bryan, for instance, used to speak of a nation "springing to arms," which excused the failure to provide a professional corps of military men. And in all our wars, even both World Wars, preparation was delayed on these very grounds. So with effective Commanders in Chief. They would materialize out of nowhere if things got bad enough.

563

In the World Wars there were bold and energetic Presidents to combat lethargy and to demand and fight for adequate appropriations. But the second Roosevelt, until crisis was upon the nation, felt it necessary to speak of "defense" and never to mention war. In the campaign of 1940, with conflict to follow in 1941, he made an impassioned speech in Boston affirming that American boys would never be sent to fight abroad.

This was recognition of a democratic dogma, respected even in so late a time. Defense did excuse a more adequate build-up than had been achieved twenty years earlier by Wilson. But 1942 was nevertheless a national shambles when war was actually entered on. Only a now-lost isolation preserved the nation while preparations went on.

It had been the same in World War I, and before that in the Spanish-American War. Because of unreadiness, more soldiers died of disease and neglect than were killed by the Spaniards.

President McKinley had not wanted that war and had not got ready for it. The "springing to arms" in 1898 had needlessly cost many lives. And the Civil War had been even worse. Its approach was presided over by doughfaces—Buchanan and his official family. Important posts in the Cabinet were occupied by plotting secessionists, calls for volunteers confused the Generals, and recruitment and training were left to the Governors of the states. Lincoln began with very little, and more was slow in coming. The War Department had been sabotaged by Jefferson Davis, and many officers who preferred their state affiliations to the defense of the Union were disloyal long before they defected. If Providence provided Buchanan in the nation's crisis, a better arrangement could have been made.

These strictures can be substantiated by incidents in every generation, some serious, some not so crucial. The democracy, given time, always rallied. The rallying was not prompt enough, however, to warrant the reliance placed by Bryan and others like him on special guardianship; and technological advance has tended to cut down the time allowed for debate, decision, and preparation. The national security soon became a matter of constant readiness. The recurrent spells of weariness, of isolationism, of withdrawal from the responsibilities of power—all these became inadmissible. A letdown of this sort could invite destruction.

It became the task of Presidents to keep the electorate sensitive to the need for ready power to support national policy. It was no job to be left to a Providence that might have a special feeling for America but might, on the other hand, just possibly be indifferent. It was a task for the ablest of leaders, seized of responsibility, intelligent, wise, and vigorous. The processes we have been discussing that lift men to the Presidency have not been revised to meet the fact of constant danger.

If it is true at all that crises provide the opportunity for leadership, this is the ninth wave for the next strong leader in the nation's history. Independence is identified with Washington; equality with Jackson; expansion with Polk; Union with Lincoln; industrial growth with Theodore Roosevelt; the abolition of poverty and the provision of social security with the second Roosevelt. That last Roosevelt was ambitious also to give the nation the organization for peace Wilson had failed to provide; but he died as it was coming into being. And when it did appear it was concurrently checked by a new imperialist threat. The Soviets were equipped with all the devices of subversion and with genocidal weapons to back them up.

This is an example. It has been the same with other national desires. There is a weakness for thinking them on the way to accomplishment when actually the leader who advocated them has been more frustrated than successful. The work that he begins is apt to remain incomplete. His successors falter, or the opposition convinces the electorate that the time for reforms is past, that relaxation is safe.

It was so with the issues at the center of the Civil War crisis. The South, even though defeated, was not reconciled to emancipation or to the principle of Union. An amendment to the Constitution guaranteeing Negro rights went for generations without implementation. And states' rights are still loudly proclaimed in the South. Expansionism took an imperialist road, and the borders of the Union were fixed short of their natural limits. Polk's great work was limited by the quarrel about the extension of slavery.

The organization of peace, whose establishment was the purpose of two vast wars and immense convulsions of effort, was attenuated and defeated by a turn after both wars to selfishness and withdrawal.

Social security and the abolition of poverty, so deep a desire in people's minds and, moreover, so essential to the working of a technological economy, was half completed in Roosevelt's time because old conceptions were successfully appealed to. After Roosevelt there came Eisenhower. There is a weakness for Eisenhowers after Roosevelts. And after eight years Kennedy had to begin again.

But the desires not gratified, or institutions embodying them not securely established, leaves successive leaders not only with new demands to gratify but with the old ones to defend or to complete.

So the competence of a President has had to expand if he is to succeed. And the qualifications he must possess have grown more complex and demanding.

If the best way to the White House is the sensing of vast desires surging through the electorate, and if our listing of them and of the leaders who became their embodiments is at all valid, then we are entitled to a conclusion. The next great President will be one who can

sustain his offer to give the nation security from the instant annihila-
tion it has been threatened with for a generation. And if, besides, he
shows promise of being able to muster the productive facilities we already possess to eliminate slums, hunger, and civil disorder, he will be
welcomed as Washington was, or Jackson, or Roosevelt.

The question, a haunting one, is whether our democratic procedures
can conceivably find and advance him to the place he must occupy if
he is to succeed, giving him preference over a Buchanan, a McKinley,
or an Eisenhower.

In the campaign of 1964, L. B. Johnson gave no sign of interest in
governmental reform. He did speak of further progress, and even of a
Great Society, but it remained to be bodied forth.

Toward Better Candidates

THE NEXT PRESIDENT is never more than eight years from the White House, and most of the time he is closer. It is a measure of human incapacity that although he is in plain sight he cannot be identified. He must indeed be highly visible because he is already at least thirty-five years old and rapidly advancing in public life. If he is forty or more he is probably the Governor of a populous state or, less probably, a member of the United States Senate. He has often appeared on television before a nationwide audience. And anyone watching and listening can tell by the signs we have outlined here that he has hopes or even expectations. And all those who may vote have had a chance to develop some sort of judgment about his qualifications and his appeal.

It is true that there are rivals, both in his own party and in the other; and all may seem to have so nearly the same characteristics that it may be difficult to choose among them. Voters will mostly maintain a reserved judgment when the distinctions are not clear. They did this when Kennedy and Nixon were matched; and in most modern elections the results are very close. When national elections are nearly always won by a majority of a few per cent, and often by a much smaller one, the delayed decisions of a few voters may be determinative. Even by the most advanced methods, poll-takers cannot predict what will happen in the voting booths.

Besides, who can say whether attractive figures of today will not have disappeared before the final heat of the race is run? They, like all of us, are vulnerable and mortal. There are many hazards.

It is one of the advantages of democracy that there may be several eligibles, perhaps many. The next President in a democracy does not have to be someone's heir and will not be designated by a dictator. True, he may be chosen by a group of insiders with interests of their own in mind; but this is a problem that can be solved.

The best way to solve it is to make sure that the way is open for those who have the needed qualifications and is closed to those who

567

do not have them. There will then always be competent candidates to choose among.

If this goes—as it does—to the improvement of all the processes of our society, our liberties, our fair-sharing, our education, our equal opportunity, we surely know by now that democracy is not conferred automatically on a people but has to be worked for and protected.

A better society will produce better leaders, and better leaders will accelerate the improvement. We have doubtless entered that spiral; but it is surely allowable to observe that as yet we are not far enough along in its evolution to ensure even the nation's safety, to say nothing of its citizens' well-being.

New Questions, New Techniques

THE CAMPAIGN of 1964 re-emphasized technical conditions the professionals had been trying to ignore—and certainly had not taken into account—for a quarter of a century. McKinley's campaign might have given a clue—his front porch technique was a serious accommodation to changes then visibly beginning; but almost at once Theodore Roosevelt, following his own bent, had begun to rampage up and down the country in the manner of Bryan rather than of his staid predecessor in the Presidency; and after this no candidate returned to the low-keyed appeal. The developing facilities for travel and addressing crowds proved more attractive than those for remote communication—the press conference, the radio, television. Candidates behaved as though they were running for local office—more demagogues than statesmen.

This seems somewhat strange to one who reviews the whole tradition of American campaigns. Washington, Jefferson and Lincoln were retiring candidates. They would have judged Roosevelt and Bryan shockingly undignified, and the way Johnson and Goldwater reduced the whole country to county size in their jet planes, speaking half a dozen times a day, would have dismayed them.

Some few candidates since 1904 had shown reluctance to bloviate so endlessly. Not many can have preferred simulating heartiness early and late and returning to base with ruined digestions, bruised hands and depleted energy; but none had the courage to refuse. Even Harding, F. D. Roosevelt and Eisenhower, who from the time of their nomination were obviously destined to win, had lacked the resolution to stop. It is true that F. D. Roosevelt did not want to stop; barnstorming was the Roosevelt family political style; besides, he had to show that lifeless legs had not reduced his vigor. Harding loved to spout, even if not the material prepared by his ghost writers; but his performance was so out of character that he must have lost rather than gained votes on the road. Eisenhower, even if he can hardly have fancied himself as an orator, was so inexperienced that he could not set himself against the professionals. For whatever reason, the Bryan-Roosevelt method

569

substituted itself for the older custom, and it became a settled but unexamined assumption that merciless exploitation of the candidate served some purpose.

Nineteen sixty-four, however, showed this to be a fallacy, and showed it so plainly that even the professionals were forced to recognize the facts they had been avoiding. There had been, it is true, three campaigns since 1900 which had seemed likely to be, and had turned out to be, close enough to have been determined by frantic appeals of the sort whipped up every four years by stables of public relations advisers, dozens of speech writers, and hordes of small politicians anxious to prove their worthiness. The close decisions—the exceptions —were the Wilson-Hughes (1916), the Truman-Dewey (1948) and the Kennedy-Nixon (1960) contests; and even in these it was arguable that the result might have been the same if both candidates had been put under wraps by agreement and had refused to make themselves ridiculous.

The Wilson-Hughes contest was always close, and neither man had any considerable advantage, nor was Wilson's victory easily explained. What won for Truman, it was said, was his last minute whistle-stop tour; but it was much more likely that the competition given him by Wallace, the third-party candidate, had forced him to take positions more acceptable to Midwest progressives. It was also said that what gave Kennedy his infinitesimal advantage over Nixon was probably his more attractive appearance in televised debating, introduced for the first time in that campaign. But even so the conclusion to be drawn from this had to be that restrained high-level debate was more effective than indiscriminate mud slinging.

The lesson of 1964 ought to have been learned in the earlier Eisenhower-Stevenson contests. The voting would have been almost exactly the same at the beginning as at the end of the campaigns, and no conceivable tactics could have changed the result. Why had the supposedly hard-headed professionals not been convinced?[1]

It is hard for a politician to admit, even if his reason is at work, that actual physical appearance in public, what he calls "contact with the people"—although a political meeting cannot honestly be called that —is not indispensable. Standing his candidate before a crowd that stamps and cheers and claps, he forgets that it is a wholly contrived performance, and that no one there remains to be convinced. But, of course, such affairs have gradually become charades to amuse or convince the voters who see them on television, and the audiences are

---

[1] Especially since the rule had first been articulated by James A. Farley who was the manager of two F. D. Roosevelt campaigns. So thoughtful a commentator as Richard Rovere had by now taken to calling it "Farley's Law." *The New Yorker*, Nov. 14, 1964, 241.

really part of the act. He also tends to forget that in such circumstances the chance of making some mistake—of words or manner—is as considerable as the chance of making a winning appeal; votes are as likely to be lost as won. The candidate's judgment is impaired by exhaustion; he is constrained to keep exactly to a manuscript he did not write and may barely have scanned; and if he does that, his personality is muffled; he is bound to be dull and repetitive; and if, in desperation, he *ad libs*, his ignorance is almost certain to be embarrassingly evident. If he were exposed only to the crowd before him, this would not be important; but since he is speaking, actually, to millions of voters sitting before their television screens at ease—and therefore at their most critical— it may be disastrous. It would be better to have him address them from some retired place away from the distractions of travel.

These unfortunate circumstances, being the same for both candidates, are presumably as difficult for one as the other. But this is not actually so. The one who is least exhausted by his schedule will appear freshest and most vigorous; the one who has tamed his speech writers will be most appealing; and if thoughtful artifice is called for, there is more chance of contriving it in seclusion than off-stage before a meeting. It is hard to admit that the cheers and tumult are useless for the main purpose; and it must be noted that their tyranny has tended to grow rather than to diminish.

Furthermore, politicians are not usually of a statistical turn of mind and this leads them to distrust the forecasts of poll-takers outfitted with an apparatus that has only gradually lost its mystery. A local leader, an editor, or a knowledgeable friend who says that Kansas or Illinois will go one way or the others seems to them more trustworthy than any scientific sampling extrapolated into a prediction. Only one election in the campaigns since poll taking had begun had really gone differently than anticipated. And this had been seized on and used as an example of poll-takers' fallibility with a persistence that in itself was betraying. Truman defeated Dewey in 1948 when the forecasts had made it seem unlikely. But actually what had been indicated was that Dewey had been ahead *when they were taken*. What accounted for the surprise was that a shift was going on; and by election day it had changed the percentages. The polls were not wrong; they had been wrongly interpreted.

Even if campaigns did affect election results, more careful watching of trends in repeated samplings had removed about 99 per cent of the uncertainty. Weeks before any election it could be told what the result would be. If it was a "squeaker" (in political talk), then frantic activity in the most profitable territories was indicated; this explains the Kennedy-Nixon bout, but not most of the others. What motivated the candidates in 1964? There was never any doubt that Goldwater was due to be rejected by an enormous outpouring of votes. Since Johnson was aware of this—he was known to carry around in his pockets the latest figures and to study them daily—why did he undertake the most strenuous campaign known to the history of elections? Not only did he not mean to engage Goldwater in debate, but his strategy was a deliberately and properly above-the-battle one. He was the Protector, Goldwater the revolutionary Pretender. He might have been expected, therefore, to stay serenely in the White House, the trustworthy custodian of power, rather than to make daily sorties to the far ends of the nation, blurring the image of reserve and dignity he meant to project. The explanation is that he accepted the now established custom of the profession. This custom had now become something more than a belief in conversion; it was a party duty fastened on the candidate.

All the Democratic Congressmen, one-third of the Senators, and numerous state and local officials were hanging onto his coattails. That he was certain to be elected made those coattails much more attractive. It was his duty to appear in every doubtful state and district, an arm thrown about the candidates, making their fortunes part of his own. He was not so much running for the Presidency as helping others gain lesser offices. There was more than this in the particular Johnson case. In 1960 he had been rejected by these same politicians who now, in 1964, begged his favor. A man from Texas had accomplished the impossible. When he had accepted the Vice-Presidential nomination, he had been written off by the professionals; he had reached the end of his progress; Kennedy's eight years would carry him beyond the favored age. Accident, however, had given him the opportunity to show these doubters what stuff he was made of. He had been a success in office and he was about to win it on his own. Indeed he was rolling toward a consensus unknown since Monroe's Era of Good Feelings. It was no time to stay in Washington; rather it was one to lead the triumph in full view of the voters—and of the doubters. Whether it was good strategy, he apparently did not ask.

If that accounts for Johnson, there remains Goldwater: why did he go on with it? Moreover, why did he compound his coming defeat by resorting to dubious means? Desperation was suggested. But could he have believed that the inflation of a few scandalous incidents, ones not certainly attachable to Johnson himself, would stem the avalanche so clearly and repeatedly predicted?

It may be that Alfred Landon, in 1936, felt that Roosevelt's defeat was possible if he worked hard enough; those closest to him said that he did; but there were not such clear indications available in 1936. With all the indicators agreeing, Goldwater cannot have thought, at any time, that he had any possibility of being elected. Yet he wallowed in the dirtiest campaign in generations. It was comprehensible only as something other than an election campaign.

And indeed for both Johnson and Goldwater the contest was something transcending an election. For Johnson it was a vindication; for Goldwater it was a crusade. This last is a syndrome developed in amateur minds. Even in what seems afterward to be comic circumstances, the escalation of a political campaign to the level of a crusade is quite possible. The unready contender who is trying to see himself as an appointed leader must have some such justification. Even if the conviction has arisen from the most cynical of sources—if he is being encouraged in it by a professional group intending only to use him—simpleminded men have a weakness for this sort of flattery. Goldwater's reactionary sponsors had found the Republican convention easy to capture. The election was something more difficult. But they either had a conviction of rightness approaching the fanatic, or they seemed to have it. Goldwater, being an innocent in a society that was bafflingly complex, allying himself with the fierce fighters of the right, lost all sense of reality—and all sense of the situation if he should be defeated. When it was over, he was again a private citizen, but one who never again would have any claim to political respectability. Arizonans might again elect him to office, but he would have a hard time regaining admission to senatorial society, easy as that admission admittedly is. Young men ought to be warned by his disgrace.

The lessons of the last generation were so obviously underlined by the campaign of 1964 that changes were quite confidently predicted after the election. Campaigns would be shortened—in the last ones the public had been bored; and in 1964 only a little more than 60 per cent of those qualified cared enough to vote. They would be conducted differently—candidates would use television as it is capable of being used, and would allow its full potential scope. Also campaign managers would be guided by the probabilities, neither ignoring them nor allowing them a domination they ought not to have. The polls would become respectable.

The consensus Johnson was drawing together was so massive that it was said by experienced oldsters that it could only be broken up in years to come by some external event—perhaps a failure to secure the nation's safety or a serious depression. But there would not be another challenge from the dark caves of reaction. Americans were coming out into the cooperative sun Roosevelt had promised them; they had no intention of retreating again to rugged individualism. If this was true, the challenger of the future was likely to have a hard time indeed. If still more prosperity and a still safer peace were wanted, why should any Republican be trusted to attain the goals so vehemently repudiated by the party and its candidates?

Any aspiring young person must clearly try to revise the party's promises and trust that what Willkie, Dewey and Nixon had so nearly won by saying, he could some day win by repeating. This was that the gains of past years were not Democratic monopolies, that Republicans had shared in making them and could be trusted to administer them better than the Democrats. This was, of course, the "me-tooism" ridiculed by Goldwater Republicans; but if the party was condemned to this confinement it was the fault of its own leaders.

As for any young and aspiring Democrat, he ought just as clearly to join enthusiastically in shaping the Great Society that was now his party's official aspiration. Such a contribution would very likely be his best claim to future preferment. He naturally ought to master the latest techniques, but techniques will not substitute—or not very often—for leadership. The Kennedy sort of tour de force with no end in view except the getting of power very rarely succeeds. There are always movements going on; becoming part of one is still a good way to the White House. Johnson could claim legitimacy in the New Deal tradition much more convincingly than Kennedy had done. His victory was Roosevelt's as much as his own. Goldwater, it is true, had tried to identify himself with Eisenhower, and that confused old gentleman had lent himself to the deception; but no one was fooled. Eisenhower had not been paying attention. And anyway heroes' coattails are not so long as those of leaders. Johnson was a young Roosevelt as Polk had been a young Hickory, and that, essentially, accounted for his victory.

The new generation, among whom potential Presidents were concealed and in whom the fires of aspiration were burning, could see, if they looked for them, the new means they must use. But they could also see that qualifications were changing. The world had become a more demanding one. The nation expected the impossible from its Presidents. To become one was more of a test than ever. For a successful leader, talents and abilities were needed that were very scarce indeed. There was still the old distinction between getting there and rising to the requirements afterward. There was glory to be had, more glory than ever before; but there was tragedy waiting for the man of doubtful capacity whose offer to lead was accepted and who fell short in wisdom or resolution. So aspirants must look inward as never before—for the country's sake, and for their own.

Index

Abilene, Kansas, 438, 446

Abolition movement, 140, 150, 153, 158, 159, 165, 170, 187, 202, 204

Acheson, Dean, 491

Adams, Abigail Smith, 31, 36

Adams, Brooks, 317

Adams, Charles Francis, 150

Adams, Henry, 317

Adams, John, 16, 17, 21, 27, 29, 31–41, 42, 44, 45, 46, 51–52, 55, 58, 68, 102

Adams, John Quincy, 17, 34, 41, 56, 57, 63, 65, 66, 73, 74, 75–85, 86, 89, 92, 93, 107, 119, 126, 128 n., 333

Adams, Louisa Catherine Johnson, 75, 83

Adams, Samuel, 41

Adams, Samuel Hopkins, 360

Albany Regency, 78, 99, 103

Alien and Sedition Acts, 31, 39–40, 44, 45

Allegheny College, 295

Allison, William Boyd, 302

Allison letters, 149–50

American Federation of Labor, 380, 381

Americans for Democratic Action, 449

American Party, *see* Know-Nothings

American System, 77, 81, 97

Amherst College, 262 n., 370, 374–75

Annapolis Conference, 27, 63

Anthony, Edward, 400 n.

Anti-Masonic Party, 94, 106, 107

Anti-poverty program, 497

Anti-Slavery Society, 153

Armstrong, John, 119

Arnold, Benedict, 68–69

Arthur, Chester Alan, 14, 17, 245, 247, 257, 259–69, 272, 275 n., 311, 319

Arthur, Ellen Lewis Herndon, 259

Babcock, General Orville B., 235

Bagehot, Walter, 348

Bank of the United States, 70, 97–98, 102, 104, 107, 108, 122, 126, 127, 128, 129, 142

Barkley, Alben, 423, 426

Barlow, S. M., 181 n.

Bates, Edward, 197 n.

Bayard, James A., 46, 75, 181, 182

Belgium, Commission for Food Relief in, 386, 393

Bell, John, 188, 196 n., 197

Benjamin, Judah P., 180, 182

Benton, Thomas Hart, 143

Bierce, Ambrose, 481

Biffle, Leslie, 433

Bill of Rights, 51, 173

Birney, James G., 138

Black Hawk War, 143, 152

Black River Academy, 370, 374

Blaine, James G., 235, 236, 238, 244, 249, 250, 254, 257, 269,

Blaine, James G., *continued*
   270, 272–73, 277, 278, 288, 290,
   293
Blair, F. P., 92 n., 219
Borah, William E., 389
Bossism, 94, 103, 105, 115, 117,
   119, 120, 124, 146, 149, 151,
   187, 276, 316, 317, 319, 322,
   342, 472
Boston police strike, 380–81
Bourne, Jonathan, 345
Bowdoin College, 166, 170
Boxer Rebellion, 386
Braddock, General Edward, 21
Bradley, General Omar, 441
Bragg, General Braxton, 146 n.
Braintree, Massachusetts, 31, 75
Brandegee, Frank B., 358
Brandeis, Louis D., 354
Breckinridge, John C., 178, 188,
   196 n., 197
Bricker, John William, 403, 489 n.
Bricker Amendment, 489
Bright, Jesse D., 181, 182
Bristow, Benjamin H., 235, 236,
   244
Britain and the British, 25, 26, 30,
   33, 37, 38, 41, 44, 57, 58, 59,
   61–62, 67, 70, 72, 78, 80, 84,
   92, 95, 118–19, 129, 131, 141,
   142, 159, 287, 497
Britton, Nan, 359
Brookline, Massachusetts, 456
Brooks, Preston, 176
Brown, George, 493
Brown, John, 176
Brown, Walter F., 400 n.
Brownell, Herbert, 453
Bryan, C. W., 370
Bryan, William Jennings, 46, 250,
   263, 267, 295, 298, 299, 303,
   304, 305, 306, 322, 323, 325,
   337, 342, 343, 345, 347, 350,
   352, 353, 375
Bryn Mawr College, 339
Buchanan, James, 85, 133, 163, 168,
   173, 177, 178–87, 193, 195, 224,
   272

Buchanan, James P., 484
Buena Vista, Battle of, 143, 145,
   146, 148, 151
Buffalo University, 162
Burr, Aaron, 16, 40, 41, 42, 45, 46,
   50, 57, 59, 69
Burchard, Samuel Dickinson, 278–
   79, 293
Burton, Harold Hitz, 400 n.
Businessmen as presidential aspir-
   ants, 525–27
Butler, William M., 176, 384
Butler, General William O., 152

Caldwell, New Jersey, 270
Calhoun, John C., 60, 71, 75, 77,
   81, 85, 89, 101, 103, 104, 112,
   117, 120, 126, 127, 130, 133,
   143, 168 n., 192, 250
Canada, 61, 164, 175, 280
Canning, George, 80
Cannon, Newton, 133
Carnegie, Andrew, 288, 303 n.
Carpetbagger governments, 232,
   235
Cary, Colonel Archibald, 68
Cass, Lewis, 133, 134–35, 143, 150,
   152, 153, 168, 181
Castlereagh, Lord, 80
Caucus, Congressional, 60, 73, 105
Cayuga County, New York, 155
Central Labor Union of Boston,
   380
Chapman, John Jay, 315
Charles City County, Virginia,
   110, 122
Chase, Salmon P., 168 n., 197 n.
Cherokee Indians, 101
Childs, Marquis, 440 n., 449
China, 175
Choate Academy, 456, 460, 461
Churchill, Winston S., 444
Cincinnati, Ohio, 323
Cincinnati Law School, 323
Civil Rights Bill, 495, 497
Civil Service Commission, 308, 312

Civil service reform, 227, 254
Civil War, 145, 157, 187, 200, 213, 224, 225–27, 242–43, 254
Clark, Champ, 351, 352, 353
Clark, Grenville, 406
Clay, Henry, 60, 71, 73, 75, 77, 81, 82, 83, 85, 86, 89, 95 n., 96, 104 n., 107, 112, 116, 120, 124, 125, 126, 127, 128, 130, 131, 134, 135, 138–39, 140, 143, 145, 150, 151, 153, 157, 159, 160, 162, 163, 165, 168 n., 250, 306
Clayton, John M., 151
Cleveland, Frances, 57
Cleveland, Grover, 17, 97, 237, 252, 263, 270–84, 285, 286, 289, 290, 292, 300, 306, 331, 359
Clifford, Clark, 435
Clinton, De Witt, 53, 58, 61, 71, 78, 99
Clinton, George, 42, 50, 53, 58, 59, 71
Clipper ships, 175
Cold Harbor, Battle of, 225
Colfax, Schuyler, 219
Columbia University, 308, 311, 326, 342, 347, 403, 438, 447–48
Commager, Henry Steele, 114–15, 116–17
Commerce Department, U. S., 396, 398
Communism and Communists, 436, 451, 452, 496
Compromise of 1850, 155, 157, 159–60, 163, 168, 169, 192
Confederate Congress, 122, 130
Confederate States of America, 225
Congress, U. S., 44, 47, 95, 119, 140, 227, 256, 322, 418, 425, 455, 480–81
Conkling, Roscoe, 235, 236, 244, 245, 249, 254, 257, 259, 261, 264, 265, 266–67, 268, 269, 272–73
Connally, Governor John B., 491
Constitutional Convention, 21, 27, 31
Constitutional Unionists, 197, 198

Constitution of the United States, 28, 48, 49, 50, 56, 95, 105, 108
Continental Congress, 21, 27, 29, 31, 48, 53, 59, 63, 69, 117
Contreras, Battle of, 166
Conventions, national, 105–06, 133–34, 151, 164, 165, 168, 169, 183, 197, 198, 236, 255, 266–67, 274, 295, 297, 320, 332, 347, 351–53, 363, 368, 383, 402, 407, 409, 412, 419 n., 441, 496, 497
Coolidge, John Calvin, 14, 17, 208, 351, 356, 370–85, 386, 388, 389, 398, 399, 400, 409, 412, 430
Cooper Union speech, Lincoln's, 192
Copperheads, 116
Cornwallis, General Lord Charles, 21, 30, 69
Correa da Serra, José Francesco, 65
Cotulla, Texas, 474, 482–83
Coxey's Army, 349
Crane, Winthrop M., 379, 382
Crawford, William H., 73, 77, 81
Crédit Mobilier scandals, 256, 277
Cresson, Margaret, 68
Crittenden, John J., 149
Crook, General George, 242
Cuba, 174, 175, 313, 314, 323, 327, 332, 333, 334–36
Culver, Erastus D., 262
Curley, James Michael, 460, 461
Curtis, Charles, 386, 388, 400, 401 n., 403
Curtis, George William, 277
Cushing, Caleb, 173, 174, 175
Cuyahoga County, Ohio, 247

Dallas, George M., 130, 131
Dana, Francis, 75
Daniels, Josephus, 352, 403, 407, 408, 409, 463
Dartmouth College, 170
Daugherty, Harry M., 359–61, 364, 367, 368, 369, 382, 397
Davis, Jefferson 143, 146 n., 168 n., 173, 174, 370

Davis, John W., 412
Dawes, Charles Gates, 388–89, 401 n., 435
Dawes, John W., 370, 383
Day, W. R., 303 n.
Dayton, William L., 178, 188
Debs, Eugene V., 349
Declaration of Independence, 48
Delaware, Ohio, 233
Democratic Party, 93, 94, 97, 104, 106–07, 108, 115–16, 125, 128–29, 130, 138, 139, 140, 141, 142, 150, 153, 168, 170, 171, 172, 183, 184, 185, 187, 196, 197, 198, 204, 214, 232, 237–38, 252, 255, 257, 278, 287, 298, 311, 353, 355, 357, 397, 406, 419, 447, 453, 470, 511–54
Democratic-Republican Party, 29, 35, 37, 39, 45, 46, 49, 56, 57, 58, 59, 60, 70, 72, 73, 81, 93, 95 n., 108, 115, 116, 157, 170
Denby, Edwin, 382, 397
Denison, Texas, 438
Depew, Chauncey M., 293
Depressions, 98, 102, 107, 389, 396, 411, 414, 416
Dever, Paul Andrew, 465, 466
Devereux, William K., 344
Devices, use of, 542–44
Dewey, Admiral George, 313
Dewey, Thomas E., 403, 421, 423, 436, 449, 451–52, 453, 454
Dickinson College, 178
Diversity, prevalence of, 528–31
Donelson, A. J., 92 n., 95 n.
Douglas, Helen Gahagan, 454
Douglas, Stephen A., 143, 168, 173–74, 176, 181, 183, 188, 192, 193, 195, 196 n., 198, 199, 202, 215
Douglas, Justice William O., 491
Duff, Senator James H., 450, 452
Dulles, John Foster, 489, 495
Dunne, Finley Peter, 313 n.

Early, Stephen, 426
Eaton, John H., 92 n., 104–05

Eisenhower, Dwight David, 50, 82 n., 88, 96, 112, 113, 438–55, 465, 466, 489
Eisenhower, Ida, 422
Eisenhower, Mamie Doud, 442
Electoral College, 37, 38, 204
Emerson, Ralph Waldo, 115, 163, 240
Emigrant Aid Society of Massachusetts, 176
Equalitarianism, 79, 84
"Era of good feelings," 72, 73, 82
Erie Canal, 78
Esberg, Milton, 400 n.
Estrada Palma, Tomás, 335
Ethics, politics and, 558–60
Everett, Edward, 188, 197
Ewing, Thomas, 129
Exactitude, uses of, 511–12
Exceptions, rules and, 503–07
Expansion, national, 79, 93, 157–58, 161, 174, 175, 321

Fagan, Mark, 345
Fairbanks, Charles Warren, 308, 339
Fairfield, Vermont, 259
Fall, Albert B., 382, 397
Farley, James A., 414, 415, 417, 418, 421
Federalists, 35, 37, 38, 39, 40, 44, 45, 46, 49, 50, 51, 52, 55, 56, 59, 60, 61, 71, 72, 73, 93, 107, 115
Fillmore, Abigail Powers, 155
Fillmore, Caroline C. McIntosh, 155
Fillmore, Millard, 14, 17, 93 n., 143, 151, 152, 153–54, 155–65, 169, 202
Fitzgerald, John F. (Honey Fitz), 461, 464
Flynn, Thomas, 344, 418
Folger, Charles J., 275
Food Administration, U.S., 394
Foraker, Joseph B., 302, 330, 361, 362, 363

Force Bill, 102
Ford, Henry, 457
Foreign relations, 39–40, 44, 56–57, 59–60, 62, 70, 72, 78, 80, 84, 129, 141, 174–75, 287
Forrestal, James, 447
Fort Donelson, 224
Fort Harrison, 143
Fort Henry, 224
Fort Meigs, 119
Fourteenth Amendment, 243
Fox, Alan, 400 n.
France and the French, 25, 26, 29, 37, 39, 44, 48, 49, 57, 60, 63, 70, 72, 78, 80
Franklin, Benjamin, 24–25, 29, 42, 49
Franklin County, Pennsylvania, 178
Free silver, 303, 305
Free-Soil Party, 103, 150, 153, 169, 171, 176, 186, 202, 204
Free trade, 193, 287
Frelingheusen, Frederick T, 131
Frémont, John Charles, 178, 183, 184, 185, 188, 202, 223, 241, 262, 287
French Revolution, 55
Freneau, Philip M., 45
Frick, Henry C., 303 n.
Fuess, Claude M., 376 n.
Fugitive Slave Law, 157, 163–64, 165, 169
Fulton, Hugh, 432

Gallatin, Albert, 50, 75
Gardiner, Henry D., 262, 408
Garfield, James A., 243, 247–58, 259, 262, 266, 269, 299, 305, 311, 441
Garfield, Lucretia Randolph, 247
Garner, John Nance, 82 n., 403, 415, 418, 433
Generals as Presidential aspirants, 525–27
George, Senator Walter F., 419
Georgetown Law School, 484

Gerry, Elbridge, 53, 58, 59
Ghent, Treaty of (1814), 62, 75, 82 n.
Goebel, Dorothy B. and Julius, 88 n.
Gold discoveries and mining, 175, 176
Goldwater, Barry M., 422, 474, 495, 496, 497, 498
Gompers, Samuel, 381
Good, James, 400 n.
Gould, Jay, 275 n.
Grady, Thomas F., 277
Graham, Philip, 493
Grand Army of the Republic, 278, 286, 300, 367, 441, 444
Grant, Julia Dent, 224
Grant, Ulysses S., 13, 17, 88, 145, 146 n., 153 n., 213, 219–32, 235, 237, 238 n., 243–44, 245, 249, 254, 256, 264, 265, 266, 273, 278, 306, 418 n., 440, 441
Greece, 80
Greeley, Horace, 219, 232 n., 264, 306
Gresham, Judge Walter Q., 288, 291
Groton School, 403, 405
Guiding suggestions for students and Presidential aspirants, 539–41

Hague, Frank, 418
Hale, John P., 169, 171
Halleck, General Henry W., 225
Hamilton, Alexander, 16, 27, 35, 36, 37, 38, 39, 40, 41, 45, 51, 52, 71
Hamlin, Hannibal, 188, 319
Hampden-Sydney College, 110, 118
Hancock, Winfield Scott, 247, 255, 266, 267
Handicaps for Presidential aspirants, 517–19
Hanna, Mark, 287, 299, 300–03, 304, 305, 317, 360, 361, 362

Hannegan, Robert, 432–33, 434
Hardin County, Kentucky, 188
Harding, Florence Kling, 365–67, 368–69
Harding, Warren Gamaliel, 13, 356–69, 370, 373, 381–82, 386, 394, 395, 398, 409, 495 n.
Harris, Levett, 65
Harrison, Anna Tuthill Symmes, 110, 118
Harrison, Benjamin, 270, 285–94, 300, 308, 312, 330
Harrison, Benjamin (father of W. H. Harrison), 117
Harrison, Pat, 426
Harrison, William Henry, 93 n., 99, 106, 107, 110–21, 124, 126, 145, 151, 152, 200, 258
Harvard University, 31, 75, 239, 308, 312, 403, 405, 456, 460, 461
Harvey, George, 342–43, 344, 346, 358
Hay, John, 303 n., 315
Hayes, Lucy Ware Webb, 233, 236
Hayes, Rutherford Birchard, 231, 233–46, 250, 251, 252, 253, 255, 257, 258, 259, 265, 272, 299, 305
Hayne, Robert Young, 101
Hearst, William Randolph, 349, 415
Heath, Ferry, 400 n.
Hendricks, Thomas A., 233, 270
Herndon, William, 191, 202
Herrick, Myron T., 303 n., 362
Hess, Jake, 311, 312
Hill, David B., 279, 281
Hillman, William, 427
Hillsborough, New Hampshire, 166
Hitler, Adolf, 420
Hoadly, George, 289–90
Hobart, Garret A., 295, 317
Hollister, John, 161 n.
Holy Alliance, 78, 80
Homestead Act, 194
Homestead mill strike, 292

Hoover, Herbert Clark, 17, 97, 384, 386–402, 403, 414, 415, 416, 421
Hoover, Lou Henry, 391
House of Representatives, 46, 128, 191, 250
Houston, Sam, 168
Howe, General Lord George A., 23, 67
Howe, George F., 261
Howe, Louis M., 409–10, 411, 413, 415
Hughes, Charles Evans, 339, 345, 394, 395, 396, 397, 398
Hull, General William, 118, 152, 175
Humphrey, Hubert, 459, 466, 470, 472, 474, 491, 497
"Hundred Days," the, 416
Hunt, Henry, 273
Huston, Claudius, 400 n.
Hyde Park, New York, 403

Independence, Missouri, 423, 427
Indiana Territory, 118
Indian wars, 118–19
Ingersoll, Jared, 61, 250
Ingersoll, Robert, 293
Interior Department, U. S., 235
Irving, Washington, 55

Jackson, Andrew, 44, 46, 50, 55, 56, 61, 75, 77–78, 81, 82, 83, 84, 85, 86–98, 101, 102, 103, 104–05, 106, 112, 125, 126, 133, 135, 137, 138, 139, 158, 170, 190, 195, 203, 211, 212, 213, 306
Jackson, Henry, 493
Jackson, Rachel Robards, 86, 104–05
Janin, Louis, 391
Jardine, William Marion, 384
Jay, John, 16, 29, 34, 35, 40, 51, 59, 265
Jefferson, Martha Wayles Skelton, 42, 49

Jefferson, Thomas, 16, 31, 35, 36, 37, 38, 39, 40, 41, 42–52, 53, 55, 56, 57, 58, 60, 63, 65, 66, 68, 69, 70, 102, 103, 190, 191, 200

Johns Hopkins University, 339

Johnson, Andrew, 14, 44, 99, 110, 133, 188, 204, 206–18, 219, 223, 226, 227, 228, 229, 238 n., 243, 245

Johnson, Claudia Taylor, 474, 477, 493

Johnson, Eliza McCardle, 206, 209

Johnson, Hiram, 339

Johnson, Hugh, 399, 418

Johnson, Lyndon Baines, 14, 208, 456, 459, 470, 472, 474–99

Johnson, Tom, 273

Johnson City, Texas, 474, 482

Jones, Golden Rule, 273

Jones, Joseph, 68

Josephson, Matthew, 317

Judd, Norman, 197 n.

Julian, G. W., 169

Kansas-Nebraska Act, 173, 176, 181, 202

Kefauver, Estes, 438, 459, 470

Kelly, John, 276, 277, 418

Kendall, Amos, 92 n.

Kennedy, Edward, 471

Kennedy, Jacqueline Bouvier, 57, 456, 468

Kennedy, John Fitzgerald, 191, 456–73, 474, 476, 477, 478, 479, 480, 490, 491, 492, 493, 494, 498

Kennedy, Joseph P., 460, 462–64, 471, 472

Kennedy, Patrick, 461

Kennedy, Robert, 471

Kennedy, Rose, 464, 465

Kenyon College, 233, 239

Kern, John W., 323

Kerney, James, 343 n., 344, 346 n.

Khrushchev, Nikita, 470, 497, 498

Kinderhook, New York, 99

King, Rufus, 42, 53, 63, 73, 99, 166

"Kitchen Cabinet," Jackson's, 92–93, 96, 103, 104, 105

Kleberg, Richard, 474, 483–84, 485

Kling, Amos, 365, 366, 367

Know-Nothings (American Party), 161, 183, 185, 198 n., 204, 242

Knox, Philander, 303 n.

Kohlsaat, H. H., 303 n.

Korean war, 451, 453–54

Krueger, General Walter, 442

Labor unions, 343, 380, 381

Lafayette, Marquis de, 69

La Follette, Robert, 343, 345, 383, 412

La Follette, Robert, Jr., 418

Lamar, Missouri, 423, 427

Landon, Alfred, 420

Lane, Franklin K., 188, 197 n.

Lawrence, David, 493

Lawyers as Presidential aspirants, 525–27

Leader, finding a, 563–66

Leadership, attraction of, 532–35

League of Nations, 382, 463

Lee, General Robert E., 146 n., 148 n., 219, 225

Lewis, Fulton, 446

Lewis, John L., 421

Lewis, W. B., 92 n., 95 n.

Lincoln, Abraham, 29, 82 n., 91, 95, 96, 138, 145, 157, 158, 188–205, 212, 213, 214, 215, 216, 217, 219, 225, 229, 306

Lincoln, Mary Todd, 188

Lincoln-Douglas debates, 188, 193, 196, 215

Link, Arthur S., 345, 346 n., 347, 349, 352

Linn, William, 52

Lodge, Henry Cabot, 314, 315, 317, 319, 382, 395, 408

Lodge, Henry Cabot, Jr., 450, 452, 456, 463, 465–66

Logan, John A., 238, 270

Louisiana Purchase, 70, 77
Lowden, Frank O., 388, 400

MacArthur, General Arthur, 333
MacArthur, General Douglas, 438, 442, 445, 447, 452, 453
Madison, Dolly Payne Todd, 53, 57–58
Madison, James, 45, 50, 53–62, 63, 65, 66, 71, 102, 119, 120, 143
Manning, Daniel, 276
Marcy, William L., 145, 146, 168, 173
Marshall, General George C., 441, 443, 444, 452, 453, 455
Marshall, John, 12, 45, 51, 67, 69 n., 71, 101
Marshall, Thomas R., 12, 339
Marshall Plan, 450, 451
McAdoo, William G., 352, 383, 412, 415
McBain, Howard Lee, 11
McCarthy, Senator Joseph R., 453, 455, 462
McClellan, General George B., 145, 188, 200, 216
McClernand, General John A., 225, 226
McClure, A. K., 184–85
McCombs, William F., 347, 352
McKinley, William, 256, 257, 258, 263, 288, 293, 295–307, 308, 312, 316, 319, 320, 321, 331, 333, 360
McKinley Tariff, 298
McLean, John, 184, 197 n.
McNary, Charles L., 403
McNary-Haugen bills, 399
Meade, General George Gordon, 146 n., 229 n.
Mecklenburg County, North Carolina, 131
Medical care program, 479
Medill, Joseph, 194–95, 196
Mellon, Andrew, 389, 395
Merit system, 91

Mexican War, 131, 142, 143, 145, 146, 147–49, 166, 170, 172, 201, 219, 224
Mexico, 134, 141, 147, 148, 149, 174, 175
Mexico City, capture of, 145, 148, 149, 172, 219
Miami University, 285, 292
Michigan Territory, 118
Mills, Ogden, 400 n.
Minnegerode, Meade, 71
Missouri Compromise (1820), 141, 151, 174, 192, 202
Monroe, James, 29, 45, 50, 55, 57, 61, 63–74, 75, 80
Monroe Doctrine, 80
Monterrey, Battle of, 149, 151, 219
Montgomery, Field Marshal Bernard, 444
Moor, Jeremiah, 48
Morgan, Edwin D., 259, 264
Morison, Samuel Eliot, 114–15, 116–17
Morris, Robert, 118
Morrow, Dwight W., 375, 378
Morton, Levi P., 244, 268, 285, 291, 302
Mugwumps, 321
Murphy, Charles F., 407, 409
Murphy, Thomas, 259, 264
Murray, Joe, 311–12
Mussolini, Benito, 420
Mutual Defense Assistance Act, 451

Napoleon, 59, 78
National Convention, French, 70
National debt, 97
National Recovery Administration, 416–17
National Youth Administration, 483, 484
Navy Department, U. S., 235, 277, 407, 408
Nebraska Territory, 174
New Deal, Roosevelt's, 95, 410,

New Deal, *continued*
416, 417, 418, 430, 431, 433, 484, 485
New Era, Harding and Coolidge's, 410–11
New Freedom, Wilson's, 354
New Orleans, Battle of, 61, 86, 92, 146 n.
New York City, 308
Nicaragua, 175
Nichols, R. F., 169, 181, 186, 187
Niles, Ohio, 295
Nixon, Richard M., 438, 455, 456, 459, 462, 469, 472, 476, 492
North Atlantic Treaty Organization (NATO), 448, 450, 451
North Bend, Ohio, 285
North Carolina University, 131, 136
Northwest Territory, 118
Nugent, James R., 342
Nullification, 101, 108, 125, 126

Oberholtzer, E. P., 249, 250 n.
Ohio Central College, 356, 364
Olney, Attorney General, 283 n.
O'Neill, Peggy, 104–05
One-term President, proposal for, 140
Oregon Territory, 131, 140, 142
Ostend Manifesto, 178

Paine, Thomas, 41
Palma, see Estrada Palma
Palmer, Frederick, 334
Palo Alto, Battle of, 146, 219
Panama, 323
Panama Canal, 175, 318
Panics, financial, 98, 107, 343
Paris Peace Conference (1919), 339
Parker, Alton B., 308, 322, 407
Patton, General George, 444
Peace Congress (1861), 130

Peek, George N., 399
Pendergast, Thomas J., 426, 428, 429–30, 431, 434
Pendleton, George H., 188
Pendleton Bill (1882), 282
Penrose, Boies, 317, 395
Pension office scandals, 292
Perry, Admiral Matthew C., 175
Philippine Islands, 313, 316, 323, 327, 331, 332, 333, 442
Philosophical Society, 49
Pierce, Franklin, 17, 145 n., 163, 166–77, 180, 181, 183
Pierce, Jane Means Appleton, 166, 171
Pinckney, Charles C., 37, 38, 40, 42, 50, 53, 58
Platt, Thomas C., 268, 302, 304, 314–15, 316, 317, 319
Platt Amendment, 335
Plymouth, Vermont, 370, 372–74
Point Pleasant, Ohio, 219
Political instruments, evolution of, 561–62
Politics, ethics and, 558–60
Polk, James Knox, 94, 130, 131–42, 145, 146, 147, 148, 171, 211, 257
Polk, Sarah Childress, 131
Pope, A. A., 303 n.
Popular sovereignty, 46
Populists, 299, 303, 342, 343, 415
Port Conway, Virginia, 53
Positions, on taking, 555–57
Post Office Star Route incidents, 277
Pratt, Ruth, 400 n.
Presidential aspirants:
advantageous conditions for, 520–24
businessmen as, 525–27
caliber of, 567–68
disadvantageous conditions for, 517–19
generals as, 525–27
guiding suggestions for, 539–41
lawyers as, 525–27
reluctance of, 545–50

Presidential aspirants, *continued*
  rules for, 503–07
  selection process for, 536–38
  uniformity among, 515–16
  willingness to work hard, 513–14
Princeton, U.S.S., 130
Princeton University, 53, 270, 339, 341, 346
Pringle, H. F., 318, 325, 327 n., 329
Progressive Party (Bull Moose), 308, 353, 355, 357, 407, 412
Progressivism, 345, 346
Public Works programs, 93, 97, 125

Quay, Matt, 302, 304, 317
Questions, new, 569–74

Railroads, 174, 176, 194, 343
Raleigh, North Carolina, 206
Randolph, John, 71
Rawlins, John A., 225
Rayburn, Sam, 484, 485
Record, George L., 345, 346
Reed, Thomas B., 302
Reid, Whitelaw, 270
Report on Manufactures, Hamilton's, 70
Republican Party, 176, 184, 185–86, 187, 193–94, 195, 197, 198, 214, 216, 219, 232, 235, 236, 239, 252, 254–55, 267, 278, 286, 289, 298, 311, 323, 353, 355, 357, 361, 367, 372, 406, 413, 416, 421, 447, 449, 453, 492, 496, 551–54
Republican Wide-Awakes, 198
Requa, Mark, 400 n.
Resaca de la Palma, Battle of, 146, 147, 151
Reuther, Walter, 493
Revolutionary War, 67–69
Rickard, Edgar, 400 n.
Robespierre, Maximilien, 70
Robinson, Charles, 386, 426
Rockefeller, Nelson, 496

Roosevelt, Eleanor, 410
Roosevelt, Franklin D., 17, 44, 82 n., 88, 95, 96, 98, 191, 250, 321 n., 356, 386, 397, 403–22, 423, 425, 426, 430, 434, 435, 443, 444, 459, 463, 467, 484–85, 492, 499
Roosevelt, Franklin D., Jr., 471
Roosevelt, James, 449
Roosevelt, Theodore, 14, 17, 44, 102, 175, 208, 295, 308–22, 323, 325, 326, 333, 334, 335, 336, 337, 339, 350, 353–54, 363, 406, 435, 458
Root, Elihu, 319, 331, 334
Rosecrans, General William S., 242
Rosenman, Samuel I., 420 n., 435
Rough Riders, 308, 313, 316, 318, 320
Rowe, James, 491, 492
Rush, Benjamin, 34
Russia and the Russians, 78, 451, 497, 498

Sackville-West, Lionel, 287
St. Clair, General Arthur, 118
St. Johnsbury Academy, 370, 374
Santa Anna, General Antonio López de, 145, 148, 149, 153 n.
Schurz, Carl, 277, 318
Scott, General Winfield, 145, 147, 149, 151, 152, 153, 165, 166, 168, 169, 172, 186, 202, 219, 241
Scranton, William, 496
Secession, 101–02, 108, 157, 159, 192, 196, 211
Sectionalism, 77, 85, 158–59, 160, 173
Seminole War, 84, 86, 143
Senate, U. S., 95, 103, 130
Sergeant, John, 86
Serra, Correa da, see Correa da Serra
Seward, William H., 143, 163, 168 n., 198–99, 203

Seymour, Horatio, 219, 223, 230, 259, 264, 306

Shadwell, Virginia, 42

Shafter, General William R., 313

Sheehan, John C., 274–75

Sheridan, General Philip H., 200, 242

Sherman, John, 265, 266, 269, 288, 293, 297, 300, 323, 331

Sherman, General William T., 200, 213, 225, 446

Shiloh, Battle of, 226

Sicily, 174

Sievers, H. J., 288

Slavery issue, 77, 108, 125, 130, 141–42, 153, 154, 157, 158–59, 161, 163–64, 168, 170, 173, 174, 175, 192, 193, 194, 195, 202, 213

Slidell, John, 180

Slocum, General Henry W., 276

Smith, Alfred E., 383, 386, 388, 399, 400, 402, 403, 412–14, 415

Smith, James, 342, 344, 345

Smith, Page, 36–37

Social Security system, 416, 417, 420, 421, 422, 479, 495, 497

"Solid South," 115

Sorensen, Theodore, 468, 470

Southwest Texas State Teachers College, 474, 482, 485–86

Spain and the Spaniards, 57, 84, 313, 333

Spanish-American War, 308, 316, 318, 331

Sparkman, John, 438

Sparrow, Thomas, 233

Spoils System, 89, 90–91

Spotsylvania, Battle of, 225

Stanford University, 386, 390

Stanton, Edwin McMasters, 218, 219

States' rights, 71, 105, 116, 125, 127, 170, 174

Staunton, Virginia, 339

Stearns, Frank W., 378–79

Steffens, Lincoln, 24, 345

Stephens, Alexander H., 149

Stevens, Thaddeus, 226, 243

Stevenson, Adlai Ewing, 270, 295

Stevenson, Adlai Ewing (grandson of the above), 438, 453, 454, 455, 459, 465, 469, 472, 491

Stirling, General Lord, 68, 69

Stockbridge, Frank Parker, 347

Stonewall, Texas, 474, 482

Sub-Treasury system, 102, 107

Sullivan, Mark, 358–59

Sumner, Charles, 174, 176, 250

Supreme Court, U. S., 95, 101, 159, 330, 331, 338, 417, 499

Swiggett, Howard, 23

Symington, Stuart, 459, 469, 470, 472, 491, 492

Symmes, John Cleves, 118

Taft, Horace, 332

Taft, Robert, 82 n., 447, 448, 449, 452, 462, 492

Taft, William Howard, 17, 97, 102, 308, 323–38, 339, 341, 350, 353, 357, 363

Tammany, 103, 104, 261, 275, 276, 277, 278, 279, 281, 282, 352, 407, 408

Tariffs, protective, 70, 71, 77, 93, 97, 101 n., 125, 126, 129, 142, 159, 193, 298, 383

Tarleton, Colonel Sir Banastre, 69

Taylor, John, 50

Taylor, Colonel Joseph P., 149

Taylor, Margaret Mackall Smith, 143

Taylor, Zachary, 93 n., 143–54, 155, 162, 163, 164, 200, 201, 219, 440, 441

Techniques, new, 569–74

Tecumseh, 110, 118

Tennessee Valley Authority, 417

Tenure of Office Act, 218, 228, 245

Texas, annexation of, 130, 134, 135, 139, 140, 141, 148, 154

Thames, Battle of the, 110, 119, 120, 152

Thomas, Benjamin P., 203 n.
Thomas, Norman, 366
Thompson, Charles Willis, 368
Thompson, William J., 344
Thurman, Allen G., 285
Tilden, Samuel Jones, 232, 233, 237, 244, 255, 276, 306
Tippecanoe, Battle of, 110, 118
Tompkins, Daniel D., 63, 99
Toombs, Robert, 149
Tories, 29
Trimble, Richard J., 311
Truman, Harry S., 14, 208, 386, 403, 419, 423–37, 447, 448, 450, 452, 453, 454, 466, 469, 470, 472, 492
Tumulty, Joseph P., 346
Turkey, 80, 174
Twenty-second Amendment, 94 n., 421, 455
Tyler, John, 14, 93 n., 110, 122–30, 134, 151, 164
Tyler, Julia Gardiner, 122

Underwood, Oscar W., 351, 352
Unemployment compensation, 421
Union College, 259, 261
Urban, George, 275
U'Ren, William S., 345

Van Buren, Hannah Hoes, 99, 105
Van Buren, Martin, 17, 78, 85, 86, 92 n., 94, 96, 98, 99–109, 110, 112, 113, 120, 124, 125, 128, 130, 133, 134, 135, 137, 150, 153, 170, 171, 203, 211, 319
Vandenberg, Arthur, 463
Vatican, 334
Vera Cruz, Battle of, 145, 149, 172, 219
Versailles Treaty, 357, 382
Vicksburg, Battle of, 219, 224, 225
Virginia University, 49, 339

Wade, Benjamin F., 218
Wakefield, Virginia, 21
Wallace, Henry A., 403, 419, 426–27, 433, 434, 435, 436
Wallace, Henry C., 399
War Hawks, 60, 61, 62, 71
Warm Springs, Georgia, 403, 410, 411, 413
War of 1812, 55, 60, 61–62, 71, 72, 118–19, 152, 175
Warren, Earl, 423
Washington, George, 11, 17, 21–30, 33, 36, 37, 38, 39, 44, 45, 48, 51, 67, 69, 70, 102, 118, 120, 357
Washington, Martha Custis, 21, 36
Washington, William, 67, 68
Waxhaw, South Carolina, 86
Wayne, General Anthony, 110, 118
Webster, Daniel, 89, 101, 103, 106 n,. 112, 114, 116, 117, 118, 120, 129, 143, 151, 157, 159, 160, 163, 165, 168 n., 250
Webster-Ashburton Treaty, 122, 129
Webster-Hayne debate, 101
Weed, Thurlow, 117, 119, 128, 140, 145–46, 149, 150, 151, 160, 161, 162–63, 164, 165, 176, 264
Welles, Sumner, 204
Wescott, John W., 344
Wesleyan University, 339
West Branch, Iowa, 386, 389
Western Reserve Eclectic Institute, 251
Westmoreland County, Virginia, 21, 63
West Point Military Academy, 171, 219, 224, 438, 441, 442
Wheeler, Burton K., 418, 431
Whigs, 93, 94, 106, 107, 112, 113, 115, 116, 124, 125, 127, 128, 129, 137, 138, 139, 140, 141, 142, 145, 149, 150, 152, 157, 159, 161, 163, 165, 168, 169, 170, 171, 172, 185, 186, 202, 204, 213, 551–54

Whiskey Ring, 277
White, General Harry, 231 n.
White, Hugh L., 89, 104, 106 n., 211
White, William Allen, 328–29, 376 n.
Whitlock, Brand, 273
Wilderness, Battle of the, 225
William and Mary College, 42, 47, 63, 66, 67, 122
Williams College, 247
Willis, Raymond E., 400
Willkie, Wendell, 403, 420
Wilmont Proviso, 141
Wilson, Edith Bolling Galt, 339
Wilson, Ellen Louise Axson, 339
Wilson, Henry, 219

Wilson, Woodrow, 11 n., 84, 97, 250, 308, 339–55, 357, 382, 394, 403, 407, 408, 409, 458
Wood, General Leonard, 388
Woodbury, Levi, 133
Worcester *vs.* Georgia, 101
Work, Hubert, 400 n.
World War I, 379, 390, 393–94, 428, 442, 445
World War II, 443–45
Wright, Silas, 162
Wythe, George, 68

Yale University, 323, 327, 337

Zhukov, Marshal Georgi, 451